HOOLIGANS 2

To Kalvin. My top boy.

– Nick Lowles

In memory of Dainton "Denton" Connell, Black Sam and Paul "The Brick" Debrick. Three true terrace legends. RIP.

– Andy Nicholls

HOOLIGANS 2

The M-Z of Britain's Football Hooligan Gangs

Nick Lowles & Andy Nicholls

MILO BOOKS LTD

First published in September 2005 by Milo Books
This edition published in September 2007

Copyright © 2005 Nick Lowles and Andy Nicholls

ISBN 978 1 903854 64 8

Design and layout by e-type

Printed and bound in Great Britain by Cox & Wyman, Reading

MILO BOOKS LTD
info@milobooks.com

Introduction

SHORTLY BEFORE THE start of the 2006 World Cup Finals in Germany, the British Home Office revealed that 3,286 football banning orders, more than ever before, had been granted. The orders forced people identified as potential troublemakers to surrender their passports for the duration of the summer tournament. At the same time, the host nation announced it was setting up courts that could expel English troublemakers within 24 hours.

As was now usual at international tournaments, a vast team of British police "spotters" – 48 in uniform and 31 in plain clothes – was assembled to travel to the event to gather intelligence and assist the German authorities. Uniquely, they were accompanied by four "flying prosecutors" from the Crown Prosecution Service (CPS), on hand to collect evidence on offenders for use in UK courts – the first time that members of the CPS had worked alongside British police in a foreign country. Their information was sent back to a network of specialist prosecutors in England and Wales who, under a change in legislation introduced in the Violent Crime Reduction Bill, would be able to use the packages of evidence to apply for even more banning orders in English courts. Other proposals in the Bill increased the maximum length of these bans and gave prosecutors the facility to appeal any decisions by magistrates to refuse their applications. The Home Office called it, "The most comprehensive range of measures ever put in place to help prevent significant football disorder among England fans."

It was proof, if any were needed, that the spectre of violence still loomed large over the domestic game. Twenty-one years after the Heysel Disaster, and after rafts of measures to prevent spectator violence, from fencing and segregation to all-seater stadia, from identity cards and stiffer sentences to CCTV and "football intelligence", significant numbers of young and not-so-young males were still intent on fighting each other on match days.

Hooligans 2: The M-Z of Britain's Football Hooligan Gangs is, along with its companion volume Hooligans: The A-L, the first-ever attempt to chart who the hooligan mobs are. Between them, these two volumes give a comprehensive overview of the soccer "firms" at English, Scottish and Welsh league clubs over the past 40 years: who they are, how they organize, what they do.

Although some of the scores of participants interviewed do give reasons for their involvement, this is not an attempt to explain why hooliganism persists, but to answer the questions: who, what, where and when.

Here are the true stories behind some of Britain's most notorious football mobs: the Red Army of Manchester United, the Millwall Bushwhackers, the 6.57 Crew of Portsmouth, Stoke City's Naughty Forty, the West Ham ICF, the Subway Army of Wolves. Here also are lesser known gangs such as the Northampton Affray team, the Swindon Active Service, the Blue Division of Peterborough United and the Kirkcaldy Soccer Casuals of Raith Rovers. *Hooligans 2* also explores infamous rivalries such as that between Wrexham's Frontline and Shrewsbury Town's English Border Front, or the conflict between the Owls Crime Squad and the Blades Business Crew in the city of Sheffield, between the two Sheffield clubs, while West Brom have their say on the Zulus of Birmingham, and Swansea "put the record straight" about their great rivals in Cardiff. Highly active northern firms like Oldham and Stockport, and forgotten mobs overshadowed by bigger neighbours, such as Port Vale and Walsall, are all included.

The authors would like to thank all of those, too numerous to mention, who gave interviews in person or over the phone, or supplied information in writing or via email. They would also like to thank all of those who generously gave photographs for inclusion.

There are signs that the current sledgehammer approach to hooliganism is working. Figures published in November 2005 showed that the marked rise in the number of banning orders was mirrored by an 11% decrease in the number of arrests. Arrests for football-related offences fell from 4,067 to 3,628 during the 2004/05 season, building on a 10% decline during 2003/2004. The 2004/05 season also saw the highest League attendances for 35 years. More than 29 million supporters attended League games and the vast majority passed trouble free, with just 2,725 arrests.

The Tony Blair Government also launched a new UK Football Policing Unit, jointly overseen by the Home Office and the Association of Chief Police Officers (ACPO). It brought together various strands of the policing-football infrastructure, including the Football Banning Orders Authority, the National Criminal Intelligence Service football intelligence section, UK National Football Information Point and the ACPO policing-football support team, and is to intended to "help ensure delivery" of English and Welsh policing operations at local, national and international level. "It is clear that the tough legislation to stamp out football hooliganism together with targeted policing and enforcement is continuing to be effective," said Home Office Minister Paul Goggins.

Opinions among the hooligans themselves vary on that last point. While many insist that the culture in which they grew up is effectively over, others warn of a rising generation of "youth" mobs undaunted by security measures and unintimidated by the police. Football hooliganism has, they say, gone full circle. Forty years ago, when soccer violence as we know it today emerged, the national press were full of lurid stories of out-of-control teenagers. Today, a generation of hooligans is emerging to replace long-established "boys" who are rapidly dropping out of the scene because of police and court action. These young hooligans are deemed uncontrollable not only by the press but also by the police and even by their peers. "They don't follow the rules of their elders," one NCIS officer told the present authors. "They do not distinguish between other hooligans and ordinary fans and they have no problem attacking the police."

One ten-year-old Portsmouth fan is a case in point. In court for throwing a brick at a police officer after a bad-tempered match against Southampton, he was asked by the magistrate if he had been scared.

"No," replied the youngster. "Why should I be? I was with my mates and I was fighting the police."

In Stockport, the newly formed Baby Squad is run by an eleven-year-old boy. In Swansea, a mob of 15 youths travelled for the away match at Yeovil, their ages ranging from 15 down to just eleven. "Some were sons of old-school hooligans," said one Swansea police officer. Few can afford to go to home matches so they mainly gather together close to the ground after the game with the aim of picking off away supporters and bricking their coaches. "It's proving a policing nightmare," the officer added. "We don't know who they are, and because they are under sixteen many of the old established forms of intelligence gathering, such as informers, cannot apply. The rules of engagement are different and we are struggling to cope."

Most of the youth firms are older than that, but are still in their late teens and early twenties. While more seasoned hooligans slip away from the scene, this next generation will keep this British sub-culture alive for some time yet. Most people accept that hooliganism as it once was is dead – the days of thousands of rival fans battling it out inside and outside the stadium are long gone – but it will never go away completely. Cup games, promotion and relegation matches and local derbies will always bring some of the old faces out. Many more games are now "police free" and some police forces are even scaling back their football intelligence units.

Attending a football match today is a more pleasant, though not necessarily more exciting, experience than 30 years ago, but the social and economic conditions that made hooliganism a cultural phenomenon that heaped shame on the country have not gone away. After more than a century of disturbances at British games, the problem is unlikely ever to disappear for good.

M

MACCLESFIELD TOWN

Ground: Moss Rose
Firm: Moss Rats
Rivals: Chester City, Altrincham

In the 2000/01 season, Macclesfield earned the accolade of having Britain's best behaved supporters, with not one single fan arrested during the year. Three years later little had changed, with their fans once again rated the friendliest around.

Despite that, Macclesfield Town have had a hooligan following dating back to the 1970s, when their non-league status brought them up against local enemies Altrincham, Wigan and Southport. A decline in footballing fortunes in the late Seventies saw a corresponding drop in hooliganism, which was only reversed in the early Eighties. An FA Cup game against Worcester proved to be the spark for further trouble.

"We lost five-one and after the match everyone seemed to lose their heads and it kicked off all over the place," recalled Dave, a Macclesfield veteran. "I felt a bit sorry for Worcester because it was one of those days when every lad turned out for trouble. The following year we got Port Vale in the Cup but this time they took over the place. No matter how much we tried to stick together they just had too many and we took a good hiding."

A Port Vale hooligan at the game agreed. "Macclesfield's ground at the time was a typical old fashioned non-league arena," he recalled. "There was no segregation and it was possible to walk all the way around the so-called stadium, in reality a poor excuse for a field surrounded by crumbling terrace and a few seats under a shed roof. An early sign of potential trouble was when one bloke was seen to climb over the wall into the ground with what looked like a hunting knife in his mouth. Hundreds of people were getting into every end by climbing the walls, and with it being such a small ground it was soon overcrowded.

"The fighting started shortly after kick-off on a small section of terracing. It wasn't just a bit of pushing and shoving and the odd punch and kick being thrown, it was so vicious the police did not dare intervene. The violence seemed to be on and off and it broke out in various areas of the ground. You could tell disaster was looming. Due to the fighting, there was constant surging towards the front of the terrace and the inevitable happened, the perimeter wall collapsed trapping lots of people under it, mainly kids.

"The game was stopped for around fifteen minutes while police, stewards and even some of the Vale players helped the injured. Luckily, the crowd was relatively small so there was no huge crush and no deaths. The match re-started and so did the fighting. The police were losing control and foolishly sent a couple of police dogs into the crowd to try to quell the violence. These dogs were never to return; they were kicked to death. I have heard and seen some pretty bad things in my time at the match but the squeals of those dogs being systematically kicked to death is one I will never forget."

The first recognised mob at Moss Road was the Bostock's Road Crew, who were active during the Eighties and into the early Nineties. The name derived from the coach company that was normally used to travel to away matches. In 1987 Macclesfield were promoted to the Conference and a few rucks brought their hooligan element a mention in the *Non-League Yearbook*. Into the Nineties, a new firm emerged called the Moss Rats. The name derived from a council estate bordering the ground, considered by many to be the roughest in the town. "All the kids on here are known as 'rats' due to being scruffy thieving bastards," laughed Dave. "So we took the name as a few of the lads live on the estate."

Macclesfield achieved Football League status in 1997, a dramatic rise for a club who not too long before were battling it out in the Cheshire County League against fierce rivals Altrincham. Even to this day Macclesfield fans continue to chant against their local rivals. A televised FA Cup tie against West Ham in 2002 featured chants of, "Are you watching Altrincham?" The two clubs were closely matched for many years, with Macclesfield having the biggest away support outside the League and Altrincham known for their giant-killing feats. By the early Nineties their fortunes diverged and the animosity between the fans grew. Several matches saw fights between their fans.

Outside this local derby, violence at the ground tended to be caused by away fans, although very few firms have Moss Road high on the list of grounds worth a visit.

Promotion into the League saw no increase in lads attending matches, largely because anyone drawn towards hooliganism was already affiliated to larger clubs, particularly Manchester City. The close bond between Macclesfield and City supporters was evident when York City played the Cheshire side, then still a non-League team.

"Macclesfield away in the Cup late 1980s was the biggest ruck I've ever seen in a ground," remembered one York lad. "It went off all through the game and on the pitch afterwards." Boosting Macclesfield's numbers that day was a mob of Manchester City.

The Moss Rats continue to be active, albeit on a very small scale. Some local lads who also ran with Manchester City dropped Macclesfield after they achieved league status. The defining moment in this relationship was when the two sides met in the old Second Division in the 1990s, much to the embarrassment and humiliation of the City boys. From that day tension and even open animosity has existed.

Dave was not too disappointed when the relationship with City came to an abrupt end. "There were some decent City lads who came with us when they had no game or one that was not worth bothering with, but their demise on the pitch meant that a few years ago we actually played them in the league. It was priceless, the so-called big club who have spent years trying to rival their more illustrious neighbours, United, suddenly find that their local derby was little old Macclesfield. How the mighty had fallen. It was too much for the City lads and they were never seen again."

Other local rivalries also became strained once Macclesfield joined the League. "We never seemed to get on with either Stockport or Rochdale for some reason," said Dave. "Stockport used to enjoy turning up and taking the piss, which to be fair they could do as they had a good following and well outnumbered us.

"We have one of the smallest firms in the league but we're honest enough to admit it. We only average about fifteen lads to an away game but we can still pull out a few more when lads can be bothered. The good thing is that the small number of lads who do go will all watch each other's backs and stand and fight. We have no runners, as some of the better-known lower league mobs have found to their expense. Doncaster took a slap when they came into town and thought it was clever to punch a local taxi driver. We fronted them outside Wetherspoons and they crumbled. They were an embarrassment and could not live with the fact that we had done them. The same thing happened after an FA Cup game at home to Walsall. They beat us seven-nil, gave it too much mouth in a pub and got trounced. Again they could not believe we turned up and smashed up the boozer with them inside it, we are only Macclesfield after all."

A "result" was claimed by the lads at Huddersfield even though not a punch was thrown. "We arrived early doors and fifteen of us went into their main pub, The Crescent," said Dave. "A couple of spotters in fake Burberry hats came in and were soon on their pay-as-you-go Nokias. After about an hour, more of their lads arrived and soon the police got on to it and escorted us to the ground in the interests of our own safety. One even asked if we had a death wish. After the game we tried to go back there but there was no chance with the full force of the Yorkshire dibble on to us. One of their lads told us we deserved credit as no other mob had done that to them all season."

Other turnouts in recent seasons have been against Bury and Chester, where they had thirty-five lads. Until the 2004/05 season, the Macclesfield and Bury mobs had got on well, but that changed after a misunderstanding between them. Bigger mobs, anything up to seventy-strong, went to matches against Coventry, Port Vale and Kettering.

With such a small crew it is no surprise that there have been no major police operations over the years, but recently undercover officers infiltrated the mob after complaints were made about an upsurge in racist behaviour at the ground. Dave admitted the problem was getting out of hand and also that the ease with which the police got into the small firm has made them very wary of any new faces that show on match days.

The first banning orders handed out to Macclesfield lads, imposed after fighting in Manchester city centre on the day England hosted Wales, decreased mob numbers further. It is common for Premiership managers to bemoan the fact that players come back from representing their country with injuries. With numbers as low as they are amongst the Rats, the last thing the firm needed was to lose members whilst on international duty.

MANCHESTER CITY

Ground: City of Manchester Stadium, formerly Maine Road
Firms: Cool Cats, Mayne Line Service Crew, Guvnors, Young Guvnors
Rivals: Manchester United, Leeds, Everton
Police operations: Omega

For many years, particularly in the 1970s, Manchester City was viewed as a family club. Perhaps it was when compared to city rivals Manchester United, whose Red Army was the scourge of football. But it still seems surprising, given that the ground was in the middle of Moss Side, which as far back as the 1960s had the reputation as a dangerous, unruly ghetto. Inside the ground, where rivals fans were often separated just by a rope, it was often no more welcoming.

"Maine Road had the potential to be a hotbed of violence," recalled Mickey Francis, once a prominent City hooligan, in his terrace classic *Guvnors*. "Crowds were huge, segregation crap, policing a joke. Away fans could easily get lost wandering around the narrow streets and dead ends, especially at night. We knew every nook and cranny, where to hide, where to wait, how to get away. Visitors were routinely escorted by the Old Bill but there were dozens of places to launch ambushes without being sussed. The police tended just to react after fights had already started, they weren't very good at preventing trouble. You could do almost anything and get away with it."

The supporters of Manchester City were involved in some of the earliest incidents of soccer violence in the modern age. Through the early Sixties, they fought rival fans on Merseyside and in Yorkshire. In September 1963, *The Times* reported how a terrified train guard watched as 200 Manchester City fans vandalised a train bringing them back from a match in Sunderland. The guard called police after he "had been threatened by the rioting mob of City fans" but the officers were unable to investigate after the guard refused to testify, saying he feared for his safety. A few months later, more than 100 light bulbs were smashed, lampshades were broken, luggage racks bent and tables torn out of a train carrying 343 City fans back from a match in Swindon. Derek Bailey, passenger manager for the Manchester division of British Rail, said they were "sick and tired" of hooligans on trains.

Home matches were marred by fans throwing objects onto the pitch, especially toilet rolls, but by the end of the 1964/65 season the club was confidently predicting that they had put an end to the trouble. They were wrong. There was disorder during City's visit to Huddersfield Town early the following season, fighting broke out with Leeds fans on a regular basis during the late Sixties, and the opening day of the 1967/68 season saw 12 people arrested after a home game against Liverpool. A trip to Stoke in September 1969 was marred with clashes during and after the match with Stoke City at the Victoria Ground. Eight people were arrested, all but two from Manchester, and several others were ejected from the ground. A police spokesman said, "We were kept busy all afternoon, but we have had more trouble at some other matches. One trouble spot after the game was at Stoke station where police were called in to separate rival groups of supporters."

Determined to take further action, in August 1970 the club announced its intention to build concrete pens at Maine Road to keep rival spectators apart. Nine pens were to be incorporated in a £350,000 stand due to be opened at the start of the next season. A Manchester police officer said, "Our main problem is preventing fans moving from one part of the ground to another. This scheme will make it easier." He said that in a capacity crowd of 60,000 fans only a few hundred caused trouble. The club and the police had recently been encouraged to identify troublemakers so their details could be distributed amongst other clubs.

Manchester derbies still guaranteed trouble. In 1970, bus companies in Manchester and Salford refused to carry football supporters to one match. City won the game 4-0 and forty-three people were ejected from the ground. Four years later, the two teams played each other twice towards the end of the season. The first was a home game at Maine Road, where the game finished goalless. The game was a dour but nasty affair, matched only by the intensity of the violence between rival fans. "Hooligan fans' trail of terror," read the headline in the *Manchester Evening News*.

> Householders and shopkeepers near Maine Road were counting the cost of the Manchester derby game violence that spread to the streets in an orgy or wrecking and terror.
>
> Rampaging mobs of fans smashed windows, damaged cars, and fought with each other. Damage is estimated at £800.
>
> Police were swamped with calls for help from frightened residents as fans went wild, hurling bricks and stones through windows.
>
> On one side of Kippax Street a long terraced row had hardly a house without a broken window.

Forty-five people were injured. The match itself was equally nasty, which was perhaps unsurprising as, in addition to it being a derby, United were languishing at the bottom of the division. An *Evening News* journalist pleaded that Manchester United's survival did not rest on the return leg at the end of the season.

"In the name of football sanity, I hope Manchester United's fate is settled before they meet Manchester City again in the final match of the season," he wrote. "Otherwise, we will be forced to witness a battle probably even more ugly than the scoreless, shameful affair at Maine Road. The prospect of a fight to the death at Old Trafford on 27 April is frightening if the situation is such that United need one or two points to stay in the First Division. The behaviour of both teams was a disgrace to these great clubs on a night when two players were sent off, four others were booked and 45 fouls committed – 22 by City, 23 by United. In addition, World Cup referee Clive Thomas called a five-minute cooling off period when

Mike Doyle and Lou Macari refused to go off after a clash in which they were both booked."

United's performances did not improve and they went into the final game, at home to City, knowing that even a win may not be enough to keep them up. It was a predictably fraught affair, played out in front of 57,000 spectators of which only 2,000 were Blues fans. With seven minutes remaining former United hero Denis Law back-heeled a goal into the United net. The City fans went ecstatic while United supporters swarmed onto the pitch to get the game cancelled. A local radio reporter described the events:

> There are now at least 4-500 supporters on the pitch on the pitch in front of us. They have their banners and their flags and they're really doing no good at all to the club that they are supposed to follow to the ends of the earth … and now there's a wall of policeman going forward, there must be all of 150 policemen and supporters are falling down … there is mayhem down there on the pitch that's meant so much to football. A policeman's helmet is lost and he's in some trouble, a policeman on the floor with three or four supporters on top, and then the wave of policemen come back again and try to make some sort of sanity and sense out of all this carnage, because it's the most wicked sight to see anywhere in the world but certainly at a ground which has meant so much, as I say, to this game … this game has been abandoned, the last that Manchester United will play in the First Division, certainly for one season, with the local club Manchester City. That's it then, the final scene at Old Trafford, a scene really of destruction and viciousness, a scene that one doesn't want to see repeated. From us all at Old Trafford, goodbye.

The game was halted shortly before the end, but the FA allowed City's 1–0 win to stand and United were relegated.

In 1975, the two sides met at Maine Road in the League Cup and there was widespread trouble. A police officer was struck on the head with a brick and 30 fans thrown out of the ground. Yet in the same season came a shortlived phenomenon known as the Manchester Coalition, which brought together City and United in a fight against common enemies, as United fan Ste Foy, aged 48, from Moston, remembered:

"In April 1975, the FA Cup final replay between Fulham and Birmingham was held at Maine Road. It was on a Wednesday night and proved to be one of the most violent encounters ever in Manchester. You had Fulham, aided by big mobs of Cockney thugs from various teams, then you had thousands of Brummie boot boys, skins, blacks and rastas, rockers and all sorts of thugs. Then you had, for the first and last time ever, a Manchester coalition: a truce was made between all the City and United gangs of Manchester. It was strange seeing Salford Reds alongside the Gorton Blues, sworn enemies for years before and after.

"All the Manc firms met in the Piccadilly Gardens at six pm. Present that night were the Reds of Stretford, Davyhulme, Chorlton, Wythenshawe, Salford, Cheetham Hill, Moston, Middleton and the City mobs from Moss Side, Gorton, Levenshulme, Denton, Failsworth, Stalybridge, Ardwick and Burnage. There must have been 500 lads all told, many wearing their respective scarves.

"All day, thousands of Brummies had been pouring into Manchester, and at five pm many of the city centre pubs were filling up with them. The Cockneys began arriving by train via Piccadilly a bit later, and there were many brawls outside the station between the Cockneys and Brummies.

"Meanwhile, this massive Manc firm of thugs marched towards Maine Road, and by the time they got to the ground many Brummies and Cockneys were already there. There was a mass punch-up on the forecourt outside the ticket office, well over 1,000 youths from all over England fighting and kicking each other. Added to this, the over-zealous Manc cops were wading in with their big sticks and many people got hurt badly. Dozens of ambulances and St John staff were tending the injured, cars were overturned, it was mayhem and this brawl lasted for twenty minutes before the cops brought some kind of sanity.

"Most of the Mancs made their way into the North Stand, a couple of hundred got into the bottom of the Kippax, whilst the Brummies soon filled most of the Kippax. Fulham and the Cockneys were in the top far corner of the Kippax. The Brummies terrorised the Cockneys for most of the game but when the gates opened for the last ten minutes, all the Mancs from the North Stand piled into the Kippax, up those huge concrete steps at the back. But the Brummies forced us back down and onto the car park. They outnumbered us greatly, they had thousands of lads. We Mancs grouped together on the car park and waited for the end of the match.

"At the final whistle, the Brummies came charging down the steps and onto the car park. They had lost one-nil and as the Cockneys celebrated, the Brummies were going apeshit, attacking the cops and any normal fans they came across who were not wearing Birmingham colours. Although we had well over 500 lads, the Brummies soon had us on our toes. Reds accused City of running and City accused Reds of running, the truth is that the coalition fell apart, and many City and United fans began attacking each other as they fled through the back streets of Moss Side. This played into the Brummies' hands, divide and rule, they really rampaged for the next couple of hours, many of them marching into the city centre smashing many bars up. The cops could not cope, although there were many arrests. City and United split up and just looked after themselves but neither made any impact against the mad Brummies.

"This failed coalition and the fact that the Brummies took over the Kippax, and indeed Manchester, really hurt. City and United fell out big time and both threatened to really turn each other over when they next played each other. Unlike the Scousers, Mancs could not stick together and the hatred between both sets of fans still exists to this day."

In 1977, United fans infiltrated the away end at Old Trafford to fight with their city rivals and then, in September 1978 there was serious disorder when City hooligans attacked United at the Brewers Arms in Market Street, central Manchester. Iron bars, lumps of concrete and bottles were thrown through the pub windows. Many of the next day's newspapers carried a picture of a City fan with a dart embedded. For the return fixture it was a policeman who was struck with a dart, though he had to share the media reports with the smoke canister that was thrown onto the pitch and the 122 people ejected as fighting broke out around the ground. Outside the ground a mob of 1,000 United chased a couple of hundred City for some distance.

There is some grudging respect from City's top lads towards their United rivals but it is also clear there is a sense of irritation at the media publicity given to them. "Let's be honest about this, they have had some tremendous turnouts at City," said Frank, who has been involved off the field at City games for three decades. "But I, like most City lads, know that they only have the same hardcore as us; the rest are sheep being led by the shepherds. Put City lads on Manc United lads and there is nothing in it whatsoever, in fact we probably shade it. It's not like that though and they come to our place with their 3-400 strong mobs and make a big show. They don't fare that well on the streets and in the pubs at night, believe me; City are a match for them once they get rid of those hanging onto their coattails.

"They brought big numbers in the Seventies and some games at Maine Road were like home games for them, they were all over the place. They always took over Platt Lane, once steamed the North Stand, but in the streets around the ground it is a different matter, they have had as many bad times outside as good times inside. At Old Trafford we have never had the ticket allocation they get at ours, so it has been hard at times. We took 250 lads about three years ago for a cup match and they were not as up for it as usual, which again proves the point that with them it is purely a numbers game."

Violence followed City around the country. A League game away at Oldham in August 1973 saw 20 arrests and dozens of ejections from the ground. In 1975 two fans were stabbed during a clash between City and Wolves fans. The same season saw 26 fans arrested at a match against Birmingham. Spurs brought one of the first firms to Maine Road in 1975 when 100 slipped into the Kippax, gathered at the back of the stand and then with a pre-arranged signal steamed down the terrace. Fighting broke out in other areas of the ground and after the match a massive City mob waited to teach the Londoners a lesson for daring to come into their end. Two years later, in April 1977, Middlesbrough brought a large firm down and they too attempted to take the Kippax. Hundreds of City lads repulsed their attack and the visitors were saved from serious injury only by the police, who escorted them around the ground. In between, there were 50 arrests as Man City fans clashed with Newcastle at the League Cup final in London.

The early City hooligans were loose alliances of young men, largely based on areas. There were the Beano Boys from Gorton, the Wythenshawe and Fallowfield firms and the Chadderton lads, who were closely aligned politically to the National Front. Despite Maine Road being in the middle of Moss Side, the emergence of black lads on the City terraces only happened from the mid-Seventies. The first recognisable mob was the Cool Cats, or Kool Kats, led by Donald Francis, the oldest of the three Francis brothers – the others were Mike and Chris. The Cool Cats were mainly black and mixed-raced lads, who found strength in unity. The NF contingent at City, led by lads like "Scotty", were a hostile bunch and the black lads from Moss Side could sometimes get picked off by their own fans if they wandered onto the Kippax on their own. According to one account, the Cool Cats finally confronted the white NF mob after Donald's youngest brother, Chris, was set upon in the toilets at one match. "We had had enough, so after the match we waited for them to leave the ground and as they came out we did them," recounted Donald in *Guvnors*. "We also stormed the Sherwood Inn, near the ground, which at the time was their pub. There was this fear factor of fifty coloured and half-caste guys. It is a psychological game."

The Cool Cats formed around 1974 and lasted until 1983. "The brothers ruled the roost," recalled Frank. "They could pull 400 lads for a big game, not just football lads. Say we were going to London, they would tell all the Moss Side lads it was going to be a big one and maybe an earner and loads would join us just to get away from their mundane lives. Like an excuse to hit back a bit at society. Same at home games, if they banged the drums the lads would respond."

There were always some white lads within the Cool Cats, but the older, more NF-orientated hooligans, kept their distance. Donald Farrar, a black City and England fan better known as "Daft Donald" because of his mad escapades (he used visitors' passports in the names Mike Tyson and Freddie Krueger and once boasted to a tabloid newspaper that he planned to "kill a Kraut" during the European Championships), described the uneasy relationship. "City had a big NF following but it was just at the time when they were prominent at the football. How the fuck can you have a big NF following when your ground is smack bang in the middle of Moss Side? There was the odd scuffle on the Kippax when we all started to go as a firm but soon the NF lads drifted away or gave it up."

For over 20 years the racial tensions were put on the back-burner until at the turn of the millennium they surprisingly reappeared. "At a night match at Stockport I saw the closest it has come to a major off between them," said Frank. "The brothers for some reason had pulled a quality firm of fifty blacks together and they went on an all-dayer in Stockport, all big blokes, all dressed immaculately, long black coats, the full hit. So it was an occasion of some sort, and in the stand they were in the Chadderton lads' faces, with all this, 'Come on nigger-haters, where's your fucking NF now.' It never went off but it was an unpleasant atmosphere and one which is very rare at City games. That night there would have been only one winner."

The Cool Cats, however, were just one of a number of mobs that followed City. Geography more than race was often the defining feature of the City gangs. The Cool Cats attracted fighters because of their growing reputation but were never able to unify all the disparate groups, and as a result City was quite disorganised. "The Kippax had the bootboys like any other club," said Frank. "They were replaced by the Cool Cats when the brothers came onto the scene, there were loads of white lads with them but the majority of the hardcore in the Cool Cats were black. We were probably one of the most disorganised mobs about, everyone did their own thing apart from the brothers' firms and because of that we never got the recognition many felt we deserved."

By the mid-Seventies, the Cool Cats were becoming widely known at a time when few big gangs had names. Its main heads would meet in the cellar of the Francis house near the ground before each game to draw up a strategy for the day. Transport would be arranged for away matches, and ambush points would be agreed for home games. One of them would even write to football grounds across the country ahead of City games, posing as a collector, to acquire match programmes and in the process get a layout of the stadiums, enabling ends to be selected for infiltration. There were even instances of "sussers" travelling to a town or city a few days before a game to suss out pubs used by local hooligans and possible meetings points for themselves.

One of the violent encounters during this period was an away tie at Everton in 1976. The Cool Cats organised six coaches for the short journey; in fact they were the only City mob to make the trip that day. Everton greatly outnumbered them as they attacked after the game, but it proved to be a defining moment for the City mob, who were told by their leader that running wasn't an option; not only would they not be allowed back on the coach but they would get a personal hiding. "We did the business but we had loads of casualties on the coach," one of them later recalled.

In September 1977, City were in hot water with UEFA after one of their supporters chased an opposing skipper who had scored the Polish team's second equalising goal in the UEFA Cup tie against Widzow Lodz. The tie ended in a draw and the one-man pitch invasion would undoubtedly have received more media attention if it had not been for Manchester United's violence in St. Etienne on the same night. As it was, City were still in trouble, as chairman Peter Swales was quick to recognise. "We have never had this sort of trouble before so the least we can hope for is a severe warning. At worst UEFA could order us to fence in the ground, something we certainly don't want to do. I don't think they could go so far as to impose a ban. That would be ridiculous."

Over the following few days, City decided to pre-empt the finding of UEFA and announced their intention to build a fence around the ground at a cost of £10,000. "It was a decision that was not taken lightly," declared Swales. "We don't want to fence in our fans but we must deter them from running on the pitch. We are certainly not happy about fences but it is a sign of the times. In fact we prefer to call them safety barriers. We already have them running along the length of the Kippax Street terraces and now work will start immediately to have them installed right around the ground."

One of the key hooligan groups at City drew its followers not from Moss Side but from an inner-city band of east and north Manchester. Though they didn't have a gang name, they included some of Maine Road's "top boys". Most are now in their mid-forties.

"It all started for us around the football season of 1974/75," recalled one of them, speaking on condition of anonymity. "We were just a group of friends from around Levenshulme, Beswick and north Manchester with one thing in common: Manchester City Football Club. We would meet in Manchester city centre in one of the amusement arcades on London Road on match days. There we would often wait for rival fans coming off trains and heading for the match buses to take them to Maine Road. If we were ever outnumbered then you'd have your belt off, because the belt was then the weapon of choice – a Levi belt buckle around the head.

"We would go to away games together, mostly by train though sometimes we would hitchhike from Knutsford Services. We would arrive in a town or city, ransack some of the shops for clothes and money, then on to the match, where sometimes we would try to get into the other fans' end for a punch-up. On a lot of journeys home there'd be someone with us who'd have clothing or money they'd made that day.

"Most of this took place from the mid-Seventies until the early Eighties. By the Eighties it was just match-day violence up and down the country. We were one of a few different groups who would watch City. All the groups knew each other but did their own thing. Now and then we would all mob up if some of the big boys arrived in town.

"Our main rivals throughout the Seventies and Eighties were Man United but some of the best planning and action was against the Scousers. Against Everton and Liverpool there was always a battle to be had, whether on Merseyside or in Manchester, and many of us older lads still carry the scars."

The East Lancs Road, and later the M62 motorway, were corridors to mayhem. From the mid-Seventies there were clashes between the four Manchester and Liverpool clubs, as the two cities competed on and off the pitch. The Manchester teams have never united to fight their Scouse foes, unlike the two Liverpool clubs, but City often used the choice of Maine Road as a regular FA Cup semi-final venue as an opportunity to ambush their fierce rivals.

Little changed in the Seventies, and if anything, as hooliganism began to get more organised and moved outside the stadiums, it got worse, as was evident in the serious disorder away at Goodison Park in 1976. There were tales aplenty of knife attacks and slashing. "Stabbed soccer fan fights for life," was the headline of the *Liverpool Echo* in March 1980 following a City game at Anfield. "A young soccer fan was fighting for his life in hospital today after a savage stabbing attack following last night's Liverpool–Manchester City Division 1 match," the article continued. "One stab plunged into 17-year-old Neil Jackson's right lung – while another deeper gash missed his heart by just an inch. The attackers also smashed a bottle over his legs and arms."

However, on this occasion the police believed that the City fan had actually been attacked by his own side after being mistaken for a Liverpool supporter because he was wearing the red scarf of his other favourite club,

Stoke City. An ambulanceman who took Neil to hospital told reporters that "he was lucky to be alive".

The following season, City played Liverpool in the League Cup and Everton in the FA Cup within a few weeks. The mayhem escalated. Liverpool won the first leg of the League Cup clash at Maine Road in a game that was overshadowed by violence away from the ground. The *Manchester Evening News* reported that rival gangs battled through the streets of Moss Side after the game. Several shops were attacked and in one instance fighting fans spilled into a sweet shop terrifying the staff.

"More than twenty Liverpool fans suddenly rushed into the shop. They wrecked the place when they played City in October and we thought we were in for the same treatment," said the owner's 37-year-old daughter. "But this time they were on the run from City fans. They said that if we didn't let them stay under cover in the shop they would take it apart. They were all men, not youngsters, but I still grabbed one round the neck," added the woman. "He was really scared and said he was just looking for somewhere to hide.

"But then a massive gang of City supporters gathered outside. There were fights going on in the road and in the shop doorway and the Liverpool fans were grabbing bottles and throwing them outside. They said some City fans were armed with knives." The only reports of knives being used, however, was the slashing of a 16-year-old City fan in the city centre.

Five people were stabbed at the second leg, on a day that saw 30 arrests. "It was a very busy night," remarked a police spokesman. "We think there may have been several more slashing incidents which were not reported."

There was further disorder when City went back to Merseyside for the FA Cup sixth round against Everton. "Rival Manchester City and Everton soccer fans fought in the streets of Liverpool this afternoon," reported one local paper. "There were ugly scenes at Lime Street station when the first train load of about 100 City supporters arrived for the FA Cup quarter-final tie. As they were leaving the station, they were charged by a mob of thugs and skirmishes broke out. Platform luggage trolleys were used as battering rams. It is believed that the attackers were Everton and Liverpool FC fans who had joined forces to do battle against the rivals from Manchester.

"One officer at the scene said, 'It's always the same when any Manchester fans come to Liverpool. The Liverpool and Everton supporters team up and go looking for trouble.'"

"Sometimes it was like a war zone there," recalled Frank. "We took one of the best mobs ever to Everton in the FA Cup. At the replay they brought a full squad and over the two games there was nothing between us. That season was the best ever in my eyes. Everton was worse than Liverpool for City because of the race thing, we would come out the ground and they would be onto us before you could even try and regroup, no hiding places for the black lads, all you could hear was, 'Get the niggers.' It was a frightening place for many of the lads, as it was pure hatred towards them." [see POLITICS AND RACISM]

Another key City rivalry was with Leeds United. There are reports of trouble between the two teams dating back from the mid-Sixties, but the hostility grew worse in the late Seventies, partly because City's black-led mob was an anathema to some of the racist Leeds boys. An FA Cup game at Leeds in 1977 saw the Cool Cats invade the pitch in an attempt to get the match postponed. It failed, and throughout most of the match Leeds fans stoned away supporters. A year later, again in the FA Cup, it was Leeds' turn to invade the pitch and the match was stopped for 16 minutes. City won the game 2-1 but after the final whistle 800 of their fans were ambushed by Leeds as they passed under a new subway on the way back to the station, causing panic.

It was an incident in September 1979, again at Elland Road, that really stirred the pot between the mobs. City fans came under attack from a barrage of missiles thrown from the home supporters, dozens were injured and 33 people arrested. Blues fan Ken Smith had taken his seven-year-old son to the game as a birthday treat but that did not prevent him being set upon by 50 hooligans, which left him with eye injuries and a suspected fractured skull. Leeds fans were dubbed "the worst in the country" and the club announced the closure of one part of the ground.

The City supporters' club reacted with understandable fury and urged their followers to boycott Elland Road for their own safety. "We are asking all Manchester City fans not to go to Elland Road – you can say we are making it a no-go area," club president and former City hero Roy Clarke told the media. "These Leeds fans want to declare tribal warfare on anyone who goes to see their matches. There was a constant stream of abuse directed at the City contingent. I faced some fearsome full-backs during my playing career but they were nothing compared to the louts who litter Elland Road."

Away from the formal club structures, the City hooligans were out for revenge and for the return fixture a reception committee was waiting. The threat of disorder led to three of Manchester's MPs following events closely on the day with a promise to send their findings to the Home Secretary. "Many City fans say they fear for their safety at places like Leeds and Liverpool. So we thought this match would be a good opportunity to see how things are done in Manchester," said Ken Marks, MP for Gorton.

The match passed off relatively peacefully. In the city centre, away from the eyes of the politicians, hundreds of rival fans battled it out near the Arndale Centre. One City fan was badly injured after being set upon by a mob of 30 Leeds supporters. He was kicked about the head and the body and had his wallet and watch stolen.

A 1–0 defeat at Halifax Town in the FA Cup in January 1980 was one of City's most embarrassing exits in recent history. Almost inevitably, some among the 7,000 travelling Mancunians caused carnage. The locals, too, were heavily involved. "A seething mass of Halifax fans marched through the town on a victory parade after Saturday's match at the Shay," reported the *Halifax Courier*. "Police made more than forty arrests, most of them after the game. Traffic was brought to a halt and shoppers left panic-stricken as Manchester City supporters were chased towards the Cross Field bus station. Wood, bottles and bricks were hurled by the visitors in George Square and only the use of dozens of police with dogs prevented a battle. The rampage lasted for more than half an hour until all the fans were persuaded to board buses and trains for home.

"At the final whistle, angry City fans chanting 'Allison out' poured out of the ground at the Shay Club end and ran out into Shaw Hill, jumping over hedges. A group of some 450 City fans headed straight for the town centre with 500 Town fans hot on their heels. Traffic came to a halt as scuffles broke out in the road and on the footpath outside the swimming baths. The two groups charged each other but no one was seriously hurt." Of 44 arrested, 23 came from Manchester and 21 from Halifax.

Away from the ground there was further trouble when a carload of City supporters stole a ball that was being used in an amateur match between the Irish Democratic Club and the Hebden Bridge Sports and Social club. The game had to be stopped nine minutes from the end after the ball went onto the road and was whisked up by the laughing fans. "The annoying thing about it is that we only bought the £25 leather ball two weeks ago and it was only the second time we had ever used it," complained the IDC team manager.

In 1983, the Cool Cats gave way to the Mayne Line Service Crew, more a change of name than of personnel. Some of the old crew did "retire" to be replaced by a new generation of casuals. The name was taken from a coach company, Mayne Line, which was regularly used. Flyers were printed under the new banner and passengers were informed that they travelled at their own risk. In common with other mobs at that time, they also circulated calling cards: "You've just been tuned in by the Mayne Line Motorway Service Crew."

However, like the Cool Cats before it, the Mayne Line was still unable to unite all the diverse mobs and, according to Frank, this is one reason why City's thugs are never talked about in the same breath as Leeds, West Ham, Chelsea and even Manchester United. "Many white lads did not want to be associated with the black gangs and went their own way. Had we have all joined maybe we would get the respect United believe they earned...."

There could not have been a more tense end to the 1982/83 season when City entertained Luton on the final Saturday. The Sky Blues were one place and one point above the drop – and bottom place was held by Luton. City had just won at Brighton and everyone thought survival was a probability, but a dreadful performance at Maine Road resulted in a 1–0 defeat, relegation and a pitch invasion that saw Luton players assaulted.

City were out of the top flight of football, but found themselves in a Premier League of hooligan mobs: Cardiff City, Portsmouth, Leeds and Chelsea were all in Division Two, while there was also the promise of northern derbies against Oldham, Blackburn, Huddersfield and Sheffield Wednesday. Over the next two seasons the Mayne Line and smaller City mobs were involved in violence at nearly all these places.

In January 1984 City fans hit the headlines when they rampaged through Blackpool. The attraction of the seaside resort made it an early start and the mob had arrived by 10.30am. Blackpool's Benny's Mob were out in force too, and got the better of at least one visiting mob near the ground before kick-off, but during and after the game the City contingent was too big to handle. The game was held up for several minutes as hundreds of City fans spilled onto the pitch and fought with the police. "It was just unbelievable that day," a member of the Young Guvnors, a City youth firm, later told the *Manchester Evening News*. "Our lads took liberties all day long. They robbed the club ticket office before the match and were selling tickets outside to City fans, so a lot of the City supporters got into the Blackpool end. When Blackpool scored their goals, all hell broke loose. The City fans turned on the police and started fighting them and the police backed off. A couple of Manchester lads had got on to the roof of the stand and were chucking the asbestos off. Chunks of it were falling down and our lads started throwing it at the police. That was going on for about forty minutes and the police could not control it."

For most City veterans, Chelsea stand out of all the London mobs as the most respected. City have struggled both home and away against the West London outfit, with the Friday night match in early May 1984, when Chelsea took up to 7,000 fans, being particularly well-remembered. "That firm was a hundred per cent the best to ever come to Maine Road," said Frank. "They were everywhere and we could not get near them that night.

No-one has ever come to City with a mob like that before and no-one ever will again. They had everything, hard men, numbers and organisation and in a nutshell we got fucked all over. They were in three ends of the ground, getting on the pitch and well up for it all day. They started arriving at midday for a night match and they ran amok, if the truth is to be told."

Of the other London firms only West Ham earned City's respect. "West Ham did very well about the same time, nowhere near as many as Chelsea but a quality firm and very well organised. Occasionally visiting firms went in the Platt Lane Stand and were not shifted, but the ICF went one better and 150 somehow made it into the Main Stand, all smartly dressed and all very game. For a few years the lads moved from the Kippax to the seats and the Platt Lane became a battleground, as a few of the braver firms came in and had a go. Leeds, Liverpool and Birmingham all showed their faces in there and did reasonably well, as did Everton who one year took us by surprise and took the piss, but they tried the same trick the following season and were chased onto the pitch. The soft cunts should have quit while they were ahead."

"Fans go on rampage at local derby," read the headline of the *Oldham Evening Chronicle* in April 1984, after a particularly violent Good Friday game. "Gangs of marauding soccer fans brought violence and terror to the streets of Oldham and Chadderton," reported the paper. "In an orgy of damage and destruction, they turned Good Friday into Black Friday. Windows were smashed, shops and pubs robbed, motorists stopped, assaulted and robbed." Ground staff in Boundary Park were attacked and four policemen were hurt inside the ground by the invading supporters, with City fans climbing over the security fence, running onto the pitch and storming the Ford Stand paddock in a bid to attack Oldham's mob. The police were powerless to stop them and home fans could be seen fleeing in terror. At one time the club chairman, Ian Stott, considered evacuating the entire stand and the game was held up for five minutes while discussions between police, club officials and the referee took place. "In the end we had to leave the entire stand to the invading fans," said Stott. "If we had tried to get them out, all hell might have broken loose and we couldn't risk that." A total of 37 people were arrested and a further 100 ejected from the ground.

The *Chronicle's* subsequent editorial was uncompromising. "If City don't win promotion to Division One, then we can only suggest, with regret, that Athletic go down to Division Three. At least that way we should be saved from the soccer animals and their mob rule."

One of the most violent incidents during the Mayne Line era was a battle against Stoke City at the Rothersthorpe service station, on the M1 in December 1984. City fans heading to Charlton Athletic arrived there just before a coachload of Stoke heading to Chelsea, and a huge ruck, lasting almost ten minutes, broke out all over the service station. Rival coaches were trashed, several people were hurt and 100 were arrested. One of those subsequently jailed was Donald Francis. This incident was followed, the next month, by an FA Cup exit at Coventry, with over 500 seats being ripped up and several stewards attacked. Two months later there was trouble at a night match against Birmingham, and the season was far from over.

In April, City played host to their old foes Leeds United. Predictably there was trouble. "Soccer hooligans went on the rampage in Manchester centre after City's clash with Leeds United," reported the *Manchester Evening News*. "A convoy of twenty-five buses carrying the Yorkshire fans from the Maine Road ground was attacked as it neared Victoria Station. Despite a heavy police escort, eleven buses were damaged and there were thirteen arrests for public order offences. A Greater Manchester Transport spokesman said seventeen windows were smashed and twenty seats were hurled from the buses."

City were still in a shout for promotion when they travelled to Notts County on the last Saturday of the 1984/85 season. However, the promotion party turned to disaster as City were routed 3-0. Their fans tore down sections of fencing and later poured onto the pitch, showering the police with an assortment of missiles. Both managers appealed for calm, with City boss Billy McNeil even telling fans that if the game was abandoned, as was obviously their hope, the points would still be awarded to County. After the match, about 40 City fans invaded the away dressing room. "I told them to behave for their fellow supporters, for themselves, and more importantly, for the team," McNeil later revealed.

"Soccer Shame!" was the front-page headline of the *Nottingham Evening Post*. "Not since 1975, when Manchester United fans ran amok, has the Meadow Lane ground witnessed such scenes." The paper's editor called for City to be relegated to Division Three as punishment. "Demotion has happened once before – to Peterborough FC in 1968 for financial irregularities," he wrote. "So why shouldn't it be done for serious law and order offences by hundreds of supporters? It would be tough on the punished club and their supporters. But we suggest that it would need to happen more than once or twice before it seeped through even the thick skulls of the morons whose animal behaviour sullies this great game."

The Mayne Line proved to be a short-lived affair, as older lads drifted away and others, like Donald were imprisoned. A few kept it going and before long the Guvnors was formed. Actually the name was stolen from a

City youth mob, the Young Guvnors, who announced themselves publicly in an interview with the *Manchester Evening News* in 1986. Under the headline: "Soccer's secret squad of scum", one of their members said, "We call ourselves the Young Guvnors because although we're the youngest, we're the best. United have always been reckoned to be the trouble club but at City it's worse. United's hooligans are living on a worn-out reputation. They're rated in London but nowhere else. City's hooligans are rated everywhere. Wherever you go, other clubs' hooligans say, 'We heard what you did last week.'"

With a full turnout of around 300, the mob moved out of the Kippax into the North Stand, where they occupied a large section virtually by themselves. However, the club's fortunes had slipped and promotion into the First Division in 1985 was quickly followed by relegation again in May 1987. Now they had to contend with matches against Bournemouth, Plymouth and Reading. Trouble, however, continued, with a number of clashes against Huddersfield, Wolves and Sheffield United – and Swindon, who surprisingly turned out in numbers at home and ran City.

The Levenshulme/Beswick lads too were still active. "By the time the Guvnors and Young Guvnors arrived on the scene, we were still doing our own thing, just a group of mates who had grown up together," said one. "We would stand on our own spot on the Kippax week in, week out, and when trouble came our way we were always up for it. The majority of other groups knew they could rely on us at City.

"Out of many good times following City, one of the best was Millwall away in 1986, because of who they were and what we did. These were the boys with the big reputation, it was the big one and most of our lot turned up. There's not many go there with 60-70 but we did and were drinking and walking around down there and had no bother until we reached the ground. There were no police with us at all during the day until we reached the Den, then there was a minor disturbance and the police got us all in the ground. We won the game 1–0.

"Some of the other groups had arrived on coaches, which by now had been smashed to bits, so the police decided to put us all together to go home on the train. With the whole group joined up there was 200-250 of us. Millwall tried to ambush us at London Bridge station but we chased them off. So we had got in and out of the Lion's Den with and without the police. Not many mobs could match that. Millwall have never liked us since that day. The few times we have played them in Manchester they've turned up with hundreds to get even but they haven't as yet."

In February 1988, 21 City hooligans were dawn-raided by Greater Manchester Police (GMP) as part of Operation Omega. For several months undercover police officers had been running with City, collecting evidence on its main faces and offences caused. The local paper revealed a catalogue of weapons seized and the *Daily Mail* noted a possible link to the National Front, a strange claim given the colour of the gang's leaders. For GMP, it was simply a case of "weeding out" the small minority of trouble-makers.

Either the problem was greater than they cared to admit or they had missed many of their targets, because only a week after this highly publi-cised raid a vicious fight erupted between City and United fans at Piccadilly station. The press dubbed it the "Battle of Piccadilly" and the hero of the day was PC John Duffy, who took on 60 thugs. For protecting his fellow officers he was struck over the head with a bottle and suffered a fractured skull.

The Omega trial was held at Liverpool Crown Court in February 1989 and in the end 20 fans were convicted. Several, including two of the Francis brothers, were sent to prison. While those convicted represented only a small number of City's mob, the trial and others pending had a sobering affect on those not arrested and many old heads suddenly adopted very low profiles.

At the same time, City were promoted back to the top flight. On their return they clashed with Bolton Wanderers inside and outside the ground, and then had two almighty tear-ups against Manchester United. The first, at home in September 1989, saw hundreds of United hooligans gain access to a home end and there was fighting throughout the match and again afterwards in the nearby streets. However hard they tried, the City lads could not budge 200 Reds from their end. The return fixture saw wide-spread trouble in the city centre. Hundreds fought pitched battles and one innocent United fan was left in a critical condition on a life support machine.

"It was absolute Wild West-style madness," said the landlady at the Crown and Kettle, a pub that was badly damaged in the mayhem. Doormen attempted to block the entrance to the pub but the fans burst their way in. "They hurled broken furniture through every one of our four-teen Victorian glass windows," she added. "There were eighty people inside, mainly women. We were all on the floors hiding under the tables and behind the bar, screaming as broken glass showered down. It lasted for seven minutes and it was sheer hell." The police estimated the damage at that pub alone at £30,000; the landlady, who had obviously checked her insurance policy, put the figure far higher. Overall, there were 20 separate incidents in the city centre alone.

"At that time we had a right firm," said City hooligan Tommy Gunn. "I was a teenager and I remember well the two firms, the Guvnors and the Young Guvnors. I was a tag-along, barely out of school, and weighed about ten stone. That operation ripped our firm apart, as it would any in the country. We, the kids at the time, were left to pick up the pieces over the next four or five years. A few older lads were left but no-one really had the leadership qualities that any of the jailed lot had, and instead of being a firm of 150 we became four or five factions of forties and fifties."

In the post-Hillsborough, post-Italia 90 era, the atmosphere around football was changing. Seating in stadia, ubiquitous CCTV, rising attendances and a middle class invasion of the game all conspired to dispel much of the old yob ethos. Families and fun were replacing wire mesh and fear. At Manchester City, this meant inflatable bananas and "Always Look on the Bright Side of Life". The hooligan or scally element, however, was never absent at a club whose roots were firmly working class.

"You had the Parkside pub firm and the Beer Monsters, who just took one or two coaches everywhere, basically a mixture of young and old lads from Wythenshawe, Moss Side, Fallowfield, Hulme and Whalley Range," said Tommy Gunn. "They were dealers, touts and weedheads who just didn't run because it wasn't in their dictionary. The Alty lot mixed and travelled with them but mixed it a lot with other firms without even looking for help. North Manchester consisted of lads from Chadderton, Moston, Failsworth, Droylsden, Hollinwood, Collyhurst. These are the lads who had to travel through the town centre for home matches and would hang about till the death for firms passing in and out.

"The Old Bill had succeeded in taking out the organisers, so we basically just met any thing that came our way home and away for the next few years. Just after this, United's raids [Operation Mars, which saw a number of alleged Manchester United hooligans arrested] hit the papers but the trial of all their big potatoes collapsed, much to the joy of their firm – stuffy cunts, as always. This left the brain of their firm well in place to organise one of the largest firms in the Nineties on the back of their success on the pitch. As much as I hate the Rags, I do respect their firm and a few things they did but to say they were invincible is laughable. As one lad once said to me, chop the head off the monster and the body falls to the floor."

In the 1992/93 season City twice clashed with Spurs in Manchester. The first was in a League game when the rival gangs battled it out behind the Kippax. The second match was an FA Cup tie, again at Maine Road, and this time hundreds of Spurs got onto the pitch and 37 people were arrested [see *Tottenham Hotspur*]. At the end of season, City hooligans and local doormen clashed with Everton thugs in Manchester City Centre. A league game at home to United in 1995 saw further trouble when the away hooligans again got into sections of the City end, causing sporadic fighting followed by more serious trouble afterwards.

A 2–2 draw at home to Liverpool in May 1996 meant that Manchester City finished in 18th position in the Premiership and so were relegated. A mid-table finish the next season was followed by further deterioration the year after, and when Man City travelled to Stoke City for the final Saturday of the season they faced almost certain relegation into the third tier of English football. While there was an outside chance of staying up, their fate lay in results elsewhere. Stoke City were in an equally precarious state, and with two of the largest hooligan gangs in the country lining up against each other, violence was always likely.

"City go down fighting," was the front-page headline in *The Sentinel*, the local paper in Stoke-on-Trent. That summed it up in several different ways. Stoke City and Manchester City were both relegated, despite a 2-5 thriller at the Britannia stadium and there was mass trouble throughout the day. Predictably, thousands of City fans made the short journey down the M6 and if that didn't prove enough for the Stoke hooligans, hundreds of City got tickets into the home end. Fighting erupted during the game and over 300 Man City fans were ejected from the home end. Play was stopped as hundreds of other fans fled across the pitch to escape the police. The intensity of the disorder grew outside the ground as Stoke mobbed up and attacked City fans and their vehicles with bricks, rocks and bottles. City fans responded by breaking down a seven foot high fence and rival gangs fought running battles on a nearby wasteland.

The violence was certainly not the worst involving City fans over the years but in the modern era it was substantial enough to hit the national press. A statement from the local police summed up the mood on what was a very difficult day for the boys in blue. "The circumstances of the fixture made it a very challenging policing and stewarding operation." It proved to be a very long day indeed. Later that evening there were serious disturbances between Port Vale and Stoke City supporters in Hanley and Kidsgrove [see *Port Vale*].

The following season, 1998/99, brought an unexpected encounter. "Eighteen of us got a mini-coach to Walsall away," said Tommy Gunn. "No mither, we thought, just a day on the piss. Anyway, we bumped into two of their lads in a pub on the outskirts. They said did we fancy a pop at their firm. We thought they were taking the piss but agreed and they said they would meet us at a pub. So twenty minutes later we pull up outside and bounce off the coach straight into the lads outside. As we're fighting in the car park it's getting sticky and we back ten yards to the road and let a few of their bods up. Then the pub empties and to be fair it was even numbers and we got fucking hammered. People on the deck, noses west, claret everywhere, we were in a right mess. I will never forget that day. We got to the ground and I was fucking ill, we were all ill: 'Fucking Walsall just minced us.' First time we had all been and we got blitzed. And we had fucking Millwall the following week!

"Anyway, the week of the Millwall game we were mobbed up all together for the first time in ages. Rumour was they were coming big style. Even Danny Baker said on his radio show that he had heard all the 'old boys' were out for that game. The friction between us and them stems from a time we got a result down theirs in the Mickey Francis and Mikey Williams days. I was too young so I cannot comment but their old boys had it in their heads that it was payback time and this was their first chance since then. They brought about 500, maybe 700, met in Stockport and then the Old Bill gripped them and walked them to the ground, closing off every street they went down and when we tried to have a go at getting near them or waiting in ambush another eighty-strong unit of TAG kicked fuck out of us and broke us up with horses. The Old Bill bung them on a train back to London so fuck-all happens.

"No! United are at Forest. Happy days. We make the call. They're on their way, then they're not, then they are. By this time it's eight bells at night. A lot of our lads are going local as they cannot see it happening. That leaves sixty or seventy of us in three different pubs. Then one of the lads from Chesterfield bells us that fifty United have just got off the facing platform.

"I walk up and have a spy and stand at the bottom of the approach at Piccadilly. They walk down with about eight robocops and that's it. It's dark, it's moody, it's right. But fifty, my arse; there was about 100. Still, United have always outnumbered us. We didn't give a fuck about numbers and never will. It's about quality, not quantity. As they get closer I walk to the Waldorf and inform the lads in there, a few in the Goose and a few in the Brunswick.

"They make their way off the concourse with O'Neill stood out like a sore thumb, holding his hand up like General Custer about ten back waiting to give the order. He can smell it – a trap. We give it the call on to United and the Old Bill are whacking a few back and the ones that get through have a bit toe-to-toe. Then the second pub empties, another bunch of City lads put up the shout. United heads turn, they're disorientated, Old Bill whacking them, City having it with them on one front and calling it on another. Heads gone, a few panic and they're split up all over the road. The Goose empties with more Blues. O'Neill's main twenty or so go for them and get stuck in as they are the ones in front of them. United's disciplined firm is fucked, fighting on four fronts. O'Neill's twenty or so go into the gardens down towards Portland Street but get fronted by the twenty we are with from the Waldorf. They come at us, a Blue to the left gets a full breeze block in the head, O'Neill's looking well with a large traffic cone over his head. More Blues from the back put up the call, then two Old Bill join in the anti-United brigade and start strapping them and they are on their toes across the Metrolink lines like greyhounds in disarray. And that is a fact – we've got the fucking CCTV.

"I respect every firm from every club but I rated Boro more than anyone in the Nineties, fifty to 100 lads max but stuck together and got results everywhere.

"United's main thirty were top notch and there's no denying it, strategic and large. But it was the fact that they never admitted when they had been done. They've spanked us a good few times but let me tell you we've returned the favour. And we have always turned up at theirs. We've been done off a good few firms, Walsall, Boro, United, Everton, Leeds, to name but a few, but we've played in three divisions in the last ten years and faced every cunt. We're not the best, never have claimed to be, but we would face any firm."

That season also saw trouble at matches against Wigan, both in the league and in the play-off semi-finals. City sneaked through and a penalty shootout at Wembley against Gillingham saw the club promoted at its first go. The other big incident during that season was a home game against Millwall. There had been some trouble at the fixture in South London earlier in the season but word soon circulated that the Londoners' trip north was the "big one". The events on the day were captured by the *MacIntyre Undercover* programme, which filmed a mob of about 1,000 lads making the trip north. There was considerable fighting that day but mainly between Millwall and the police. Despite the newspaper headlines, City were largely unimpressed with their visitors.

"Another load who believe their own hype," said Donald Farrar. "We went there a few years ago and they steamed onto the tube at London Bridge, there was nowhere for us to go and we fought back like fuck, it was a proper battle but I tell you something, when we fought back they lost it in the end and we chased them off the tube and out the station."

In January 2000, City were drawn at home to Leeds in the FA Cup. An NCIS report noted: "A group of 60 Manchester City supporters attempted to attack a group of Leeds supporters who were being escorted to the ground. Police kept the rival groups apart. At the end of the fixture Manchester City supporters attacked police officers with bottles and other missiles. A van belonging to visiting Leeds supporters was overturned and damaged."

The following month there was trouble at an away match at Huddersfield. "They have a good mob, they always had numbers out for us and City respect them," says Frank. "It's more of a big game for them but we would take a good size firm there as it was local and we knew they would be out for us." Donald Farrar agrees, but says on that day, like most others, City simply had the numbers. "We took some great mobs to places like that. We turned up there and took it to them and went through them all down that big long road on the way to the ground. They were typical of those type of small towns, hard, game lads but they could not cope with the numbers City took to places like that."

City were promoted back into the Premiership and the final game of their first season was at home to Chelsea. "At the final whistle home fans invaded the pitch and there was an exchange of insults between them and the visitors, which worsened," noted the NCIS report. "Police struggled to keep them apart and some disorder took place as rival fans fought across the segregation area in the North Stand. There was some damage caused and seats were broken and used as missiles. Police eventually restored order and the Chelsea fans were taken to the train station under escort. Large groups of City fans loitered in side streets adjacent to the ground and confronted the police. But they were eventually dispersed and order restored."

The trouble made the national press, though most City hooligans believe it was over-rated. "It was an incident that in this day and age warranted national news," said Frank, "but I suppose it was quite bad for today. They did not seem that up for it. City did all the hard work, getting on the pitch, getting into their seats, bit of a kick-off but nothing special."

"Chelsea were poor," bemoaned Farrar. "We piled on the pitch and steamed into them. Some lads broke the segregation in the seats and went into them. Well overrated, Chelsea. They shit themselves that day, they have always been good with the numbers game, like the year they came on a Friday and took most of the ground but even numbers I don't and never have rated them and that day was a perfect example of how bad they are."

The return to the Premiership brought City up against their old foes United once again. The mutual acrimony had never gone away, with mobs clashing regularly in the city on match days, but there was nothing like a Manchester derby to pull out the numbers. In November 2000, police escorted a 400-strong United mob to Maine Road, whilst separately, a coachload of United fans was attacked with bricks and bottles. After the game, hundreds of City hooligans attempted to attack the United escort, some throwing smoke bombs and distress flares, which the police admitted "added to the confusion".

Two months later, the two mobs clashed again. City were playing Leeds at home, and Manchester United were away at Bradford. Afterwards, about 400 City supporters gathered in a city centre pub to await the return of United. Shortly after 9pm, word reached them that their enemy was back in town and the mob left en masse. An attempt by police to halt their progress was met with bricks and bottles. "The disorder continued for some time," recorded the police. "Incidents of disorder were reported all around the city centre until 2am involving both City and United factions."

The same season saw 70 United hooligans attempt to pass themselves off as City fans in a bid to get into their rival's home game against Southampton. Detected, they decided to head for a pub near Oxford Road. At a public house further down the road a similar number of City fans had gathered. It was only the swift intervention of the police that prevented the two groups clashing halfway along the street.

City played away at Old Trafford in late April 2001 and took a mob of 150-200 to the ground. Some did not have tickets so after being turned away from the stadium they returned to the pub. Their movements were known to United and a short time later the two mobs clashed and a number of arrests were made. "The groups then moved into the city centre where several attempted confrontations were prevented by police," noted the police report. "The City group then attacked a public house containing around 40 United supporters, windows were damaged and missiles thrown, resulting in further arrests. Later in the evening there were a number of running battles and further arrests were made."

At around the same time, magistrates in Manchester temporarily forced a city centre bar, the Athenaeum, to close on Saturdays because it was used as a base by City hooligans. On one match day, according to police, a mob of 60 left the pub carrying weapons, intent on confronting United fans. "We have been called at least four times in the last year because large numbers of Manchester City fans have been helping themselves to alcohol from behind the bar or, on one occasion, trying to steal money from the till," said an officer.

Violence involving City is nowhere near as bad as previous decades, but it does still occur, particularly at matches with United. The last derby at Maine Road before its closure saw one such clash, as a City hooligan describes: "United wanted this result more than anyone. Early in the day, they had numbers as usual, with good organisation, whilst in the City camp every lad possible was in attendance. The South Manchester firm turned out with a lot of older lads who really wanted a few scalps and were never going to let the Men in Black have an easy day.

"Before the match the police were all over both firms, with City stationed on Wilmslow Road near the Clarence and Sherwood pubs while

United were bringing attention to themselves by hassling scarfers in the Beehive. The Guvnors organised a split and meet at the Salutation in Hulme, a boozer off the beaten track but a good location to regroup. United moved on to the Denmark pub thinking it was going to be an easy day, as they had a good 200 lads. At the Salutation, City's numbers were about 200 also, but with lads who were experienced, fit and game as fuck.

"City spotters saw United coming towards the Science Park in Hulme. The shout was given to the Salutation and the Guvnors stayed calm and walked, with tactics being shouted by the older heads. Darkness had crept in and the MiBs were showing up as shadows in the distance. Both firms ran into each other, with the dark firm of City throwing a few large airbombs into the MiBs, one lifting a MiB about two feet off the floor. United's firm were split by a four-foot hedge and, with Old Bill steaming them from behind, this put the Guvnors on the front foot, ploughing into United and splitting their ranks. One unlucky rag received a full log of wood right across his napper as the Guvnors took no prisoners. The front 40 or 50 United fought and fought and none of them ran, but they were constantly fighting on their back foot, picking their mates up. This was City's day, on and off the pitch."

The 2006/07 season saw City and United's firms again battle it out, this time at the King's Head in Ardwick, after the derby at the City of Manchester Stadium. The police closed all pubs near the ground after the match so made it impossible to drink locally. "The route the MiBs had to take back to town in taxis passed the King's Head where a mixture of old and young City fans and old lads were sat outside in the beer garden," said a City lad who was there. "City noticed taxi after taxi floating past. The older City agreed not to go looking for trouble as it would just lead to charge sheets and sentences that no-one could afford. If United were going to come then City would have it, but they weren't going to leave the pub and go looking for it in a city flooded with CCTV cameras. City numbered about 60 in total with about 40 good lads, and the rest just straight-going fans.

"United arrived at the pub, with many of them tooled up to the max, bricks, bottles, wheel braces, metal pipes, the lot. A shiny fella was pulled out at one point. United walked to the pub with possibly the same numbers, maybe more, but none of City were counting, just fighting like fuck. United blitzed the pub with cries of 'War! War!' while City stood, taking blow after blow. Some City ran into the pub to escape the bombard-ment of bricks, bottles and scaffolding clips, and after two minutes of mayhem, City were left with probably 15 lads outside the battered pub, surrounded by up to 60 of the MiB's main firm."

Another City lad recalled, "The Blues I stood with outside that pub were the bravest lads I have ever had the honour of being friends with. We were outnumbered due to City lads going in the pub due to the ferocity of the bricks and bottles thrown. In my eyes there was no shame in that. The pub and a silver Astra were blitzed. It looked like a bomb had gone off in the street.

"After two minutes I think the MiBs were so shocked that the fifteen City actually stood that they froze due to the intensity of this battle. While they did, the fifteen City, most covered in blood, were well past the pain barrier. They just carried on by picking up dropped tools and regrouped and ran into United again and again, battling and battling. Twice the fifteen had the front United running back into their rear ranks. I have never seen or been involved in anything as mental in all my days. If anyone has ever seen the Ducky Boys fight with the Wanderers at the end of the film, times that by two. One City fan was in a coma for thirty-six hours and put on a life support machine and nearly died. The battle lasted for over twelve minutes and police sealed the area off for forensics for twenty-four hours. The City fan recovered but his son nearly lost a father.

"I saw Reds and Blues throwing up during the fight. I myself was sick during and after. Your adrenalin was rushing that much that your stomach turned. Also the horrific injuries sustained by both sides were like something out of a war film. These were two sets of lads from Manchester set on killing each other over football. It made me sit down at home for a solid week and look at my kids and think what the fuck was I doing. What the fuck were we all doing? What was it for? Was I proud of it? What did anyone achieve?

"I had actually grown up with lads in United's firm, for fuck's sake. In fact some were even related. What I do know is a young boy nearly lost his father, and a man lost sight in one eye, all over football. The weird thing is, after the battle most lads from both firms involved in this have walked away from football totally. I think it was the mother of all battles and no one involved wanted to witness those scenes ever again. A lot of people from both sets of fans were scarred for life mentally and physically."

The 2007/08 season saw a visit from Birmingham City's Zulu Warriors, on the twenty-fifth anniversary of the day they had first come together and used their "Zulu" chant – at a game at Maine Road. A big firm of old Zulu heads turned out to celebrate. Coincidentally, it was also the twenty-first anniversary of the formation of the Guvnors and needless to say, when the clubs met in October 2007, it went off with some style. "Although quite a few lads from both firms may eventually regret getting involved, it was a cracking party," said one Zulu veteran. "We picked the City game as that's where the first Zulu chant went up all those years ago and we knew we'd be sure of a quality turnout. City returned the compliment and we had trouble not seen in the ground for years. It was all a bit daft really, as it is all on film and every knock on the door sends alarm bells ringing. Outside City had a good go and at times the local OB seemed to lose control. The trouble went on for ages."

Yet most are of the opinion that the old days are gone. "Association banning orders, three years' jail for throwing a punch, it's time to call it a day," said Tommy Gunn. "It was a buzz and a rush, especially when you were outnumbered. You find out who the men are in your firm. But the Old Bill and the courts have too much power. If you're still doing it, you must be mad."

Further reading: *Guvnors*, Mickey Francis (Milo Books)

MANCHESTER UNITED

Ground: Old Trafford
Firms: Red Army, Cockney Reds, Inter-City Jibbers, Men in Black
Rivals: Manchester City, Liverpool, Tottenham
Police operations: Mars

An atmosphere of fear hangs over the residents who live near Hillsborough football ground as the countdown to the Cup clash between Manchester United and Leeds begins.

The picture is grim and distressing as families and elderly people who live by themselves remember last year when Manchester's notorious fans were in town for a FA Cup semi-final.

- Young married women are going on a course of Librium because of their nerves according to a local councillor.
- Windows of many homes will be boarded up.
- Children and pets will be kept inside.
- People with cars are making plans to leave their vehicles with friends, well away from the ground.
- Housewives are having to alter shopping plans because they know local traders will be closed on Saturday afternoon.

The *Sheffield Star*, which devoted three pages to the terror generated by the impending arrival of Manchester United in the Seventies, was not alone.

Across the country, Manchester United, or more aptly their vast, travelling Red Army, were pariahs, unwelcome visitors who left a trail of devastation wherever they went. Violence followed them virtually everywhere they went throughout the late Sixties and Seventies. Any absence of conflict was normally only because the locals were too scared to show their face.

Reports of trouble involving United supporters date from the late Fifties when, like their Merseyside counterparts, they were involved in train wrecking and vandalism. By the mid-Sixties, with a successful and glamorous team on the pitch, they were starting to develop the country's biggest support, with a reputation for rowdiness, and the massive Stretford End at Old Trafford became one of the best known and most notorious "ends". But it was probably a match at Upton Park in 1967 that brought hooliganism into the popular consciousness and the Red Army to near mythical status. The match against West Ham was overshadowed by mass disorder by Manchester United fans before, during and after the match [see: West Ham] in what was regarded by many as the "taking of the East End" – something no other crowd had ever done.

By now there were also regular battles closer to home, particularly with the supporters of Northern rivals Liverpool, Everton and Leeds, all three of which had successful teams of their own in this period and big travelling support. Disorder became so common that in 1967 the club banned flags and banners from the ground. "They are a great source of provocation to visiting supporters," noted a local police officer, "and they can be used as weapons."

A match at the beginning of the 1970/71 season saw Manchester United play away at Wolverhampton Wanderers, then one of England's top teams. The match was accompanied by mass disorder and 31 arrests. The sight of "football special" trains disgorging thousands of drunken, scarf-bedecked juveniles was starting to become common on Saturday afternoons and policing methods were constantly evolving to contain them. At home, United fans turned Old Trafford, and more particularly the Stretford End, into a fortress. What was special about this, David Robins concluded in his book *We Hate Humans*, was that, contrary to other clubs, the fans were not drawn from one location. "The Stretford was a new phenomenon – a non-territory-based mob, with nationwide connections from the Cockney Reds and the Tartans of Belfast to branches as far away from Manchester as Dover and Deal in Kent," he wrote. "The Stretford regularly picked up ... tearaway elements from the disparate fighting crews in the cities they invaded. If you were out of work, a school failure, with little to do and nowhere to go in your area, there was great appeal in joining up with the Red Army."

United's main rivalry over the years has of course been with Manchester City, a rivalry in which the Red side of the city claims to have always had the upper hand. "When it comes to City I can honestly say the best fights were always in their Kippax," remembered Colin Blaney, author of the book *Grafters*, who comes from Collyhurst on the north side of Manchester. "I really believe the Kippax was the most popular end in the UK [for invasion], with only Arsenal's North Bank seeing as much action. When I think back to the Sixties and the Kippax, the first thugs I ever saw were all Mods and it was an Amateur Cup final replay and was Cockneys versus Scouse, Enfield versus Skelmersdale. No weapons, just small mob fights. The real street fighting went on for over an hour. I was well impressed with the day but never had a clue who won, on or off the field.

"Years later, when we were all active fighting City in the middle of the Kippax Street, police used to put a rope right down the centre thinking this, with a few Dibble down the side, would quell the boots flying in. Even better fights happened at twelve bells in Albert Square every New Year. If City didn't turn up we'd fight north side Manchester versus Salford. Brutal fights and I can't remember winning one."

There were reports of serious disorder at Manchester derbies from 1970 onwards but it was a match in April, 1974, that saw the mighty United relegated, that really grabbed the headlines. Manchester United fans swarmed onto the pitch towards the end of the game in the hope of getting the match abandoned [see MANCHESTER CITY].

With United already down, the authorities in Stoke-on-Trent braced themselves for the final match of the season. "Dozens of extra police have been drafted into Stoke and all leave has been cancelled in a bid to ward off any trouble at tonight's match," reported one newspaper. Shops near the ground were advised to close and police ringed the pitch to prevent fans from storming the pitch. Meanwhile, Sports Minister Denis Howell condemned the incidents at Old Trafford the week before as "outrageous". Despite the police's best plans there was still trouble and 15 people were arrested. After the game, rivals pelted each other with bricks as United fans rampaged through the city.

Life in the Second Division proved to be no disaster for Tommy Docherty's rejuvenated team and also brought the Red Army to smaller towns and grounds, and at almost all there was trouble. Placed a clear first in the *Daily Mirror*'s "League of Violence" as "the team whose visit is most dreaded", an estimated 10,000 United fans descended on London for their opening game against Leyton Orient, clashing with Arsenal who were on their way out to a game at Leicester. At Orient, thousands of Reds stormed the gates and invaded the pitch twice, forcing Sir Matt Busby to make appeals for calm over the ground's loudspeaker. United's next game was at home to Millwall, who unlike most teams, brought a mob to Old Trafford but were run ragged – some were allegedly unable even to leave the confines of Piccadilly train station, so big was the mob waiting for them. The Red Army weren't quite so brash at the return fixture in South London, when a traditional Cold Blow Lane welcome terrified many of them.

For the next game, Manchester United played away at Cardiff, a fixture that evoked mixed emotions. For the authorities it was a nightmare, for the hooligans it was heaven. There was a media frenzy in the days running up to the match which, some would argue, made trouble more likely. For the hooligans however, there was little need for encouragement; as soon as the fixtures were announced, both sets of fans began preparing.

United veteran Colin Blaney was part of the massive Red Army mob – sometimes referred to as Red Devils – who made the trip to Wales. "I can still remember clear," he said. "Cardiff all looked like my cousins from Northern Ireland: suedeheads with slick long lamb chop sideburns, all the spit of the paramilitary, with braces and those huge Doc Marten twenty-something laceholes."

Almost as soon as they arrived in the Welsh capital there was aggro. "We agreed to meet at the massive swimming baths but were immediately ambushed. The first mistake was that the Collyhurst crew had forgotten to take off the Salford Van Hire stickers and our vehicle was trashed. The second mistake was that we had no tools when we got attacked and ambushed. What saved my bacon, being first one out, was a steel comb, I was just lashing out wild. They backed off thinking we all had blades but within seconds they had twigged and were all now steaming back into us.

"We snapped off the nearest car aerials then lashed out with them when the pack got near. Then we legged it full pelt right through the High Street all the way to the train station. Then what a sight, all incoming trains full with hordes of Bluebirds from the Valleys baying for English blood.

"The police were trying to keep things together but very soon it was all gonna kick. Lots of Devils had already been busted up and were almost ready to jump the first train out. Then just at the right time the Cockney Reds' train came in and they restored order on the approach. Reports of running battles and locked or smashed up pubs came flooding in as the Manchester special arrived.

"Fuck me. When it came in the noise was something else. 'Tommy Doc's red and white army!' First off were all the lads, George Lyons, Gaftney and Rosko, all ready to rumble. The waiting Cardiff mob was huge, all at the bottom of the ramp, but we were 1,000 strong and we just

burst through the police lines and shattered Cardiff and it was a-mobbin'
and a-robbin' all the way to the ground – we got that saying after Leyton
Orient when we'd steamed all the offies, but this day we done almost every
shop and it was on par with the feeling of really taking over, 'Shag your
women and drink your beer,' et cetera.

"We all jumped the turnstiles into their end but we soon realised it was
a no-go, as they'd spent fortunes on the fencing and barbed wire. So we
were caged into this stupid corner with Cardiff a stone's throw away – and
plenty of stones, half bricks, bottles and missiles did rain down on us."

The Red Army had brought 8-10,000 followers and most were placed
in the huge open end. The first half kicked off only for fighting to break
out on the terraces and punches soon gave way to darts and kung fu stars.
One catalyst was the sick chanting on both sides, with United fans
responding to taunts about the Munich Air disaster by singing about
Aberfan, the tragedy when a coal slag heap engulfed a village school, killing
many children. This raised the mutual animosity to boiling point.

"At the end of the game we all knew it was gonna kick off and to get us
in the mood Willis cracked a copper full on the chin as we left the ground,"
continued Blaney. "Then it went mad. I'd never seen or been involved in
mob fighting on this level. It went on all around the stadium. We even ran
back into the ground on the other side and attacked any cunt, as it seemed
that day it was all about national pride.

"Outside the mobs were still full on fighting. It was ultra-violence. It
was also a culture shock for their heads. Taffs were really in a time warp.
The Red Army was a mixed lot, all done up in boneheads, butchers' coats,
bovver boots and braces, while our lot sported Rod Stewart barnets called
carrot tops or pineapple heads, all had beards or bushy porkchop sideburns, long hair, polo necks, tartan scarves, tank tops, semi and full flares
over our suede desert boots from Clarke's. Cockneys wore the top sheepies
and some even wore Afghans.

"No mob has ever been able to claim the result from that day. I can only
speak for the north side lads who were there and we had the best day of
our lives, even though half of us were in need of hospital treatment."

United literally took over smaller grounds and town centres. An estimated 20,000 were locked out of Blackpool's ground when United played
there and at least 10,000 packed into Hull's ground during the same
season. Another 20,000 made up more than half the crowd when the team
played at Hillsborough in December 1974; there was widespread trouble
and over 100 arrests, and for a time it appeared that the game might be
abandoned. The violence erupted 30 minutes into the game when Man
United fans climbed over the barriers and ran across the pitch to join in a

fight at the opposite end of the ground. "Fighting spread on to the corner of the pitch as scores of police, some on horseback and others wearing white crash helmets, battled with fans," reported the *Sheffield Star*. "At one time, more than a dozen fans were lying injured on the grass waiting for stretchers to take them to the first aid room."

After similar clashes at Oldham, Oxford and Bolton, the Red Army travelled to Notts County in May for the final game of the season, with promotion secured. Once again, their fans took over the area and on the final whistle they stormed the pitch while others ripped up seats.

United were back up and with them returned old rivalries. In October 1975, they played Man City in the fourth round of the League Cup. "City had built up a reputation whilst we had been in the Second Division and thought they were Manchester's top team both on and off the pitch, but United took their end off them, the famous Kippax," recalled 49-year-old Martin "Psycho" Sykes from Ashton-under-Lyne. "The word had been doing the rounds for weeks prior to this match that United must take the Kippax to shut the fuckers up once and for all. We knew City had a tough crowd but we would have far too many for them, and every Red firm for miles around were going to this match.

"Our firm were the Ashton Reds. Only five miles from Manchester, Ashton-under-Lyne was a Red stronghold surrounded by the Blue strongholds of Droylsden, Stalybridge and Denton. We had a mob of fifty-plus lads, aged seventeen to twenty-two. Our dress code for the night was donkey jackets and working boots, as most of us worked on various building sites, and we met up at five pm and began boozing before jumping on the bus into Manchester. On the bus we kicked fuck out of any City getting on, which was quite a few as we passed through many City areas. We got into Manchester City centre for six pm and Piccadilly Gardens were full of Red mobs from Salford, Collyhurst, Middleton, Wythenshawe, Oldham and Eccles. Altogether we had a mob of 600 and we marched as one mob the two miles to Maine Road.

"We smacked loads of City fans on the way, but they could only muster mobs of fiftyish. We did not even have a police escort and just ran amok, robbing all the Asian shops and off licences on the way. As we approached Maine Road, we saw a mob of 300 City, who came at us, but our greater numbers soon had them on their toes and we rampaged around the ground for half an hour, overturning hot dog stalls. Our mob had now swelled to over 1,000 lads. The cops could not cope with us and many shops and houses had their windows smashed.

"Half of us got into the Kippax and the cops shoved us all in the top far corner. By kick-off, though, City had a massive mob in and outnumbered us greatly. They came charging into us every few minutes and though we fought back many of us got hammered. Meanwhile, United were all around the ground, with one of the biggest turnouts of lads at any football match in Britain, literally thousands of lads. City were being very brave, picking off lone Reds.

"At half-time, we charged across the Kippax and into the City mob and we gained half the Kippax and we could not be budged. When the gates opened at three-quarter-time, hundreds more Reds came piling up the steps at the back of the Kippax, and most of the City mob fled towards the bottom of the pitch, many climbing onto the pitch. Within a couple of minutes we had taken the Kippax. City still had more than us but they bottled it, apart from a couple of hundred diehards who fought bravely but were soon overwhelmed. By the end of the game United had control of most of the Kippax as hundreds more joined us. It was a great feeling and one that we have boasted about ever since, and that cannot be denied. A mob of over 2,000 lads then marched victoriously back into Manchester city centre, proving without any doubt who the 'kings' of Manchester really were."

The same month saw United play at Upton Park for the first time in years. With the memory of their visit in 1967 still raw in the minds of the East Londoners, a siege mentality gripped the area. Underground staff went on strike rather than ferry United fans across London and hundreds of police and stewards were employed. More significantly, the area's thugs turned out in force to attack the visitors, in particular in Upton Park's South Bank, where they launched a series of assaults on United supporters. One national newspaper reporter spent the afternoon with the police officers trying to contain them:

Even before the game began the lines of policemen knew something was going to happen when they heard that chillingly prophetic chant echo around the ground.

'There's gonna be a nasty accident,' chorused the Manchester United fans. Well-versed in sensing impending crowd violence, they waved hundreds of red and white scarves aloft like an army of medieval knights twirling maces before a battle.

And it wasn't just the little boys in bobble hats who looked frightened – the police were throwing nervous glances at each other as well.

'Christ, if I have to go in among that lot, I'll nick the first one I see causing any bother and then he'll be out and I'll be out too,' said [a PC] as he faced the supporters glaring down from the South Bank.

Every five minutes the sea of heads in the South Bank parts as another fight breaks out.

A harassed policeman back from the South Bank says: 'The West Ham supporters are goading the Manchester lot. They're pushing them back into the corner to force a fight. It's evil in there.'

Evil it was. The game was held up for 19 minutes as fans seeking to escape the fighting became crushed against barriers and had to be helped on the pitch. Injured children were carried out on stretchers and more than three dozen people were arrested. Newspaper headlines highlighted the Red Army's comeuppance: "The Day The Terrace Terrors Were Hunted Like Animals and *Hammered!*" gloated the *Sun*. Not surprisingly, the London club banned away supporters for United's next visit to Upton Park.

The 1976/77 season was one of the most violent in United's history. The August Bank Holiday weekend saw a short trip to Derby County and once again the newspaper reports were full of the violence that erupted inside the ground. "Derby Riot!" ran the headline in one.

Manchester United fans resorted to the behaviour which has disgraced their club's great name by inciting a pitched battle at Derby yesterday.

At the end of their side's goalless but captivating game a horde of United followers swarmed over the barriers.

They hurled bottles and tin cans and aimed punches and kicks at everybody who got in their way as Derby's fans accepted their challenge to fight it out.

It took the police 10 minutes to get anything like order as they struggled to clear the area.

But then the fighting started up almost as terrier-like on the terraces. Girls screamed as the boot was going in and the goalmouths, which only minutes earlier had been the scene of fine football action, were used as clearing stations for the injured.

By now, any fixture against Manchester United brought fear and trepidation to the home police force. United's visit to West Brom in October 1976 saw 1,000 police mobilised for the game in the expectation that the 20,000 United fans would cause trouble. "People left their homes, boarded up their property and closed shops and pubs as the 'Red Army' descended," noted one Midlands newspaper, for what became the largest ever police operation conducted by West Midlands Police around a single football match. With the memory of United's previous visit in 1974, when their fans rampaged through the local area, the police were determined to prevent United fans arriving early and getting drunk. "Coaches and trains carrying United supporters to the match against Albion were banned from the town until an hour before kick-off in a bid to keep the centres of West Bromwich and Smethwick peaceful," the paper continued. "People carrying bottles or cans or wearing 'bovver boots' or steel helmets will not be allowed into the ground," commented one senior police officer. The game passed off relatively peacefully with "only" 79 arrests, down from the 100 for United's last visit. "They were outmanoeuvred, and out-generalled by our officers," said one policeman.

But it was a game away at Norwich City, in April 1977, that was to signal the crackdown that ended the Red Army heyday. A stand was damaged, 30 people were hurt and 19 arrested as United fans went on the rampage. One youth was filmed falling 40 feet from the roof of the away stand and then was attacked as he was led away on a stretcher. In an attempt to restore order, United boss Tommy Docherty came onto the pitch before even a ball had been kicked but he too became a target, as he was showered by missiles including a lump of concrete. Sheets of asbestos were ripped from the roof of the stand and hurled onto the pitch.

"Red Alert: Howell is ready to act," ran the front-page banner headline in the *Manchester Evening News* the following Monday. As Sports Minister Denis Howell threatened to impose new curbs on United's supporters, the club, its supporters' club and the manager lined up to condemn the minority causing trouble. The Norwich disorder came after major disturbances earlier in the season at Tottenham and Southampton. On the back page there was an interesting story highlighting the dilemma for United's opponents. "'War' or peace? That's the choice for clubs. Do they want to risk the trail of destruction that the bandits in the huge Red Army are capable of leaving? Or do they want to boost their attendances and pick up the extra gate receipts involved with entertaining Manchester United?"

The prospect of action against United proved to be correct as the football authorities met the Sports Minister and decided to make their future away matches all-ticket affairs, with all terracing being given to local fans. In the meantime, some clubs were answering the "war or peace" question themselves. Bristol City was the first to announce a ban on all United supporters for the early May fixture, and they were soon followed by QPR, though this was not to apply for that current season as they had already allotted 8,000 away tickets for the game. United reacted with fury, with Tommy Docherty leading the chorus of protest. "By banning our fans from travelling," he claimed, "Denis Howell is helping some clubs along the road to extinction."

Docherty went out of his way to praise the Red Army at United's next game, at home to Stoke City. Sending a special Easter message to the club's fans, he said, "The gates at Old Trafford have been the key to making Manchester United so strong and confident. Many clubs are up to their eyes in debt but thanks to you people, we have been able to stand independently in a game beset by financial worries." Not everyone shared his faith in the Red Army. Two hundred miles away, police in Sunderland were preparing for United's next game. "The 220,000 people of Sunderland held their breath, crossed their fingers and hoped for the best," cited one newspaper report. However, much to everyone's relief the game passed off peacefully, with just one arrest.

The restrictions on travelling fans did not apply to Manchester United's FA Cup semi-final with Leeds at Hillsborough, and predictably the Red Army travelled over in their thousands. In fact there were far too many for the ground, so thousands were locked outside, which itself became a cause for trouble. "Hillsborough's angry residents pick up the pieces," headlined the *Sheffield Star*. The police reported damage to cars and houses "caused by hundreds of rampaging and ticketless Manchester United fans". There was further trouble inside the ground after attempts to segregate the rival fans failed completely. Celebrations from Leeds fans after their side scored was the signal for further trouble, again inside and outside the ground. After the match Leeds fans were attacked as they left the ground.

With United fans facing increasing restrictions in Britain, their trips to Europe became increasingly attractive. There was rarely a United match on the continent which was not accompanied by some disorder. In 1974, United fans rampaged through Ostend, smashing windows and damaging cars. But it was a match against St Etienne in the Cup Winners' Cup in September 1977 that received most attention. Fighting on the terraces led to 33 people requiring hospital attention and initially the club was kicked out of the competition. The *Manchester Evening News* ran an editorial headlined: "The Shame of St Etienne."

Once again groups of alleged Manchester United fans bring their great club's name into disrepute by their wild acts of hooliganism – this time in France.

The shame of St Etienne cannot easily be cast aside. And it is all the more sad when the team itself plays such exemplary football on the field.

Now another First Division club has decided to ban Red fans from the terraces and it is possible United could be banned from the Cup Winners' Cup.

The club is suffering deeply. Blame cannot be escaped, although many Red fans say the French started the trouble.

Continental Europe presented easy pickings to the United hardcore, as Colin Blaney remembered. "Me and Rab-eye from Salford stole a Van Gils suit each, sold them on, got ourselves bit of shady ID, just got into the Post Office before it closed and came away with two snide visitors' passports. We jibbed the Rattler to Euston, then the Tube over to Victoria, another train down to Dover, then ferry over the pond, onto a coach to Gay Paris, met a firm at Gare du Nord and cruised all the way on a first-class double-decker super-something. Not one hector [ticket collector] came round right through to Lyons main square. I remember as we were coming into the city looking around then thinking, fuck me, even their car parks are outstanding.

"The Reds had taken over all the main bars. Hard to believe but I still had enough money left from the sale of the Van Gils suit to get the beer in. Coco had a mega hotel room for us to crash.

"Next day, first thing on the menu, meet the main face who ran the south of England's inter-city, Coventry Rob. He'd put all the plans together, then we were all ready to go bang at it. Lois jeans, Kicker boots and shoes, Lacoste tops and a good few tills were banged or robbed. Then we got together with all the barmies in the fountain in the square. It felt like we'd won the cup already, everyone was drinking local wine in the red hot sunshine, singing and waving flags. It was going to be some day.

"At some point Eddie Beef shouts out, 'It's time for a-mobbin' and a-robbin'.' All the way to the ground cash boxes got snatched from the food and drink stalls. Once at the stadium, Devils were all wearing green tops, scarves and hats – they had robbed the club shop – so Rab and I got a St Etienne tracksuit top each in return for a few drinks.

"The atmosphere in the ground was very continental, with all the klaxon horns. St Etienne were a top team who'd never been beaten at home in Europe. Over 2,000 went straight into their end. Plenty of French were throwing stupid things like plastic bottles of water and wine, which we just drank. They were even throwing huge bread rolls, so United whizzed back coins and things started to build up.

"Then it kicked off. Reds were pulling the sticks out of their homemade flags and using them as weapons, forcing hundreds of Froggies to run to the front, where they scaled the huge wire fence separating the terraces from the pitch. Some climbed to the top then fell off the fence and came crashing down, with bones broken and busted bad.

"The exodus continued even when the game kicked off and the riot police steamed in swinging batons and cracking heads. They chased around 500 Reds out the ground and all the way back to the train station. While the police steamed in the locals also took bits of revenge, with the dibble looking the other way. They didn't give a toss and can you blame them?"

United fans got support from a surprising quarter when they were backed by Chief Supt Graham, head of GMP's M Division. Relaying a report from a sergeant at the match, he told the press, "The United fans were completely searched before the game so where did all those bottles and cans which were thrown come from? The indications are that the United fans were trying to get away from the aggravation. But there was no segregation inside the ground."

The unfortunate timing of football fixtures can often create problems. Three days after St Etienne, United were at home to Chelsea, a side whose supporters were creating similar fear and loathing across the country. For the police it was clear that the match posed a problem, coming as it did on the day of the Lord Mayor's Parade through the city centre. While hundreds of police were to cope with any possible football disorder, another 200 were drafted in to protect the parade in case of an attack from football fans.

As it was the parade passed off peacefully and while there wasn't the feared mayhem, that was certainly not for the want of trying on United's part.

It took 1,200 Chelsea fans 15 minutes to shuffle 400 yards to safety after their team had beaten Manchester United 1-0 at Old Trafford on Saturday (reported the *Manchester Evening News*).

And they only made it because a thin blue line of 200 police officers kept at bay a howling 3,000 strong mob of fanatics who regard themselves as United's 'Red Army'.

Like a guerrilla army the United hooligans melted away when squads of police cleared the quarter-mile route from the ground to Warwick Road station.

But they hid in side streets, down back entries, behind parked cars and at nearby blocks of flats ready to ambush the Chelsea supporters on their way back to their trains.

The Chelsea fans were held at the ground for thirty minutes after the final whistle as the police enacted a carefully planned operation to clear the route ahead of locals. Only then, under a heavy escort and with mounted horses and dog handlers acting as outriders, were they allowed to move. One group of Chelsea fans stopped for a drink on the way home and must have wished they hadn't. They were attacked by a group of 20 men, shouting, "Let's get the bastards," at the Royal Thorn Hotel, in Wythenshawe, a tough council estate south of the city. "Everything was chaos," recalled the pub landlord. "I went to phone the police and when I came back a young chap was lying in a pool of blood, so I went to phone for an ambulance. It only lasted about three minutes but thirteen windows were broken along with twelve chairs, six tables and six stools. I think the troublemakers were a gang of hooligans from the local estate."

Five days later, Manchester United fans learnt that their team had been booted out of the Cup Winners' Cup, following a UEFA report into events in Paris. "As a result of the excesses which were caused by the supporters of Manchester United on September 14 at the match in St Etienne, and in order to safeguard the interests of European football and the security of the football public, the commission resolved to exclude the English club from the current competition and to declare St Etienne to have qualified for the next round," read the UEFA statement. The commission were of the opinion that the violent behaviour of the supporters of Manchester United seriously endangered the public security and physical well-being of the spectators.

United secretary Les Olive immediately declared he would appeal the ban, and was backed by David Smith, the chairman of the supporters' club. "I am amazed at the decision," said Smith. "We have always understood that the home club was responsible for the security on its own ground. I appreciate that the presence of red and white colours and United's reputation inflamed the situation and brought about the incidents. However, the whole root of the problem was the non-segregation of French and English supporters." His view was shared by many United fans, and the European ban was subsequently rescinded by UEFA, who took into account the "excellent behaviour of the United players". Their condition was that the return game be played at a neutral venue in England.

The late Seventies witnessed an explosion of violence in games between Man United and Leeds United, a rivalry that had first emerged in a series of FA Cup semi-finals in the Sixties and worsened as Don Revie's Leeds took over from Matt Busby's United as the country's dominant team in the early Seventies. One harrowing trip to Elland Road in 1978 will never be forgotten by some of the Red Army.

"I have been kicked to fuck several times whilst following Manchester United, but the worst kicking I got, and I have no doubt it was the same for many United fans that day, was when we went to Leeds in 1978," said 47-year-old Ronnie McClelland, from Middleton. "We took over 10,000 fans, with possibly 3,000 lads, but we got hammered from ten in the morning, before the game, during the game and after the game. All day, battered to fuck.

"Our mob from Middleton arrived in Leeds at ten on the train. We met up with loads of Reds and had at least 200 on the first service train. We piled off the platform and made the short journey into the city centre, but within a couple of minutes we were ambushed by hundreds of Leeds fans, and not just lads; many blokes in their twenties and thirties came wading into us. We were easily sussed out because hardly any of us were wearing scarves at that time, whereas every Leeds fan wore a scarf, many still wearing them hanging from their wrists or wrapped around their heads. Most of the cunts wore donkey jackets with NCB [National Coal Board] on the back in orange and they still wore half-mast jeans with cherry red Docs. It really was Timewarp City, most of them still had bleached blond feather cuts *a la* Rod Stewart and homemade Indian ink tattoos with 'LOVE' and 'HATE' across the knuckles, and every second word was, 'Munich cunts'.

"Even the Leeds birds were attacking us with bottles and brollies. I have never experienced such hatred, we got blitzed and tried to fight back but we had no chance, they came from every angle and out of every shop. I got dragged down an alleyway and got stomped off two skinheads. Finally the police sirens wailing had the Leeds fans scattering. Out of the fifty lads that left Middleton that morning, we were down to twenty by eleven o'clock. We later found out that the rest had got the next train back out of Leeds.

"We kept our heads down by going into the shopping centre and mingling with the shoppers. At 11.30am we made our way back to the station to meet the next train full of Reds. Over 500 came bouncing off this train, but as the mob was walking under the big railway bridge outside the station, Leeds fans once more attacked us, only this time they really went to town on us, many brandishing knives and broken bottles. Loads got cut up. They outnumbered us two to one at least, with many shoppers joining in the assaults. The cops herded us back into the station and we had to wait an hour for the next train, which was also full of Reds. When this arrived at 12.30pm, the cops escorted this huge mob to the ground, which was over two miles. Every street corner there were mobs of Leeds thugs bricking us and throwing bottles. The cops did fuck all and lots got cut up. We tried breaking the escort but the cops had it sorted.

"As we approached the ground it was like Custer's Last Stand. There were thousands of Leeds fans on these big hills overlooking us, many wearing scarves around their nappers like Indian warriors. 'Kill the Munichs!' they were screaming as bricks rained down on us and eventually the cops shoved us into the opposite end to the Leeds Gelderd End. The ground was a sellout, and all through the game Leeds fans in the paddocks were climbing into our ends on suicide missions. They got leathered but more and more would come jumping in and take their beatings. It was a fucking eerie atmosphere.

"After the match, the cops once more escorted us back to the station, but every fifty yards or so we got attacked by mad mobs of Leeds fans, with the cops turning a blind eye, and many of the cops were laughing at our predicament and calling us 'Munich' and 'Manc wankers'. At one stage the cops left us to the mercy of hundreds of Leeds thugs near the station, who came at us with scaffold tubes and iron bars. The few who fought back were arrested. It was a fucking sham.

"When we finally get onto the station there were still Leeds fans on the opposite platform stoning us and the cops did fuck all. I got on the first train and within two miles every single window on our train got put through by stones and other missiles. The next four trains all got smashed up by Leeds thugs as we left their godforsaken City of Hell. It was the very worst kicking many Reds had experienced, and I know many have never returned since that day, so as much as it pains me to say it, Leeds hammered Man United that day, big time."

The Red Army consisted of groups drawn from across the country. Greater Manchester contained numerous separate contingents, while slightly further afield there was Dave and his Warrington Reds. On the East Coast there was a sizeable group from Hull, while the Midlands and the South West also turned out numerous Devils. But undoubtedly the most famous United mob outside Manchester was the Cockney Reds, led by characters like Banana Bob.

"The Cockney Reds, well all the ones I knew, were just as hardcore as any Manc," said Colin Blaney. "Maybe because they have to put up with plenty down South. Their history seems to be that they were all born mid-Fifties, early Sixties, and many of their old fellas had moved down South to the big car plants and better jobs. You must remember the Busby Babes were the first team that all the UK loved, and them being a glamour team it was only normal in a way that these Cockneys who'd been brought up hearing their older lot bigging up Man U all went like rebels in the capital."

A lesser-known group, who were only around briefly, were the Young Munichs. "They were mainly white, with a few mixed-race kids on the firm all from Moss Side and Hulme's bullring flats," said Blaney. "They never really travelled much, partly because of some of them being class-A drug users. They were a nightmare for quick, in-and-out, stabbing-and-gassing tactics, always around the Chester Road area. They never mixed in the town much so they really were looked down on and it was no surprise they soon faded away. Their main lad was Macca, who was nicknamed Munchen because he was always abroad grafting.

"Cockney Sam took them under his wing one year. He had been in and out of nut homes. When I first met him he'd just got out from Brixton and was going through a period of looking like a nutter or a weirdo by wearing really over the top thick glasses and one of those sky blue rain tops that you'd wear on the Blackpool front when it's pissing down. When he sussed the away firms he'd turn into a General asking Munchen and Co. to bring the tools out. Munchen and the Young Munichs were all blade merchants and true to say around this time period Man U were the only ones giving it back to the Mickeys tit for tat with the cutting at that time. Even Scousers will admit we never got to match their level but were the closest."

With Leeds United and Man City spending much of the mid-Eighties in Division Two, United's most violent confrontations were against the hated Scousers of Liverpool and, to a lesser extent, Everton. A terrible series of mutual slashings and stabbings began, especially after the attack on teenage United fan and amateur boxer Jobe Henry in 1982, which left him needing more than 200 stitches. Over the following years dozens of hooligans and innocent fans alike would suffer wounds from carpet and craft knives wielded by cowardly attackers. It was also a period of great frustration for United on the pitch as they could not seem to break the duopoly of the two Merseyside teams.

The death of a Tottenham fan during an altercation on the escalators at Seven Sisters Tube station also led to enduring recriminations with the Tottenham mob, who blamed a prominent black member of the Cockney Reds for the tragedy. United also clashed several times in this period with West Ham's notorious ICF, most infamously during the making of the seminal TV documentary *Hooligan* and on a cross-Channel ferry taking rival fans abroad for a pre-season tournament.

In 1987, Greater Manchester Police formed the undercover Omega Squad to target football hooligan gangs. Their first success came against Manchester City's Guvnors and Young Guvnors, and United were next on the list. Mass brawling at the derby at Maine Road in September 1989 – when United's main firm infiltrated the North Stand with tickets bought from touts – was described by senior police officers as the worst violence at a Manchester football ground for years, and was the final straw. "They were fighting like dogs in the Kippax, the Main Stand and the back of the North Stand," said an exasperated chief superintendent.

Three months later, Operation Mars was launched. Police spotters in plain clothes attempted to mingle with the United firm over the next few months to build up a picture of who was who and to collect evidence. The person they identified as the ringleader was Tony O'Neill, a long-standing United face from Wythenshawe who even as a teenager in the mid-Seventies had been invited to a meeting with the then-Sports Minister Denis Howell to discuss the hooligan problem at Old Trafford.

Though the officers were never able to infiltrate United's inner circle, on 22 November 1990 more than 30 suspected hooligans were arrested at addresses in Manchester, London and elsewhere. Most were eventually charged with hooligan-related offences. After legal argument that dragged on until May 1993, the case against them collapsed when the courts refused to allow undercover officers to give their evidence anonymously from behind screens. It was a humiliating blow for Greater Manchester Police but it had also temporarily knocked the stuffing out of the mob.

One of those rounded up in Operation Mars was Gary Powell, a former soldier who was obsessive about football violence and everything that went with it. Powell would come into his own in the Nineties and was largely responsible for the modern United mob, who would become known as the Men in Black, a name that reflected the all-black clothing they favoured. "Powell gave us the name and gets credit from other Reds for that," said one of the firm. "He doesn't get the credit he deserves though for rebuilding the firm from scratch. Tony [O'Neill] was always the number one at United and he is a game, loyal man but for whatever reason United had lost their way like many firms in the early Nineties and there were United fans and lads getting slapped all over the place by muppet firms who years ago we would go through.

"Gary started getting everyone together and was in people's faces every week, saying, 'Are you coming here?' or 'Are you going there, and if not, why not?' He would say, 'If we don't have tickets we will still go and have it regardless. We will put ourselves on show and if we don't get it at Derby we will stop off at Chesterfield, if Boro don't have a go we will get off at Darlington, et cetera, et cetera.'

"It was a one-man recruitment campaign that snowballed and exploded. With Tony's firm and the Cockney Reds we were all of a sudden 300-strong, whether it be a trip to Goodison, West Ham or fucking Coventry. One well-known Cockney Red said 'Gary Powell deserves a medal for what he has done for United's firm,' and there are very few who will argue with that. Gary used to say, 'We will take it to everyone, if they want it we will give it them, we must go to every game, not just pick and choose like some firms. Give no firm the chance to say we never showed.' It was mad but one season he pulled it off and we went firm-handed to every game and came unstuck nowhere. Yes, the odd breakaway group would get a slap or put on their toes, but the main firm that season had nothing but home and away wins. Home was easy, no one came, Everton, Boro and Barnsley to give them credit did, no other firm bothered. Everton were game, they showed a few years running at Old Trafford and always seemed to be on a bit of a suicide mission numbers wise, while Boro are Boro and have demanded respect over the years."

A memorable trip to Upton Park for a night game saw United's firm pull on a job lot of balaclavas and charge through the streets like a gang of ninjas, startling both police and West Ham fans. It was around this time that people started to refer to them by a new name. "The Men in Black name was a bit of a joke but it stuck," said the United lad. "Twice at West Ham we did them, and apart from the balaclava game the lads always wore dark clothes, as Powell said there was less chance of being picked out by the police and people listened to what he said. He was nicknamed the Wing Commander and he did believe in planning things like a military operation. Without him United would not have been what they were during that purple patch throughout the Nineties and into the Millennium.

"Gary had some great one-liners that were legendary. My favourite was after one poor showing at somewhere like Newcastle, when we were split into two sections on opposite sides of the ground. After we went out and for them and it came on top, Powell said, 'There is no shame in getting done. You have to show to get done. There are firms who claim never to get done and it's because they don't fucking show.' Tony was not impressed and bollocked us all for not mobbing up before getting into the Geordies. He was right, as when we got together we went through them all the way to town.

"A day when we let the country know what we were made of was the Scotland vs England game at Hampden in the World Cup play-offs. We got on the train at Warrington eighty-handed and told every firm that day that if they wanted it we would give it them. Chelsea, Birmingham, the Yids, all declined. In the end only Preston had the balls to have a go when we got off there on the way home. Give them credit, they had lads phone the police to say it had gone off in a pub then attacked us coming out of the station while the dibble shot to a false fight in some pub. They got done in but had more balls than the rest of England's so-called finest that day."

United became once again perhaps the most formidable hooligan outfit in the country. Few rivals had the respect of their top lads, largely because so few were prepared to "take it" to Old Trafford, while United turned out everywhere. Liverpool were generally dismissed as "has-beens", despite the high-profile slashing of a United lad at Salford Quays in the mid-Nineties (which led to an equally nasty reprisal outside Salford Magistrates Court), while Man City are also held in low esteem. "The cherry pickers," said the United lad, dismissively. "They are a fucking joke. They never turn up mob-handed against us, never call it on firm on firm and have never had a result against us as long as I have been going. But they fucking harp on about ruling town because all they do is snide attacks on pockets of Reds when they have the numbers in their favour. They swoop on stragglers late at night, picking people off and then claim to be the top firm in Manchester. As for proper violence at the derby, seriously, apart from minor bits and pieces over the past ten years, nothing, because they don't show, home or away."

Opinion is divided on Leeds. Whilst many United hooligans are dismissive, others have more respect. "Despite what many Man United lads say, I rate Leeds," said the United lad. "At home, they are a different animal when they play us and you have to respect the kind of firms they pull when we come to town. At Old Trafford they have been generally a waste of time and for years it was one no-show after another. We had every excuse in the book from them, how many times can the Pennines be blocked by snow for fuck's sake, and why is it that our trains to Leeds are never cancelled due to leaves on the track? We go there every game and they cannot deny it.

"We went three times in a week once, Sunday game we had it with them, Gary Powell had his nose broken in a brawl under the subway. We only used to get that small corner of the ground while the cunts gave the Scousers 6,000 tickets. Still we went firmed up and it was not all pleasant, but we went. Three days after the Sunday game, Powell steamed into them outside the Wheatsheaf pub, still had the plaster on his nose from the Sunday. They were mental rows but respect to them, they were game as they come when they had the numbers, and their frontline were tough bastards.

"The one that changed it was when we got out and our main man took a fence to bits and we squeezed through it one by one. Sixteen of us slid across a local football pitch and bumped into their firm on the Holbeck Estate who were about sixty-handed and emptying a skip into us. Standard lamps, old sofa bits the lot came at us but we stood and when the rest of the firm showed they were wasted and did not stand for long. It was all filmed and a few did a bit of jail for it but that was the one when we knew they could not live with us. The year after we had it again and they were badly done after. We had an inner strength that made us better than them. They outnumbered us but we did them and I remember Powell saying after the battle that that was our best ever showing at Leeds."

In recent years Arsenal's rivalry on the pitch spilled over off it and there have been several clashes between the Gooners and United's boys.

While these were certainly not the large-scale battles that accompanied United on their travels to London in the 1970s, it was a fierce rivalry nonetheless. "It is more of a Cockney Red thing," said one of the Cockney mob. "We battered them at Villa Park at a cup semi and the year later they got it back when thirty Reds went on a bit of a suicide mission up Holloway Road. Our lads were fighting for their lives that day but overall Arsenal are nothing special and I suppose the same thing will happen with Chelsea now they are starting to take us on on the pitch, the same way Arsenal did a few years ago. London was always lively but for years we have had the run of the place and very few dents were put into our armour. West Ham were more show without punch, Chelsea living on past reputations, Millwall were here once and did nothing, so I suppose over the years Arsenal were about the best of a very average bunch."

One mob they do respect, however, are Tottenham, who over the years have caused some surprises against United, motivated partly by the bad blood that lingers from the Tube station death of a Spurs fan in 1981. On one occasion, Man United are keen to stress, the perpetrators were actually locals from the Broadwater Farm estate, as the Cockney Red recalled. "We went into Broadwater Farm by mistake and United got slaughtered. All the lads say it was the worst experience ever. It was nothing to do with football for the locals, just hatred towards a load of Northern cunts, but the firm got done and it has to go down as a bad day for us."

One of United's biggest European rows in recent times was a Champions League match against Feyenoord in Holland in 1997. Followers of the Rotterdam side were regarded as the bad boys of Dutch football and a large police operation was mounted to prevent them clashing with the Men in Black before the game. It fell apart, however, when United's mob simply walked through a line of riot police at Rotterdam Station and headed into town, much to the bemusement of the British police spotters present. They stormed the square where Feyenoord hooligans were gathering and destroyed several bars.

Outside the ground, the angry Dutch amassed a huge mob and bricked coaches bringing United fans to the stadium. "It was payback time for them bars done in the day," said Colin Blaney. "I couldn't believe it when just at that moment a tasty firm of Reds had jibbed right through a massive police line, around 150, and it was United who steamed in. I had no choice even at my age in my fifties. It's a fact, once a thug, always one.

"We got scattered and slapped all the way back to the train platform which is only used on match days or for concerts. Black Henry was screaming at them all to wise up and pointed out the fact that they'd not pulled tools out, so there was fuck all to worry about. In fact we were all very lucky but that pride needs restoring, so we all got tight – but second time round was even worse. Half the Reds jumped on buses but what stayed with us all that night was how soft we all looked to their firm as no weapons were on show. They see that day as theirs, and I would agree."

It was a rare setback, however. United's thugs were in their pomp, exemplified by their appearance at an England international at Anfield in 2001, when 250-350 Men in Black marched around the ground unopposed. They probably reached their apex in October 2003, at a Champions League fixture against Rangers in Glasgow. Few younger United thugs would have remembered the visit of Rangers to Old Trafford in 1974, and the carnage unleashed that day by the Scottish hordes, but some of the older heads obviously did, and were determined to make amends. It was like a throwback to the old days.

"The cream of all firms," said the Cockney Red, proudly. "No firm in the history of football would have come near what we had that day. A Rangers lad posted that it was 'sinister and frightening' and he was not wrong. Five hundred lads, no hangers on. Rangers never came near and who can blame them. Their showing at Old Trafford was pathetic though and that was a massive letdown after the show we put on up there. Feyenoord came around about that time with 300 loons, sat off in town and did not have a care for the police or CCTV. If they can do it why not Rangers?"

Fifty-one people were arrested after clashes around Ibrox Park. "It is understood Manchester United 'casuals' had gathered in a bar on Paisley Road West, where they spent much of the day drinking," noted one report.

At around 6pm they left the pub and ran riot down the busy road, attacking rival supporters and the public at random. Passers-by took refuge in doorways. Much of the violence took place outside the District Bar, a favourite haunt of Rangers fans.

Police, who had been monitoring the fans' movements, moved in with raised batons to quell the trouble and mounted police helped to disperse the fighting fans.

Further along Paisley Road West, at the Park Bar, an ambulance took an injured fan to the Southern General Hospital, but he was not thought to have been badly hurt.

Manchester United fans – who had sung Celtic songs and waved green and white flags during the game – were kept inside the stadium for more than an hour after the match in an attempt to allow the Rangers support to disperse.

United in this period were even labelled "the superfirm", especially when they were joined by some heavy hitters from Edinburgh team Hibs and by incorrigible hooligan Lee Spence, who had previously led Oldham's Fine Young Casuals. But as seems to be the case with all football firms, their rise was followed by a fall. Tony O'Neill was jailed for an incident involving Stoke City before the England World Cup qualifier against Greece at Old Trafford and was subsequently banned from all football grounds. Gary Powell, meanwhile, moved to Thailand, where he was joined by a number of other prominent boys, including Spence.

The United firm might have dwindled but that is not to say that they are completely dead. When Wayne Rooney returned to Goodison Park for his first match for United, the Reds took a mob numbering close to 600. One United hooligan summed up the present situation.

"There are signs that things are not as they were. It has just as much to do with the fact that nobody shows at Old Trafford though, rather than the fact that Tony and Gary are no longer involved. We still have a very tasty hardcore but things like Everton recently [where a group of United left their escort from Goodison and were caught by a large Everton ambush] would have been better organised if those two were still with us. Give Everton their due, they were well up for it that night and were, for this day and age, very, very decent, but the numbers involved were hugely exaggerated and in the end there were minor casualties, so was it as bad as the papers and media made out? Okay, the United lads that came out the escort got had off. Big deal. If it was the other way around it would have been business as usual and not an eyelid would have been blinked. No one is invincible, we never said we were, but you would think Everton had run us all the way back up the M62 the way the fucking internet was buzzing. We got a slap, big fucking deal."

United still continue to show at most games, although Old Trafford is now one of the safest grounds for visiting fans, as one of the Men in Black described: "OT is boxed off by the Dibble, but there's no point really, who comes looking for it? It takes a big cup match for any real chance of an off, we had Coventry in the FA Cup and they brought over ten thousand fans and a decent firm of lads, they beat us on the pitch, when Sir Alex gave our kids a chance to prove themselves. Off the pitch, let's just say our younger lot did a lot better."

A trip to Roma made the headlines when millions on TV watched the local Italian riot police batter any Red within striking reach as rival fans attempted to get at each other inside the ground. However, it was the violence outside which the lads will remember. Indeed, some regard it as their most memorable football violence experience ever.

"For those of us not the wrong side of forty, Roma was the one," said one veteran. "Lads who have been at it for years will agree it was mental. We had been there the day before and, apart from the odd incident, which we get everywhere, it was business as usual: United drinking all over the city without a care in the world. The night before, we were in their bar, the same one where they chopped up Boro the season before, and a few came for a nose and clearly did not fancy it.

"The day of the game was not so straightforward. After watching them buzzing around on their fucking mopeds all day, we took up the offer to meet them at the ground. We set off with about three hundred and got to the bridge they had told us they would be at. They did not disappoint. We went straight for it and I know people reading this will think it's exaggerated, well I can swear it isn't, in front of us was over a thousand ultras. Now these are not all fighters but it's still a scary situation. Everyone knows the Italians are tooled up and I honestly doubt many firms would have tried it on like we did. It went on for about thirty minutes, back and forth, and we covered about a few hundred yards at the most. They were pulling up in cars and blokes were jumping out, opening the boot and running at us with wheel braces and anything else they could get their hands on, it was full-on violence and I'm sorry to say a lot of the younger lot did not have the guts for it.

"The outcome was never going to go in our favour, we had no chance of moving them. Every time we got in front the police would wade into us, when they were on top they would stand back laughing. We had brollies, they had machetes and axes. The end count was thirteen of our good lads were stabbed. Despite that, when we made it to the ground their main lad, complete with his silver motorbike helmet, wanted to shake our hands. We did as well as we could have done and I doubt any firm could have done any better.

"As we were going in, over half the firm arrived under escort. We had done what we did with about a hundred, the rest had crumbled. That's something they have to live with, when we needed them they failed to deliver. After the game we were kept in for about two hours and I will hold my hand up, a few wanted to go back for more but most said they would take the escort back and get the fuck out of there.

"Give Roma credit, they turned up for the second leg and had a couple of hundred making a nuisance of themselves up by the ground all day. The touts were well pissed off, they were taxed, punched and chased off. By the time we got to OT, the police had them wrapped up and for an hour there was a bottle- and brick-throwing competition. As luck had it we drew them again the following year but they failed to show, a couple of hundred tucked up inside the ground two hours before kick-off shitting themselves."

Further reading: *We Hate Humans*, David Robins (Penguin), *The Red Army Years*, Richard Kurt and Chris Nickeas (Headline), *Red Army General* and *The Men In Black*, Tony O'Neill (Milo Books), *Scum Airways*, John Sugden (Mainstream), *Grafters*, Colin Blaney (Milo Books)

MANSFIELD TOWN

Ground: Field Mill Ground
Firms: Psycho Express, SAS, Carrot Crew, the Cucumbers, Mansfield Shady Express
Rivals: Chesterfield, Lincoln, Shrewsbury

The 1975 season kicked off as the previous one ended – with trouble. Mansfield Town's home game against Hull City in the Anglo-Scottish Cup saw fighting between rival fans before, during and after the match in the town centre and both inside and outside the ground. Passing sentence later on a number of those involved, magistrate A. Barnes said, "It seems to be the order of the day to go and cause as much trouble as you can at a football match."

A week later, and in Nottingham Crown Court his sentiment was being repeated. "Hardly a Saturday goes by without newspapers being filled the following day with some hooliganism or other misbehaviour on the part of football supporters," said Judge Ellis as he passed sentence on a local man following the visit of Shrewsbury Town. The court heard how away supporters were attacked after a "crowd of about 400 supporters walked in a tight bunch through the town" chanting, "You're going to get your heads kicked in." A number of other youths were up in front of Mansfield magistrates, and their behaviour was also condemned, with threats of custodial sentences in appropriate cases.

This new "get tough" approach from the bench was welcomed. "The remarks will be appreciated not only by the police but by the directors and officials of Mansfield Town Football Club, all those supporters of the club whose pleasure is spoilt by a hooligan element in the crowd, and by local businessmen and persons residing near to the ground," responded Chief Supt Buckley. He also announced several initiatives that he hoped would reduce violence seen regularly towards the end of matches, particularly the hooligan ploy of leaving one stand minutes before the end of the match only to re-enter in another to attack opposing fans. "In future we shall have a key to the gate and nobody will get back into the ground," he said.

Trouble had followed Mansfield Town since the late Sixties. Sometimes this involved clashes with supporters of rival teams but on other occasions there was trouble between Mansfield supporters from different pit towns in its catchment area, including Worksop, Kirkby, Sutton and Ashfield. "At that time Mansfield were not well organised, basically whoever was there and was interested just got stuck in," remembered one longstanding Stags fan. "A guy called Ray Ball was the leading light around this time, but basically gangs came together based on the estate or pit village they lived in. If no opposition fans turned up we would just fight among ourselves."

The strong words from the courts appeared to do nothing to quell disorder around the club. Frightened Grimsby fans had to shelter from attacking Mansfield youths in February 1976. There was also serious disorder despite a strong police presence for the local derby with Lincoln City in November 1976. Fighting broke out on the terraces but the worst incident took place outside the ground when a Mansfield fan threw a missile at the visiting team coach, seriously injuring the driver.

Much worse was to come with the arrival of Stoke City in August 1977. Mansfield had just been promoted into the Second Division and were given an immediate taste of life with the big boys. "Black Saturday – Football thugs run riot in Mansfield" was the headline in the local paper. It continued:

A terrified Mansfield watched in horror on Saturday and witnessed the effects of their football team's entry into the Second Division.

In one riotous, violent day, two policemen were rushed to Mansfield Hospital with blood streaming from head wounds.

A police chief was so covered in spit from rival fans that he had to be cleaned up. A car was overturned near Mansfield town centre in the street fighting that broke out before the match.

Horrified shoppers watched about 60 Stoke City supporters charge through the Four Seasons Centre, which had to close.

Mounted policemen had to be drafted in from a Notts County match to help their four colleagues. Police helmets were trampled, police uniforms ripped, their wearers' wristwatches wrenched from their arms. Pubs closed.

Two heavy iron bars were retrieved from the Stoke section of the crowd. Street-fighting broke out not only in the centre of Mansfield but on some of the peripheral roads.

White Hart Street, Nottingham Road and the Market Place all witnessed ugly scenes. But Albert Street was subjected to an onslaught that left two premises filled with broken glass and debris.

The trouble erupted after 200 Stoke fans arrived in town early on the Saturday morning and embarked on a two-hour orgy of violence. Inside the ground the trouble continued. For many Mansfield fans this game was the big one and chants of "Come and have a go if you think you're hard enough" from home supporters in the North End provoked hundreds of Stoke to stream out of the Quarry Lane end to take up battle. They were joined by a large group of Stoke who had already infiltrated the Mansfield end – and Stoke emphatically proved that they *were* hard enough. In fact they were to be the only club to completely take the North End.

It took the deployment of mounted officers to restore order. Chief Inspector Culley, who was in charge on the day, was hit by a missile and covered in so much spit that he had to beat a hasty retreat into the club secretary's office to clean up. The police later found two iron bars hidden amongst the Stoke fans and expressed disbelief that they had been smuggled in; ten uniformed and plainclothes officers had searched away fans as they entered the ground by having them "up against a wall in a manner that you could liken to what is seen on American television shows," one officer told a subsequent court case.

Mansfield's chairman called for tougher action. "We must have extra police, and police dogs must be brought on duty. That would deter a lot of the troublemakers." He also suggested making those people brought up before the courts report to police stations on match days to prevent them causing more trouble in the future. He was obviously a man ahead of his time.

The Stoke game was the exception and soon Mansfield's supporters returned to their small-scale skirmishes with smaller teams. There were regularly outbreaks of violence at the end of the 1970s and a steady stream of Mansfield fans came up before the courts. During the late Sixties and early Seventies, Mansfield was a "grebo" club – many of its hooligans were greasers or heavy rockers – so they had to fight a lot, as everybody else was skinhead, suedehead or just scruffy. Fights broke out with Spurs, Newcastle, Sheffield Wednesday, Hull, Lincoln, Bournemouth and Grimsby to name just a few.

The early Eighties saw the emergence of the Psycho Express, home to Mad Alfie, Russ, State, Brough, Rigger and many more. They came together just before the Miners' Strike, ran until the early Nineties and were the first identifiable hooligan gang at Mansfield. Mad Alfie was the main face in the group, as one veteran recalled: "Mad Alfie was a character. He was a great person to have a day out with and a pint, totally loyal to his friends, and seemingly indestructible when it came to fighting, drinking and certain substances. In fact even in the most trying of circumstances he would always have a smile on his face. I do remember going down to Brentford and we had stopped at the services. As we went back to the coach there was a Rolls-Royce parked nearby, with the bloke looking at us as if we were scum. Alfie climbed on the bonnet of the Roller, dropped his trousers and had a crap. The guy's face was a picture. I don't think Alfie gave a fuck about anything other than the Stags, his mates and booze."

The Psycho Express emerged from a group of supporters who drank in the Queens Head and who travelled together for away games. They would meet at 6am, have a few pints and then set off at eight to be wherever in time for the pub opening. Drinking led to fighting and it wasn't long before the name "Psycho Express" had been attached to the travel party. They were soon to be joined by the SAS, a group of Mansfield fans drawn largely from the satellite town of Sutton who enjoyed wearing SAS-style balaclavas before going into battle. Their speciality was going into opposing ends, something they did on a number of occasions.

In November 1983, the FA Cup match against Doncaster Rovers was marred by fighting that left one Mansfield supporter unconscious on the terraces. The trouble began when a group of Doncaster fans got into the Mansfield end and clashed with locals. Brawling spilled onto the pitch and one Doncaster supporter was beaten so badly he was unable to stand.

By the mid-Eighties a new generation of hooligans was emerging. The Psychos were getting older and many young Mansfield supporters wanted to join the national trend for more organised hooligan firms. A meeting was arranged in a local Italian restaurant to discuss the group's name. Many wanted something imaginative, a name that would amuse people. They divided themselves into two groups, the older group coining the name "The Cucumbers" while the younger lads became "The Carrot Crew". Together, they were to take the name of the ITV – "Intertown Vegetables". Perhaps it was something to do with the menu.

The Carrot Crew's core was about 30 lads, though they could number two or three times more. Mansfield is typical of many small towns where local hooligans often attach themselves to larger clubs, in their case Leeds, Derby, Man U, Newcastle, Forest and Spurs. For really big matches, however, the Carrot Crew, the SAS and the Psycho Express would come together, as was often the case when Mansfield played local rivals Chesterfield, home of the Chesterfield Bastard Squad (CBS). Almost every game between the two clubs has seen trouble.

In 1983, over 100 Mansfield ran amok in Chesterfield town centre but 50 were arrested on their return journey for trashing a service bus. The following year Chesterfield invaded Mansfield's main stand and later police horses were used to separate hundreds of fans after the final whistle. The largest Mansfield turnout was in 1985, when between 200-300 of them clashed first with Chesterfield and then with the police. In 1988, 60 Chesterfield ambushed 35 Mansfield with bricks and bottles as they descended an escalator near Chesterfield bus station. More recently, it was only the swift intervention of police in January 2003 that stopped 130 Mansfield making a pre-arranged clash with the CBS.

The 1984 Miners' Strike gave local rivalries a new intensity. Many of the miners from pits around Mansfield continued to work and the chants of "scab" at matches against teams from Derbyshire and Yorkshire continue to be heard to this day. While this just provided new ammunition to long-standing opponents like Chesterfield, new enemies emerged, most noticeably Hartlepool and Darlington, and several nasty fights took place during the late Eighties. The trouble was not just restricted to Stags' matches. With many of Mansfield's lads being drawn from neighbouring smaller towns, post-strike hostilities were continued in non-league fixtures. The irony is that many of the Psycho Express followers stayed loyal to the striking National Union of Mineworkers during the strike but facts like that are often overlooked when football rivalries kick in.

The period 1985-87 saw the Carrot Crew at their most active. In the first three months of the 1985/86 season they clashed with Port Vale, Hartlepool, Southend, Middlesbrough, Northampton, Swindon and Burnley. The following season carried on in much the same way, but now, with the club doing well on the pitch, their numbers and confidence grew. In October, 30 Mansfield fans attacked visiting Bolton fans at the Red Lion pub with bricks and bottles. The confrontation lasted for several minutes as Mansfield tried to get into the pub, smashing windows in the process.

In March 1987, the Carrot Crew organised a double-decker bus to take 80 of their firm to a midweek Sherpa Van Trophy match at Middlesbrough. Boro's Frontline had begun to establish a fierce reputation and Mansfield, probably at the peak of their activity, decided that they could not let the match pass off without at least an effort. The Carrot Crew began meeting up at midday but it was not until three in the afternoon that the bus set off. From the beginning something did not seem right and their suspicions were confirmed when the bus headed straight for the depot, where they were greeted by the police. The Mansfield lads were taken off one at a time and searched and an array of weapons, including knives, blades, pool balls and even a metal-handled screwdriver sharpened down like a dart, were found. A dozen lads were nicked, some for the weapons, others for possessing their mob's calling cards, and two for travelling to a sporting event in possession of alcohol. A few were later released but eight were held overnight on the charge of "suspicion of conspiracy to organise an affray with intent to harm". They were eventually committed to Nottingham Crown Court on the charge of "unlawful assembly" but this was dismissed by the judge, who deemed boarding a bus as not being unlawful assembly. The defendants were finally bound over for a year for £500, which seemed small beer considering their armoury.

The season saw Mansfield win the Freight Rover Trophy at Wembley, but what should have been a victory parade to welcome home the victorious players was overshadowed by running battles between 400 local youths and the police. Bottles, cans and bricks were just some of the weapons thrown in an hour of violence. The trouble began when some lads left the Sir John Cockle pub furious that they were "not being served quickly enough". The club and police quickly tried to dismiss the incident as "isolated" and "nothing to do with football". Twenty-seven people were arrested and 47 were injured, including 17 police officers.

In 1988, Mansfield played host to Birmingham City, whose supporters were rarely out of the news for their hooliganism. One would have thought that the opportunity to have a crack at the mighty Zulus would have brought the Carrot Crew out in droves, but quite the reverse. Some believed that Birmingham would not bother with such a small, midweek fixture, while others probably decided to find other things to occupy their time out of fear. As it was, a large firm of 300 Zulus arrived to be met by a paltry firm of twelve locals, and unsurprisingly it did not take long for the Brummies to control the town centre. Mansfield's humiliation was matched six years later when they took the same number, an embarrassing dozen, away to arch rivals Chesterfield, with the bulk of the mob, about 40, deciding to travel to Leicester with Nottingham Forest's mob.

Convictions, marriage and age took its toll on all three groups, while the Carrot Crew in particular was decimated by a local feud. To many in the town they had become too cocky and had begun to throw their weight around. This included the cutting up of two local bouncers and a Hell's Angel, which was a seriously bad move. The bouncers in Mansfield worked for a pair of notorious Nottingham-based heavies, and one Sunday lunchtime they sought retribution, mob-handed, at the Swan pub. Carnage was the only way to describe what took place. The Hell's Angels were more subtle; they hunted down the Carrot Crew in small groups but the result was the same.

The remnants of all three groups merged to form the Mansfield Shady Express, though for some time the police and others continued to refer to them as the Carrot Crew. The title "Shady" was taken from the name local "dressers" or casuals were known by. It was as the MSE that a bitter rivalry emerged with Shrewsbury's English Border Front. In 1992, 30 MSE took the fight to Shrewsbury for an FA Cup tie. They had been drinking in the town all day but deliberately missed the game, preferring to pass the time in the EBF's main pub, the Elephant & Castle. They were about to leave when they bumped into one of Shrewsbury's top boys, who directed them to another pub. It was game on as the EBF, also numbering about 30, attacked Mansfield with fence posts, beer crates and planks of wood. The MSE returned the attack but ended up with 27 arrested and four hospitalised.

Hostilities were resumed at a service station following England's home game with Holland in October 1993. The following August, Mansfield hosted Shrewsbury on the first day of the season. Once again there was serious trouble, with the rival groups clashing several times before the police intervened. However the police had to back off after a Shrewsbury lad gassed them and fighting commenced. There was still trouble between the two clubs ten years later when 100 lads clashed before and after the game. One local publican described it as "absolute bedlam". The rivalry with Shrewsbury continues to this day.

The early Nineties saw the MSE clash with other gangs around the country. In October 1990, disorder broke out in a local pub after the home game against Preston North End. "Soccer hooligans went on rampage" was the headline after 40-50 Mansfield supporters stopped off in Newark from a match in Lincoln in March 1992, where they had earlier caused trouble. The police were aware of Mansfield's arrival but their presence did not prevent a fight breaking out with locals. The police stepped in and as they were attempting to shepherd the visitors back to the station they too came under attack. Seven were arrested in Newark, adding to the eleven who had been picked up earlier in the day. A few months later, nine football fans were arrested following trouble at Mansfield's home game against Stoke City.

Lincoln was another team the Carrot Crew and later the MSE fought regularly. Mansfield were badly turned over in 1981 when loads of their lads were attacked by small groups of the Lincoln Transit Elite. After the game the LTE mobbed up and invaded the pitch from three sides, armed with pieces of broken terrace, and proceeded to run amok amongst the Mansfield fans. It was another ten years before Mansfield next visited Lincoln and while their hosts were no less hospitable, Mansfield exacted some revenge. The police were waiting as a sizeable mob arrived in town but a bit of ingenuity lost their escort. There were small "offs" all over the place before the MSE began mobbing up in the Still pub. Lincoln tried twice to take the pub but were beaten away on both occasions.

Buoyed up by that success, the MSE decided to take the battle to the LTE and marched on the Green Dragon pub, though not without casualties as several Mansfield were attacked with pool cues and stools. Unfortunately for the away firm, some of this violence was caught by police evidence gatherers and used in subsequent court cases. It was 9pm before the police were finally able to get Mansfield out of town. While Mansfield would claim a victory for that day they did acknowledge that some of the LTE's more experienced lads were away watching one of their friends box in Northampton.

Lincoln are not known to be good travellers but for an FA Cup game in 1987 they turned up in style. Having just been relegated to the Conference, it was not only a big game for them but they felt they had something to prove. The LTE turned up early, parked at a disused hospital and entered Mansfield unnoticed. Nothing happened before the game but after, as Mansfield were preparing to ambush their guests, they found themselves ambushed. This happened not once but on three or four occasions, including one where a top Mansfield face was bounced off a shop window. While Mansfield accept that Lincoln came out on top that day, a few visitors did become acquainted with a shopping trolley and drainpipes.

Increased police surveillance and town centre CCTV have restricted the activities of the MSE, but incidents have not stopped completely. In mid-November 1997, Mansfield were drawn at Oldham in the first round of the FA Cup. It was to be a day of frustration and surprises, as one of their number recalled.

"Around fifty of us travelled to Oldham on November 15, 1997. It was the FA Cup first round. We arrived around twelve and a call was made to Oldham telling them we'd arrived. Their response was that they only had twenty-five or so out, so we agreed to give them half an hour to sort themselves out. They told us where they were drinking, so one of ours jumped into a car and drove off to find the pub. When he returned he told us it was just down the road, about a mile away.

"We waited half an hour, then left our pub, caught a service bus and got off at the pub because it had a stop right outside. We piled off and went into the pub through the side and front doors, but they weren't there. We had a look around for them and found they had gone to a pub called the Hope and Glory. Six of us stumbled upon it and their mob, still around twenty-five, steamed us with bottles and chairs. Luckily the rest of our lot, who had gone down a different street, heard the commotion and came to our help and we steamed them back into the pub, where they locked the doors.

"After the game we made our way back to the first pub we had visited because the landlord agreed we could watch the England v Cameroon game being played that evening. Unfortunately the local plod were having none of it and with the help of the GMP riot squad we were evicted. So we decided where to go and watch it. We ended up in Brighouse and watched the first half there but the giant screen was fucking awful to watch, it was all snowy, so we then drove into Huddersfield, which is what some of the lads had wanted all along. We went to a pub we knew they used called the Pen and Sty, I think. Some local lads made contact very quickly and word must have spread; well, the locals turned up and it kicked off. Even though we had the numbers, only around fifteen or twenty of us had a running battle with an even number of local lads. Some of ours watched from the bottom of the road giving off about the CCTV, but fuck it. The Hudders lads were game and we had a decent brawl before the OB turned up. We all fucked off sharpish and there was a bit of arguing with some of our lot making excuses up about not getting involved because of the cameras.

"On November 25 the doors went in – the CCTV *had* filmed the parts of the fighting, though it only caught the beginning of the incident. Which was a good thing really. Six lads were charged with violent disorder but all went no comment. The case took nearly two years to get into Bradford Crown Court. Instantly the charges were dropped to threatening behaviour, but only if we admitted to the charge. One lad got twenty-eight days, two lads got 200 hours' community service, two got £300 fines and the last one got his charge dropped."

Mansfield's location automatically attracted some of their lads to Forest, and from the early Nineties this trickle became an organised stream. It began with Mansfield travelling with the Nottingham lads to England matches but soon the favour was reciprocated, with Forest coming through to Mansfield to back them up at home games against Preston, Cardiff and Chesterfield. Forest rarely travelled to Mansfield's away matches, but an exception was the FA Cup game at Leicester when 20 made the journey. Forest's biggest turnout was to Mansfield's derby with Chesterfield in 2001 and this coincided with an upsurge in local interest in the MSE. The 30 hardcore swelled to 100. Word of a major clash spread around the hooligan scene well before the match and while 80-100 Forest linked up with 300 MSE, hooligans from Leicester, Derby and Man City swelled Chesterfield's ranks. In truth, the Forest lads were motivated more by a desire to get Derby than simply out of benevolence towards their Mansfield friends.

"Very little happened on the day," recounted one lad who was there. "Chesterfield's main lads were supposed to be in Bolsover organising their travel to us. Mansfield had a massive mob out, one of the biggest ever. The thing was, in the local paper the headline was stating that Chesterfields hooligans were coming to smash our town up, something they have never done and never will. So every nutter turned up hoping for some fun.

"By one o clock, around seventy to 100 Forest turned up. They had been told by both Derby and Leicester that they would have lads present who were travelling with Chesterfield to have a pop at us. Mansfield themselves had over 300 boys out. In the NCIS report it states that Mansfield attacked the Chesterfield escort near the Village nightclub. What really happened was a mob of Mansfield had attempted to get into the Village but were moved on, and when they got near the Vic pub, Mansfield steamed out and into them thinking they were Chesterfield. After the game a large mob of 4-500 Mansfield were being forced into town. They bumped into some Mansfield and Forest who had not been to the game and it kicked off until people realised who they were. Then near the bus station there was a series of scuffles and some Derby lads were battered as they and the Chesterfield lads present ran. The NCIS reported that Chesterfield had over 400 lads there; no way whatsoever, they had 100 max in the ground."

Mansfield's largest mob they took away for anything other than a game against Chesterfield was surprisingly in the 2002/03 season when they played at QPR. There was a mark of respect after the West Londoners had brought a mob of 90-100 lads into the centre of Mansfield by 11am earlier in the season. On that occasion most of the main Mansfield faces had been at Villa Park watching England and the 15 or so who were around town were no match for QPR. Instead of humiliating the small group, some of the older QPR lads had a chat with them, an act of friendship that was appreciated and not forgotten. The return fixture saw 150 travel down, with about 100 being drawn from the 35-50 age group. Few QPR were around and the only clash was outside a pub near the ground between 15-20 younger QPR and ten Mansfield.

In their 2004 *Annual Report*, Nottinghamshire Police estimated MSE strength at 120 and noted the emergence of the 40-strong "Mansfield Youth Group". Together, it concluded, "they make a formidable group for Mansfield games". The report also stated that 18 Mansfield fans were on banning orders and 49 were banned from the ground.

On 21 January 2006, Yates's Wine Lodge in Nottingham was the scene of an apparently arranged clash between the MSE and Shrewsbury Town. Mansfield were playing at home, while Shrewsbury were at Notts County. "A group of about thirty Mansfield Town supporters went to the Cross Keys pub beforehand, and around eighty per cent of those are known to me and my colleagues," related local PC Jon Harris. "They went to Yates's, where the Shrewsbury fans had arrived just before them, and there was a huge amount of mobile phone activity between the two groups."

The two gangs met at about 2pm in a family area of the pub. "Families enjoying a meal out on a quiet Saturday afternoon had no idea that terrifying violence was about to break out," reported the *Nottingham Evening Post*. "Chairs and tables were hurled through the air as fifty men waged a pitched battle in the upstairs family area of Yates's Wine Lodge in Old Market Square. Pensioners and children fled for cover and one diner was left unconscious after the horrific brawl – one of the worst incidents of football violence in the city in recent times."

The scale of the fighting took police by such surprise that they had to focus on dispersing the two factions and leave the investigation for later. The Shrewsbury mob were monitored and escorted out of the county on their coach two hours later. However, the brawl, had been captured on the pub's CCTV. PC Harris later spent 200 hours examining the footage, and in May 2006, eight suspected hooligans were arrested in a series of early morning raids coordinated from Mansfield police station.

Yet less than four months later, the MSE were at it again. On a Bank Holiday Saturday that August, they were due to play Lincoln City at home when a group from Chesterfield turned up as well, many of them banned from the centre of their own town. It led to a mass brawl in Mansfield Market Place before the game. A heavy advertising sign was hurled and punches were thrown before a large Mansfield group chased a smaller Chesterfield group along Leeming Street, past a children's bouncy castle set-up as part of a funfair in the market place. "The incident happened on a busy Saturday afternoon in the town centre where there were children playing and babies in push chairs," said one police officer. "They could have easily become caught up in the horrendous display of violence but those involved did not stop to think about anybody else."

It led to Operation Grindstone to track down those responsible and in December 2006 and January 2007, police arrested 34 suspects in Mansfield, Ashfield and Chesterfield as well as in Leicestershire and Lincolnshire. In September 2007, Nottingham Crown Court sentenced eleven hooligans for their part in the disturbance after they all admitted affray.

MIDDLESBROUGH

Ground: Riverside Stadium, formerly Ayresome Park
Firm: Ayresome Angels, The Beer Belly Crew, NTP, Boro Joeys, Frontline
Rivals: Sunderland, Everton

"Boro should not have the mob they've got," wrote Portsmouth's Rob Silvester in his book *Rolling With The 6.57 Crew*. "They must put something in the baby milk up there." That sums up how many view Middlesbrough's soccer firm. From the Ayresome Angels to the Beer Belly Crew, the Frontline and all the small mobs in between, Boro have long had a reputation for toughness. The city was once dominated by steel mills, docks and the huge ICI plant on its outskirts, and while these have shrunk or disappeared, it remains a rugged community. The old ground was in the middle of an estate of terraced housing, surrounded by alleys and dead-end streets, adding to the feeling of entrapment many visiting fans have had over the years. The new Riverside Stadium might have relieved some of this claustrophobia but it still retains an unfriendly feel for those seeking trouble.

The bleak industrial landscape has over the years been etched on the faces of the burly followers of the football club. The hardest lads stood in the Holgate End, and during the 1960s and 1970s, dressed in red and white hardhats, long butchers' coats adorned with players' names and the obligatory hobnail boots, they became known as the Ayresome Angels. Fiercely proud, Boro have always hated local rivals Sunderland and Newcastle but also the "gobby" Cockneys with their fancy clothes and arrogant swagger. There was little better feeling than turning over Southerners.

Arsenal was just one team that found out what an unpleasant place Middlesbrough could be when they travelled there in 1976. The North Londoners were a top mob and many believed that the trip to the barbarian country would be a walkover. They had recently disposed of the likes of Chelsea, Portsmouth and Villa and few thought that Boro would be any different. They not only met their match but some were literally lucky to get away with their lives. Colin Ward, in his book *Steaming In,* describes how Boro fans bombarded Arsenal with first bricks and then darts, one of which stuck in the eye of a fan close by. The police appeared well acquainted in this sort of behaviour and raised some protective canvas screens on top of the away end terrace.

The season before, Leeds had suffered an even more torrid time in what Boro fan John Theone, in his book *The Frontline*, considered the "most comprehensive hidings it has ever been my pleasure to witness". On the morning of the game Boro began mobbing up in the Zetland pub, close to the train station. By midday the pub was overflowing and it wasn't long before the police sirens signalled the arrival of the train from Leeds. Hundreds of men downed their drinks, grabbed whatever weapon they could and headed out for a clash. The police were well prepared and despite repeated attempts the Boro could not breach the escort. The same could not be said for after the game as Leeds were chased, beaten and robbed of their hats and scarves.

Trapped between two groups of Boro, Leeds fled into a wooded park, where only a few months before Man City had taken a hammering. Unbeknown to them an even bigger mob of Boro were waiting. "It was already fairly dark," wrote Theone, "giving us perfect cover. Now it was pure carnage; even I was amazed at what I saw. I am not talking handful of lads here, more like hundreds getting the shite kicked out of them. It was a massacre." From then on the wooded area became known as "Suicide Park".

Not all teams were so easy to turn over; indeed, Boro may have been earning themselves a reputation among northern teams but they were still some way off challenging for the position of Britain's worst hooligans. When Millwall travelled up to Ayresome Park in 1970 the young and disorganised Boro firms were taught a severe lesson from the big boys. "Miiillwaaal" went up the shout from just 50 Londoners into the middle of the Boro end. "You'll never take the Millwall," they chanted, arms outstretching, beckoning the home supporters forward. Few wanted to mix it with these grown men in their donkey jackets, jeans and heavy boots.

The return fixture was a chance for Boro to test themselves at London's best and a mob of 300 made the journey by train, coach and van. The euphoria and excitement at the size of their mob evaporated as they reached the ground. "I practically shit my pants on the spot," recalls Theone, who was only young at the time. "I mean, these were not lads in their mid-teens, they were all big fuck-off dockers and they were literally laughing at the state of our crew, calling us babies and kids." Theone and his friend found themselves isolated amongst Millwall fans and as if to emphasise their superiority a small group of Londoners decided to humiliate the intruders by pissing up the trouser leg of his mate.

During the early Seventies, Boro's bootboys would congregate in the Holgate End of the ground. There was no single mob but a collection of groups usually relating to specific areas. Topping the pecking order were the lads from Middlesbrough and Grangetown (the area directly outside the Holgate End) and they occupied the central section of the terrace. Around them stood the B Farm boys (Brambles Farm estate); the Border bootboys (St Hilda's estate); the Park End crew (Park End estate); the Whinny Bank boys (Whinny Banks estate); the Newport gang; and the Doggy boys, who represented North Ormesby. Also on the Holgate End were the Redcar Reds, the Stockton firm, the Haverton Hill mob and the Port Boys. Other firms were the Bob End Crew and the NTP. The Bob End Crew took their name from a section of the ground, while NTP was the initials of three neighbouring estates – Netherfields, Thorntree and Priestfields.

Usually the mobs co-existed peacefully, united in their desire to hold their end against outsiders, but sometimes there were clashes as top boys vied for the title of King of the Holgate. Like any other team at the time, Boro's first priority was to keep control of the Holgate End. Rarely did it come under threat but this made it even more attractive to the mighty mobs of Chelsea and West Ham. Boro might have had the numbers willing to brawl but they did not have the organisation to match the big London mobs.

In 1975, a couple of hundred West Ham travelled up to Ayresome Park with a fair amount of trepidation. "At a service station, Newcastle fans warned us that Boro had a firm to be reckoned with," recalled Cass Pennant in his book on the ICF. "The area certainly looked rough enough." After the match, the small West Ham contingent were pelted with bricks and bottles from a huge Boro mob who had gathered in a park close to the ground. "A hail of bricks whistles through the air and over the railings, landing in the street where we stand," wrote Pennant. "There are too many to dodge completely; they've got us trapped. Run or go forward? Running isn't an option."

Instead West Ham charged towards their attackers, scaling fences despite salvoes of missiles to run at Boro. "As we drop and fling ourselves off the railings into the park, the red sea wall breaks and runs. We pursue them to the open gates of the far end of the park. You can almost see their fear at the thought of what might happen to them if the maddened Cockneys catch them."

The change to the casual era was late reaching Middlesbrough. When their fans came across the new look among visiting teams they perceived it as typical southern femininity. In the fanzine *Red Issue*, one Manchester United fan recounted a fraught journey to Boro in the 1979/80 season, when the smartly dressed Mancs were confronted by 3-400 locals. "What's with all the clothes and trainers? You look like poofs," sneered one, while inside the ground the Boro faithful greeted their team in their customary fashion: "Ayresome Boys, Ayresome Boys, laced-up boots and corduroys."

United's mob, however, proceeded to chase the motley collection of punks, skinheads and steelworkers around the streets of Middlesbrough, and it was with new-found respect that one of the donkey jacket-wearing Teessiders asked a United lad, "What's all this clobber you've got on?" "It's just something that's taken off in Manchester" came the reply.

Boro's young lads eventually did latch on to the casual fashion, much to the amusement of the older lads who mocked them as "joeys" because of their wedge haircuts. They in turn would sneer at their elders who they referred to as the "fossils" or the "Beer Belly Crew". In time the teasing stopped as the young casuals began earning a name as the gamest and best organised of the Boro boys. Their emergence also brought together Boro's young lads and the inter-group rivalry on the Holgate dissipated.

Once the casual era kicked in it was hip to give your firm a name and a handful of young Boro lads came up with the moniker "the Frontline". Paul Debrick, known as "The Brick", rose from gang member to become one of the leaders of the firm. "It was important for some mobs to have a daft name," he said, in his blunt manner. "Personally I didn't give two fucks about Boro on the pitch or some fancy gang name off it. I was there to vent my violence on anyone we played and as a few of us were always in the front line, some started to go under that banner. Later on some Wrexham lads were claiming that we had nicked their name. We went there in the cup and funnily enough none of the cunts wanted to meet me and discuss it."

There was nothing to rouse the passion of a Boro fan than a local match against Sunderland or Newcastle. Over the years there have been a number of titanic battles between their fans and the rivalry continues to this day, even if the outbreaks of violence are few and far between. Sunderland ranks as their main rivals though many Boro feel more than irritated that the feeling is not mutual, with the "Mackems" more concerned with their own hatred of Newcastle. Even more annoying for Boro is the description by their North East rivals of there being two and a half clubs in the region, with Boro counting as the half.

The Frontline helped to unite the lads from Middlesbrough proper with mobs from outlying towns such as the Redcar Casuals and the Stockton Wrecking Crew, so named for their youthful activity of ransacking gaming machines. Perhaps best known among the Stockton lads is the hulking Lee "Oathead" Owens, one of the hooligan world's most instantly recognisable characters. The photograph of him being arrested by Belgian police at Euro 200 in Brussels, with his huge beer belly and hideous tattoos, was published around the world as an icon of the British soccer hooligan (and is unapologetically reproduced here).

The Eighties began badly for Boro when one of their number died after a fight outside the ground with Forest. It had been an innocuous spat between small groups of casuals but 18-year-old Craig French received a mighty blow and buckled and collapsed in a heap, cracking his head on the pavement. The death caused many of the Boro lads to rethink their involvement, but for most these thoughts were quickly dispelled as it was Sunderland away the following Saturday. The game passed off relatively peacefully but the same could not be said of the return fixture a few months later. Over 10,000 Mackems made the journey and piled into every stand in the ground. While they got chased in several incidents, it was an awesome show of strength that Boro were never able to repeat at Roker Park.

Relegation in 1981 saw Boro up against a different set of teams; an opportunity to renew old acquaintances. One such rivalry was against Chelsea whom Boro played on the last game of the season with the Londoners still fighting to stay in the division. Chelsea got the point they needed and hundreds of their lads steamed across the pitch at the final whistle. It was only the lines of police and tall fencing that kept them from Boro and prevented a riot.

Boro's young firm was still on a learning curve when Chelsea made a surprise appearance in the Holgate in January 1984. Numbers differ, with Boro claiming 300 and Chelsea 100, but either way an experienced mob travelled up by train intent on taking Boro's end. With the clock ticking down towards the final whistle, Chelsea slipped out only to reappear at the back of the Holgate, scattering fans in every direction. As if to prove their invincibility, they then stood there, arms folded, taking in the atmosphere. The Londoners were quickly rounded up and a police escort took them towards the station but even here Boro were not safe. A section of the Chelsea mob slipped their escort and steamed through the bus station. A week later, Boro played host to Arsenal in a cup game and this time a group of 70 Gooners ran amok inside the ground. It was a timely reminder, if one was needed, that Boro still had some way to go before they could take on the best.

By the mid-Eighties, the Frontline had a growing reputation in the hooligan world, even if the London-based media was still obsessed with the West Hams and Chelseas. Northern firms like the Frontline were growing in stature and organisation, while at home Ayresome Park continued to be a frightening place to visit.

The viciousness of the Boro mob was experienced most terrifyingly by Barnsley in February 1984. Up to 200 of the Barnsley Five-O, their biggest ever away mob, arrived in town but for Boro they were just another group to attack and sure enough the visitors were butchered by knife-wielding loons. Seven Barnsley men were badly cut, the worst requiring 100 stitches to a head and neck wound.

"We thought there would be no trouble, although I always went just on the off-chance there would be," remembered Paul Debrick, who would be jailed for his part in the carnage. "Barnsley had never been associated with football violence, however this particular Saturday they would be associated with it whether they liked it or not. It must have been about 12pm and some of the lads told me that Barnsley had a large mob in the Wellington Pub on Albert Road. I was shocked that Barnsley had brought a proper mob to our town and had arrived so early, because not many teams have done this at Middlesbrough.

"There must have been forty of us at the most. We didn't have the numbers to match Barnsley but the mob that we did have would have stood their own against anyone. As we were stood just outside the pub it was around 1.30pm and we could hear banging coming from the Wellington. All of a sudden the doors burst open. The Barnsley mob came spilling out onto the pavement and were now spreading out into Albert Road. We met in the middle of Albert Road head-on, fists and feet were flying and there was a lot of shouting. A few more of our lads had come up from behind them so were now on both sides of their mob and they were trapped in the middle; a Barnsley sandwich if you like and they were the filling.

"All the lads were going at it and then all of a sudden there seemed to be a panic amongst the Barnsley mob. I could hear people shouting, 'He's been stabbed, he's been stabbed,' and the Barnsley mob were now starting to back off to make a retreat back into the Wellington. While we were still attacking them I can remember one lad stood in front of me and he was in total panic. He had been slashed right across his forehead and he had a gaping wound from one side to the other. The blood was pissing out of the wound and he was covered from head to foot. As I turned I could see another lad running about like a chicken with no head. He had also been slashed right down his arm from top to bottom and he was screaming for help."

Thirteen Boro lads later received a total of 39 years in jail for what the judge said was the worst case of football violence he had ever encountered. During the 16-day trial some 200 witnesses were called, ranging from the full Barnsley mob to Saturday shoppers and shopkeepers, and it remains one of the heaviest total sentences handed out for a single football hooligan-related incident.

The last game of the 1984/85 season saw Middlesbrough travel to

Shrewsbury facing the humiliation of a drop to Division Three. It was the second consecutive season that Boro had travelled to the Gay Meadow on the final day of the season with relegation a possibility. In May 1984 they had secured the necessary points and their fans rioted in celebration but this year the outcome was not so rosy. When Shrewsbury went ahead Boro fans responded by scaling the fences and ripping up seats and throwing them first onto the pitch and then later at the police who waded in to restore order. A kiosk at the back of the stand was demolished and the pieces thrown onto the pitch. After the final whistle, and with relegation confirmed, the police kept the home fans locked in the ground for their own safety and desperately tried to get Boro out of town as quickly as they could. Much of the trouble had been caught on camera and this was used as evidence to send 20 Boro to prison.

The Third Division brought new grounds for Boro to visit. One such trip was away at Hull City, a club with a tough hooligan reputation but until that point considered on friendly terms with Boro – some of their main faces knew each other well from the Northern Soul scene. There had been serious trouble between the two clubs back in the early 1970s but they had not played one another for several years until 1986, when the Frontline made a surprise visit. A coachload of them surprised some Hull boys in the seats and ragged them onto the pitch.

Whilst the relative proximity of Sunderland, Newcastle and even Hull can explain the rivalry between their mobs and the Frontline, surprisingly some of Boro's most violent clashes have involved Everton. Their feud dates to 1977, when Boro hosted an FA Cup tie which they won 3–2. There was some trouble before the game, and after Everton raised the stakes, and as one Boro lad climbed over a wall to get away from the chasing away mob, he was stabbed straight up the anus and came within an inch of death. That incident sparked off almost a quarter of a century of violence which saw pitched battles home and away and left scores injured.

The two sides met infrequently after the FA Cup match but in 1985 it was Everton's turn to host Middlesbrough in the same competition. They brought down 200 lads and attacked an Everton-frequented pub near Lime Street station. The intensity of the assault prevented Everton from getting out and it was only when one of the Everton lads threw a stool through a window that they were able to confront the Boro mob. Everton were humiliated, as it had been years since any firm had shown like that so early in the day, and as word went round Everton's mob was joined by lads from the other pubs around the station and even men out shopping. For several minutes a large-scale disturbance continued in full view of hundreds of shoppers and cinema-goers and one youth was thrown through a clothes shop window. Police eventually escorted Boro to the ground and afterwards were stretched to their limit in an attempt to keep the warring factions apart. The game finished a draw, and for the replay Everton took a huge mob, but the Teesside police were not so naïve as their Merseyside counterparts and kept firm control.

The two sides could still not be separated and a second replay was played in Liverpool. Once again there was trouble, but the outcome was far more serious as knife-wielding local youths took revenge for the liberties taken by Boro at the first game and seven Boro were admitted to hospital having been either stabbed or slashed, with one victim losing an eye.

Everton travelled up to Boro for a nondescript game towards the end of the 1989 season. They were doing poorly in the League but still took a mob of 100. Small groups of Boro came out to meet them and despite being heavily outnumbered on each individual occasion they battled with Everton all the way to the ground. The tiny back streets made it perfect for ambushes and a nightmare for away fans. To many Everton, Middlesbrough was the nastiest place to visit. As Boro yo-yoed between divisions, Everton's mob went into a decline, at least in terms of numbers. So when the Toffees next travelled north they were a much smaller unit. It was to be a memorable trip and one in which a new Everton mob was formed.

The visitors parked up in Darlington and, undetected by police, made the short hop by train into Middlesbrough and went straight into the home pub. The Frontline must have thought Everton had big numbers, as the few lads in there were forced to kick the fire door open and escape. But by the time the Blues made their way to the ground they were confronted by mobs from all sides and fights broke out at every junction and crossing. "The Boro lads had the mentality that the police did not exist," said one Evertonian. "The local bizzies would say, 'Pack it in, Billy' or 'Stop it, Joe.' The police knew every one of them but rather than nick them, they'd dish out the odd slap."

The new Riverside Stadium was slightly more hospitable to away fans than Ayresome Park and Everton survived everything Boro could throw at them. The group of 40 visitors – who were to become known as the Snorty Forty from that day on – fought their way to the ground, and even the blunt-speaking Paul Debrick was impressed: "Everton, what can I say? They were always a formidable mob to come across whether we played them at home or at Goodison Park and they always turned out for us, and were always game as fuck; bit like us. I've lost count how many times I've been there over the years but every trip had one thing in common, you got what you went for – trouble. Everton were pretty similar to ourselves, loved the element of surprise, always came early, and loved an off. In short, game."

Boro played at Everton early in the next season, and after the game the home mob phoned the visitors to try to arrange a meeting. They were told that the police were with the Boro crowd, so quite a few Everton headed home. Half an hour later, Boro rang back and said that they were on the move without a police escort. A fight was arranged though most Everton were sceptical and so refused to move. To their surprise, Boro were there, and out piled the depleted Everton mob. They charged but Boro stood their ground. This is how the event was remembered in *Scally*, by Andy Nicholls:

We went straight into them. They stood firm, as I had expected, and from the back of their mob came a load of lads with big rocks. One had a fence pole. Had they kept hold of them we would have been in lumber, but they threw them at us and backed off. I picked up the fence pole and I ran forward and hit the biggest fucker they had clean over the head. It snapped in two. I rammed the broken stake into his chest and waited for him to crumble, and waited. He shook his head, picked up the other half and came into us with it. How the Boro lad stayed up I will never know, but he did. He was the hardest bastard I have ever fought. They battled like mad but in the end they went. We chased them before they stopped and fronted it again, but this time they had casualties and got done in. One lad was stabbed in the arm and a couple more were unconscious on the pavement.

Middlesbrough against Everton was now more of a grudge match than ever. The return fixture was on Boxing Day, normally a big day out for any mob, but on this particular bank holiday many Evertonians decided to make themselves busy. Boro had come off badly at the previous encounter and everyone knew they would be out for revenge. Again, *Scally* takes up the story:

If you need an excuse to bottle out of a game that could be a bit tasty, Christmas is the ideal one. Quite a few used it that day, and expectations of 150 going up were well off the mark as we failed to even fill a coach ... We got there nice and early at about twelve and made it to the centre of town without a bizzie in sight ... A lad came out of a pub, one of their boys I had seen loads of times. He was sound and asked, 'How many?' I told him fifty-odd, but a good fifty, and he laughed; not a sly piss-taking laugh, but a 'don't fucking bother' laugh. I asked him what Boro had out and he said, 'Hundreds.' I nodded and walked away shaking my head. He shouted back at me. I will never forget him saying, 'Nicholls, six hundred an hour ago, get your lads back on the bus and fuck off home. You're gonna get killed, the whole town is out for this one.' Seconds earlier I thought he was blagging but this time his tone was different. Although I didn't want to believe him I knew I had to.

I caught up with our mob and came to a boozer full of them. We fronted the main door – we had been there less than a minute and it was ready to go. A few came out and there was a massive roar, but they turned and pushed their way back in ... Boro steamed out, and we were forced back under the bridge as wave after wave of glasses and bottles landed around us. I was screaming for our mob to hold our ground, as if Boro got out tooled up, we were finished. Briefly we got them back in the pub ... and we regrouped before heading off to the next boozer.

As we looked up the hill, it was a sight to forget but I never will. There was a ... car driving slowly towards us with a mob of hundreds behind. I thought it was a police car, albeit a clapped out one, but it revved up and drove straight at us ... and within seconds our mob was scattered. They were behind us, at both sides of us and the road in front was still full of them. You could not see an inch of tarmac, just masses of lads piling down the road ... I thought I was going to die.

At last the police arrived. I'm sure that they had let it go on as they did to teach us a lesson. They surrounded us but Boro went through them and we were chased back to our coach ... We were silent all the way to the ground and Boro left us alone. I was embarrassed that our stupidity had cost us and the myth that our forty could go anywhere and do it was blown out of the water.

The Brick agreed. "We were to get our revenge that Boxing Day. They'd been told to come to the Whicker's World pub and to get there early doors. I was head doorman at the pub at the time, so I knew I'd be there, which was convenient. I'd just returned from the toilets and had a massive line of coke to get me charged up when one of our lads came bursting through the door. 'They're here, they're fucking here,' he was screaming. I thought it was a wind-up at first, but to my delight I could see around fifty lads outside coming straight for the door. One of the Everton lads ran forward and sprayed the door with CS gas and there was a slight stand-off for a few seconds, then the other lads in the pub with me all came steaming out, and I was shouting, 'These fuckers are tooled up.'

"By now our entire mob was bearing down on Everton and, to give them their due, they stood their ground, and under the circumstances were game on. Three or four hundred lads, all fighting like fuck to get at them, was not the kind of Christmas present the Scouse bastards had asked Santa for. I could hear sirens screaming everywhere now, and it was only a matter of minutes before the inevitable swarm of police came. We quickly attacked again and there was lads laid out in the middle of the road, getting kicked all over. When order was restored they put a massive police line between us and the Everton lads so we couldn't attack again.

"A short while later I walked straight over to their mob near the ground, and I was screaming abuse at them. Pointless really, but it made me feel better at the time. Everyone was happy how things had gone, except one of our lads had been slashed across the chest and later needed thirty stitches. I think they thought they'd surprise us but we were ready for them and turned the tables. Victory was ours that day, but respect where respect is due, and Everton have my respect all day long."

Boro probably reached their peak in the 1989/90 season. While several other more well-known firms, such as the ICF, Leeds Service Crew and Zulus, virtually went to the wall largely because of police operations, the Frontline prospered. Many of the better-known firms became victims of their own notoriety and the fact that most of their violence was conducted outside the stadia meant there was not the same public pressure for the police to act on Teesside. The pinnacle of this period was Boro's dominance in the North East. At one evening game at Newcastle, 150 Boro marched through their opponent's city centre unscathed before the game and scattered their rivals afterwards. "Doing the biz twice in a row at Newcastle was the icing on the cake," wrote John Theone. "We had finally arrived as a respected firm and our reputation was second to none."

Others agreed. Everton had nothing but respect for Boro, and this was a view shared by, among others, Portsmouth 6.57 Crew, who see similarities between themselves and the Frontline. The two firms have had several confrontations over the years, dating back to 1977 when around 100 Boro made the long trek south for an evening game and had to fight for their lives in the Milton End at Fratton Park in the days before it was segregated. In the early Nineties furious fighting between the two mobs saw one Pompey lad suffer a badly broken leg.

Another firm to have the utmost respect for the Frontline were Cardiff City, who played Boro in the FA Cup in the 1993/94 season. Boro set off at four in the morning and were in Cardiff, 100-strong, by pub opening time. Cardiff were caught unawares and even when Boro's presence was noted, they failed to get a proper mob together. "Middlesbrough had a reputation as one of the best firms in England," said David Jones and Tony Rivers in their book *Soul Crew*. "They were a real firm who did things right: they made sure we knew where they were but kept quiet about it, not making a fuss, just waiting for us to get a firm big enough to have a crack. This is why they have got tons of respect in the hooligan netherworld." Cardiff finally put a mob together but it could not handle Boro, who steamed out of the Albert pub tooled up and chased the locals. Many of the older South Wales lads said that not since Chelsea or Portsmouth had they seen a firm so organised or game.

Chelsea were regarded by many as top dogs towards the end of the Eighties and Boro more than obliged when the chance came to clash in London. The two clubs played each other in a number of crucial fixtures in the late Eighties and early Nineties, beginning with the 1988 Division Two promotion play-off final when Boro won and sent Chelsea down. Boro took an enormous mob, estimated at up to 1,000 strong, that marched through west London to the ground and was far too much for any Chelsea groups hoping to snipe them from pubs en route.

Middlesbrough went into the game with a 2–0 lead from the first leg and though Chelsea pulled a goal back early on, the visitors held on to win promotion. A few Boro climbed onto the fences but were beaten back by the stewards. At the other end of the ground hundreds of Chelsea poured onto the pitch and headed straight towards the away end. Subsequent TV and newspaper footage showed Chelsea's boys baiting Boro and throwing missiles at them from the pitch, but had the Teesside mob been able to join them the story would have been very different. Boro fans were kept in until Chelsea had been cleared from the surrounding streets, and a potential battle royal was averted.

Two smaller groups did manage to stage a toe-to-toe encounter two years later when they met in the Zenith Data System Final at Wembley. After the game the two mobs clashed down a side street near the ground in a punch-up that seemed to last forever to those involved.

Middlesbrough's fortunes fluctuated on the pitch as their slide coincided with a deep financial crisis that almost crippled the club. In 1986 they were put into receivership and many thought the club would fold. In came a saviour in the shape of local fan and wealthy businessman Steve Gibson, who during the Nineties was to revolutionise the club. Gibson brought in Brian Robson, pumped in millions of his own money and within a year they were back in the Premiership.

Life in the top league also brought a move to a new stadium, the Riverside, and before a ball had even been kicked over 18,500 season tickets had been sold. Middlesbrough survived in the Premiership and the following season enjoyed arguably their best year to date. Adding flair to the team were foreign imports Fabrizio Ravanelli and Emerson. In 1997, Boro had the most successful season in their history and reached the FA

Cup final, where they lost to old rivals Chelsea. On the way to the final the Frontline had, in Paul Debrick's words, "fucking good chew" at Man City.

"I always regarded Man City as being one of the top firms in the country," he said. "They had the numbers, they were always up for it and we always got trouble whenever we went to Maine Road. We decided to go by train for the cup match and when we arrived in Manchester Piccadilly there must have been around about 150 of us, all charged up on alcohol and cocaine. The same day fifty Hibs casuals also showed, as they knew several of our lads and had arranged to come into Mancland because they knew there was fun to be had by all.

"No chew before the game, we got escorted to the ground and the police kept us in a tight group so we had no chance of escaping and doing what we came for. Just before full-time it was arranged that we would meet at the main exit and get off together, but as we left the ground there was some fuck-up because 120 of our lads came out and turned left, and myself and about thirty others turned right. Before we realised what had happened it was too late and the thirty of us were on our own in the middle of Moss Side, where half the city wanted to kill us.

"I looked at our small mob and there were about fifteen good lads with us; the rest of the numbers were made up by younger lads. I thought to myself, if these young lads want to be game, now is the time to show it. We approached the main road at the top of the street and were coming close to a T-junction and there were City lads everywhere, I turned and said to everyone, 'Keep it tight, stay together, we'll do what we can,' and seconds later they came at us straight across the road. This is it, I thought, I am going to that big terrace in the sky. As the first few approached I hit the first one with a left hook and the second one with a right. I continued throwing punches like they were going out of fashion and was surprised how easy they were going down. The other lads with me were all doing the same and I was quite pleased with how we were doing until suddenly the whole road just seemed to attack us. It was like Custer's Last Stand. Suddenly two police vans crashed into one another on the way to sort the trouble out and that diverted everybody's attention just long enough for the road to be swarming with police. It was the one time at the match that I thought I was going to be killed.

"We were escorted back to the station and City followed us all the way, about 300 of them. We met up with our main mob and they had had it with another mob of Mancs; City must have had some mob out that day. Our lads had also bumped into the firm of Hibs who wanted to join up with Boro but they were told to fuck off and were also attacked, leaving three mobs going for it in the same place. The police didn't have a fucking clue what was going on."

The Frontline also turned out in force for a visit to Old Trafford in 2001. As is the case when an away mob claims a major result at one of the so called "top firms", the rivals have different slants to the day's events and this game was no different, as one respected Frontline member explained.

"We took Man United away, it's as simple as that. They admitted that we turned them over but they're slightly more reluctant to admit that both sides had a full mob out. We got there early, were drinking in their city, and they came down with numbers and got done. The reason United are hated as a firm is that whenever they come unstuck they never admit it. At the end of the day they came to us and got done; they know it, we know it and they would be respected a lot more if once in their blinkered fucking lifetimes they admitted it. Anyone can get done by anyone on the day and United were not the first or last firm to come off second best against Boro, so they should get over it. Shit happens." Needless to say, many United hooligans disagree with this version of events.

While members of the Frontline openly respect fellow mobs and are quite complimentary about the strength of some major rivals, in recent years Sunderland have gained little respect and as other feuds die out the Mackems' return to the Premiership rekindled the hatred towards them from most Boro fans and thugs alike. This has existed since an incident which saw Sunderland thugs attack a disabled coach load of Middlesbrough supporters as one Boro lad recalled.

"Any mob that blatantly attacks pensioners, kids, women, and even bricks a disabled supporters' coach, deserves fuck-all respect. This was after a cup game up there, and rightly or wrongly we took revenge in bricking their team coach at the return leg. We have taken a mob up there the last three times we have played them and the spur for all the Boro is the attack on the disabled coach. The last time we played them they only gave us 1,000 seats but that didn't bother us too much, as we went up before the game and bought tickets for all over the ground. It was going off everywhere during the game."

Over the past few years, Boro hooligans have established themselves as a major force on the England scene, both home and away. Over 100 Boro lads made the short trip to Glasgow for one recent international, and according to one Frontline lad, "the fear on the faces of smaller English mobs when we boarded the train at Darlington was worth the trip alone. From arriving in Scotland, to leaving after the game, our lot misbehaved. One of the lads had a Union Jack with 'Middlesbrough' painted across it. He held it up, when we got off the train, and shouted, 'Right lads, these colours don't fuckin' run.' What he was saying was, any one gets shitty and runs during any conflicts, and they'll be sorted at a later date. So off we went. Any jocks we saw, either 'lads' or the silly kilt-wearing types, were considered fair game, and as we approached them, out would come the flag, to show them who we were. Then in we'd go, hitting them with anything we could. A few smaller groups from England latched onto us, and this 'Boro' mob was now growing into a small army, but we were still running the show. We hit small mobs of jocks, large mobs of jocks, pubs, buses, anything Scottish we could find. The police finally sussed us and took us up to the ground, and word soon got round who we were and what we'd done. We tried to settle a few scores with English mobs that day as well and with the London firms still considered the best about, we fancied it with any of them, but no one had the numbers to even consider it."

When England played their crucial Euro 2004 qualifier at the Stadium of Light, Sunderland, in April 2002, many English thugs were intent on seeking 'revenge' for two Leeds fans who had been killed in Istanbul a couple of years before. Boro, however, had a more pressing score to settle – with Sunderland. About 100 Frontline made the short trip and clashed twice with Sunderland before the game. One of the police spotters noted that this included some of the worst hand-to-hand fighting he had experienced. When he expressed his surprise that neither of these incidents had been logged on the police system, a local officer told him that this was so routine when the two clubs met that it didn't warrant a mention.

A couple of years later, England played a home match against Albania at the Riverside, but much to the disappointment of locals, including virtually every Boro lad who had been active in the past thirty years, no other firm put in an appearance. "Lads from the old days, the new Frontline lads, old beer bellies, lads like myself who just wanted to hit someone, all came out in antic-ipation," said Paul Debrick. "Every pub in town must have had a little Boro mob of at least twenty in it, ready to go. We ended up disappointed as there wasn't much chew anywhere. It's still considered a dodgy place to come."

The England scene has brought about the strangest of alliances in foot-ball, often between once bitter enemies. Boro, however, have never linked up with anyone, though a few individuals have sometimes travelled abroad with Chelsea. This changed in Euro 2000 when they went to aid some Arsenal lads. Since then the two groups have been fairly friendly, much to the annoyance of the old school. "It came to a head at Old Trafford in the FA cup semi a couple of seasons back," admitted one Frontliner. "The current Frontline met up with the Arsenal lads in a boozer, but the old Boro were also in there. The new Boro decided to leave, and after they left an Arsenal lad said, 'We'll be kicking fuck out of them cunts tomorrow.' This was heard by the old Boro, who got straight into them and gave them a kicking. I thought this might cause some shit between Boro, old and new, but nothing came of it, though there's a lot of bad feeling between the two sets of Boro lads, even now."

Today's Frontline probably have a hardcore of about 60 and for big games will see 150-200 turn out. At the Coca Cola Cup final in Cardiff, where old and new mixed together, they numbered around 500. However, like many other mobs the Frontline have been badly hit by banning orders. Despite this, Middlesbrough always has been and always will be regarded as a tough place to visit and the locals are always happy to oblige if you go there looking for trouble, or in their own words, are "after some chew".

In the past few years the most violent clashes involving Boro have been in Europe. According to Boro lad Craig, "It went off at nearly every game in Europe, Ostrava 2005 was mental, Zurich 2006, only had 20 lads but went mad before the game. Roma attacked normal fans. At one stage we had over 130 lads banned but no fucker comes to Boro now anyway."

The club's European match against Banik Ostrava, in the Czech Republic, was marred by fighting in the stands. In November 2005, supporter Brendan O'Connor, 36, was killed and his friend, Howard Boville, 38, was seriously injured in a stabbing after Boro's game against AZ Alkmaar in Amsterdam, which they had watched in a bar after failing to get tickets. A Dutch drug dealer was later jailed for four years for Mr O'Connor's manslaughter, which was not football-related. The following year brought clashes in Zurich, and then in March 2006 Boro travelled to play AS Roma in the Uefa Cup. It was the scene of a horrific attack.

"Terrified British football fans fled for their lives early yesterday as a mob of 80 Italian hooligans attacked them with knives, axes and baseball bats," *The Mirror* reported. "The Middlesbrough supporters, including mums and dads with children, were ambushed by notorious Ultra thugs in Rome's picture-postcard Campo di Fiori square. Three Boro fans were knifed and many more battered in the well-planned, unprovoked attack before baton-armed Italian police waded in to chase the Ultras away."

The English fans were drinking in the square when the armed Ultras, wearing black and ski masks, arrived and attacked 30 of them in the Drunken Ship pub. A handful of Boro fought back but were not to blame for the violence. Peter Green, 43, from Stockton-on-Tees, and his son Andrew, 18, were among those wounded. Peter said, "I heard an enormous explosion. It was so loud I thought a bomb had gone off. I dashed outside and ran straight into a huge gang of Ultras. They were running up the street towards the Boro fans and pulling out clubs, coshes and batons. As I was trying to get through them to get back to my sons I was hit over the head with a cosh. My head was split open and blood was pouring down my face. I had to put up my hands to ward off more blows, then someone hit me over the back with a chair. It was surreal. All the pub's shutters had come down. I could not see any of the Boro fans or either of my sons and I was shouting out for them. Then a shutter on the Drunken Ship flew up and Andrew and the other Boro fans came running out. Andrew had a stab wound above his backside where a knife had gone straight in."

Mirror sports writer Simon Bird watched as the Ultras lashed out. He said, "They attacked wearing crash helmets and balaclavas, wielding knives, flares, fireworks and sticks. One lunatic even had an axe. It was only good fortune that prevented any deaths." Cleveland police Superintendent Steve Swales, in Rome for the match, said, "The Ultras were clearly well-organised and had an identified leader. He was wearing a shiny fireman's-type helmet with a bandana across his face that meant only his eyes were visible. Boro fans were mainly in family groups with younger children, some with their wives." One of those stabbed was David "Allo" Allison, aged 39, a well-known Boro fan who 15 years earlier had been acquitted of killing notorious Teesside gangster Lee Duffy. Allison was knifed in the back and chest and later underwent surgery.

The most stunning news for the Frontline was the sudden death in August 2007 of Paul Debrick. Larger than life and seemingly indestructible, Paul was at home during a break from his work on offshore oil rigs when he collapsed and died, at the age of only forty-two. Tributes poured in to the Frontline website from all over the world for one of the true characters of the football terraces. "There will never be another Brick," said one of his friends. "He was a hard man but also very funny, always joking and taking the mick, and he would stand by his mates till the end. He will be sadly missed."

Further reading: *The Frontline*, John Theone (Milo Books), *The Brick*, Paul Debrick (Milo Books), *Scally*, Andy Nicholls (Milo Books)

MILLWALL

Ground: The New Den, formerly the Den
Firms: Treatment, F-Troop, Bushwhackers
Rivals: West Ham, Portsmouth
Police operations: Dirty Den

Neil MacPherson is a decent bloke, and that was his downfall. Almost 1,000 Millwall fans had just rioted for several hours, injuring 57 police officers and 26 horses. It was probably the worst outbreak of football disorder London had ever seen. "It was worse than the Brixton and Poll Tax riots," MacPherson whispered. And he was a man who knew; he was, after all, Millwall's football intelligence officer. The infamous Lions had just lost their play-off semi-final to Birmingham and their fans reacted in the only way they knew how. A lamp-post was literally pulled out of the ground and used as a weapon, paving slabs were ripped up and brick walls knocked down and thrown, brick by brick, at the police.

MacPherson watched in a mixture of disbelief and angst. Millwall fans had misbehaved on at least ten other occasions that season, including five riots against the police, but nothing on this scale. "What can I do?" he sighed to a BBC television crew who had been following the club, and him, around all season. He looked as though he was about to cry; perhaps at that moment he knew that he was about to lose his job.

Earlier in the season, he had predicted a match at Wolves would be skipped by the hardcore, only for 250 to catch a midday train out of Euston, some armed with baseball bats and knives. A couple of weeks before that, a South London newspaper had run a series of photographs of Millwall fans wanted for attacking police at a home game against Notts Forest. The mother of one twelve-year-old took her son by the ear into the local police station. "You fuckin' cunt," she screamed, pushing her son forward. MacPherson looked on. "A new generation is being born," he would later comment. The young lad was released and later that evening, with a confidence and swagger that had been lacking in front of his mother and the police, he sauntered into a local youth club wearing his caution as a badge of honour. He had made it into the ranks of Millwall and for him and his peers there was no better accolade.

Neil MacPherson proved no match for Millwall. They had, after all, been fighting the police and officialdom since the 1920s.

The mere mention of Millwall invokes football hooliganism in the minds of many. No other club has, for such a long period, been so associated with crowd disorder. From ransacking mobs at Luton, to assaults on referees and officials, sledgehammers and pickaxes used to smash down pub doors to lamp-posts being ripped from the ground, Millwall's followers ooze trouble. When *Panorama* investigated football hooliganism in 1977, it was to Millwall – and "Harry the Dog" – that they turned. When the BBC returned to the topic with a three-part series in 2002, again Millwall were the stars of the show.

It is not just the media who have contrived to give this folkloric status to the fans of the South East London club. "When it comes to fear, there are few things to match being bushwhacked in a dark subway by several hundred Millwall boys," wrote Manchester City hooligan leader Mickey Francis in *Guvnors*. "It makes you wonder why you ever became a football hooligan."

"The word [Millwall] sent shivers down my spine; the hardest fans in the land," wrote Colin Ward in *Steaming In*. "I practically shit my pants on the spot," recalls Middlesbrough's John Theone, in his book *Frontline*, about a trip to Millwall in the 1970s. "I mean, these were not lads in their mid-teens, they were all big fuck-off dockers and they were literally laughing at the state of our crew, calling us babies and kids." The image repeatedly conjured up, in these and many other hooligan memoirs, is of a tough and fanatical fan base, derived from London's docks and with a universal hatred of all outsiders.

As early as Christmas 1919, the club was warning spectators of their behaviour. "Don't swear or use bad language of any description in the hearing of others," a match-day programme advised. "It is not nice for ladies to hear, and it does not raise you in the estimation of other would-be friends." The programme also asked for fans not to "give advice to the referee. He has to give decisions quickly, and like the rest of us, he makes mistakes." The appeal did little to reduce the hostility shown at the Den and the following year the club was reported to the FA after a Newport County goalkeeper was "flattened by a useful right hook". The ground was closed after an FA meeting was "satisfied that missiles were thrown by a section of spectators and that there was a considerable amount of disorderly conduct, bad language and intimidation of visiting players."

During the 1934/35 season, a match against Bradford Park Avenue again saw the Den closed after away players were pelted with missiles. At the end of the match, a 4000-strong crowd gathered outside the ground chanting, "We want the referee." The club was closed for a third time in 1948 after a game at home to Barnsley. Fury at refereeing decisions again appeared to be the spark, as the away team was awarded a penalty late into the game. "After the spot kick made it 3-3, a number of Millwall supporters cleared the wall and ran onto the pitch to remonstrate with the referee," noted James Murray in his book, *Millwall: Lions of the South*. "One was stopped only seconds before he could reach the man who had so infuriated the crowd all afternoon. The official was also the target of missile throwers within the ground and as he departed Cold Blow Lane made another wrong decision by admitting his identity to one pent up fan, who tried to hit him."

Garry Robson, in *No One Likes Us, We Don't Care*, notes that programmes during this period would refer to the troublemakers as "ultra-keen supporters" rather than hooligans or any other derogatory term. "These individuals were thus acknowledged as genuine supporters overcome by zeal," he adds. A game the following season saw yet more trouble after three of Exeter City's goals were hotly disputed. "After the game a gang of between 150 and 200 spectators ambushed referee Meade and linesmen Day and Turner," noted Murray. "Mr Meade claimed he was struck on the back and teacups were thrown." The ground was closed for another seven days and the club fined £100.

Conventional wisdom holds that modern football hooliganism began when Manchester United fans ran amok at Upton Park in May 1967, but for Millwall fans that was old news. Eighteen months before, in November 1965, at an away at Brentford, one Millwall fan threw a hand grenade on to the pitch. "A copper picked it up and puts it in a bucket of sand and places it behind the touch line," recalls one Millwall fan present that day. "It was a dummy grenade and it landed in front of Chic Brodie, their keeper. He ran for his life. He was an unlucky cunt, as his career was later ended by a dog that invaded the pitch." Millwall's keeper, a young Alex Stepney, told the press immediately afterwards that if it had landed near him he would have been the first person out of the ground. "Soccer marches to war," said the *Sun*'s headline shortly after.

Later that season, Millwall played a crunch promotion clash at QPR. Both teams had a chance of going up but a magnificent display by the young Rodney Marsh saw the home side romp home 6-1 winners. Many of the QPR goals were followed by good-natured pitch invasions but the atmosphere turned ugly when a coin struck Millwall forward Len Juliens on the head and he immediately threw it back into the crowd. Via the public address system, the crowd were told that any further crowd disturbance or pitch invasion would result in the game being abandoned. It was not the sort of thing to tell Millwall fans when their team was being hammered. Thirty away fans ran onto the pitch and proceeded to sit down in the expectation that the game would be ended. It took the Millwall manager Billy Gray to plead with his own supporters, who he referred to as "hotheads", to acknowledge Rangers as "the better team on the day" and leave the field. They complied.

There was worse to come. At the next home game, smoke bombs were thrown onto the Cold Blow Lane terrace, and the following month saw trouble during Millwall's match at Oxford. Former Millwall player Eamon Dunphy recalled the game vividly as being the first he had experienced where the police were out in force. "In those days the team travelled by train, and the fans travelled with us," he later wrote. "The decent supporters, plus a small group of young toughs, numbering no more than two dozen, were met by about 20 policemen who escorted them on foot through the town to the Oxford United ground. On this day the hooligan was noticed, his presence felt, and he grew a little in stature. Saturday afternoon shoppers in a provincial English town were ushered off the pavement by the forces of law and order to allow the London Boys – the Millwall Boys – free passage to our game."

The Millwall Boys and others like them found that by banding together, chanting and generally misbehaving in an intimidating manner, they could "take over" town centres and make national headlines. They also found that fines for football-related crimes were derisory and policing often ineffectual. A match programme shortly after the Oxford game gave spectators yet another warning about their behaviour. "Once again we are seriously perturbed by the irresponsible behaviour of certain groups of unruly teenage supporters. This sort of thing must be stamped out for the good of Millwall and the game. We are not exaggerating in any way the unruliness of these young people. Even our own genuine supporters have been shocked and shamed by their behaviour and unless it is nipped in the bud now, decent civilised supporters will stay away and this is something we cannot afford to happen."

Millwall fans were beginning to earn a reputation outside their home turf. From 1966, every visit to Portsmouth for the rest of the decade brought trouble, which until that point had been unknown on the South Coast. The ferocity of the repeated Millwall invasions, often by men in their forties, created such fear in the young Portsmouth hooligans that most would not even consider a trip away to South East London. "Millwall away was a no-no," recalled one Pompey fan in the book *Rolling with the 6.57 Crew*. "We went the first year in 1967 but nobody went again after that. I'd go Millwall away but I'd go incognito. I went twice and I kept very quiet and low, it's as simple as that."

On the field the Millwall team was improving, and during the 1966/67 season they went more than five months without losing a match, until they lost 2-1 at home to Plymouth, who ironically enough had not won away all season. The home supporters reacted furiously and pelted the Plymouth goalkeeper during the game and attacked the visiting players' coach after the game, smashing several windows.

Later that year, Millwall were again in hot water after a pitch invasion left the referee unconscious and needing to be carried from the pitch by six policemen. "The wild, unruly elements of the British soccer public must be fenced in," screamed *The Sun* the following Monday. "If they are going to behave like animals, they must be treated like animals – and put in wire cages. Closing troublesome grounds is not the answer. Millwall's ground has been closed twice since the War. This sadly did not stop the fastest and worst pitch invasion at the Den after Saturday's 2-1 defeat by Aston Villa."

While there remained an initial mystery as to whether the referee was hit or simply collapsed through fear, there was no confusing the behaviour of some of the crowd. "Some of these people here are just plain savages," retorted an angry police officer. The Football League Management Committee launched an investigation but it came to "no conclusion because of a lack of facts". Len Shipman, President of the Football League, said, "Control of spectators is entirely the club's responsibility, but it is difficult to see what more we can do. I think the police will eventually stamp out hooliganism." Millwall FC was fined £1000, an amount that outraged *The Sun*. "Those Cold Blow Lane louts will laugh at the FA after this," said the paper following the FA decision. The fine, it declared, "will be as effective as stopping sixpence from a boy's pocket money for kicking his sister".

The referees were even less impressed and believed the sentence, which also included posting notices up around the ground, was too lenient. Leading the protest was the Association of Football League Referees and Linesmen, which advised members to not work at the ground until security could be ensured. It looked as though Millwall's next home game, against Portsmouth, would have to be called off but last-minute talks between the League and the Association came to a compromise and the revolt was averted. While referee Dennis Brady said that he was not in the least bit worried about overseeing the next match, the compromise appeared hollow. Millwall admitted to the press that no extra police, or other security measures, would be put in place. The whole affair was monitored closely in the media, and it was another major signpost of what appeared to be a worsening hooligan problem, particularly at the Den.

The Millwall myth began a long time before Millwall FC was formed by Bermondsey dockers in 1885. The area of South East London which encompasses Bermondsey, Southwark, Peckham, Lewisham and Deptford had a reputation of toughness dating back to the early Middle Ages. "If there is a modern equivalent to early Southwark it might well be Tijuana, the seedy town just south of the Mexican-American border," wrote Richard Byrne in his book *Prisons and Punishments of London*. "The Thames might not be the Rio Grande, but medieval Southwark certainly had a Wild West atmosphere. In the taverns, brothels and gaming-houses of Bankside sudden violence was common and its causes were the stuff of cowboy films. Stagecoaches would arrive with their passengers robbed or wounded, after an ambush by masked men lurking by the roadside. This was the flavour of Southwark life for centuries."

This close association with crime and a place to fear by the more affluent middle classes north of the River continues to this day. "From medieval criminal quarter and pleasure ground to Fagin and the definitive Dickensian criminal warren at Jacob's Island in Bermondsey, from the original nineteenth-century Hooligan to the first 'Teddy Boys', from classical gangland enclave to home of the archetypal football thug at Millwall, marks south-east London out as a very particular and historically significant place," wrote Garry Robson in *No One Likes Us, We Don't Care.*

The central role of criminality and the seeming acceptance of organised crime within much of the community, together with a long-standing tradition of working class masculinity, meant Millwall fans were more willing to use violence to articulate their frustrations than fans at most other football grounds. While Burnley fans complained to local papers about rowdy teenagers singing songs in 1966, and the Arsenal North Bank was formed in 1967, Millwall fans, young and old, had been enacting many of these "new" practices since the 1920s. By the late 1960s, while most early hooligans were teenagers, Millwall's already included men in their forties.

In the 1950s, the Teddy Boys, Britain's first modern youth sub-culture, emerged from the slums of the Elephant and Castle, a stone's throw from Millwall's ground. One of its sons, Michael Caine, described the area in his autobiography as "rough and dangerous as it was possible to get without anybody actually declaring war. If you were asked where you came from, you only said 'the Elephant', and if you could keep a reasonably straight face, this was usually enough to strike terror into anyone from outside the area."

If East London had the Krays, South East London had Charlie and Eddie Richardson and Frankie Fraser, local gangsters who ran protection rackets across London in the 1960s and achieved almost cult status in the area. Charlie Richardson's straddling of the line between street-trading and criminality, epitomised by his scrap-metal business, and his refusal to undertake National Service because he claimed that he didn't need to be in the Army to prove he was a man, were common values in South East London dating back to the 11th century. The TV comedy *Only Fools And Horses,* set in Peckham, was a parody on this sort of dodgy geezer. Eddie Richardson was also known as "King of the Teds".

This part of London has spawned a host of other major criminals over the years. Most of the Great Train Robbers, and more recently the Brinks Mat robbers, came from the area, as did the Arifs, a Turkish family who by the early 1990s ran many rackets in South London; when police finally brought their activities to a halt, the operation looked more like a NATO manoeuvre, such was the weaponry employed to arrest the suspects. In 1987, a senior Met Police Flying Squad officer noted that "some 60 per cent of all armed robberies in this country take place in London, and about three quarters of those which take place elsewhere are committed by Londoners. Proportionally, the chances are high that an armed robber is from South East London."

This violent culture spilled over to the terraces, and like the early West Ham days, big matches would bring out the criminal underworld. As recently as the mid-1990s, a major face at Millwall was a relative of George Cornell, the gangster killed by the Krays at the Blind Beggar pub in East London. The man, who was in his early fifties and missing several front teeth, certainly looked the part.

The close association with criminality was accompanied by a strong anti-police attitude and probably explains why Millwall fans have confronted the police more than any other set of supporters in the country. As recently as 2001, young Millwall fans were firing rockets at police lines, while hundreds of older supporters, in between supplying the rockets to the kids, were singing the "Harry Roberts" song. Roberts shot dead two police officers (his accomplice killed a third) during an armed robbery in the late 1960s and showed no remorse for his actions during his trial. Though Roberts was a West Londoner, his actions have been eulogised by Millwall supporters as though he was one of their own.

Harry Roberts is our friend,
Is our friend,
Harry Roberts is our friend
He kills coppers

Let him out to kill some more
Kill some more
Let him out to kill some more
He kills coppers.

Millwall had the unenviable title of being the only London team never to have played in the top flight of English football, but that looked like ending in early 1972, with the club playing some of its best-ever football. But trouble off the field continued. An FA Cup game at home to Notts Forest saw away supporters attempt to get into the Cold Blow Lane end. They only got to the top of the stairs when they were, in the words of one eyewitness, "absolutely smashed". Some of the Forest fans then tried to enter the Ilderton End, and while some made it, others had to run for their lives.

The team's final game of the season was at home to Preston. As they were coasting to a 2–0 win, news reached the fans that Birmingham, their closest rivals, were losing at Sheffield Wednesday. The news quickly spread, and at the final whistle the players were carried shoulder high to the dressing room and a champagne celebration. But the joy was brief, as the real result from Sheffield came through that Birmingham had won and so could overtake Millwall with their final game, away at Leyton Orient a few days later. The team captain reacted in perhaps typical Millwall style by smashing the radio against the wall.

In an attempt to influence the result, some Millwall fans travelled over to Leyton's ground, swelling the attendance to an incredible 33,383 fans. "The three-way interest in the game created an atmosphere that even the FA Cup Final on Saturday would be hard to equal," noted *The Times*. "Sometimes the voices of Orient's supporters seemed nearly lost in the roars from the huge contingent of Birmingham. But fortified by the Millwall choirs, Orient attacked the evening's task as if their own future depended on success here." It was not enough, and in the 58th minute Birmingham scored, giving them the points to leapfrog Millwall into the First Division. As thousands of Blues fans swarmed onto the pitch, hundreds from the opposite end of the ground were doing likewise due to a large firecracker exploding on the terrace. All fingers pointed at the Millwall fans.

In February 1973, Millwall were drawn away at Everton in the FA Cup, and for many in South East London it was their first crack at a top team, and a top mob. Two football specials crammed full of Millwall fans, numbering almost 2,000, made the trip. It was not to be one of their better away days. Liverpool had been drawn at home to Manchester City, and with kick-off at the same time both Scouse mobs lurked around Lime Street. Mounted police were deployed, with sticks flailing, to keep the rival sets of fans apart. There are differing accounts of what happened that day, with many saying Millwall were run, but a few saying the opposite. One Sunday newspaper even concurred with this minority view, leading with the headline, "Everton started it, Millwall finished it." What is certain is that a group of Millwall got into the home end only to be attacked from all sides. Ten were stabbed, one critically. "They were like lambs to the slaughter," recalled a Millwall fan. However, their team ran out 2–0 winners, so for those who escaped unscathed the day was remembered as a success. Everton hooligans do accept that Millwall were the first and only firm to ever attempt to take their end. [See *Everton* in *Hooligans* Vol. 1]

Goodison Park was not the only venue where Millwall came unstuck during this period, giving credence to the view that no firm is unbeatable. "For me [Everton] wasn't the worst," remembered one Millwall fan. "Man United away 1974, Bolton away 1975 and a Newcastle night game in 1976 were a lot worse. I think it was all the stabbings and slashings that makes Everton sound worse, but for the firm actually getting done/run, them last three were a lot worse."

The Bolton game is remembered by another Millwall fan as the day the police came to their rescue. "It was one of the few occasions when I've been with a proper firm of Wall, 150-plus including lot of older lads, and it has come on top. When we came out of the ground, Bolton came at us. We had our backs to the wall with nowhere to go. If it hadn't been for plod they would have slaughtered us. The rumour was that Man Utd and City were with them that day swelling their numbers, but I spoke to Bolton on England trips over the following years and said it was all their firm, one of the biggest I've seen come at Wall." Surprisingly enough Bolton never showed at Millwall for the following few seasons.

Millwall drew Wolves away in the next round, a team that had its own reputation for trouble. "There was complete mayhem behind the goal under the stand," one Millwall fan recalled on an Internet forum. "I remember a burger bar being used as a battering ram to try to get at a Wolves' firm that took the piss out of one of our black lads, not our famous one. That day there was a small group of Wolves lads wearing long leather coats. We went back to Wolves in about 1977 when they were in the old Second Division and I remember seeing a group of lads in long leather coats, the same lot. They were tooled up at that second game, they had it with Wall after the game, well game, well outnumbered but stood before getting done."

The following season it was business as usual at home. The first game was against Aston Villa, though their hardcore didn't even make it out of New Cross station before they were attacked and then sent straight back to Birmingham by police. Shortly after kick-off, a Millwall fan threw a rock at the Villa goalkeeper.

The final game of the following season saw Millwall host a Bristol Rovers side who needed to win to stay up. About 30 Rovers sneaked into the Ilderton End but before long were sussed out and badly beaten. The police escorted them out but somehow they returned, shortly after half-time and stood in the same spot. "They were bruised and bleeding, some of them with bandages and plasters," recalled one Millwall fan. "They were battered to fuck. The Wall round them left them alone and stood with them the rest of the game, a few even apologised and got a bit chummy."

A Sunderland mob suffered the same fate in a game a couple of seasons before. "A little mob started singing in the Cold Blow Lane in the first half," recounted the same Millwall fan. "They had hundreds on them straight away, with loads more surging round from the halfway. People from all round the ground were lining up to get at them. Absolutely hammered. I recall seeing some of them sitting on the CBL steps at half time nursing their wounds and getting seen to by the St John's. Some of them were in a right state. But they'd had their pasting and were being left alone after that, more or less. All these clowns that go to the New Den and act up behind plod in the country's safest ground have no idea how lucky they are. No idea at all."

As mentioned earlier, Millwall had an unpleasant trip to Old Trafford in the 1974/75 season, but this was nothing compared to the hostility faced by the Red Army when they went to South East London a few weeks later. "Millwall away was changed at short notice to cut down on the numbers travelling," remembered Mancunian Colin Blaney, author of *Grafters*. "We only had the train half full, yet it was still one of the best firms I'd ever seen. No colours were on show, we were all in work clothes. Thirty hardcore Cockney Reds met us as we all cut through over to Euston Square tube but the dibble [police] blocked us all in, only letting small groups onto any tube. We all ended up slipping into the ground in dribs and drabs. One side of the ground was like the Kippax at Man City and at the two ends you could gain entrance to no problems, and it meant that as soon as United grouped together Millwall mullered the Reds from all sides.

"Steve Coppell scored the winner and we never even jumped up or let out a peep, we were still all in our teens and surrounded by docker thugs in their thirties and forties. After the game, we kept our heads down and were so lucky to avoid a good beating. All the way to the tube, Reds walking with us were picked off and dragged into the alleyways for a shoeing. It was without a doubt our shadiest trip to the Smoke in the Seventies. No wonder they call it Bandit Country; more like Jack the Ripper Manor, I'd say."

Few away firms travelled to Millwall, such was their infamy at home. Those who did were made to pay and each story frightened off others. Apparently the first large mob ever to appear was Tottenham when the two sides met in the Second Division in the 1976/77 season. "A massive away firm showed at the Den," recounted one Millwall fan. "To this day I rate them for size and quality with West Ham as one of the best that ever came to the old or new Den."

Cardiff also brought a mob down to Millwall during the same period but came badly unstuck when the appearance of the players signalled a home charge into the away end. A few Cardiff stood and fought but most legged to other parts of the ground, even if it meant having to pay in again. Like many others before and after, the Cardiff fans didn't even dare raise a cheer when their third goal went in; they were more concerned with survival. The tables were turned the following April, when 150-200 Millwall piled out of Ninian Park ready for a fight, only to be attacked by wave after wave of Cardiff, some wielding scaffolding poles from building work at the Ninian Park pub.

"That game at Cardiff was unbelievable," recalled one Millwall fan. "When we came out of the ground Cardiff came at us from across some park, I remember the big Cardiff half caste fella, a certain Wall lad pulled a small machete and whacked him across the gut. Seeing that, most Cardiff backed off and Wall steamed into them.

"I was only about sixteen and that journey back to the station was the scariest and most exciting ever. I recall about 100 Wall – probably less – being ringed by plod and marched back through an absolute sea of Taffs, hundreds and hundreds of them. Every now and then they or us would break through the plod and it'd be off like there was no tomorrow. All sorts bouncing off our heads. At one point near the station the plod dissolved and I was fronted by a bird with some sort of carving knife. Couldn't believe it. I thought I'd make a name for myself with one or two other young 'uns and got to the car park in front of the station first. Half a dozen Taffs appeared from behind a van and mullered us. I went down and took the kicking of my life. Limping around with bruised nuts for weeks and my swede cut to fuck. Always rated Cardiff after that – how could you not? It was what I imagined coming to the Den must have been like. Except we held our own. I think we got the result that day, not many firms could claim that back in the Seventies, Cardiff were and still are a top firm. That was Wall at their best. Most firms would've folded up under that onslaught."

Paul Roberts is one former player who is not fondly remembered down the Den. During Millwall's 1979 end of season dinner, partly to celebrate the youth team winning the FA Youth Cup, he grabbed the microphone and began singing the West Ham anthem "I'm Forever Blowing Bubbles". An angry Millwall fan lobbed a bottle at him and he had to be bundled out of the back door for his own safety. Roberts moved to Brentford but on his next visit to the Den he was abused throughout the match and a few fans even leapt onto the pitch to attack him. Other victims of the Millwall fans were two Sheffield United fans who were captured after their mob had been badly turned over. "We tortured them by making them sing Millwall songs," one fan recalled. "We convinced 'em we were going to take 'em to a warehouse in Rotherhithe and hang 'em upside down."

Despite popular misconceptions, Millwall has never been one organised firm like the West Hams, Birminghams or Leeds of the hooligan world. Rather it has always been a collection of small mobs drawn from the various communities of South East London. Bermondsey, Peckham, Eltham, Deptford and so on have always tended to operate alone and this separatism has often made Millwall disorganised, and apparently weak, especially away from home. A few firms have transcended these geographical divides, such as the F Troop, Treatment and Bushwhackers, but these have tended to be small mobs of hardcore hooligans rather than any unifying force. "It's always when these small groups from all the areas get together when you see Millwall in full," said Lee, a 40-year-old Millwall veteran. "It all depends what team it is, or was. We like to be a bit unpredictable, so one week we will take fuck-all to, say, Sheff United when everyone and their dog is expecting a massive turnout from us, and the next week take 250 over-thirties to Sunderland. We've had some right fun and games at Derby, Forest, Stoke, Brum, Burnley, Man City, Blades – and had them on the back foot.

"We are the one that everyone else likes to knock, so everyone's got a gripe about Wall 'not showing in force', but they tend to keep schtum when we turn them over on their own doorsteps."

The British public was introduced to some of the Millwall gangs by a BBC documentary in 1977. The origins of the programme were in the failure to secure promotion five seasons before, which caused a mass trauma within the club. Within a year, many of the team had left. A year later Herbert Burnige, a director at the club since 1969 and a lifelong and passionate Millwall fan, became chairman. Gradually the club got itself back on its feet, and with Burnige's drive and money began to improve its image. One of his early signings was Gordon Jago, who Eamon Dunphy described as "a bright young football manager with progressive marketing ideas". The two set about transforming the club, with Jago even suggesting changing the name of the ground to Montego Bay. When that proved impossible, he invited in the television crews to record the transformation. Jago saw the *Panorama* documentary as an opportunity to kill the Millwall myth.

The BBC, and for that matter many Millwall supporters, had other ideas. Both contrived to promote the very image the club wanted to bury. The BBC also interviewed National Front leader Martin Webster as proof that political groups were exploiting and whipping up the violence. The one outstanding personality in the programme was Harry the Dog, a prominent Millwall face who epitomised its support. His one-man assault on Bristol Rovers' Tote End became the stuff of legend.

The club was furious at the programme and saw it as an act of bad faith, and Jago resigned soon after. There was an even more stinging rebuke from the Sports Minister Dennis Howell, who described it as the most irresponsible journalism that he had seen in a long while. On the terraces, however, the Millwall myth had not only been restored but enhanced. Across the country, football fans were introduced to the comical, but also scary, sight of Millwall fans wearing surgical masks.

It was still an era when few football gangs had names, and there is debate even amongst Millwall fans as to the exact origin of the "Treatment". One fan says the masks came from two Millwall lads who worked at St. Thomas's Hospital, and were first worn at Brighton in the mid-Seventies. Other Millwall fans started singing, "Treatment, Treatment," and the name stuck. "It was never really a name of a firm as far as I was concerned," said Lee. "It was a load of lads, most from the Peckham area, who stood on the halfway line who would call themselves Treatment." Not so, says another Millwall fan, who insists that the name came from the hiding the fans got at Bolton in the early Seventies. "Wall were hugely outnumbered and basically had to fight all the way back to the station. A copper who seemed important said, 'For fuck's sake you've given them some treatment.'"

Millwall's next match after the *Panorama* programme was away at Oldham and the lads in the North West mill town simply couldn't wait. "We were licking our lips at the prospect of taking on the feared Millwall," remembered Carl Spiers, one of Oldham's leaders. "We had played them a couple of times in previous seasons and they had attempted to take our Chaddy End twice but failed both times, our greater numbers giving us the advantage. We knew, though, that they would be up for this game mob-handed. They had set a precedent, declaring themselves as the country's top mob. Every crew in Oldham was talking about this match and every mob had at least double its numbers for this match. Rumours that Man United's Red Army was coming up also fired everybody's imagination.

"On the day our kop, the Chaddy End, was packed to the rafters a full hour before kick-off. All the lads were bouncing up and down and chanting songs of war, 'Millwall where are you?' being the most popular. Meanwhile the away end was filling up with Millwall as dozens of coaches began arriving. The mood was ugly. At about quarter to three, a big gap appeared in the Chaddy End, and a mob of about fifty Millwall fans dressed in donkey jackets and most wearing flat caps stepped forward, arms outstretched, chanting, 'Millwall, Millwall,' in that slow Cockney drawl. I forced myself to the front and came face to face with this big ugly mob of Cockney thugs. Most of them were big bastards. A tall, gangly fucker stepped forward, beckoning us, 'I'm Harry the facking Dog, who wants to know?' My mates urged me to do him. There was a deathly hush, and I stepped forward dressed in my Crombie overcoat, straight-leg Levi jeans and cherry red Doc Martens, plus a number two crewcut complete with razor side parting, and I shouted back at him, 'I'm Carl the Cat, you fucking Cockney cunt!'

"With that I did a diving headbutt which connected with Harry and dropped him. His flat cap went flying. I dived onto him and we began brawling, both mobs piled into each other and a mass brawl broke out. Oldham soon overwhelmed them, having at least ten times as many lads, only the coppers with snarling dogs and big sticks separated the scrapping thugs.

"Fair play to Millwall, every one of them fought gallantly and they were still fighting the cops as they were dragged around the pitch. Meanwhile I was getting all the backslaps and congratulations off the boys for sticking the nut on Harry, and my best buddy Paul grabbed Harry's cap and proudly wore it for the rest of the match. A lot of Oldham fans thought Paul had done Harry, and not surprisingly he wasn't denying anything.

"At half-time, Millwall's mob in the away end surged forward down the huge bank of open terracing and a big gap appeared. We wondered what the fuck was going on. Surely Oldham did not attempt to take that many Millwall on? As it happened, a big mob of Man United fans, some 200-strong, came charging into Millwall from the top of the end. Most Millwall bolted and only got back into them once they realised that there were only 200. Millwall eventually routed the United fans. We were licking our lips at the prospect of taking Millwall and United on after the match but unfortunately United had vanished by the end of the game.

"After the match, Millwall mobbed up and really gave it to us. They were all blokes, many of them in works vans and many of them tooled up with shovels, pickaxe handles and iron bars. A lot of Oldham got twatted badly and a few ended up in hospital, though some Millwall got sorted out also. But they were really in a different league after the match. At least they did not take our end, though they probably would have done if all their boys has got into it before the game."

The club's protests at the TV programme looked even more hollow less than three months later when a full-scale riot erupted at an FA Cup match at home to Ipswich. The trouble was sparked by a sole Ipswich fan who ran onto the pitch, but what the visitors started, the home fans finished. "Fighting began on the terraces, then spilled out on to the pitch and into the narrow streets around the ground," recalled former player Eamon Dunphy. "Bottles, knives, iron bars, fists, boots and concrete slabs rained from the sky. Dozens of innocent people, real Millwall fans, were injured."

The day was symbolised by the head injuries to 72-year-old Joe Hale, a lifelong Millwall supporter. It was all too much for Herbert Burnige, who resigned as chairman. The club once again found itself in front of an FA hearing, which closed its ground for two games and banned FA Cup games at home for the following season.

The late Seventies saw Millwall repeatedly clash with London rivals West Ham and Chelsea. A fight with West Ham at a London train station in 1976 left one Millwall dead, while another clash with Chelsea on the London Underground a year later saw over 60 people arrested. "Our future is in your hands," was the plea from Millwall manager George Petchley to the fans shortly before a crunch league game at Upton Park in October 1978. "Now is the time … for every true supporter of Millwall to help rid us once and for all of the small mindless element who are slowly choking the life out of our club by their constant misbehaviour."

The *Evening Standard* carried the headline "War fear in game of hatred" as it reported that an estimated 2,500 Millwall bootboys were intending to travel to Upton Park. The paper claimed the hooligans were going to meet in a housing estate near the Den in the morning before heading off to the pubs around New Cross. "The hooligan army will then move across river towards Upton Park to engage the enemy." The feared violence did not occur, largely because the police launched its largest-ever football operation involving over 500 officers [see *West Ham*].

There was also no love lost between Millwall and Chelsea, and the two sides met in the 1977-78 season. Martins King and Knight give a lurid description of the match at the Den in *Hoolifan*. Two mobs of Chelsea, one led by Eccles and the other led by Babs, got into the home end, but both were eventually expelled after a violent onslaught. "The team came out and the Millwall came in," they record. "A second's diversion and they attacked from all sides; the police were lost somewhere in the middle. We found ourselves in the far corner of the end, not only fighting for Chelsea but fighting for our very lives." At least, they insist, Chelsea put up an appearance and got two mobs into the Millwall end, something few other firms managed to do, and Babs' mob lasted until ten minutes from the end. An amusing story from that day related to some Chelsea lads who were approached by a rag and bone man. As the cart drew level, a small mob of Millwall, who had been hiding under the sacking at the back, leapt up and attacked. One leading Chelsea face was smashed across the head with a china vase.

Little changed over the next couple of seasons: Millwall attacked rival fans, the police and officials. A match at Barnsley in September 1979 saw them fight with police inside the ground, leading to several officers being injured. At Burnley, a Millwall fan off the notorious Aylesbury estate attacked the referee over a disputed decision, and at a Cup game against Shrewsbury in 1980 a linesman was hit by a bag of concrete. There were serious clashes with Portsmouth at virtually every game between the two sides between 1978 and 1985 (see *Portsmouth*).

By the early Eighties, Millwall's reputation was being matched or even overtaken by others. Leeds, Chelsea and West Ham were making more headlines in the national press, partly a reflection of how the more organised mobs were able to circumvent tighter policing. Millwall's lowly position in Division Three meant meetings with the bigger clubs were unlikely, and morale and attendances declined at the Den. This changed when Millwall were promoted back into the Second Division in 1984, thus bringing them face to face with many of the big mobs.

A clash between Millwall and Newcastle fans at a motorway service station left one Geordie fighting for his life after being slashed across his neck and head by six Millwall fans wielding Stanley knives. A calling card saying, "Congratulations! You've just met Millwall," was left by the victim. Fighting had broken out when three coachloads of Millwall supporters on their way home from a match in Sunderland pulled up at Woodhall service area on the M1. Hordes of them ran across the footbridge spanning the motorway, then laid into Geordie fans returning from a game in London. The police were called and 47 Millwall fans on one coach were arrested but they were all eventually released after the authorities met with a wall of silence.

In autumn 1984, Millwall played Chelsea in the Milk Cup. The first leg, at Stamford Bridge, was marred by trouble after a mob of West Ham got into the ground to add to the fray. Further trouble was expected for the second leg, as one police officer told the press: "It is pretty obvious that it's not just another football match." He was proved correct, with one of the worst casualties of the night being a Chelsea youth team player Bobby Issacs, who was confronted by a mob of Millwall as he was heading to the Den to watch his teammates. He tried to pretend he was a Millwall player but when he failed to name the Millwall goalkeeper correctly he was slashed badly all the way down his back.

Millwall were playing some of their best football for years and in March 1985 the club was drawn away at Luton in the quarter-finals of the FA Cup. "The date will be recalled in any history of English soccer ever written," wrote Eamon Dunphy later. "The glory at Kenilworth Road that night, a distinction of unimaginable horror, belonged to a mob some several hundred strong, the elite of London's football hooligan gangs who infiltrated the 17,470 crowd. They arrived in Luton early, drunk and armed with weapons now familiar in every town and city on the bloody Football League map. A grim fortress had been erected, but the barbed-wire, steel fencing and video cameras which were designed to keep the hooligans out served only as props in their theatre of violent fantasy."

The first stoppage occurred after only a quarter of an hour's play, when the referee took the players off for 25 minutes after hundreds of fans spilled onto the pitch from the Kenilworth Road end. The game continued but it was just a question of when trouble would erupt again. That was answered when the referee blew the final whistle and this time thousands went over the fences. Seats were ripped out and hurled at police, and just when it appeared that the authorities were regaining control, another block of Millwall entered the fray from another stand. "As a true Millwall fan it was impossible not to feel shame, not to feel sorrow for the game of football," concluded Eamon Dunphy. "And not to despair at how low life had sunk; for these were not fans, they were not people, they were animals."

The riot dominated the media and political debate. Mrs Thatcher declared war on hooliganism, saying "that the time has come for the courts to impose sentences which may deter those who are minded to use violence, at, or near, football grounds". An FA inquiry found Millwall guilty of not taking "all reasonable precautions" to control their fans and the club was fined £7,500, though this was later rescinded on appeal. Internally, just as the Ipswich riot had ended the tenure of Herbert Burnige, so Luton caused the resignation of then-chairman Alan Thorn.

The players were less affected, and a few weeks later they won promotion into the Second Division. However, their jubilation was short-lived. Extra security at the Den cost the club £1m and a lack of money for players, plus the sale of some existing stars, such as Justin Fashanu, meant George Graham had little hesitation in accepting an offer to manage Arsenal. The club appeared in freefall, with debts approaching £5m, no manager and only eight professionals on the books, but in the summer of 1986 a saviour was found in Jeff Burnige, son of the late Herbert, who formed a new, three-man board with City financier Reg Burr and PR consultant Brian Mitchell. Slowly but surely attempts were made to rebuild the team and the club's image and in May 1988 the club achieved it goal of promotion to the First Division.

Hooliganism continued but Millwall did not receive the same publicity as it had in previous years. Increasingly the trouble was outside the ground, with vicious fights against Bristol City and West Ham United. A West Ham fan told reporters of the terror of facing Millwall thugs during a meeting of the two sides in 1986. "They were slashing at us with knives, and I saw an axe being waved," he recalled. "I have never been so scared in my life." A match at the Den in 1991 saw one of the longest and most intense battles of recent times. "Four thousand football fans clashed yesterday, smashing cars and hurling missiles," noted one newspaper report. "Police said the battle raged between about 2,000 fans from each side near Millwall's Cold Blow Lane ground. Officers took 20 minutes to contain the trouble and the match was delayed by 15 minutes." A confrontation with Arsenal fans in January 1988 saw 73 people ejected from Highbury and 41 arrests. A spokesman for Scotland Yard told reporters that "a substantial number of so-called Millwall fans were a disgrace to themselves and the club."

Police were now working undercover amid the hooligans and in August 1986 Operation Dirty Den was launched to identify the ringleaders. In January 1987, the first of several dawn raids netted over 20 alleged Millwall hooligans. The subsequent court cases heard how "police mingled with the thugs during matches, guaranteeing their acts of violence were caught by video cameras".

Several of the defendants were prosecuted for an assault on a train carrying Arsenal and Charlton fans at New Cross station in November 1986. Chanting "Kill, kill, kill," a mob of 50 Millwall attacked the train with ammonia spray, bottles, knives, wooden staves and lumps of concrete. "The mob rampaged through the station ripping benches from the platforms to use as battering rams to try to force their way on to the train," the court was told. One British Transport Police officer was badly injured after he was attacked by a group of 15. Mark Nicholls was sentenced to seven years for his part in the attack and moments after being told his sentence he leapt out of the dock and made a dash for freedom. He was caught before he could escape, though not before his friends and family attempted to come to his assistance. A third Millwall trial collapsed in May 1988 after doubts over evidence collected by undercover officers.

Hooliganism didn't disappear with the police operations but days out were certainly less frequent. Big games against West Ham and Chelsea would bring out large numbers of fighters but there were other games when there was hardly a mob in sight, and the loose make-up of the Millwall firm contributed to its diminishing presence, though it also meant the police could not "behead" it like they had done to West Ham. There were occasions when Millwall would be surprised by a visiting mob, but fans would group together during the game before taking the fight to their opponents afterwards. This was the case against Hibs in a pre-season friendly in 1993, when Millwall were caught by surprise.

"We didn't have a firm out before the game as no-one was expecting them to turn out," recalled Lee. "I was drinking in the Crown and Anchor on the Old Kent Road and there must've been fifteen to twenty of us at the most. All of a sudden a fella rushes in shouting, 'They're here! Hibs are outside!' The next thing the windows start going through and a firm of about 100 of them are outside slinging anything they could get their hands on at the pub. We did our best to retaliate with pool balls and bottles that were being handed to us by the barman but we were severely outnumbered. I was surprised at the time that they didn't make an attempt to come into the pub, as there were enough of them, but they didn't, they just carried on down to the ground, tipping a few cars over and smashing windows on the way.

"After the game it was a different story. We had loads out. We were in a group of about 150 at the top end of the Ilderton and as Hibs came out they were facing us about 400 yards away. We charged at them and the majority legged it down Ilderton Road, where there was another mob of Millwall waiting for them. The surreal thing about it was at the end of the game there were loads of police everywhere but they just seemed to 'disappear' for ten minutes. When they did reappear it was game over and one cozzer said to one of ours that the cunts had got what they deserved for taking the piss on our manor – he said it as if it was ours *and* the OB's manor."

End of season disappointments continued to be a source of trouble at Millwall. In May 1994, the club lost a play-off semi-final against Derby County and once again the newspaper headlines were dominated by lurid accounts of misbehaviour. "A 200-strong cadre of Millwall's most notorious thugs sparked off a night of shameful violence at South London's £20 million New Den stadium," reported the London *Evening Standard*. "Armed with forged or stolen tickets, the foul-mouthed and aggressive gatecrashers, many high on drink and drugs, overwhelmed stewards in the East Stand upper tier minutes before kick-off when they poured into the ground. They had come straight from a pre-arranged street battle with Derby's worst hooligans in Rotherhithe during which CS gas and ammonia was used."

There was further trouble inside the ground as fans traded insults, coins and other missiles. "The situation rapidly deteriorated further as the Millwall fans, good and bad alike, howled abuse at police who were obscuring their view," the paper continued. "Within minutes they were pouring over the small perimeter wall, grappling with police and invading the playing surface."

Eventually the extra fans were taken across the other side of the pitch, where they were placed in the largely empty West Stand, but many continued their behaviour as before. During the second half, as Derby scored the goal that ended Millwall's promotion chances, hundreds of fans poured onto the pitch and several opposing players were confronted. Two black Derby players were substituted to save them from almost continuous racist abuse. After the game, Millwall fans clashed with police, a Radio Derby van was overturned and an armoured police vehicle was rocked violently back and forth. "But they were robbed of their ultimate goal, an all-out assault on the main body of Derby supporters, by saturation policing," the paper concluded.

It was the same old story. The FA ordered an investigation, the Millwall chairman Reg Burr considered resigning, the ground was threatened with closure but in the end there was a fine and nothing much else. After all, what more could actually be done? The following season saw yet another FA investigation, this time after fans clashed on the pitch during Millwall's cup tie at Chelsea. The previous season there had been disturbances, and 20 arrests, during a tie at Southend.

The 1998/99 season saw trouble at both matches against Manchester City. Large outbreaks of disorder were becoming increasingly uncommon but one-off games against teams with their own hooligan tradition brought out the troublemakers. The match at the New Den saw 14 arrests and two pitch invasions, with a mob of almost 1,000 Millwall trying to attack their rivals after the game. The return leg saw one of the largest hooligan mobs travelling in recent times when an estimated 1,000 Millwall hooligans made their way up by train. They alighted at Stockport before causing trouble in Moss Side, setting several cars ablaze and smashing windows. "Over 30 arrests were made and several police were injured during the disturbances which required police to enter the stand in full riot gear," noted a police report.

The following season saw a Millwall mob of almost 500 hooligans set off by train to Cardiff for what was one of the worst outbreaks of disorder in recent times. Trouble spanned eight hours as rival fans clashed and Cardiff ran the police [see *Cardiff* in *Hooligans Vol. 1*]. The season after saw an equally large mob travel to Swansea [see *Swansea*] and a fight with Cambridge United during which one youth was thrown onto a live rail track.

All of this was a prelude to the 2001/02 season, possibly Millwall's most violent ever. The season had not even begun before trouble occurred, with rival Millwall and Spurs hooligans clashing at a pre-season friendly in South East London [see *Tottenham Hotspur*]. The season proper began with an away match against Birmingham. West Midlands Police mounted a huge operation after intelligence suggested Millwall hooligans were travelling in large numbers to take on the Birmingham City Zulus. "Under massive escort the Millwall group was escorted from New Street Station to the ground," noted a police report. "On the way back Birmingham City fans attempted to attack Millwall at the station."

Two days later Millwall hosted Cardiff at the New Den in a potentially explosive Worthington Cup tie. Fortunately for the authorities, few Cardiff hooligans travelled, though that did not prevent young Millwall fans from rioting in the streets afterwards. Cars and shops were attacked and bricks and bottles were thrown at police long into the night. It was to prove to be the first of five major clashes with the police over the season, the second of which was only four days later after a match against Burnley. "Around 250 Millwall fans repeatedly attacked Burnley fans as they were escorted by police back to South Bermondsey Station," noted NCIS. "The hooligans fought with police for a further hour once the Burnley fans were gone."

Another major police operation was required to prevent hundreds of Millwall and Nottingham Forest hooligans from fighting during a game in late October. Over 150 Forest made the trip down and unbeknown to each mob they ended up drinking only a few hundred metres apart. After the game there was serious disorder as Millwall fans attempted to attack Forest fans making their way to Bermondsey station. Then hundreds of yobs turned their attention to the police. They fired numerous rockets and flares at police lines. Ten days later, 250 Millwall travelled up to Wolverhampton by train, catching the police unawares and attacking their Wolves counterparts, leaving several with stab wounds. One Wolverhampton police officer told a BBC team who were following Millwall that season that some Londoners were wearing trench coats from which they drew baseball bats.

"Millwall supporters attacked a group of Portsmouth fans in the Windmill Pub near Waterloo Station," recorded the police after a league match between the two sides in mid-December. "Eye-witnesses told how Portsmouth appeared to summon Millwall by mobile telephone. When Millwall arrived, they attacked the pub with bottles, bricks and dustbin lids. Portsmouth responded by throwing back everything they could lay their hands on. Every window of the pub was smashed while most of the furniture in the pub was either broken or ended up outside. Of the 100 people involved, all got away. After the match the BBC crew filmed in horror as a lone Portsmouth supporter was brutally attacked outside the New Den."

Police described a private wheel clamper as either "the bravest or most stupid man alive" after he attempted to clamp several Millwall fans' cars on a local estate during the home game against Blackburn in late January. When the owners returned to their vehicles, police had to order the man to release the cars immediately in order to prevent a riot. For good measure, the Millwall fans overturned the clamper's vehicle.

A fortnight later, 300 police were on duty, 36 pubs shut their doors and kick-off was moved to noon to prevent clashes during Millwall's away match at Forest. About 300 Millwall hooligans made the trip up by train, and in a further manoeuvre to head off disorder, the authorities delayed its arrival because a second train, carrying hundreds of Forest hooligans, was due to arrive at the station at the same time.

Millwall's game at Portsmouth was also brought forward to noon in the hope of preventing trouble, but to little avail. "Before and after the match groups of fans tried to get at each other but were kept apart by a wall of police wearing riot helmets and wielding batons," read the police report. "The two groups of hooligans taunted each other and threw missiles along Goldsmith Avenue and Frogmore Road. Goldsmith Avenue was closed to traffic and pubs were shut." A home game against Sheffield Wednesday a week later saw away fans attacked as they left the ground. Millwall fans then turned on the police with bricks and bottles, sending at least two to hospital. Police were again the target three weeks later when Millwall were prevented from attacking Wolves fans after another game.

Millwall's season of hooliganism was, oddly enough, also their most successful on the pitch, with the club reaching the play-offs for the second time in eight years. This time they met Birmingham City and it proved to be, in the words of the Deputy Commissioner of Scotland Yard, "the most serious street violence ever seen in London". Millwall lost and over 900 fans ran amok for several hours. The level and intensity of the violence was almost incomprehensible. A wall in a children's playground was knocked down for use as ammunition, paving slabs were ripped up and thrown, wheelie-bins were used to construct burning barricades and even a lamp-post was torn out and used as a battering ram. The police were bombarded with volleys of missiles, often in salvos of 15, for over an hour, and many cars in the vicinity were overturned or set alight. There were simply not enough police officers on duty to deal with the situation and extra officers were roused, some from their beds, and rushed to the area.

One resident watched the riot unfold from her window as helicopters hovered overhead and flares and thunder flashes were fired at police lines. "There were only about eight riot police in the road and they were trying to contain about 150 Millwall fans," she told reporters. "They would charge the fans trying to drive them back. But they were outnumbered and the fans would rush them back and the police would retreat. This went on for about two and a half hours. Then the police numbers grew. It went on back and forth until the Millwall fans dispersed."

"The police were on one charge going down, lots of them, and the bricks were flying," another witness told the press. "One horse hit a car. The rider fell off and smashed the screen. The horse rolled over, and was on the deck. It got back up and was limping, jumping around. After that the police had to run. There were more supporters turning up and they all had bricks."

Chief Superintendent Mike Humphrey, who led 250 police against the thugs, said, "There could have been a fatality. We weren't prepared for the ferocity and viciousness of the attack. It was far beyond anything we imagined. We believe it was premeditated," he added. "The hooligans were there to cause as much injury as they could. It was absolutely disgraceful. This was not a normal incident, this was toe-to-toe fighting and they weren't running away. The fans were furious and ready to strike. It was sheer hell. Millwall has always been a difficult club but last night it disgraced itself."

The streets around the New Den looked like a battlefield the following morning. Sixteen people had been arrested, 47 police officers and 26 police horses had been injured. The trouble was a bitter blow for Theo Paphitis, the club's latest chairman, who had done much to improve its image and crack down on the troublemakers. While he had been largely successful inside the ground, including secretly recording fans hurling racist abuse (evidence that was later used in court), there was little he could do outside. "We will see off the scum," he told the next edition of the *South London Press*, showing a united front with manager Mark McGhee. "We have both worked incredibly hard to stop this and we have not succeeded and we both feel like shit – I'm afraid there is no other word to describe the distaste we felt at what happened.

"But now we feel more positive. We do not want to abandon the people that have helped us all this time. We want to make it work. We won't let a tiny minority spoil everything we have worked for."

Few people were arrested on the night, but in the weeks and months that followed the list grew ever longer as hours of video footage and photographs were studied. To date over 100 people have been convicted, imprisoned and banned from Millwall FC for life. They included grey-haired Raymond Everett, dubbed by the press as Britain's oldest hooligan at 56, who received five years for attacking a police horse. Millwall banned away fans for six high-profile games during the following season and refused to take tickets for the corresponding away fixtures. This, together with the 100-plus imprisoned, dramatically improved the situation at the club. Twelve months after the riot, Millwall played in the FA Cup final in Cardiff against Manchester United and there were no reports of trouble. Many felt the tide was finally turning.

In truth, the threat of violence remains, given the right circumstances. The

FA Cup appearance took Millwall into Europe for the first time in its history and 3,000 travelled to Hungary to watch their team play Ferencvaros. The club sold tickets only to members of its supporters' club, but 600 travelled independently and picked up tickets on the black market. Ferencvaros fans are reportedly Hungary's worst hooligans and the stage was set for a show-down. "There were skirmishes a full one-and-a-half hours before kick-off, with stewards clashing with a small number of supporters, who were immediately ejected," reported the BBC. "This followed the events of late afternoon in central Budapest, when police were called to curtail running battles around the area of Vorosmarty Ter square. Nine Millwall followers were believed to have been arrested, following the two arrested yesterday outside a restaurant. There were also clashes at two nearby underground stations, Ferenciek Tere and Nepliget. There was also a considerable police presence outside the ground, with some officers carrying CS gas canisters and riot shields and mounted police also deployed." Two Millwall fans were stabbed and several others injured.

"There have always been downsides as well as upsides to Millwall, which the recent away trip to Budapest highlighted on the first day there," said Lee. "But it also highlighted Millwall at its best, with everyone sticking together to do 'the best firm in Hungary' on their home manor. Millwall have suffered at the hands of the OB and courts probably more than any other single team. There is a reluctance from a lot of the older heads to put ourselves on offer for a long stretch, especially when we've had our pictures taken more times than the Queen. So it's quiet at the moment. All I will say is Millwall is not dead, we are just having a doze."

Certainly the Metropolitan Police did not believe Millwall had gone to sleep. In 2006, they launched Operation Devine to tackle violent disorder at Millwall football matches by both home and away supporters. Phase one of the operation saw ten men arrested in March that year and charged with violent disorder. Phase two saw dawn swoops that May by Lewisham and Croydon officers after the identification of more suspects from CCTV footage inside Millwall football ground. All of those arrested were seen at disturbances during the Millwall v Wolves game in January and Millwall v Crystal Palace in February. "Those identified and arrested used the veneer of football to legitimise senseless violence," said the superintendent leading Operation Devine.

Away from the New Den, Millwall continued to make the occasional large showing at grounds like Blackpool, Swansea and Leeds. A large reception committee was waiting for them at the latter game. "We were out in city centre from around 10.30 and plotted up in a number of boozers around the city," said a Leeds hooligan. "Phone call comes in Wall have just arrived, Wall get off train and wrapped up straight away and taken to Yates's. We get a phone call that Wall have with them some Aberdeen lads and some lads from abroad. Another phone call comes in saying that there are some Wall in minibuses meeting at a pub not far from the ground, so it's taxis to the pub and by one o'clock there must have been three hundred Leeds in there. We walk down to the ground where Leeds have attacked the Millwall escort of four double-decker buses outside the Peacock. I didn't see this happen but I was told that the windows on the buses were smashed and some doors ripped off and Wall did not get off the buses until they were around the side of the ground.

"In the game there were taunts from the South Stand, a few bottles and things thrown, Leeds score the fourth goal Millwall make the charge at the South Stand Upper, fights with OB, more objects thrown, one Leeds lad goes over the top into the Millwall end and hats off to him but Millwall where more than happy to have a go. At the end of the game they were kept in for around a hour."

However, an experienced Millwall hooligan is dismissive of the current scene and of the security circus that surrounds every high profile fixture. "We have got a mob of young idiots from Bexley who consider themselves as Wall Youth but even QPR had them on their toes," he sneered. "There's Wall Youth and then there's these Bexley plums, they are absolute fucking clowns but it's down to the proper youth to sort, not us old cunts. However, anyone claiming a result against Wall that turns out to be that load of muppets needs to have a re-think if they think that they've gone up against proper Wall."

Another veteran added, "We ain't living on past rep. We've been doing the business for the past thirty-five-plus years consistently, unlike many who have got all active in the past few years. Our lot can't be bothered week in week out, we've got nothing to prove. But when the need arises we can still turn it on. Anyway, that's by the by. Football hooliganism has had its day. It's dead now, had it. The OB have got it too sewn up and a few spotty brats watching *Football Factory*, pulling on jekyll Stone Island jackets and gobbing off on message boards ain't gonna change that."

Further reading: *Millwall: Lions of the South*, James Murray (Indispensable Publications), *No One Likes Us, We Don't Care*, Garry Robson (Berg Publishers), *Only A Game?* Eamon Dunphy (Penguin), *We Fear No Foe*, Colin Johnson (S.T. Publishing)

MOTHERWELL

Ground: Fir Park
Firms: Motherwell Saturday Service, Tufty Club, Soccer Shorties, Nu-Kru
Rivals: Aberdeen, Rangers, Airdrie

There are many myths in football terrace culture: Everton and Liverpool fans love each other, want each other's teams to win when they are not facing each other, and join up to fight visiting fans; all Manchester City fans live five minutes from their ground; Chelsea/Manchester United/ West Ham have never been run, and so on. One that does the rounds in Scotland that is taken a little more seriously is the claim that Motherwell and Aberdeen mobs hate each other, as both claim to be the first casual mob in Scotland.

It is a myth dispelled by Motherwell, who are happy to concede that the ASC were indeed the first soccer casual mob north of the border. That does not mean they get on, and it is no myth that both firms hate each other with a passion. In 1981/82, Motherwell stormed to the First Division title, securing trips to Aberdeen and the other major Scottish clubs in the following season.

An early visit to Pittodrie acted as a catalyst in the formation of the Saturday Service as the skins and bootboys from Motherwell were confronted on the terraces by gangs of lads "dressed like poofs, with bleached jeans, patterned jumpers and big wedge haircuts," according to Callum Bell in his book *Saturday Is Service Day*. When fighting broke out after a late Dons winner the "poofs" proved to be far gamer than they looked and, in the words of Bell, "The casuals had been well and truly noticed."

Around this time, a Leeds lad who moved north wearing the casual clobber was mates with a few sixteen-year-old Motherwell fans. They cottoned on and started "dressing". Before that, skinheads had ruled the roost at Fir Park, but most of the skins soon adopted the new style as it was easier to avoid police attention, not to mention pull women. Later that season the first Motherwell casuals began making a name for themselves at a game at St Mirren when they entered the home end and fought with locals, having been viewed initially by police as young, smartly dressed lads.

The name Saturday Service came from the reduced transport timetables at the weekends, which were called Saturday or Sunday Service, and it stayed with the firm for many years despite several short term changes and attempts to introduce a new theme to the firm. One lad, Scott, explained, "Saturday Service was the name of the firm but several times individuals formed splinter groups, just for the hell of it, or through boredom tried to rename it. We had the Tufty Club, which was taken from the road traffic club for kids in the 1970s, while Soccer Shorties was aimed at keeping the SS theme as was the ladies gang, the Soccer Sisters. I haven't a clue where Nu-Kru came from but it's not very imaginative."

As the Scottish press picked up on the casual football fans, Motherwell featured prominently in a magazine article. "Aberdeen fans were quick to pick up on the casual phenomenon and the ASC quickly acquired a fearsome reputation throughout Scotland," it read. "But strangely it was nearly two years later before any other team in Scotland had a casual following. Motherwell were the next team to have a casual mob appear, their name being the 'Motherwell Saturday Service', their younger casuals (under16s) went by the name of the 'Tufty Club'. During the two previous years Aberdeen Soccer Casuals had been involved in disorder in cities up and down Scotland but had been fighting rival fans and skinheads of other clubs due to no other clubs in Scotland having casuals, even though in England the casual scene was now in full swing with gangs attached to most clubs, skinheads were almost not existent at football grounds.

"With Motherwell now having a mob of casuals, a rivalry quickly developed between Aberdeen and Motherwell casuals resulting in a number of incidents. One of the worst being in 1983 when the ASC entered the Motherwell section of the ground at Motherwell's Fir Park ground and chased their mob on to the pitch, resulting in the game being held up. There's even a story that Aberdeen's legendary club captain Willie Miller went into the stand to try and calm things down.

"Then in 1985, 47 ASC were arrested after trying to ambush Motherwell casuals on their way to the stadium for a match in Aberdeen, resulting in a number of jail sentences. The casual scene had become such a problem that in the early days Motherwell FC even tried to ban fans wearing Kappa cagoules from entering the stadium."

The SS grew quickly. "When the mob was formed it was only a dozen strong but soon the skins were into it and before long we had seventy or eighty regulars but turnouts for bigger games usually reached 150, and for show games we could bring out 400," said Scott. "The good thing about the mob was that plenty of lads stood the test of time, unlike me, and although we had a few legends the strength of the mob was in the unit rather than one or two individuals. We liked to be called 'trendies' or 'dressers' rather than casuals, the ASC were the original casuals and from day one we wanted to be alienated from them.

"The other thing that people get wrong is the use of the initials SS. Many believe we were a right-wing firm, as we used to spray SS all over the place. That is bollocks. Some lads professed an alliance to right-wing groups, as did many lads involved in football culture, but the majority had little or no political persuasions whatsoever."

The same can be said for religion and one Motherwell hooligan was quick to point out that the religious bigotry which causes so much unrest at many games in Scotland was never an agenda for the SS. "Most clubs in Scotland have mainly Protestant supporters, for the simple reason many Catholics, all over the country, are indoctrinated from birth to support Celtic," he said. "It stands to reason those left were Protestants, so the local club would see few Catholics among its support. We did have some Catholics and the ones I knew were great lads, no discrimination against them whatsoever. At one time it was noticeable, as most fans would sing songs against Celtic, which gave their background away, but it normally only happened at Celtic games. We'd annoy Rangers in different ways but religion was definitely a tool for the firm to use against Celtic. It rarely reared its head against other sides though, so I'd say overall, no, religion was unimportant to most of the boys."

However, a letter sent to one Scottish newspaper and to the chief executive at Motherwell proved that there were people at Fir Park with agendas outside of football rivalries. It read, "I am writing this letter to inform you of the disgraceful way I was treated at the match v Celtic this afternoon. I was invited to attend by my friend who lives in Motherwell and, although not a season ticket holder, goes to a number of matches each season. As a neutral supporter I was looking forward to being at the final league game of the season, as the championship had not been decided.

"As soon as I took my seat (East stand, Row B, 107) I was verbally abused by a group of four so-called Motherwell supporters. I was called a 'Fenian bastard' as I was not wearing colours of any description. I refused to talk to or even look at these people. For the first twenty minutes this continued. The abuse was not only directed at myself and those beside me but towards some of the Celtic players as well. Agathe and Balde were told to 'get back to their mud huts' and called 'black bastards'. Lennon was called a 'Fenian bastard' and Bellamy a 'Welsh coke-sniffing bastard'.

"On a number of occasions these so-called supporters called over stewards to complain that we were Celtic supporters. One steward asked me if I followed Celtic and I informed him that I was simply a football fan wanting to watch a game. The steward told these people that there was nothing he could do, as we were quietly watching the match and causing no trouble. The abuse continued and eventually another steward, an elderly man with a hearing aid, was called over by the fans who verbally abused him for not ejecting us.

"He then approached me and stated, 'You will have to leave as I have been watching you abuse the Motherwell supporters for the last twenty minutes.' I could not believe what I was hearing. A police officer was called and advised us to go with him 'for your own safety'. We duly did and were advised that we were being ejected from the ground. I explained to the officer and senior steward my position and the fact that it was us who had been abused. This fell on deaf ears and I was advised to either leave the ground or be arrested. I was also advised to put my complaint in writing and send it to you ... When the focus, quite rightly, is on stamping out racism and sectarianism from our society it is sad to see a football club such as yours doing nothing and indeed allowing these people a forum to express their appalling views in public."

As the casual scene took off in Scotland, so rivalries grew and clashes became more fierce. A few years earlier, a punch-up on the terraces or in the streets after the match was all the lads wanted; now things grew more sinister and the level of violence escalated. Scott recalled, "Obviously, Aberdeen were a main rival as we were the only casual mobs in Scotland for a couple of years. Rangers and Celtic always had plenty of scarfers who fancied their chances and Airdrie, being local rivals, were always up for it, but before long the days of a punch-up were replaced with running street battles with weapons. It was common practice for games to be held up, as the police were still years behind the times and we were getting away with things up here which had been long clamped down on down south. There were some great days. Aberdeen came in our end twice in the mid-Eighties, both incidents ending with fans on the pitch, stopping the game on the second occasion."

One of the major clashes, not only for the SS but in the history of hooliganism north of the border, was before another game at Aberdeen when both firms believe the police set up the ASC. Bell told his version of the story in *Saturday Is Service Day*:

The history between us included their infamous ambush of our mob up there when 47 were arrested in a carefully planned police operation. On the train on the way up the mood was jovial until we hit Stonehaven again, when the occasion started to produce the inevitable butterflies. The train arrived in Aberdeen with ASC conspicuous by their absence. A couple of spotters were clocked but they kept their distance. Again I hung back with some of the older ones just in case an attack came from the rear. I was right at the back, eyes darting back and forth, as well as sideways. Going past the docks there were a few streets leading off to our left, at the top of which I could see some ASC tracking our progress along a parallel street. It was obvious something was going on and others had clocked it as well. I had a copper walking right beside me being rather chatty for a change. They usually took great delight in telling us we were scum and they had enough to deal with without us going up there. This one surprised me by telling me the ASC plans. 'They're going to hit you at the top of this road, where the two streets come to a point, better get your boys ready.' I looked at him, puzzled. 'You lot better not shit it, they'll have a right team and we're going to be outnumbered so tell your boys.'

. I passed the word up to the front, immediately a buzz formed among our lads. We were heading up a slight incline. 'This is where it's going to happen, just at the top of the road. You ready?' asked the screw. I nodded and passed the word again, he took out his truncheon and quickened his pace.

'Come on then, get ready.' The ones at the front had speeded up as well, sparking a chain reaction down the ranks. Some ASC came into view at the top of the hill, prompting a few verbals. The front runners started up a narrow path towards ASC as more of them appeared at the top. 'This is it,' my new pal shouted. 'Let's go.' And off he went. Some missiles rained down on us from further up, some of our lot returned fire as they built up pace into a full sprint. We charged up the path and some ASC started down towards us but, before a punch could be thrown, more OB appeared and charged into ASC, nicking quite a few. Vans appeared from everywhere, herding the lads at the top into the side, and more charged down towards us to head us off. More ASC came into view from the other side of the road but the OB were well on top by now and any chance of an off had disappeared. They were obviously well informed as to the intentions of their mob. Forty-seven were arrested, including one of ours who got a bit too lippy on the way to the ground whilst exchanging pleasantries with ASC across the road. Unfortunately for him, his name and address was printed in the local paper and he received all sorts of abusive letters over the following months.

There were also manic days out which are fondly remembered by the lads. "Yes, there was violence, but we also had a good laugh," recalled Scott. "We were loose cannons and it is amazing how we all came through the early years without being killed or jailed. Once, Aberdeen had us penned in at Waverley Station in Edinburgh, outnumbered ten to one, with one policeman and one policewoman in-between us. I reckon Aberdeen felt sorry for those of us who stood, but a couple of lads raided a cleaner's cupboard and came charging round the corner armed with buckets and mops, ready to clean up.

"Another one was after the Airdrie League Cup game, when the OB played a game of Grand Old Duke of York, marching us up the road then back down towards the train station, before turning us back up towards the outskirts of town, eventually taking us down to the station where we pleaded poverty to try and get off with the fare. Our bluff failed and we were ordered to walk the twelve miles home under escort, only for every passing taxi to be flagged down in order to get home in time for a beer.

"We wrecked a bus on the way back from a Scottish Cup semi-final replay against Celtic. After a few windows had been kicked out, a police inspector brought an intact window back on the bus trying to threaten us with jail. When he realised he was being ignored and jeered, he ordered the driver to get us out of Glasgow. On the way home, the entire contents of the bus went out of the windows. One guy asked the driver, as calmly as you like, to stand up for a moment so his seat could join the others. No big deal perhaps, except we were on the motorway at the time. The poor driver was to be heard muttering to himself hours later whilst waiting at a bus stop for his own transport home, 'Fuckin' worst ever. All I wanted was a bit of overtime. Not worth it, that, no chance. Never again, never again I tell ye.'"

There were also days which were not so funny. "There was a near riot outside Ibrox when we were hemmed in on all sides by scarfers," said Scott. "It was a major result for us to get away almost unscathed considering the odds our 150 faced were at least five to one. Some Rangers ICF boy claimed a result on a TV documentary for that day because they slashed one of our lads. Truth be told, ICF were backed off twice and our lad was slashed only because he forgot to stop chasing them and found himself on his own. We hammered Airdrie on their own patch following a midweek League Cup tie, no disputing that one was satisfying."

Apart from the usual clashes, smaller, more surprising rivalries began and Scott has respect for some of the less-renowned firms north of the border. "When we were in the First Division in 1984/85 we had some right good goes against smaller clubs. Queen of the South always gave us a challenge no matter when we faced them. I remember Arbroath going for it as well, as the local nutters would turn out just for a pop. I always had a thing for St Johnstone after I got my nose burst at the age of fourteen at a game in Perth, but Motherwell aren't a big club so I suppose we did most of the surprising, and that's what got us our name."

Like many Scottish firms, the SS have not bothered much following the national side and also refused to join the so-called Scottish Alliance when it was recruiting. "I never bothered with Scotland much," said Scott. "A few did, maybe forty was the most that ever took part in one go, never a big mob out to do the business. As for the joint firm nonsense, no way. We're Motherwell and never join up. Always staying independent was our strength but I'm not sure that we all stayed true to that aim."

That view is reflected in an article written by *Trainspotting* author Irvine Welsh about the international scene when England and Scotland were drawn to play each other in a World Cup qualifier in 1999. "Many followers of the Scotland team now are not so much football supporters as professional celebrators," he wrote. "If they do go regularly to club matches, they tend to follow the smaller clubs or junior football. The atmosphere is boisterous but friendly, with fans over anxious to behave well in order to show their alleged differences from the 'hooligan' English. Even given the hateful atmosphere of this fixture, it's difficult to envisage serious numbers of Hibernian, Aberdeen, Rangers or Motherwell 'hooligans' fighting side by side against anyone."

The small number of clubs with significant mobs in Scotland and the fact that the Scottish Premier League teams meet each other four times a year makes the participants more easily identifiable, the aggro more personal, and forced unity for an international fixture a lot harder to achieve. It also makes the whole scene easier to police and the Scottish forces have been far more successful than their English counterparts in controlling football hooliganism. Yet the police never managed to come down hard on the Saturday Service and to this day the firm has remained undeterred by the police presence that reputation attracted.

"The old-timers who still turn out have mostly been the subject of some kind of operation at one time or another but surprisingly there have been no major prosecutions," said Scott. "We found out in the early days about the tabs being kept on us when one lad was arrested. His father was a senior plod and blew his top, shouting, "You do realise that's you on file with the rest of your pals." This was the first we knew of intelligence gathering and was probably around 1984.

"The SS is still going under that name. Lads like myself jacked it in, others have never faltered, they're still there today. The SS have a good name and lads want to be part of that, although not in the same numbers as we had when I was active. The Tufty Club name has been revived though. That fell by the wayside when the younger lads graduated into the SS proper but there's some youth there and they want to be part of the recognised scene."

Despite a few of the original members still being active and the younger lads coming through the ranks, the SS have declined over the past few years and Scott admitted the scene, although not dead, is in decline. "There are still some old faces kicking about and a lot of new blood has come in so they're active to a point. But can anyone can be active in this climate? Scottish Cup away days usually bring out good numbers and some tasty lads. If there's any opposition on those days it can be fun, but normally it's just a piss-up. One or two little rivalries are being built back up, I've noticed, due to piss-takes, but whether it evolves further is anyone's guess because, like it or not, the police have finally copied the OB down south and seem to have it so tight on match days."

The Saturday Service have an excellent website and the following passage features on the introduction page. The moderator kindly let us reproduce it as he believes it sums up perfectly the state of play today.

The SS continues to this day. Although not in the same form, they can still be found if you look hard enough at Fir Park of a Saturday, or whichever day of the week the authorities wish to choose to play a game. You might also see many of the original SS still kicking about, looking for all the world like current members. They might not be active participants anymore, but the dress sense survives, in fact it's kind of difficult to determine the active hooligans at times.

One or two of the original mob gave up football altogether to go and watch Rangers. They might as well have gone to Coventry, which is exactly where they were sent. Shut out completely by their own treason and rightly so. As the mob might have said at the time, 'We Are Motherwell,' nothing else is acceptable. The biggest majority have carried on watching the team and, should the need arise, be available to lend a hand. It's a difficult thing to give up completely, the pride in the mob will always be there, especially for those who were there at the beginning and watched it develop into arguably the best in the country, which they had absolutely no right to expect or demand. In keeping with their team, they were a relatively small outfit who can be a match for anyone on their day, only the days came around fairly quickly for the Saturday, Saturday, Saturday Service!

And we had the best name tae!

Further reading: *Saturday Is Service Day*, Callum Bell (self-published)

N

NEWCASTLE UNITED

Ground: St James' Park
Firms: The Leazes End, the Bender Squad, Mental Central, Newcastle
  Mainline Express, the Gremlins
Rivals: Sunderland, Middlesbrough
Police operations: Harvest, Crusade

All day they had been streaming in: by car from Ostend and Rotterdam, by train from Brussels, by taxi and bus from the airport. Six thousand Geordies descended on the Belgian City of Antwerp for Newcastle United's UEFA cup match against FC Royal Antwerp. From daybreak the Toon Army were making themselves known. The local mob had been looking forward to this game for a while. They were at the time Belgium's biggest mob but the chance to pit themselves against an English team surpassed local rivalries.

"This is where it all started," one of the Antwerp leaders said in great excitement. "England is the home of hooliganism." Their affinity to England was probably all the stronger with the fact that Royal Antwerp had been founded by an Englishman.

On a good day Antwerp would raise a mob of 2-300 lads, many well-versed in martial arts. They had a couple of recruits who were in the Belgium Para-commandos and even an ex-policeman who doubled up as a cage fighter. They were, by anyone's standards, a hard mob and could pit themselves against most mobs in Britain. But something about English hooligans fascinated the locals. Throughout the day, the Antwerp crew quietly watched the invasion of their city, looking out for "lads" like them, hoping for a ruck.

At some stage in the afternoon, a couple of Antwerp struck up a conversation with a couple of the Gremlins, Newcastle United's mob. A fight was arranged for 6.30pm. Excitedly, the locals rushed off to tell the others of the meet, and to prepare.

At 6.30 on the dot, Antwerp were ready but also apprehensive. Two hundred and fifty lads were packed in and around their pub, on a corner of a major junction close to the ground. Spotters were keeping an eye out, waiting for their rivals to emerge among the seemingly endless sea of black and white football shirts.

And then they arrived, the Gremlins – all 25 of them.

"We couldn't believe it," said one Antwerp lad. "To tell you the truth we were gutted. We expected an army of them but there was just this small group. We thought they were joking. Every bar in Antwerp was packed with Newcastle and their mob was just this."

Antwerp offered to call off the fight but the Newcastle lads were having none of it. They had come to battle and battle they did.

"The fight went on for a few minutes," said the Antwerp lad. "Two hundred and fifty lads against twenty-five, and yet they all fought. Not one of them bottled it."

Numbers told in the end but not before Antwerp took casualties. Any feeling of being cheated soon disappeared. "Wow, the English," says Stevie, another leading Antwerp lad. "They're great. They're men and they all want to fight." Since then he has followed the English national side whenever he can.

The common image of the typical Toon Army member is of a fanatical, soccer crazy, beer-bellied monster decked out in the famous black and white stripes and willing to travel the earth to see his beloved team. Yet strip away the stereotype and you have another underneath: the rugged Geordie who needs little invitation to join in a punch-up. Any town that has experienced a visit from the Toon Army would know the second image as well as the first: tough, often burly men who love a beer and their football but they will never shirk a fight. Yet Newcastle have a mixed reputation amongst the hooligan world. No-one doubts their toughness, but as a mob and organisationally, they have been called into question.

"The Geordies, we felt, did not have the football firm mentality," wrote Manchester United's Tony O'Neill in his book *Red Army General*. "They would come to Old Trafford and fight but never as a big unit, always in small groups on coaches or in vans, so they often copped for it. They were hardcases in the main – in fact every one seemed to be a raving lunatic – but weren't organised."

"They were always one firm we had always given some amount of respect to," admitted former West Ham hooligan Cass Pennant in his book on the ICF. "The Geordies also had respect in London when they used to come down for Wembley finals. They would come down on the Friday night and hang out in the West End, just like the Jocks would. The London lads would form various alliances and carefully pick the pubs to hit.

"The one thing I could never get over with the Geordies was the size of 'em. They were pretty big lads, all seemingly living in a time warp. Long after the world had gone casual and started wearing designer labels, Geordie geezers could still be seen on open terraces sporting a threadbare faded jean jacket with badge patches sewn on or going to football matches in donkey jackets. As far as the Geordies are concerned, clothes and style were for southern poofs, along with our bottled lager."

The home of the Newcastle bootboys was the Leazes End and it was there around 1967 that the club's first mob emerged, bringing together like-minded youths from areas such as Big Lamp, Scotswood, Long Benton, North Kenton, Heaton, Walker and West Denton. The fashion was skinheads, donkey jacket and steel-toed boots, a dress sense that Southerners would claim lasted longer there than anywhere else in the country.

There were several arrests at Newcastle's home match to Everton in February 1967 and the following season there was six hours of trouble during the visit by Celtic. The Scots literally invaded. Over 200 coaches brought the bulk of 15,000 fans south of the border for what the local police chief described as "a night of sheer, simple hooliganism and vandalism". Fifty-seven people were arrested and 61 treated in hospital as hordes of Scots battled it out with locals throughout the evening.

Newcastle United were known for their fanatical support. Regardless of the fortunes of their team, the fans would turn up in their thousands all over the country and swamp towns and cities, especially when the club was playing out of the top division. Ironically, some of the worst trouble at Newcastle came when another team did the same to them. In May 1969 Newcastle played Glasgow Rangers in the semi-final of the Fairs Cup and the Scottish hordes caused mayhem, to the point that their own chairman branded them "lunatics". Eighty-nine people were injured and thirty arrested. Play was held up for 17 minutes as thousands of Scots swarmed onto the pitch, many brandishing bottles and other weapons. Many of the 20,000 Scots who had made the trip had earlier rampaged through the city centre and smashed down the gates of St James Park.

A front-page *Evening Chronicle* editorial summed up the mood of the shocked city.

It is hoped that the drunken, bottle-brandishing barbarians from Glasgow who disgraced their club and their team last night have subtle retribution in the form of a hangover today.

The disgusting exhibition of soccer savagery by a minority of Scots supporters proved three major points:

1 The commendable restraint, under great provocation, of the newly-constituted Northumberland police force in its first real 'blooding';
2 The cool efficiency of the voluntary services and the energy of the army of workmen who moved in at dawn to clear up the carpet of broken glass, empty beer cans and debris from the city streets;
3 That Newcastle United supporters retain their standing as Britain's 'best-behaved,' in the face of sheer animal behaviour from some of the visitors.

The "best-behaved" supporters in Britain, or simply overrun and over-whelmed? Certainly there was little best behaviour when Newcastle played Wolverhampton Wanderers a short time later. Three hundred Newcastle lads, mostly skinheads, mobbed up after the game and attacked away fans as they made their way back to their coaches.

One of the most controversial days in Newcastle United's history occurred in March 1974, when they played Nottingham Forest in the fifth round of the FA Cup. Forest were winning 3–1 when a tackle saw Newcastle centre-half Pat Howard sent off. The home crowd, packed in the Leazes End, howled in protest and surged forward. When a free-kick was awarded to Forest three minutes later, ten yards outside the Newcastle box, hundreds spilled out of the Leazes onto the pitch and fighting broke out between rival fans throughout the ground. The game was held up for eight minutes as police battled with home fans on the pitch and in the terraces. The final tally was 39 arrested, 23 taken to hospital and another 100 needing pitch-side medical treatment. There was pressure on the referee to call off the game but after consulting with both managers he continued. Forest's concentration was gone, and to the delight of the home fans Newcastle battled back to win the game 4–3.

Few of those involved in the incidents were unmoved by the events that March day. "I have not got over it, even after twenty-four hours," the shaken referee Gordon Kew told the media the following day. "It was a traumatic experience I am not likely to forget but I never thought of aban-doning the game."

"Even if we had 1000 men on duty at the ground we could not have stopped an invasion of the pitch like that," said Chief Supt David Chester.

"I still feel sick," said defender Pat Howard.

Nottingham Forest lodged a protest with the FA stating that the game should have been abandoned at the outbreak of the trouble with either the score at that moment being made the result or the last 30 minutes being replayed with the score restored to 3-1 in their favour. Five hundred Forest fans signed a petition criticising the policing of the game and expressing concern at the danger they faced.

On the Tuesday after the match, an FA delegation travelled to Newcastle to meet club officials and Northumbria Police. If any of the five-man team had picked up the local evening paper they would have found an open letter addressed to them on the front page.

What happened on Saturday? Newcastle United FC played Nottingham Forest FC under the control of a referee appointed by the FA.

During the game fans invaded the pitch. The referee rightly stopped the match and led the players off the field.

When police restored order the referee quite rightly checked that no player had been injured and then spoke to both team managers. His official report to the FA says: 'Both team managers agreed to resume the game.'

The score at that point was irrelevant. The score at the end of the match is relevant. The only facts that matter is that both managers agreed to play on.

Now one of those managers has decided that he made a mistake and should not have played on. That is his problem. It should not be a problem for the FA. The FA MUST allow the result to stand.

Forest's position softened over the next 48 hours to simply calling for a replay. And that was the decision of the FA inquiry, though they said that a choice of a neutral venue should not be viewed as a punishment against Newcastle United. "What unmitigated twaddle," said another front-page editorial in the *Evening Chronicle*. "It's a travesty. It's an outrage. Not only have they taken away Newcastle's home advantage but they say Pat Howard's suspension must stand – despite the fact the match was void. One begins to wonder why they did not order that Newcastle should play the match blindfolded." The game was replayed at Goodison Park and Newcastle won by a single goal.

A fortnight later, there was further trouble at St. James' Park when 30,000 fans queued overnight for 12,000 FA Cup semi-final tickets. Four people were injured after disturbances in which supporters had uprooted fences and lit fires as they waited. A win over Burnley set up a Wembley final against Liverpool but they were to go down by three goals. Two years later, Newcastle were at Wembley again, this time in the League Cup Final against Manchester City and there was serious trouble before and after the game.

The violence against Forest had the FA force Newcastle to play all the following season's FA Cup ties away from home, and the club, fearful of further trouble and increased sanctions, put its own fans on probation at the beginning of the season. "Our reputation was tarnished last season by a lunatic minority who seemed hellbent on making football an excuse for hooliganism," said club chairman Lord Westwood. "These people are our enemies and unless we combine to eradicate them they will eventually deprive us of our local sport." He announced that if Newcastle fans misbehaved in their first five games of the season, he would be "forced" to authorise the building of fences around the ground.

The Seventies saw the emergence of the Bender Squad, Newcastle's first identifiable hooligan mob. Unlike the Leazes End mob, it was not specifically attached to one area of the ground. "Like most mobs at the time it was just the lads who went to the match, loved a drink and a fight," said John, a well-known Geordie hooligan. "It was nothing organised like today. Newcastle has about a twenty-five-mile catchment area for the lads and we all got together on a match day. Home games we would turn up every game, hundreds strong, very few obliged, Pompey, Man United, Everton once or twice. Away games were all about turning up en masse trying to get on the home end, in the home boozers. Mad, mad days, never to return."

St James' Park was an unfriendly place for any travelling fan to visit. What Newcastle's yobbos lacked in organisation they made up for in numbers and aggression. This was, after all, a city where the men wore T-shirts in sub-zero temperatures. Even Manchester United's Red Army struggled there in the Seventies on more than one occasion, with one of their legends, Jeff Lewis, being hospitalised with an iron bar as his heavily outnumbered mob were attacked before the match. He returned to the fray at half-time with his head bandaged, only to see the Red Army being terrorised inside the ground by thousands upon thousands of crazed Geordies.

Eight years after Glasgow Rangers ran amok in Newcastle, fans of another Scottish team tried a repeat performance. In September 1977 Newcastle played a home match against Hibs and there was again total chaos. "They just wouldn't stop fighting both inside and outside the ground," remembered one fan.

A week later Newcastle travelled to Dublin for a UEFA Cup game against Bohemians. "Frightening – United stars flee field after riot," declared the headline of the local paper. The match was stopped for eleven minutes after violence erupted in the stadium and the Newcastle goalkeeper was struck by a missile thrown by home supporters. Player Stewart Barrowclough described how a half-brick flew just past a fellow player's head while fellow United star Irving Nattrass described it as the most frightening night of his life. The team were locked in their dressing room for their own safety, only to be deafened by stamping feet above them and the occasional brick that smashed into the window.

The spark for the trouble was the raising of a Union Jack amongst the Newcastle fans. "Unfortunately memories die hard and waving a Union Jack to these hooligans is like a red rag to a bull," said a senior Dublin police officer. "Any excuse does and the sight of three Union Jacks among the Newcastle fans was enough." Police said that 1,000 people out of a bumper 25,000 crowd were involved in the trouble.

Referee Glyn Owens took the players off early in the second half after the Newcastle keeper was struck on the head and needed medical attention. The referee went into the Newcastle dressing room to reassure them that as long as they were happy to continue he wanted throw-ins, corners and free-kicks to be taken quickly so the game would be kept flowing. He also arranged to give them a five-second warning of the final whistle so they could be as close to the tunnel as possible in order to reduce the possibility of fans attacking them at the end. "He was as good as his word," said Northern Ireland international Tommy Cassidy. "When the final whistle went, play was bang in front of the tunnel down by the right-hand corner flag and we were off the field like a shot."

By the late Seventies, the London firms were changing the nature of football hooliganism. Smaller but more organised, the gangs that followed the likes of Chelsea, Arsenal and West Ham were taking ends more by guile than brute force. There was perhaps no better contrast in hooligan styles than the slick, lean Headhunters or ICF and the massed beer boys of Newcastle. The London firms were far more confident and cocky but their obsession with taking the North East footballing bastions reflected a grudging admiration.

In the 1979/80 season, Chelsea, West Ham and Newcastle United were all in the Second Division. In March 1980, a sizeable West Ham mob travelled on the train to Newcastle, arriving a couple of hours before the match. A few small skirmishes brought them to the attention of the police but as the mob divided into smaller groups and spread out they became difficult to contain. Only after a serious clash at a main Newcastle pub were the police able to round up the Londoners and take them to the ground. It was for an event inside that this game would be remembered. Tensions began to grow as Newcastle and West Ham traded insults. Darts flew into the away end, crammed between sizeable gatherings of home support. And then it happened: a petrol bomb was launched into the West Ham crowd and two away fans caught the brunt of the blast.

"Just how callous can you get?" asked the editorial of one local paper the following Monday. "Saturday's firebomb attack on West Ham supporters at Newcastle's Leazes End has brought a new and horrific dimension to what amounts to warfare at football matches." Newcastle hero Jackie Milburn added, "That, without doubt, is the worse thing I have ever seen at a football match. The game is being destroyed by thugs like these. Thousands are being kept away from St James' Park because of violence. It's sick, there's just no respect for law and order – and it's ruining football."

Police quickly caught an 18-year-old for the incident and within two months he had been convicted at Newcastle Crown Court. Andrew Smith, a labourer in a local metal spinning factory, told police that he was sick of his club being in the Second Division and wanted to put them back on the map. It wasn't the best defence and it came as no surprise when he was jailed.

Hooligan gangs like to seize on such incidents as motives for "revenge", and West Ham did not have to wait long, as a week later Newcastle were playing in the capital at QPR. With Newcastle fans being banned for the next match at Upton Park, the ICF did not pass over the opportunity for retribution. "The Geordies immediately started in front of us, in the middle of the street, thinking we were QPR," recalled one ICF follower. "As soon as we told them we were West Ham, that was it. They just ran everywhere."

Newcastle lads remember the petrol bombing incident with huge regret. "Every trip to London after that was murder," said John, a Newcastle terrace veteran. "No matter where we were playing, West Ham would turn up and cause murder with us. The fella that threw the petrol bomb was a complete loon. He had nothing to do with the football lads, he was just a local loon who fucked us up for years.

"The first game we had in London after the bomb was at QPR, but they were there and it was the same every game down there for a few years: midweek at Orient, they'd be there, Saturday at Arsenal, Fulham, or QPR, they'd be at the ground or the station. It never stopped us going though, not once did we not show in London and in the end they respected us for it, they will tell you that. They came up to us for a couple of years after as well so the respect is mutual."

The early Eighties saw the birth of the Newcastle Mainline Express, an offshoot of the Bender Squad. Made up of slightly younger lads who were more into the casual fashion than the older boys, they chose the name because such gang tags seemed to be in vogue at the time. "We were a bit of a breakaway group from the Benders," said John. "We were just another big drinking squad who would not walk away from trouble if it came our way. We went everywhere on the train for a few years, there were no specific fights, just the same trouble everywhere we went."

Five thousand of the Toon Army travelled down to Sheffield Wednesday for the first game of the 1980/81 season. The team lost but the fans sang their hearts out from beginning to the end. At the end of the game, hundreds of Newcastle fans, led by the Bender Squad, burst out of the ground and attacked the home supporters. The police quickly moved in and in the ensuing chaos, nine police officers were hospitalised.

Six hundred miles might divide the two cities but one of the best mobs to travel to Newcastle was Portsmouth in October 1983. Hundreds of the infamous 6.57 Crew made the journey up overnight and were strutting through the city by early morning. The two mobs clashed an hour before the game, sending Saturday shoppers fleeing in every direction. In one incident, a half-brick was thrown through a pub window, striking an elderly lady on the leg. Fourteen fans were arrested, equally divided between home and away supporters. Local magistrates dished out fines totalling £1200, an amount welcomed by the local newspaper. Under the headline "Nasty Fans", the editorial of the *Evening Chronicle* hoped that the severity of the fines would deter future potential trouble-makers "for the sake of other citizens and the police".

One Newcastle supporter fined for threatening behaviour that day was Terry Mann, then 24 years old. Known locally as "Mr Newcastle", Mann has been the city's best known hooligan over the years. Small but burly, Mann is also the landlord of the Adelphi, a city centre pub which is almost a shrine to his team. Adorning the walls and shelves is a veritable museum of Newcastle United memorabilia, what he calls his "pride and joy".

Mann's first recollection of trouble at Newcastle was as a ten-year-old at the visit of Glasgow Rangers in 1969. He remembers those early days in his interview in *Terrace Legends*. "I used to like the Gallowgate End where I used to go with my dad, and all the kids were passed over people's heads to the front where we could see. Those were the days, at the proper old terraces. It was magic times." By the mid-seventies he was in the thick of the trouble, at home and increasingly away. "I've been in the Fulwell and at Sunderland's Roker Park a few times when we've cleared it," he recalled. "It's a great feeling going through the turnstile, up the steps, and into their end. They back off, and we've had a right result. It's a lovely feeling walking round the edge of the pitch with the job done – I'm five feet tall but now I'm twenty feet!"

He soon became a leading face in first the Bender Squad and later the Newcastle Mainline Express. By the turn of the Millennium he simply ran with "The Adelphi". Despite his advancing years, Mann remained active until receiving a football banning order in 2004 after being involved in trouble in Holland during Newcastle's UEFA Cup visit to Breda. Giving evidence to secure his ban, the local football intelligence officer reeled off a catalogue of offences involving Mann.

In December 1999, he was arrested at Newcastle's home match against AS Roma and was subsequently stripped of his season ticket. A year later he broke the nose of a Sunderland fan during a local derby, for which he was convicted of assault at Carlisle Crown Court. In November 2000, he was banned from St James' Park for a second time and the following April was one of 79 Newcastle fans arrested before a match at the Stadium of Light. In November 2002, he was spotted by police boozing and chanting offensive songs at the club's away fixture with Feyenoord. In April 2003 he was arrested twice, at Fulham and Sunderland, but on both occasions was released without charge. Mann was also one of 89 Newcastle fans arrested in the infamous "Battle of Breda", for which he was stripped of his season ticket for the third time. Even then, and with the police trying to secure a banning order against him, Mann couldn't resist involvement. In March 2004, he was arrested at an away match against Tottenham and finally, two months later, police claimed that he charged at police lines in Marseille, repeatedly kicking out at their riot shields.

Terry Mann will be almost 50 when his ban ends but it is hard to believe that he will steer clear of trouble. Asked by Cass Pennant what would have stopped him getting involved with the lads at football, he replied, "Nothing. It's just the buzz. I live, eat and drink football."

The years between 1980 and 1984 brought several violent games between Newcastle and Chelsea, whose hooligans were then at their most active. One match saw a big fight outside the ground that went on for about five minutes. "Newcastle away games became a bit of a crusade for some Chelsea fans," recalled Headhunter Chris Henderson in his book *Who Wants It?* "Perhaps it stemmed from the fact that the London press always used them as a benchmark for the fans' loyal support, or perhaps it was because the Geordies genuinely hated us. We had everything they despised, especially jobs and money, and we were flash with it."

After having been bricked all the way back to the train station one year, the Chelsea Headhunters returned the following season and launched a merciless attack on a group of men outside a pub called the Strawberry. Several were badly hurt in an incident that was graphically remembered by Ginger Terry, a Chelsea lad who was rounded up in the first of the Own Goal trials [see CHELSEA in *Hooligans*]. He kept a diary, used in his prosecution, in which he described the fight: "Done a pub load of Geordies … We done well against the Geordies, they were terrified."

Tensions between the two firms worsened as Newcastle vowed revenge. On their next trip to London, some of the bigger lads walked into Chelsea pubs and offered out their opponents in one-on-one fights. The Londoners returned mob-handed for the return fixture and in a clash at a motorway service station, a Newcastle fan was so badly cut up that he needed 140 stitches. Henderson crowed that the Chelsea had upped the ante by "introducing the Geordies to a surgeon's knife".

Newcastle lads accept that the battles with Chelsea were amongst the fiercest they faced in the 1980s, though they are keen to stress that they got the upper hand from time to time. "The NME had some right ding-dongs with Chelsea, including travelling to Darlington in order to have it with them on the train on the way up to Newcastle," said John. "We also did them at the Trafalgar in Gateshead in revenge for the time Chelsea slashed a few blokes who were waiting for a pub to open after they'd been fishing. I also remember the headline Motorway Madness in the local *Sunday Sun* after one game against Chelsea in the early Eighties, where there was a picture of lads dodging cars on the central motorway in Newcastle trying to get across to attack Chelsea at Manors Station.

"To read the flash cunts' books they make out they are the elite force of feared Headhunters, but when you see what they have actually achieved it comes to very little. They have bricked a few buses and smashed a couple of pub windows, made a lot of noise and slashed a couple of fishermen minding their own business. Is it any wonder most fans despise the fucking idiots?"

Newcastle might have had growing feuds with the London firms but their real "enemy" remained Sunderland. In late August 1979, the two teams faced each other in the League Cup. The first match, at Roker Park, saw 19 people arrested during trouble at the ground and a further 21 ejected. One of those injured at the match was Supt David Lander, who was struck in the face by a brick. The game was a thriller and ended 2–2, setting up a second leg at St James' Park a week later. The fans were not to be disappointed. Seventeen goals were scored as Sunderland went through 7-6 on penalties and there was surprisingly little trouble, with only 3,500 away fans making the trip.

It was to be several years until the two sides met again but in 1985 they faced each other twice in four months. The first match was on New Year's Day, with Newcastle romping home 3-1 winners. Trouble before and during the match brought 34 arrests. The game at Roker Park was played in early April and 300 Geordies infiltrated Sunderland's home end. The game was halted briefly while police escorted the mob back to the away end, where they were greeted by the customary applause. Newcastle did not have it all their own way. Among the 28 fans arrested was 21-year-old George Howard, a Sunderland supporter, who was sent to prison for participating in an attack on a group of Newcastle fans. While he argued in court that he was retaliating for a beating he had taken at St James' Park earlier in the season, his cause was not helped by the fact that one of his victims was an off-duty police officer.

During the 1986/87 season, the Gremlins were formed. They were a younger generation of lads more in keeping with the smaller tight-knit hooligan groups found elsewhere in the country. The name was given to them by the older lads after the film about aggressive little creatures who take over a small town.

Newcastle found themselves in the play-offs against arch-rivals Sunderland in May 1990, having missed out on automatic promotion on the final day of the season with a 4-1 defeat at Middlesbrough. The first leg, at Roker Park, ended goalless, and so the two great rivals battled it out at St James' Park four days later. When Sunderland took a 2–0 lead in the 85th minute, seemingly placing the tie beyond Newcastle's reach, some fans stormed the pitch to get the match abandoned. What began as a trickle soon grew and hundreds of United fans swarmed out of the Gallowgate and East Stand seats onto the grass. Play was held up for 21 minutes. "And they were not without support from the Grandstand," reported the local paper. "Even in the expensive seats of the Milburn Stand, apparently responsible and respectable people urged on the invaders, some even screaming for them to breach the police cordon and reach the Sunderland supporters' enclosure." Fifty-two people were arrested and 20 needed hospital treatment, including seven police officers.

Police would later claim that they had received "information through a series of intelligence sources" that a call had gone out for Newcastle fans to invade the pitch to try to get the game abandoned if Sunderland appeared to be heading for victory. This has been strongly denied by the Newcastle lads themselves. "It was just loads of loons and not the firm," said John.

The Gremlins' excursions abroad with England brought them into contact with other mobs and friendships and enmities emerged. Two groups that the Gremlins were to forge close links with were Shrewsbury's EBF and Notts Forest's FEC. The link with Shrewsbury was formed in 1990 and for the next decade the two mobs linked up at England games abroad. In 1993, a combined group of 150 Shrewsbury and Newcastle lads were present in Holland for the crucial World Cup qualifier. In 1997, some Newcastle lads were travelling with Shrewsbury when a couple of EBF lads badly stabbed a North African man in Berlin.

"A load of Newcastle met up with some Shrewsbury lads on the camp site in Sardinia at Italia 90," said John. "They were all good lads and started to come up for weekends. They always came when we played Sunderland and were with us when, after a game at West Ham, we had a massive off with Leicester at Kings Cross the weekend they played Spurs in the League Cup final. With Forest, Boatsy [real name Gary Clarke, author of the book *Inside The Forest Executive Crew*] got mates with one of our main lads and they used to come up, like Shrewsbury, for the odd weekend, I went with them to Cardiff a couple of seasons ago and they were a top firm that day. We meet up at the odd England game. Forest and Newcastle went across the river to the Turkey game at the Stadium of Light in April 2002 and we had it with Hull and Sunderland that night."

Newcastle got over the bitter disappointment of the 1990 play-off defeat, and under the stewardship of Kevin Keegan, went into the last game of the 1991/2 season requiring a win at Leicester to go up. United ran out 2–1 winners thanks to a Leicester own goal but the game hit the headlines for the violence that accompanied it.

"This was mental," said John. "We needed a result to go up and they needed one to stay up or something. It was one-each and then we scored and the other results went against them. It went off to fuck; we were on the pitch more than the players. They had a right firm and kept piling on the pitch, every time they came on we were on with them, total bedlam. We had turned up before and had it with them, after was on top with the bizzies and was pretty quiet compared to the game. The Bender Squad were behind the trouble. The Gremlins had started about that time but that firm at Leicester was Bender Squad and all the old heads were at it."

Newcastle were in the Premiership. But while their ground capacity expanded dramatically, the Gremlins and Bender Squad found it increasingly hard to swamp other towns and cities. Limited tickets and much more effective policing meant that they could no longer run amok without serious legal consequences. That's not to say that there was no more trouble – there was – but it was less frequent and more organised away from the ground.

One new rivalry that emerged was with Sheffield United, and the two mobs clashed in 1994 and 1998. The second confrontation took place in the semi-final of the FA Cup, with 150 Newcastle, a combined Gremlins and old school mob, scattering Sheffield outside the Wetherspoons pub in Piccadilly Gardens, central Manchester. Considering the reputation the Blades had earned, many Newcastle lads expressed surprise at how quick they crumbled.

From a footballing perspective, the 1995/96 season was Newcastle's best for many years. For much of the season they led the Premier League, and home wins against Liverpool, Arsenal and Leeds saw them go into the Christmas period with a ten-point lead. Though they slipped back in the New Year, the outcome was still in their hands at the end of April. The Toon Army was going crazy, believing at long last that silverware was coming to St James' Park. But they slipped on the final straight, allowing Manchester United to come through on the rails and prompting a memorably emotional rant from Kevin Keegan directed towards Alex Ferguson after another disappointing performance.

Newcastle went into the final game at home to Tottenham needing to win and for Man United to lose. It didn't happen and a 1-1 draw saw them pipped at the last. Their fans, who had experienced the emotional roller-coaster of years of underachievement and false dawns, erupted into spontaneous violence. Almost 1,000 rampaged through the city, smashing shop windows and attacking the police after the match finished. At one stage ten ambulances were ferrying the injured to hospital. "It was a disturbance on a large scale and we got a big shock," said a spokeswoman for Northumbria Ambulance Service. "We expected it to be busy but we were very surprised with how busy. We were dealing with incidents well into the night, the last one coming just before one am."

Twenty-nine people were arrested on the night but dozens more were netted after the local paper ran pictures of 100 people taken from CCTV footage. Two weeks after the riot, Northumbria Police conducted a series of dawn raids across the region, netting several prominent members of the Gremlins. Operation Harvest saw the homes of 26 men raided, with 120 officers using battering rams to smash down doors in the early hours of Friday, May 24.

The police were jubilant at their catch. "So far we've recovered machetes, air pistols, a lot of knives, coshes, souvenirs of tours abroad and literature relating to the Gremlins," boasted Det Chief Inspector Derek Scougal, the officer in charge of Operation Harvest. "By the end of the day we expect to have arrested more than twenty people and have recovered a lot of useful information relating to organised football violence."

The local *Evening Chronicle* was in no doubt that the police had nabbed the men behind the end-of-season riot, a charge the Gremlins themselves reject. "The Gremlins were nothing to do with it," insisted John. "It was just a big piss-up with every fucker out on the town. Things got out of hand and loads of local lunatics went on the rampage. All the place was CCTV'd up and quite a few Gremlins were seen associating or playing up in the incident. It was nothing, absolutely fuck-all, yet they got hammered for it by the police and courts."

An even bigger catch for the police came four years later, when one of the most vicious hooligan fights of recent years led to the imprisonment of the leadership of both Newcastle and Sunderland mobs. John, one of the Newcastle lads imprisoned for the incident, tells the story:

"It was the night before we went to Everton, and Sunderland were at home to Boro. The Mackems had been on the phone to one of the lads with the usual bollocks that they were coming over, and were we up for it? We'd heard it so many times before so no-one took any notice at first. After a while it was looking like they were serious, so about fifty of us got together in a pub and waited. Then it went off on the 'you come to us' nonsense, so at eight o'clock we all split up and fucked it off. There was only about ten football lads left when, about quarter to ten, they phoned and said, 'We're here, fifty of us.'

"They were filmed getting off the ferry and it was used in court and they were forty-four-handed, to be exact. To this day I think they just were there for the show, march past a couple of bars, play up and jump on the last ferry home claiming a result. Well their plan went to fuck because we told them to hang on and give us five minutes to get there. In total there were just sixteen of us and six were blokes out of the pub who didn't like the cunts coming across the river taking the piss.

"They expected us to come down the bank towards them but we went behind them through the disused docks, spread across the road to make it look like we had more and just steamed into them. We ran them straight back to the ferry, they tried to come back at us when they realised our numbers but were chased back on and we had to do one quick when the police turned up from nowhere."

The fight was short but fierce. Pool cues, pool balls, ashtrays, CS gas spray canisters, broken chairs and table legs and bottles were all found littered around the scene of the fight. Knives were also used and a trail of blood spread across the ferry landing quayside. Three Sunderland fans were rushed to intensive care, including one who was put on a life support system and was so badly brain-damaged that he was unfit for trial. One of the ferry crew was even attacked as he tried to help one of the football lads who lay injured on the floor. "It could so easily have been a murder inquiry," acting Det Chief Insp John Ramshaw, who led the police investigation, told the press. "One of the two men we found unconscious on the Quayside had severe head injuries and had also been stabbed in the back."

The police were alerted to the trouble by dozens of calls from a terrified public. By the time the Sunderland group arrived back in South Shields, a fleet of vans were waiting. Meanwhile, other police were removing CCTV footage which had captured the whole event. But Northumberland Police did not want to stop there. The leaders of both groups were involved and the police knew they would never get a better opportunity to decapitate the local hooligan hierarchy. Their investigation was boosted a couple of days later when rival hooligans began boasting about the fight over the Internet site set up by Carlisle hooligan Paul Dodd. Under the header, "Casuals v Gremlins; the truth any firm needs to know," the posting gave an incredibly detailed account of the build up to the fight and the contact between the rival hooligan firms. The information appeared to come from Sunderland's Seaburn Casuals.

After the Boro game, the Gremlins were supposed to come to Roker Avenue. We got a phone call to tell us that they would not be coming on the Avenue but to the Blue Bell and they were at Heworth waiting for a train. A taxi ride later, we were in the Blue Bell only to receive another phone call to say that the Gremlins were now in South Shields and at the County pub waiting for us.

...To get to North Shields from Sunderland involves getting a ferry from South Shields over the Tyne. Anyone familiar with the North East will tell you it is a Mag stronghold. Eighteen of our boys and by no means our top boys went across. When they got off the ferry they were confronted by about 40 Gremlins backed by about 100 locals. It had been agreed beforehand that no-one would be tooled up; we were going toe to toe to see who the best firm was.

The Mags had conveniently forgot about this and came at Sunderland with sticks, bricks and bars. A couple of our lads ran back on to the ferry but most of them stood and fought the best they could.

With lads boasting about the fight being arranged, the police knew they had a chance to prove conspiracy. They were able to prove this in court by examination of the mobile phones seized from those arrested. During the build-up to the fight, Gremlin leader Graham Russell made ten calls to his Sunderland rival James Jameson and also sent a text message arranging the time and the place. A complex diagram of telephone contact between the rival groups was presented to the court and helped obtain the guilty verdicts. Thirty people were convicted, with Russell and Jameson getting four years. The average age of those involved was 30, with the youngest being in his 20s and the oldest in his 40s.

The arrests and intensive police investigation did little to reduce the violence between the two mobs. For the next game at the Stadium of Light, over 300 Newcastle lads made the short journey. The police were determined to prevent a repeat of the trouble the previous year, when fifty-five people had been arrested, and decided that their best tactic was to bus in all the away fans straight to the ground and then straight back again at the end. This, they hoped, would prevent Newcastle and Sunderland fans clashing across the city. It sounded good but they had not accounted for the resourcefulness of the hooligans.

The Gremlins booked a coach through a Glasgow-based firm claiming that they were going to the races at Thirsk but with a "pick-up" in Sunderland. "Once he reached Sunderland, the coach driver was paid off and told to do one, but he allegedly told the bizzies instead," said Gremlin John. The police quickly surrounded the pub and all 60 occupants were arrested.

Elsewhere, a mob of up to 250 "veterans", aged from their mid-30s to their 50s, eschewed the free buses laid on from St James' Park and went on the train. It took the police an hour to herd them the ten-minute walk to the ground, such was their intent to cause trouble. A total of 160 fans were arrested before the game and there were sporadic instances of disorder on the Wearmouth Bridge. After the match, away fans were held in until the Sunderland crowd had dispersed. Despite the huge arrest figure, the police were happy with the day, though well away from the ground groups clashed in several pubs in Washington, a large but distinct area within the Sunderland city boundaries.

The convictions following the ferry fight in 2002 did nothing to dampen the rivalry between Newcastle and their Sunderland counter-parts. A year later, a firm of Newcastle thugs waited in the Centurion bar, at Central Station, for Sunderland fans returning from a friendly against Hibs in Edinburgh. There had been talk about a possible confrontation for several days but still the police appeared unprepared. Sunderland disembarked their train at 9pm, and as a small group of police attempted to shepherd them down into the Metro they were confronted by a group of Gremlins.

"You could see they were winding each other up and were just dying to get at each other like a pack of animals," said Tracey Vicreck, manager of the Centurion, later. "They managed to break free and the two groups went at each other right in the middle of the pub. It was terrifying. The pub was crowded with about 400 punters and these yobs just began flying at each other. Glasses were going everywhere and they were using bar stools to smash things up. It was absolute mayhem. We had young staff who'd never dealt with anything like this before."

Up to 150 people were involved in the fight but only four Sunderland fans were arrested. Later that evening a Seaburn Casual posted on the internet: "What a day! What a turnout! If Sunderland can get numbers like that more often then no one can touch us! Keep it up lads. This was a great day with SAFC untouchable off the pitch! We showed the Gremlin bottle-throwers how to break police cordons and showed them up in their own backyard. Their plan backfired and the Gremlins ran, ran and ran and as far as I know are still running."

Newcastle's recent forays into Europe have seen the team play the Dutch teams Feyenoord and Breda and both games saw large mobs travel. Three hundred lads made the trip to Rotterdam but tight police prevented any trouble. The following season, in 2003, Newcastle played Breda in the second round of the UEFA Cup. A fight before the match saw 87 Newcastle fans arrested, many of them known to the British police. The incident was caught on CCTV and that, together with eyewitness police evidence, formed the basis of a police operation to secure banning orders against dozens of lads.

Newcastle now struggle to raise a large hooligan mob. Where once they could rely on 200-300 for each game, they are now left with a hard-core of 40-50. Changing football culture, the redevelopment of the ground and banning orders have had a debilitating impact on the lads. The Gremlins continues to be the name most associated with Newcastle but few of the main lads concur. "I would say no name now," said John. "The Gremlins were the youth firm that started going together in about 1986/87."

Even when yobs do turn out, which is usually for a local derby, they are unlikely to do so as one mob anymore. The fans of many clubs now turn up and enjoy the hospitality on Tyneside, now rated one of the top night-time destinations in the country, without any knowledge of how intimidating it once could be. "The place is full of day-trippers and stag parties nowadays," said John. "After home games there are literally scores of lads wandering around dressed like pop idols, thinking they are the cock of the North. Good luck to them. I bet their dads have different memories of the old place though."

One group of supporters, however, found the city centre decidedly unwelcoming. According to the *Newcastle Chronicle*:

Violence erupted inside the Three Bulls Heads, in Newcastle city centre, after an FA Cup clash between Newcastle United and Coventry City on January 29, 2005.

The thugs, members of the notorious Newcastle Gremlins, desperately tried to find hooligans from Coventry to fight. But they failed to organise a clash and turned on genuine Coventry fans, men and women, who had been enjoying a quiet drink in the Percy Street pub.

Caught on CCTV, the gang steamed into the bar shortly after 6pm. They attacked the startled visitors, throwing bottles and glasses at them. Then they waded in kicking and punching like a scene from a Wild West saloon.

According to police, the Gremlins entered the pub after being tipped off when to strike and ran across the room to attack the Coventry supporters. They first hurled bottles and glasses at the visitors, many of whom were standing with female partners, before wading into them. Some 44 seconds later, the fight spilled out on to the streets, as those under attack tried to escape from another door into Percy Street. "Dozens of innocent people were passing by when the melee spilled out," said one intelligence officer. "It was down to pure chance that no-one was more seriously injured."

Although innocent fans were targeted in the ambush, police found messages about the attack posted on websites of Coventry City's hooligans, the Legion. Football intelligence officers began tracking the suspects who fled the scene and three months later they swooped on houses in a series of raids. Seven men subsequently pleaded guilty to affray at Newcastle Crown Court. Three of those arrested had already been on banning orders, including one who had been arrested and booted out of Portugal during Euro 2004. He had protested his innocence but his home computer contained photographs and him and his friends at other matches, under files entitled "Gremlins".

Further reading: *Terrace Legends*, Cass Pennant and Martin King (John Blake Publishing)

NORTHAMPTON TOWN

Ground: Sixfields Stadium, formerly the County Ground
Firms: County Tavern Mob, Elly boys, Northampton Affray Team
Rivals: Brighton, Luton, Oxford, Peterborough, Shrewsbury Town

It was called the "Battle of Abington Park". On April 13, 1974, 500 Northampton and Peter-borough lads fought before, during and after a vital top-of-the-table clash. "'County Ground Battle' – Several fans need treatment," ran the headline in the evening paper on the day of the trouble. It continued:

"Fighting broke out on the pitch at Northampton's County Ground this afternoon before the start of the vital Cobblers v Peterborough local derby clash. Two spectators were dragged off the pitch by police 15 minutes before the start of the game. Several supporters needed treatment, and one boy had head injuries following a fight.

"The tension and electric atmosphere spilled over into crowd trouble and the small band of police was kept at full strength, dealing with trouble which flared mainly from the Hotel End behind the goal. Today's violence on the terraces was the worst since the Bristol Rovers cup tie earlier this season. But it had been quelled by kick-off time; when the Posh started the match rolling comparative peace reigned throughout the ground."

The newspaper went to print shortly after kick-off and so was not able to report the serious violence after the match. If it had known of what was to come it would not have ended the article so positively. The account of the post-match violence was left to the next edition.

Forty-four youths, mostly teenagers, will appear before Northampton Borough magistrates tomorrow following the 'Battle of Abington Park', in which two policemen were hurt.

A pitched battle involving hundreds of youths raged for nearly an hour after Saturday's Cobblers v Peterborough match at the County Ground which attracted more than 11,000 spectators, the biggest crowd for years.

Spasmodic clashes between rival gangs of youths broke out in Abington Avenue and in the ground before the match but these were quickly quelled by police and comparative peace reigned during the match which Peterborough won 1-0.

But pent up emotions erupted into greater violence after the match and hundreds of youths converged in Abington Park for what were some of the ugliest scenes ever seen in Northampton.

Police said a "considerable number of youths" were involved in a whole series of fights in the park. One eye witness put the number at well over 500 at the height of the fighting.

"It was like a battle scene from a film where everyone converged to carry out personal duels. I have never seen anything like it," he said. "The police were hard pushed at one stage but eventually broke up the groups. The police did a splendid job."

…Before the start of the match police frisked youths entering the ground and took possession of a wide range of weapons which included bottles, sticks and scarves in which stones were wrapped.

Chief Superintendent George Swain said today: "There were some deplorable scenes before and after the match. The affair in Abington Park was a disgrace but at no time did the police lose control. Most of the people involved are young teenagers. I hope the parents of these youngsters will look to their responsibilities in these matters."

The battle continued to dominate the front page of the *Chronicle & Echo* five days after the match. "'Battle of Park' – Now the fines," ran a headline. "Sticks with nails embedded in the end, part of a brick, broken bottles, a large beer can and a pint mug were displayed before Northampton Borough magistrates today, when 44 youths, the youngest 13, appeared on charges arising from, and before, the 'Battle of Abington Park'." Of the 42 people eventually convicted, only three were over 20, with the oldest being 22. The rest were teenagers.

The Northampton Town hooligan firm around at the time was the County Tavern Mob, named after the pub which was their base on match days. They were around from the early 1970s until the end of the decade, when they were replaced by the Elly Boys, again named after a pub, who in keeping with the times, were younger and identified with the emerging casual scene. Many of the early Elly Boys had lived in London and were attached to some of the bigger mobs, and with them came new fashions and trends. Their numbers averaged 100, though up to 200 could be mobilised for big games. Arguably their biggest row was a home match against Swindon. Away fans attacked the Elly Boys in the White Elephant pub, and during vicious fighting several people were stabbed. One Northampton lad was sentenced to seven years' imprisonment, though many insist he did not commit the offence he was found guilty of.

The Northampton mob has always consisted of lads from not only the town but also surrounding towns such as Wellingborough and even Milton Keynes. There have been many prominent figures over the years, none more so than Paddy R, a legend to Town fans. "What can I say about Paddy R – apart from being small!" said Northampton lad Barry. "But what he lacked in build he certainly made up in bottle. He was the gamest lad you will ever have met surrounding football, a true legend in this town."

An early battle for the young Northampton firm came at Gillingham in 1981. A vanload of 20 lads, most aged between 17 and 19, made the trip. They were a new mob, cocky, and drunk. They mouthed off to an older group of 50 Gillingham after the game from the comfort of the van before speeding off before the home firm could respond. Unfortunately for the visitors they were held up at a railway crossing and the chasing Gillingham gleefully smashed them and the van to pieces. During a cold and painful journey home the Northampton lads reflected on the lesson they had just learned.

In 1983, a large mob of Chesterfield travelled to Northampton tooled up to the eyeballs. Two local lads were stabbed and Northampton were well and truly "turned over". The return fixture was a revenge mission and a huge mob made the journey. They entered the home end, forced Chesterfield onto the pitch and the game was held up for 20 minutes. This was not to be the last violence involving Northampton and Chesterfield, for eleven years later the Cobblers travelled up to Derbyshire on the final Saturday of the season needing a win to stay in the Football League. Their position was secured but once again violence spilled onto the pitch and held up the game.

It was another away trip, this time to Cambridge in 1985, that had a major influence on the future of Northampton's hooligans. "There was major fighting all day," remembered Barry, "but the biggest incident happened on the way home. We stopped off in St Neots, where the lads had agreed to meet for a drink. There were thirty of us in a Luton van and though we were late we expected the others still to be waiting for us. They were not but we went for a drink all the same. We were happily supping away as more and more locals started to come in.

"Inevitably, it kicks off. We run the locals out of the pub and into the next one and that too gets smashed to bits and two stabbed in doorway. Emboldened by our success we then try to attack the next pub down only to be met with a very tasty set of lads who turn out to be very well known Chelsea, and it starts to really come on top for us. We retreat to the van to get away when an empty beer barrel is launched through our windscreen. One of theirs stands in front of the van to stop us, only for our driver to dispatch him over the bonnet in first gear. We get just outside the town when the police pull us over and nick all thirty of us. We are held for two days and while twenty were eventually released, ten were charged with affray."

The case came to court in September 1986 and two Northampton and two locals were convicted, with one of the Northampton lads receiving 21 months. It was the events on that day in St. Neots that led to the formation of the Northampton Affray Team, the name the lads still use.

The NAT are a small but tight mob, with a hardcore of between 30 and 50 lads. On a good day, against fierce opponents, they have pulled out 150 bodies and their best ever turnout was 400 for the club's two Wembley play-offs against Swansea in 1997 and Grimsby the following season. Local rivals include Luton and Peterborough, but over the years the Northampton mob has also had repeated run-ins with Chesterfield, Brighton, Lincoln, Shrewsbury and Oxford. As previously mentioned, perhaps their worst violence in recent years was the home match against Swindon, which began with the Wiltshire mob attacking a pub of Northampton and then a retaliatory strike. There were serious injuries on both sides.

Another nasty battle was the home fixture against Brighton in 1988, when a large mob travelled up from the South Coast and really turned Northampton over in several incidents during the day. "The worst by far took place outside the ground where there was a massive battle on the park near the ground," said Barry. "Hats off to Brighton for that. For the return fixture we went there and completely reversed it, taking liberties everywhere. Overall, it was a definite one-one draw."

Every firm has stories where the lads travel away and get a taste of trouble but want more. Often this results in the mob stopping off on their way home to have a drink and a fight. That's exactly what happened in 1987 when two coachloads of lads on their way back from a match in Peterborough stopped off in Kettering. A few Northampton had been given a hiding in Kettering some time before and this was a revenge mission. Over 100 lads attacked and wrecked the Traders pub. The police came but the fighting continued, with one officer later requiring twelve stitches and a police car overturned. Thirty people were arrested, and 14 Northampton and five Kettering were charged. At the subsequent trial, eight Northampton lads and three locals were jailed for between six and 30 months.

This was not the only time Northampton caused havoc on the way home from a match. In 1991, 150 Northampton travelled to Birmingham City unannounced. Many saw this as payback for the trouble Birmingham had caused when they visited Northampton in October 1989. The police scrabbled to control the situation and while they were able to round up the bulk of the mob, about 30 slipped the net and headed to a known Zulu pub near New Street. Two lads nonchalantly walked through the pub emptying the contents of CS gas canisters while the others watched in amusement as the other customers stumbled out. Buoyed up by their mischief, most of the main Northampton mob decided to stop at Rugby on their return for a few beers and no doubt try their luck against the locals. Their presence was quickly picked up by local lads and soon their every movement was being shadowed. Eventually it kicked off in the Merry Minstrel pub, with locals again gassed and the pub smashed up. Outside the pub a furious local mob gathered and Northampton had to fight their way back to the train station.

Some time before the Birmingham trip, a mob of Northampton had travelled up to Rochdale and clashed with a combined mob of locals and Manchester City. Before the game the away firm got the upper hand and a local pub was badly damaged, but afterwards Rochdale got their act together and fought back. "This was probably the best toe-to-toe fighting we have ever had and full respect goes to Rochdale that day," said Barry.

Northampton were struggling on the pitch during the early 1990s and for two consecutive seasons they found themselves going into the last Saturday fearing the drop into the Conference. The first was in May 1993, when they travelled to Shrewsbury. The stakes were raised because Shrewsbury Town still had an outside chance of making the play-offs.

Thousands of Northampton fans made the journey to Shropshire, including a mob of 200 lads. They were the ones cheering at the final whistle as Northampton took the game 3-2. Hundreds of away fans stormed across the pitch in jubilation, with the NAT heading to the Shrewsbury end. Shrewsbury did not respond, but outside the ground there was mayhem. "There was serious fighting outside the station," remembered Barry. "There was a much smaller but very game bunch of Shrewsbury lads who got done that day, but fair play to them for the effort."

> Hundreds of football fans charged through Shrewsbury terrorising local people, smashing windows and attacking a pub [reported the *Shropshire Star*].
>
> Marauding supporters were involved in several punch-ups before the match but the main trouble came after Northampton had snatched victory from Shrewsbury in a vital Division Three game.
>
> After the final whistle, jubilant Northampton fans stormed through the town, clashing with Shrewsbury supporters in an afternoon which saw 16 arrests.
>
> Northampton fans ran riot up Wyle Cop, engulfing the Nags Head pub, after the match.

The newspaper also reported that one supporter headbutted a window, while others hurled missiles.

This was to spark off a series of spats between the two teams, as Ryan from Shrewsbury confirmed. "We had a couple of proper ding-dongs with Northampton. They came to our place needing a win to stay up one year and brought loads, it went off all day and they were decent. They came in the home end and it was going off all game and after was a free-for-all. The following year we met a few Northampton lads at an England game and told them we would turn up at their place. We took about forty in minibuses and holed up in some pub called the King Billy. They came down firmed up, at least 100-odd, and started smashing the pub to bits. The windows went through and then two lads, total nutters, came jumping through the window. They got battered and one was in a bad way, in a coma and someone said he ended up in a wheelchair, not sure how true that is but we knew he was in a bad way. They gassed the pub and eventually the police came in and took us out but we had thrown everything we could at them and did well. It was a mental experience."

The following season, Northampton travelled to Chesterfield again fearing the drop. There was trouble almost as soon as the Cobblers arrived. "There was fighting all day long with a very game bunch of Chesterfield," said Barry. "There was trouble before the game and during half-time, where

Stewards try to break up fighting between Manchester City fans (left) and Chelsea supporters in the seats at Maine Road in the late Nineties.

An unconscious and bleeding fan is tended at the roadside by a police officer at a Stoke City-Manchester United game in September 1983.

Feyenoord supporters (left) try to defend themselves with chairs against an attacking mob of Manchester United hooligans outside a bar in Rotterdam in 1997.

Millwall yobs storm across the pitch during their infamous televised riot in the FA Cup against Luton Town in 1985, a watershed event in football hooliganism.

Distinctive Middlesbrough hooligan Lee "Oathead" Owens being arrested in Belgium after disturbances at the Euro 2000 tournament.

The late Paul Debrick, once a leading figure in Boro's Frontline gang and author of the memoir *The Brick*. He died suddenly in 2007 at the age of 42.

Members of the Motherwell Saturday Service. The casual fashion was embraced as a way of life in many Scottish cities as new football gangs sprang up north of the border.

A petrol bomb explodes among away fans at the Newcastle United–West Ham game, one of the most notorious hooligan incidents inside a UK football ground, in March 1980.

The outspoken Nottingham Forest and England yob Paul Scarrott became for a while the most notorious soccer thug in Britain, his exploits luridly covered in national newspapers.

Former Oldham Athletic hooligan Carl Spiers has chronicled the exploits of forgotten terrace gangs such as the Sewer Mob, the Crossley Leathers and the Sholver Skins.

An Oxford United mob attack pubs in the Irish area of Kilburn, north London, before an England international at Wembley. Anti-Irish and pro-loyalist sentiment among English football gangs has often led to violence directed, as here, at innocent members of the public.

Portsmouth fans clash with police in the seats at Cardiff City in 1983, at the height of the casual culture. Pompey's 6.57 Crew were one of the most active travelling firms in the early Eighties, their name taken from the time of the train they would catch to away games.

Andy Frain (centre), who received a lengthy jail term after an investigation by the *Macintyre Undercover* television series, may be the most notorious football hooligan in Reading but he actually follows Chelsea FC. His nickname is "Nightmare".

Mounted police chase a mob through the streets of South London before a high-profile Millwall-Cardiff fixture at the New Den in the 1999/2000 season.

Corbis

Members of the Blades Business Crew of Sheffield United fight it out with their Middles-brough Frontline rivals in the seats at Ayresome Park.

the game was held up for twenty minutes while fierce battles happened on the pitch, during which our manager John Barnwell pleaded with us to get off but to no avail. After the game they didn't have the numbers but certainly gained our respect for keep coming back time and time again."

Northampton once again survived and gradually their playing fortunes improved.

Nineteen ninety-seven was to be an active year for the NAT. A home match against Cardiff saw 40 battle with 100 Soul Crew outside the ground before the game. Afterwards there were further clashes when a group of 40 Cardiff left the match early and bumped into a much larger Northampton firm. Cardiff initially stood their ground but the greater numbers soon had them on the run. "Eventually they got turned over, but still hats off to them," says Barry. "It was a good ten minutes toe-to-toe, with both sides getting put down but getting stuck straight back in. They won't admit to getting done, but there you go."

The same season saw Millwall bring 150 lads up from London and get a result against just forty Northampton outside a pub near the ground. Then there was an away trip to Brighton when thirty Northampton caught Brighton completely by surprise and in the process smashed up their pub. Brighton got their act together after the game and attacked small groups of away fans but in the eyes of the NAT, the result was already theirs.

The hooligan scene went quiet in Northampton for a number of years as increased policing, jail sentences, and hooligan fatigue took its toll. However, there was a big turnout for the home game against Luton Town in late 2002. Thirty NAT were drinking in a pub close to the train station when news filtered through that a similar-sized group of Luton were about to arrive. The Northampton lads supped up and headed to the closest pub to the station, where they hid in the back room. The unsuspecting Luton mob casually wandered into the pub, only to be caught by surprise. "Northampton threw everything out at Luton," recalled Barry. "We charged through two doors and they quickly ran, leaving behind a street littered with glass and stools.

"Then, about an hour later, word reached us that Luton had gone to a pub about fifteen minutes away. Northampton headed straight there, taking side streets to avoid the Old Bill and then mounted a full frontal attack on the pub. For a good ten minutes Northampton repeatedly tried to get in, but fair play to Luton, they held us at bay, at great cost to them. One game Spurs lad who was with Luton tried to glass one of us but caught his hand in the door frame and severed his fingers. He was not alone; a few of theirs were bleeding heavily."

Twenty Luton were arrested on the day and in a series of dawn raids some time later. However, by the time the cases came to court, only four had been charged with violent disorder. Three were acquitted, while the fourth was jailed for 21 months. Interestingly, the Northampton newspaper described the trouble extensively, though in their eyes Luton had been the instigators.

Members of the Northampton Affray Team have been prominent on the England scene and are never far from trouble. In 1990, a small group, including a couple of their main faces, joined up with lads from Oldham, Wigan and Southend, in a fight against 200 Italians in Sardinia in what became known as the Battle of Pula. Some notorious Northampton lads were also involved in fighting at Frankfurt the evening before a Germany–England World Cup qualifier in Munich.

According to an Oldham lad interviewed for this book, "I met some Northampton lads through the BNP scene and then went to an England game with them. They may not have the most famous mob about but those lads who follow England are up there with the very best of the prominents at England games." Similar testimonies from other hooligans, and the admission by the Cardiff Soul Crew that they nearly came unstuck there, may surprise a few who have never crossed swords with Northampton. Those who have will know where their reputation comes from.

In 2007, three Northampton Town fans were banned from all football stadiums in the country until 2013 and given lengthy jail sentences for their part in a violent brawl after an FA Cup tie. David Mobley, Mark Arbery and Craig Mabee got involved in a fight in the Kings Cross area of London after the Cobblers' third round FA Cup defeat by Crystal Palace in December 2006. They were followed by officers from the Metropolitan Police after the fight, and then arrested by Northamptonshire officers. They were subsequently found guilty of violent disorder, along with fans from Charlton Athletic and Cardiff City. Mobley and Arbery were convicted after a two-day trial and were both jailed for 18 months. Mabee pleaded guilty and was jailed for a year.

NORWICH CITY

Ground: Carrow Road
Firms: C Squad, Steins, Magnificent Seven, Norwich Hit Squad (NHS)
Rivals: Ipswich Town

"Every town has its nutters and hardmen, and every football team is much the same, although it would be a struggle to find a punch-up in Norwich," wrote Colin Ward in his seminal terrace autobiography *Steaming In*. He was articulating the views of many. Norwich, a hooligan mob? Surely its off-the-pitch antics owe more to Delia Smith than anything its firm has done over the years?

That, of course, would be to understate the activities of the hooligan minority at Norwich City. While they've never been in the Premier League of thugs, they have often been active. And the city's close proximity to the coastal resort of Great Yarmouth and relative closeness to London has always ensured a steady stream of travelling mobs coming into town.

The two early mobs at Norwich were Steins and C Squad. Steins came from a greeting used by one of the older lads to another, "Alright stein", which was picked up by other lads. They also had their own song, set to the tune *Lord of the Dance*: "Image free, wherever you may be, we are the mental Stein army, and we smash the Old Bill wherever we may be, we are the mental Stein army." One of the lads, Hue, sneaked into the ground and sprayed "Steins" in the corner of the River End Stand where the lads stood, to mark their territory. This mob had members from all the local estates and could pull good numbers together. There was also a close-knit crew of scooter boys called the Magnificent Seven, who were always together and proved their worth in many a scrape both home and away.

Football disorder was first nationally noted at Norwich in 1967, when home fans clashed with Crystal Palace supporters. However, it was in December 1975 that Norwich hit the national news in a big way. The visitors were West Ham and their fans ran amok after Norwich were awarded a penalty late on in the game. Dozens of Hammers had infiltrated the home Barclay Stand and remained unnoticed until the referee's decision. They then broke into song and charged the home crowd. Thirty-one people were arrested and 34 injured. The local paper said the scenes resembled a "battlefield", noting that it was "probably the worst instance of crowd trouble ever seen at Norwich".

Hundreds of Norwich fans were forced onto the pitch to escape the fighting, though many of the injuries were caused when fans were crushed by the stand barrier. Fighting also broke out on the pitch as a ground steward was attacked by a group of youths, and one youngster in the claret and blue of West Ham was chased the length of the pitch by a group of 30. He was cornered in front of the main stand and punched and kicked repeatedly before a policeman rescued him. One fifteen-year-old Norwich fan said, "The trouble seemed to be all over the Barclay stand but mainly towards the middle. West Ham supporters were all over the place inside the Norwich section. The police were telling people to get back, but they could not."

The police ordered Anglia TV to hand over their footage of the game. After viewing it in court seven months later, Judge Beezley described the violence as "the worst that ground has ever seen or will see again. If you wear Norwich colours you get attacked by the visitors. If you wear visiting colours you get attacked by Norwich. Wear no colours and you get attacked by both."

Had Judge Beezley known much of football, he might have foreseen that the impending visit of Manchester United's infamous Red Army was likely to be even worse. United were the scourge of English football and their fans were laying waste to grounds around the country. Desperate pleas were made by officials of both clubs urging fans without tickets not to make the journey. Some might have listened but most did not, as hundreds of United fans began arriving in Norwich early on the Friday morning. Fighting broke out with locals soon after their arrival and continued well into the night, with a United fan being stabbed during one clash.

Fighting resumed around the ground prior to kick-off as police tried, unsuccessfully, to separate the fans. Hundreds of United supporters stormed the Barclay Stand, forcing home fans to flee onto the pitch. As police moved in to prevent further Red Army chaos, they were attacked. One United fan famously scaled the stand roof and then fell through it and plummeted to the concrete terrace, only to be attacked by home fans as he lay injured on the ground and again as he was stretchered away.

United boss Tommy Docherty appealed to his fans to stop but he too was showered with missiles, including a lump of concrete. Further fighting broke out at the end of the game as police tried to stop hundreds of United fans from leaving early. The Red Army swarmed up the grass bank at the back of the Barclay Stand, ripped large pieces of corrugated asbestos sheeting down and hurled them at police. Thirty people, including eight police officers, were injured and 19 United fans were later convicted.

There was universal outrage, not least from the two clubs themselves. Norwich boss John Bond called for tougher prison sentences for offenders and suggested that Man United supporters could soon be banned for away games. "That would be tragic for such a great club but it may be the only way to stop these sickening incidents," he said. Tommy Docherty called for the retun of the birch, while Norwich director Ian Courts described the incident as "nothing short of a riot" and demanded the use of water cannons, riot batons and shields to deal with similar situations. "I think the time has come when law and order has to exist in a football stadium just as much as anywhere else," he said.

The debate about hooliganism continued in the pages of the local newspaper. An editorial dismissed hand-wringing politicians for seeing the trouble as just another isolated incident rather than as part of a wider malaise in society. Several readers also called for far tougher action, including one hardliner who wrote, "Any reasonably fit young thug can stand a mild birching and come back for another vandal session later in the hope that he will not be caught. The British Army in the last century and earlier knew how to deal with types like this. You got a thrashing that would deter you for the rest of your life. During the American War of Independence, the rapist or looter got 1,000 lashes. These were normally given in batches of 250, since 1,000 at one session might kill you."

A week later, the authorities were braced for more trouble with the visit of local rivals and league leaders Ipswich. Pleas from both clubs for calm went out before match day, and although 26 people were arrested and charged, there was no repeat of the disorder witnessed during United's visit. Police escorted the thousands of Ipswich fans from Norwich station to the ground, where a fence and a line of officers kept them away from home fans. Most of the arrests were shortly before kick-off after a number of isolated incidents in the streets around the ground.

Violence at Norwich continued, though on most occasions it was caused by visiting fans. John Bond called for compulsory ID cards to be introduced at the ground and for away supporters to be banned. Speaking at the club's annual meeting in September 1980, he said, "I don't think ID cards would be too much of a problem. It would be like buying a ticket for a match and, if any supporter steps out of line, then the card would be withdrawn. Obviously, innocent supporters will suffer because of this ban, and I'm sorry about that, but I hope they realise that something has to be done if we are to cure a sickness that has gone on far too long. We have to be firmer and stronger in our discipline. There has been so much talk about hooliganism that it's now time to stop the talking and start the action. Too many people are evading their responsibilities. And too many managers are covering up their footballers, pretending they don't see things going on."

By the early 1980s, a new mob was emerging. The C Squad was about 30 lads living near the main hospital. They were around at the same time as the Steins, and though not all followed Norwich, they all came out together for big games. More recently, the main hooligan group has been known as the Norwich Hit Squad (NHS).

The Norwich firm's biggest ever turnout was probably an away game at Grimsby in 1985. Two hundred lads travelled up to Skegness on the Friday night. Norwich were not alone in town; a small Nottingham Forest group were also staying and two similar-sized groups clashed outside The Smugglers pub. By morning, lads from Kings Lynn, Downham Market, Wisbech and Yarmouth swelled the group's numbers to more than 300. A large convoy of cars, coaches and minibuses set off for the short hop to Grimsby, arriving in the town soon after eleven. The police quickly arrived and surrounded the pub holding the Norwich crew. Undeterred, someone found a back door and, giggling like little children, the lads filed out into the empty streets.

Inside the ground, a fairly drunk Norwich mob kicked off with the police, forcing then-manager Ken Brown to come onto the pitch and appeal for calm. Several Norwich would later tell the Press that police provocation ignited the trouble. After the match there was further disorder, this time between rival fans. "Grimsby were well game but our mob was top notch and gave a good account of themselves," said Norwich veteran JC. "I was arrested almost as soon as I left the ground. A lot of the lads went to the Old Bill station to wait for their mates and it kicked off all evening until the last of the lads was let out and we were escorted all the way home."

When the Norwich lads returned to Grimsby for their court case, a Grimsby mob was waiting for them. For a moment it looked as though it could get nasty but then JC recognised a face from his time at Watton Detention Centre, and with a handshake and a little wink the tension subsided. JC was fined £450 for insulting behaviour but was pleased to retain his liberty.

"The thing about Norwich is that unless it's a big game or a game in London, we don't travel well," admitted JC. "Saying that, when we do turn out, we turn out. One such game was the FA Cup semi-final at Villa Park against Everton. This was like the Grimsby game and anyone who was anyone was out. There was a mob of about 200 before the game but, afterwards, there must have been 400 and it kicked off big style. I think we surprised Everton that day."

The scale of violence that day is debatable though. While a few lads remember brief skirmishes before and after the game, Everton have never regarded it as nearly as good, or bad, as the semi-finals in '84 and '95, against Southampton and Spurs respectively, when fighting spilled onto the pitch.

Another big turnout was for the club's away match at Arnhem in 1993, when 150 lads sailed on the ferry from Felixstowe, but there was little trouble, not least because most people were either drunk or stoned. There was more trouble when Norwich played Inter Milan in a match fondly remembered by the Canaries because one of the lads hired a plane for the trip.

At various times in the Eighties and Nineties there have been rivalries with QPR, Sheffield United, Cambridge United and, more surprising,

Wolves. The latter stems back to play-off semi-finals when it is alleged that Wolves thugs attacked large numbers of normal Norwich supporters, including women. These spats, however, pale into insignificance compared to the hatred of local rivals Ipswich.

In 1985, Norwich were drawn against Ipswich in the semi-final of the Milk Cup. Any game against Ipswich brought trouble but a cup semi had extra spice. Loads of Norwich managed to get into the Pioneer Stand, where the Ipswich mob based themselves, and before long their presence brought a violent response. Ipswich won the game by a single goal and the scene was set for the return leg at Carrow Road. Ipswich turned out an impressive crew and commandeered the Woolpack pub before the game, but a heavy police presence prevented anything more than a few bottles being thrown.

"Over the years there have been many battles," said JC. "I can remember being in the Potter Gate pub and one of the lads was handing out craft knives. I never felt the need for them myself but this day saw a scum [Ipswich] fan get cut up opposite the old cattle market. It was all a bit naughty but they were the times we lived in."

One of Norwich's best results against Ipswich dates back to an away match in the early 1980s, when Norwich occupied a pub close to the railway station and tooled up courtesy of some rubble from roadworks. Suddenly word swept the pub that Ipswich were in sight and Norwich bounded out to be faced by a mob of 150 locals. Missiles were exchanged and Norwich were forced into a rearguard defensive action back to a big roundabout. There, another Norwich crew joined them and together they charged back at Ipswich, forcing the locals to flee.

Another big game saw Norwich travel to Ipswich for a night match. After full-time, the Norwich mob decided not to go straight to the train station but to seek out Ipswich. About 200 walked apprehensively into the dark streets, aware that their every move was being watched by Ipswich spotters. As they reached a roundabout, on the way into the town centre, they met an equal number of home fans. Both mobs charged but soon Norwich were being backed off and split up. One group ended up on the Whitton estate, and even though they had a police escort they received little hospitality from locals. "People were coming out of the flats shouting abuse and throwing gear at us, and I do mean anything they could get their hands on," recalled JC. "Even the police with us looked worried. This was a bloody experience I never want to repeat."

A further clash with Ipswich took place at Cambridge. City did not have a game but 30 of the younger lads decided to travel over to the famous university town for a match involving their two East Anglian rivals. The

Norwich lads settled in to a town centre pub, and despite a Cambridge firm of eighty and an Ipswich firm also in the vicinity, there was no trouble before the game. However, all three mobs converged on the ground together and it took the police some time to work out who was who. Eventually the factions were separated and Norwich were escorted back to the station.

Cambridge has been a regular stopping off point for Norwich fans returning from games in London. On one trip back from QPR, 60-70 lads occupied the Sugar Loaf, a three-storey pub next to a cinema. An argument with a squaddie soon exploded into violence, with Norwich battling it out with British Army regulars and locals. The visitors were on the back foot but as they were forced upstairs they found themselves in an excellent defensive position and for the next few minutes were able to repel anyone attempting to climb the stairs. Outside, a Norwich lad took the ladder of a cinema worker who was changing the billing and threw it through a window. The worker was left stranded several metres above the ground until help arrived. Meanwhile, the police turned up and more than 50 lads were arrested. "The Sugar Loaf went down in city's history," said JC. "Cambridge was always a good trip."

The QPR rivalry is largely because of the mutual hatred for "Gregor", a peripatetic hooligan and one of the West Londoners' main faces. "In fact we hate any club that Gregor latches onto," said JC. "I don't know where this all started, but I heard a rumour he had family living in Norwich and that's how he knew his way about."

The first remembered clash between the two teams was in the early Eighties when a young mob of 50 Norwich ran QPR through the cattle market. A little later, according to Norwich, an older mob ran 100-150 QPR back towards the train station. Another fight saw a small but impressive group battle it out with an equal number of QPR outside a local nightclub. A Norwich lad knocked out a lad who was with Gregor, and as he went down he dropped a bottle of pills. While a copper was forced to give the victim mouth-to-mouth resuscitation, the lad who was responsible was chased all over Norwich by fellow officers. To hasten his arrest, one police officer even commandeered a pushbike.

The following season, QPR brought another large mob down to Carrow Road. There were a few skirmishes before the game but most of the trouble was afterwards, when two groups, both numbering about 100, battled outside the train station. Several of the Londoners were armed and one, a large black lad, stabbed a couple of Norwich before being knocked out with a fence post.

If there was an award for ingenuity, Norwich would be entered for their trip to Fulham. A mob disembarked their coach at London Bridge and stopped in The George for a few, where they were joined by some Norwich who lived in London. Someone had the idea of taking the boat along the river, so went to commandeer a vessel. Feeling pleased with themselves, helped by the on-board bar, they set off for West London.

"I was near the back of the boat on the lower deck taking in the sights when I saw this little ship in the distance," said JC. "It was a police boat but I thought it was nothing to worry about. As we got closer I could see our spotter, Chris, on board with a video camera. At Putney Bridge we are greeted by the biggest welcoming party I have ever seen. All we needed were a few cannons and to be piped ashore! Instead we got snarling dogs and big, ugly Met OB accompanying Chris. I'm sure I saw him smile and wink at me. It was top class of us for sorting a boat out and for him for doing the same. I would love to see that video."

On the way to an Exeter game, JC and another lad first headed down to Torquay on a Friday night. "We had a close shave because West Ham were playing Torquay the following day and a few locals thought we were Londoners. When we said we were Norwich and going to Exeter they were our best mates, as they hated Exeter and really looked after us. On the Saturday morning I woke up with a stinking headache but the prospects of the day ahead soon cheered me up. It's amazing but, in those pre-mobile days, you always seemed to be able to find your mob in some pub. There were about thirty of us, all good lads. The landlord could not have been nicer but we found out later he was a tosser. The lads were playing pool and having a drink when a few local lads came in. Another twenty pence went in the pool table but this time the balls don't get put in the triangle. I can't really remember how or even why it started but a few moments later the pub resembled a Western movie. Balls, cues, glasses, the lot went in. We then ran straight into them and chased them out of the pub just as the club coaches were going past. We beat a hasty exit and headed to the ground. A bit later we saw the landlord pointing us out to the police. Lads went everywhere changing clothes hiding behind people. It was as funny as fuck, but not for those who got nicked."

Different firms have greatly different memories of fights, and so it is over a confrontation between Norwich and Sheffield United. One Sheffield account has it that 25 Norwich attacked three non-hooligan United supporters. This was not the case, insists a Norwich "under-five" – the name given to young hooligans. "There was a lad with a crash helmet, Big Gary, a bit of a legend in and around the city. He was walking through the city after parking his scooter when he saw some Blades steaming into some scarfers. So he steamed into them alone, and not accompanied by the other twenty-four the book imagined.

"Later, about thirty of us were walking behind the train station near the coach park when a minibus came down the road towards us. One of the lads noticed it was Sheff Utd and smashed the wing mirror off. We waited in the road and about twelve lads in their mid-twenties came running straight into us. We outnumbered them but they were game boys and there was toe-to-toe fighting for what seemed like ages, but of course it wasn't. Suddenly the OB came from everywhere and let the dogs go. One lad got bitten to fuck while the rest of us scattered."

Over the years, Norwich have also had a bit of a rivalry with Luton. In one away trip in the early 1980s, twenty-five Steins and an equal number of C Squad travelled up by coach and were dropped off at the bottom of a hill by the main Luton shopping centre. Luton's Men In Gear (MIG) crew came bowling over to the coach but didn't realise it was the top Norwich mob and were soon on their toes. Norwich walked triumphantly up the hill towards the ground, but halfway up Luton attacked again, picking off stragglers. The visitors regrouped and soon the tables were turned once more, with Luton being run. After the game, Norwich were escorted out of town, but their coach stopped in Chase, where they clashed with some soldiers. A pub was wrecked and at least two people glassed. The following morning several fans were woken in dawn raids but only two were eventually charged and prosecuted. Norwich did not always find it so easy against Luton and there were occasions when they came off worst.

The police have tried their best to curtail the hooligan mob, though there have been a number of embarrassing failures. Some years ago, a plain clothes officer attempted to follow the lads around. However, the team scarf he wore was a giveaway and he lasted only a couple of games. More recently, Norfolk Police were given £50,000 to obtain banning orders against their core hooligan group prior to the 2004 European Championships in Portugal. Eight alleged hooligans were targeted but the judge threw out every case and demanded the Chief Constable pay all the legal costs.

Despite this debacle, the police are now firmly on top, especially for high-risk games. In 1999, they received information that Norwich fans had made petrol bombs for their derby against Ipswich. A search of wasteland near the train station found two and a bomb disposal team was called to deal with them. However, the match proved to be one of the quietest in the history of the East Anglia derby, with only two arrests all day. "It is now important that this successful match is built upon so that future derby matches between the two clubs can be even more friendly," said Chief Superintendent Roger Sandall, the match commander.

However highly Chief Supt Sandall rates his force, it seems that the continual yo-yoing between the top flight by both clubs prevents their hooligans clashing, rather than the officers he has at his disposal.

In August 2006, two lifelong Norwich fans became the first to be convicted of chanting homophobic abuse during a Carrow Road match. A magistrates' court heard how the pair taunted Brighton fans with anti-gay chants at a match on St Valentine's Day. Football intelligence officer PC Chris Watts said they had previously been warned about their behaviour and there was a round of applause from Brighton fans when he asked the defendants to follow him out of the Barclay stand. "I know that historically Brighton have been subject to these kinds of taunts before," he said.

The two men aged 28, and 24, pleaded not guilty but were convicted of disorderly behaviour and each given a one-year conditional discharge. Both admitted using the word "queers" but said it was just football banter. They said they had been responding to Brighton fans chanting, "You're just a town full of inbreds." Both men denied being homophobic and said they had gay friends who used the word queer.

NOTTINGHAM FOREST

Ground: City Ground
Firms: Forest Mad Squad, Forest Young Lads, Forest Executive Crew
Rivals: Derby County, Millwall, Birmingham City

To the national Press, he was Public Enemy Number One. Not bad for a man who worked to drink. Paul Scarrott was publicly pilloried as the personification of the English hooligan – and he loved it. In fact, he revelled in it. He would peel back his lower lip to reveal his Forest tattoo for snap-happy photographers, gave ridiculous and shocking sound bites to headline-seeking journalists, and just in case anyone forgot about him, would send postcards to the British police taunting them about the ease with which he could slip out of the country for international games. He claimed that one of his many passports was in the name "Al Capone". Regardless of whether or not it was a wind-up, the media went along for the ride and once again Paul Scarrott's face was plastered across the tabloids.

Scarrott was born in 1956, and by the late 1980s had become the most infamous hooligan in the land. He was arrested in Denmark, imprisoned in Scotland and Belgium, deported from Germany and evaded police detection in Italy. By the age of 32, he had been incarcerated 13 times for soccer violence. He may not have been the greatest fighter around but he was certainly game – or mad, depending on your view. Stories abound about him. His collection of "blag" passports always got him an audience and he once shouted, "Touché, dirty dago," at Spanish fans as his sombrero saved him from being drenched in their piss. On another occasion, he was arrested when he threw a takeaway container out of a window only to injure an elderly woman walking by.

At an away game at Portsmouth, he single-handedly charged into the opposing firm. He got whacked and whacked badly, but after dishing out a beating, his attackers stopped, shook his hand and bought him a drink. He turned up in Glasgow's Barrowland before an England v Scotland game draped in a St George's Cross flag and wearing a First World War helmet. But it was the 1988 European Championships in Germany where Scarrott first got his "most evil" tag when, just days after he teamed up with a firm from Bradford and attacked Irish fans drinking in bars in Stuttgart, he was arrested and deported after leading England into battle in Dusseldorf. The picture of a handcuffed and sneering English loon was plastered on almost every front page the following day.

Scarrott, who died in a bar in Spain in 1999 from alleged alcohol and steroid abuse, was one of English hooliganism's real characters, despised by the majority but loved by his own. He became known for his drunken, violent and crazy exploits with the English national team, but his bread and butter was Nottingham Forest where he was a respected member of the Forest Executive Crew.

Even before Forest had a football firm with a name, opposing fans found their way into the River Trent. Surely it could not have been in the mind of the ground's designer but its layout, on the banks of the river, gave home fans a perfect way to humiliate their opponents. Time and again, Forest would come up behind opposing fans and charge at them, forcing them back towards the river. Bigger numbers and better organisation meant the away fans either got pummelled or had to jump into the water for their own safety. Fans of Spurs, Villa and Derby all got soaked, to their eternal embarrassment. Several Derby fans ended up in the Trent in the first home game of the 1993 season and had to endure the chants from home fans as they dried their clothes at the back of the stand. On the odd occasion, fans were even thrown into the water from the bridge.

Newspaper stories of violence at Forest date back to the mid-Sixties. In 1965, when Chelsea played there, a group of Forest fans made a line across the street in preparation for an attack on a small group of away supporters who had come off the train. The Chelsea fans were just that – fans, not thugs – and as away support was so rare in those days, the group even included some of the players' families. The attack was averted when Chelsea terrace legend Mick Greenaway stepped forward, let out an ear-shattering chant of "Zigger zagger," and charged at the Forest line, clearing a path for the others. In 1969, hundreds of Forest fans ran wild at local rivals Derby County before and during the game. In September 1971, seven Forest fans were arrested after serious crowd disorder broke out at Wolves.

A year later, nine fans were arrested after Forest and Villa clashed outside the City Ground. Hooliganism, said the local magistrate, was making Nottingham "a dangerous place to go". When the two sides met again a year later, Forest clearly came out on top. One Villa lad recalls it was one of their most comprehensive beatings, as they were run ragged outside the ground, although vengeance came at the Boxing Day return fixture.

Gary "Boatsy" Clarke was a young lad watching the game with his dad at this time who later went on to become one of the main lads at Forest. "The earliest fighting mob was around in the late 1960s and early 1970s and they were all greasers," he said. "Loads of leather-clad bikers in the town used to take on anyone who wanted it at the match. That changed in the early to mid 1970s when the Mad Squad was formed, led by a bloke called Ronnie, a true Forest legend. Scarrott was a main figure in the mob, mad, daft, call him what you want, but he was game, he went into anyone and everyone. Wilmot was a young lad who went with them. They wore green flying jackets and ended the bikers' hold of the mob. Loads of skins joined and there were a good two hundred of them most games. At Wembley in the 1980 League Cup final, two hundred Mad Squad, all in jackets, chased Wolves all around Wembley."

At this time, Forest were regarded as perhaps the toughest hooligan proposition in the Midlands, but they still lagged behind the Londoners for organisation. In 1976, Chelsea came to town and there was almost ten hours of disorder as rival fans were involved in fighting before, during and after the league clash. As seven people were convicted for assault, threatening behaviour and possessing offensive weapons, the chairman of the magistrates told them, "You must realise that no one can expect to come into the city of Nottingham to attend football matches principally for the pleasure of causing disruption." Thirty-four people, mostly Chelsea supporters, were arrested at the game, which local police described as the worst day of violence in Nottingham that season.

Trouble first erupted as Chelsea were being escorted off the train and it continued in the ground. The referee was forced to take the players off after only four minutes while police broke up fighting amongst fans. After the match, 200 police attempted to contain widespread trouble across the city centre. Three police cars were rocked, shop windows smashed and pubs damaged in violence that continued well into the night.

"They behaved like animals on the way to the ground and during and after the game," said the prosecuting solicitor. "But perhaps we are doing an injustice to animals in the jungle, because they, at least, have a certain code of conduct which they obey and conventions they observe." Senior police joined the criticism, describing the Chelsea fans as "ugly visitors". Hooliganism was "putting football in jeopardy," they said. "Society as a whole will not stand for it."

In 1975, Brian Clough was appointed manager in the best acquisition in the club's history. Forest had been languishing in Division Two, but under the stewardship of Clough and Peter Taylor, who joined six months later, they became the best in Europe. In a glorious three-year period, Forest won the League Championship, the European Cup twice, the League Cup twice, the Super Cup and were runners-up in both the League and League Cup. They dominated British football, much to the horror and jealously of rivals Derby, who Clough had previously managed. Amid their glory years, Forest set a record for the longest unbeaten run in the League when they went 42 games undefeated from November 26, 1977, until November 25, 1978, a record which stood for 26 years until Arsenal's 49 games from 2002–04. One of the highlights of Forest's unbeaten spell was a 4–0 victory over Manchester United at Old Trafford, and the club won the 1978 championship with four matches remaining. It was in the middle of this run that Forest travelled to Derby. Clough had left County after a fallout with their chairman and the fans resented Forest's success. Many away supporters were ambushed before the game and pitched battles were fought in the streets afterwards. Thirty-three people were arrested.

In May 1979, Forest won the European Cup by beating Malmo. Their journey to the final had taken them past Liverpool, AEK Athens, Grasshoppers of Zurich and FC Cologne. Forest had been underdogs who no-one expected to get past the mighty Liverpool, let alone go on and win the biggest prize in club football. Against Cologne, they came back from 2–0 down to draw the first leg 3–3, and in the return leg at the City Ground they won by a single goal. Trevor Francis, Britain's first £1 million player (though Clough insisted that he paid £1 short of that on principle), scored the only goal in the final. Clough later said that winger John Robertson's cross was the most satisfying moment in his career. "When I sit in my garden and close my eyes I can still see the moment in Munich when Robertson made his move," he reminisced shortly before his death. "Peter Taylor stiffened beside me and grabbed my arm. Robertson is not far from the corner flag. There are half a dozen Malmo players in the box. Trevor Francis is hurtling towards the far post and Robbo sends over the perfect cross. One-nil. Pass me the European Cup. Thank you!"

At the beginning of the 1978/79 season, Forest played host to Tottenham. A massive 8,000 made the journey up, some arriving in town by mid-morning, catching both the police and the club by surprise. Fighting broke out between rival fans three hours before kick-off and the game itself was held up for 14 minutes as 400 Spurs fans, angered at being separated from the rest of the travelling contingent, poured onto the pitch. Fifty people were injured and 43 arrested during the day.

The police later acknowledged that they had been caught unawares. "We didn't expect wolf packs of idiots to be descending on the area of the ground and rampaging some three hours before a ball was kicked," admitted Supt John Yarnell. He conceded that the police operation had not even begun when the trouble first occurred. The police had hoped the game would show that their new operational headquarters worked successfully, the match commander watched the game from a new "crow's nest" in the roof of a stand and the ground was covered by CCTV cameras. Instead, it was their shortcomings that dominated the headlines. In a straw-clutching exercise three weeks later, Chief Constable Charles McLachlan called for a shorter football season "for the sake of my men" because of the growing pressures of policing the sport. He wanted a return to the four-month summer break because his officers did not get a day off for much of the year. He made these comments on the day Forest played Arsenal and 36 people were arrested after the match in which a police officer was kicked in the face.

By the turn of the decade, the casual look had reached Nottingham and a younger generation of hooligans appeared. Alongside their wedge haircuts and tracksuit tops was a move off the Kop and into the stands. It was a sign of their perceived superiority over the scarf-wearing herd, and on a practical level it provided easy access to away fans. The Forest Executive Crew (FEC) was born the following season with the opening of the Executive Stand, later renamed the Brian Clough Stand. At every game, hundreds of lads would take up their seats in the stand and then, at a given moment, clamber over the fence into the adjoining away end. It was these lads who transformed themselves from the Forest Mad Squad into the Executive Crew. Several years later a new, younger firm emerged, and out of deference to the older FEC they decided to call themselves the Forest Young Lads (FYL). As the FYL began to perform, the distinction became blurred and today Forest's mob is simply the FEC.

One of the FEC's early opponents were West Ham's infamous Inter City Firm. Between 1980 and 1982, the two mobs clashed several times. A twenty-seven-year-old Nottingham man, William Adams, required 21 stitches for a cut running from his right ear to his jaw after a razor-wielding yob attacked him after Forest's home game with West Ham in November 1981. What police later described as an "unprovoked" attack came ten minutes after the game. "A bunch of West Ham fans came up," Adams later recalled. "They surrounded us and we were split up. I felt a blow to the side of my face but did not realise what the injury was like." A few days later, Adams and another witness accompanied police as they mingled with West Ham fans at their home League Cup tie with West Brom, but failed to find the knifeman. The attack was just one of a series of incidents that marred the First Division match. Twenty-one arrests were made, most of them West Ham supporters.

A photograph of the horrifically injured man was displayed prominently on the front page of the *Nottingham Evening Post*. Understandably, there was public revulsion. The chairman of the Parole Board, Lord Harris of Greenwich, in Nottingham for a meeting, said that it was important for people not to be desensitised by football violence. With the images fresh in everyone's mind, a local magistrate handed out fines totalling more than £4,000 to 13 men convicted of soccer-related violence following Forest's home games against Leeds and West Ham. Never one to hold back, Forest boss Brian Clough reiterated his determination to beat hooliganism after the home fixture with West Ham, claiming the behaviour of home fans in the Trent End was partly to blame for the attack on Adams. He said that he was fed up with the violence and foul language in the stand, and reaffirmed an earlier threat to close down that terraced area of the ground. "The 'fans' responsible for the jibbing at West Ham supporters last Saturday should hang their heads in shame," he said. "They are the people who encourage violence. They either stop it or we will take our own action." In Forest's next home game the club displayed anti-violence messages on their electronic scoreboards. This was not the first intervention by Clough. In the 1977/78 season he posted a "no swearing please" notice behind the goal.

Forest were out for revenge when they took a mob of 600 to Upton Park for the return game. Their arrival surprised the ICF, but soon the hosts got their act together and Forest needed a large police escort to the ground. As West Ham gathered along the pavements, a sizeable number slipped into the escort and into the away end, and when Forest began chanting their team's name the ICF attacked. "Forest were getting forced out and people were getting chucked out on to the pitch," remembered Cass Pennant in his book *Congratulations You Have Just Met The ICF*. "They tried running on to the pitch, but the Old Bill put them back. Then, within five minutes, West Ham had steamed them all back on the pitch again. This time it was like an avalanche. It started with a few and then quickly became the entire Forest travelling support clambering to seek safety on the pitch." They were escorted out of the ground for their own safety. Forest might have been humiliated but they had showed at West Ham, unlike a lot of other firms during this period.

There was continued trouble with arch-rivals Derby. At a game in 1983, 20 were arrested during fighting at the Baseball Ground. Nine police officers were injured, three vans damaged, and a mounted officer was struck with a brick. Two years later, 400 police were required at a cup-tie to prevent a repeat of the trouble, and in 1988 Derby fans took refuge in a pub as 80 Forest fans used hockey sticks, pool cues and bricks to attack it. In 1993, 100 FEC went to Derby and stoned cars and smashed windows before and after the match. In 2002, Forest hooligans were arrested in a police operation after information that rival gangs were to clash on the outskirts of Derby, ahead of the sell-out game at Pride Park. The Derby troublemakers didn't turn up for the anticipated showdown but scores of known Forest descended on Ilkeston Social Club to watch the game on television. Police moved in after fighting broke out towards the end of the match. Bottles were thrown at officers and many of the group refused to disperse, leading to 27 arrests for public order and breach of the peace.

Forest still take a mob to Derby but there are rarely problems, as the police appear to be firmly in control. The police have even taken to sending known hooligans letters advising them not to attend the fixture. "We have told them in no uncertain terms they are not welcome," said Inspector Greg Drozdowski. "If the hooligans are spotted by police, they may be arrested if we anticipate trouble."

In June 1984, Derby took the unusual step of linking up with hooligans from Forest's other key rivals, Leicester City, and together 150 of them travelled to Nottingham looking for revenge after regular FEC incursions into their cities. Forest were by far the biggest mob in the East Midlands and a desire to turn them over proved stronger than regional loyalties. The combined force arrived in the city centre unannounced, but before long their presence attracted the hostile attention of lads, ordinary fans and Saturday afternoon drinkers alike, particularly a large group of FEC who were on a stag do. At the battle's height, more than 400 men were fighting, while just five police officers were trying to deal with the situation. Sixty-three people were later convicted, 30 receiving custodial sentences. One officer, a former soldier, told the court that in all his tours of duty to Northern Ireland he had never witnessed such violence. This turn out by Derby, although bolstered by their Leicester allies, was rare, and in recent years they have not shown the same bravado. This may be a wise move, as at the time of writing (2006) a mob of 400 Forest, including veteran FEC members, turned out for their last visit in the hope that hostilities could be resumed.

There is nothing like an FA Cup tie to re-ignite local rivalries and past hatreds and this was certainly the case when Forest were drawn away at Birmingham City in the fourth round. The Birmingham Zulus were rarely out of the Press, and the FEC were keen to try their luck. Up to 400 made the journey across the Midlands and there were clashes almost as soon as they arrived. The worst flared after the game when Blues supporters, their team defeated, charged the barriers keeping them from the Forest fans and fights broke out in the streets around St Andrews.

"The police were bombarded with bottles and bricks and you could see their helmets flying in the air amongst the missiles," said one witness. "The thugs were throwing lumps of concrete, planks of wood, clods of earth – anything they could get their hands on. Six mounted police charged the fans and I dashed for my life. A disabled couple in wheelchairs had to be held back against a wall to prevent them from being hurt by the fans." Fifty were injured, including eight police officers, and more than 100 were arrested. Even Zulus admit that the FEC won the day, but they point out that several of their leaders had recently been rounded up in a police operation.

"It was one of the all time great days at the match," declared main Forest face Boatsy. "Those were the good old days! Eighty-seven arrested at the match, none of this six-months-later bollocks. Loads from both firms were nicked. We went in two mobs, the first lot of a hundred-odd got there by train and fifty of us went in cars and got to the city centre about 11am. Forest were in a pub and the Zulus attacked them. It went off all the way to the ground after that. Before kick-off they attacked the first lot of Forest by the ground and our lot came behind them and they were sandwiched between us. It was mental, one of the best rows ever. They had lads arriving in taxis and joining in. In the end, as taxis were pulling up Forest were ready and were pulling them out as they were slowing down.

"During the game they were outside slinging bricks into the seats we were in, so afterwards we went behind them and it was the same mob by the coach park, slinging everything they had into the Forest fans coming out. It was on top and we were backed off by more than 100 of them, Ronnie went through us and sparked their big black lad clean out, and from then on we had them backing off all the way to some bridge, when the police finally split us all up. We were taken back to the Bullring and it was to and fro all the way, both mobs trying to break the escort. When we landed they came again down the escalators into us again. It went from eleven in the morning till nearly seven at night. Unbelievable. Unforgettable."

In 1998, four Forest lads required hospital attention after another visit to Birmingham. It was a crucial game, with both sides going for promotion.

Forest arrived two hours early and clashed with the Zulus in the Sparkbrook area of the city, some distance from St Andrews. More than 100 lads were involved in the disturbances.

The following season, Forest drew Man United away in the Cup. A mob of 250 FEC made the journey and fought toe-to-toe outside Old Trafford after the game. When stewards opened the gates at the end of the match, Forest fans were greeted by a mob of 500 United massed on the forecourt. Realising the danger, the stewards closed the gates, leaving 50 FEC outside to fend for themselves. The Forest lads grouped together in a half-circle and fought for their lives against wave after wave of United attacks. Somehow, they survived until police moved in to separate the groups.

Silverware returned to Forest when they won the League Cup in both 1989 and 1990. They had two third places in the League and twice reached FA Cup semi-finals, on both occasions losing to Liverpool. It was at the second of these encounters that the tragic Hillsborough Disaster occurred, and to their credit, the support and compassion shown by both the club and its supporters is still remembered fondly on Merseyside, although once again Clough was not backward coming forward and comments he made in his autobiography about the Liverpool fans that day made him a despised figure at Anfield even after his death.

In their first victorious League Cup campaign, Forest played Huddersfield Town. After winning the first leg at home, they took a tidy mob of 150 up to West Yorkshire and violence broke out from the moment they arrived at four in the afternoon.

In 1994, 100 FEC travelled down to South London for a ruck with Millwall. "It was our first time at Millwall for many years and we were right up for it the minute we arrived at the Warrior pub," recalled Forest veteran Nick Stevenson. "We were walking around Surrey Quays as if we owned the place and nothing really happened beforehand, but it was very lively in the ground as we tried to get at Millwall, while they mobbed up in our corner. We came out of the ground and got escorted through the estates, it was Easy Street and to be honest I wondered what all this bollocks was about Millwall. We turned a corner and, fuck me, at the top of the road were a few hundred of the cunts.

"We started to jog towards them but then just thought, fuck it, and steamed straight into them. It was do that or crumble, so we went for it. They were dropping like flies as our frontline went to work and after a minute or so they turned and ran, which I couldn't believe. They got it together and came back at us and now it was real hand-to-hand combat. This second wave contained many old faces and although no-one claimed it was their top boys we still got the better of them. To be honest, they disappointed me. The Old Bill finally separated us and took us to our vans. Millwall had very kindly petrol bombed a couple of them, they always had their own special way of getting even. I didn't give a fuck and would have walked back to Nottingham if I'd had to. We'd just done Millwall on their manor."

The liberties taken by Forest at that clash were the beginning of a long-running feud between the two mobs. In 2001, more than 200 Forest plotted up in a pub in Surrey Quays, knowing that this time Millwall's main firm would be ready to accommodate them. They were oblivious to the fact that the Bushwhackers were only a hundred yards up the road in a separate pub. After the game, police in riot gear fought running battles with hundreds of Millwall fans as they attempted to attack Forest.

The police were out in force for the return fixture as word spread that Millwall were planning to put on a show, and with the match being moved to a noon kick-off on police advice, 36 city centre pubs were closed to prevent trouble. Double the normal number of officers was on duty and good intelligence meant the match commander was able to control events throughout the day. Before the game, nearly 200 Forest drank at Carlton railway station, from where they intended to board a local train to arrive at Nottingham's Midland Station at the same time as the 350 Millwall hooligans aboard. A huge police operation prevented the group boarding the train and the FEC had to watch in frustration as the impressive Millwall mob was escorted out of the station. After the match, the Londoners were detained for 15 minutes outside the stadium until the police had cleared the area of Forest lads.

More than twenty years had passed since Supt John Yarnell had sat on top of the main stand in a crow's nest, admiring his new CCTV system as fans rioted in the streets away from the ground. It seemed that the Notts constabulary had finally cracked it.

The FEC emerged a top mob in the 1990s, with a hardcore of 150 to 250 lads who were quite prepared to take the fight to anyone. Generally they claimed "results", although there were times when they came unstuck. One was at Birmingham in 1998, although this was not on the scale of the hammering they took from Man United before the League Cup Final in 1992. That pre-arranged meet took place in Kilburn, North London, and turned out to be one of the mob's darkest hours. Turning up 100-strong they were ambushed from all sides as every pub in the street contained huge numbers of United's thugs.

"It was a perfectly timed attack. Forest were proper hammered," Gary Clarke remembered ruefully. "It was a very bad day at the office. The week before, we were at QPR. A couple of our lads were drinking in a boozer after the game and United's firm walked in. Powell [of United] saved them from a beating but told them to tell me to get our firm into Kilburn the next week. I told everyone it was going to happen but loads of the older lot didn't listen and we ended up taking about 100 down, a tidy firm, but is it ever enough for United? Not in London it wasn't!

"We got to the Dolphin at St Pancras and then on to meet United. They came out of every pub on that road, hundreds of them. Glasses, bottles, chairs, it must have only been the fucking jukebox that never came into us. Some stood until we got backed off by sheer numbers, another load ran into some dark Irish pub and we had to watch as it got smashed to pieces. Five hundred United smashing us, a bad, bad day. Still, we went and had a go, unlike many firms who would not have even turned up knowing what United can pull for those games."

Nick Stevenson agreed he'd had better days out with the FEC. "We didn't realise they had scouts on the train station," he said. "As we came out I looked up the road and it was like the start of the Olympic fucking Games. The lot went and we got legged everywhere. Our lot were chased into a pub under the bridge and United just smashed it, proper smashed it to bits." To rub salt in the wounds, the attack was filmed by a bystander and the footage shown on a *World In Action* documentary, much to the dismay of the FEC, who would have preferred the humiliation to have been kept between the two mobs and not shared with twelve million television viewers.

Time, they say, is a great healer, and undeterred by the thrashing at the hands of United, in 1996 70 FEC tried their luck away at Middlesbrough. They met up in Darlington and made their way into Middlesbrough without much police attention. They had a couple of minor skirmishes before, and after the match Wilmot, one of Forest's top boys, rang a Boro lad to tell him of their intention to stop in Darlington again. It was an invitation, but as Forest boarded the train out of Middlesbrough they had no idea whether their offer would be accepted.

Three stops down the line, as the train pulled in to Thornaby station, they found out. More than 100 Boro were there to greet them. The train stopped and out poured Forest. "This was proper," remembered Stevenson. "No-one gave an inch for what seemed like twenty minutes which in reality was probably less than five. I'm not saying we hammered Boro, but I think we got the better of them in the end. There are two sides to every story and I am sure they have their own, but regardless of what anyone says it was a fucking great off."

Also in 1996, 150 Forest made the trip to Stoke for yet another mouth-watering Cup game. There was little to report before the match but the same could not be said at its conclusion. "At the end of the game we spotted a gate to our right", said Stevenson. "We steamed straight into their Main Stand just as some of their boys were coming out and ran them back into the ground before we moved on to their streets. The Old Bill were panicking, wondering how we had got there. We went down three streets, bumped into three different mobs and ran them all. We were well on top and the police, angry at losing control, turned on us in a graveyard. I took a right kicking and ended up with truncheon marks all over my back. It kicked off non-stop for about half an hour, and by the end I was fucked. We eventually got back to our car and slumped in the back, sweating and out of breath. Two Stoke approached and after a few iffy looks between both sides they shook my hand and told us we were awesome."

The 1990s also saw a number of clashes with Leeds. In a Premiership match in 1994, 150 Forest travelled to Bradford, where they transferred to a local service train into Leeds. Greeting them was a mob of 250 and it went off immediately. The home supporters were backed off, most running back to the two pubs where they had mobbed up. One landlady said, "We were enjoying a laugh with the lads when a hundred and fifty Nottingham supporters charged in each door chanting, 'Come on, come on.' They kept goading the lads to go outside to fight. I immediately set off the panic alarms and the Forest supporters ran off. We locked our customers in the pub for safety and suddenly two of the big windows were smashed in."

Leeds were out for vengeance, and as Forest were escorted to the ground, a huge mob of locals shadowed their movements. "They came charging at us," said Stevenson. "We just spread out and stood. I got sparked right out with a flying headbutt that fucking hurt. As I struggled to my feet, I took a look around and every one of our lads was engaged in a one-on-one fight. The Old Bill finally separated us, but what a performance. Outnumbered in their town and we did better than most. It doesn't get much better."

The rivalry festered, and when the sides played in a FA Cup tie in 1998 the FEC attacked Leeds supporters after the game. Two police officers were injured and 13 people arrested. Two years later, in a pre-season friendly, Forest again attacked Leeds fans as they returned to their cars. It was a ploy often used by Forest mobs and has earned them little respect from many firms who see those travelling by road in small numbers as soft targets. Several Forest supporters were arrested as a result of this incident and a Leeds fan was taken to hospital after being hit with a bottle.

Over the past fifteen years, Forest have developed a close friendship with the Mansfield Shady Express, which is unsurprising as many Forest fans live in the former mining towns around Mansfield. On the England scene, Forest formed a friendship with Newcastle, and in 2002 the two mobs battled with Sunderland before England's Euro qualifier against Turkey at the Stadium of Light.

Games involving Forest have seen tragedies other than the one at

Hillsborough. In September 1980, Forest took a large mob up to Middlesbrough and fighting broke out after the game in a small side street. The trouble did not last long but it was vicious enough to cause the death of one 15-year-old Boro lad who was laid out with a single punch and smacked his head on the kerb. Twenty-five Forest were jailed for between six months and five years as a result. Twenty-two years later, 17-year-old Forest fan Nathan Shaw was killed after being hit with a bottle in a pub in Burnley. When Forest were due to make their return to Burnley the following season, officers from Lancashire Constabulary visited key FEC hooligans to warn them against travelling.

In December 2004, Nottinghamshire Police produced a report that identified two groups of hooligans at Forest, the long-established Forest Executive Crew and the younger Forest Nasty Squad. The older group could total more than 250 for high-profile games, while there were about 50 of the younger group. The report said that the groups associated with each other at some matches, but some of the older members did not like the attention that the younger group could bring. It concluded that the number of incidents of disorder was falling, with arrests down 40 per cent at home games and 31 per cent away, and put this down to the success of banning orders and a local initiative, PACT – Police and Clubs Together (Against Violence). At the time of writing, there were 37 football banning orders against Forest fans, with a further 15 pending. There were also 159 Forest and Notts County supporters banned under the PACT agreement, which restricts supporters from entering a stadium and from being within a certain radius of grounds on match days.

Police intelligence files consider the "general" of the FEC to have been active for nearly 30 years. He was jailed for his part in the Middlesbrough fight that led to the death of the teenager in 1980, returned to action on his release and, say police, remains active. Other well-known targets looked upon as organisers are Wilmot and Gary Clarke, who was interviewed for this chapter.

In early 2004, a huge mob of Forest travelled to Cardiff and a new name emerged when 43-year-old David Kelly was arrested with explosives shortly before the match. Kelly later claimed in court that he was simply going to ignite the device outside the ground for Forest fans to "announce their presence". Not surprisingly, the jury was unimpressed and he was jailed for 18 months. Kelly's was the sort of stunt of which Scarrott would have been proud.

In October 2007, football disorder described as "the worst since the 1980s" erupted between rival fans attending Forest's match at Luton Town. Disturbances were reported in several areas of Luton before and after the fixture, and two Forest fans required hospital treatment, one for a head injury. The skirmishes centred on Bury Park Road and Dunstable Road, near the ground, as well as on High Town Road. "Elements from both sides looked to engage in disorder, and without doubt there are indications that this was organised in advance," said Bedfordshire Police football liaison officer Peter Palmer. Police arrested six fans on the day and later released CCTV images of 11 more men they were keen to trace.

Further reading: *Inside the Forest Executive Crew*, Gary Clarke and Martin King (Headhunter Books)

NOTTS COUNTY

Ground: Meadow Lane
Firms: The Lane Enders, Roadsiders.
Rivals: Mansfield Town, Bristol Rovers

Officially the oldest club in the Football League, Notts County are largely overshadowed by their local rivals in both fan base and the size and contents of their trophy cabinet. They are also often dismissed as "the posh club", one hooligan book referring to their support as "middle class".

This sneering attitude infuriates many of County's hardcore. "I read that bit about County being more middle class, no way," insisted Curtis, a County legend. "In fact, when County were formed they had a following from a notorious gang from the now demolished Narrow Marsh part of the city, which at the time was one of the worst slums in the country. County and Forest support is spread throughout Nottingham with no geographical difference."

As far back as May 1969, 49 County supporters were arrested after causing trouble after a Cup match with local rivals Mansfield. "Mr M Davies, prosecuting, said that at about 5pm, Nottingham football supporters returning from the match at the Quarry Lane ground, Mansfield, were shouting, throwing stones and generally making a pest of themselves," reported the local paper. "A gang was seen near the Dukeries garage on Nottingham Road, acting in a disorderly manner. Some youths were in the road, causing motorists to swerve in order to avoid them. A resident on Nottingham Road was showered with glass when a stone was thrown through her window. Another resident, frightened at the attitude of the youths, hid in her hallway."

Those convicted were bound over for two years in sums of £25. "Let it ring loud and clear that we in Mansfield will not tolerate such behaviour as you have admitted this morning," Mr D. Childs, Chairman of the Magistrates, told the defendants. "We are quite sure that people concerned in the organisation of professional football have no desire to encourage your type of hooligan support."

In the 1970s, the County hooligans were called the Lane Enders after the Meadow Lane end behind the goal. It is now the family stand. From 1978 onwards, the County Road side of the ground became popular and the lads there were known as Roadsiders.

"I was about fourteen when I started to hang round next to them," recalled another County fan, Taff. "They had some good lads then, one who became a good mate was Dean Barsby, game as fuck and smart with it, with the best wedge I have ever seen. A few of the old Lane Enders started using the Main Stand while the young lads I knew used County Road (renamed the Jimmy Sirrell Stand), called themselves Roadside Casuals and were game lads who were building a bit of a reputation."

County's relatively small fan base has meant their ground, and in turn their mob, has often been overrun. During the late Seventies and early Eighties, most games against Stoke City proved difficult affairs. There were more than 23 arrests at one game and a far more serious incident three years later.

Mark Chester, the legendary Stoke supporter and best-selling author, gave an insight into why his firm always caused mayhem at Notts County when they knew that the Midlands rivals were not in a position to come near them. "I feel for Notts County a bit, as the truth is we have no problems with them whatsoever, but always seem to turn their place upside down. Our issue is with Forest and every time we played County it was get the [Pools] coupons out and see if there was a chance of bumping into Forest. In 1979, we took more than 17,000 there for a game when we were promoted from the old Second Division to the First. It was not organised football violence that led to the arrests, it was pure mischief, lads playing up at a promotion party. Sunderland lost at Brighton so we were up, and some got arrested for celebrating a little too boisterously."

In May 1982, at the Victoria Ground, one County fan was stabbed twice in the lower back. Twenty-year-old David Wilson was heading back to the station to catch the soccer special when he was set upon. A big police hunt commenced, with dozens of County and Stoke fans pulled in for questioning. Nottinghamshire Police detached a four-strong detective squad to Stoke to continue investigations. They issued descriptions of two suspects, both aged between 17 and 19. A youth was arrested, charged, found guilty and sent to prison for several years. "It was a stupid incident and the lad convicted lost some of the best years of his life," said Chester. "It was a pointless stabbing, he was a quiet lad but ended up getting involved in no end of trouble whilst in prison and probably did double the original sentence he was given."

Nottingham's pubs also suffered at the hands of Stoke, as did many other clubs' hostelries, and on more than one occasion were set on fire. "Stoke and fires are a bit like Scousers and knives; we were made for each other," quipped Mark. "We have a thing about fires and on many occasions have seen fit to set pubs alight. One year we set fire to a pub at County and the riot police were brought in to sort us out. They were heavy-handed at the ground with Stoke supporters – not thugs, normal fans – and were knocking shit out of them so the lads attacked them and scores of Old Bill needed hospital treatment."

County's FA Cup clash with Bristol City in January 1984 was also overshadowed by violence, though the bulk of it appeared to be caused by visiting fans. Seventeen people were arrested, all but two from the Bristol area. A win for County set up a home tie with Middlesbrough and there was considerably more trouble.

The *Nottingham Evening Post* reported, "At the White Hart in Arnold, Middlesbrough fans – who had seen their team lose 1-0 at Notts County – attacked a group of locals with chains after an hour of drinking and chanting football songs. Manager Trevor Cox said the attack, which was totally unprovoked, could have resulted in serious injury if the police had not arrived so quickly. At the Old Spot Inn at Daybrook, another group smashed a window, broke into the jukebox and phone box and stole cash from the till. 'Some were singing football songs to divert our attention while others did the stealing,' said manager David Samples. Ten Middlesbrough supporters are to be charged with breach of the peace and actual bodily harm after an incident at the Woodville hotel on Mansfield Road."

Curtis rated the Boro firm that day as the best he has ever seen in Nottingham. "They were awesome, small mobs of them were everywhere, in the seats in our end, all over town, fucking awesome. We had a mob of sorts out that day but it was a token gesture, a lot bigger and badder firms than us would not have lived with Boro that day."

County were two games away from Wembley and Everton were the visitors for a quarter-final tie played in torrential rain. It was another takeover, with the Scousers having three sides of the ground. The cup run came to an end as Everton ran out winners thanks to an Andy Gray diving header. Even the commentator on *Match Of The Day* said the game would be remembered for the size of the Everton support. "That was some following they had that day," Curtis agreed. "Thousands of them were all over the place, we have no history with Everton but it was hard watching hundreds of the fuckers sliding all over the pitch at the end of the match covered in mud."

The opening game of the following season was at home to Leeds. The Miners' Strike was dividing the nation and politicising communities, and football supporters were no exception: Yorkshire was solidly behind the strike, Nottinghamshire was not, and much bad blood ensued. The widespread disorder led one local reporter to comment, "It wasn't just the 'mindless few' who were out for trouble." Amazed journalists reported afterwards that 3–4,000 Leeds fans were set on causing trouble. County were clearly outnumbered.

"It started early," remembered one lad. "I went for a drink in a pub near my home in Bulwell, where there was a coachload of locals on their way to Sheff Wednesday for Forest's first game of the season. All of a sudden, a coach of Leeds pulls in and in seconds it had kicked off good. At the ground there were literally thousands of Leeds, all giving the 'scab' shouts.

"After the game we get a few together and started with any Leeds we could find. We did a group of about the same size in the Meadows Estate next to the ground, then made our way to the city centre and spotted this big fuck-off crew of Leeds making their way to us from the Meadows, hell-bent on revenge. We thought this is it, a good kicking was coming, but we said, 'Fuck it, stand.' Just then we were joined by this large gang of black lads from the Meadows who called themselves 'the Riffs'. These Leeds fans come bombing up the road, tooled up, ignored us, and headed straight for the Riffs shouting, 'Kill the black bastards.' We couldn't stop laughing."

Seven months later, Nottingham was invaded again, this time by Man City fans. "It was like being at Maine Road," said Taff. "There were Mancs all over the place. At half-time we were three-one up so off it goes. The fences came down, seats ripped up and coppers smacked. City got some resistance from a firm of our lads in the Main Stand but to be honest, it was their day."

Taff was not kidding. City fans ran amok and County were overwhelmed. "Soccer Shame – City fans on the rampage," declared the front-page headline in the local paper. Hundreds of City fans invaded the pitch and held up the game for almost 30 minutes. It took public appeals by both managers to finally quell the disturbances enough for the game to restart. A group of 40 City fans even invaded their team's dressing room. For older County fans, there was a feeling of déjà vu; ten years before Manchester United fans had conducted themselves in similar fashion.

An unusual rivalry has developed between Notts County and Bristol Rovers. This first emerged on the pitch in the semi-finals of the Leyland Daf

Cup in 1990 and was followed by trouble off it after the game. Curtis remembers it as one of the better showings by the County lads.

"At the end of the game they took a tidy little mob on to the pitch, right in the corner and started handing out a few slaps," he said. "They must have thought we would be a walkover but in a matter of minutes an eighty-man brawl broke out and we had the upper hand. It was not that much at the time, as there were hundreds rampaging all over the country, but it was a wake-up call to the likes of Rovers that we were not going to let mobs take liberties at County.

"Don't get me wrong, when the likes of United, Everton and Boro came and basically took the ground, what the fuck can you do? But if a smaller firm came and started giving it out, this was a reminder that they had to take a bit back. That day we done Rovers and from then on it was regarded as a grudge match."

Seven years later hostilities were renewed, this time at a League match in Bristol, where several arrests were made. Trouble erupted again in 2000, when Notts County equalised in the final minute from a throw-in which should have been given to the opposition following an injury. Bristol Rovers demanded a replay but the FA refused.

Notts County played Brescia away in the Anglo-Italian Cup in the early 1990s and there was trouble throughout the trip. "There were scuffles throughout the day and virtually non-stop with police during the game, and more trouble with police and locals afterwards," remembered Taff. "One good memory of that night is Curtis, all five feet seven of him, running about like some loony, wearing his trademark over-sized Stone Island coat with some sort of large Arab scarf wrapped round his face, with his long black mop of hair hanging over it. Another is of a bloke we call Big John punching all comers, Italians and English, and Eddie, the biggest loon of all, doing his best to behave until he was insulted by an Italian after the game."

It also went off with Brescia after the final at Wembley. "I'll give them every respect at that game," said Curtis. "They turned out a tidy mob. It went off in the car park about sixty-a-side and they were a proper firm. They had blade men, which was no surprise, but County were solid and it was a definite result for our lads."

More recently, there has been continuing trouble at Meadow Lane. In August 1997, referee Phil Richards was attacked by a County fan late during the game with Lincoln, following the sending off of a home player and an away goal less than a minute later. To make matters worse for the home fans, there was a serious claim that the goal scorer was offside. The attack on the referee was just one of a series of incidents at that bad-tempered game. Eight fans were arrested, six from Lincoln. The FA demanded an inquiry as the local police, club and stewards promised to meet to review security inside the ground. Fearing a repeat of the trouble, a shaken Richards had to be given a police escort off the field at the final whistle.

Hooliganism at County has been greatly reduced by strong police action in recent years, and in addition to the civil bans, a recent agreement between clubs and the police (PACT – see *Nottingham Forest*) has led to even more fans being excluded from the ground even if they do not have court bans or convictions.

While this has curtailed trouble, it has not stopped it altogether. A new, younger generation of hooligans has begun to emerge at County in recent years. Sixty made the trip to a League Cup game away at Chelsea in October 2003, and there have been clashes with Chester City, Oxford United and Mansfield, who, for the younger lads, are re-emerging as fierce rivals.

There is little hostility between County and Forest, partly because it is so long since they played one another. A report into hooliganism by Nottinghamshire Police in 2004 even stated that County and Forest hooligans had linked up to cause trouble together. It is no surprise, as both Forest and County lads have respect for each other. "I have no problem with Forest whatsoever," said Taff. "In fact I quite like them. They are a good firm who have to be respected and on their day can be a match for anyone."

A well known Forest lad agreed. "County have some good lads, there is little or no animosity between us, they do their thing and we do ours. It's not quite like Dundee, where they actually join forces, but if a firm turned up in town playing up and we bumped into them, we would not hesitate to give the County lads a hand and send the fuckers packing."

O

OLDHAM ATHLETIC

Ground: Boundary Park
Firms: Sewer Mob, Sholver Leathers, Crossley Skins, Werneth Mob,
   Glodwick, Fine Young Casuals
Rivals: Manchester United, Bolton, Blackburn, Wrexham

"Europe is our goal," said Ken Bates. "It's the start of a new era for the club and the fans who for too long have had to be content with half-forgotten memories of long-ago triumphs of once having been a First Division club, and once having got to the semi-final of the Cup. All that is really behind us now. It's to the future we must look. Not next year, or even the year after but as far ahead as the shining Seventies. And in that time, if well-laid plans go according to schedule, Athletic will be firmly implanted on the bigger and more attractive map of European soccer."

No-one could accuse Bates, then chairman of Oldham, of a lack of optimism, but it was never going to happen. However, off the pitch Oldham were hitting the headlines as far back as 1964. The club might have been languishing in the old Third Division, but its close proximity to Manchester meant that the newly emerging fad of football violence was to come to Oldham long before it reached far bigger clubs.

In January 1966, Oldham were drawn at home to Wolves in the FA Cup. Wolves were one of the biggest teams around at the time and everyone knew it would be a tough game, on and off the pitch. By 2pm, hundreds of Wolves fans, a mixture of Mods, rockers and black youths, had taken over the home Chaddy End. It took some time for Oldham to get organised but by kick-off they had not only reclaimed their end but forced Wolves onto the pitch.

The Oldham hardcore was the Sewer Mob, a Chadderton-based gang that had emerged a couple of years before. "They were a hundred-strong mob of rockers, all Oldham Athletic fans," said Carl Spiers, a leading

Oldham hooligan during the 1970s and 1980s. "Between 1964 and 1968, the Sewer Mob followed Oldham all over the country and took over many away teams' ends, including QPR on a night match, Doncaster, Mansfield, Rochdale, Bury, Stockport and many others. The Sewer Mob was led by a huge, powerful youth called Gill Doc."

Gill Doc was born in the late 1940s and by the time he was 13 he was a renowned gang leader. "He was a huge, powerfully built youth and already the cock [hardest] of his school. He soon gained a fearsome reputation throughout the Oldham area," recalled Spiers. "He had also begun taking his big gang to Oldham Athletic and beating up away supporters. These were the early days of football violence, and in those days rival fans leaders would challenge each other. This happened many times and Gill Doc never lost a fight. By the time he was sixteen he was fighting grown men in the town centre many years older than him. Gill's greatest moment came when he singlehandedly led the charge to retrieve the Chaddy End in January 1966 after Wolves had taken it over. He punched and pummelled his way through this vast mob of Wolves fans, who eventually fled across the pitch. Gill was known as the King of the Chaddy End for the next few seasons."

In one of Oldham's most infamous battles, Gill led a 50-strong mob into Manchester United's Stretford End for a Lancashire Senior Cup tie in January 1969. Most of the 24,000 crowd was packed in to the Stretford End and shortly after kick off Gill and his boys roared and chanted and the famous Stretford Enders scattered, leaving the Oldham mob standing alone. Only when the United fans realised how few Oldham there were did they counter-charge but there was no shifting Gill, who stayed put until half-time, when he and his cohorts were escorted around the pitch to the away end, where they were greeted like returning heroes. "This battle has gone down in Oldham folklore," said Spiers. "Gill retired from the scene by 1970 and would just make the odd appearance. He has worked in the construction industry in the Oldham area all of his life and is now in his late fifties."

Gill's retirement left a void on the Oldham terraces, but before long the Sewer Mob had been replaced by the Glodwick Mob, again mainly rockers, who by now were known as grebos. "These were the hardest mob in the Oldham area during the early Seventies, and retrieved the Chaddy End several times after it had been taken. They always arrived just after kick-off, drunk and rowdy," said Spiers. The Glodwick Mob went home and away and during the 1970s took the home ends of Chester, Crewe, Rochdale, York, Bury, Halifax, Wrexham, Southport, Notts County and Chesterfield, among others.

Spiers's right hand man was Lloyd Scan, a mixed-race lad who he had known since childhood. "He went to school with me and was a strong athletic youth, a top-class amateur footballer," said Spiers. "He had great courage and was often targeted by away mobs. 'Get the nigger,' they would shout, and make for Lloyd, who loved the challenge and just laughed at them. He had tons of bottle and he could fight, individually or in a gang situation, but he got arrested quite a few times because the cops also targeted him and he did a bit of bird. He was a doorman for a few years and gained a big reputation around Oldham and indeed Manchester in his twenties. At one time he was banned from all the town centre's public houses. He has been settled down though for a while and is now a successful businessman with property in England and the USA."

Oldham earned a reputation during this period, but through the 1970s several visiting groups actually took the Chaddy End. In January 1974, Oldham played host to Burnley and were overrun. "Burnley took the Chaddy End in great style. We were then in the old Third Division, Burnley were second in the old First Division and 22,000 packed into the ground, the biggest crowd for years at Oldham. At two-thirty, the Chaddy End was packed out but hundreds of Burnley fans came charging across the pitch towards us and while many Oldham fans fled a few of us stayed and met them head-on. Burnley fans leapt from the pitch right amongst us, and soon overwhelmed us and surged up the terracing. Within five minutes they had taken the Chaddy End and they were soon joined by hundreds more Burnley fans who also came across the pitch. They soon filled most of the end and it was a very impressive takeover." To add insult to injury, Burnley won the game 4–1. "Others to have taken the Chaddy End included Bolton twice, Blackburn, Stockport in 1968, Bristol Rovers, Sheff Wed, Sunderland, Man City, and finally Sheffield United in December 1977, the last team to take us."

In October 1974, Hearts brought hundreds down from Scotland for a mid-season friendly and initially took the Chaddy End only for it to be reclaimed by the home fans, with the Glodwick Mob playing a major role. For bigger matches the Chaddy End was shared with away fans, which might have increased receipts for the club but it also meant almost constant fighting between rival fans. Battles occurred with clubs such as Bolton, West Ham, Chelsea, Spurs, Man Utd, Cardiff, Bristol City, Aston Villa, Stoke, Preston and Notts Forest.

Ask any Oldham fan about their most hated team and almost every one will say Manchester United; that was partly why the decision of Oldham's hooligan leader, Lee Spence, to switch allegiance to the Reds in the late Nineties disgusted some of his fellow Oldham lads even more than a move to virtually any other firm. Since the beginning of football violence there has always been increased animosity at Oldham's match against United. Even away from games, there have been numerous clashes between the two sets of supporters.

"We have had many battles against Manchester United over the last forty years," said Spiers, "ranging from the 'Battle of the Stretford End' by Gill Doc's mob to the December 1974 match at Boundary Park when United failed to take the Chaddy End. Oldham stood firm, although after the match United rampaged through the town with their thousands of thugs. Throughout the Seventies we often attacked United fans in Manchester city centre after returning from away games on the train. In the early Seventies, United had a big firm called the Oldham Reds but they did not show their face much after 1974, as the Oldham Athletic mob grew and grew.

"In the mid-Eighties, we played United in a mid-season friendly at Boundary Park when United tried to take the Chaddy End but got whacked all over the place, and we also ran them after the match. In 1990, we played them in the FA Cup semi-final at Maine Road, where we were allocated the Platt Lane end of the ground. Many United got tickets for this end and there was much brawling throughout the whole match. Oldham's bigger numbers gave them the advantage inside the ground but after the match United ran us everywhere. The game ended 3-3 and at the replay a few days later United hammered us before and after the match. Oldham were too disorganised that night.

"We played United a few times over the next few seasons in the Premier, and they never did anything at Boundary Park, with Oldham fans just picking off infiltrators. We always went to Old Trafford but the cops had it sorted down there so we got away unscathed. We played United at Wembley in 1994 for the semi-final of the FA Cup and hundreds of United fans got tickets for our end, but once they were sussed Oldham fans attacked them and every one of the United fans fled, many climbing onto the pitch. It was a tremendous result for the Oldham fans. After the match there were many brawls on the way down Wembley Way and to the train station.

"More recently, the Fine Young Casuals trashed the Cockney Reds' pub in Kings Cross after the match. I would say ninety per cent of Oldham fans would choose Manchester United as the team they hate the most, although the younger fans have clashed more with Man City fans since the late Eighties."

One of Oldham's fiercest battles was the home game against Sheffield Wednesday in January 1980. "This match was arguably Oldham's mob's finest moment," recalled Spiers. "It was certainly one of my proudest times on the terraces. Sheff Wed were a massive club with a huge following, and during their previous visit, for the first game of the 1974/75 season, they took over our end. Most of our mob were thirteen-to-fifteen-year-old kids back then, but now we were all aged twenty-plus, veterans of the hooligan scene, and had faced all the country's top mobs and defended our kop against them.

"As expected, there were hundreds of Wednesday fans in the Chaddy End, and as usual with most Yorkshiremen they were big, ugly bastards. We repelled them time and time again. Every five minutes, big mobs of Wednesdayites were coming into our end and charging into us, and for a full hour we fought them but held onto our end. There were many hand-to-hand fights and many mass brawls, but we stood firm, eventually chasing them onto the pitch. It was a tremendous victory. We were outnumbered two-to-one for most of the time, but the courage and pride we had helped us no end. By kick-off, every one of the hundreds of Wednesday fans who had come into our end was out. They marched up the pitch towards the away end, which was also full of thousands of Sheff Wed fans, got their round of applause, then spent the next hour or so rioting with the cops and invading the pitch. They wrecked the Rochdale Road End and attacked the coppers, injuring many, but they would not come across the pitch into our end again."

The violence received national media attention. Play was halted, lumps of concrete terracing ripped up and hurled at police and a lottery kiosk was shattered and used as ammunition. When Wednesday manager Jack Charlton pleaded with his own supporters for calm, he too was pelted with stones. Greater Manchester Police came in for considerable criticism in the Press for being unprepared but its Chief Constable, James Anderton, who later boasted of having a hotline to God, claimed everyone was over-reacting.

"It was unfortunate from every point of view, but it has been blown out of proportion," he said. "It is not true to say there was an uncontrollable riot or that the police arrangements were unsatisfactory or inappropriate. There were approximately five thousand Sheffield Wednesday supporters. There were seventy police officers inside the ground, which in our opinion was adequate, and thirty officers outside the ground were also available. When the trouble started, a further sixty officers were dispatched to the ground. They were not needed, as the incident was adequately controlled by the officers already there."

Some papers described it as the worst soccer violence for many years but Anderton remained defiant. "No members of the public, ground staff or players were injured. The pitch invasion took place after an incident involving players, which was being dealt with by the referee, ten to fifteen minutes after kick-off. It was close to where the Sheffield supporters were and the crowd became excited and angry. They surged forward, pressing younger supporters against a safety barrier. The officer on duty at that point – quite rightly in my opinion – opened the built-in safety gate in the barrier to ensure that the children were not crushed. I suppose you could say that the police uncorked the bottle." One hundred Sheff Wed supporters burst through the open gate and it took 30 minutes for them to be put back.

While Anderton played down the trouble, his Oldham divisional commander was less sure. "We tried to treat the Sheffield fans like civilised human beings but they behaved like animals," said Chief Superintendent Bert Hoy. He absolved the police and the club and placed the entire responsibility on the shoulders of the two players whose booking sparked the trouble. "If they had listened to the referee and walked away after they had been cautioned, none of this would have happened. The blame is entirely theirs."

Oldham boss Jimmy Frizzell became the latest in a long line of football managers to call for the birch for hooligans. "We should take a leaf out of Saudi Arabia's book and bring back the lash," he opined. "It is the only sort of treatment these people understand." He was backed by the Latics chairman, Harry Wilde, who said, "The last time Wednesday fans were at Boundary Park they wrecked our social club, and now they have wrecked our reputation. It is a disaster." He seemed unaware of the trouble caused by Oldham's own supporters.

The Football Association ordered an inquiry into the trouble. Instead of the usual three-man team, five were picked, which the FA said showed the seriousness of the matter, and both clubs were charged with bringing the game into disrepute. While the Latics waited for the inquiry results, they made their next home game, against local rivals Bolton Wanderers, an all-ticket affair for the Ford Stand paddock. "We are determined that this section of the ground in particular will be reserved entirely for our supporters, especially for those people with young children." The club had tried such a scheme for the Wednesday game but it failed pitifully. "The response to this scheme was so bad for the Sheffield Wednesday game that we allowed people to pay on the day and, unfortunately, some visiting fans got in there. That won't happen again." In Parliament, MPs passed new legislation forcing clubs to erect fences.

By the late Seventies, no away firm took the Chaddy End, though a few did try. The Glodwick Mob had developed into a strong, tightly knit group with bags of fighting experience, though as the early Eighties arrived, some of their core group began to drop out. New rivals, including Man City and Huddersfield, replaced some of their old adversaries, and the casual scene was taking hold.

"The Fine Young Casuals was formed in the mid-Eighties by a group of about a dozen sixteen-year-old fans," remembers Oldham lad Fraz. "We would follow the bigger lads about at the match but they were not into the fashion and we would break away from the main mob, forming our own crew, which built over the next few years. We began drinking in the Grapes in Oldham town centre and soon could muster a mob of fifty lads. We began fighting rival fans, but very rarely at the match; the older mobs were still into that but we were more organised and arranged fights away from the grounds. The older lads could never understand this, they were all about taking ends or defending their end, but things were changing. There were many dawn raids in the Eighties and early Nineties, so we had to get more organised and tight."

The FYC were led by "Spence", a well-known local youth who was one of the original teenage founders in 1985. Lee William Spence was born in 1968 and claimed that he was drawn to the scene as a schoolboy after he watched the infamous *Hooligan* TV documentary about West Ham's Inter City Firm. He soon began following England and formed friendships with many similar youths from several clubs, which resulted in his name cropping up whenever Oldham were mentioned in hooligan circles. Regarded by many as "game" rather than a hardcase, there is no disputing that he marshalled Oldham's hooligan element and turned them into one of the most active smaller mobs during the period when many of the bigger football firms were in decline.

Not content with being a big fish in a little pond, and being blighted with the police attention such status can attract, Spence was attracted to higher-profile games. After witnessing how a huge mob could operate while travelling with England, he took a chance and started to attend games with Oldham's hated rivals Manchester United in 1999. Initially he was not accepted by the United hooligans, as he had been involved in several clashes with them previously, but soon he formed a close friendship with one of the leading members and gradually was taken on board. At the time of writing he was living in Thailand with a mixture of United and Hibs lads and was rarely seen at games in this country.

"By 1990 most of the older lads had retired," said Fraz. "We did respect them very much, we know what they had been through, most of us were little boys in the 1970s and saw what they had to go through when other teams came into the Chaddy End. They were very brave and it was a lot rougher back then and on a much larger scale. But from 1990, it was us

FYC who represented Oldham. We were a tight-knit firm and had some right results, including doing Leeds' main firm in Leeds centre, and we hammered City and United fans many times in Manchester city centre pubs. At our peak in the mid Nineties we could muster over one hundred good lads, and when some of the old boys turned out we were a serious mob."

According to the FYCs, three of their most famous victories were taking Spurs in London, turning over the Cockney Reds' pub, and doing a number on Stoke's mob in Manchester. Fraz remembered the Stoke game.

"Stoke brought a massive mob up to Oldham that day and took over many of the town centre pubs. We tried to get at them several times but the cops had it boxed off. It was the same at the ground. We had a good-sized firm out and were desperate to get at Stoke. At 5.30pm we ordered twelve taxis to take us the seven miles down to Manchester Victoria Station, as a Stoke lad told us they were due there. We got out of our taxis in Manchester and headed towards Victoria, where we spotted the much bigger Stoke mob from about fifty yards and began to charge towards them. A few of our lads aimed flares at them, which scattered most of them, but they regrouped and we had it toe-to-toe with them. It was a good brawl but we deffo got the better of them before the cops came; ten of our lads got arrested plus a few Stoke. The Stoke lads gave us plenty of credit for taking the fight to them and travelling so far to have it with them, and it was one of the better FYC battles. We were proud of ourselves."

It is rare that a major mob admits it got turned over, but Stoke admit that they were second best. "It was one of those days when our firm was too big and it all went horribly wrong" said Mark Chester, who was marshalling Stoke's troops that day.

"We came out of the ground and at the time were in our prime, so there were a good few hundred lads in the mob. There was no way we could all go back to Manchester at the same time and meet Oldham, who in fairness were up for it despite inferior numbers. We decided to split into three mobs, and the first firm, mainly the younger lot, set off for Victoria, as we thought they could get there early, have a scout round and let us know what was on the cards when we got there. Fair play to Oldham, they clocked what was happening and a load of them jumped taxis and were there before the first train got in. As our lads came out, they walked into a classic ambush. Oldham came out of the shadows and hit them hard. Distress flares, the lot, went into them and it was a result for Oldham but at the same time a good experience for our younger lot. In those days we were as good as most at it, but hey, who ever said we were invincible?"

One new rivalry that emerged during the 1990s was with Wrexham's Frontline. Asked about this, Fraz recalled the day that Oldham bumped into Wrexham on returning from the final game of the season at Huddersfield. "We had rampaged around Huddersfield that day, chasing their mob everywhere. We had a good-sized crew on the train going back, which stopped at Manchester Piccadilly, and as we got off the train we noticed a mob of Wrexham who had been to Bury. We piled into them. Most of them stayed and slugged it out but we overwhelmed them. The cops were soon on the case and one lad known as Winkle ended up getting sent down for his part in the affray.

"We have had a few battles with Wrexham these past few years and most of the time we have done them. One time they did us over but they had seventy-odd lads against our mob of thirty. We went team-handed recently but they would not come to meet us and they ended up getting turned over by our 'booze cruiser' lads, many being ex-Seventies hoolies who arrange a boozers' coach to every away game. The FYC turned over a few pubs in Chester, sorting out the bouncers who put one of our lads in hospital." [See *Wrexham* for a different take on this feud.]

The Fine Young Casuals were not everyone's cup of tea on the Oldham terraces and some gave them the nickname "Farm Yard Chickens". Carl Spiers, the Seventies hooligan, however defends them. "A few of the older lads think that the FYC are a joke but most agree there are a few really good lads amongst them. The thing that pisses a lot of the old-timers off is when you have some of them turning to other teams, but today it is deemed acceptable at many clubs, so although I get on with many of them, some old-school veterans still ask me, 'What the fuck is all that about?' When these casual mobs came on the scene in the mid-Eighties, they made us lot laugh. They would arrive half an hour after kick-off, make a big entrance, then fuck off with ten minutes to go in a big exit. Wow.

"Like I said, they have good lads but you talk to any of the FYC lads and they can tell you of only about a dozen major battles that they have had over the last twenty years. Fuck me, we had ten major battles in one day against Bolton, Sheff Wed, Sheff Utd, Burnley, Hearts, Chelsea, West Ham, Stoke, Forest, Newcastle, Spurs, et cetera, at the big games in the Seventies. We began battling as early as 10.30am on a Saturday morning, running battles in the town centres, many times getting kicked to fuck, then we had to fight outside the grounds, then fight throughout most of the match, then fight after the match!

"I am not sure very many of the current hooligans across the country dressed in their flash clobber could have handled that. Of course it was a different era and I accept that, you can only do what you can only do, but we saw so much more violence than they could ever imagine. We were fighting lads much older than ourselves most of the time and sometimes blokes, but all this organised fighting crap, fuck me, I can't imagine phoning some Bolton loony up in 1976 and saying, 'Err, how many you got mate? We'll have fifty good lads on such a car park miles away from the ground.' He would reply, 'Fuck off you Oldham bastards, we are coming with a mob of a thousand lads,' and they did, plenty of times. The FYC can muster fifty-to-seventy lads on a good day but occasionally we guest at the odd game and Oldham took 150 lads down to QPR a couple of seasons ago. Half of them lads were over forty and the old mob out on the piss; most of the FYC are in their thirties, whereas ninety per cent of us had jacked it in by the time we were twenty-two because we had seen enough.

"To tell you the truth, most of the firms today, the 'casuals', are not really football fans, they are more interested in their silly Burberry and Paul & Shark snides than the football. It's just a game to them. In our day, passion and courage took us well beyond the call of duty. The FYC's CV of 'major battles' includes Wrexham, Wigan, Mansfield, Rochdale and a couple of respected results at Leeds and Stoke. We had to contend with Sheff Wed and United, Bolton when they were tough, Burnley when they were tough, Wolves, Forest, West Ham, Millwall, Chelsea, Spurs, Bradford, Villa, Stoke, Bristol Rovers, Cardiff, Everton, Liverpool, United, City, Newcastle, Sunderland, Middlesbrough, Hearts, Preston when they were tough, Derby, Leicester, all these home and away. The FYC can only do what they can in this day and age, but I would only take about thirty lads from the last twenty seasons back in time if I could, and ninety per cent of my ultimate Oldham firm would come from the Seventies and early Eighties."

During the Nineties, Oldham became firmly established on the England scene and large numbers would follow the national team abroad. It was on these trips that they came to form an alliance with Shrewsbury and Stockport, while during one of Oldham's regular pre-season tournaments on the Isle of Man they met Hibs. The four firms would link up at big domestic games, with sometimes as many as thirty Shrewsbury travelling up to Oldham and vice versa.

"Football has changed and most teams have friendships and links with other teams, we have links with Hibs, Shrewsbury and Stockport," said Fraz. "They are all good lads and we have helped each other out many times. You have to remember most of us original FYC have been active for almost twenty seasons, and have met many other lads and made lasting friendships. We are proud to be associated with Hibs, who are recognised as one of the best firms in Britain, and they respect us. We always make each other welcome when we visit each other's manors. Once again, a lot of the older lads cannot understand these friendships and cannot understand the need for the 'look', which is also important to us. Most of the older mob were ex-skins, greasers and Mods and by the Eighties most of them sported the mullet look."

This antagonism from older lads is most evident in Carl Spiers. "Most old-school hooligans find it inconceivable that any other teams should join up with each other. Without sounding like Oldham's version of Uncle Albert, it would never have happened in my day. In the Seventies, Man United once came to supposedly help us out when Aston Villa came up, but they got turned on by Oldham fans and never came back. Many are very critical of a lot of the so-called casual scene and this joining up shit really pisses some people off. I have no doubt that some of these Hibs, Shrewsbury and Stockport boys are good lads but I have never spoke to them and would never dream of asking for their help. We let them get on with it but it happens all over the country not just at our club and shows just how weak the hooligan scene has become. Most of your courage comes from the pride of supporting your home team and fighting for your team and your mates."

At the turn of the millennium, the FYC almost folded after Lee Spence switched his loyalties to Manchester United. Five years later and the resentment lingers. "[He] did a disappointing act when he turned his back on his hometown team and linked up to Manchester United's firm," said Fraz. "This upset a lot of Oldham fans. This lad was one of the originals and had gone through so much with so many Oldham lads, and now he had done the dirty. He lost a lot of respect in Oldham and he had plenty. The thing was, he hated Man United and had been with us many times when we had attacked their boys." The FYC reeled under the humiliation but slowly they recovered, partly with some of the older lads regrouping but also as a new generation emerged. Fraz says that the FYC can now pull a regular mob of seventy lads out, and more for a big game.

In recent years, Oldham's mob has become better known in the general media for its right-wing connections than football exploits. Oldham has long been a town divided along racial lines. Asian youths believe they are the victims of white racism while many white youths believe Asian gangs target them. Since the late 1970s, many of the Oldham lads have been linked to far-right groups. Carl Spiers remembers many of the active lads in his time associating with the National Front, but as he points out, with the involvement of mixed-race lads like Lloyd, few took it seriously.

In recent years, racial tit-for-tat violence in Oldham has become more pronounced, culminating in 2001 in several days of rioting by both white and Asian youths. Several of the FYC aligned with the hardline neo-nazi group Combat 18. A minibus full of the FYC lads, which for a relatively small mob is a sizeable proportion, attended a C18 gig in Coventry in 1999, as well as other events around the country and even in Europe. This politically motivated mob, combined with a number of high-profile attacks on white lads and the town becoming the electoral priority for the British National Party, formed an explosive concoction.

In April 2001, a 78-year-old pensioner was mugged and attacked by four teenage Asian lads. It was a wicked and unprovoked incident and received national media attention. Two days later, BNP leader Nick Griffin announced his intention to stand in Oldham in the General Election only a few weeks away. This increased the tensions between the communities. A week after the attack, Stoke City were in town and the balloon really went up.

A Stoke crew had been turned over by the FYC the previous season and they came mobbed up. Events took over and they ended up rampaging through a predominantly Asian area close to the ground. Mark Chester, in his book on the Naughty Forty and in their chapter in this book, says that targeting Asians was not the intention of the 450 Stoke lads who had journeyed north that day, but admits that the media coverage of the attack on Walter Chamberlain "combined with tales and rumours that were emanating from this part of the country, fuelled much conversation and further rumour mongering on the journey". As beer flowed among the Stoke fans who had got into Oldham, the pensioner's name was repeatedly chanted. They were soon joined by locals and a football escort became a political march. Asian street traders had their stalls attacked. The police moved in and divided the Stoke lads into three groups but this only spread the violence. "At this point Stoke's lads and some locals started to attack anything ethnic: businesses, taxis, houses," recalled Chester. "Local residents were even standing on their doorsteps pointing out neighbours who were Asian."

Inside the ground the racist chanting continued, but outside the local Asian youth, furious at the actions of the Stoke lads, began to prepare a reception committee for their return. There was yet more trouble as the two rival groups clashed, with the police once again making a hash of policing.

Word spread round the hooligan scene like a bushfire as phone calls and internet messages organised reprisals. The following Saturday, the FYC tried to carry on where Stoke had left off and organised a mob to go back into an Asian area. Hooligans from across the country promised to show but in truth few turned up. Nevertheless, there were still over 100 lads, mainly FYC with small groups from Huddersfield, Stockport, Man City, Shrewsbury and Everton. The police were firmly in control, holding 40-50 lads outside a Barclays Bank for several hours, though later that evening a small group of FYC and Stockport clashed with some Asians and a Stockport lad was stabbed.

Three weeks later, and with tension continuing to rise in the town, the FYC tried again, though this time they arranged to meet outside of the town centre to avoid the police. On this occasion there were about 65 lads, a mix of Oldham, Stockport, Shrewsbury and Combat 18 from London. The police kept a close eye on the group, and at one stage moved in in numbers to prevent them from entering an Asian estate. Mysteriously, the police stood down in the early evening and an altercation between the nephew of one of the main FYC/C18 lads and a local Asian saw three carloads of lads run down a street attacking Asians and their property. Local Asians reacted in fury and so occurred an evening of rioting and mayhem. Nine white men were sent to prison for this trouble, including the 43-year-old leader of the FYC, who had the nickname "the General".

While the riot actually made worldwide headlines, less widely reported was an attempt to disrupt the England and Pakistan cricket match at Old Trafford a week later. A 40-strong group, led by the FYC and Combat 18, planned to get into the ground to fight with Pakistani supporters. There was even a plan, to be carried out by an Oldham lad, to run on the pitch and stick a Combat 18 flag into the wicket. However, the police were alerted to this plot and rounded up the group outside the ground.

Following the riots, the lad who set up the FYC website boasted that Oldham was "the most right-wing mob in the country". Carl Spiers is one of those who is less than impressed. "Had they been top of the league for taking home team ends and scattering away mobs all over Oldham town centre I would get my pension book out and buy the lads a drink," he joked. They are not, and even Carl who is fiercely proud of the town's football club and supporters, knows he may never have to dig that deep in his lifetime.

Further reading: *We Are the Famous Football Hooligans*, Carl H. Spiers

OXFORD UNITED

Ground: Kassam Stadium, formerly the Manor Ground
Firms: The Business, South Midlands Hit Squad, Oxford Youth Outfit
Rivals: Reading, Swindon, Brighton

Think of Oxford and one thinks of the academia, historic buildings and the Boat Race, a middle class vision of England where former Prime Minister John Major could easily have found his warm beer and cricket image. But strip away the surface and there is another Oxford, tough, poor and fiercely proud of its football team. The Oxford United of the 1970s was a community club drawing its support from the huge estates like Blackbird Leys and Barton, which for so many years supplied the bulk of the British Leyland workforce at the Cowley car plant.

This was the Oxford whose young supporters stoned two coaches taking QPR fans back to London in September 1971. "Supporters left the coaches and chased the gang who fled through the Barton estate," reported the *Oxford Mail.* The QPR supporters' club secretary, Mrs Daphne Biggs, couldn't understand it. "Oxford had just won and won well, so what possible reason could they have to attack us?" She went on to complain that the hour-long journey home was "very draughty".

A few months later, Oxford fans were involved in trouble at Aldershot. The match was held up twice as rival fans clashed on the terraces and then on the pitch. The first pitch invasion was quickly dealt with by the police, but the second, after Aldershot scored their second and winning goal, lasted longer. Fifty fans were involved in a running battle along the pitch and play was held up for two minutes.

The rest of the season passed off relatively peacefully but the same could not be said of the following one. On the opening Saturday, Oxford played at Leyton Orient and one coachload of supporters was abandoned in London by their driver. "The coach was hired by a private party and forty-nine youths were picked up at Gloucester Green," explained a spokesman for the coach company. "They stopped at Stokenchurch, where they went to a public house. By the time they arrived in London the coach was littered with broken bottles and empties and the driver had had enough. He asked the police for advice and apparently they suggested he return home because they could not be responsible for the coach."

The club's supporters group quickly distanced themselves from the trip. "This was nothing to do with the supporters' club or the coach we ran to London," said its secretary, Jim Hunt. "These people seem to be an unruly element who go to matches with the sole purpose of causing trouble."

During the match several people were ejected but no arrests were made. After the game, a gang of youths smashed a number of car windscreens.

A week later Oxford played host to Middlesbrough. "Police had to create a no-man's land between rival football supporters at the Manor Ground," reported the local paper in its coverage of several subsequent court cases. "Mr Brian Heath, prosecuting, said the Oxford fans were responsible for a great deal of provocation by shouting obscenities and waving their fists towards Middlesbrough supporters."

The visit of Manchester United was eagerly awaited by Oxford United fans and the city alike. The local paper produced a special edition and a maximum crowd saw their club hold the mighty United to a 2–2 draw. Eleven people were arrested, mainly Oxford fans, in incidents before and after the game. Most of the arrests came when gangs clashed along Headington Road after the game. Nine people were treated for minor injuries, the worst being a suspected fractured wrist. The local police felt pleased with the way the events unfolded. "The situation was under control at all times," said Superintendent James Hipgrove. "It was quieter than expected. The Manchester fans by reputation are supposed to be fairly lively, but so few came."

Next up at the Manor Ground was Millwall, a fixture laced with potential for disorder. Sure enough, it came, despite a larger than average police presence inside the ground. A number of arrests were made inside the ground and the local paper reported serious trouble after the game as "packs of fans from both sides began a pitched battle near the junction of Headington Road and Gypsy Lane. But police intervened quickly, driving cars and vans into the crowd and dispersing it."

There was further trouble a fortnight later when Preston manager Alan Ball was hit by sand thrown by an Oxford fan. He turned to face the stand but police and the linesman moved in quickly and ushered Ball back to the bench. Four fans invaded the pitch after Preston scored a penalty. Oxford travelled to Brighton for their next and there were nine arrests after clashes inside the ground.

The visit of Aston Villa in late November 1972 was a big game for Oxford. Villa had been relegated and their huge away following was tormenting home fans and police forces across the country. Perhaps complacency had set in or perhaps they were simply arrogant enough to believe they were invincible. Either way, it proved to be a torrid afternoon for the claret fans.

"Villa were top of the league, or thereabouts, and were *the* team in the division," recalled Col, an Oxford terrace veteran. "They were pulling 40,000-plus crowds at home and had a massive away following. This included, as was the norm in those days, a very large hooligan following. We knew it would be tough to defend our turf, but we felt confident we could put on a good show as we were no pushovers, particularly at home.

"I arrived fairly early in the city centre and there were already tales of lads having small offs with Villa fans and it was obvious there were going to be a lot of them around. We made our way to Headington and as we got off the bus opposite the ground there were already hordes of Villa. We went into the Britannia Arms opposite the London Road entrance to the ground and met some mates. It was rammed with Oxford and more were arriving by the minute. I was with a mob of older lads, all in their twenties. Most lads involved in football violence at the time were, like me, teenagers, so I felt confident with the company I was in. The adrenalin was really beginning to buzz.

"As we got closer to kick-off, some lads drifted off to the ground and some of us stayed put and went in about half two in a group. As we left the pub, we could see large numbers of fans, many of them Villa, queuing to get in through the London Road entrance which was our end. We decided to go in the Osler Road, to the side, and as there was no segregation in those days, enter the London Road from there. We eventually got in about quarter to three and when I looked immediately to my left at the packed London Road terrace I could not believe my eyes. It was full of Villa, many wearing the *Clockwork Orange*-style eye make-up and garb. There must have been at least 5,000 of them crammed in there with just a small mob of Oxford immediately behind the goal near the bottom of the terrace. We had been outmanoeuvred, as the Villa had got in early and packed our end. They were taunting us and the Oxford who were in there were coming under a lot of pressure. Could this be the first ever taking of the London Road?

"It was decided to go to the opposite end of the ground, the Cuckoo Lane End, as there were more Oxford there and we could plan what to do. As we walked along the terrace, more and more lads who had been unable to get in the London Road joined us and by the time we got to the Cuckoo Lane we were a sizeable number. It was decided that we would go down the opposite side of the ground, the Beech Road, where it was possible to walk behind the stand, and try to get into the London Road from that position. We walked purposefully until we reached an area where players' cars and other vehicles were parked. Unfortunately, the police were blocking our way and formed a barrier by linking their arms, as was often the way in those days. We stopped dead, then someone shouted, 'CHARGE!' and everyone rushed the OB and broke their lines.

"We were now immediately behind the London Road where there were other Oxford who had just entered from the gate at that end. We split into four groups and rushed into the London Road from the four rear entrances. This gave us the element of surprise as we rushed into the back of the Villa near the entrances and sent them scattering. At the same time the Oxford lads on the two sides of the London Road took this as their cue to charge in at the now panicking Villa. The lads who had been in the London Road all the time were also doing their bit. What happened next was amazing, something I will never forget and lads of today will probably never experience. As the Villa lads fled in panic, there was only one route of escape for them and that was on to the pitch. They poured over the wall and some were trampled by others in their haste to get away. To see 5,000 people fleeing in this way was a sight to behold and those Villa that were unlucky enough to get caught took a kicking.

"The players were taken off the pitch and the game was held up as police and the ambulance people tried to restore order and treat the injured. We had shifted 5,000 people in a matter of minutes and regained our end. The London Road was now full of Oxford and it was our turn to taunt the sorry-looking Villa wandering around the pitch.

"They eventually climbed over the walls and watched the game from the other end of the ground. Some left and went home with their tails between their legs. There were a lot of injuries, with some taken to hospital, and that evening my parents told me that there had actually been a national newsflash on the television, such was the severity of the trouble. It was an amazing day, the sort of thing that stays with you for life."

The match statistics made grim reading. The game had been held up for eleven minutes, there were ten arrests and 17 people needed medical treatment. The worst was a 13-year-old who was still in intensive care 48 hours later. And the trouble could have been worse if it had not been for a strong police presence preventing 500 Villa fans from running through the city centre before the game.

The finger of blame was pointed at young Oxford fans. "It is the youngsters who cause all the trouble," said the Oxford United chairman. "If the youngsters are not going to appreciate the game of football like the average spectator does, we shall have to give serious thought to whether we allow youngsters in at reduced prices." He warned of strong action against young fans if there was a repeat of the unprecedented incident.

The *Oxford Mail* reviewed the options open to the club and the police. One suggestion from Superintendent James Hipgrove was for numbered enclosures so fans would go from a marked entrance to a marked area on the terrace. A senior St John Ambulance officer suggested crash barriers would stop the full weight of a crowd surge forcing fans on to the pitch, while the club insisted on barring people from the ground who had been convicted of hooliganism. The FA Disciplinary Commission ordered Oxford United to post warnings around the ground and in their programmes for a month threatening severe repercussions if the trouble was repeated. After the hearing, Oxford's chairman commented, "It was an unfortunate affair. It was the case of two rival factions occupying the same piece of ground."

In a bid to prevent further trouble, the club organised a meeting with the younger fans to stress the seriousness of the situation. Club director Vic Couling told the audience that future pitch invasions would not be tolerated by police. Waving one of the notices in the air, he said, "They'll close the ground. We've had this warning. If anything goes wrong during the time of this warning we've had it." In a sop to the fans, the club announced free tickets to a new penned in section of the ground. However, only 14 young people attended the meeting and the club was shocked at the strong anti-police attitude many held.

The youth of the troublemakers was a problem all over the country and Oxford was no exception. On a website dedicated to Oxford supporters, several people active in the early 1970s reminisced about their activities. One remembered hitching to York in January 1973 for an FA Cup match. "I was eleven and went with about fifty others from Cowley Road, the oldest being maybe thirteen. I sometimes despair when I look at the kids in the Oxford Mail Stand now. Could you imagine these kids of ten or eleven taking off to away games on their tods? We often went on crime sprees to Swindon mob-handed, bunked the train, stole and fought and went home very happy. Once our lot did the windows of the Swindon ground in the middle of the morning."

Any hopes that Oxford fans would behave themselves were dashed only four days after the FA reported on the Villa game. There was trouble before, during and after an FA Cup game away at York City. Trains carrying Oxford fans to Yorkshire were damaged, several houses and cars were attacked outside the ground and play was held up when a barrier collapsed. Local people were enraged, especially as the damaged properties were almshouses and many of the broken windows opened straight into the bedrooms of the elderly. "Oxford supporters are notorious troublemakers and we were out to see they did not cause any trouble here," said a police spokesman. "We succeeded apart from a 50-yard stretch where the flats are."

The club played down the trouble. "I don't think our fans are notorious troublemakers," responded manger Gerry Summers. "I think the police would have taken the same sort of precautions whoever was playing there.

In fact I did not notice any crowd trouble apart from the fence coming down, which was unfortunate. I thought we had a very good following at the match and they certainly supported the team well." Jim Hunt, secretary of the Supporters Club added, "Like all teams, there is a hooligan element, but I don't think we are any worse than any other." Two special trains carried 1,085 Oxford fans to the game. Hunt claimed that they could have sold more tickets but "we bar people whom we think might be undesirable".

Many Oxford fans recited stories of police brutality to the *Oxford Mail*, with three fans needing hospital treatment after being bitten by police dogs. One of those was 18-year-old Steven Rand, who was bitten 20 times. His mother told the paper, "Steven was bitten on his leg from behind and he turned round to try and get the dog away. It bit him all over his arms and legs and tore his clothes to shreds. Steven says that he was then pushed to the ground by the police and although he told them he had been badly bitten by a police dog, they just left him outside the ground."

A home clash against London giants Chelsea in February was almost guaranteed to be accompanied by violence. Twenty-two people aged 14-22 were arrested. Chelsea supporters damaged a car and threw a bicycle through the large front window of a local ironmonger. "It was a bunch of hooligans who had been running up and down St. Ebbes on the rampage," the shop owner said. "They were wearing Chelsea scarves." There had earlier been trouble on the two special trains bringing the Chelsea fans to Oxford and on arrival many refused to board the double-decker buses the police had laid on to transport them to the ground. Instead, they chose to walk through the city centre in a large group. However, given Chelsea's reputation, the police, who had drafted in an extra 80 officers to escort fans to and from the ground, believed their operation was a success.

Unreported in the press was the behaviour of some Oxford fans who threw paint bombs and stones from the footbridge across Headington Hill on to the Chelsea escort below. There were also hit-and-run squads hiding out in the numerous alleys near St Clements, who melted away as quickly as they emerged to attack Chelsea coaches caught up in the heavy traffic. Another incident involved a couple of Oxford taunting a group of 20 Chelsea into chasing them, only for a larger group of locals to be lying in wait.

Oxford's Manor Ground was a formidable place for rival hooligans. Though a small club with a relatively small crowd, they included a large section of hard nuts. This is partly explained by the council estates many of these young men were drawn from, but also because of the nature of the ground and its community feel. "We all knew each other through United," recalled one veteran. "There was more of an identity with the Manor, your club, your team. You knew most other United fans. United were a small club that had won nothing and on our journeys every team seemed bigger than us, so we stuck together. Then there always was the London Road. The memory still makes the hairs on the back of my neck stand up. Being in a packed terrace, singing and chanting, shoulder to shoulder, roaring your team on. Or getting to an away match somehow with all the lads there supporting United together. You could not wait for the weekend to come, win or lose we would keep on coming."

The nature of Oxford's hooligan base was examined by local academic Peter Marsh. In 1974, the club increased security inside the ground. A dry moat had been created around the pitch and barriers erected to divide rival fans. Police patrolled the no-man's land between them. "The net effect of the fortifications around the end and the strategies to keep people in them, is, or course, the highlighting of their distinctive nature," noted Marsh and his co-authors in *Rules of Disorder*, a seminal work on soccer hooliganism. "The police and officials have succeeded in delineating fans' territories in a way the fans themselves could never have done. Another by-product of official strategy is one which involves the fans and the police acting in a concerted and co-operative manner. The maintenance of territorial integrity has become a joint enterprise. Invading fans are not only repulsed by the occupants in defence of their own 'turf', but also by the police in their pursuit of law and order and the status quo."

The academics studied the Oxford hardcore and found three distinct groups in the London Road End: the Novices, aged about ten, whose job was to watch the antics of the rest; the Rowdies, aged between twelve and 17, who carried the banners, made most of the noise and were the most aggressive; and the Town Boys, aged up to 25, the tribal elders. Each group stood in a specific place on the terrace behind the goal, and the youngest aspired to rise through the ranks.

Oxford's footballing fortunes were such that they rarely played the big teams in the 1970s. Most of their hostility, as it remains today, was aimed at Reading and Swindon. Few matches against those two went ahead without any sort of trouble, though some were far more violent than others. In April 1977, Oxford played both rivals on consecutive days. Thirty-three people were arrested at a home match against Swindon, most when rival fans clashed inside the London Road End. The following day, Easter Saturday, a paltry 6,000 attended the game in Reading. The home club put the disappointing crowd down to the hype given to hooliganism in the media during the previous few days.

In addition to Oxford's game against Swindon, hooliganism was in the news with Portsmouth causing trouble at Brighton, Chelsea wrecking Charlton's ground, the decision to ban Manchester United fans from away matches and indeed Reading's previous match against Portsmouth, all within the previous few days. Despite the small crowd and extra police being drawn from across Berkshire and Oxfordshire, there was still disorder and 13 arrests.

Oxford United's chairman wished that hooligans would stay away but admitted he was clueless how this was to be achieved. "I would sooner they did not pay to come to matches," he sighed. "We don't want them throwing beer cans, stones and coins and causing trouble." Supporters' club secretary Jim Hunt added that the club had spent as much as £20,000 on barriers, a moat and other general improvements to crowd control. He also said that about ten per cent of the average £2,000 home gate was spent on policing an estimated 20-30 hardcore troublemakers inside the ground. Their frustration was mirrored by George Curill, chairman of the Oxford City Magistrates' juvenile panel and a United season ticket holder. "I would like to see an attendance centre being set up in Oxfordshire or Thames Valley where juvenile offenders could report or even to do hobbies on Saturdays," he said.

By the beginning of the following season, the police and the club knew something had to change. There was too much trouble far too often. Under a suggestion from the police, the club now put away fans in the Cuckoo Lane End, on the other side of the pitch from the home London Road End. This didn't completely stop trouble but it reduced the likelihood of spontaneous outbreaks of violence that often occurred when rival fans both occupied the same end. While there was still trouble, the six arrests at the home game against Portsmouth in September 1977 were considered by the police to be a good day at the office.

The next target was away matches and a few days later a United director, the famous zoologist Dr Desmond Morris, announced plans to form a travel club with badges and identification cards which had to be carried at all games. "It is the duty of every club to do as much as they can for the fans instead of bleating about them," he said. "If all the clubs had this attitude it might change the situation concerning hooliganism. Any member who is proved to have caused trouble at home or away matches will have his travel card confiscated and will have to make his own way to away matches. We want to weed out the troublemakers and let the vast majority get on with what they are there for, to enjoy themselves."

The scheme was launched at Oxford's away match at Cambridge in late October, but nothing went according to plan. "Fans riot as match finishes," bellowed the front-page headline in the *Oxford Mail*. More than

£2,000-worth of damage to Cambridge's ground included one broken crossbar, mangled railings and crash barriers, two car windscreens smashed and a broken advertising board. Oxford's manager, Mick Brown, was struck on the chin by a bottle and the game was interrupted as Oxford fans threw fireworks and rampaged through the ground. Cambridge manager Ron Atkinson said the incident was the worst he had seen during his three years at the club. "Some of the Oxford fans were just looking for trouble," he said. And he told his opposite number, "Don't send any coaches to the next match. We don't want your troublemakers."

Morris was quick to point out that none of those arrested were members of his new Travel Club, and claimed the scheme had been successful. He was also critical of the police for holding the away fans in until after the home supporters had been cleared from the ground. "United fans were penned in like cattle. Such action is calculated to increase violence and damage, and as far as I know is illegal. If people want to leave a place of entertainment it seems to me that they should be allowed to do so."

Cambridge Police defended their actions. "We used the same tactics we have used for over 18 months," said Chief Insp Jack Cole. "The only problem was that many Oxford fans behaved like animals. They were disgusting. They pelted us with coins when we tried to clear the pitch during the first half and I was hit near the eye by a 10p piece. There is only one exit to the ground and there would be a good chance of trouble if we allowed home and away fans to leave at the same time."

Many of those involved would never forget the day. "That was the first ever 'Varsity' league meeting and the crossbar was broken in two at the end of the game," reminisced one Oxford supporter on a fan forum. "There were several battles off the field throughout the game and the Blackbird Leys coach was bricked afterwards. I seem to remember a Cambridge 'hard man' offering to fight a few Oxford lads without realising there was one behind him. Cue a pale face of fear and a sprint to safety with a bruised arse!"

"The [bus] driver was a fucking loon," added a fellow veteran. "He stopped on a main road for a mass urination and when everyone was lined up along the coach the bastard drove off and at least twenty knobs were exposed to shocked drivers on the other side of the road. We were stopped just outside Cambridge by the police who searched us all and played the delaying game before taking our supply of beer. I have to say there were some serious psychos on the bus that day. By the time we got to the ground I think most of us were oiled up and then the fun began. The coach going back was minus a few boys too. Ron Atkinson stood on a box and tried to calm things down but soon retreated when he was pelted with stones. Also his Merc got smashed up in the car park. I remember seeing the Blackbird coach arriving at the ground, recognised a few people onboard and thought, 'That's some fucking gang.'"

Those scenes were not to be repeated for a while as the police and club action appeared to have an impact. Trouble still occurred but pitches were not invaded and goalposts were not broken. On the pitch, however, the club's fortunes were taking a turn for the worse. After eight consecutive seasons in Division Two they were relegated in May 1976 and their fortunes continued to decline for several years. Managers Mick Brown and Bill Asprey came and went and off the field financial troubles saw the club teeter on the edge of extinction. Into the breach came newspaper proprietor Robert Maxwell, and while he saved the club from folding, he hardly won many fans with his idea of joining up with Reading to form the Thames Valley Royals. In the 1983/84 season, Jim Smith replaced Ian Greaves as manager and the club entered the best period in its history, culminating in a Milk Cup Final win over QPR in 1986, two consecutive Championships and three seasons in the top flight.

Trouble had not been eradicated completely. Better policing and improving performances were changing the nature of the Oxford crowd and many of the areas that had once spawned the Oxford hardcore, like Cowley Road and Headington, where the ground was, were rapidly becoming student strongholds.

In February 1982, Oxford played away at Coventry in the FA Cup. Oxford lost the game 4–0 but it was the behaviour of their fans that dominated the headlines. Thirty-five people were arrested in trouble before, during and after the match, though a police spokesman said that 100-plus arrests would have been a fairer reflection of the trouble. Fighting broke out in a pub opposite the ground and continued inside when small groups of Coventry supporters found themselves in the middle of the Oxford end. The spark for the trouble was when police moved in to make fans sit down, but as there appeared too many supporters for seats available, and given their team's poor showing, many Oxford supporters appeared disinclined to cooperate.

The *Coventry Evening Telegraph* was not impressed with proceedings and described how "fighting broke out during the game, first as rival fans clashed, then as police tried to make fans in the cheapest seats sit down. The fans, many of whom could not find their way to their own seats, stood on the chairs and later stripped them of their plastic covers and hurled them on to the pitch. The soothing voice that came over the intercom no doubt meant well. It urged fans in the Sky Blue stand to sit down and watch the match. 'We are seeing some good football,' it said in the reassuring tones of a peacemaker. The effect was like pouring kerosene on to a bonfire in the hope it would be put out. Oxford were 3-0 down at the time and Coventry fans were yelling their taunts across the right angle which separated the main bulk of fans. In the Sky Blue stand nearest to the pitch there was a struggling mass of fans and police. Moments later the much-vaunted seats in the Coventry stadium were stripped of their plastic covers which began spinning like Frisbees out on to the pitch. It was the culmination of an hour of chaos in the Oxford crowd where the all-seater policy almost broke down completely."

There was worse to come for Oxford during their last away match of the season at Swindon. "Night of Shame on the Terraces of Terror," ran the headline in the *Oxford Mail*. "Smoke bombs, rocks and planks of wood were thrown as violence exploded on the terraces. Steel crush barriers were ripped up and used as battering rams and the referee fell injured as coins showered on to the pitch."

The trouble began at the start of the second half when two smoke bombs were thrown into the Oxford goalmouth from the Swindon supporters' end, and while the smoke poured on to the pitch, Swindon scored. Furious Oxford fans responded by bombarding the pitch with coins and other makeshift weapons, several hitting the referee, Eric Read. He fell to the ground clutching his head and was immediately surrounded by policemen, forcing a six minute hold up of the match. The violence grew in intensity as police rushed into the away end. While they managed to keep the warring factions apart, Oxford supporters ripped up steel barriers and used them to batter down a fence.

One young Oxford fan said, "I'm never going to an Oxford away match again. Swindon supporters got behind the Oxford stand and starting throwing rocks – and I mean rocks – into the Oxford crowd. Oxford supporters picked up the rocks and threw them at the police."

Oxford's image as a welcoming family club was being strained by the yobs. Promotion into the old Second Division in 1984 brought them up against some of the country's hooligan giants. The first home match was against Portsmouth and nineteen people were arrested after 200 Pompey got into the home end and fighting spilled on to the pitch even before a ball had been kicked. "If we have pitch invasions, that will bring the day forward when we have to have fences," said club secretary Jim Hunt.

An editorial in the local paper raised the prospect of further trouble. "Hooliganism at Oxford United's ground, before the first home game of the season had got under way, is an inauspicious beginning. Let us hope that it is a freak curtain-raiser and not a portent of things to come."

In November 1984, Oxford United hosted Leeds United in a game that was marred with violence and mass vandalism. Six-foot planks were ripped from a TV gantry and thrown on to the pitch and the home goalkeeper was struck on the head with a missile. While Oxford were cleared of responsibility for the trouble, life in the higher division was attracting attention for all the wrong reasons.

Worse was still to come. "Fans on the Rampage" was the front-page headline in the local paper following Oxford's home game against Birmingham City in March 1985. Trouble began the night before the match when between 50 and 100 Birmingham fans arrived early and clashed with locals in a city centre club. There was further trouble in surrounding streets and as police arrived to quell the violence, a police car was overturned. There was even worse trouble on the day of the game and fourteen people were arrested in what turned out to be a bad-tempered top-of-the-table match. Birmingham's three-nil victory solidified their own promotion chances while pushing Oxford from third to fourth in the League.

Police had hoped that the travelling supporters would agree to travel on specially chartered coaches from the train station to the ground but a mob of up to 400 decided to ignore this request and march through town. As locals tried to pick off stragglers, it took a huge police operation to round up the Zulus and escort them to the ground. Inside, the police had an even more difficult time as away fans spilled on to the pitch and taunted their rivals after the third goal. "Several Oxford fans came over the moat wall and ran to meet them in an ugly clash with fists and flying kicks," reported the *Oxford Mail*. "Officers who lined the front of the visitors' end to stop a further pitch invasion were pelted with coins. After the match, Birmingham fans leaving the visitors' Cuckoo Lane End smashed down fencing in the narrow passage behind the stand. They spilled into the John Radcliffe Hospital grounds where two unattended police Transit vans were overturned. Police also quelled trouble between opposing fans in the Headley Way area, close to where Birmingham City coaches were parked. There were several other disturbances across the city."

In January 1987, Oxford were drawn away at Aldershot in the FA Cup. The clubs played one another several times in the 1970s but the games had been few and far between since. "United fans on rampage," ran the front-page headline of the *Oxford Mail*. The trouble happened after about 50 Oxford fans tried to break their way into the ground. The group jumped off the train before they could be herded in by police, ran across a live line, through a goods yard and into the town centre. Several Oxford fans were injured and fourteen arrested. During the melee, the Oxford mob stormed the Next shop and stole a quantity of clothes. Ten Aldershot fans were also arrested.

The 1980s saw the birth of the South Midlands Hit Squad, Oxford's casual firm, which replaced the short-lived mob The Business. The SMHS soon attracted the interest of the local police and in the mid-Eighties became one of the first hooligan mobs to be successfully targeted, leading to the jailing of its alleged leader in May 1988. Kevin Clarke, then aged 30, was said to have led 150 soccer hooligans into a pitched battle with 80 Queens Park Rangers fans, terrifying city-centre shoppers and children. Clarke, a married man, was convicted of violent disorder at Oxford Crown Court and was jailed for three years. "I am quite satisfied you led a gang of youths into this violence," said Judge Richard May. The police told the court there had been six main incidents of soccer violence in Oxford over the previous season. Three younger men were also given custodial sentences for violent disorder.

Later that year, it was also revealed that a new system devised by Hitachi to take frames from CCTV cameras and reproduce them on a colour thermal printer was to be used by Oxford United FC to more rapidly identify and arrest hooligans. Oxford FC's CCTV operator, the unfortunately named PC Dick Cockhead, said the new system would give police "instant irrefutable evidence and the means to effect an immediate arrest".

Despite this, the SMHS survived. "The Hit Squad has a hardcore of about forty lads," said one current member, "but for a local derby our numbers have hit 200-plus. Our heyday, like most clubs, was in the Eighties and early Nineties, but we are starting to get back on form with some old faces coming back and some new ones coming through."

The FA Cup again proved to be a catalyst for trouble after Oxford were drawn at home to Chelsea in February 1994. In what the local paper reported as a "cowardly attack", at half time home supporters attacked travelling fans who were in the home end. Between 3,000 and 4,000 Chelsea fans had turned up without tickets and touts had done a thriving trade for all parts of the ground. As the fighting broke out, police were forced to use horses and dogs to bring the situation under control. Ground commander Insp Steve Wilson laid the blame firmly at the door of Oxford fans. "At half-time it appears that a lot of Oxford hard-core fans went round the back of the stand to these Chelsea supporters and launched what was a cowardly attack on, effectively, kids. There were families with some children in there. They were causing no problem whatsoever."

A long-standing Oxford rivalry has been with Brighton, with regular fights dating back to the 1980s. "It culminated in an excellent thirty-on-thirty row while a game was going on in 1996," recalled Oxford yob Tommy. "There were no OB and it went on for fucking ages."

Another rivalry is with Oldham after a particular violent attack in the

1990s. "They stopped off with Hibs one night and flare gunned one of ours in the head from five yards," said Tommy. "Any further and the flare would have gathered speed and could have killed him. It transpires it was a Hibs lad showing off, but we hunted Oldham at every England game afterwards. We bumped into them at Rome in 1997, they were on the back foot and called on Newcastle, Pompey and Northampton in the pub to bail them out."

Travelling abroad with England has long been a feature of the Oxford firm. There were 45 Oxford in Dublin in 1995 and in Rome in 1997, and 60 went to the Euro '96 clash with Scotland in London. "We've had great battles with England home and away," said Tommy. "We've taken small mobs to Turkey twice, Dublin twice, Norway, Poland, France, Glasgow, Rotterdam, as well as the World Cups and Euros, and made lots of good acquaintances, mainly with Mansfield, Bristol City and Hull."

The Millennium saw an upsurge in violence with a rise in the number of people willing to get involved in trouble. The South Midland Hit Squad was joined by the Oxford Youth Outfit. In October 2000 there was serious disorder before Oxford's away match at Reading. Two home supporters were rushed to hospital after an Oxford attack in the town centre. The incident was the culmination of several years of growing frustration with the ability of the police to prevent disorder at Oxford and Reading matches.

"Throughout the late 1990s home and away both clubs turned out decent crews," said Tommy. "But a few scuffles apart, Plod always had it sewn up, so we knew we had to do something special to get to them. We put 70 on the train, which Plod thought was our lot, but another 50 went by road, the back way in. Plod even managed to split up our 50, but ten escaped. They holed up in a back street pub and a few more left the ground to join us, giving us sixteen in total. We had been on the phone from 10am, but they did not believe that we had brought the 50 by road and said we were shit coming by train straight into Plod's arms. They didn't believe that we were at the other end of their town centre.

"This mug kept giving it the, 'I'm gonna cut you up' one. I was saying 'well come down and it's on a plate for you,' but he just kept up the abuse. We were being led about by one of our very game loons from Henley, which is half way between Oxford and Reading, and he took us to one of their pubs. We ran straight in but there was only a few of them so we threw a few things and did one before Plod arrived. About 4.15, three of our sixteen were down the road from the pub when suddenly 25 Reading appeared out of the dark and chased them to where we were. At last, a dark back street, no coppers and 25 Reading with some of their known faces at the pointed end.

"Out we went, leaving pool cues and balls behind. A couple took bottles but in the main it was a toe to toe. Our sixteen were almost all main faces, so even though they were a game bunch it was no surprise when we started to get the better of them. Two of them were down and being vultured, the rest of them had that look, turned and literally ran for their lives. We were hot on their heels, we did not want to let this one go easily and the adrenalin was motoring, but so were they. They hurdled barriers across a very busy road faster than Colin Jackson and with complete disregard for the cars. These boys were fucking scared. Eventually we gave up and started chanting 'Run run run run … Reading' as they became smaller figures in the distance, apart from the two they had left for dead in the street. We split up and headed for home, knowing that we had settled the score. I very much doubt if an occasion like that will happen again, our intelligence OB were fucking gutted."

There was further trouble only a few weeks later, this time at an FA Cup game away at Macclesfield. "Oxford supporters held up the game for about five minutes when they pulled the net down from one of the goals," noted an NCIS report. "At the end of the match around 40 Oxford supporters left the train at Stoke. They then went to the buffet at the railway station where they were attacked by a group of around 50 Stoke supporters. The buffet was seriously damaged and a number of Oxford supporters were assaulted. A British Transport Police officer was injured during the disorder."

It was becoming a very violent season. In late February, a home game against Millwall saw a mob of 60 Oxford, who had not gone to the game, attempt to reach the train station to ambush the away fans as they returned. The police were at full stretch to contain the group, but some slipped the police cordon and clashed with Millwall.

A fortnight later there was more trouble, this time with the visit of Swindon. Rival groups clashed outside a pub, which was then closed and the away mob were escorted by police to the ground. An NCIS report continued, "During the game, when Swindon scored their opening goal in the first half, Oxford supporters reacted angrily towards a Swindon player, who, they alleged, gestured towards them. When Oxford had a second player sent off the London Road crowd began throwing bottles and coins at the Swindon goalkeeper. This was brought to the attention of the referee who consulted with the police and stewards before restarting the match. About ten minutes later the incident re-occurred with more bottles and coins being thrown by Oxford fans. Swindon fans at the Cuckoo Lane End of the ground copied this action. The referee at this point consulted with the police and stewards and halted the game for five minutes until it had stopped.

"After the match, two arrests took place at the rear of the London Road stand for incidents that occurred during the match. Officers required assistance during these arrests due to the nature of the home crowd in the area.

Batons were drawn to move back a group of about 40 home fans. Oxford supporters at a public house had exited and were making their way down London Road towards the bus stops for the city. Three Swindon players who were parked at this pub needed to be moved on by police as they were targeted by Oxford fans.

"About 70 Oxford supporters ran down Park End Street towards the station. Officers placed a cordon across the road and this displaced the group into Hythe Bridge Street. Officers drew batons in an attempt to push the group away from the station area. Some of the group ran down a towpath that exits near to the station but they did not get near enough to the station to cause any problems. Swindon supporters were placed without incident on to the train and left the area. A small number of Swindon supporters were placed on a later train to Swindon via Reading after hiding in the railway station toilets."

Recently, better policing and the move to a new out-of-town stadium has reduced the opportunities for hooligans to cause trouble, but they have not completely eradicated the problem. In January 2002, Oxford and Swindon hooligans clashed at Banbury railway station and the same year there was serious violence at the home game against Exeter. In February 2004, the police issued images of people they claimed were responsible for disorder at Oxford's game against Reading.

And in July 2004, a planned pre-season friendly at Havant & Waterlooville was cancelled after police received intelligence that 20-40 United supporters had arranged with the same number of Portsmouth fans to meet at Havant's ground for a fight.

The Noughties also saw the emergence of a new gang, the Oxford Youth Outfit, one of whose leaders was banned from the Kassam Stadium after disorder at an away fixture at Bristol Rovers. In November 2006, a group of young Oxford fans were involved in a fight when they played Chester City in a League Two match in November 2004. The brawl, in a wine bar, spilled into the street and was caught on CCTV. Eleven Oxford fans were later banned from attending matches, while four others were acquitted at Chester Crown Court after denying affray.

In July 2007, a football fan described as a "top dog" in the South Midlands Hit Squad was handed the longest ever banning order in Oxfordshire. Patrick Vigilante, then aged 40, of Witney, was said by police to be one of the orchestrators of the gang. A court banned him from attending any United or England match for four years after police said they had been aware of his role in the local hooligan movement since the early 1990s. Vigilante had been arrested after trouble between about 100 United and York City fans in September 2006, when children and residents were forced to run for cover after bottles were hurled, insults traded and punches thrown in Blackbird Leys [see *York City*].

DC Huw James, Oxford's football intelligence officer, said, "He has involved himself in football hooliganism now for fifteen or twenty years. He has built up an association with a number of other hooligans and within that group he has a certain status which enables him to organise or be involved in football disorder." Dc James added there were up to 50 fans considered to be in the group. "Vigilante has an influence in Oxford's risk group and if he is there on a given day it will add an extra element to that risk," he said. "In the supporters' risk group a lot of them are, by association, or aspire to be, in the South Midlands Hit Squad, but then deny it exists."

Vigilante was convicted at Oxford Magistrates' Court of a public order offence and given the four-year ban. By then, five others from Oxford United had been convicted following the trouble. Vigilante, the director of a building firm, denied he was a leading hooligan. "Sure, I have been in trouble in the past, but as far as being one of the organisers of football violence, that is ridiculous," he told the *Oxford Mail*. "I find it hard to believe police say this stuff with no evidence. Which fights, where and when do I organise them? If organising trouble was my day job I would be out of work because there hasn't been any trouble for ages."

Vigilante said he was on the fringes of the trouble against York after walking past the two rival gangs on the way to the match, but was spotted by police because of his reputation. He also denied the South Midlands Hit Squad existed. "I've never been a member of any firm. I laugh about it now, but when you read about it in the papers it affects my children, my wife and my life. I don't get into trouble, I pay my taxes and go to work. I can't believe I'm supposed to be this person who I am reading about. Nine times out of ten on a Saturday afternoon I'm outside in my garden or playing golf, so I must be organising it from miles away."

However, the court heard his football violence convictions included: 1991, a 12-month ban for a public order offence at a match; 1994, fined for fighting with Chelsea fans after an FA Cup tie; 1996, fined for threatening a rival supporter; 1997, banned from matches for 18 months; 1999, admitted causing actual bodily harm to a Stockport County fan; 1999: banned from Premiership and Football League games for two years; 2000, fined £5,000 after being convicted of fighting rival supporters when England played Scotland.

Further reading: *Rules of Disorder*, Peter Marsh, Elizabeth Rosser and Rom Harre (Routledge)

P

PETERBOROUGH UNITED

Ground: London Road
Firms: Peterborough Terrace Squad, Saturday Service, Under 5s, Blue
  Division
Rivals: Northampton, Cambridge

The *Northampton Town* entry in this volume opens with what was arguably
one of the biggest lower league battles of the 1970s: Northampton v.
Peterborough in April 1974. Hundreds of Northampton fans launched a
ferocious attack on Posh fans in what the local paper dubbed "The Battle
of Abington Park" and 44 people were arrested. It is fitting to start the
history of hooliganism at Peterborough at that point too. While most of
the Posh troublemakers admit that they were run ragged after the match,
they are quick to insist that their bitter rivals did not have it all their own
way.

"We were near the top," recalled one Peterborough old-timer on an
Internet forum. "They were just below us. The Posh boys were out in force
yet again but this time some had gone over the night before and stayed in a
B&B. By 10.30am Posh were everywhere in the town centre, we had been
told that the Cobblers were going to sort us this year, however, as per usual
so far it was all mouth. Again, we did the business in the town centre. We
were there, they weren't. We eventually got a police escort to the ground
where we found it far too easy to give them the slip. It had been agreed that
we would meet up at 2pm outside a used car garage just up the road from
the ground as it was our intention to have a pop at the infamous County
Tavern.

"Like flies converging on a piece of dead meat, 30 of us turned up virtually at once and had a quiet walk to the County Tavern so they didn't know
we were about. One of ours from Whittlesey threw a chair into the bar. I
remember a mate of mine from Deeping saying, 'Here we go,' and the
mayhem only lasted for about two minutes but it was manic.

"As we left to find our way to the Kop, Boro came cascading down from the home end, yet again we had taken the mighty Hotel End. In we went, in ones and twos. It was full with Posh giving various accounts of the day's fun. At 2.40 all hell let loose, the word went up that a few Cobblers were gaining entrance to the ground via the cricket side. There must have been 1,000 and we got smacked up big time. A few of us refused to run. Most of the lads who had some sense had long gone, jumped the fence into the enclosure. There were only about 50 of us left. We had no alternative but to jump the fence, but not before we gave Cobblers the big one! At the front of the terrace a few black guys were throwing bottles at us. The police had lost it."

By the early Seventies, games between the two were regular flashpoints. In the 1972/73 season, a mob of 300 Peterborough caused trouble in Northampton before the game and took the Hotel End. Fortunately, contrasting footballing fortunes meant the next game between the two teams after the infamous 1974 clash was not for several seasons. The police were on high alert for the game at Peterborough and proudly showed the Press their Polaroid camera, which they claimed would help them avoid identification mix-ups. The derby resulted in only two arrests despite more than 1,000 Northampton fans travelling in 16 coaches for the game.

Another local rivalry which was often accompanied by trouble was Peterborough v. Cambridge. Another Peterborough fan recounted one trip to the University city in the mid-Seventies. "Coaches containing Boro lads arrived in Cambridge mid-afternoon for what was to be an evening kick-off. Smaller numbers of about 100 split up into two groups and had some fun at around 5.30pm in Cambridge city centre with a group of skins who were soon dispatched.

"We met up with another Boro mob with numbers now at about 300. We walked to the ground with a pub opposite getting smashed to bits. We then entered the Abbey Stadium, filtering into Cambridge's Newmarket Road End in twos and threes where we congregated near to where (we thought) the Cambridge lads were standing.

"When our numbers were at thirty-to-forty, one Peterborough lad said, 'OK then, let's do 'em now before we get sussed.' We all waded in and kicked it off with what we thought was Cambridge's main mob, but after about thirty seconds of manic fighting we realised that we were having it with other Boro lads in the Cambridge end."

There was trouble at both games in the 1977-78 season. Five police were hurt when Cambridge travelled to Peterborough on November 7, 1977, however, according to the local newspaper, most of the fighting took place between Cambridge fans themselves. Still, the twenty arrests made sent shockwaves through the club and the board. The Peterborough manager and club secretary met a few days later to discuss the trouble and a letter calling for tougher action against soccer thugs was sent to Sports Minister Denis Howell. The author was Dr Brian Mawhinney, prospective Tory candidate for the city, who happened to have presented the match ball on the day of the game. He suggested to the minister that "spartan" detention camps should be formed to deal with hooligans. "The time has come to take strong action," he wrote. "There should be bigger fines for these hooligans."

Initially, he was supported by Posh manager John Barnwell. However, a few days later he distanced himself from Mawhinney, saying that there was a danger of scaring away decent fans by talking up the trouble. "I personally feel that he is making himself an expert after only one match. I would like to know just how often he comes. I don't think it helps when people from the outside look at a 'one-off' and make snap judgements." Barnwell denied trying to gloss over the events and said that outbreaks of violence were very rare at London Road.

Concern over a repeat of "the ugly scenes" meant a large police operation was in place for the return fixture. While there was some bottle throwing and "fence bashing" there was no significant disorder between the two sets of fans and there were only seven arrests.

When Peterborough next visited Cambridge, in March 1984, the police commended both sets of supporters for their behaviour. Given that hooliganism was probably then at its height, the police feared the worst, not least because only a few weeks before a Chelsea fan had almost died in serious disorder in Cambridge. The normal match day police numbers had been swelled from 40 to 250 but with the leadership of the Cambridge firm awaiting trial for the Chelsea incident, perhaps there was simply no-one for Peterborough to fight. "We planned to keep thugs under control and the only trouble was very quickly nipped in the bud," said one senior police officer.

The first organised firms at Peterborough were the Peterborough Terrace Squad, the Saturday Service and the Under 5s, although the latter two names are more closely associated with Motherwell and West Ham respectively. "Legendary lads include several head-cases, now retired, from the Westwood area of Peterborough who even had a mention in a book following the exploits of England lads at the World Cup in Spain in 1982," said one Posh lad who wished to remain anonymous. "Others include several well-respected lads who have turned out for Boro but have made their name at clubs such as Chelsea and Rangers. Several older lads still running with Boro are looked up to by many of the younger element as role models.

"In the Seventies Posh had the biggest numbers of the Peterborough, Cambridge, and Northampton triangle, with turnouts of anything up to 300 for derby games. During the Eighties and Nineties numbers varied from fifty to 150, but numbers declined at the turn of the century, mostly due to banning orders."

Clashes with other clubs included a nasty encounter in the early Eighties during a visit from Darlington, who had one of the bigger mobs in the lower divisions. There was serious disorder in Peterborough city centre before the game and an attempted assault on the home kop during the match which culminated in a pitch invasion by both sets of hooligans. "As they walked toward the away end, the Stan Ground Mob decide to have a pop," recalled Pete, a veteran Posh hooligan. "A milk crate in some Darlo's gob started a fracas on the pitch, then the Enclosure hardcore jumped on to the pitch to lend a hand to sort them out well proper.

"Posh also took a mob to Wigan in 1982 where despite being heavily outnumbered they gained massive respect from Wigan lads of that time for having a good go at them down their High Street. Twenty Boro lads went to Wigan on the train and got there shortly before 11am. We had a few beers in the first boozer we came to, then went down the road. Some of their boys were shadowing us, so we steamed into them and then went to the next pub, which was in the middle of a road. One of our lads went to the bookie's and came back to say that we were in deep shit as there was about 100 Wigan lads at each end of the road. I picked up two bar stools and took them into the bogs, where we pulled off the legs. I was wearing a long leather coat and managed to hide one of the legs inside it.

"We rounded up all the boys at the door and got the landlord to open it for us. He said that when the last one was out he would lock up, so we left the pub. Ten of us went one way and ten the other way down the street and Wigan came at us from both ends. One Wigan lad was running straight at me. When he got about ten feet away, out came the stool leg and he began putting on the brakes. He couldn't stop in time so I said, 'Tough shit,' and whacked him around the head. It then went ballistic. We smacked every one that came at us and we were fighting for fifteen minutes before the Old Bill got there. By this time, every one of us was covered in cuts and bruises. The police rounded us all up and escorted us to the Ground with the Wigan lads walking on the other side of the road. Wigan stopped and all together applauded us as if to say, 'Fair play, boys.' What a great feeling that was."

In 1984, fighting in the crowd held up Peterborough's FA Cup tie against Dagenham for five minutes. The FA Cup proved to be a catalyst for further trouble in the 1990s. Peterborough's home tie against Spurs in

January 1994 was the club's biggest match for years. A capacity 19,169 crowd packed into the Ground. There was equal excitement, though of a different kind, amongst the Blue Division, and dozens were out early doors to greet their Premiership Rivals. There was little trouble before the game but serious violence erupted afterwards as rival gangs clashed in the city centre. A WPc was hurt after she was hit by a dustbin and a Spurs fan suffered a broken leg. The trouble lasted well into the evening, with reports of disorder at pubs more than three hours after the end of the match. Fifteen people were arrested, though six were released without charge. The four Posh fans charged were all in their twenties while the five Spurs fans ranged from 29 to 43.

Peterborough almost pulled off a shock win but the London club equalised with only four minutes remaining. Thousands travelled to White Hart Lane for the replay, which Spurs sneaked through by a single goal, but all those charged from the first match were barred.

During the 1990s the numerous clashes between Peterborough and Stoke left a lasting impression on the Potteries team's Naughty Forty. "Peterborough are very well respected by Stoke as a home firm," said the N40's Mark "Jasper" Chester. "I have never known them to travel very well but in the early 1990s we had it with them on three occasions and they stood and fought every time. We went there with huge numbers at one game and they could not get anywhere near us but a few of us who were on bans had to get off from the ground and walked into a very decent mob of about twenty Peterborough who were bang into it. They were good lads as well, when the police showed up they got us out of the place without a second thought."

There was further trouble at another FA Cup tie, this time with the visit of Wrexham in January 1997. "Fans arrested after cup match trouble," reported one local paper. "Extra police had to be drafted in during Peterborough United's FA Cup match after a series of pitch invasions by away fans. Officers arrested 27 people, the majority Wrexham supporters." The first pitch invasion came after Wrexham's equaliser. Some of their fans jumped over the advertising boards in an attempt to get at their rivals. Sixteen were arrested for being on the pitch and others for public order and actual bodily harm offences. "We were aware of the likelihood of possible problems, but did not anticipate the extent of the trouble which ensued," noted Inspector Paul Phillipson, one of the match commanders. "We don't usually get pitch invasions."

It seemed that the police had turned the corner at Peterborough. Their hooligan mob was certainly less active than in the past and fewer opposing teams were bringing troublemakers in any great number. In November

1998 a home game against Cambridge passed off relatively peacefully with only six arrests which, given the rivalry such a fixture had in the past, was considered a good day by police.

While trouble-free games were becoming the norm there was the odd exception. One such match was against Cambridge in March 2001 where ten people were arrested during trouble before, during and after the game. A crowd of 10,000 packed the ground to watch Posh hammer their rivals four-one and ease their own relegation fears. The arrested men, aged from 24 to 39, were picked up for a variety of offences including pitch invasion and throwing missiles.

"A minute before kick-off, Posh and Cambridge fans tried to come together and were shouting abuse and taunting each other, but the police kept them apart," said an eye-witness at the game. "Then, five minutes into the game, some Posh fans were winding up the Cambridge fans. They were moved on by police, who, I think, handled it well."

Peterborough's chairman, Peter Boizot, said, "I thought we had built up a friendly crowd, and I would be disappointed if any of our fans were involved in any trouble. I'd like to see fewer police at football matches and a friendly crowd, so it is disappointing when there are arrests."

These arrests coincided with an upsurge in trouble involving Peterborough fans. During the 2000/01 season, 49 Posh fans were arrested, with only Millwall, Swansea, Bristol City and Stoke City having more. The figure probably exaggerated the level of trouble at the club and when 144 Peterborough fans travelled to Cardiff mid-way through the following season, there was more than a little apprehension. It came only a week after Cardiff City's highly publicised FA Cup match at home to Leeds United, and TV images of pitch invasions, contorted faces and menacing jibes at their opponents made the Welsh capital an inhospitable place to visit.

"En route, some Peterborough fans had admitted to feeling nervous about visiting this supposed cauldron of hate," noted *The Observer*'s sports correspondent Denis Campbell, who travelled on the one supporters' coach. "One said the trip to Cardiff was the one he looked for first, and dreaded most, when the fixtures came out. Fortunately, heavy policing, including scores of police officers, horses and dogs, ensured yesterday passed peacefully despite Peterborough's two-nil win."

"These days things have started to look up, with several old faces coming out of retirement and a fresh youth element turning out," said Pete. "Numbers have risen to a reasonable forty to fifty for home games and anything up to 200 for the big games, such as the away cup ties at Coventry and Forest and Lincoln away in the League. For Cambridge away in the late Nineties, we had a good 200, and recently for Coventry and

Forest away in the Cup we turned out with a decent 100-odd lads. In 2000 we had a good mob out for Millwall at home."

The resurgence of hooliganism at Peterborough coincided with the birth of the Blue Division. "The Blue Division is an adaptation of Joy Division and has been in use since 2001," said another member of the gang. "PTS and SS are self explanatory, and the Under 5s were a youth mob from the late Nineties who eventually earned their stripes to form the Blue Division with several older heads. These days a new set of young ones are looking to gain recognition and are known as the Peterborough Youth Outfit."

Forty-five Peterborough hooligans boarded a coach for their team's first home match of the 2002/03 season away at Luton. Conscious that the old bill would be keeping a look-out for them, the coach went to Bedford where, after a quick drink, they caught the local service into Luton. To their surprise, there was no police welcoming committee and before long there was a brief but nasty clash with the local gang. Bricks, broom handles and wood were just some of the makeshift weapons flying around the street. The police quickly broke up the trouble and the Peterborough group were escorted to a nearby pub where they proceeded to help themselves to drinks from behind the bar. For some strange reason the police were never fully on top of the situation and on their way to the ground another clash occurred with Luton. This time a bookcase, holding dozens of paperbacks, was used as a weapon, much to the horror of the bookshop owner.

In more recent seasons, Peterborough have developed a rivalry with Notts Forest, a mob who even Blue Division hooligans admit are normally out of their league. The rivalry began with a pre-season friendly match in 2001. There were several clashes around town that day but, as the area was covered with extensive CCTV, the police had a relatively easy job of identifying and prosecuting the culprits. Of the 40 Peterborough fans currently on football banning orders, 18 were banned after this game, of which 14 were imprisoned.

In February 2003, Peterborough hooligans returning from a match at Chesterfield decided to stop off in Nottingham and notified the locals. "Forest lads quickly sent a firm out to confront the Peterborough lot at a pub next to the train station," recalled one Posh lad. "Ten Forest got into the pub but doormen quickly sensed trouble and locked the doors and bolted the windows before the Forest lads outside, including a few Mansfield, attempted to smash the windows and kick in the doors, with Peterborough inside doing the same. Police arrived on the scene and forced Peterborough out of the pub. A few scuffles took place and Peterborough were taken to the station and shoved on the next train out of Notts."

"Ten of us got in the pub and the doorman locked the doors," recalled one Forest lad, "leaving us in there with twenty Boro, mostly older lads who looked mean as fuck. Cue a big stand-off in the pub with everyone wary of the cameras all over. It could have got a bit hairy but fair play to Peterborough for leaving it, as we were outnumbered. Outside there were a few more Forest who were joined by some older Mansfield. Thinking we were gonna get battered in the pub they started putting the windows in and kicking the doors. The Old Bill arrived and took the Boro lads to the train station, where apparently they ran at the few Palace who had been waiting for us."

Asked what they think of the boys from the Posh, Peterborough's rivals give a mixed response. "Things have been frustrating with them over the last few years," said a Northampton hooligan. "We are always showing there and getting OB on top. The closest we had was three years ago when they came here by coach and we arranged to meet them twenty miles away an hour after the game. We went there, ran at each other but the police came from everywhere and I ended up on a conspiracy charge. We went there eighty-strong five years ago and took the piss, bowled round all day and did as we pleased. We had a proper toe-to-toe on the bridge by the ground, ten on ten, and smashed them to bits. Then we marched round their town for a good hour and fifteen of us went into about forty of them and stood and did well until our friends in blue turned up. They turned up forty-strong for a mid-week LDV game when none of us were out and that's the only result they claim in fifteen years."

This view is predictably not shared by the Peterborough lads. "The way I see it, Boro and the Cobblers have always been pretty even over the years," wrote one hooligan on the Internet. "The Blues came out on top after a couple of notorious battles in the 1970s, including Posh lads taking their Hotel End back in 1974. The Cobblers bought a good mob up here back in 2000 and it went off big style in Cathedral Square. Despite all the rivalry there has always been a mutual respect between us two, but Boro are edging away now."

The most recent attempted clash between the two firms occurred in January 2003. Coming soon after the away trip to Luton, rumours about a big Peterborough turnout had been circulating for a while but few Northampton believed it and their turnout reflected this. Up to 40 Peterborough travelled to Milton Keynes on a coach and then took the local train into Northampton. However, they quickly ran into the local police and were given a large escort to the ground and back again after the match. Calls were made and Peterborough promised to wait in Milton Keynes for their opponents. About twenty Northampton made the journey down, but it appeared that the police were fully aware of what was occurring and were there in force to escort both mobs back to their respective towns.

Lincoln City are another mob who have few kind words to say about the Peterborough of today, though they accept that this has not always been the case. "Peterborough used to have a really good set of lads in the Eighties but when we went there a few years back they only had about forty out and we took 150 on the train, so it was a bit of a waste," said one. "That same season they came to us with about forty lads but not that much happened, just the odd skirmish here and there."

Bristol City, however, have been more complimentary. They took a very large mob to Peterborough several seasons ago and while the locals were heavily outnumbered they put up a stand outside the Verve pub, which earned them some respect from the City boys. "I think it was lucky for us the police turned up within seconds or else we would have taken a pasting," admitted one Peterborough lad.

PLYMOUTH ARGYLE

Ground: Home Park.
Firms: A38 Crew, The Central Element, Plymouth Youth Firm, Plymouth Youth Element
Rivals: Exeter City, Cardiff, Bristol City, Bristol Rovers, Burnley, QPR and Luton
Police operations: Ewood

With its huge naval base and dockyards, its sailors, soldiers and the marines, Plymouth is not unaccustomed to violence. It is no surprise that newspapers have been reporting soccer violence in the city as far back as Boxing Day 1967. In January 1968, the Football Association wrote to the club ordering it to post notices around the ground demanding that the pitch invasion that held up the Yuletide home game against QPR for six minutes was not repeated. The referee noted in his match report that fans "adopted an aggressive attitude to him" after he awarded Rangers a penalty. The FA warned of "serious consequences, which could result from a reoccurrence of misconduct".

An insight into Plymouth's emerging hooligan problem came in a court case involving several young men in October 1972, relating to a home game against Bristol Rovers the previous season. Eleven Plymouth fans were convicted of attacking a small group of away supporters, most for riotous assembly and assault. Eight were sentenced to three months in a detention centre, two 16-year-olds were each fined £40, with their parents ordered to pay the fines, and one 13-year-old boy was given a conditional discharge. The oldest of the group was just 19 and the court identified the ringleader as a 17-year-old mill boy who had already amassed eight previous convictions.

"What happened was a disgrace to this city," said Mr. Justice Mais, passing sentence. "You terrorised many citizens, and you put fear into Bristol Rovers supporters. You were a rabble and many of you behaved like wild animals. Many of you are cowards. Some of you kicked boys who were already down and someone kicked a girl. Violence is all too prevalent in Plymouth and I have been made aware of it since I have been sitting here. This conduct has got to stop." The judge also had praise for the three police officers who led the case. "If people are thrown out of the ground for their behaviour, their names and addresses are taken by the police and sent to Argyle, who in turn send them a letter saying that they are not welcome on the ground," he added.

So as well as having one of the first active "youth" firms in the country, Argyle also can claim to have the first hooligan intelligence force in the country, although the sending of a letter saying that you are not welcome back was hardly going to stop the "hardcore" from returning to the Home Park hot spots.

The early Plymouth mob, active in the 1970s, was called the A38 Crew after the main trunk road that passed the ground. In August 1973, ten fans were arrested when Plymouth played Stoke, and the following April, 14 were arrested after further clashes in the city centre. The trouble at Home Park became serious enough for the club to erect fencing inside the ground.

In the book *Armed For The Match*, Chelsea hooligan leader Steve Hickmott recalled a visit to Plymouth in the 1976/77 season. Chelsea ran the home end but outside a huge reception committee was waiting and mass brawling broke out all around until the police loosed their dogs to restore order.

During the early 1980s, Plymouth faced a torrid time at the hands of Portsmouth, both on and off the pitch. Both might have been rowdy naval ports but Plymouth has never been able to emulate the hooligan exploits of its coastal neighbour. "Pompey Animals Caged" ran a newspaper headline after one visit from Portsmouth in March 1981. "Honours may elude Pompey this season, but according to the Plymouth police, their fans retained one title, they are the worst behaved supporters in the land," read the article. "Their unruly behaviour at Plymouth on Saturday frightened locals and shocked West Country police. We've branded them animals. They now have the worst reputation in the country and, according to a senior police officer on duty at Home Park, Portsmouth fans are 100 times worse than the once-feared Manchester United."

Two years later, Portsmouth travelled to Plymouth needing a win to clinch the Third Division title. More than 10,000 Pompey fans made the trip and simply took over the ground. They had been allocated both ends behind the goals and one side of the stands but even this was not enough for the numerous mobs that made up the 6.57 Crew. Their focus was Plymouth's home end, a large open terrace along one side of the pitch. "We got in there," remembered one 6.57 veteran. "About twenty-five of us ran straight into Plymouth, fighting, and once we were in their end, Plymouth all turned round. They had a good go for a bit and came charging at us, there were various scuffles and it was quite amusing to see the different mobs of Pompey going into the Plymouth terrace to have a crack at them. At one stage Plymouth were all huddled at the back of their main terrace."

The Central Element (TCE) was formed in the mid-Eighties when a younger generation came on the scene, replacing the older A38 Crew. Their name came from the Central Park, a large open area which visiting fans are forced to walk through on their way to the ground. "The Central Element" was once famously spray-painted at the entrance to the park as a warning to away fans. The mob has kept the name to today, though a new group emerged in 2002 called the Plymouth Youth Element.

The Central Element's heyday was in the Eighties. In 1984, they surprised Burnley by turning up there, running off a couple of local mobs and claiming the "result" for the day. A home game against Leeds in 1986 saw a mob of 300-400 mobilised. Over 500 turned out for a play-off final at Wembley, but this game was marred by fighting within the Plymouth crew. Numbers gradually dropped but at least 350 made the short trip to Exeter in 1993 and 250 went to Cardiff a couple of seasons later. In 2002, Plymouth still managed to raise 250 lads for a top-of-the-table clash at Luton, and 150 went to QPR a season later. However, the Central Element hardcore remains a steady 100, with the Youth Element another 40.

"Back in the early days, we always used to meet in the Noah's Ark pub in the city centre", remembered one Plymouth lad. "It was in a prime location for any visiting mob but the arrival of CCTV cameras across the city in 1988 ended the days of patrolling the city centre in mobs of fifty or more looking for away fans."

Changing youth culture took its toll in the early Nineties as many of the original Central Element switched focus to the emerging rave scene. As was the case in many cities, drugs took precedence over football and the hooligan scene virtually died. This coincided with declining fortunes of the team following relegation in 1992 into the old Third Division. But by the mid-Nineties, fortunes were on the up again, as the rave scene quietened and some of the older lads returned to football at the same time as a new generation also emerged. The resurgence was aided by numerous derby games against Exeter, Bristol City and Cardiff. The latter two obviously were their bigger opponents but Exeter was Plymouth's real derby, so the lads rarely missed an opportunity to take liberties. The fights were often one-sided but the very nature of derbies meant that Exeter would regularly put up resistance.

Any game involving Plymouth and Exeter would see a large police operation and in recent years it has been an all-ticket affair. Exeter's hooligans would rarely go in force to Plymouth but Argyle would always go up in large numbers. In 1987, Plymouth fans staged repeated charges against Exeter fans following their 1–0 away victory, and more recently police made 24 arrests after trouble erupted before the local derby. Further bother was averted after police ejected some Plymouth fans who had entered the Exeter end nearly an hour before kick-off to be met by the home mob already there. Another recent match saw 19 arrested after 200 Plymouth got into the Exeter end. Police moved in to separate the warring firms, but at the final whistle 100 Plymouth swarmed onto the pitch to celebrate their team's 3–2 victory and once again police had to intervene after the Plymouth crowd began moving towards the Cowshed to taunt and goad home fans.

As Plymouth languished in the lower divisions during the Nineties, their most eagerly awaited fixture was against Cardiff. But, as in many bitter rivalries over the years, some of their leading players became friends. In February 1994, a small but tight mob of 33 Cardiff travelled to the South West and clashed with a much bigger mob of Plymouth outside the Britannia pub in Milehouse, near the ground. "Outnumbered three to one, we had Plymouth on the run," remembered Cardiff hooligan Tony Rivers in his book *Soul Crew*. "A couple of our boys got nicked and the police watched in wonder as we started clapping each other, shaking each other's hands and hugging. Later Plymouth said it was the gamest little firm they had ever seen." As a mark of respect, ten Plymouth lads waited outside the court hearing the Cardiff lads' case and afterwards went together for a drink.

The following season, Cardiff came again and as before headed straight for the Britannia, but this time the police were waiting to intercept and arrest the Welshmen. While there was to be no trouble, it did re-affirm the antagonism between the two firms. Any remaining doubts were eradicated the following season when a large group of Plymouth jumped eight Cardiff, including "Neath Punk", a prominent Soul Crew face. When Plymouth turned up in the Welsh capital later in the same season, the Soul Crew were only too willing to accept the challenge. "Everyone wanted this badly for Neath Punk", remembered Rivers. "As we got near the pub a few Plymouth spotted us. They threw some bottles as we sprinted towards them, and I do mean sprinted. About twenty-five of them were outside and started to back off straight away. Needless to say Neath Punk was right at the front gaining revenge. Maybe ten Plymouth were bloodied, with two lying unconscious as we made our way back to the pub. Six Plymouth later had to be taken to hospital."

After the game, Plymouth attacked a Cardiff pub. News of the incident quickly spread and Cardiff regrouped and assaulted Plymouth as they were leaving in their mini-buses. Every window was put through and Plymouth were even forced to drive up a street the wrong way. A week later, some Cardiff at Maine Road for an Oasis gig had a drink with three Plymouth, who said it was the worst time they had ever had.

The rave scene probably did more to quell hooliganism than the Popplewell Report, heavy fines and the threat of the birch all put together. But it was never dead and buried, and while many popped pills, attended love-ins and swapped strong lager for chilled water, some of the faithful stayed loyal to the Central Element ethos. The FA Cup was always a hooligan magnet and brought Plymouth into contact with bigger teams. A game at Nottingham Forest saw 80 make the journey and catch the Forest Executive Crew unaware. Those numbers were rare though – Plymouth were never the greatest travellers – and the following tale from one of their lads highlights how difficult it was to protect their reputation once people had discovered "disco biscuits" and "doves".

On the last Saturday of November, 1996, Plymouth played at home to Burnley. This had long been a grudge game, on and off the pitch. Burnley had relegated the Devon side on one occasion and prevented them from reaching a Wembley play-off final on another. Mike, a Central Element veteran, said, "I will always remember this one. It was never going to make *News At Ten* but it was lively and went on long into the night. It was a cold day and on leaving the Britannia pub we walked up to the ground as usual at about ten to three and came across three Burnley lads. A few words were exchanged but it secured the fact that they knew we were out and we knew that they were down. When I say we were out, we were only about fifteen strong, as it was during that lull period that all clubs get. The football was crap and off the field it was probably during the change of generations where the older lads have stopped or are certainly not as active as they had been.

"The game was a classic nil-nil draw, played in front of 6,500 passionate spectators. We decided to leave about ten minutes early. I was right up for it, more so than my mates, but for the life of me I can't remember why. We made our way to the end of the car park, which separates the ground from the main road. Through the car park runs a lane with two high hedges that separate it from a football pitch. Five of us milled about at the end of the lane and noticed two groups of about ten lads, walking towards us. One of the groups lashed out at some younger lads on the football field but when we fronted them up they disappeared. The second group stayed aloof and just disappeared, then the police turned up and the situation calmed down.

"The other four in our group seemed content with that, but not me. I just went off on one and stormed off up the street. Ahead of me, by a bank on one side of a dual carriageway, I could see a group of Burnley strutting around, so I went back to our small group and remonstrated that we catch them up. This we did, and before the Burnley group knew anything we steamed straight into them. As we were fighting, we edged closer to the road until it spilled across the four lanes to the opposite bank. Anyway, the fight fizzled out and one of the Burnley lads told us that they were staying down for the night and drinking in the Barbican area of the city centre. They told us that they were meeting some others and were more than happy to meet at nine that evening to continue the fight. That was fine by us, so we agreed to meet later. We named a pub and a deal was clinched.

"Our group split up and we agreed to meet again a short distance from where we had agreed to meet Burnley. We all went off to find some more decent lads. I actually went for a meal with my missus but told her that I had to be gone by 8.15pm and to her credit she dropped me off!

"By 8.45pm, we realised that we were at full strength, with a massive seven lads! As we drank up and began to file out of the pub, we were clocked by a Burnley lad walking past, who scuttled back to their pub to alert them. There was no way back now, as twenty-five Burnley poured out of the pub, throwing stools, pint glasses, bottles, ashtrays, all to the air of that fucking annoying 'Soo, Soo, Suicide' chant.

"We fronted them off for a good few seconds as objects rained down on us. One of ours was caught full on by a pint glass and his face turned claret. As objects continued to fall around us, we decided to charge into them. The Barbican on a Saturday is normally full of people enjoying an evening out, but it was now empty, such was the seriousness of the trouble. We rushed forward, took a bit of a pounding and were backed off thirty yards down the road by the numbers and supply of weapons. I can remember the looks of disbelief on the faces of people sitting in restaurants and wine bars as objects flew around like a firework display and bins were hoisted above our heads and thrown in anger.

"We regrouped and attacked again, using many of the weapons that had originally been thrown at us. There was still no Old Bill, and we later found they were already overstretched covering a large rave with a celebrity DJ. The battles continued for about five minutes, which is a long time for anyone's fitness levels.

"Eventually the police did arrive and Burnley retreated to their pub. We temporarily disappeared down the side streets only to gather again in a nearby pub. Word had gone out that Burnley were still in the area and a few of the older nasties, having heard of the trouble, joined us. The usual, 'What do those cunts think they are doing drinking here,' and, 'They're taking fucking liberties,' do the rounds. Within an hour our numbers had grown to eighteen-to-twenty lads and, fuelled by this added confidence and drink, we marched back on Burnley's pub. Burnley filed out thinking they would be up against the same seven lads and many stayed indoors. They looked more than a little shell-shocked as they were smashed into cars and walls and generally knocked all over the floor.

"This is not trying to give it the big 'un, nor meant to be detrimental to Burnley, it's just what any firm would do if you stay in their town at night. I saw it when we tried it at Forest and Cardiff and I know it happened a few years at Shrewsbury. It's pride, you see."

In 1997, the home and away fixtures against Bristol Rovers were accompanied by trouble. Returning from Bristol, the Central Element stopped off in Exeter and clashed with locals. The final game of the 1998 season saw Plymouth travel up to Burnley staring relegation in the face. There was trouble inside and outside the ground and the mood of the Devon supporters was made worse with the result. Plymouth were at the pinnacle of their off-the-field strength, but increasing violence brought greater police attention.

In November 1999, Plymouth clashed with police in a pub in Cheltenham. A couple of hundred Central Element made the journey for what police later described as a pre-planned meet with Cheltenham hooligans, although it was not that well planned, as the locals failed to show. Thirty Plymouth clashed with police in the Cat and Fiddle, just outside the ground, while in a separate incident 100 tried to barricade the doors of the Sudeley Arms to stop the police from entering. In an obvious attempt to destabilise the gang, the police told the press that they prevented trouble because of informers within the group.

The incident provoked an analysis of Plymouth's hooligan problem in the local paper. "Plymouth Argyle have a hardcore hooligan element of fans intent on wreaking havoc across the country, or that's what some people would have you believe after Tuesday night's trip to Cheltenham," it said. "Plymouth has never been badly affected by the hooligan problem, and outbreaks of trouble are extremely rare. Officers say the troublemakers were members of Plymouth Argyle's Central Element, otherwise known as the TCE. But any suggestion that the TCE is a highly-organised gang is probably way off the mark, more a name that has survived from the 1980s, which is used by various thugs on the rare occasions trouble flares."

The police were not quite so dismissive of the TCE and it was not long before plans were being put in place to curtail their activities. It was not only the domestic league where Plymouth were active. Their resurrection in the Nineties was accompanied by a return in large numbers to the England scene, where often they linked up with Wolves. The catalyst for police action, in the form of the on-going Operation Ewood, came from Plymouth's increasing activity on the domestic front, and the Government's desire to prevent English hooligans marring Euro 2004.

Domestically, Plymouth's biggest turnout in recent years proved to be the Easter Monday match at Luton towards the end of the 2002 season, billed as the Third Division championship decider, with Plymouth at the top of the league and Luton Town second. "Everyone decided to make a big show for this one and about 250 Plymouth lads turned up", said Mike. "The main TCE group met up in London before catching a local train to Luton. Various phone calls were made between the two firms and a plan was hatched. Approximately 100-130 went on the first two trains out of London but were met on arrival by Luton Old Bill and mounted officers from the Met. There were no major games in London that day so, unluckily for us, large numbers were dispatched to Luton. We were then escorted to an away pub in Luton where a lot of other lads were already drinking. Another group had travelled up unnoticed in minibuses and as they parked up near the place we had arranged to meet it went off immediately, as a small firm of [Luton] MIGs attacked, the pub was trashed and our lads had the result."

Meanwhile, Luton's main mob was trying to reach the pub earmarked for away fans but the police were there in large numbers. As kick-off approached, the Plymouth pub emptied and the mob was escorted to the ground. Luton peppered the route and, while tensions were running high, there was nothing more than the exchange of coins and abuse. After the game the police were stretched as both mobs split up to avoid detection and minor skirmishes were breaking out all over the place.

A group of Central Element managed to evade the police cordon and slip away through the numerous side streets and alleys surrounding Luton's ground. They found themselves in a predominantly Asian area where they broke out with renditions of "God Save the Queen" and "Rule Britannia", much to the annoyance and distress of locals. As they entered a shopping area on Dunstable Road, fights broke out. "Luton are famous for being tooled up, but that day it was nothing to do with the football lads," said Mike. "The locals they excelled themselves: they had knives, screwdrivers, bats and even an axe was seen." One Plymouth lad was stabbed in the chest and the fighting escalated. Eventually large numbers of police arrived and a number of Plymouth were arrested. The rest were rounded up, taken back to the station and put on trains to London. On hearing of the trouble, Luton rang Plymouth and suggested that they come back up and the two mobs join together to fight Asians. The police had other ideas and ensured that the away firm headed nowhere but home.

Eighteen people were arrested, all but three from Plymouth. The Luton paper called it a "day of shame for football", and went on, "Fans had spent several weeks baiting each other on the message boards of their clubs' Internet websites. But despite the huge police presence, the outbreak of hooliganism was the worst in the town for more than a decade."

Plymouth were promoted and were becoming more active off the pitch, with a younger crowd of hooligans emerging. An impressive 150 travelled to QPR, and a further promotion saw them move into the old Division One, with matches against the likes of Millwall, West Ham, Cardiff and Leeds ensuring that big turnouts were regarded as essential if these respected firms were to be tackled. The Central Element responded and in 2002 Plymouth topped the league for arrests. There was little let-up in the 2003/04 season, when 91 Argyle fans were arrested, the seventh highest in the country. In response, the police spotting team was expanded from two to eight, police surveillance at games increased, including extra funding for a force helicopter, and banning orders were dished out.

Operation Ewood, aimed at reducing football-related disorder, had it biggest success with the arrest of a large number of young men at addresses across the city after trouble in the Britannia pub before a game against Leeds United in September 2004. Five alleged members of the Central Element, including an amateur boxer, were subsequently jailed after a court heard they repeatedly attacked door staff at the pub in a four-minute "tide of violence" as they attempted to get at Leeds fans inside. One of the mob even held up his mobile phone to film the fighting. Bouncers formed a protective wall despite being punched, kicked and hit with bottles, while pub staff were ordered into the cellar for their own protection and the landlady pressed a panic button linked to the nearest police station. The assault was caught on CCTV and TCE calling cards were found at the house of one of those arrested, though the others denied being members. The TCE was described in court as a 200-strong, all-male collective "intent on criminal activity". Officers said they could be recognised by their "designer uniform", with the most popular brands being Burberry, Stone Island and Aquascutum. Five others who played a lesser part in the attack were given community punishment or rehabilitation orders.

"Members of The Central Element, or TCE, have long had a notorious name in Plymouth, but the extent of their vile behaviour, as revealed by the police, Plymouth Argyle, football fans and members of the gang, has not been widely realised – until now," said the editorial in the *Plymouth Evening Herald* after their convictions. "This repulsive violence is the trademark of Plymouth's TCE, a gang of men who follow Argyle at home and away. To call its members football supporters is an insult to Plymouth's many loyal, law-abiding fans. They are enemies of the game, causing injury and even death, and do not necessarily attend the matches. Disturbingly, members as young as 15 are welcomed in to learn the same hate and violence as their seniors who, themselves, are often married men and fathers. On websites members post details of their 'victories', but it is the police who are winning the fight. These yobs can no longer hide behind their designer clothes. We applaud the work of officers who are bringing these men to justice – leaving the sport for the real fans to enjoy."

Although the firm continues to be active, the measures taken by the police – including the banning of almost 50 fans from Home Park by the end of 2005 – mean it is much more selective in its choice of games.

POLITICS AND RACISM

To many people, the image of the football hooligan remains that of a racist, xenophobic skinhead wearing big boots, tight jeans, tattoos and a snarl. More than 20 years after the skinhead fashion virtually disappeared from the terraces, fascism and football hooliganism remain closely intertwined in popular consciousness. Hardly a major riot has occurred without the far-right being blamed. From Heysel and Birmingham in 1985 to Dublin in 1995, the media and football authorities have blamed neo-nazis. All too often this has been well wide of the mark. While some hooligan gangs have been closely aligned to such groups as the National Front and Combat 18, most hooligans have little interest in "politics", while some have even been politically left-wing.

Hooligans, like any other football fans, live in a society where no-one can be completely immune from the politics of the day. From the racist attacks and "Paki-bashing" of the Sixties, to the Miners' Strike of the mid-Eighties, to Republican and Loyalist paramilitarism, to the emergence of an increasingly confident urban black generation who refused to take the racism lying down.

Skinhead culture swept through British inner-cities and housing estates in the late Sixties. Aggressive and proudly working class, they were the antithesis of the more middle class, peace-loving hippies. Most were also avowedly racist, with Paki-bashing a regular pastime of many young skinheads. "I saw my first skinhead in late 1968," recalled Man United lad Colin Blaney, who lived in the rundown Collyhurst Flats, in his memoir *Grafters*. "I was terrified ... I'd seen the lad around previously and thought nothing of him, but his newly cropped hair, his clothes and his attitude suddenly made him a somebody. Soon more skins appeared in the Flats, aping the behaviour of others they'd seen or read about in the papers. One Friday night I was in the chippie when I heard them all walking past singing, 'Hey ho, the lights are flashing, we're all going Paki bashing.' And that's what they did."

Micky Smith, in his book on the early West Ham years, recounts how Paki-bashing was an integral part of his early skinhead days, though he is quick to stress how they found a common bond with West Indian lads, many of whom were also skinheads who professed to hate Asians. The racial violence was, however, disorganised and there was little attempt by the National Front after its formation in 1967 to harness this aggressive racism into the political field.

All this began to change in the late Seventies. The initial skinhead phenomenon was shortlived, with most of the initial gangs dying out by the early Seventies. In 1976, the skinheads re-emerged, though this time closely associated with racist and fascist politics and imagery. "Oi", a raucous, cranked-up version of punk rock, was born and racist bands like Skrewdriver had large football followings. London continued to be the centre of this musical trend, with most terrace ends having their own favourite Oi band. West Ham had the Cockney Rejects, while Chelsea had Combat 84, whose lead singer, Chris "Chubby" Henderson was to become a major face in the Headhunters. Violence continued between them, including at skinhead music concerts, but rivals were often united when attacking their political rivals.

Far-right organisations began targeting football in the 1979/80 season as part of a concerted effort to – in the words of Derek Holland, a leading National Front organiser at the time – "win the hearts and minds of young people". The NF, then Britain's leading fascist organisation, was on the decline. Having once attracted thousands of members and hundreds of thousands of votes across the country, it was a shadow of the organisation it had been only three years before. Margaret Thatcher had stolen some of their clothes and anti-fascists had driven many of them off the streets.

The NF was joined on the terraces by the British Movement, a hardline nazi group formed in 1968 and which had already abandoned the electoral process. The BM was smaller than the NF but its membership contained a high concentration of young men, particularly in London, many of whom were already involved in soccer violence.

The increasing activity of racist hooligans coincided with the skinhead revival between 1976 and 1980 in London. Chelsea, West Ham, Charlton, Arsenal and Millwall all had significant groups of BM-affiliated skins. A vocal and visible mob of nazi skins were regulars at West Ham's Upton Park. Numbering at least 200, they stood and chanted together and would give nazi salutes in unison. Some fledgling West Ham casuals initially were attracted to the image and the message. At Millwall, meanwhile, a fire in New Cross which killed 13 black people in 1981 was met with the regular chant around the Den of, "We all agree, niggers burn better than petrol."

In 1981, the National Front launched *Bulldog*, a magazine aimed at attracting young people through race and politics. One page was always dedicated to football violence, with reports of racist chanting and accounts of hooliganism. Catching the imagination of many hooligans was the "League of Louts", a table charting racism within the game. Leeds United, Chelsea and Newcastle United fans would regularly battle it out for the title of Britain's most racist fans.

Liverpool was widely considered by many black football fans as the most racist footballing city in the country. Whereas groups of young Afro-Caribbean lads were beginning to attach themselves to hooligan groups in many urban areas, this was certainly not the case on Merseyside, where the football clubs and their gangs were the preserve of white people. Everton, in particular, was considered a hostile place for black fans to visit.

"Sometimes you would have to blend in and if many white lads are honest very few would stick close to a black kid, as you knew it would come on top," said a Manchester City fan. "As the years went by and numbers grew, the black lads used to be buzzing going there knowing they were going to get a fight. Anfield was no walk in the park but they never had the same agenda as Everton, so it was probably less intimidating. They brought some great firms to City though and there were some very bad slashings on both sides. City would not hesitate to fight fire with fire when the mickeys were in town and if that meant a few getting cut up, that was life in that era."

"We always did alright at Liverpool but to be honest for the black lads like myself Goodison was like *Nightmare on Elm Street*," said another City hooligan, Donald Farrer. "It was one on-top place. We never used to take the numbers there and a lot of it was to do with the racist thing, if you got collared at Goodison and you were a black kid you were in serious trouble. Only once or twice did we turn up mob handed. I kid you not, we would take better mobs to London than what we took to Goodison."

The alleged leader of the Leeds Service Crew, the hooligan gang that followed Leeds United, once wrote an angry letter to *Bulldog* complaining at its apparent London bias. "Isn't it about time that those who organise the Racist League should play the White man? I am talking about putting the true Whites of Leeds United Service Crew on top where they rightfully belong." He ended the letter by adding, "We have a lot of respect for *Bulldog*."

The racism at Leeds' Elland Road ground was extraordinary. Thousands would join in the racist chanting at opposition players and fans. "Elland Road is the worst ground of the lot," said Crystal Palace's black player Andy Gray in 1987, while Watford's Luther Blissett told the *Daily Mirror*, "Normally the abuse is from the terraces, but at one Leeds game whole groups in the stand were doing nazi salutes and shouting, 'Sieg heil'."

The fans in the stands were the Service Crew, and their move into seats followed a national trend to avoid the police, get closer to their opponents and illustrate, as with their expensive designer-label clothes, that they had money and style. The National Front was quick to exploit the racism of Leeds fans. There were regular paper sales and Leeds United/NF badges widely on display. Racist abuse was encouraged by *Bulldog* as well as the throwing of bananas.

Another ground that saw heavy fascist activity during the 1980s was Stamford Bridge, the home of Chelsea. A National Front contingent emerged in its hooligan ranks in the late Seventies, based around Hounslow and Feltham, the core of which remained active into the late Nineties. This group of Chelsea hooligans formed the backbone of the London far-right for several decades, joining the NF on demonstrations in London, defending meetings hosted by Holocaust denier David Irving and attacking left-wing meetings and demonstrations. Even into the early Nineties, the BNP would boast of selling 200 newspapers in the neighbouring pubs on match days. Racism really hit the headlines in the mid-Eighties when Chelsea fans booed Paul Canoville, their team's first black player. Even Leeds fans never stooped to this depth when black players were brought into the team. As many as 50 Chelsea Headhunters, including most of the top faces, were in some way affiliated to or supported Combat 18, another violent neo-nazi caucus, in the early Nineties.

The widespread racism at Chelsea and Leeds in the early Eighties coincided with declining performances on the pitch. Both sides languished near the bottom of the Second Division and, for the thugs, football violence and racism became alternative routes to infamy. The shock value and the moral outrage of the media and opposing clubs only encouraged them into further excess.

Darren Wells was a leading Combat 18 member who had come up through the ranks of the Chelsea Headhunters. "It's natural to rebel," he said. "If you have nothing and are from a working class estate, you say, what's wrong with that? I am white, I am working class. I haven't got a job, and it's you're way of rebelling back. Rather than just taking it you hit back. The right-wing is the most shocking thing because it's constantly put to us through the television, the press, everything, that the worse thing ever to happen is the Nazis. So the biggest way to rebel is to be seen to endorse it."

During the early Nineties, Wells, along with other C18 hooligans, used trips to see England play Poland to stop off at former concentration camps. There they posed for photographs, ripped up artefacts and generally insulted tourists paying respects to those who died in the death camps. "We did it because it was a laugh. No one really believed that the Holocaust never happened but we knew that to say so would infuriate people. Going to the camps was just the final straw. There was nothing more insulting than that. It was all just being provocative – it was us sticking two fingers up at a society we didn't like."

Many other clubs experienced racism amongst their fans. In Lancashire, Rochdale, Burnley and Blackburn Rovers were all intermittently targeted by NF and BNP paper sellers. Wigan, Newcastle, Aston Villa, Charlton, Exeter City and Darlington were just some of the English clubs where hooligans were linked to the NF or other fascist groups. Portsmouth, Sunderland and Hartlepool all had strong Loyalist links. Glasgow Rangers, Chelsea and Hearts combined the two.

However, despite the activity of fascist groups at many football grounds around the country, there is little evidence to show that many people were recruited into political activity. Hooligans, on the whole, have proved to be too ill-disciplined or uninterested for party politics. While some have always turned out for fascist demonstrations or as stewards for meetings and rallies, most find ordinary campaigning boring. Even among the mobs where the NF, C18 and more recently the BNP have had a base, few have got involved in political campaigns.

The influence of far-right groups at football grounds declined markedly in the early Eighties, with exceptions such as Leeds and

Chelsea. The BM collapsed and the NF switched its attention away from football. The changing demographics of our cities drastically altered the fan base of many clubs, and while few black and Asian people attended football matches many did go into the hooligan gangs. This was particularly the case with the Afro-Caribbean youth, who began to follow football instead of cricket.

In the early Seventies, the football gangs of Birmingham City, Manchester City and even Arsenal were the preserve of white lads only. Birmingham and Man City had big NF support while Arsenal was British Movement. By the late Seventies that began to change, coinciding as it did with changing hooligan fashion from skins to casuals. The Zulu Warriors (Birmingham City), Cool Cats (Manchester City) and the Gooners (Arsenal) were all led by large groups of black lads.

There were initially clashes between the new multi-racial mobs and the older white mobs but age, numbers and even toughness soon marginalized the racists. Many other mobs followed suit. Manchester United and Spurs had always had black lads involved, and Sheffield United, Wolves, Leicester, Bradford and Derby soon were also mixed-race mobs. Even some of the gangs normally associated with the NF, including Newcastle and later Leeds, had prominent black lads.

There have long been black hooligans active at Chelsea, despite the racist views of some of their fans. In the Seventies the most famous Chelsea hooligan leader was a one-armed black man known as Babs. His fearsome reputation and loyalty to the club meant he had little hassle from the racists. More recently, the Combat 18 influence at Chelsea suffered a major setback in 1994 when a C18 leaflet was stuck under the windscreen of a veteran black hooligan. He was Chelsea through and through and this was seen by many as unacceptable.

The changing fashion also had an impact. The Eighties saw several violent clashes between the traditional nazi bonehead gangs and football casuals even when they shared similar political outlooks. This simmering tension continued into the late Nineties when Chelsea's Andy Frain and other casuals were involved in fighting at Blood and Honour gigs.

The only time fascists have had much influence on hooligans since the early Eighties came with the emergence of Combat 18. C18 was basically a fascist football hooligan mob, attracting supporters from Spurs, West Ham, Charlton and Millwall. However, it was linked most with Chelsea. This initially gave it strength and respect around the country, especially because during this period Chelsea took on the mantle as leaders of England abroad, but it also brought it difficulties. When C18 tried to recruit in Millwall following BNP success in council elections, they were told in no uncertain terms to go away because they were a Chelsea mob.

The increasing involvement of black hooligans did not please everyone. At Aston Villa and more recently Sheffield Wednesday, previously multi-racial firms have become racist mobs. In both cases this has led to increased hostility with their city rivals, who have multi-racial firms, and, in the case of Villa, brought them into conflict with other mobs solely on the issue of race. It is clear from the recent Birmingham City book *Zulus* that race has given Birmingham-Villa clashes an added edge. During an England match in Poland in the Nineties, Villa confronted a Huddersfield mob who contained many black lads. They came badly unstuck, facing the wrath not just of the Yorkshire hooligans but also of other hooligans angered at Villa's stance. Huddersfield's mob has also clashed with Stoke City over race. In 1995, on their way to Dublin, the two mobs fought after Stoke hooligans racially abused their rivals.

One of the few mobs to have significant numbers of Asian lads involved has been Bradford City's Ointment. Sikhs and Muslims are an integral part of the gang, as are Afro-Caribbeans and whites. During the Bradford race riots of 2001, the Ointment made a conscious decision not to get involved in the trouble.

The changing climate and fan base has also had an effect on fascist involvement at football. Many of the older white mobs were targeted by police operations in the late Eighties, and the anti-racist campaigns and rising influence of the supporters groups marginalized racism in the stadium. By the Nineties, with Leeds United back in the top flight and relatively successful, mass racism virtually disappeared within the stadium.

The new political avenue for many hooligans was Loyalism, and in the early 1990s, with Loyalist fears that a future Labour government would create a united Ireland, the Ulster Defence Association brought the struggle to the mainland. Support for Ulster Loyalism had long been a central element of hooligan mentality through songs and regalia but now they were willing to get further involved.

In January 1993 over 600 hooligans, Loyalists and fascists took to the streets of London in a bid to disrupt the annual Bloody Sunday march. The intention of the UDA organisers had been then to march on to Kilburn, home of London's Irish community. They were only prevented from doing so with the arrest of 396 people. Hooligans from over 20 different gangs were out on the day.

Two years later, English hooligans forced the abandonment of a friendly fixture in Dublin. This was not the work of organised fascists, as some in the media claimed, but a mixture of spontaneous hooliganism, England's first away fixture for some time, strong pro-Loyalist sentiments at a time when some nationalist hooligans believed the Irish peace process favoured Republicans, and appalling stewarding and policing. The Irish police refused any collaboration with their English counterparts for internal political reasons and this, combined with the added memory of a game in 1991 when those arrested were only fined £1, proved irresistible to the English yobs. Whilst many later identified themselves as Combat 18 supporters to the media, few were. In fact, only one major London C18 activist was present that day, having travelled over with just one Chelsea Headhunter.

Irish republicanism, linked to Celtic and to a lesser extent Manchester United, is the closest thing there has been to left-wing hooliganism. The hard-left group Red Action, which was also central to the confrontational anti-fascist group Anti-Fascist Action, was active in Glasgow and Manchester, often against Glasgow Rangers fans. They would also clash with their Loyalist rivals on political demonstrations, such as the annual Bloody Sunday march in Glasgow or the James Connolly march in Edinburgh. There was also a strong Republican tradition among Hibs hooligans until the late Nineties, but the formation of the so-called Scottish National Firm, an attempt to create a unified national mob, pulled in some of the Hibs casuals and resulted in a split in the group.

Of course, there have been many other hooligans around the country who would consider themselves politically liberal or on the left. Some of the early Birmingham City hooligans came together in the late Seventies in a response to the National Front, which was active at the time. There were also other occasions when an opportunity to clash with their rivals brought hooligan gangs out on demonstrations. In 1977, some Millwall hooligans appeared at an Anti-Nazi League demonstration, alongside the Socialist Workers Party, to attack West Ham.

The bulk of football hooligans are drawn from working class communities and so anything that impacts on their lives and jobs obviously has a knock-on effect on hooliganism. In 1981, Sheffield United fans reacted violently to taunting by opposing fans at Reading during the Steel Strike. With so many of the Blades either working in steelworks or coming from neighbourhoods where most people did, the issue was raw and hatred against the police was strong. West Ham and Millwall hooligans were also active on the regularly violent picket lines at Wapping, East London, four years later. However, it was the Miners' Strike, in 1984/85, where trade union radicalism really crossed over into the football field. Football provided an outlet for communities that were being ripped apart. Hooligan gangs in areas representing mining communities came together, with those still in work often subsidising those on strike, while new rivalries emerged with areas where miners were still working. Nottingham Forest, Notts County and Mansfield Town had a torrid time when playing Yorkshire or North East teams like Hartlepool and Darlington. Ironically, in the case of Mansfield, many of their hooligans who had to run the gauntlet of abuse were actually on strike themselves.

Many Forest fans also feel unfairly picked on. "Let's get this straight," said Forest's Gary Clarke, author of *Inside The Forest Executive Crew*. "Nottinghamshire is a big fucking county. I don't know more than a handful of people who have ever been down the pit, yet still other firms call us scabs. It does wind us up because they are fucking thick, not because it hits the spot! Mansfield, Hucknall, Calverton are pit towns, not Nottingham. More Geordies work the pits than Forest lads, scores of them moved to Calverton. Be honest if you have been to Nottingham, you ever seen a mine, ever seen coal, ever seen lads in donkey jackets covered in dust? Have you fuck. I tell you what, if any of the lads I know had worked down the pits they would have been fighting to go on strike as it's one shit job."

The anger was also felt in non-league football. An FA Cup match between South Yorkshire's Frickley Athletic and the working miners' area of Stalybridge Celtic in late 1984 was held up for 24 minutes as seemingly the entire crowd spilled on to the pitch to confront one another. Lumps of concrete, bricks and planks of wood were all used as rival mining factions battled it out.

The Miners' Strike also reinforced a hatred and loathing of the police, never a friend of the hooligan anyway. When Sheffield United failed to win promotion in May 1984, they signed off their last home game of the season by mass fighting with the police inside and outside the ground. At its height, according to the *Sheffield Star*, over 500 people were fighting. When Leeds United fans battled with police in Bournemouth, including riot police drawn from the Met, in May 1990, chants of "Yorkshire miners" rang out. It was London officers who were often blamed for the worst excesses of police violence during the strike, and 20 years later bitterness lingers, with chants of "scabs" still heard at certain games.

Football hooligans have also been involved in urban riots. In Leicester, a match at home to Derby County was followed by two nights of disorder. In Wolverhampton, the death of a black man in police custody in 1987 sparked riots which, according to Wolves leader Gilly Shaw, involved many hooligans. Even when hooligans were not directly involved in city riots, the atmosphere of discontent and hostility towards the authorities spilled over onto the terraces. While the Toxteth riots in

Liverpool had nothing to do with football hooligans, Everton's first away game of the following season saw undisguised venom directed at police in Birmingham.

More recently, issues around asylum seekers and Britain's Muslim communities have aroused the interests of hooligan gangs. In 2001, Oldham erupted after weeks of rising tensions between local Asian and white youths, largely organised around the Fine Young Casuals (FYC). Burnley followed suit a month later and again football hooligans were heavily involved. However, in Bradford, which saw the worst disorder, the local hooligan gang stayed out of the troubles, largely because it has always been a multi-racial firm; local racist hooligans have largely associated themselves with Leeds United. More recently, Plymouth's hooligans clashed with local Asians in Luton following a match in the town. They were encouraged by Luton's own gang, which itself has had many black lads involved but who have their own differences with Asian youths.

Anti-Muslim sentiments are often heard but most of the time it extends little beyond internet chat rooms and message boards. During the Oldham riots, dozens of hooligans expressed support for the FYC's "battle for Britishness" but few seemed prepared to do anything about it. The recent formation of the United British Alliance (UBA) probably more accurately reflects the political views of many hooligans, namely anti-Islamic rather than anti-black or anti-Arab. Indeed, the UBA, which has attracted support of hooligans in the Midlands and London, stresses its anti-racist credentials and at least one former anti-fascist activist is believed to be centrally involved. At a protest in Trafalgar Square last year, the UBA clashed with the National Front over the presence of black or mixed-race hooligans.

The British National Party has, in more recent times, attracted support from hooligan groups keen to defend their "British way of life". Hooligans from Stoke City, Swansea, Blackburn, Burnley, Oldham, Halifax and Leeds are among those who have been BNP candidates or played influential roles in local BNP branches. But like the NF in the past, there are few places where active support has extended beyond one or two keen people. And with the BNP striving to distance itself from violence, what racist hooliganism that does occur tends to be unorganised or spontaneous.

The initial trouble in Oldham in 2001, caused by hundreds of Stoke City hooligans going through a largely Asian area, was not pre-planned. The Stoke mob had arrived to settle a score with the FYC, who had got the better of some of their number in Manchester the previous year. When Stoke City hooligans tried to repeat their actions the following year, there certainly was co-ordination between Stoke and Oldham hooligans, with the knowledge of the BNP leadership. On this occasion it took a huge police presence to contain the 350 Stoke hooligans and divert them away from any Asian areas [see OLDHAM].

Football hooligans were also central to disturbances in Burnley a month after Oldham. While most of the media focused on the Asian trouble, in another part of the town young white men were also causing disorder. The riots, plus growing activity from the so-called Burnley Youth, led to Operation Fixture, funded by the Home Office. "A minority of racist thugs affiliating themselves to Burnley FC were posing a threat of disorder which reached far beyond the arena of football," said an internal police report. "The so-called 'Burnley Youth' were engaged in organised and spontaneous violence on match days in and around town centre pubs where the negative impact on public reassurance was often dramatic. The wider threat included their potential involvement in the ever-present risk of large-scale disorder between Asian heritage and white offenders in the Burnley area. During the riots of summer 2001 a significant proportion of the white offenders were known football hooligans."

Under the headline "The Racist Threat", the report continued, "The hooligan element at Burnley is overtly racist and holds extreme right wing views that present an ongoing threat of disorder in the town. Evidence to support this statement includes: the key involvement of known hooligans during the riots of 2001 and intelligence that Chelsea and Burnley hooligans agreed and planned a joint attack on Asians in Burnley in September 2001 during a friendly fixture. A major policing operation involving more than 300 officers was required to prevent disorder. There was intelligence that Stoke and Burnley hooligans agreed and planned a joint attack on Asians in Burnley in 2002. A vicious, alcohol-fuelled attack on Asian taxi drivers in Burnley followed the Sweden game during the 2002 World Cup. There are racist and inflammatory entries on the Burnley hooligan website, 'burnley-lads.com', and there have been numerous arrests for racist chanting and a notable arrest of a prominent member of the Burnley Youth for Nazi saluting at Tottenham fans. On arrest the offender's bedroom was found to be a shrine to the National Front and BNP." During the Burnley riots, the report concluded, "a significant proportion of the white offenders were known football hooligans."

Football hooligans are always likely to be involved in local racial disturbances because they draw supporters from the working class communities which are likely to be involved in trouble. However, it is also clear to say that the role of organised fascists has often been exaggerated. The National

Front were not responsible for the Heysel Disaster or the riots at Birmingham City in 1985. Certainly in the latter instance there was NF support amongst the Leeds Service Crew but it was a football affair, an end of season match with both clubs in with a promotion chance and two of the country's leading hooligan gangs facing off. Combat 18 did not cause the Dublin football riot, though their extreme nationalist and pro-Loyalist links gave them an aura with which some hooligans liked to associate themselves.

In the Nineties, anti-Turkish sentiment also became a feature of British hooliganism. In part it was another aspect of the anti-Muslim feeling stoked by the Gulf wars, but it took on a new intensity after a series of vicious clashes between English and Turkish soccer supporters, especially those of the Istanbul side Galatasaray. In 1993, visiting Manchester United fans were greeted at the airport with "Welcome to Hell" banners and at their hotel by a baying Turkish mob, whipped up in part by some United heavies who provocatively draped an Israeli flag from their hotel room window.

The antagonism took a quantum leap, however, when, in April 2000, two Leeds United fans were horrifically stabbed to death in an Istanbul street before their team was due to play a UEFA Cup semi-final against Galatasaray (see LEEDS UNITED in *Hooligans*]. In the subsequent final, Galatasaray faced Arsenal in the Danish capital Copenhagen, and hooligans from all over England made the trip to indulge in further serious disturbance. Since then, fights with local Turkish residents have become a feature in major European cities when England have played there.

Three years after the killings in Istanbul, a group of Leeds United fans were jailed and banned from future matches for six years for affray before the Euro 2004 qualifier against Turkey at Sunderland's Stadium of Light. Trouble flared between the gang of six men and Turkey fans at a car park when, according to evidence given at Newcastle Crown Court, the group were taunted about the deaths of the two Leeds fans. All six men admitted affray. Five were jailed for 18 months and the sixth man for 21 months.

The tribal, aggressive and nationalist nature of football, and in particular football hooliganism, has meant that more participants have leant politically to the right than left. However, hooligans are ordinary members of society and share the same stresses, strains and concerns as everyone else. In periods where racism and divisions within communities are strong, so this racism will be reflected within the hooligan groups. Where there are strong economic and social upheavals, such as that caused by the Miners' Strike, so hooligans will be dominated by more collective and anti-police political actions.

Further reading: *White Riot,* Nick Lowles (Milo Books)

PORTSMOUTH

Ground: Fratton Park
Firms: 6.57 Crew
Rivals: Southampton, Millwall
Police operations: Market

"The hooligans who shamed the city," was the heading of a statement issued by the Portsmouth Supporters' Club in August 1969. "The antics of a mob of hooligans at Blackpool last Saturday brought shame not only on the football club and its supporters but on the city as well. Fortunately, no members of the Supporters' Club were involved in the incidents, nor were supporters travelling on the excursion organized by the football club. Supporters' Club members are reminded that under club rules they are liable to expulsion if they become involved in acts of hooliganism."

The match in question was Portsmouth's opening game of the season away to Blackpool and it was the first time that hooliganism associated with the club had been reported in the national press. What gave the media added interested was the description of those behind the violence. According to a chief inspector who later gave evidence at Blackpool magistrates court, the arrested Portsmouth fans were "in a large group of Portsmouth fans who adopted a peculiar style of dress similar to the Royal Navy's fatigue wear. Most of them had close-cropped hair, wore thin braces supporting jeans which were in a 'half mast' position, and all [were] in heavy brown boots".

These were the fledgling "Pompey Skins" and must have been a formidable sight in a northern town not used to mass incursions from strange-looking southern invaders. Some reports put their numbers at 100, others 200, but what is certain is that a large group of them arrived in three coaches in the seaside resort early and ran amok. Tables and chairs were thrown about and, according to the local paper, "a beach ice-cream cart was extensively damaged and a promenade rock stall was overturned." "It is a disgraceful state of affairs that innocent people cannot enjoy a football match and honest traders cannot conduct their business without being set upon by a crowd of hooligans," said the chairman of the bench, fining six of them a total of £375 for their part in the "trail of destruction".

Blackpool '69 is still talked about today when the oldest heads start rambling down Memory Lane after a few pints. After spending the money mucking around on the seafront and the pleasure beach, they headed for a home section of the ground and scattered any fans in their way. Before long, Blackpool's own hooligans began to re-group and retaliate, but the

Portsmouth men claim they were never budged for the entire game. After the match it was basically a riot as the Pompey bootboys fought with anyone and everyone on the prom: football fans, local pub-goers, tourists, deckchair sellers and fairground workers. Later that night a huge mob of Millwall skins, who had been to see their team play at Bolton, turned up in Blackpool, yet surprisingly the two groups didn't fight. Some say it was mutual respect at the skinhead gathering of both firms, but things would never be so amicable again between the two mobs.

The fear of violent young skins caused a panic down at Fratton Park, a week later. The local paper carried a picture of one, with the headline, "Police frisk youth". The paper went on to report how young skinheads were searched for offensive weapons before entering the ground. "Police removed steel combs, studded belts, heavy rings – and anything that could be used as weapons," it noted. "Spectators were asked to finish their canned drinks before entering Fratton Park to prevent the empty cans being used as ammunition by rowdies. The police were also on the lookout for heavy boots. They left them in the supporters' club room and went into Fratton Park in their socks!"

Hooliganism first arrived at Portsmouth in 1966 with visits from northern teams such as Manchester City. The home fans were disorganised but would fight shoulder to shoulder to keep away fans out of their end. A team that Portsmouth was to have most problems with over the years was the aforementioned Millwall, whose fans took Fratton Park by storm during the 1966/67 season. "They all came in one group and it was led by men of about forty years of age," recalled one eyewitness. "They were massive."

One man with more reason than most to remember Millwall's invasion of Fratton Park was Ginger Howard, arguably the first Portsmouth face back in the Sixties. Ginger was regarded as fearless, and led a rearguard action to defend Pompey ground, but after several minutes in the thick of the battling he re-emerged with his clothes virtually hanging off his back. "I'm not having any more of that," he said, and promptly walked off. Portsmouth's resistance quickly crumbled and Millwall were triumphant. On another occasion, Ginger was almost drowned by Millwall fans in an ornamental fish pond near the railway station.

Portsmouth's hardcore grew in confidence even before the trip to Blackpool. In 1967, some 20,000 Pompey fans travelled up to White Hart Lane for a cup match against Spurs and walked through their end without even having to throw a punch. The first crew to emerge were the Southsea boys, led by Dinksy, who by February 1968 was beginning to organise coaches to away matches. Early trips included Rotherham, Hull and Blackpool, with the coach setting off from a pub after closing time on the

Friday night, arriving in the early morning at their destination. It was to be a pattern often followed by Portsmouth hooligans over the next 20 years.

The first game of the following season saw a coach organised to Birmingham where, according to Pompey veterans, a mob of 250 Portsmouth ran the home fans up to the ground. That season saw a particularly treacherous trip up to Blackburn whose biker and grebo look contrasted with the skinhead fashion that had been quickly embraced by some Portsmouth fans after visits to West Ham and Spurs, two clubs Pompey fans were to have close links with over the years.

A trip to Rovers at that time could be considered mixing it with the big boys, both on the pitch and off it, and some Pompey had been forewarned by Manchester United fans about their own battles with their Lancashire rivals. True to form the home fans attempted to take the away end of the ground but were repulsed by only two coachloads of lads, the special train having been delayed, only for its passengers to arrive at the ground at half-time. During the game, Blackburn tried again, this time with far bigger numbers. They came up behind the Pompey fans, and from the sides, some chucking sharpened coins while others squirted ammonia. But Portsmouth, against greatly superior numbers, held their own. Several Portsmouth fans say this was the day that the young hard nuts turned from boys to men.

The skinhead fashion took off at Portsmouth in the summer of 1969, as stories swept the national media of clashes at seaside resorts and pop concerts. A pre-season friendly against Leicester City saw hundreds of lads dressed in this fashion run the visitors. The next week, the beginning of the season, saw the trip to Blackpool and it was this game which really set hooliganism alight at Portsmouth. To have travelled all that way, had such a rampage, then come home and find your exploits all over the national newspapers, was an addictive thrill for many of those present.

There was further trouble at Portsmouth's next away game at Norwich, with 150 drunken skinheads wandering around the town in the early hours of the morning after another overnight trip. Inside Carrow Road, the visitors took the home end, understandably riling the home fans, who regrouped after the game with the intention of teaching them a lesson. A full-scale riot broke out in the town centre and for the second time in a fortnight Portsmouth fans were national news. The Pompey Skins had arrived.

Skinhead fashion proved to be a passing fad and by 1972 it had been replaced by the suedeheads and smoothies; however, the legacy of football violence remained, as did many of the same people who had caused the trouble a few years before. On 1 September 1973, Portsmouth travelled to

Cardiff for a league match and became the first mob to turn the Welshmen over at home. Over 600 Pompey yobs battled it out with home fans and local police during the game, heralding the start of a long-lasting rivalry. "Pompey always turn out for them and them for Pompey," said one fan. Several Portsmouth louts were arrested, much to the annoyance of the local magistrates. "You are going to learn that it does not pay to come to Cardiff and behave like a hooligan," the chairman of the bench told them.

Two and a half years later, Portsmouth played a home league game against Southampton. It was the first clash between the two sides for several years and their first meeting during the modern hooligan era. For 89 minutes, concern about trouble seemed unfounded – until Mick Channon scored Southampton's winner. "Scores of Pompey supporters evacuated the Fratton end of the ground, and descended on their rivals transforming the terraces into a mass of people, mostly terrified innocents, scattering in every direction," noted the *Portsmouth News*. "Fists and boots flew indiscriminately as the minority thug element of the crowd imposed its violence on an otherwise peaceful evening."

The slightly old-fashioned language of that report was not mirrored by the *Reading Evening Post* in March 1977, after its town's worst experience of hooliganism during a visit from Portsmouth. "Animals!" was the stark front-page headline. Hundreds of Portsmouth fans had arrived unsupervised by train as much as three hours before the game and wandered freely around town, drinking heavily. Others, who arrived by coach, were dropped outside a stand for home supporters and there were instantly clashes. "Shoppers fled in terror, clutching their frightened children, as hordes of screaming fans charged through the streets near Elm Park, leaving a trail of shattered glass, splintered fences and bloodstains," continued the paper. In addition to fighting amongst themselves, the soccer hooligans attacked police and bystanders. They overturned cars and smashed windows in an orgy of destruction in the streets leading to Elm Park. In one house, a boy was hit by a brick thrown through his window."

One victim of the Pompey violence was 30-year-old Reading supporter Leslie Cross, a father of two. He was beaten senseless by half a dozen fans, just after Reading scored their second goal, and even two days later his condition was given as "seriously ill". Reading's second goal signalled the start of a huge pitch invasion by their fans in what was a clear bid to try to force the game – a very clean contest – to be abandoned. "As top international referee Clive Thomas was forced to halt the game for three minutes, police chased hundreds of fans across the turf. Fighting spilled on to the grass from the terraces and ambulance men rushed to tend to the injured," added the paper. Sixty-two people were arrested, 56 from Portsmouth, and dozens of people were hurt, including many policemen.

"The behaviour was diabolical and disgusting and the club is determined to stamp it out one way or another," said Portsmouth FC commercial manager Bill Davis. He handed police 600 passport photographs of members of the Portsmouth Travel Club. "If those responsible for the attack on Mr Cross belong to the Travel Club they will be in the book. We had a lot of new members for a recent away game and it is likely that the attackers were amongst those who joined."

There was further trouble when Portsmouth went back to Reading two seasons later, with 69 arrests. However, the disorder was not on the scale of 1977 and the police described themselves as happy overall. Local residents were taking no chances however, and many of them stood guard in front of their homes and shops armed with broom handles in case of a repetition of the previous trouble.

Portsmouth fans were now making headlines with increasing frequency. The same season as their riot in Reading, there was trouble in Swindon, including death threats against former Pompey player Chris Kamara. When the sides met again in August 1978, there were ten arrests for a match which the local Portsmouth newspaper said "produced its expected flash-points of violence". Most of those picked up were Portsmouth fans, with charges against them of criminal damage and various public order offences. A further 15 people were ejected from the ground.

Another city that was to be on the receiving end of repeated Portsmouth incursions was Plymouth. Between 1980 and 1983, three visits to the Devon city saw trouble. The first was in August 1980 and again Portsmouth fans were described as "animals" by the local newspaper, which also related "the worst hooliganism at Plymouth for many years". Twenty people were arrested as Portsmouth invaded the pitch to get at their rivals. Earlier, fans had clashed throughout the city centre after visitors began arriving in the early hours. "Just before the game," said the local paper, "as police rushed to a big punch-up outside the ground, 200 Pompey followers surged on to the Home Park pitch and stampeded towards the nearby Plymouth contingent. A corner flag was ripped from the pitch and used as a spear while hooligans tore apart chairs at the side of the pitch to form makeshift weapons. Police with dogs moved in and formed a human wedge between them."

When Portsmouth returned to Plymouth later that season for the league fixture, there must have been more than a little trepidation on the part of the Devon club and police. They hoped to have learned lessons from the trouble earlier in the season but nothing could be certain until the Pompey fans arrived. The home club had spent £800 on new fencing to prevent fans invading the pitch. The game did indeed go peacefully but only, as the local newspaper was keen to point out, "because the police were there in force – and they knew what to expect". Chief Inspector Alan Jones promised not to have a repeat of what he described as the worst scenes he had witnessed at Home Park. "We had a carefully drawn up plan of how to control the fans this time, and this was a major police operation."

The police were determined not to give the Portsmouth fans any freedom to wander around the city and so police with dogs herded the fans together as they arrived and then, under a heavy escort, took them on the 20-minute walk to the ground. Inside the ground, the mesh fences, aptly called "the cage", were held in place by scaffolding poles and there were always 40-50 police officers on hand to nip trouble in the bud. There were a few scuffles outside but considering what had gone on before, this was mild. Altogether, twelve fans were arrested and eight ejected from the ground.

Their third visit, in May 1983, saw Portsmouth gain promotion from the Third Division. Over 10,000 Pompey fans made the trip over, taking over three stands in the ground. The home fans could offer little resistance.

As the hooligan minority grew in confidence, so their wariness of other firms diminished. Back in the late Sixties, the mention of Millwall struck terror into the hearts of many Pompey fans, but by the early Eighties, with hooliganism at its peak at Portsmouth, matches between the two clubs were eagerly awaited. In 1978, after Millwall were forced to play their next home FA Cup tie at a neutral venue because of crowd trouble at a previous match, Portsmouth's Fratton Park was the chosen venue. This was a red rag to a bull and hundreds of Pompey fans turned up to defend their end from Millwall. This marked the opening of hostilities in what was to become one of the most violent rivalries of the period.

On another occasion, three coachloads of Portsmouth hooligans descended on a Southampton–Millwall match after their own game away at Swindon had been called off. The rivalry was mutual. "You know how it is, we do not like Portsmouth fans and they do not like us," a Millwall fan told magistrates before being sentenced to 42 days' imprisonment. Eventually both clubs banned away fans during their respective fixtures for two seasons in a bid to stop the trouble.

Portsmouth first took a mob to the Den in December 1980, but with Millwall not expecting them to show there was little local opposition. However, their presence had thrown down a gauntlet, so when Millwall travelled south the following April, they were determined to put on a show.

Millwall fans spilled over the wall, into the moat, and from there onto the pitch to fight the police. The game was held up for eight minutes in what was described as the worst outbreak of hooliganism inside Fratton Park. The final toll was 23 arrests, three policemen needing hospital treatment, windows smashed and hundreds of pounds' worth of damage.

The first outbreak of trouble occurred when 200 Millwall came off a train, broke through police lines and clashed with youths in the city centre. "Sirens wailed in the Fratton area as match time approached. But the trouble, so far, was to prove only a prelude of things to come," reported the *Portsmouth News*. Tension built throughout the game as rival fans traded insults and threats until, ten minutes into the second half, the Millwall crowd surged forward, several jumping into the moat separating the pitch from the terrace. Police rushed onto the pitch, with reinforcements called in from outside, as Millwall fans began ripping down hoardings and using them as makeshift weapons.

"Play had temporarily stopped as a group of policemen climbed in front of the mass in a bid to restore order and players and crowd watched aghast as the officers were savagely attacked by scores of thugs," continued the *News*. "In scenes of chaos, dazed fans were carried out of the seething throng, police hats flew on to the pitch, stretchers were brought to the trouble-point, and the referee decided he had seen enough. He called the players away from that end of the pitch as the violence raged on."

After the game, hundreds of Millwall fans rampaged through Haslemere Road, smashing windows, jumping on cars and leaving terrified and weeping residents to clear up the damage. "My window will cost £50 to mend," one resident told reporters. "I had just gone out to buy the local paper. I left my wife in the sitting room. When I got back she was crying and surrounded by neighbours. She said the window was smashed when 200 of these youths ran through the street. They pulled off a bike wing-mirror and just chucked it through my window, showering my wife with glass. I've never known football violence in this road in the twelve years we've lived here."

Whilst a £50 bill for new glass and a replacement pushbike wing mirror were causing the local resident concern, the club faced more pressing matters. There was no fencing for the Milton End behind one goal because it was usually occupied by home supporters but on this occasion the police decided to give it to away fans. "The trouble will almost certainly mean steel fences go up for the next season. There seems to be no alternative, although it is an unpalatable prospect," said the Pompey chairman. Club manager Frank Burrows refused to discuss the violence with the media, except to say, "I wouldn't dignify it by talking about it ...that had nothing to do with football. But it did ask a lot of my defence and goalkeeper to play with that lot at their backs, hurling everything they could find at them, but they got on with the job very well."

The incident was referred to the FA, and while Portsmouth feared punishment they hoped to escape the worst by proving that the trouble came from away fans. To help their case they enlisted the help of independent assessors to report on the trouble.

There was further disorder when Millwall visited again six months later, as police battled to keep rival factions apart after the game. Hooligans picked up stones and bricks and hurled them at the officers. Forty-seven were arrested and seven officers were injured. Local journalist Mike Newsom witnessed one of the most violent incidents as fans headed out of the ground. "I was halfway down the staircase when a fight broke out at the bottom. It was sparked off by one hooligan standing on a table who suddenly kicked someone. Within seconds, seven or eight people were involved in a vicious fight while people on the stairs were unable to move back because of the press of fans moving towards the exit. It was extremely frightening and could easily have led to a major disaster."

Despite several officers being taken to hospital, the police were happy with how their operation had gone. "There were pockets of trouble which were extremely nasty but we managed to keep the rival fans apart," said a superintendent. "We escorted the Millwall fans – about 2,000 of them – to and from Fratton Station, but the trouble that did occur was unfortunately unavoidable." He said that the level of violence was nothing compared to that experienced a year before.

Not everyone was convinced. One policeman's wife, speaking to the media on the agreement of anonymity, disagreed. "I am speaking on behalf of other people's wives, and I want to dispute the official statement that they have contained the trouble well at Fratton Park. The time has come when positive action is taken to prevent Millwall fans and others coming here. Why should our husbands have to risk serious injury stopping people who are hell bent on fighting? We have to sit at home on Saturdays like this waiting for the phone to ring to say our husbands are in hospital or perhaps even worse. These people are sub-human, and they should not be allowed to come to a city like Portsmouth to terrify and injure innocent people."

Neighbours were equally furious that another football match had brought trouble and came together shortly after the game to discuss action. "It is intolerable that residents of this area should have to endure behaviour of this nature," said one town councillor. "They are rightly outraged and fully justified in applying pressure on the authorities to do something about it." A petition was drawn up and the organisers promised to set up a large public meeting where the mood of the local community would be apparent to the police, council and club.

So concerned was he about the prospect of further trouble that the leader of the council even considered legal action to prevent Millwall coming back to Fratton Park the following January. Meanwhile the Portsmouth chairman announced his own investigation, looking into the club's security operation. To placate residents, he invited them to write to him with details of damage to their property. "While not promising anything," he stressed, "we will consider each case to see if anything can be done."

While the council and lawyers pondered a possible injunction, one councillor decided to take matters into his own hands by demanding that the Chief Constable refuse to police Pompey's next home match against Huddersfield. That way, he said, the club would have to cancel the game and that would be punishment for the disturbances at the Millwall game. He also demanded that the police withdraw cover for the New Year fixture against Millwall.

Meanwhile there was still the small matter of the cup replay. The authorities were taking no chances and 160 officers were being deployed to prevent a repeat of the trouble. The Met announced that Pompey fans would be escorted to and from the ground and would be kept in the ground whilst home fans were cleared. Inside the ground they were to be held together in "the cage". It seemed the strategy worked, as there were just five arrests during the evening, though the game was punctuated with a smoke bomb and coin throwing. "The small amount of trouble was no more than normal," commented a police spokesman.

Portsmouth is a naval town with a proud working class tradition. It is also, to a degree, an insular place, surrounded by sea on three sides, and a dislike of outsiders is combined with the tight bond forged between locals. Many of the club's hooligans were drawn from estates such as Paulsgrove, which was built as an overspill to take people who had lost their homes during the War. Forty years on, when Portsmouth's hooligans were at their most active, many of these temporary prefabricated flats and houses remained. It was no surprise when the various street and estate gangs who fought for the town at the football latched onto the hooligan scene.

Pompey's football firm are now regarded as one of the most infamous mobs to come out of the casual era, and it is well documented that the name given to them was derived from the train that the lads took to many away games. If you caught the 6.57 from Portsmouth to Waterloo, you could get a connection to virtually any town or city with a Football League club and be there by 1pm. The 6.57 Crew were Pompey's main mob and the name became synonymous with hooliganism when most gangs were "branded" in the early Eighites, but the 6.57 train had been used by the hooligans long before the name was adopted. The Air Balloon were another mob who involved themselves in all things naughty in Portsmouth, and were named after the pub they drank in. They were involved in everything from football to thieving to the local drug trade. Smaller gangs came from Eastney, Somers Town, Cosham and Paulsgrove, but on a match day they would all be labelled as the 6.57 Crew, whether they wanted to or not.

Prior to uniting under the 6.57 banner, and even once the majority did, they often described themselves as the most disorganised firm ever to exist. Despite having massive numbers they would often split up and drink in separate pubs, dissipating their forces. Had they stayed together more often, many believe they could have been the number one firm in the country.

The first proper clash between Portsmouth and Millwall hooligan mobs in London occurred in May 1982, when hundreds battled it out around London Bridge Station. Fortunately for the authorities, resources were on hand to quell the trouble when officers were diverted from a Bobby Sands demonstration in the capital. With trouble breaking out at every foot-balling encounter, the police made the next match in London, in 1983, a "high risk" game and ordered a Sunday noon kick-off. "Undeterred, over 500 lads made the trip," recalled one terrace veteran. "It was an awesome mob, no hangers-on, full of the old boys and swelled by the younger lot all smartly dressed in the Pringle jumpers and many wearing deerstalker hats.

"We got off at Waterloo and got a train across to London Bridge, where someone shouted that Millwall were here. You could not see them as our full mob sprinted across the platform, and the lads who were near the front told us not-so-fast runners that Millwall were battered, well the few hard cases out of 100-odd who stood were anyway, the rest were off. Years later, one of their lads told us they could not believe the size of the firm that piled out of the station that day.

"We got to New Cross and were escorted to the ground but a huge mob of us got into their seats, and before kick-off there were no Millwall in there to move us. Just after the game kicked off, there was a bit of a scuffle and Millwall had come onto the pitch, having noticed we were mobbed up in the seats. They tried to force us out but never had enough and we kept there all game. I doubt if anyone has done that, even to this day. After the game, we had a huge escort all the way back. By now our numbers were double and we were basically untouchable. Still, a hard core fifty of their old blokes had a go, no other firm would have come near our mob but you have to give Wall credit, outnumbered to fuck they did not care and always had a go."

With Portsmouth having to travel through London for most away games, there was always the chance of a planned or accidental encounter with Millwall on the transport system. "One of the best battles with Millwall was when we played Chelsea on a Boxing Day," said another Pompey hooligan. "It was a morning kick-off to prevent trouble, well it wasn't as fucking as easy as that! Millwall had a shit game at Wimbledon, and after we came from Chelsea a small mob went up there and there was a bit of bother before the OB sussed it out and sent our lot packing. Most Pompey went on the drink, and about seven o'clock about 200 of us were at Waterloo when Wall showed up with a mob about the same size and it went off solid for about fifteen minutes. They would back us off, we would be back into them, running battles all over the station long before the OB got onto it.

"It was, to many, one of our best ever battles with Millwall. We won't claim a win, but they shouldn't either as there was nothing between us that day. Quite a few times we had split up and it was always Millwall's trademark to turn up after the pubs shut and bushwhack the stragglers catching the last train back to Portsmouth, which left just before midnight. This time we all agreed to stay put and true to form about eighty Wall turn up like vultures looking for some easy pickings. Well it was a bad move, by now there were about 500 Pompey waiting for the train and we slaughtered Millwall, absolutely massacred them. Happy Christmas."

The loyalty and resilience of Portsmouth fans saw them travel in large numbers over great distances. Fans often either caught the 6.57am train out on a Saturday morning, or headed off by other means after the pubs and clubs closed on a Friday night, arriving in cars, vans and coaches at their destination early the following morning. Along the way it was normal for them to come across rival mobs similarly travelling the transport system and on the odd occasion they would make a slight detour in the hope of bumping into a rival firm.

On 1 October 1983, Portsmouth were away to Newcastle and as usual the hardcore of the 6.57 Crew left town on the first train to London. They clashed with 50 Millwall at Waterloo Station, and then with Chelsea, who were travelling up to Huddersfield, at Kings Cross. The Portsmouth mob got split at the station, with half catching the 10am train to Newcastle while the remainder were forced to catch one 30 minutes later.

"Portsmouth caught everyone out by coming into the city centre and nobody really did that," recalled Newcastle fan Alan Montgomery. "It took a while for everyone to greet them properly and, yes, I was very impressed with the Portsmouth numbers." The two mobs clashed an hour before the game, sending Saturday shoppers fleeing in every direction. In one incident, a half-brick was thrown through a pub window, striking an elderly lady on the leg. Fourteen fans were arrested, equally divided between home and away supporters. Local magistrates dished out fines totalling £1,200, an amount welcomed by the local *Evening Chronicle* under the headline "Nasty Fans".

On the way home, the Portsmouth fans again clashed with Chelsea, this time at Doncaster Station. This was no coincidence, as many Pompey fans knew that Chelsea leader Steven Hickmott would be out for revenge after the pasting he had taken at Kings Cross earlier in the morning. As the train pulled in, the Pompey mob surged out of the carriages and chased the Chelsea lads off the platform. There was a further clash between the two sets of supporters back at Kings Cross. So, one away day saw five separate clashes.

Cardiff City and Portsmouth clashed several times in the early Eighties [see *Hooligans*] and earned both mobs mutual respect. The first major battle came when Portsmouth played a cup game at Newport County and a mob of Cardiff decided to make the trip. It was shortly after the Falklands War, and in response to Pompey chants about some Welsh Guards being killed, the home fans chanted, "Argentina," which did not please the fans from the naval town. There was much worse trouble at Portsmouth's game against Cardiff the following season, with Pompey claiming a victory against the Soul Crew before the game. Fifty people were arrested and the intensity of the fighting caused the police to order a noon kick-off for the return match, which saw a massive Cardiff mob, with as many as 1,000 lads, turn up.

The scene was set for Portsmouth's return the following year, as one 6.57 Crew fan remembered. "The year before had been mental at Cardiff and although we knew that they would be up for it again, we also knew that the police would be ready for us this time, so decided on a different approach. One lad suggested that we all dress up smart as if we were going to a wedding and see how we got on, so we agreed to get the train as usual but be dressed in Farah pants, blazers, shirts and ties. We even got some fake wedding invitations printed, and true to form a good tidy crew appeared on the station looking the dog's bollocks.

"We got to Cardiff about twelve. There was a massive police presence there and we were walking through and they were asking, "Football?" and we were saying, "No, wedding." About thirty of us got away with it before a couple of Pompey spotters turned up and started pointing out known faces and it all went a bit pear-shaped. That was one of the first games the spotters were at and was the start of the new-style policing at football. Very little happened at the match, but once again Cardiff could not question our efforts."

January 1984 saw Portsmouth drawn against local rivals Southampton in the FA Cup. Portsmouth like to belittle Southampton but there is no mistaking the historic rivalry between the two sets of supporters, which continues to this day [see *Southampton*]. From the moment the draw for the fourth round of the FA Cup was made in early January 1984, there were concerns over possible crowd disorder. The police promised to use every available resource, local councillors demanded neighbouring building sites be cleaned up to prevent them becoming "ammunition dumps" and representatives of both clubs urged calm.

Three days before the match, the police unveiled their "battle plans". These included closing certain roads to traffic around the Portsmouth ground to allow the shepherding of Saints fans along "wide corridors" without home fans getting at them. "We are expecting that the vast majority of fans will co-operate with our requests," noted Supt Ron West. "But we have laid on contingency plans to cope with any problem caused by the small minority who will try to disrupt other people's enjoyment."

The editor of the local paper urged fans to "make it a match to remember":

> With all this talk of 'armies of fans' and 'battle plans' being drawn up by police, it is easy to forget that Pompey and Saints are meeting in a football match tomorrow – not rehearsing for World War III.
>
> There was a time when a match between these two clubs would have attracted true fans who were content to cheer on their own team – not abuse their opponents.
>
> There was a time when any policeman in the city would have considered duty at a Pompey-Saints match a bonus.
>
> Now they must dread the prospect of marshalling two groups, many of whom masquerade as supporters, but whose loathsome antics have stained the reputations of their cities and clubs.
>
> But just for once, wouldn't it be great if the cynics could be proved wrong. Wouldn't it be marvellous if the prophets of doom got their comeuppance?

The editor did not appear to know the history of Portsmouth v. Southampton football matches, and predictably, the events during and after the match made for grim reading. "A city licking its wounds," was the headline in the *News,* with shops and cars damaged, 18 people in hospital, 32 ejected and 59 fans arrested – and, for Pompey, a match thrown away.

They lost in the extra minutes added on for an injury to Saints player Mark Dennis, who had been felled by a coin thrown from the crowd. Not able to reach their rivals, the Pompey fans turned their anger on the police.

One shopkeeper near the ground described how a brick "exploded like a bomb" as it struck her window. "I thought World War III had broken out," she added. The workers in the Alive 'n' Kicking café demanded that the club be shut down. "It's terrible," said one employee, "someone could have been killed. They should not let them have football if they are going to behave like that." Eddie Burns, a worker at a decorating shop agreed. "It's pathetic and disgusting that a game of football should cause so much trouble and terror. If police cannot control the crowd, they should stop the cause of the trouble – the football itself. It's the only way."

More than 40 fans appeared in court the following Monday and immediately the presiding magistrates indicated their mood by sending the first two people to prison. "We in this court listen to advice from higher courts," chairman of the bench Maurice Smith told the defendants. "The position is that these courts are fed up, and the general public is fed up, with this activity." Of 21 fans who pleaded guilty, 15 were sent to prison.

The club quickly distanced itself from the trouble, with the chairman John Deacon denouncing the "moronic actions" of the hardcore hooligans. He promised to crack down on future trouble and asked amateur cameramen, who might have caught some of the disorder on film, to hand the tapes over to the police. He also announced a £100 reward for information leading to the identification and conviction of "the coin-throwing louts". This was instantly doubled by the *News*, who, in a special back-page editorial, declared, "Some of the morons who masquerade as Portsmouth supporters have done the club an enormous disservice over the years – but they hit an all-time low on Saturday. And they must go down as the first bunch of 'fans' in the League to actively contribute to the defeat of their own team ... You cannot legislate for the mentality of morons whose idea of Saturday afternoon entertainment is to throw bananas at black players, coins at linesmen – and the reputation of their club out of the window."

While Millwall were Portsmouth's main London rivals, they also often fought with Tottenham and Chelsea in particular. In 1985, Pompey played Spurs in the Milk Cup and there was fighting at both legs. More trouble followed when the sides met again in 1991 [see *Tottenham Hotspur*]. Some of the worst football violence witnessed in Portsmouth, however, was at the visit of Chelsea in April 1984. Two Chelsea fans were stabbed after they were set upon by a 20-strong Portsmouth mob, with one requiring emergency surgery to save his life. A third man was temporarily blinded by chemicals thrown in his face. In clashes earlier in the day, police broke up one large brawl on Southsea Common, and heavy patrolling of the Commercial Road shopping precinct kept the factions apart. To the east of the ground, street violence flared with cars and shop windows the main target for rampaging fans. Nine police were injured in the evening's troubles, most being hit by flying seats inside the ground.

After the match, a massive police operation successfully shepherded the bulk of thousands of Chelsea fans on to 23 police-escorted coaches and special trains out of the city, but not before 140 seats had been ripped up by fans angry at being kept in the ground long after the game. Others attacked the scoreboard, pulled up part of a big advertisement hoarding, smashed three large doors at the Milton End and damaged fencing supports.

The 6.57 Crew become national news in March 1987 after a fight at an Afro-Caribbean club in Derby ignited the city's worst race riots. There is a difference of opinion about the motives behind the 6.57's involvement but what is clear is that at 7pm a group of 60 Portsmouth fans attacked the Texas Goldmine Afro-Caribbean club "smashing windows and yelling abuse". There were 30-35 black youths in the community centre at the time and they quickly retaliated. Fighting spilled out onto the street, but as the police arrived and arrested some Portsmouth, while shepherding others to the ground, the local youths were not finished and were soon on the rampage themselves. "They were showing their frustration and wishing to inflict some revenge," said Chief Constable Don Davidson later. Before long the local mob had risen to 400-strong and was smashing windows and cars and besieging pubs.

They were still rioting as the game finished, and one minibus of Portsmouth fans was caught and chased after the match. Some managed to get into the van and get away but its owner was caught outside and had to run for his life. "It was like street warfare," he told the press. "I saw the mob attacking my van. I panicked and leapt over the wall to avoid being beaten up. This lot drove off without me and I just heard the screech of tyres as it disappeared round the corner." Portsmouth fans and local youths also clashed near the railway station after the match and it wasn't until 11.30pm that order was fully restored.

The media put almost total blame on the Portsmouth fans, who they believed had deliberately targeted the community centre for racist motives. This view was shared by the police who, at a midnight press conference, seemed almost to excuse the rioters. "It was an understandable reaction to an orchestrated and planned attack by Portsmouth youths," said the Chief Constable. "I don't condone what happened but I can understand their frustration." He went on to claim that his force had "intelligence" that the Portsmouth attack was planned in advance and race was a motive.

Portsmouth Council issued an apology to their counterparts in Derby, as did Portsmouth FC. "I am sure I speak for Pompey as I say that we are utterly tired of having mud flung at us at football for incidents in which the clubs have no control," said club secretary Mike Dunfold. The *News* carried a front-page editorial which condemned the "peddlers of hate" and called for no effort to be spared in "exposing these people for what they are – mindless thugs seeking a fix of violence".

The following day the paper started this exposé itself with an investigation into the 6.57 Crew. It claimed the mob had developed almost a "cult-like following – despite frantic efforts by club and police to weed them out". The paper quoted police officers as saying that "several hardcore" members of the gang were involved in the attack on the club and that the 6.57 was a growing problem. "Two years ago," the paper noted, "the group was said to have a hardcore of up to 50 hooligans, with another 150 in its fringe element." In response the local police sent in plain clothes officers to identify the ringleaders. The paper also reported that in April 1985 an internal police report claimed that the 6.57 Crew had become known as "some of the worst troublemakers in the Football League" and had links to the National Front.

The hooligans themselves have always denied the Derby attack was racist, claiming that before the big promotion game, which saw 2,500 Pompey fans travel, a small group of 60 hooligans who were looking for their Derby Lunatic Fringe counterparts bumped into a black man and ask where the firm was. They were pointed towards Pear Tree Road, where they saw a bunch of youths outside the Texas Goldmine. It immediately kicked off, but the lads did not realise it was an Afro-Caribbean Centre. Some of them threw a drainpipe and a For Sale sign through the windows, a mob came out carrying knives and the Pompey tried to rip a fence down to protect themselves just as the police arrived.

After the game, the Pompey lads were identified and arrested and were locked up for criminal damage. Their situation grew more depressing when the following day the news filtered through that the attack had caused the worst ever race riot in Derby. Three days later, the suspects were released after being charged with affray, but when their cases came to court, all were either dismissed or the defendants were bound over.

To this day, well-known Pompey lads stress they thought it was a mob of Derby hooligans they were fronting, although they agree they did not pick the right time to attack the meeting in the Texas Goldmine – unbeknown to them, tensions were running high within the community after the death in custody of a black Wolverhampton man a few days before, which had sparked disorder in that city.

The same month saw another round in the Portsmouth–Birmingham City conflict, which had been raging over the previous few years. Both had big hooligan mobs who never shied away from a conflict, and probably because of their similarities there is mutual respect. Three hundred Zulus had travelled to Portsmouth in 1985 and a fight was arranged for the Guild Hall. Journalist Caroline Gall, in her book *Zulus*, recounts the Brummie mob wandering up to the spot and dancing on the steps to the sounds of reggae on a ghetto blaster. "Those [shoppers] who stopped and clapped were soon in for a shock when a huge roar went up, signalling the arrival of Pompey," she wrote. "A flare was immediately fired and bounced off the steps followed by a volley of bricks, and a rocket put a stop to the music as it landed on the speakers. There was a stand-off and the Zulu chant went up, but the Old Bill arrived and put a stop to any major fighting. They were the only ones that could claim a result that day."

At Birmingham's next visit, in October 1986, the main trouble happened after the game, with both sides accepting that the Zulus won. "The police were starting to sew things up and dawn raids were commonplace around the country," recalled Rob Silvester in his book on the 6.57 Crew. "The Zulus didn't seem to give a fuck about any of this and brought a good mob down who did the business in some style on Fratton Bridge after the game. Against the odds they broke up some fencing and went to work with some pieces of wood, and to be fair we took a slapping. They battled really well that day and continued this all the way up to the Air Balloon, where again a small but bang-up-for-it crew of them really performed. They had jogged all the way from Fratton Bridge to the pub for a fight, a distance of about three miles. The Zulus were like men possessed that day and we were second best ... You have to say that Birmingham gave the best man-for-man display ever seen at Fratton."

There was further trouble when Portsmouth went up to Birmingham later in the season. Over £3,000 of damage was done when 100 Zulus attacked the Fox pub, containing away fans, with pool cues, bricks and bottles.

1987 was General Election year and while most football hooligans seemed to care little for politics, in Portsmouth the 6.57 crew was in full campaign mode. After all, they had their own 6.57 Party candidate. Matty Hughes, better known as "Docker", stood on a platform demanding that all magistrates serve time themselves and that dockers should have their own community policing; Portsmouth be taken out of Hampshire and duty-free be made available on the Gosport ferry; a social policy to help war widows and a programme to expel Southampton folk from the city; a banning on curly perms or mullet hairstyles as sported at the time by Bryan Robson and Chris Waddle; and the creation of a race track on Southsea Common. The final manifesto pledge was to help Loyalist prisoners in Northern Ireland and for an annual Derry Apprentice Boys march in the city.

Some of the 6.57 crew took this seriously. Posters were made, leaflets distributed and a battle bus hired, decked out in "Vote Docker" banners. A public meeting was organised, which of course ended with the police being called after Docker Hughes decided to set off fire extinguishers instead of making a speech. Docker ended up with 455 votes, which for some of his campaign team was a disappointment. However, election day saw his 30 selected representatives drink the bar dry at the count.

Pompey made national headlines once again when the club arranged a friendly against French side Le Havre in Honfleur. Weeks before the trip, organised supporters' groups had planned to demonstrate at the game in protest at how the club was being run. They had not bargained for the 500 drunken 6.57 members who joined in and invaded the pitch, causing the game to be abandoned. One lad told how the firm calmly walked onto the pitch, kicked the ball around and drank beer in the penalty area while ignoring appeals from home officials. The game was called off and the rest of the trip saw widespread disorder.

Rave music killed off the 6.57 Crew. "For whatever the reason, nearly everyone got into it, and of those who didn't many stopped going to the football as it was never the same," said one Portsmouth veteran. "There are always the odd days out like the one at Coventry [see *Coventry City* in *Hooligans* Vol. 1] but they are few and far between. That game made the headlines as the match was held up but it wasn't a planned event, just one of those days where everyone decides to go for the crack and to have a good day out. They are the ones which usually end up going pear-shaped though and that was the case that day. Loads were nicked but only one got jail so it was a result really."

Trouble has continued sporadically, but nothing like in the past. When it did plumb the depths of previous years, the police were waiting. In March 2004, Portsmouth fans rioted at their home game with Southampton. On a wet and miserable Sunday evening, hundreds of Portsmouth fans battled it out with police in the hope of reaching their bitter rivals who were being kept in the ground for their own safety. Bricks, bottles and rocks were hurled at police, and car windscreens and shops were also attacked. Masonry and other building equipment was collected up by some rioters in wheelbarrows to be later used as weapons against the police.

"It's a sad day for Portsmouth that thugs had to take away the focus of the team's 1-0 victory," said Hampshire's Assistant Chief Constable Colin

Smith. "These thugs just wanted confrontation with the away supporters and with the police. This was just mindless violence that achieved nothing." The following day the police claimed that the trouble was orchestrated via mobiles. "There's evidence that there were a number of people in different parts of the city communicating with each other about what they were going to do," said Chief Supt Dan Clacher. He also issued a warning that his force would track down the culprits. "It doesn't matter how long it takes – we're going to get every last one of them."

He was true to his word. Over the next year, dozens of people were identified from CCTV and other film footage in Operation Market, and were hauled before the courts. Almost 60 people have since been imprisoned, and in one swoop an emerging mob of Portsmouth hooligans was virtually wiped out. "But for that game we would probably have a tidy little firm again now, as there were plenty of them and they were game little fuckers," reflected one Pompey lad. "But that one game wiped out the firm a lot quicker than Ecstasy wiped out the 6.57. The Premiership is finished for football violence. All-seater grounds and the ticketing policy makes it near impossible to play up, although Pompey still take good numbers to England away games and are very well respected."

With a Russian part-owner investing millions, and Harry Redknapp returning to the club he left in turmoil, Portsmouth are finally making national news for footballing reasons. But ask any football "lad" what they remember of Pompey and apart from a few who may mention the "nutter with the tattoos and bell", most will respond, "The 6.57 Crew," undoubtedly one of the most notorious and, within their world, well respected football gangs of the modern era.

Further reading: *Rolling With The 6.57 Crew*, Cass Pennant and Rob Silvester (Blake Publishing), *The Pompey Boys*, John Payne (PB Publishing)

PORT VALE

Ground: Vale Park
Firms: Vale Lunatic Fringe, Vale Young Casuals
Rivals: Stoke City, Wrexham, Walsall
Police operations: Scorpion

When football fans talk of the Potteries, they usually mention Stoke City. But only a couple of miles away from the Britannia Stadium is Vale Park, the home of Port Vale. Often overlooked, Port Vale's hooligans have been busy over the years. In the 1970s Port Vale's mob was a collection of smaller firms, based on housing estates. There were the Smallthorne Clampets, Corbridge Mafia and the Norton Normals – all separate mobs but who would join together for the bigger games. In those days, fierce rivalries existed against Bolton Wanderers and Walsall, but they had not played Stoke City since 1957. "We hate Walsall more than Stoke," was a regular chant on the terraces in the Seventies.

"Every season the Walsall fixture was the one everybody looked for, and often it did not disappoint, with violence occurring at most meetings," says Fletch, a Vale veteran. "There is a lot of respect for the old Walsall lads at Vale for what has happened over the years. Unfortunately this rivalry has cooled down over the last few years due mainly to their lack of numbers."

The Vale Lunatic Fringe was born during the 1980/81 season when fifty lads made the trip to Bradford and had a nasty fight with a similar-sized group. One of the Vale lads later commented that they were "lunatics", and the name stuck. An early battle was the home fixture against Bolton, which saw the visiting mob take over the Foaming Quart pub, then a key VLF drinking hole. About 100 VLF broke into two groups and stormed the pub, smashing every window in the process. Fighting continued outside in the surrounding streets and one man was slashed across the face.

A couple of years later, Port Vale played host to Spurs in the FA Cup. This eagerly awaited tie saw a large mob of Londoners arrive in Burslem, and fighting broke out all over town. "Although the violence was not organised," remembered "CP", one of the firm members, "it was the most severe spontaneous scenes of fighting ever seen at the small club. The fighting lasted all day and night and it even resulted in a small mob of Stoke taking a beating in Longport, for the sheer cheek of turning up."

Six thousand Wolves fans made the short trip to Port Vale during their promotion push in 1996 and filled most of the small ground. Trouble flared as the visitors went 2–0 up. A group of Wolves tried to leave the ground but were pushed back by the police. After the game, fighting broke out in Burslem town centre as up to 100 fans battled one another. The police totally lost control for several minutes and traffic was brought to a halt as brawling spilled into the busy streets. Other Vale fans and locals poured out of pubs, many armed with bottles and glasses, but eventually police regained control.

Much of the worst trouble happens when fewer lads get together. In 1998, 40 Vale made the short trip to West Brom by train. They avoided police observation and after a quick drink in Wolverhampton continued on to Sandwell and Dudley station, where they crossed over the track.

They headed to the Hawthorn pub, where they were confronted by a similar number of home lads and battle commenced. "Several West Brom left in ambulances," recollected CP. "After the game, both firms tried to give it to each other outside the ground with missiles being thrown from everywhere." Several arrests were made.

In 1989, after an absence of 32 years, Port Vale were once again in the Second Division and this brought them up against their fierce city rivals Stoke. "Around 200 lads marched from Burslem town centre into Hanley where fighting broke out with Stoke at the Market Tavern pub," remembered Fletch. "Sporadic fighting took place all day around Stoke-on-Trent, but considering the large numbers of lads from both sides, nothing major happened. After the game, and unknown to the Vale lads, Stoke had made their way to Vale's main boozer. At the time Vale were half a mile away in Middleport and upon hearing the news soon surrounded the pub with big numbers. Once again the police prevented any major disturbance."

Almost every game between the two close neighbours saw trouble, with some of the worst coming in 1995. "The plan was to get on to the outskirts of Stoke and then make our way in undetected," said Fletch, "It was arranged to make our way in small groups to the Bell & Bear pub, which is approximately a mile from Stoke town centre. Around ten lads had made their way to the pub and were waiting for the others. One lad then ran into the pub and shouted, 'They are fucking here.' We had been spotted and we had only been in there five minutes. With only ten in the pub, a mob of Stoke were fast approaching and things were looking grim.

"There was only one option and that was to make sure that they did not get into the pub. Fighting broke out at the door as all attempts were made to stop them from entering. In the meantime every window on the pub was going through. You name it and it was coming through the windows: tins of beans, soup, road signs, bricks, kerb stones. We managed to keep them out, and they fled down the road.

"More and more Vale lads started to turn up. In the meantime, Stoke were reloading with ammo. They came back a second time and all attempts to empty the pub were repelled by missile attack. A lone copper accidentally stumbled across the incident and in no time the OB were there in big numbers. We were escorted to the ground through the middle of Stoke, how the police kept Stoke at bay is a mystery to this day. As we turned the corner to walk up to the Vic pub, opposite the away end, you could see that there were hundreds of them waiting to pounce. Minor scuffles took place near the away enclosure fence but that was about it for the day, other than Vale winning the game one-nil."

A couple of seasons later, local rivalries were heightened as Port Vale and

Stoke City languished near the bottom of the old First Division. Both teams went into the final game with their future uncertain. Vale travelled to Huddersfield and sealed their survival with a 1–0 win. Stoke City, meanwhile, lost 5–2 to Manchester City in a game marred by mass disorder and were relegated. An angry mob of 40 Stoke travelled to Burslem later that evening intent on exacting at least a physical revenge. Port Vale heard of Stoke's imminent arrival and the pubs emptied. Waterloo Road became a battleground as the two firms clashed. However, the area was under CCTV surveillance and several lads were later arrested, convicted and banned.

"At the height of last night's violence," commented the local newspaper, the following day, "more than 100 Stoke City and Port Vale fans clashed in Waterloo Road, hurling bottles and stones at each other as police intervened. Other incidents took place across the city and emergency services struggled to attend every outbreak of violence. A police spokesperson said that every available officer in North Staffordshire, including the force's dog handlers, were called to cope with the violence."

Stoke City made a quick return to the second flight and hostilities with Port Vale were renewed. In September 2000, trouble erupted before the derby game when Stoke attacked a pub holding Vale fans with smoke canisters and a variety of other weapons. Police arrived and eight people were arrested.

The following season saw some of the worst ever trouble between the VLF and Stoke's Under-5s, resulting in 84 arrests. Three hundred police officers could not prevent fighting before or during the game. Twenty people invaded the pitch after Vale scored and four Stoke fans had to seek refuge in a ticket office after going into the opposition end of the ground. "Bottles and cans were hurled during the game, which resulted in a press photographer suffering facial injuries," reported the local paper. But the real trouble occurred much later, as both mobs retreated to their respective heartlands, as Fletch recalled.

"News was filtering through that Stoke were waiting in Hanley town centre with 200-plus lads, but also with a large police presence. A decision was made to travel to the other nightlife location, which was Newcastle-under-Lyme. After a lot of talking between the lads, only twenty-four were up for making the trip, a disappointing number. With such small numbers this was going to be a dangerous trip and there was a feeling that it was going to get messy. We were not wrong.

"We made our way into town with a certain pub in our sights. It wasn't long before all hell broke loose, smoke bombs and pool balls were soon smashing the windows of the pub. Fighting then broke out as Stoke piled out of a couple of pubs. Vale had the upper hand in the early exchanges but were then backed off as more and more Stoke appeared. Vale by now had backed off to some road works on a dual carriageway where the opportunity was not wasted by both sets of lads to unleash as many road signs and cones as possible. Vale then ran at Stoke again and backed them off towards the town centre.

"With what seemed like more Stoke coming from the town centre Vale backed off again. The fighting must have lasted for at least ten minutes, there was no OB as they were all monitoring Stoke's big mob up Hanley. Vale eventually backed off further up the road but scuffles were still taking place. Some serious casualties were taken on both sides and after what seemed like an eternity the police turned up with dogs. As mentioned in so many books, people go on about 100 versus 100, but believe me small fights like this are far more dangerous."

In recent years, Port Vale lads have clashed with several other firms. There was a 40-a-side fight in Tunstall town centre after their home game with Wigan. "We left Burslem hearing Wigan were in Tunstall," remembered CP. "We headed to the Sneyd Arms pub where they were and it went off for a good thirty minutes before the OB turned up. Mops, buckets, brushes, pots and even frying pans were used in a battle that both sides did well in. The police finally appeared and both mobs disappeared."

In 1993, Vale was still languishing in the Second (old Third) Division, having lost to West Brom in the play-off final the previous season. The fixture list handed them a Bank Holiday game at Plymouth and many of the lads lost no time in organising a weekend of it. However, with no real history between the two teams many took their families. About 1,000 fans made the journey down, which considering the size of Vale support at that time was impressive.

The holiday atmosphere was not to last. The game was Plymouth's first police-free, and that proved to be a mistake. "We were in the old shallow terracing at Plymouth which was surrounded by a high fence," said Fletch. "Their mob was to our right and seemed to realise that fun could be had due to the lack of police. During the game, taunting a lad wearing a Stoke top who was giving it the big one in the home end was the only thing of interest. Vale lost the game and the final whistle saw Plymouth's mob come on to the pitch goading, spitting and throwing coins at the Vale fans stuck behind the high fence. This incensed the lads, as kids and women who were standing at the front were in the firing line.

"It had to be done and within seconds scores of Vale had climbed over the fence and were fighting on the pitch with Plymouth. More and more spilled onto the pitch until Plymouth retreated to a corner terrace bit at their own end. Vale now had them penned in, the roles reversed. Both sets of lads were fighting on the fences until Vale forced open the gate, which saw Plymouth make a hasty retreat. Outside the ground they were nowhere to be seen. The police arrived around ten minutes after the fighting had stopped. Plymouth had called it on and had come off far worse."

A few years later, Vale played an end-of-season home game against QPR. Both teams were on the verge of relegation and over 4,000 travelled up from London. During the match there were attempted pitch invasions and missile-throwing but most of it was quickly contained by the police. Vale won, securing survival while leaving QPR above the drop zone only on goal difference. After the game, fighting broke out in the surrounding streets and numerous arrests were made. The away fans were shepherded off home and Vale retreated to their pubs to swap stories and compare battle wounds.

Unbeknown to them, fifteen QPR had booked into a local hotel, just down the road from the main Vale pub. The game had been over for almost three hours when QPR struck, storming into the pub and clashing with a similar number of Vale. Reinforcements were called in, swelling the VLF mob to 50. After several minutes of "serious fighting" the police finally appeared, restored order and escorted the visitors out of town.

Other games involving the VLF included a vicious 60-a-side battle with Barnsley which led to eight arrests. In December 2000, 50 Vale clashed with 40 Rotherham fans in Burslem prior to their league game. Two Rotherham needed medical treatment and the deployment of police was needed to separate the warring mobs. A few months later, at a police-free, low risk game against Swansea, trouble broke out after Vale discovered that six Stoke were with the away supporters. After the game, about 130 Vale gathered at the away exit but stewards escorted the Stoke fans out through another gate. That did little to placate the angry home mob, who continued to search through the away fans for their prey. Police were eventually called and in an ensuing battle ten arrests were made.

More recently, 50 Vale lads travelled to their team's game at Luton. "We plotted up in a boozer," said CP. "Calls were made and Luton said they were coming. Bang on cue, ten minutes later, they were at the front and back of the pub. The Vale inside armed themselves with pool cues and pool balls as the pub windows got put through. Some of the Vale lads managed to get out the back and a confrontation took place with the Luton MIGs. During the fracas, one of the Vale lads threw a sound system out of the window straight into a group of Luton outside. Police turned up and all was calmed down." The police gathered up the away fans and escorted them out of town. On their arrival back in Stoke-on-Trent, about twenty of the Vale lads attacked a mosque, provoking an angry response from local Muslims.

The racist side of Vale's support was evident when the club played at home to Oldham. Over 100 home fans began chanting, "You're just a town full of Pakis," at the away supporters. A police intelligence officer watching the crowd spotted 21-year-old Sean Ratcliffe, and two weeks later he was arrested. He admitted he had taken part and conceded, "It's racist, innit?" But he denied starting the chanting, asked whether 'all the women and children" who joined in would be prosecuted, and said he had been picked up because "he looked like a hooligan". At his subsequent trial the defendant's lawyers argued that the phrase was not insulting, a position agreed by the district judge, and he was acquitted. However, the CPS appealed and a High Court judge concluded that the term was indeed insulting and racist and ordered the district judge to overturn his judgement. After the hearing, Maureen Shea, of the Crown Prosecution Service, said, "This is the first case we have had of this kind. If any football crowd is chanting and the word Paki, or Pakis, is in the chant, it is going to contravene the act."

Away from the bread and butter of the league, Vale love a run in cup competitions and the chance to clash with some of the so-called big boys of the hooligan world. In 1996 they were drawn to play Everton away and during the interview about this fixture (conducted by co-author and Everton fan Andy Nicholls), a rarity in hooligan circles occurred: both sides agreed with each other's accounts of the day!

Fletch gave the Vale view of the two games. "Heavy snow and a big freeze had put paid to ninety per cent of the fixtures that day. This didn't put off over 100 lads making the trip to the FA Cup holders and a well-established top flight club. The weather had caused travel chaos but eventually the train rolled up at Lime Street to be greeted by no other than the Merseyside OB. Most lads were put in an escort, while a handful broke away and made it to the Punch and Judy pub near Lime Street station.

"Very little happened before the game. A late Vale equalizer put everybody on a high and small scuffles broke out outside the ground between small groups of Vale and Everton. Everyone then mobbed together and did a right turn down the road from the ground, where a mob of approximately fifty Everton were waiting. Brief skirmishes were going off all over the place until the OB intervened and stopped the fighting. At this point Vale split into two groups. One group made their way to a back-street boozer, where they were to see no more action. The other group were escorted towards Lime Street, where the police were picking off and arresting certain individuals. The actions of the OB split the group even more, as some went their own way to avoid arrest. Around thirty lads made it to Lime Street, where they were confronted by a group of Everton. Taken by surprise, they legged it to the steps of Lime Street where there was a bit of a stand off before the OB intervened."

Everton's view is no different, though they complained that 100 Vale sat in a boozer at the back end of Lime Street with cameras all around rather than try the pubs around Goodison. "Fair play to the thirty who did make it to town unescorted, but why walk for miles in the freezing cold if the minute you are taken by surprise you leg it?" was one Scouse comment.

At the replay, a massive police presence, and some enthusiastic use of the truncheon, reduced any conflict to a few minor skirmishes. "After the problems we'd had at Goodison Park, a good Vale turnout was guaranteed for the return leg," said Fletch. "Everton had sold over 7,000 tickets for the game and it wasn't long before it kicked off, this time in one of the pubs near the ground. With a mob of Everton at one end and approximately twenty 20 Vale at the other, the inevitable happened with glasses, chairs and stools raining down on each other. The police were called to break up the incident, which left the pub in a bad state of repair.

"The next incident happened as we were walking up towards the ground near a block of flats. An Everton mob were seen grouping together on the car park of the flats and some faces were recognized from the game at Everton. It wasn't long before Vale were over at them and small skirmishes took place before the massive police presence intervened."

Vale's biggest battle in recent years has been with Wrexham in 2003, as CP recounted: "The day had started well. By the time we had reached Crewe Station, one train with seventy-plus lads was already on its way to Chester. With another seventy waiting for the next train, all was going to plan. We arrived in Chester and soon met up with the rest of the lads. It wasn't long before the police had spotted us but surprisingly they kept their distance and were only monitoring the situation.

"The decision was made to catch the 12.30pm train in to Wrexham. As we got off the train, numerous OB attempted to block off the road to the town centre. Many lads made it through and made their way to the town; other unfortunate ones were taken to a pub well out of the way. Not much happened before the game other than some Wrexham mouthing off behind the OB lines as we marched past the Racecourse pub. It was their town and we had taken liberties and as yet had met no resistance. However things were soon to change.

"The game finished two-one to Wrexham. From the atmosphere in the ground it was obvious something had to happen and things weren't helped when a Welsh flag was set on fire and thrown onto the pitch. We could see in the ground that they had around 50 lads to our right who would be up for it after the match. The match finished and all the lads bowled out to get stuck in, only for the road to be completely blocked by lines of OB. Approximately 30 lads then ran up a side street to try to get to Wrexham but funnily the police didn't follow. This put most lads off, thinking it was either a dead end or a set-up, so the majority of the lads were stuck behind the lines of OB.

"The 30 who had made a sprint for it eventually found a small alleyway where they clashed with the Wrexham lot. Punches, sticks, bricks, kicks and anything that could be found was used until the police eventually broke it up. Unfortunately most of the 30 or so eventually received prison terms for their endeavours that day, as it was all captured on the police helicopter cameras."

One newspaper reported, "Vale fans dodged police by running up a side street, forced their way through the garden of a private house, and then hurled bricks at Wrexham supporters. They reacted by running up another street and violence erupted in an alley joining the two roads, with rival fans kicking and punching each other, and hurling bricks, pieces of wood – and possibly gnomes from gardens – at each other." The two mobs clashed for fifteen minutes on a council estate near the Racecourse Ground, apparently unaware that the whole area was covered by CCTV cameras and was also captured by a quickly scrambled police helicopter.

Thirty-two arrests were subsequently made and nine men were sent to prison, with a further twelve receiving community service orders. All but three were from Port Vale, their ages ranging from 18-44. Interestingly, eleven were over 30 and four over 40 years of age. The judge concluded, "Members of the public on the streets or in their own houses would have been truly terrified by the scale of the public disorder." The police inquiry that led to the arrests came under the remit of Operation Scorpion, set up by Staffordshire Police to crack down on hooliganism within their force boundary. By the spring of 2004, over 115 hooligans had been caught. The arrests also boosted the overall arrest figures at Port Vale to 48, almost double that of Stoke City.

The following season, the Port Vale chairman Bill Bratt expressed his fear of a repeat of the disorder and urged the club's supporters to stay out of trouble. He said that the violence had led to an increase in policing costs at the ground, at a time when the club could ill-afford them, and noted that the next home match against Wrexham saw a police bill of £19,000. He told the local paper: "I am asking the fans not to give in to provocation. It was because of the trouble at Wrexham last season that we ended up with a larger police bill. I am asking them to behave themselves, even though I know the majority of Port Vale supporters are law abiding."

According to CP, "This was the biggest number of arrests at Vale for several years. Twelve prison sentences and numerous bans were handed out to Vale and Wrexham hooligans. The punishment was harsh, as the incident was blown out of proportion, but typical of what happens at present. The lads knew the risks, and as they say, if you can't do the time don't do the crime."

Today, the VLF has a hardcore of around 40-50, though for bigger games this number can reach 80 or, with hangers-on, up to 150. "The biggest turnouts are for big games at home against the likes of Stoke, Wolves, Birmingham, West Brom, QPR, and basically any other team with a decent reputation," said Fletch. The firm has been hit hard by the police, with 67 people currently on bans at the club. For a club with an average home gate of less than 5,000, this must rate as one of the highest ratios in the country.

It's a statistic in which Fletch shows a perverse pride. "We may not have the numbers or get the publicity they do, but like Stoke we don't lie down if firms come here and try and take the piss. We have one of the biggest percentage bans per attendance average in the league, and even away from the football have had some good battles with our neighbours. I respect their main firm lads 100 per cent but they don't get it all their own way with us, although I doubt if any of them will admit it."

PRESTON NORTH END

Ground: Deepdale
Firms: Spotty Dog crew, Town End mob, Preston Para Soccer, Preston Foot Patrol
Rivals: Blackpool, Wigan, Stoke City

If there were any 150-year-old Preston fans still alive, they would laugh at claims that modern football hooliganism was started by the followers of the Merseyside clubs in the 1950s. "The 1950s?" they might mock. "We were seasoned veterans of disorder by then."

For some reason, the newspaper archives are full of stories of Preston fans misbehaving over 150 years ago. Perhaps there was similar trouble elsewhere, but no club had the same number of documented disorders than Preston. In 1843, 200 soldiers and 50 policemen were needed to patrol the ropes at a Preston North End v Sunderland match. Almost forty years later, in 1881, two railway officials were knocked unconscious at Wigan Station by a group travelling to an away match at Newton Heath (later Manchester United). Three years later Preston fans attacked Bolton Wanderers players and spectators at the end of the game, and in 1885 a mob of "roughs" attacked a visiting Aston Villa team with sticks, stones and other missiles. The following year brought a violent clash between rival PNE and Queens Park fans at a railway station. Finally, in 1905, several fans were tried for hooliganism including a "drunk and disorderly" 70-year-old woman.

In more recent times most of the trouble involving Preston has been against local rivals Blackpool, Blackburn, Burnley, Wigan and Bolton. It is bad enough being relegated, it is even worse being relegated by your local rivals, but the feeling is almost indescribable when your team is relegated by your local rivals in a match that also sees them get promoted. That was what happened to Preston on Monday, 13 April 1970, when a 3–0 home defeat by Blackpool saw the complete polarisation of fortunes.

"The agony and the ecstasy!" shouted the headline in the *Lancashire Evening Post*. As Blackpool fans poured onto the pitch at the end of the game, the bulk of the 35,000 people inside the ground watched in utter disbelief. A comment piece in the same newspaper summed up the emotions of a town built upon footballing greats. "The harsh realities of modern day soccer finally caught up with, and indeed overtook, PNE last night. As one who has avidly followed the fortunes of this once proud club for many years, I am afraid that like many others, I found those 90 humiliating minutes almost too much to bear."

"It was a humiliation," remembered Billy, a long-time Preston supporter. "Blackpool kicked the gates in and flooded the Kop."

Saturday, 17 October 1970, is another date that will not be forgotten by many Preston fans around in that time. That was the day when Preston North End travelled to Halifax and manager Alan Ball referred to the away fans as "The Gentry". Whether Ball was referring to a quote from an unknown 18th century historian who described Preston as "a pretty town with an abundance of gentry in it, commonly called Proud Preston" is unclear. What is certain is that Preston fans loved the title and for the next few years they would turn up at away matches wearing bowler hats (made fashionable by John Steed in *The Avengers* – and John Cleese of *Monty Python*) and umbrellas.

Billy remembers the trend. "When PNE were relegated in 1969/70, Alan Ball senior was appointed and used to salute the fans at the away matches. Most away games that year were walkovers, as PNE took mobs everywhere. Notable exceptions were Mansfield and Port Vale, who fought back. These grounds were fairly new, as this was the first time we had been out of the top two divisions. One notable trip was when a furniture van pulled up in Plymouth city centre, dropped its tailgate, and out walked about twenty-five blokes in bowler hats.

"This was early Seventies and so a bit early for me, but I can remember getting on the train with a lot of older lads who were up for a good laugh, a bit of thieving, fighting and lots of drinking. Always attracting a police presence, but always running through town centres, smashing up pubs, having a go at any locals who fancied themselves. They were usually glad to get home in one piece. These guys were often encouraged by Alan Ball, who used to come on the pitch before the game and bow to them. Everyone in those days wore the bowler hat."

The Gentry became the general name given to Preston fans, bootboys and ordinary supporters alike. There were, however, several small gangs operating during the period, each with their own legends. "I remember Frankie Rizz, King of the Kop," says Billy. "Illy, a feared Jamaican – there were a good gang of Jamaican lads around in the early Seventies. Johnny and Joey F were always in there, and well feared. JC once hammered a Rolls Royce windscreen in Taunton, on the way back from a game at Exeter, after a big fight in a chip shop with locals. Then later we had the Spotty Dog, and a team of lunatics who would go on any end away from home. There were several gangs on the go at this time: Jacko from the Chorley mob, a Leyland crew who always caused trouble wherever they went."

In August 1971, Preston played at Barrow in the League Cup, in a game marred by serious disorder. While they won the game comfortably, the newspapers were more concerned with the violence. "A 'bit of bovver' is bad enough, but the scenes in the streets of Barrow near the railway station and on the terraces at the ground were absolutely disgusting," noted a reporter in the *Lancashire Evening Post*.

They completely overshadowed the match itself, starting before the kick-off and going on for an hour afterwards, and I lost count of the boys I saw clutching blood-stained faces, some with seriously cut eyes or ears from fights or broken glass.

Gangs of alleged supporters of the two teams went wild, with the boot going in on many occasions, and there was a constant stream of ejections from the terraces by the police in a running battle.

The Barrow youths are notorious, I was told, and it may be that they were the instigators, but the problem is a general one with boys of this low mentality.

Obviously, all they want to do is to get down to the 'aggro' as soon as they can – and it is quite clear that something drastic will have to be done to stop their activities.

... I don't know whether the crowd of nearly 4,319 enjoyed the fixture but I do know some of them should not have been allowed to see it.

North End have many genuine young supporters who Ball calls 'The Gentry' and who do a great job cheering the team on. Surely it's time the 'bovver boys' were sorted out and not allowed to ruin their enjoyment.

Preston fans did not have it all their own way, and in October 1973 it was their turn to be overrun. The visitors were Sunderland and their usual large following was swelled by the euphoria of their FA victory over Leeds the previous May. "They brought about 7,000 fans," recalled Billy. "They were massed on the Town end, and about 100 were getting a kicking on the Kop. They then ran across the pitch, swarmed all over the Kop beating up any remaining PNE, and then ran back across the pitch. We were annihilated by sheer weight of numbers." It was several years later, in the 1980s, when Preston could claim to take any sort of revenge. "We gave Sunderland a fright when about 3,000 turned up at Roker for a New Year's Day game. Police expected 300 and had to open a paddock at the side to accommodate us all. The Sunderland fans came round for a do at the end but quickly got chased off without too much bother."

Four years after the horrific scenes at Barrow, Preston were again shamed in the national press after an FA Cup defeat at non-League Scarborough. The Lancashire club crashed out 3-2 but once again it was the behaviour of their fans which received most national attention. Sports journalist Norman Shakeshaft, who had penned the outburst following the Barrow match, was once again in indignant mood. "A disgrace to the town," the headline of his column read:

Saturday was the blackest day in Preston North End's history for several reasons. But the worst aspect of all was the behaviour of some of the club's young supporters at Scarborough's Seamer Road ground.

'This is proud Preston, is it?' asked new social club steward Eddie Adams as he looked at the damage caused by the fans.

I felt embarrassed to be a Prestonian and could not make a reply.

The hooligans who smashed the windows of the boardroom and the club extension specially opened ahead of schedule to offer hospitality to Preston people, had disgraced the name of the town.

The North End directors, officials and players were also terribly upset. 'We do not want fans who behave like this,' said Chairman Alan Jones. 'We would rather have no support at all.'

Mr Jones has my sympathy and I hope something positive can now be done to stop vandals from seeing games at Deepdale and from travelling to away matches.

Only last week, outside Deepdale, a window of the Wrexham team coach was smashed after Preston had lost to the Welsh club – and the follow-up at Scarborough has again shown that some youngsters do not know what sport is all about.

If they cannot accept disappointment they should not be involved in any way with football.

It is often said that many trouble makers are not interested in any case and that they only go to matches to cause bother and do as much damage as possible. If that is so, it is time other football followers rooted them out and gave the police much more help in identifying the culprits.

The result on Saturday was also the worst ever, with the team beaten by a non-league club. But it is up to everyone connected with North End to act with dignity.

The young fans should prove that they are capable of being men and not morons. That is the only way the town can salvage its reputation and become proud Preston again.

The autumn of 1976 saw Preston fans in further trouble in cup ties, first against Crewe and then, a fortnight later, away at Halifax. The disorder at the Crewe game was largely with Liverpudlians, as the third-round replay was held at Anfield after two earlier score draws. "There was a mass battle with Scousers for the Kop," recalled Billy, "which ended with PNE being led away by police into the paddock. However many scuffles remained and the city centre looked like a war scene as we travelled back to the trains."

A win over Crewe set up Preston with an away tie at Halifax, a team well below them in the league. In what should have been a comfortable formality, Preston were humbled – and their fans ran wild. It started when the home side scored the only goal of the game in the second half. "Opposing fans ran to meet each other in the centre of the ground," reported the *Halifax Courier*. "Police, who managed to separate them and return them to their own areas, had to cope with a shower of 200 beer cans thrown by Preston fans." A policeman was struck on the head with a can and had his uniform torn. After the game, some of the 400 Preston fans escorted to the train station smashed windows in the waiting room and pushed trolleys on the line.

By the late Seventies, a new generation of hooligans were emerging at Preston, though more a gang for whom drinking appeared compulsory and violence was an added bonus. "We were mainly train travellers who would go to most away games," recalled Billy. "I was one of these, and the players in our mob were Breck, Bowser, Pouch, Eric the Viking, Harold, Greggy, Jacko, Rhodesian Frank and several others whose names I can't remember.

"One match that stands out was at Swindon. We arrived by coach and were drinking in the supporters' club. A bit of banter turned into a singing match but when a pint pot came across the floor the response was immediate and about fifty glasses from our mob put paid to their mob. They mustered a huge gang after the game, and as we were depleted, they charged. A brave few turned round to have a do. Breck, me, Bowser, Rhodesian Frank, Steve C, all gave our best against far superior numbers. We escaped any serious injury only to get the upper hand back at the coach when Bowser (also known as the Black Panther for his looks) launched his famous ear kick from a standing position, bringing the Swindon lad down on the floor. Breck actually left the front of one of his famous yellow boots in Swindon that day."

This mob never missed a match, home or away and all too often became embroiled in trouble. "Harold was famous for putting his foot through the Villa drum whilst PNE were assaulting the Holte End," said Billy. "Another good set-to was at Peterborough. The train was full of beer when we left, and everyone was pissed when we got off. There were about 1,000 lads on the train, and we all headed for the city centre. On approaching the ground, several of us were set upon by about twenty Peterborough. Little did they know that the group in front were PNE, and as I approached the bridge, one PNE fan, Bambs, was throwing one in the canal from the bridge. As our group approached the ground we were getting 'V' signs from their first-floor supporters' club. Someone broke the big window in the club, scattering the occupants all over the place."

Trouble became more than harmless fun on 6 May 1978, when a fight between two rival football gangs in a Preston nightclub ended with the death of 22-year-old Henry Bailey. "The fight erupted during the final number by punk group The Depressions," reported the local paper. "Chanting between rival gangs of Blackpool and Preston youths developed into a full-scale battle as fans throwing chairs, metal crash barriers, glasses and ash trays waded into each other."

One punk fan told the paper, "Someone grabbed the mike and started singing, 'Sham 69,' and then there was trouble between the Blackpool and Preston lot. It was like a football fight. The Blackpool lot started singing, 'Seaside aggro,' and the Preston lot started singing back. Chairs were being flung about and even metal barriers that are used to stop people getting on the stage. Most punks are football supporters and there is big rivalry between Blackpool and Preston." Another eyewitness recalled chants of

"Preston are magic" shortly before the brawl erupted, while a bouncer said there was little that he and a colleague could do. "There were only two of us on stage to control 600 howling fans. It was absolutely ridiculous." He himself was dragged off the stage and kicked and punched repeatedly around the head and body.

A massive murder investigation was launched, involving over 100 detectives, and five days later a 22-year-old man was arrested and charged with Bailey's death. The accused was a Preston man, who was later acquitted of the murder. Suspicion remained focused on the culprit being a Blackpool fan. "Harry was a good mate of mine," remembered Billy quietly, "and he was a well-known PNE boy. However, all the locals thought it was the Blackpool crew who had done it. This had serious repercussions for future games and it did worsen the battles with them for a while."

The death of Bailey did not stop the trouble at PNE. Early into the new season, the visit of Millwall saw serious disorder, largely caused by the Londoners. The game itself was described as "the worst display of the season", with the only bright spot the penalty awarded to Preston ten minutes from the end. But, in keeping with the overall poor showing, the spot kick was easily saved by the keeper.

A fortnight later, it was the turn of Stoke City to instigate trouble. "There was a big fight on the Kop with the over-forties mob," said Billy. "They all had bald heads and were mean." It was also a day remembered by Stoke hooligan Mark Chester. "The game was one of my first memories of Stoke taking an end and handing out a good hiding," he said. The local paper reported that a Preston supporter was stabbed in the chest after rivals clashed in Preston town centre after the game. Sixteen people were arrested, five of them from the Preston area. Despite mounted police being used on the terraces at Deepdale, the trouble was not actually as bad as expected. "Most of the problems came afterwards when the supporters came into town," a police spokesman said. "There was a lot of shouting and messing around. The most serious incident was the stabbing, but the boy was not badly hurt." Another officer said that most of the trouble at Deepdale was caused by younger supporters. "Most of the time it was just bunches of kids hanging round looking for fights," he said.

When they played that season at Stoke, Preston insist they avenged the hiding they got at home. "We surprised them at Stoke in a night fixture when we had a running battle outside," said Billy. "There was a fight in a cemetery." The *Stoke Sentinel* reported on a particularly bad injury.

A Stoke City fan may have lost sight of an eye following an attack after last night's match.

And today, police were appealing for witnesses to the soccer violence flare-up outside St. Peter's Church, Church Street, Stoke.

Doctors carried out an emergency operation to remove teeth from a metal Afro-style comb embedded in 2-inch deep wounds.

Police said: "It would appear the Afro-style comb was pushed into the face of the lad, causing serious injuries.

"The incident happened as PNE supporters were among the Stoke city fans making their way up Church Street at the same time.

"They were seen to jump over the wall into the graveyard."

"Since those do's with Stoke back then it's always been bitter when we play each other," added Billy, "and I have witnessed incidents on railway stations when the two mobs have met on their travels."

Blackpool were Preston's most hated rivals and one match, in 1976, saw the Seasiders start a fire on the Deepdale terraces, to the chant of "Preston's stand is burning down, burning down, burning down." Another match, an FA Cup tie, saw running battles all around the town. "There was a good mob from Blackpool and they did seem to have the upper hand on the way back to the station," recollected Billy. "But plenty of them got hammered around Meadow Street before the game. I remember one big do outside the bus depot on Deepdale Road about five minutes before kick-off, when a group of Blackpool were attacked by a PNE mob led by a deaf guy, who could not hear the police sirens. He was lifted. I never knew his name – he couldn't speak." Trouble between the two continued into the Eighties, with a particularly lively encounter at Deepdale on Boxing Day, 1987 [see *Blackpool* in *Hooligans 1*].

Other derbies against Blackburn, Bolton and Burnley were also violent affairs and there are reports of disorder with these clubs going back to 1966. Other, less obvious rivalries exist with Wigan, Gillingham, Chester and Wrexham. "Wigan – they hate us much more than we hate them," said Billy. "This is based on us always discounting them, as they were, in our opinion, still a non-league club. How times change, eh.

"Gillingham, they list us as their worst enemy, don't know why except that a mob arrived early in the town a number of years ago and set fire to a load of tyres and rolled them down a hill into the centre. Also Wrexham and Chester, born out of the fact that we used to overrun them every time we went there. At Wrexham, when they won the old Third Division in 1978, about 2,000 PNE turned up to support them, as they had to avoid losing against Peterborough so PNE went up. After the end of the game, the result was positive and the Wrexham fans were singing, 'Wrexham and Preston,' only to be treated shamelessly by a mob from Preston. We never got on after that."

Preston's promotion from the Third Division in May 1978 saw them swap the likes of Shrewsbury, Chester, Bury and Exeter with West Ham, Sheffield United and Newcastle. A respectable seventh place finish in the division saw them play Chelsea the following season, after the West London giants were relegated. It was always going to be a game where trouble was likely and for the PNE lads it was one of the most eagerly awaited of the season. "This match was billed as one of the worst possible games for hooliganism for a long time," said Billy. "Gangs of PNE were out early, and the expected Chelsea mob arrived in good voice. They were chased and harried throughout town."

The result was the death of one Chelsea fan. "Soccer fan in bridge plunge riddle," declared the front page of the *Lancashire Evening Post*. "A soccer fan took a short cut to death when he leapt from a road bridge. Gary Blissett-Lee slipped and plunged nearly twenty feet as a group of his friends watched in horror." He had been on his way to the match when the accident happened. "He was walking along Preston's Ringway opposite the town's magistrates courts when he tried to jump across a five-feet gap from the road bridge on the first floor of the Market Car Park," added the paper. "Police believe he was taking a short cut back into town before going to the match when he lost his footing and fell into market's service area." Two days later Det Insp Roy Slater of Fulwood CID said police inquiries into the incident were finished and there were no suspicious circumstances. "It was a pure accident. We don't know what exactly he was thinking about but he lost his foothold and fell."

What no-one reported was that Blissett-Lee was actually fleeing Preston fans when he was cornered and felt he had no alternative but to jump over a small gap. He misjudged and slipped to his death. "The news of the death spread like wildfire," remembered Billy. "It seemed to put a dampener on the proceedings, which quickly quietened down. The return at the Bridge seemed to pass off peacefully, however two PNE fans were ejected from the Shed after singing North End songs as the teams emerged."

Chelsea's next visit to Deepdale was to be an anxious affair for the authorities. In addition to memories of Blissett-Lee's death, the London side were chasing promotion, and as a result were expected to be followed by 5,000 supporters. The police drafted in extra officers and in the days leading up to the game repeatedly reassured the public that order would be maintained. Preston police had been liaising with the Metropolitan Police over potential trouble. The operation paid off and only a dozen were arrested, mostly for minor offences. A specially assembled taskforce, incorporating mounted officers and others with dogs, led the Chelsea fans under a heavy escort from the railway station to Deepdale. "Things were reasonable, there was nothing we could not handle," a police spokesman said. "We arrested both Chelsea and North End supporters, but mainly for minor public order offences." However, fifteen Chelsea fans were arrested in Blackpool after many decided to stay in the seaside resort for the weekend.

The early 1980s saw a new mob emerge when casuals, sick of the Kopites, began the Town End mob. Over the first few seasons they battled with, among others, Sheff Wed, QPR, Crystal Palace and Birmingham. Later, segregation took over and battles inside the ground reduced. "Funnily enough," said Billy, "the Town End mob grew in size after that."

The casuals might have arrived but there was still life in the beer boys yet and the late Seventies and early Eighties saw the formation of the DO Mob. "This was a bunch of lads who drank more beer than any crew I've ever come across," laughed Billy, an active follower of the DO Mob. "It was while I was working at the Royal Mail and we had between fifteen and twenty-five to a lot of away games and we would nearly always travel on the service train. We couldn't give a fuck about any crew and we could drink for England. We were always late for the game because we stayed in the pub for the last several rounds of shorts before staggering usually onto the home end. Always too pissed for anything serious, but not many would tackle us due to the nature of the mob. Sometimes we would go straight from the night shift with regulation GPO black donkey jackets on.

"We had various accepted drinking holes in different towns, always had the crack, kissed the policewomen, always had cans or bottles of spirit on trains, and usually got away with murder. Only a few of us ever got nicked but we did end up in some rather strange places, like locked in a train in sidings on the Wirral after a trip to Wrexham. We once went to Burnley for a night game at 10.30am, proceeded to have a lock-in at the Waggoners on Colne Road, and then stopped a Burnley coach from Nelson. The driver thought we were Burnley but we ended up stood up right along the coach singing PNE songs and snarling in their faces. No-one on the bus moved or murmured a word. When we got to the ground we marched into their pub and demanded more drink, and got it, taking the piss out of Burnley fans till kick-off time.

"We also had a good do at Shrewsbury one year. Two groups had gone for meals after the game, and the Indian meal lot ran out without paying, taking a huge Indian flag with them. As we met up with the other crew, who incidentally were running towards us from another direction, one of the lads produced the flag and said, 'Look at that bastard.' The other team then produced a massive ornamental lamp they had nicked off the restaurant bar. We then continued to serenade some grandmothers before kissing the policewomen goodbye as we were ejected from Shrewsbury. This team were really mad, and could always be found drinking, and gambling on the train. Never really started fights, but were a force in the PNE chapter."

While Preston's footballing fortunes declined, off the pitch names were being made. "Mad Mick is infamous at Preston after he tried to take on the Colchester crew and was only rescued at the last minute by a couple of heroes who dragged him into the stand to safety. Hereford away the night they won the championship, then came across the pitch, about 2,000 of them onto forty, and they ran away after Bowser led the charge over the second wall on the away end. Reading away, home fans invaded the pitch and about fifty very drunk PNE chased them off led by a certain JC holding an empty bottle of Pernod. He had previously walked through their mob threatening anybody who might have wanted to challenge him and his mate."

The club hit rock bottom in the mid-Eighties, falling from mid-table in the Second Division at the start of the decade to twenty-third place in the Fourth Division in 1986. Yet their hooligan following did not significantly diminish – in fact this period saw the mob emerge who would become known as Preston Para Soccer (PPS), a late acknowledgment, perhaps, that football gangs now needed catchy names. Inevitably they produced their own calling cards, with the catchphrase, "We came in peace, we left you in pieces."

In 1988, 200 PPS leapt out of the Town End section and stormed onto the pitch at the end of a Sherpa Van Trophy semi-final at Hartlepool. Thirty Hartlepool jumped on to confront them. "One of the Pool fans then charged into the Preston crowd before being dragged to the ground and given a beating," noted one eyewitness, the sports editor of the *Hartlepool Mail*.

The club remained in a perilous financial state and form on the pitch was uninspiring. In 1994, a local magistrate, sentencing five men charged with various offences after a game at home to Carlisle, told the defendants that he wouldn't ban them from Deepdale because watching Preston North End was punishment enough!

In the mid-Nineties, PNE fans ran amok at Scarborough, smashing windows and fighting outside night clubs after 2,000 supporters made the trip to the seaside resort. And a Coca-Cola Cup game at neighbours Blackburn Rovers in 1997 saw fans fighting outside Blackburn train station after the game. Police had to escort the away fans on their train home. "I was disappointed with some Preston supporters whose behaviour deteriorated after the match because of drink," said Inspector Stuart Caley.

Several Preston fans were sent to prison after fighting broke out in a pub in Mansfield after a league game in October 1990. A fight between rival fans broke out in the Plough public house, with one customer getting struck on the head with a stool. The fight spilled outside and continued in the car park but a passing police van was able to prevent the trouble worsening. A subsequent court case heard from the Preston police spotter that Preston fans were "gesticulating to Mansfield fans on the terraces, indicating that they should meet outside." Four men were sent to jail, while a further three Preston fans who pleaded not guilty were acquitted.

Preston's location as a railway hub proved to be bad news for the town and local police after several hooligan mobs decided to stop off there for a fight on their return from England's match in Scotland in November 1999. "Soccer hooligans turned Preston town centre into a bloody battlefield in a series of pre-arranged riots," reported the local paper. "Party-goers fled as dozens of fights broke out in crowded pubs last Saturday night following England's victory over Scotland. The fights – between sets of thugs from four local football teams – culminated in a 100-strong brawl on Preston's railway station at 10.30pm."

The violence was described by police officers as the worst the town had experienced in several years. Police told the *Citizen* newspaper that dozens of followers of four local clubs – PNE, Manchester United, Burnley and Wigan – had set up the clashes to coincide with their return home from England's Euro 2000 qualifying game, as some of their trains terminated at Preston. PC Philip Bilsborough, from the town's football intelligence unit, said, "In total there were twenty-seven incidents reported in the town's pubs, which culminated in the main incident on Preston Railway Station."

A well-known Manchester United hooligan, Fran, acknowledged the Preston lads that day: "We had took the piss all day long, offered it on a plate to every firm who travelled to Scotland that day and there were no takers. On the way home Preston were on the phones and planned a meet, and although they were done, had the balls to take on what was a very impressive United firm that day."

The first few months of 2001 was a busy period for Preston hooligans. In mid-January, their team played at neighbouring Blackburn Rovers and "a large fight took place between rival Blackburn and Preston supporters," noted the NCIS intelligence report. "Police used batons to disperse the rival supporters. Outside a local public house further disorder took place as Blackburn supporters inside tried to force their way past mounted officers blocking the door in an attempt to attack the Preston supporters being escorted by police."

Three weeks later, Preston travelled to Portsmouth, where their mob attacked their Pompey rivals in a local pub. "A fight took place with glasses and bottles being thrown," reported NCIS. "One of the Preston supporters sustained a broken cheekbone. Both groups were separated and taken into the ground via different routes. After the match, the home supporters congregated outside the away end and tried to bait the Preston supporters. Both groups were kept apart and the Preston supporters were escorted to their coach with the Portsmouth supporters trying to ambush them through the side streets. They were prevented from doing so by police cordons. Later that evening, away from the ground, a Preston supporter was assaulted in a local pub and sustained a serious injury to his eye."

"This was an arranged scrap," said Billy. "There were lots of injuries and local pride hurt. There were threats of revenge from Pompey but they never showed at Deepdale." The day was not over yet for the Preston lads. A coachload of their hooligans decided to stop for a drink in Stafford town centre on their way home, but before long their presence attracted the attention of locals and a fight followed. Police, some with dogs, were rushed to the area and the Preston mob were herded onto their coach and escorted away. One Preston fan, who suffered facial injuries, was left behind in the local hospital.

Towards the end of the season there was further disorder with the visit to Deepdale of Nottingham Forest. A group of 30 Forest left the ground ten minutes before half-time and headed to a nearby pub where 20 Preston fans were based. Police moved in quickly to block the path of the Forest group but while they were doing so the Preston group got out of the pub via a side door and attacked their rivals. Chaos ensued, with the police trying to force Preston back into the pub whilst battling to keep Forest out. Order was eventually restored, with the police escorting the away mob out of town. However, a group of 40 Preston clashed with other Forest fans after the game.

In May 2003, the *Lancashire Evening Post* introduced its readers to a new threat at Deepdale:

Football hooligans are planning to set up a violent new "firm", the Evening Post can reveal The thugs are using the Internet to target key Preston North End matches next season.

The sinister motives of the so-called Preston Youth Firm (PYF) are laid out in a website chat room where violence at matches is celebrated.

One entry on the site says: "...never really had a proper ruck apart from a minor incident at Rotherham. I think we should take it to them as there is some scores to settle there."

Entries on the website discuss tactics and ways of arranging fights with rival gangs without being detected.

The derby against Wigan Athletic, Yorkshire rivals Bradford City and a possible friendly with Blackpool are earmarked for possible clashes.

One of the main topics on the site is the possibility of setting up a new "youth firm" for teenagers.

An entry under the title, New Firm, says: "If anyone is really interested about going to a few away games next season hopefully we can get something sorted.

"I'll be going to place(s) like Sheff Utd, Notts Forest… anyone who's serious (and) wants to join up then they can.

"If enough lads get to know each other then we could organise things by mobile. After all, these sites are for things that have happened, not what are going to happen."

More recently, Preston greeted Leeds United's return to the second tier by taking a large mob to Yorkshire and there were clashes in the city centre before the match. Three weeks later, seven Preston hooligans were arrested in early morning raids in connection with the incident. The police action was immediately welcomed by the club and the official supporters' club, whose secretary, Karen Wolstenholme said, "Hooliganism seems to be on the rise and it has to be stamped out, anyone who carries out violence when following our team is not a real PNE fan."

A hundred and fifty years after Preston fans started misbehaving, some things have not changed.

Q

QUEENS PARK RANGERS

Ground: Loftus Road
Firms: C Mob, The Hardcore, Naughty 40,
Rivals: Luton, Norwich, Fulham, Oxford

Many hooligans believe QPR have one of the most underrated firms in the country. They are too quickly dismissed as either a family club or even a "feeder" mob for nearby Chelsea. Both views are wrong, as many opposing mobs have found out to their cost, especially in more recent years. The vast White City estate, visible to anyone who has travelled into London on the A40, coupled with the long-standing gang culture of Ladbroke Grove and Notting Hill, have given the club some violent followers. With the recent gentrification of Chelsea and Fulham, QPR have increasingly been seen by local lads as "their team". Today, QPR are possibly the most active firm in the capital, something that will not surprise those clubs that have fallen foul of them in recent years.

The Times was reporting trouble at QPR back in 1968. By the mid-Seventies, pitch invasions and fighting by young fans caused the club to first raise the ticket prices for young fans and eventually to stop special fares altogether. It failed to contain trouble. In the early 1980s, QPR had a number of clashes with Crystal Palace, culminating in an FA Cup match at Loftus Road in 1982 at which serious fighting on the terraces spilled on to the pitch and saw several players attacked.

Mention QPR to most seasoned hooligans and one name crops up: that of Mark Gregory, or "Gregor", as he is better known. Now 45, Gregor has been on the QPR scene for nearly 30 years but is also known to have run with Chelsea, Millwall and Spurs. His first trip to Loftus Road was an end-of-season home game against Burnley, which erupted into violence as the visitors twice attempted to take the Loft, the end frequented by QPR's hardcore. During the late 1980s, he was a keen mover behind attempts to form a London-wide mob to meet the threat of some larger northern mobs.

"Mark is a legend at Rangers, at least among the older lads," said Darren, one of QPR's football firm. "His exploits are well known and his reputation among other firms and even at England games has made him one of the most well known names on the football violence scene, attracting respect and ridicule in equal measure. Norwich in particular seem obsessed with him and always ask where he is whenever our two firms meet. However having such a high profile has worked against him, attracting a lot of police attention, and for much of the last eighteen years he has been banned or even inside, so that has limited the influence he has had during his sporadic appearances. It's also made him a particular target for opposing firms and he's received many a slap or had narrow escapes, though to be fair he's pretty irrepressible and gives as good as he gets.

"Whenever he's been around though, he's been in the thick of things. Lads gather round him and he's used his network of contacts to organise trouble. I remember in 1987/88 he even used his girlfriend to try to organise a meet with Pompey after our home fixture. However this doesn't mean he was always the top boy and often it was in tandem with other, older faces. Nowadays he appears every so often but only really speaks to the older lads. I don't know if many of the Youth are even aware of who he is, although he has been present at trouble involving them at Loftus Road."

The first hooligan mob at QPR was the C-Mob, who were active in the early 1980s. "They used to go everywhere and they always stuck tight," recalled Gregor in the book *Top Boys* by Cass Pennant. Next up was the Hardcore, which existed from the mid-to-late 1980s. "As far as I know it was Gregor's idea," said Darren. "A couple of lads had some calling cards printed, but I never saw them used. Very occasionally the name was chanted by us at away games. One occasion was Charlton away, which was the last game of the 1986/87 season. We had a good 150 there that day, there were some scuffles with the home firm and a long walk after the game which ended up at Elmers End station, where we got the train to Victoria and about eighty waited for Leeds to return from Brighton. Unfortunately very few Leeds had taken that route, but a good drink was had opposite the station in Shakes."

The mid-Eighties also saw regular fights with Ipswich, including a League Cup match which included a big punch-up in the ground. But this rivalry was nothing compared to the trouble QPR regularly had with Luton Town. "You were always guaranteed a warm welcome at Luton," remembered one QPR veteran who is now in his forties. "I think they thought that we were the only London club with any sort of reputation that they could take on. Same place every year – by the underpass at that dual carriageway going back to the station. We always more than held our own.

"I remember a game at Easter in 1981 when Rangers went into the 'triangle', Luton's gathering point at the time. Took about ten minutes for the police to bring things under control and I'm sure I saw a copper's helmet fly towards the centre circle at one point. The next year was just before our FA Cup final appearance and the night Luton won the Second Division championship. It went mental afterwards, particularly in the alleyway along the side of the ground. When we played them again a couple of years later, the OB had finally started using escorts. This didn't stop them attacking us with missiles from the top of a multi-storey car-park."

Luton then banned away fans – to little effect. "We never had any problems getting in. I remember about half a dozen of us celebrating a Les Ferdinand last minute winner in the Kenilworth Road end. No-one said a word to us.

"Although away fans were banned for league games, Luton had to let them in for cup ties. Rangers had a fifth-round FA Cup replay there in the mid-Eighties. This was nasty. They were picking people off as they left the station, using knives, ammonia, pool balls, the lot. We really got it together after the game and marched up Dunstable Road. People were really angry after six stabbings beforehand. They were waiting for us in Bury Park, but threw a few missiles and ran when they saw the Rangers mob."

Their most violent encounter in London was on 11 April 1987, a battle at St Pancras train station that was one of the first fights captured by CCTV cameras. Darren, who was convicted as a result of the fight, recounted the day: "At that time I sat in R Block of the Ellerslie Road Stand, which is next to the away end. For the last couple of seasons that was where a lot of our boys had been gathering. That day there were Luton in our seats and right from the off there was a very tense atmosphere. There were several scuffles in the first half and at half-time, which resulted in the Luton lads getting taken out of our seats and put into the away end. Gregor slashed a Luton lad, which resulted in his arrest outside and was the reason he wasn't at St Pancras later. This led to a prison sentence and ban, which to all intents and purposes ended his career as QPR's number one. Things were quiet in the second half, but I could tell this wasn't the end of the violence for the day.

"As soon as the game finished those of us in R Block went outside looking for Luton's firm, but they were nowhere to be found. About forty of us boarded the Tube at Shepherd's Bush, then when we got to Paddington some more lads joined the train and yet more at Edgware Road, so by the time we got off at Euston Square there were around eighty of us. We walked a short way down Euston Road, then cut away into the back streets to avoid detection by the OB. Eventually we arrived opposite St Pancras Station. Everyone hid round the corner out of sight, and a couple of lads were told to go into the station, draw out any Luton and run across the road with them in pursuit. We would then ambush them.

"The lads did as they were told, we waited for a little while, but nothing happened. All of a sudden people started shouting, 'Come on R's, let's do it,' and before I knew what was happening everyone charged across Euston Road up the steps and into the station's main entrance. I was toward the back and as I ran in I could see our lot going toe-to toe with Luton by a platform entrance.

"Luton, who were well outnumbered, backed off onto the platform itself and with nowhere to go a vicious brawl broke out. I saw a luggage trolley used as a battering ram and dumped on someone who hit the deck, and one Luton lad was swinging a broom around hitting anything in range. People were dropping like flies as the boots and fists went in. Later on the police video I saw one of our lads stab and slash a couple of Luton, I think he was arrested and put on trial for this but got away with it. It was so intense at the front and space was so limited that those of us towards the back couldn't get a look in and I just stood there watching the fighting whilst looking for an opportunity to get a punch in. It must have gone on for about a minute or two – as always, it seemed a lot longer – but our numbers told and the Luton lads started jumping off the platform to get away.

"As the police turned up in numbers, everyone started to scatter, running across the tracks on both sides. I decided to run back through the gates and was rugby-tackled by a copper as I did so. I was cuffed and taken to a meat wagon waiting at the side entrance to the station. While I was in the back of the van, an old lady approached the police and out of earshot started remonstrating with them.

"For years I thought she was grassing me up, however now I think she might have been saying that I hadn't actually thrown a punch, or was one of the Luton lads that had been attacked, because a copper got in and asked who I supported. I had a QPR badge on my jacket so saw no point in lying and replied, 'QPR.' He said, 'Suit yourself then,' and that was that. I'm sure if I'd said 'Luton' I would have been let off, but *c'est la vie*. I was taken to Kentish Town police station, photographed, fingerprinted and spent three hours in the cells before being let out and bailed to appear in court on the Monday morning."

The St. Pancras station incident had a debilitating affect on the QPR, with the arrests and subsequent prison sentences coinciding with a general downturn in hooliganism around the country. For a brief period the name Naughty Forty was given to the QPR mob but this proved to be shortlived and was to be their mob's last name. Now they are simply QPR.

"Our turnouts were few and far between and the numbers much reduced," recalled Darren, "so the name Naughty Forty was pretty apt. I think it sprung up among the lads who were frequenting Chelsea games at the time with Gregor, and may have been an attempt to create come kind of small 'elite' who all knew each other, because at this time there were lots of stories and incidents of undercover OB infiltrating mobs."

Shortly before the St Pancras fight, QPR fought Notts Forest in a park close to the ground. Both sides numbered between 150-200 and incredibly someone was able to shut the park gates, trapping in both mobs. With few police on hand, a battle raged for three to four minutes, in what Gregor later described as "proper toe-to-toe".

There was further trouble at St Pancras station after the game, as Darren, who was then new to the QPR mob, remembered. "At this stage I was just tagging along on my own and didn't really know anyone in our firm, as all my other football-going mates were Chelsea, Watford or Arsenal. I was at Euston waiting for my train home when about fifty lads emerged from the tube exit. I recognised them and went over to ask one what was happening. He said that they were looking for other firms and as none were at Euston were going to try their luck at St Pancras with Forest again, so I decided to tag along.

"As we walked down Euston Road to St Pancras, some of the lads up the front spotted some Forest and ran to confront them. The Forest lads, about six of them, sprinted for the safety of the station. When the bulk of us arrived there, the OB were outside and prevented us from entering the station. Likewise though, they were holding back a huge Forest mob, which well outnumbered us. I later heard Forest had 300 boys down that day. I'm not sure if that was the case, but it was an impressive firm nonetheless. There was one Forest lad, however, who had slipped the escort and was mouthing off big time. A copper grabbed him and said, 'Who are you?' to which he replied, 'Forest.' But some of our lads were shouting, 'He's Rangers, let him go, he's with us.' I could see the lad shitting bricks, as it was obvious what would happen if he was passed over to our side. Anyway his protests worked and he was shoved back into the station.

"We were then told to 'Fuck off or you're all getting nicked,' which needed no repeating. Just as we made our way back up the road, a strange incident occurred. A tasty-looking group about 30-strong ran from the bar over the road, then called Drummonds, now the Euston Flyer and confronted us, with a couple of glasses thrown, shouting, 'Who are ya?'

"'We're Rangers, QPR' came the response and I prepared for a battle. All of a sudden the oncoming lads stopped. 'We're Arsenal,' a lad said. 'We've got no quarrel with you, we're here to have a pop at Forest.' Our main lad explained that this was why we were there too. Some lads from both mobs had recognised each other, there were a few pleasantries exchanged and that was that, both firms went their separate ways."

The relationship between QPR and Arsenal was not always so friendly. For many years there was mutual antagonism stemming from Friday nights at the Lyceum in London. Gregor would be up there with a small team from Ladbroke Grove and Notting Hill and a small altercation led to a long-running feud which soon spread to matches. "At one time," recalled Gregor in the book *Top Boys*, "we had about 400 waiting for them to get off and it was like we was all going to the Falklands, we had everything you could think of and they didn't come that way. But give them their due, they did get off after the game, about 300-400, and it went through the market and there must have been about 700 people just having it in the market stalls."

Another of QPR's rivals are Norwich, though the East Anglians largely personalise it to a hatred of Mark Gregory. "In fact we hate any club that Gregor latches onto," said John in the *Norwich* section of this book, a reference to Gregor travelling through to Norwich with several London teams. From QPR's point of view, they hate Norwich, pure and simple. "I've been to Norwich on many occasions and have had some good days out there," says Darren. "Nearly every time we've played them at Carrow Road they have had a good turnout and I've got a lot of respect for them. In turn we've taken some of our best away firms to Norwich.

"One year that stands out is 1988/89. Our firm met at Liverpool Street and boarded the train about ten o'clock. After we arrived in Norwich we made our way to a pub near the Castle about sixty-strong, and waited for other lads to join us. After about an hour the pub was heaving and we were up to 100. All of a sudden there was a commotion in the street. Looking out the window I could see a small group of Norwich, probably ten or so bouncing across the street at the few Rangers who were outside. In particular, I remember a black lad wearing dungarees, which were briefly fashionable then. They were in the usual 'come on' pose with hands spread wide and were making lots of noise. Gregor went out of the pub to have a word with them. One of the Norwich lads had got a road cone from somewhere and threw it towards him.

"They had underestimated how many Rangers were inside, and the pub emptied with a roar. Everyone charged outside lobbing glasses and other items in their direction. There were a few punches exchanged but the outnumbered Norwich soon beat a hasty retreat. This attracted the attention of the Old Bill, who arrived and stood guard outside the pub. On the way to the ground we had a police escort, there were a few more stand-offs and minor scuffles back and forth as Norwich's firm appeared and disappeared at various points along the way.

"The game ended in the usual one-nil victory for the home team and everyone gathered at the back of the away end for the walk to the station. Now we were all together our firm probably numbered around 120-150. As we headed back into town along the river Wensum, the main Norwich mob appeared, equal numbers at least and went on the attack. The road was also full of normal supporters, the situation was confused and this helped the two mobs while the police struggled to identify who was who. At first Rangers were taken a bit by surprise and backed off and a little bit of panic ensued, then came the familiar, 'Stand! Stand Rangers,' cries. We regrouped and charged back in, plenty of action was now going on and Norwich were thrown back.

"The OB now restored some order to separate the two groups, but with everyone strung out along the road, fighting broke out at the front as Rangers chased some Norwich in the direction of town. As the police ran to deal with this, Norwich came at us again. Good blows were landed on both sides and I remember an amusing incident with a Norwich lad getting a proper hard kick up the arse.

"Eventually OB managed to intervene and for the rest of the journey the two firms walked parallel down the road, with a bit of to and fro as they tried to break police lines. As we reached the station, a large car park gave more space to manoeuvre and once more the police found themselves rushing around to deal with fights breaking out among the parked cars. Police numbers increased and Rangers were forced into the station, where they were prevented from going back out as the Norwich mob were dispersed. Some who had slipped the escort came into the station in dribs and drabs with tales of more fighting. In my own opinion Rangers just shaded it the exchanges but Norwich were very game."

The late Eighties was an active period for hooligans at QPR, with feuds with Norwich, Luton, Charlton, Southampton and Oxford. Games against each of these teams brought out big numbers, including mobs of over 200 to Norwich on at least two occasions, with the same turning out for matches at Oxford, Luton and Spurs. One hundred and fifty "boys" travelled up to Blackpool for an FA Cup game in 1990, and a similar number turned out for another Cup tie at Southampton in 1992.

Between 1986 and 1989, QPR clashed several times with Charlton. "They brought some decent firms to Loftus Road, particularly for a League Cup game in '89 where they more or less took the piss," admitted Darren. The final key rivalry of this period was with Oxford United, which is unsurprising given the closeness of the two grounds. "The rivalry began with the Milk Cup final in April 1986. QPR had defeated Notts Forest, Chelsea and Liverpool to reach the final and were widely tipped as favourites. On the day the team froze and were thrashed three-nil, in one of the worst performances seen in a major final at Wembley.

"That day QPR had a huge turnout of boys – I've heard figures of 600 – with the ranks being swelled by lads from Ladbroke Grove, Notting Hill and other areas of West London who weren't dyed in the wool QPR fans but would turn out for big occasions such as this. It's also fair to say there were probably lads from other firms such as Chelsea who had QPR mates, but their numbers should not be overestimated.

"At the same time Oxford had one of their best firms ever, with groups from towns across the county of Oxfordshire and even Bucks showing up to form a mob of around 300. I've heard from an Oxford lad with whom I became good friends that they were very impressed and even a little over-awed by Rangers' firm that day, but in the event the only incident of note was at Wembley Park tube station, which seems to have been pretty even, though both sides claimed a result.

"This set the scene for the next two seasons. Both away fixtures attracted large firms from QPR, the biggest I have personally seen at an away game, 200-300 strong. With the famous long walk from United's Headington ground to Oxford Station there were ample locations for attacks from the home fans and it was a battle all the way, with Oxford's South Midlands Hit Squad taking full advantage of this.

"Both clubs had victories and defeats. On one occasion a group of us came unstuck not far into the walk back to the station, and fighting among the busy traffic resulted in us scattering, with some taking shelter on local buses to avoid being picked off. All this time further incidents were occurring up and down the London Road with an ebb and flow of fighting. By the same token, I remember Rangers clearing the road behind the away end of Oxford's firm, running them back toward the city centre, where they regrouped and resumed the fray only to be backed off again.

"The fixtures at Loftus Road were less eventful, however in the 1987/88 season, with the fixture on a Christmas Bank Holiday Monday, Oxford brought a very respectable firm through and acquitted themselves very well in skirmishes along Uxbridge Road. I remember the contents of a skip being found in a side road and put to good use."

The rivalry fizzled out in May 1988 when Oxford was relegated and the two clubs were not to meet again until the League Cup in 1995. Neither mob was as big as it had been and the game passed off quietly. QPR were relegated during the same season, which meant the clubs played each other in three consecutive seasons, and while the feud was rekindled it was never to be as intense as before.

"We had firms of around fifty-to-seventy at the away games, but I would have to say that Oxford were the more aggressive at the Manor during this period," said Darren. "Few supporters now travelled by train so incidents were restricted to the area surrounding the ground. They turned up at Loftus Road on each occasion, but had suffered badly themselves from bans and police operations, reducing the numbers who came and there were only very minor skirmishes. Oxford's own decline saw them lose Division One status in 1999, and we haven't played them since."

QPR's increasing links with Chelsea coincided with a decline in their own mob. The rave scene, more intensive policing, a changing football culture and prison for many lads for the St Pancras fight led to the virtual collapse of their firm in the early Nineties. "Gregor started to take a few lads from Rangers to Chelsea games, this was around the time of the so-called Naughty Forty," said Darren.

"There have always been links between the two clubs' firms and Chelsea lads quite often made an appearance at our games, especially 'Fat Pat' Dolan, who knew a lot of our top lads well. Indeed it sometimes became an excuse for some of the more well-known firms, who came unstuck at QPR on a fair few occasions, that Chelsea had turned up to augment our mob. Perhaps it sounded less embarrassing than admitting that they had been done by 'little' QPR. Chelsea were present on some occasions but never in numbers exceeding single figures.

"Likewise the number of Rangers boys that were going to Chelsea games at this time probably didn't exceed fifteen, if that. This never caused any problems at Rangers. I did hear some stories that not all the Chelsea lot were best pleased, but I didn't hear of any incidents where QPR lads were told to stop coming or were attacked, so on the whole it was an amicable thing."

As mentioned earlier, QPR are arguably the most active mob in London at the time of writing, something which even their old hands have some trouble explaining. "After our slide from Premiership to Division Two and going into administration, a real fighting spirit developed at the club under Ian Holloway as we fought our way back up," said Darren. "People realised we were in danger of going bust and rediscovered their passion for the club. This brought a lot of old faces back as crowds grew, we were now a big fish in Division Two and seen as a challenge for the firms following teams in that division, so there were plenty of opportunities for trouble. At the same time the 'Youth' phenomenon took off countrywide and we had a group of lads at the right age who came through all at the same time.

"There has been no involvement from outside clubs unless someone's brought a mate along now and then. The firm as it is today is all QPR, with a mixture of older lads and the new Youth lot." While the older lads remain in contact with Chelsea there is no such relationship amongst the younger generation and the youth firms of the respective mobs have clashed several times over the last few years.

A similar situation exists with Brentford, with the older faces of both getting on well but animosity between the younger mobs. Fulham, however, are despised by all, while a new London rivalry emerged during the 2004/05 season between QPR and Millwall, a club that until then they had seen little trouble with. "We took the best QPR firm I've seen in the last fifteen years to The New Den," said Darren. "However a very heavy police presence scuppered any chance of a confrontation. This incident certainly upped the stakes between us and put us on their radar, though they don't care to admit it. The comeback from it has yet to be determined."

The last five years has seen a resurgence in the QPR firm, with old-timers returning and young hooligans emerging. In 1999, QPR's mob of 100 lads was supplemented by hundreds of others willing to have a go during an away match with Fulham. "Before and after the game QPR fans walked in their thousands along Fulham Palace Road to and from the Bush," recalled Darren. Two away games at Luton at the beginning of this decade saw turnouts of over 100 on each occasion, while about 120 travelled up to Grimsby for an FA Cup game in 2003, a few weeks after an incident between the two sets of supporters in London.

The White City estate remains their principal recruiting ground and as a result they have a tough, tight unit. The estate has long been racially mixed, and this has been reflected in QPR's mobs over the years. "Being so close to the ground, anyone there who cares about football is staunch QPR," said Darren, "and with many of our boys having connections either historical, through friendship or even crime, to the place, the local inhabitants have always been happy to help see off invaders in support of our firm, whether or not they are football fans. The same can be said of Ladbroke Grove and Notting Hill, where locals who are not necessarily QPR or even football fans have been involved in football violence in the past.

"In my time there have been several occasions where opposing firms were invited to go there as a place which would be away from the immediate attention of OB, but there haven't been any takers. I recall a story that Arsenal did turn up there in the early Eighties but were thoroughly trounced and petrol bombs were among the weapons used that day."

In April, an NCIS report noted trouble at a QPR match at Huddersfield. "There was continual baiting between each group during the game. In extra time, Huddersfield scored the winning goal and supporters celebrated by coming to the front of the seated area and baiting QPR supporters. Stewards and police moved in to Huddersfield supporters and attempted to move them into the seating area. QPR supporters overran the steward lines and attempted to move towards the Huddersfield area. Police were deployed with batons and supporters were driven back into the away area and out of the stadium. Huddersfield and QPR supporters moved out of the Stadium and attempted disorder which was prevented by police officers. Two officers were injured, resulting in two arrests for disorder and assault."

Two years later there was trouble after a bizarre incident in Cheltenham. A small QPR mob stayed in a pub near the station well after the end of the game, unaware that Plymouth and Cheltenham had arranged a fight for the same area. "The QPR lads were basically me, a couple of mates and a group of older lads in their forties we know who'll get stuck in if necessary but aren't boys," said one man present. "We were all drinking in the pub waiting for the train back and when we saw it kicking off we all thought it was their Youth and ours. Everyone ran out of the pub and a couple of punches were thrown but when we realised who was fighting everyone just stood and watched.

"A couple of us tried to help a lad whose ear had been mangled, but we couldn't get any sense out of him as he'd had a right hiding and just wandered off. In any case it was a nasty little fight and after it was broken up there was a bit of scuffling between some Rangers and Plymouth on the station – but there definitely weren't two unconscious QPR lads on the deck, as one report said."

Later that season QPR reached the play-offs, where they faced Oldham in the semi-finals. Oldham veteran Carl Spiers was there. "Although we expected a good crowd up from London, we did not expect much trouble as QPR did not have a rep for aggro," he said, "although having been down there a few times I knew that Shepherds Bush was a rough area. Anyway, no word had reached the Oldham hooligan firms of any QPR show, so even though the pubs were full of various mobs of Oldham lads, it was to support our team in their hour of need. However on the lane leading down to the ground before kick-off there was a big mob of QPR thugs picking off small mobs of Oldham fans. This QPR mob was noticeable for two reasons: they were a mixed-raced mob, with half them being blacks or half-castes, and they were all dressed to the max with Burberry and Aquascutum overcoats and with most of the blacks wearing trilbies. Amongst this QPR mob was none other than a renowned and famous London promoter, Soul DJ and radio personality. He did not get involved in the trouble but was close to it and his mates definitely did.

"QPR bossed it before the game and Oldham fans were both shocked and livid at such a show of strength. During the game, which was watched by a capacity crowd, Oldham's hooligans swore revenge and to attack the QPR mob after the game. The game ended one-all and Oldham fans swooped out seeking the QPR mob, but the QPR were equally as keen and both mobs met head-on outside the ground, with QPR getting the better of the mass brawl before police boxed it all off.

"The second leg was only three day later. Oldham's pride was hurt and the word was all the lads were going down to London for what was the most important game for years. All day hundreds of Oldham fans poured into the capital, and all the bars around Shepherds Bush were full of Oldham fans, a great turnout with many old faces and former Seventies and Eighties hooligans out in force. There were a few scuffles with QPR lads in the Australian bar before the game, but Oldham were well oiled and well up for it. A mob of 300 lads marched to the ground through that horrible council estate and a few blacks tried attacking us but were repelled.

"The game itself was very tense. Oldham, buoyed up by 2,500 fans, played their hearts out, only to lose by the single goal, which sparked great celebration from the West Londoners. Outside the ground big mobs of black lads attacked Oldham as we made our way back to the coaches, vans and cars. Because it was dark many Oldham fans got lost and strayed onto that god-awful council estate, many getting filled in by locals. To tell you the truth it was one place most of us were glad to get away from. QPR were very much underestimated, certainly no mugs."

Further reading: *Top Boys*, Cass Pennant (John Blake Publishing)

R

RAITH ROVERS

Ground: Starks Park
Firms: Kirkcaldy Soccer Casuals (KSC), Kirkcaldy Baby Crew (KBC)
Rivals: Dunfermline, St Johnstone, East Fife

Raith Rovers FC is the only football club in Kirkcaldy, which has a population of only about 60,000 and is the largest town in Fife. Like many smaller clubs it has had its highs and lows: the former include beating Celtic on penalties in the 1994 League Cup final, which meant they would play in Europe for the first and possibly the last time, while the latter include being on the verge of closing down due to financial problems. Off the pitch, their hooligans have tangles with some of Scotland's top firms, including Hibs, Aberdeen, Kilmarnock, Dundee United, Airdrie, Morton, Partick, Ayr, St Johnstone, Cowdenbeath, Arbroath, Falkirk, St Mirren and East Fife.

The following account was provided by Nick, a Raith soccer casual who has been present at many of their most violent encounters:

"I first became involved in the casual movement in 1984, this was with Rangers. The first time I had witnessed serious crowd disorder had been at the 1980 Scottish Cup final between Rangers and Celtic at Hampden Park, though I had seen some disturbances at Raith games in the late Seventies. One in particular was against Hearts, a midweek game, when there was disorder before and after the game.

"In the early Eighties, St Johnstone had a group of skins called the 'Perth Pack' and every time they played Raith there was violent clashes, probably due to the fact that there was a scooter club in Kirkcaldy and everybody knows that skins and mods don't get on. This rivalry was to carry on through the Eighties and Nineties and even in the 2004/05 season there was a violent clash before a game in Kirkcaldy. St Johnstone is Raith's number one rival but they have never done us, home or away.

"We started to get things together about 1984/85. At the time a lot of our boys were running with Rangers and Hearts, while a couple of lads also ran with Hibs, Celtic and Motherwell. About twenty lads from Fife ran with Rangers, so every week we were getting involved with violence either at Rangers games or Raith games. We had about forty lads in our firm in the early days. Over the years we've had anything from twenty-five to 150 lads, but we've had a hardcore of about fifty. I would say that we had an advantage because a lot of our boys were running with teams from the Premier League as well as with Raith. It gave us an edge. With a lot running with Rangers and Hearts, our firm tended to support the far-right, but most of the lads kept their views to themselves and didn't really talk about politics.

"Word soon got around that we had a good firm and we were getting results.

"This was to be our undoing on a couple of occasions. We've had bad days just like everybody else and Hibs and Aberdeen were both to teach us a lesson. On one occasion, twelve of Hibs's top boys came through to Kirkcaldy one Saturday when Raith were playing Arbroath at home. We had about thirty boys out because we didn't expect Arbroath to show. One of our young lads said that he had seen a mob of about fifteen boys at the train station, so we went to the station, no joy. As we were heading back to the town centre we passed the Station Hotel, there was a couple of lads standing outside. The next minute a shout of 'CCS' went up and the rest of their firm [the Capital City Service] ran out of the hotel. All I can say is they ran us ragged, we got well turned over.

"On another occasion, Aberdeen were playing in Edinburgh in a cup semi against Hearts and we were playing Dunfermline away. Seemingly Aberdeen had heard that Raith had a mob of about 200, this was because we had played Peterhead earlier in the season and had 150 lads out for the game because we were told that Aberdeen had joined up with Peterhead, though on the day Peterhead only brought about forty lads. Anyway, Aberdeen must have caught one of the early trains on their way to Edinburgh because they were in Kirkcaldy at about eleven o'clock, and as we were only travelling fourteen miles to Dunfermline there weren't a lot of our lads about, forty at most, in groups of four and five. I reckon 100 Aberdeen must have got off the train, and they took over the town. A few of our lads got a good doing. Even if we'd had our full mob together I reckon we would have struggled. Aberdeen were Scotland's top firm at the time."

A Scottish Cup quarter-final at home to St Mirren in March 1987 saw the KSC's biggest turnout of 150 lads. "We had been planning this game for weeks," said Nick. "We had heard that some Celtic lads were coming with the St Mirren mob, the Love Street Division, and any chance of a ruck with Celtic made things even more interesting. We decided to meet at several locations to try to keep a low profile. The Starks Bar, a pub just down the road from the football ground, was where our main firm drank, our top fifty lads. Along the road from the Starks Bar was the Football Arms, where some of the other lads drank. The younger KBC would usually split up into smaller groups and just act as spotters or hang around the Beveridge Park, where the away coaches were parked.

"At about one o'clock it all started to kick off. There was about sixty of us in the Starks Bar and about forty outside when about 100 LSD came down Pratt Street. One of the younger lads came running in the pub and shouted, 'It's Saint Mirren!' Next minute, the pub windows went in. So everything that could be lifted – pool cues, pool balls, ashtrays, tumblers and bottles – were removed from the pub and everybody charged out.

"The KBC, who had been outside when the LSD had attacked, had done themselves proud and stood their ground. The Old Bill didn't have a clue. They had never seen anything like it, 200 lads battling it out in the middle of a busy street on a Saturday afternoon. It took the police about fifteen minutes to get everything under control. The rest of the lads that missed the scrap at the pub were gutted, but there was still more to come. Seemingly there had been minor scuffles all over the town involving groups of ten and twenty lads.

"Eventually everybody went to the game. Nobody was interested in the game, more what was going to happen after. As soon as the final whistle went, everybody was buzzing. As soon as we got outside the ground, everybody made their way towards the St Mirren end, but the police managed to split us into two groups. St Mirren had left the ground early and made their way through the back streets around the ground and managed to get to the home end. So with our mob split in two we ended up being confronted with their full mob of about 150. Our mob consisted of about forty KBC and sixty KSC. We just went for it. We stood our ground, then the Old Bill appeared. One of our lads got two broken arms, he ran into twenty LSD and got a severe doing.

"St Mirren had three buses parked at the Beveridge Park, so we grouped and made our way there. Just as we were at the park, the police arrived. We could see the St Mirren mob, so we made the decision, just to go for it. Two hundred lads, twenty Old Bill, do the old bill and have a major off. Just as we were charging at the Old Bill, police and CID appeared everywhere, riot vans, the works. About twenty of our lads were arrested. But a good day for all."

Dunfermline are Raith Rovers' derby rivals, and over the years the two hooligan mobs have fought on many occasions. "In the Eighties we would always have a good day when we played Dunfermline," said Nick. "But Dunfermline got a wake-up call from Hibs and never really recovered from it. They have had some good mobs over the years but they never really got a result against us. On two occasions we had major confrontation with them, the first being in Kirkcaldy. There was about thirty of our top boys and thirty of their top boys. We bumped into each other on the way to the ground and had a running battle in the back streets for about thirty minutes, with no Old Bill seen.

"On the second occasion, Dunfermline joined up with Cowdenbeath, a small town next to Dunfermline. We got the train early and sat in a pub on Cowdenbeath High Street. There was about sixty of our firm. Soon Dunfermline were out and about looking for us, and they found us. We clashed with them in the High Street. A few shop windows were smashed and the High Street came to a standstill. There were a few arrests, but we got a result. There was another incident when we did Dunfermline's full mob in Cowdenbeath's ground."

Dunfermline might be Raith's nearest opponents but their most fierce rivalry is with St Johnstone. "They have never had a result against us, though they keep trying," claimed Nick. "Our first encounter with them was 1986/87 at their ground, Muirton Park. We took two buses up to Perth, a thirty-seater of KSC and a twenty-five-seater of KBC.

"There were no incidents before the game but that was about to change when we got inside the ground. We were all inside at the segregation fence when all of a sudden there were St Johnstone lads in our end. It kicked off and there were lads scrapping all over the terrace. The next minute, I was lying on the ground with blood pouring from my head. I had been hit with a golf ball with a nail in it. The game was held up for fifteen minutes but the best was yet to come.

"As soon as the final whistle went, our lads grouped up, we knew that it would kick off again outside, as there were hardly any Old Bill at the game. When we got out we headed for their end. All of a sudden their mob came round the corner, there must have been 100 lads. We were outnumbered. Then the shout went up, 'KSC, let's do it!' We ran at their mob and they backed off. Bad move. We steamed right in. A few of their top boys stood but we got a major result. The only bad point was I got arrested and spent the weekend in Perth police station and up at court on Monday along with a split head.

"Over the years we clashed with St Johnstone several times, always getting a result. We done them in their own end in Starks Park in the Eighties, and more recently in 2004/05 there was a violent clash in Kirkcaldy. The season before, St Johnstone had come to Kirkcaldy and wrecked one of the pubs on the high street, so we decided to get a mob together. We had thirty-five lads, mostly in their thirties, a tidy group of boys. We met in the pub at twelve o'clock and by near two o'clock we had heard nothing, so we decided to have a walk to the ground.

"We went through the back streets to avoid the police and had just come up Alison Street near the ground when we spotted them. We went for it and they got leathered. One of their mob got hospitalised. After the game they were nowhere to be seen and the next time we played them they didn't want to know. Rumour has it they asked the police for a lift to the train station. I'll give them their due though, they travel to every game with thirty to forty boys and in 2006 were involved in disorder in Inverness. Twenty-two of them were arrested and given banning orders from St Johnstone ground.

"Over the years we have come up against most of Scotland's mobs from the lower leagues. The ones I rate the most are Airdire Section B, the Falkirk Fear, St Mirren's Love Street Division and the Dundee Utility."

READING

Ground: Madejski Stadium, formerly Elm Park
Firms: New Inn Steamers, Berkshire Bovver Boys, Dirty Thirty, Reading Youth **Rivals**: Oxford United, Swindon Town

Reading's hooligans have received a bad press from the hooligan fraternity. Mocked as invisible or dismissed as a "feeder unit" for Chelsea, they are not regarded as having a large or significant mob. While that is not borne out by newspaper reports of trouble dating back to the mid-Sixties, there is an element of truth in these widely held views. Reading has never had the history of hooliganism of say, Oxford United, and the town's most infamous hooligan, Andy "Nightmare" Frain, is a leading face at Chelsea.

Still, the Reading lads resent the commonly held view. "When most lads across the country talk about Reading, most make some kind of comment that goes something along the lines of, 'But you're all Chelsea'," said M, one of Reading's younger generation of hooligans. "For the record, Reading is thirty-five miles west of London and a twenty-five-minute train ride away. We will not deny there are links, but that's no different than saying to a Bradford fan, 'You're Leeds,' because some of their lads live in Bradford and travel twenty-five minutes by train to watch their team.

"It's also true to say that when you stand on Reading train station on a match day morning, the platform is full of locals supporting London teams, a mixture of 'barmies' and lads. Nearly all of these are local boys and grew up with most of the Dirty Thirty [Reading's gang] and still are growing up with the RYF [Reading Youth Firm]. It's disappointing from a 'lad' perspective that so many leave when, say, Plymouth are in town 150-handed, but who are we to decide which team they want to support? We have to like it or lump it. So for the record, the Dirty Thirty and RYF are not Chelsea, Arsenal, West Ham, Spurs or whoever people may think we are. We are Reading. Matter closed."

The FA Cup is always an opportunity for smaller mobs to put on a show. When Arsenal were drawn away at Reading in February 1972, they were riding on the crest of a wave. The Double-winning side was the best in England and on the terraces the likes of Johnny Hoy had made the North Bank almost impregnable. That is why it is all the more surprising that some Arsenal old-timers rate the trip to Reading as one of their most unpleasant. Reading was then a bikers' town, and tales of attacks by leather-clad grizzlies armed with bike chains, baseball bats, petrol bombs and even an air rifle still circulate to this day. Nearly 30 people were arrested and a further 20 were ejected from the ground after fighting at the Tilehurst End. "The majority of the fans at that end were Arsenal supporters and it was at this same end that a crash barrier gave way ten minutes after the game started," the local paper reported.

The 1970s and early 1980s saw regular invasions from Oxford, Bristol Rovers and Cardiff. In fact most games against Oxford saw trouble, with the home mob coming off worst on most occasions. Travelling away could be even more dangerous. In late February 1976, Reading played at Huddersfield, a game painfully remembered by Pete, a semi-retired Reading lad. "Seventy-five Reading made their way to Huddersfield," he said. "On our arrival we gave it a bit of a big one and really had the run of the town. For some reason we entered the home side of the ground at about two o' clock and what was there at that time was run all over the place. We were the kings of Leeds Road.

"Well that was only to last for about 40 minutes before half of Yorkshire descended on the ground wanting to kill us. Every one of the 75 got a continuous battering until they got back to the station in dribs and drabs after hiding in gardens, under cars and so on."

In March 1977, the visit of Portsmouth resulted in the following front-page headline in the *Reading Evening Post*: "Animals – Worst day of soccer terror hits Reading." The story went on:

A Reading fan is still seriously ill in Battle Hospital today, a victim of soccer savagery.

Reading supporter Leslie Cross, a father of two, was beaten senseless by half a dozen fans just after Reading scored their second goal. That goal signalled the start of a huge pitch invasion by Portsmouth fans in what was a clear bid to try to force the game – a very clean contest – to be abandoned.

Top international referee Clive Thomas was forced to halt the game for three minutes as police chased hundreds of fans across the turf.

Fighting spilled on to the grass from the terraces and ambulance men rushed to tend to the injured.

Sixty-two people were arrested, 56 from Portsmouth, and dozens were hurt, including many policemen. Hundreds of Pompey bootboys had arrived unsupervised by train as much as three hours before the game and were able to wander freely around town, drinking heavily. Others, who arrived by coach, were dropped outside a stand for home supporters and there were instantly clashes. The Portsmouth hooligans fought amongst themselves and attacked police and bystanders, overturning cars and smashing windows in the streets leading to Elm Park. A boy was hit by a brick thrown through his house window and shoppers fled in terror, clutching their frightened children, as hordes of screaming fans charged through the streets, leaving a trail of shattered glass, splintered fences and bloodstains.

There was universal outrage at the scenes. "The behaviour was diabolical and disgusting and the club is determined to stamp it out one way or another," said Portsmouth FC commercial manager Bill Davis. To assist police with their inquiries, he handed over 600 passport photographs of members of the Portsmouth Travel Club. "If those responsible for the attack on Mr Cross belong to the Travel Club they will be in the book. We had a lot of new members for a recent away game and it is likely that the attackers were amongst those who joined."

The *Post*'s editorial noted, "Whatever the causes the result was a scene in which a large number of people behaved like animals. The reputation of Reading, whose own supporters are on the whole good tempered and not given to violence, was besmirched ... How to stop this appalling behaviour on football grounds has so far baffled all the minds that have been applied to the question. The animals who go to fight, not watch, may in the long run supply the answer – by killing professional football altogether."

Five days after the match, the paper reproduced a picture of the stand where Mr Cross was attacked. "Are the thugs in this picture?" readers were asked. "Help solve this mystery." Police subsequently made three arrests. Mr Cross's wife was understandably distraught as she sat by her husband in his hospital bed. She told reporters, "The first thing he said to me was, 'Are the children all right?' He is that sort of man. It just seems so ridiculous that someone could go along to a football match and end up like this. I cannot understand the brutality of these people who go along just to spoil a football match."

Local residents and traders were furious at what they saw as poor policing. "There were not enough police," said one. "But what could they do? There were at least 200 of these hooligans." Another woman, whose window was smashed, said, "It is terrible. People in their right senses don't do things like this." Harry Gale, whose front window was smashed with a milk bottle, added angrily, "They should fetch the troops out with batons and tear them apart."

Residents of Wantage Road, who had often borne the brunt of trouble at the football ground, began a petition demanding action. Similar calls came from traders along Oxford Road after thousands of pounds of damage was caused to their businesses. A few days later, residents were demanding a cut in their rates to compensate them for the continuing soccer violence. "We are already paying over £200 in rates a year and it is going up again," said one. "Why should we have to pay so much with all this violence going on? Mounted police are the answer."

Two years later, Portsmouth were back, and while the level of violence was not on the same scale, there were still 69 arrests, mostly of visiting fans. The majority were inside the ground as fans tried to climb over the barriers separating them. "Local residents were taking no chances and many of them stood guard in front of their homes and shops armed with broom handles in case of trouble," reported the *Evening Post*. "Portsmouth fans did leave their mark on the town yesterday when they caused trouble in the Bugle pub in Friar Street. Landlord Richard Baker said, 'The fans piled in. I must have had 200 Portsmouth fans drinking in here until the police got them out. They smashed a window and pulled light switches off the walls. They were jumping all over the place.'"

But Portsmouth didn't get it all their own way. "About 500 Portsmouth arrived in Reading town centre early in the morning," recalled Pete. "They plotted up in the Blargrave Arms and a number of pubs around the town. About 150 Reading were milling around the Jolly Porter, which had been closed for the day. On seeing the Pompey mob arrive, the Reading mob started to move away from the railway station towards the bus station. The Pompey mob started to follow and Reading ran, but only as far as the Top Rank bingo hall, where there were a load of milk bottles at the top of the steps. These were launched into the pursuing Pompey mob. This attack forced them to back off right into the train station. The Reading mob were on a high and after turning Pompey into the station made their way to the Rising Sun.

"The main bulk of the Pompey mob had made their way to the ground and were already plotted up in the Reading South Bank. The 150 Reading made their way round to the Blargrave Arms, where about 70 Pompey were finishing their drinks. The Reading attacked the pub, putting all of the windows through and battering everyone inside. Pompey made a brave attempt to regain some face by attacking the Reading mob, but eventually they were backed into the pub. It was later reported in the local press that a number of Pompey had locked themselves in the toilets.

"The Reading mob then made their way to the ground and entered the South Bank just after the kick-off, to be met by the main bulk of Pompey. A huge terrace battle erupted and it took the police more than thirty minutes to bring the crowds under control."

It was a busy few days for the local police. Three days later, Reading were drawn at home to Aldershot, another fierce local rival. There had been trouble at games between the clubs dating back to the early Seventies, and Reading usually got the upper hand, but in April 1979 Aldershot arrived mob-handed.

"Police seize fans' weapons" reported the local paper. It said 62 fans had been arrested and dozens of weapons confiscated. Police leave had once again been cancelled and 200 officers were on duty. Trouble earlier on in the day, coupled with rumours of a major clash inside the ground, led police to search fans as they entered. It was here that most of the weapons were discovered and arrests made. Many more weapons were dumped in side streets once fans saw the searches taking place. "It is difficult to imagine what would happen if people actually got on to the terraces with these things," said Chief Inspector Peter Winship.

For the first time ever, some Aldershot fans were bussed directly from the train station to the ground and back again afterwards. Normally, trainloads of fans arrived at Reading West Station and were escorted on foot by police. There was some fighting inside the ground but officers quickly moved in. Reading won the game 4–0 to retain their grip on the top of the league. "Over the years Aldershot never really provided much competition for the Reading mob, and we thought this Bank Holiday would be no different," remembered Pete.

"Aldershot arrived early about 100-handed, with Reading totalling about seventy in the Jolly Porter. There were no police and Reading left their pub to confront Aldershot. Although there was a small difference in numbers, the sight of a rampaging Reading mob was usually enough to have the Shots on their toes. Not this time. They stood their ground and the battle commenced across the front of the station, with neither side budging an inch until the police arrived. This was unheard of after all the years of Reading taking their

East Bank, but they had come to town and stood their ground. Word soon spread through the town and we all agreed to enter the away end at the old Elm Park, known as the Town End.

"The Aldershot mob was well protected by the Old Bill, who were also extremely busy arresting any Reading fan they could find entering the Town End. The Aldershot mob were continually attacked on their way to Elm Park and were eventually put into the ground for their own safety, but instead they were met by another Reading mob, ensuring another terrace battle until the police regained control."

The consolation for Reading was that seven wins in the last nine games, with the other two matches drawn, saw them win the Fourth Division title. Aldershot and Portsmouth, two promotion contenders, both missed out, finishing fifth and eighth respectively.

The first recognised Reading mob was the New Inn Steamers, their name taken from the pub along the route from the station to the ground where most of the Reading hardcore gathered. "During the Seventies and Eighties, travelling to Reading could be a nightmare, as a number of clubs will testify," said Pete. "On the long walk from Reading train station to the old Elm Park you had to march up the Oxford Road past the New Inn pub. As the away mob walked by, the windows and doors would open and Reading would steam out.

"The pub was very much a local hostelry, and other mobs, whether from Reading or the away team, were never welcome. There were a number of battles between the New Inn boys and the Woodley mob. As Reading became a multi-cultural town, particularly along the Oxford Road, the New Inn boys disbanded in the late Eighties. Some of the Dirty Thirty still about today used the New Inn through the Nineties until Elm Park was knocked down, but the pub was never as active as it was through earlier decades."

The Eighties saw continuing trouble with the likes of Swindon and Oxford. One match remembered during that period is an away game at Wigan in March 1983, when sixty Reading travelled on the train. "No one really expected much trouble and all of the lads were just out for a few beers and a good crack," said Pete. "As the Reading mob were walking past a park on their way to town, what they thought was a load of kids playing football turned out to be a mob of Wigan.

"Battle commenced with neither side budging. As both sets of lads started to flag and there was no Old Bill in sight, things started to slow a little. After half an hour of running fights, the battleground had moved to the town's market. It went on for a further thirty minutes. Saturday shoppers watched in amazement as lads hit each other with rolls of wallpaper and paint brushes. Eventually the police split the two groups and arrested a few from both sides.

"The game passed off with no real incident, until a huge brawl happened in the car park directly after the match with more nickings from both sides. Eventually, the Reading mob were escorted back to the station minus those that had been arrested after what has been described as one of the longest incidents any had ever been involved in. After they left town, the Wigan boys plotted up in a pub near the train station. At about 11pm, the Reading who had been arrested were taken back to the station and left on the platform. The Wigan boys gave them a good kicking and then sent them on their way home."

The early Nineties was a boom time for Reading FC. In May 1994,the club won the Third Division title, then a Second Division play-off win at Wembley against Bolton Wanderers saw the club in Division One. The good times didn't last and for two seasons Reading struggled. In 1998, with 16 defeats in their last 18 games, they finished bottom and were relegated.

Off the field a new mob emerged. About 15 Reading hooligans travelled to Dublin for the ill-fated Ireland v England international which had to be abandoned when English supporters ripped up seating and hurled it onto the pitch. A couple of the Reading group were arrested and when quizzed by reporters after their release, they claimed to be from the "Berkshire Boot Boys". One journalist was kicked up the backside for good measure. The retro name stuck for a short while.

There were more clashes with both Oxford and Swindon in the 1997/98 season, though the fight against the former occurred at Didcot train station when their rivals were travelling away to Swindon. "In a moment of madness it was decided that on the evening of the game we would take a tidy little firm to have a pop at our local rivals," recalled another hooligan, who requested anonymity and asked to be known only as "M". "It had been reported that Oxford were 150-handed in the morning, with a very tidy mob of lads. Prior to our home game with Charlton we totalled about forty, all of whom were up for the fifteen-minute train ride to Didcot.

"Our spotter made his way to Didcot and plotted up in one of the pubs opposite the station. He had also worked out that if our mob caught the 19:38 train from Reading we would arrive in Didcot at 19:53 and if all went to plan we could catch the 20:05 back to Reading. This gave the lads twelve minutes to do the business and jump back on a train straight back home. We knew from previous information that the main Oxford lads always stayed in Didcot before returning to Oxford and we were sure that at this time they would still be about and the Old Bill would have left.

"Our plan went like clockwork. Twenty-eight lads left Reading on the 19:38 Bristol train, having lost a few from the lunchtime drinking session. Our spotter had confirmed that a mob of about thirty Oxford were drinking in the Prince of Wales. As we disembarked our train, a few Oxford lads were chased off the station and ran for the pub, alerting those inside. They came out and a full-scale battle took place in the middle of the road, with boots and fists flying everywhere. Eventually, the Oxford were backed off into the pub, where our lads continued to attack them with flower pots. Then the shout went up, 'Train's in,' and with that our mob returned to Reading on the 20:05 with limited injuries and no nickings.

"We knew that we had met the main hardcore of the South Midlands Hit Squad as many of the faces were known to ours. This was confirmed later that evening when one of our lads, who was working on the door in Oxford, received a number of visits and was told how out of order we were for the attack and that he was to blame. This was not the case."

The same season saw the visit of Cardiff in the FA Cup. It was a mid-week fixture but that did little to calm the fears of many. Their concerns were justified as fighting broke out across the town. The media and Reading FC both blamed Cardiff fans for the trouble. Reading hooligans insist their mob actually got the better of the visitors, a view challenged by Cardiff.

"It's true to say that Cardiff arrived about midday in great numbers and in all fairness they took over the town centre," said M. "Our firm decided that meeting out of the town centre was the best option, as not only was it crawling with Cardiff but nearly all of Thames Valley Police were also there. At about four in the afternoon, we decided in dribs and drabs to move to the Nags Head just off the Oxford Road, the main route to Elm Park. We were aware of Cardiff's numbers and that several incidents had taken place. It sounded like a toilet-smashing competition, as all we were hearing about were pubs and toilets being broken up.

"At the time we totalled about forty lads. The main bulk of Cardiff were being escorted to the game and it would have been murder for us to attempt anything. At the time we thought it was game over, but one of our spotters came in and informed us that about forty Cardiff were making their way towards the pub we were in. We walked outside and met them head-on.

"As soon as we arrived they started to back off and run. We scattered them everywhere. Some were spotted hiding behind skips and one was even pulled out of a bush by our very own Alan Titchmarsh. A few good digs were given out and Cardiff were all over the place. Next we saw the blue flashing lights, along with the police spotters trying to take their pictures while running at full pelt. Seven of ours were locked up in a meat wagon and Cardiff got a little braver and started rocking the van with our lads inside. They took more of a battering in the van than they did outside."

The continuing violence in Reading was of growing concern to Thames Valley police and in late 1998 they issued local pubs and clubs with photographs of 30 people they believed were most likely to cause trouble. While the police were initially concerned with town centre violence, all the 30 pictures were linked to the Berkshire Boot Boys. It was from this police notice that the Dirty Thirty was born.

Two years later, the nation learnt of a new mob at Reading, courtesy of BBC reporter Donal MacIntyre. His undercover investigation into the Chelsea Headhunters, in which he posed as a wannabe hooligan to infiltrate and secretly film some of the gang, brought him into contact with a young lad from Reading, Danny, who was a hooligan associate of Chelsea's Andy Frain and a leading face in the Reading Youth Firm. The Macintyre team filmed him in London and attending Millwall's game in Manchester in 1999. Many people were critical of the "stitch-up" and the foolishness of those who fell for MacIntyre's adopted persona, but M says anyone could have been caught out.

The Dirty Thirty name accurately described its strength, though for a big game its numbers could rise considerably, swelled by the likes of Andy Frain and other London-linked hooligans who lived in the area. The RYF could pull out as many as 60 lads, though they were younger and less experienced. The largest turnout in recent years was the 100 mobilised for an Oxford game who travelled in a fleet of taxis at 11am for an evening kick-off.

In 2001, Reading played Millwall. The Dirty Thirty met at 8.30am at the Cattle Market café but already the police were hot on their trail. By pub opening time, the Reading mob had moved into the Firkin pub, close to the station. While the bulk soon left to make their way to the ground, a dozen were left behind before heading off to the Red Lion in Great Knolly. By now the police had also gone to the match and the small group was alone.

"Shit, shit! There's Millwall in the pub," shouted one of the Reading lads who had gone on ahead. Behind him and advancing fast were more than twenty South London heavies.

"They let fly with bottles and glasses and were armed with pool cues, chairs and anything else they could lay their hands on including a shovel," recalled M. "After a bit of ducking and diving, we then retaliated with every-thing they had thrown at us, including the shovel. About five of the Millwall stood and the rest backed off around the side of the pub. The call went up, 'Millwall, stand.' But the rest of their mob were all over the place. In hind-sight we felt sorry for the five that did stand as they took a right battering, including a few digs with the shovel. All told, the whole incident lasted about five minutes, but for the lads who were there it felt like ages. The furious onslaught was punctuated by the arrival of the father of one of the Reading lads, who proceeded to tell off his son. The Millwall lads he was fighting just stood there in bewilderment. Pure comedy."

The culprits split before the police arrived and there were no Reading injuries or arrests. However, by every rise there is a fall and for Reading there were two the following year. A home match against Oxford saw a clash between the rival mobs during the game at the Queens pub on Great Knolly Street. As Reading approached the pub the visitors piled out, launching much of the premises' contents. The 40 Reading quickly shrunk to just five and they received a battering, with two getting slashed. The incident caused a fallout within the mob and 15 of the 40 have not been seen at football since.

An even lower point in the firm's history was when they were turned over by Yeovil. "At a time when Yeovil were still non-league they came to the Madejski Stadium for an FA Cup clash," remembered M. "They arrived in the town by coach about eleven o' clock and caught everyone by surprise. There was no real trouble before the game but afterwards they steamed straight into the waiting Reading mob and ran us everywhere, throwing manhole covers on the way."

There were further problems for the Reading mob after a game at Colchester United. Sixty Reading made the trip to Essex with few expecting any real problems. "After a brief scouting mission around the town it was reported that about twenty-five Colchester were drinking in Yates's, just around the corner from where we were," said M. "About twenty-five of us left to introduce ourselves. The Colchester lads were last seen jumping behind the bar and hiding under tables as the Reading firm attacked. We then just left and returned to the pub, still with no Old Bill evident. The police eventually caught up with us and escorted us to the ground. The escort totalled about 150, with seventy lads well up for it after the earlier event.

"The game passed off with no further incidents and the main bulk of lads were escorted back to the station and sent home. About twenty-five had managed to slip the escort and were plotted up in a pub at the bottom of a hill just outside the town centre. A few lads had split away from the main group and were drinking in the Tin Cup. These were just normal fans out for a few beers but they were in the know and overheard a number of Colchester talking about the day's events and saying that there were still some Reading drinking in a pub at the bottom of the hill. Some of the Colchester came down to where we were and called it on. We agreed and followed their directions and both mobs met head-on, with a number of Colchester taking a severe kicking and returning to the pub they had come from rather more quickly than they had left it."

However, fighting outside a magistrates' court was perhaps not their wisest move, as it was caught on CCTV. Three Reading supporters were arrested on the day and a further twelve nine months later. All of the lads were found guilty of affray and threatening behaviour. Two received custodial sentences and the rest were given community service orders, along with fines up to nearly £2,000. This, coupled with a spate of civil bans, has severely impacted on the Reading mob.

This section would not be complete without mention of a pre-season friendly against West Ham in 1996, one of the most serious outbreaks of disorder in Reading for many years. "There were two major battles and a number of scuffles which continued until late in the evening," said M. "The first was outside the Three Gunnies. About twenty-five West Ham left the main concourse of the station and approached the front of the pub, where thirty Reading and six Chelsea were drinking. As they approached, the Reading mob went straight into them and the majority of West Ham backed off in to the station. The police were present within seconds and split the rival groups.

"The second incident took place in the Flyer and Firkin. West Ham were in there, calling for a number of well-known faces from the local area. They were being a general nuisance, so six Chelsea and three Reading went to the pub in reply to their calls. A full-scale battle took place resulting in a number of injuries, including a heavy-duty slashing. The West Ham in the pub took a real hammering."

The knife victim, Barry Lewis, required 368 stitches [see *Chelsea* in *Hooligans Vol. 1*] and a week after the incident, dawn raids saw eight people charged with involvement in the attack. But here was the rub: for what was one of Reading's most violent incidents in recent hooligan history, all but one of the defendants were known Chelsea supporters.

ROTHERHAM UNITED

Ground: Millmoor
Firms: East Dene Mafia, Tivoli Boot Boys, the Friday Crew, Rotherham Casuals, Rotherham Express Crew, Section 5
Rivals: Sheffield Wednesday, Sheffield United, Doncaster, Barnsley, Chesterfield

For almost its entire existence, the supporters of Rotherham United have lived in the shadow of bigger rivals. Many young lads in Rotherham support one of the two Sheffield clubs, a few give their loyalty to Barnsley or even Leeds United. What is left is a small but loyal following. It was from this group that hooliganism first emerged in the late Sixties, coinciding with the arrival of the skinhead and bootboy scene.

We are indebted to two Rotherham hooligans for the following background information: "Mobs arose from different areas in Rotherham. The East Dene Mafia, the Kimberworth Park Skins and Maltby Millers came from particularly rough areas. These all joined up and fought under the collective name of the Tivoli Boot Boys, who met on the Kop end at Millmoor, which the lads took great pleasure in defending. Away fans may have tried to get on the Tivoli, but no firm ever took it." The opposite end of the ground was occupied by the Railway Enders, who stood alongside the away supporters.

During the Eighties, the Friday Crew emerged after a particularly lively away game at Grimsby Town. The mid- to late-Eighties saw other little firms emerge: the Rotherham Casuals and Rotherham Express Crew. But the largest, most active and most violent was a gang of casuals who called themselves Section 5, the name coming from the criminal charge of Section 5, Public Disorder. Over recent years, newer recruits have flirted with new names such as the Rotherham Youth Firm (RYF) and Masbrough Street Casuals, but the name Section 5 has remained at the forefront.

Today there are very few "veterans" around. Section 5 brought a group of young lads onto the scene and they replaced those who had gone before. There is a core of about 50-60 lads, with 100 for big games. One of the biggest turnouts in recent years was a home game against Manchester City, when a mob of over 130 was put together. The return fixture saw a mob of 70 Rotherham travel. Another 100 travelled to a recent match at Sheffield Wednesday. These numbers are way down on the Seventies but 30 years ago organisation was poorer and big numbers were mainly seen at home when a large away following came to town.

Rotherham are awash with local rivals: within a fifteen-mile radius they have Sheffield United, Sheffield Wednesday, Barnsley, Doncaster and Chesterfield. As the town is also home to so many fans who follow other teams, it is not uncommon for rivalries to spill over in the town centre at night. Doncaster Rovers are probably Rotherham's main rivals. Both towns are a similar size and they have played each other more frequently than the others. But Rotherham's rise to the Championship (the old Second Division) gave Section 5 a chance to test the Sheffield clubs.

In December 2001, just after Rotherham were promoted, they played at Bramall Lane. The game went peacefully but afterwards the Blades Business Crew decided to go into Rotherham. In the ensuing street battle, a number of lads from each side were arrested and later sent to prison.

The Blades, in truth, are in a different hooligan league but in recent years Rotherham have had several run-ins with Wednesday, which probably says more about how Wednesday have declined as a mob in recent years than the growing strength of Section 5. The first in a series of clashes between the two saw a group of Rotherham stopping off in Sheffield on their return from a league match at Notts County in January 2001. One Rotherham fan was so badly hurt that he was rushed to hospital with head injuries. Twelve months later, Rotherham played at Hillsborough and stewards and riot police had to be mobilised to prevent 50 Rotherham from climbing out of the main stand and into the Leppings Lane end. The game was to see Rotherham's largest travelling mob for many years as over 100 thugs clashed with Wednesday during and after the game.

Rotherham were feeling increasingly confident against Wednesday when the two teams met again on New Year's Day, 2003. Again there was no show from the Owls Crime Squad, so after a few phone calls a mob of 50 Rotherham decided to take the battle to Wednesday. They travelled without a police escort into Sheffield and smashed up a number of Wednesday pubs. Some time later, a group of Rotherham decided on a repeat performance but this time a group of Blades were drinking near the station. Despite Rotherham's intention to attack their arch-rivals, the BBC made their displeasure clear. "Coming into Sheffield to smash Wednesday once was a laugh," said one BBC lad. "But doing it a second time was not on. Even though it was against the Pigs, we couldn't let Toytown have a free run around the city. We told them that if they remained in Sheffield then United would deal with them. They went home."

Rotherham have also had other rivalries with clubs further afield, Stockport and Shrewsbury being two examples. In 1996, Rotherham met Shrewsbury in the Autoglass Windscreen Cup final at Wembley and battles went on all evening in London. There is nothing like an end-of-season decider to galvanise the interest of the opposing firms.

In May 2000 Rotherham played host to Swansea in what was a championship decider. There was trouble before, during and after the game as both mobs turned out in force. However, it was the tragic death of 41-year-old Terry Cole, from Swansea, that grabbed the headlines the following day. Coles died in hospital after suffering a fractured skull when he was trampled by a police horse as officers tried to separate fans before the game. The father-of-two was near a 100-strong Swansea group who were being escorted by police to the ground when they were confronted by Rotherham hooligans. The two groups exchanged missiles, and as three police horses cantered down a slope towards them, one collided with Mr Coles. "The victim had not seen the horse and he appeared to be walking into the line of the animal," said Mr Hollis, South Yorkshire Police's Assistant Chief Constable. Nineteen people were arrested before the game, which finished a 1–1 draw. That proved enough for Swansea to take the title. Play was stopped twice following pitch invasions after each goal, and there was further fighting after the game.

Rotherham's promotion to the First Division brought them bigger crowds, two Sheffield derbies and larger mobs. In their first season, disorder broke out between rival fans before Rotherham's away game at Port Vale. Two Rotherham supporters needed first aid. A few weeks later, they clashed with Sheffield Wednesday on their return from Notts County and in April a minibus of Rotherham fans were attacked after the away game at Wigan. The windscreen was shattered and the driver injured. Fighting took place and further up the street a group of five Rotherham fans were also attacked; two of this group required hospital treatment. Rotherham and Wigan fans also battled it out in a town centre pub.

The following season Rotherham intensified their feud with Wednesday, and also clashed with Gillingham, West Brom and Man City. The trip to Gillingham was not one of Rotherham's favourites, as they were attacked on their way back to the train station in the Kent town, then bumped into a group of Sheffield United fans on the train. A few weeks later it took a large presence of police to prevent Rotherham and West Brom fans from fighting in Rotherham town centre. However, after the game there was some trouble as the visitors were being escorted back to the station. The away match at Manchester City saw possibly the largest Rotherham away turnout in recent years. They attacked City fans inside the ground, resulting in the police locking out other away fans. There was further trouble after the game as Section 5 headed back to their bus. After ten minutes of trouble, the police had to escort Rotherham out of Manchester.

Away from football grounds, Section 5 have had regular run-ins with doormen. A group of 50 recently went on a stag night in York and clashed with local bouncers and Darlington lads. There were casualties on both sides, with several people needing hospital treatment after ten minutes of intense fighting. In December, a few Section 5 lads were drinking in Wakefield when a few local bouncers got stroppy about football lads drinking in their boozers. A scuffle took place and the bouncers came out on top with the help of other pubs' doormen. As luck would have it, Rotherham were playing at Bradford the next week, so 50 Section 5 made the short trip to exact revenge. The local "hardmen" were no longer so hard as the Rotherham lads chased them up and down their own high street, as locals looked on in amazement.

S

SCUNTHORPE UNITED

Ground: Glanford Park
Firms: True Irons
Rivals: Grimsby Town, Lincoln City, Hull City
Police operations: Trapper

It wasn't until the arrival of the internet that the football lads from Scunthorpe finally ran under a collective name. "True Irons" is the name of their website, and it quickly became adopted as the name of their mob. Until then, they were simply Scunthorpe, though small groups within their support have called themselves the Ashby Riot Squad and various other tags adapting the name of the River Trent.

Scunthorpe's rivals are Grimsby, Lincoln and Hull, with hostilities slightly further afield being with Mansfield and Doncaster. "For all of the above we always seemed to get the best turnouts and it's difficult to say which was hated the most," said one of the True Irons, Shane. "Our main rivalry seemed to alternate between Grimsby (Codheads) and Hull depending on the division. You could also count Lincoln, especially in recent years, and Doncaster, notably in the Eighties, as big games."

The *Scunthorpe Evening Telegraph* was reporting trouble between the home team and Grimsby and Lincoln in the late Sixties, and few derby games passed without some sort of trouble. Into the Eighties, Scunthorpe's casual mob grew rapidly. For a town of its size it took an impressive 150 lads to an FA Cup match at Spurs in 1986 and three years later a similar number away to Grimsby. "We took 150 on an early train and caught the police by surprise," said Shane. "They hadn't planned on us arriving that early so let us go. We trotted down to a boozer miles from the station and were having a beer when a couple of Cods wandered in, to get the shock of their lives. Next thing we know, we are running towards the pier area, where similar numbers of Cods are awaiting our arrival. Over the next hour or so there were running battles all over the place. Some Cods will disagree, but we surprised them that day and legged them back to their ground."

There were victories and defeats against Grimsby. "We have had a few bad days," Shane admitted. "The Cods have shown mob-handed on occasions and taken the piss."

The same year also saw hundreds out for the cup visit of Sunderland. "We shocked the life out of them," said Shane. "We were battling all over the town centre, with a few pubs getting trashed. I have chatted to a few older hands from Sunderland who gave us a lot of respect for that day. I remember twatting some bloke when this fucking monster came running at me shouting, 'I'll have you, you little cunt.' As I was only seventeen at the time I shit myself and buggered off sharpish."

One tragic occasion involved a group of Scunthorpe travelling to Doncaster on a stag night in the Eighties. Fighting broke out over several hours before the police rounded up the visitors and escorted them out of town. "A load of Donny lads got wind of their presence, went down there, and kicked it off big time," recalled a Doncaster lad. "One of the Scunny lads got killed in the ensuing fight. A few weeks after that incident, a coachload of Scunthorpe lads were stopped by the police *en route* to Doncaster. On board the coach were axes and other weapons."

Doncaster's relegation from the Football League kept the two sides apart for several years, but in November 2001 they were drawn together in the FA Cup. A mob of up to 70 Scunthorpe made the short trip across and were drinking in Yates's Wine Lodge when 25 Doncaster burst in. The *Doncaster Star* reported that "an elderly woman suffered a gash to her head and needed hospital treatment when she was hit by a flying beer glass, and a man was also injured but declined medical assistance". Dozens of police were quickly there and the Scunthorpe mob was escorted to the ground. Three years later was Doncaster's first visit to Scunthorpe since their return to the Football League and this time the police were taking no chances. Sgt Brian Burns, of Scunthorpe Police, said a couple of days before the game, "The police presence will be strong, with staffing increased due to intelligence and the potential for disorder. This should ensure this fixture goes smoothly and police resources are able to respond to any developing tension." The policing appeared to work as there was no report of trouble.

One of the worst outbreaks of disorder involving Scunthorpe in the late Eighties was an away match at Scarborough. "42 held as fans go wild," ran the headline in one newspaper. It continued, "Scunthorpe United fans went on the rampage in Bridlington last night as they waited for the kick-off of this afternoon's game against Scarborough. Police in the resort arrested 42 people – the majority of them from the Scunthorpe area. A total of 39 are still being detained awaiting charges of public disorder, damage and assault. Police in Bridlington had to call on help from a Unit Support Group after they attended various incidents between 10pm and 2am."

Another newspaper report of trouble between Scunthorpe and Scarborough during the Eighties referred to something called the Scunthorpe Utility Fighting Crew, and reproduced a calling card depicting gravestones with the caption, "In Loving Memory to Scarborough". Scunthorpe's club secretary was quick to condemn the cards. "It is a shame they have to waste their lives on such petty things," he said. "Life is to be enjoyed and if that is the maximum they can get out of life then I feel very sorry for them."

There have been several battles over the years with northern sides Darlington and Hartlepool. On two occasions, in 1982 and 1996, Darlington took major mobs to Scunthorpe, each time towards the end of the respective seasons. "In 1982, a coach load of 50 lads travelled down, causing grief," remembered Andy from Darlington. "There were a couple of arrests and fat Granty broke his leg trying to Fosbury Flop a terrace barrier."

In May 1996, Darlington went south again for the final game of the season needing a win to clinch promotion. "Trouble flared in the opening minutes," reported the *Scunthorpe Evening Telegraph*. Several people were arrested and others ejected as fighting and pitch invasions marred the game. However, it was a snooker ball hurled at the referee that received the front-page headlines the following day. "I presumed it was aimed at me," referee Roger Furnandiz told the paper, "because it landed relatively close to me. I wondered what it was at first, but when I realised it was a snooker ball I was a bit concerned. I can't say who threw it but it came from an area where the Doncaster supporters were sat." The referee decided not to tell the other match officials or the police until after the match for fear that it might incite further trouble.

Darlington are slightly dismissive of Scunthorpe. "If Scunthorpe have Darlo down as main rivals, it's only due to us going there, because I don't recall a half decent mob of Scunthorpe paying us a return visit," said Andy.

Hartlepool, at least, acknowledge some serious fights. "Yeah, there's been a bit of history over the years with them," admitted Ian, a member of Hartlepool's Blue Order. "In 2003, we went there on a double-decker bus and were in town for 11am. Couldn't get served anyway and no Scunny about. They made a show just before kick-off but there was OB everywhere. We took around sixty in the FA Cup about two years before that as well. Just one of those teams we seem to travel to and normally have them waiting. Some good scraps in the Eighties and late Nineties ensured it was always a good day."

Scunthorpe's Shane said, "We have a lot of respect for both Hartlepool and Darlo, as they have both shown at Glanford Park over the years and had a go. We won some and lost some. One funny memory was Hartlepool coming down and trying to avoid OB by taking an unusual route. They ended up getting sussed and walked about ten miles into a pub at the bottom of town through the steelworks."

Scunthorpe's mob have also had their humorous moments. "There was one match against Halifax and four of us decided to go late on the train," said Shane. "We got to the ground five minutes after kick-off and the other three decided to get in over the wall. I walked round to the turnstiles, paid in and wandered on to the terrace just in time to see the daft cunts jump straight into their lads. As expected, they were getting backed off by the mob and not looking behind them. One lad fell arse over face over a low wall onto the pitch. Needless to say, they all got lifted, one lad had lost some cash from his pocket and when they went to court he decided to go look for it. He went to the ground, jumped the wall in the same spot, found his money and climbed back out again. The amount was less than £5, the tight bastard!"

The Halifax match also made the local paper as the arrested Scunthorpe fans appeared before magistrates. "There had been several incidents in Halifax town centre before the start of the game," the prosecution noted. "Police reinforcements had to be brought in from other divisions. During the game it became apparent that the visiting supporters were intent on causing trouble. There was an atmosphere of hostility and several arrests had already been made by police."

The same man who fell over the barrier was involved in another incident, this time with Cardiff. "He was battling Cardiff in Scunny when he decided to jump on to this car," recalled Shane. "He jumped onto a Sierra and over the roof on to the back, went straight through the rear window and ended up sat between two Cardiff lads. A quick headbutt and a punch and he was out of the car quicker than a ferret.

"Another memorable match was away to Mansfield. A few of us had gone in cars and a minibus. Some of us decided to fuck the game off and went for a wander – bumping into Mansfield's firm as we did. Instead of smashing us to pieces they had the good grace to arrange a meet later in the day when we had decent numbers – there were only four of us at the time.

"After the game, we met the rest of the lads in a pub near the ground. One had spent the whole day drinking and was hammered, so we laid him down in the back of the van whilst we went to meet the Mansfield lot. We found them and a stand-off occurred until the said lad woke from his stupor and charged down the road and straight into their firm. Ten minutes before, he couldn't even stand, never mind fight."

East Yorkshire/Humberside/Lincolnshire has been one of the most active hooligan regions over the past few years, with Hull City, Lincoln, Grimsby and Scunthorpe all regularly turning out mobs, especially against each other. During the 1999/2000 season, 75 Scunthorpe surprised Hull City by turning up for an away game. The following season, Hull were determined not to be caught unprepared and attacked a bus carrying Scunthorpe's mob as it stopped at traffic lights. "The Scunthorpe supporters got off the bus and a fight ensued," noted an NCIS report. "After twenty minutes, police restored order. Fourteen were arrested. During the game, two arrests were made for pitch invasion. After the match, police deployment prevented any disorder."

In early 2003, Scunthorpe played host to Leeds United in the FA Cup. It was a big game for the home fans and a large mob turned out – but not enough to repel their West Yorkshire rivals. "There were 150 out and we did well before the game but they would have fucking murdered us afterwards," admitted Shane.

A few months later, Scunthorpe were drawn against Lincoln City in the Third Division play-offs, a draw that was always likely to be tarnished. And so it turned out, as an eight-goal thriller, with Lincoln taking their home tie 5–3, was overshadowed by violence during and after the game. "At its height about 400 people were fighting inside the ground," reported the *Lincolnshire Echo*. "Trouble began shortly after the final whistle. Hundreds of City fans invaded the pitch, running to the tunnel to praise their heroes. Moments later they ran to the south end of the Community Stand to taunt rival fans over their five-three defeat. Stewards and police successfully kept the two groups of spectators apart while they were inside the ground. Outside, however, police had their work cut out in dealing with troublemakers. Traffic in the area came to a standstill as gangs paraded up and down the High Street. Shortly afterwards there were sporadic outbreaks of violence as Lincoln and Scunthorpe fans came to blows."

With the second leg only four days later, the police in Scunthorpe were determined there wouldn't be a repeat of the violence. "Any hooligans will be subjected to our zero-tolerance policy," said a spokesman. "If they step out of line they will be arrested. We will have a large police presence in and around the ground on Wednesday evening and this should ensure that events go smoothly and everybody enjoys the day."

Predictions like that have a habit of coming back to haunt the person who makes them. Ten fans were arrested following scenes that were described as "absolutely disgraceful". There was trouble before, during and after the match, which Scunthorpe lost 1–0. The most serious incident occurred in the Doncaster Road and Hilton Avenue area of the town, where rival gangs pelted each other with missiles before turning on the police. Officers dressed in protective clothing, including helmets and vests, were forced to use shields for protection. The violence amused most of the Scunthorpe hooligans precisely because the police had promised a trouble-free game.

On 24 April 2004, however, came a street battle that police would describe as the worst incident of football violence ever seen in the region and which would spark a crackdown on United's thug element. Scunthorpe were at home to Macclesfield Town while Grimsby Town were at Stockport County. Police received intelligence that the Grimsby mob planned to visit Scunthorpe on their way home and a fight had been arranged. As a result, an officer went that day to Bar Rendezvous, described in court as "a prominent meeting place for members of the Scunthorpe United hooligan element", and noted that the windows had been boarded up as if in expectation of trouble. He gave the drinkers inside a public order warning but was told by one that they could go where they liked.

Some time later, a train carrying Grimsby supporters arrived at Scunthorpe Station. Some of the Irons mob had moved there to wait for them and were watching from outside Bondz Bar. At the same time, other Grimsby lads arrived by road and entered Der Schnapps bar. The Scunthorpe lads learned of this, went to Der Schnapps and banged on the windows. Grimsby piled out and chased them down the road.

The Scunthorpe regrouped on Mary Street and battle began in earnest. "Fighting broke out between the two groups," said Gordon Staples, who later prosecuted many of those involved at Hull Crown Court. "The fighting involved physical attacks, including punches and kicks, and a pool cue was used. Many glasses and bottles were used." One Mariners fan, Paul Carter, of Cleethorpes, was beaten with pool cues and savagely kicked on the ground. As his friends backed off from the Scunthorpe assault, Carter managed to get up and tried to escape but was attacked again. The Grimsby crew started hurling full bricks and other missiles but Scunthorpe maintained the upper hand. When they eventually returned to Britannia Corner they were seen to raise their fists in triumph.

Almost inevitably, the brawl was captured on CCTV. Humberside Police subsequently launched Operation Trapper to identify those involved and 42 defendants subsequently appeared in court. Most were either convicted or pleaded guilty and were given fines, community punishment orders and bans. They included a serving soldier due to go to Afghanistan and a £4 million lottery winner.

However, an NCIS report from a subsequent game in April 2005 showed how the problems between the two mobs continued. "A police officer was squirted in the eye with a noxious substance – believed to be CS liquid – as hardcore hooligans came out in force for Saturday's Grimsby v Scunthorpe clash," it read. "While on the pitch the rival teams played out a dull, goalless ninety minutes at Blundell Park on Saturday, off the pitch a meticulously planned police operation prevented any major disorder with just twelve arrests."

Police said a large contingent of Scunthorpe fans descended on Cleethorpes four hours before kick-off, intent on causing trouble. Intelligence had indicated the away following would invade the pitch at the final whistle. This was stamped out by stewards, police and the dog section. After the game, pockets of fighting broke out as hooligans were led back to Cleethorpes train station. "The hooligans saw it as an opportunity to have a good set-to and fortunately we prevented that. That is down to the presence and bravery of the police officers," said Superintendent Stuart Donald, the match commander.

It is a report which normal fans claimed was wildly exaggerated, and some complained to the clubs and authorities about their treatment that day. According to newspaper reports, police struggled to contain a Scunthorpe mob of more than 400. This was widely ridiculed by many innocent Irons fans, who argued that they were rounded up and treated the same as the much smaller hooligan group.

As the 2005/06 season kicked off, the local police promised an even more uncompromising attitude to hooliganism. "If we've got to arrest them, let's have them locked up and get the evidence we need for a banning order," said Inspector Neil Pattison during his pre-match message to officers policing a League Cup game against Birmingham City. The match commander now uses a DVD of the ground and surrounding area to help officers visualise their role and potential flashpoints.

SHEFFIELD UNITED

Ground: Bramall Lane
Firms: Shoreham Republican Army, Suicide Squad, Blades Business Crew, Darnall Massive
Rivals: Sheffield Wednesday, Leeds United

It is one of the fiercest rivalries around. Even now, in the age when police generally control the streets on match days, a Sheffield derby brings out the worst in hundreds of men – especially for a Blade. The hatred shown towards Wednesday fans, or "Pigs" as they are commonly known by United fans, seems more intense than the other way round. And this is despite the Blades dominating the streets for the best part of the past 20 years and having a far superior team.

Reports of trouble between the two sets of fans date back to at least the mid-Sixties, though throughout the same decade there were accounts of fans mixing happily on the terraces and even attending each other's matches. But the mid-Sixties saw the development of the "ends" of two clubs and the seasonal attempt by one set of supporters to take the others.

Wednesday were not the only team to find a hostile reception at United's ground. As early as 1964, *The Times* newspaper reported trouble at Sheffield's home match against Burnley. The first identifiable mob on the terraces was the Shoreham Republican Army, so-called after the home Shoreham End. "The Shoreham Republican Army had some loony tunes all right," recalled Zack, a veteran Blade. "In the late Sixties and early Seventies it was pretty much even-stevens with our foes from across the city. It wasn't until the mid to late Seventies that Wednesday became the more potent force.

"In those days anyone who went to football was fair game, it wasn't just lads who wanted it. I used to collect scarves from the opposition and go to work on Monday morning with them on. West Ham, Chelsea, Arsenal, Leeds, et cetera, have all hung around my neck. The problem was keeping your own and mine got nicked at Fulham of all places. I got put on my arse and relieved of my prized silky.

"The biggest rumble I can recall was in 1974 at Birmingham. We took thousands as we needed a win to secure a place in Europe. Tony Currie and Alan Woodward were playing and at least 15,000 Unitedites travelled. We ended up on their end and all the match it was murder as we battled it out with Birmingham. We were still in there at the end though. I returned home with a black eye and United only got a point, thus missing out on that magic prize. The other big tear-up I can recall was 1971 when Man United came on the kop. The game passed by with us trying to regain the kop time and time again, running battles for the whole ninety minutes, a bit surreal looking back."

The early Seventies saw regular outbreaks of disorder at Bramall Lane. An April Fool's Day game against Newcastle United saw 50 fans charged after fans clashed. "Fighting between rival gangs of supporters broke out on the Spion Kop at Bramall Lane and a series of running battles took place, with bottles and bricks being thrown," reported the *Sheffield Star*. "There were further clashes as fans made for the city centre after the match."

Three days later the typewriters at the local newspaper were busy again, this time after the home visit of Manchester United. It was to be one of several Man United incursions at Sheffield's ground. "Soccer fans riot in City," ran the front page headline.

A gang of football fans ran riot in Sheffield city centre on an orgy of destruction after last night's match between the Blades and Manchester United.

Traders off The Moor faced a £1,000 bill for damage after the gang went on the rampage smashing plate-glass shop windows.

Police called to the scene found a trail of vandalism from Broomhall Redevelopment to Charter Square.

Iron bars, bricks and concrete slabs were taken from a Corporation roadworks site in Charter Row as the fans, who had seen Sheffield United draw with the visiting team, went from shop to shop shattering display windows.

Mrs Shirley Thompson, who has a hairdressing salon in Headford Parade, said: "The football fans started running riot in the nearby flats. They were running all over and dropping milk bottles from the top."

In 1972 Leeds United fans took over the United kop, one of only a handful of mobs ever to achieve this. In August of the same year, a coach carrying Sheffield United fans to Birmingham was attacked by home supporters. The fans inside ducked for cover as bricks hit the sides and shattered four windows. The Brummie mob also daubed the outside of the coach with black paint. "I have been carrying football fans for three years and this is the first time any of my vehicles has been damaged but it won't happen again," the coach owner said afterwards. "Some of my coaches cost £9,000 and I am not risking sending them to football matches."

A week after the trip to Birmingham, United entertained Newcastle, and 18 fans were fined a total of £900 after supporters fought on the terraces. The police created a space between the two sets of supporters but even this did not deter the hooligans, as repeated charges occurred throughout the game. "We think it is disgusting that ordinary people can't go to a football match without finding people upsetting the match," said magistrates' chairman Mr J.C. Phillips. "It seems a pity ordinary people can't attend football matches without going in fear. The bench are going to make an example. Up to now we have dealt with cases inside the ground. Outside the ground we feel it is much more serious because you are bringing in members of the public."

United's hooligans lost ground to some of their fiercest rivals from the mid-Seventies onwards. Wednesday's mob was growing and regularly took Bramall Lane, as Zack admits. "We still got a few results but as our firm got fewer in numbers, Wednesday's firm was on the rise. They had some lumps with them and also had numbers on us. It's fair to say that the Seventies belonged to Wednesday's firm in Sheffield. Although United had the odd result it was more or less one-way traffic."

In March 1974, the visit of Manchester United once again saw trouble, this time with 48 arrests. Several spectators were treated for head injuries after fighting broke out inside the ground. When the crowd went on the march into the city centre, police were called out with dogs to turn them back to the Midland Station.

Arguably the worst outbreak of disorder, however, occurred with the visit of Notts Forest in March 1977. "Streets besieged in fans' battle of Bramall Lane," said the front page of the *Sheffield Star*.

> Policemen were injured and residents fled to safety during a Battle of Bramall Lane which erupted after Sheffield United and Nottingham Forest fans clashed in ugly scenes.
>
> As Operation Clear-up was underway in the area today, an appalling new picture of soccer violence came to light.
>
> Battling and rioting fans put the Charlotte Road, Shoreham Street and Margaret Street areas in a state of siege after the Blades' 2-0 home win.
>
> They left in their wake a trail of destruction and injuries.

A policeman was seriously hurt after being hit in the face with a house brick, while another officer was badly injured outside the ground. A Sheffield United fan was admitted to hospital with a broken jaw and an 83-year-old woman's house was bombarded with stones as she cowered in the back room. "Residents looked on helplessly as gangs of youths brandishing uprooted railings smashed house and shop windows and damaged parked cars," the paper added. Nine people were arrested and another 16 were ejected from the ground.

Several residents demanded greater police protection against hooliganism and a local vicar organised a petition to complain to the club, the council and the Chief Constable. Heather Bladger, who ran a corner shop in the vicinity, told the press, "In Charlotte Road one group of supporters gathered at one end of the road and another set at the other end. Then one youth in the middle shouted, 'Charge,' and they just clashed in the centre of the road. There must have been more than 500 fans. One policeman tried to get in the middle, but they just knocked him down."

Geoff and Jackie Feetham were sitting in their front room when a stave came hurtling through their four-foot, double-glazed window, while the owner of a nearby antiques shop said it had been the third time in recent years that his windows had been smashed.

There was further bad news for the city when it was announced, two days after the game, that Hillsborough was to host the FA Cup semi-final between Manchester United and Leeds United in late April. The League Cup Final replay between Everton and Aston Villa in mid-March had seen widespread violence throughout the city centre and two Everton fans stabbed. Now the prospect of another high profile cup tie between two clubs with fans with long records of disorder was too much for some.

"We appreciate that there are strong reasons for being pleased about the decision [to hold the game in Sheffield]," noted the editorial in the *Star*. "Not only will the city gain considerably in terms of prestige – so will Sheffield Wednesday, for the club's share will be fifteen percent of the receipts. But what about the people living nearby? There was a time when their only problem was noise and the inconvenience they suffered from thoughtless fans who parked their cars without consideration in any available space. Now, inconsiderate car parking is the least of their worries."

The local newspaper ran a rash of football hooligan-related stories in the days following the Forest game. West Yorkshire Police released a report detailing the cost of policing football in the area, and soccer yobs were also singled out by the paper for vandalism and drunken violence on local buses. "Particularly in Sheffield," noted the *Star*, "buses seem to attract a considerable number of attacks by football hooligans."

Six days later, local MP Fred Mulley, who was also the Defence Minister, announced that he intended to attend Sheffield United's next home game to judge for himself the threat of hooliganism. He had received several letters of complaint from residents demanding action be taken. "I will discuss the problem with my ministerial colleagues and see if there are any steps that can be taken nationally that would also help us with our problem in Sheffield," he said.

Meanwhile the Reverend Tony Lowe's petition calling for a month-long closure of Bramall Lane after every instance of disorder was signed by more than 700 people. The petition also called for more police cover in the area around the ground and an assurance that the club would pay financial compensation for damage to property. "People are sick and tired of the violence that accompanies Sheffield United's games," Lowe told the press. "People who live in the Bramall Lane area are now very frightened and very angry and we want to make our streets safe on Saturday afternoon." An action group was formed and links were made with a similar residents' group in Derby, which was exploring the possibility of obtaining a high court injunction to prevent First Division football at the Baseball Ground.

Residents near Sheffield Wednesday's ground launched a similar petition. The furore over the Notts Forest game, coupled with the announcement over the hosting of the FA Cup semi-final, had gripped the city in hooligan panic. "Hillsbro' scared to death at Red Army visit," ran the front-page headline in the *Star* on April 7. "Save us from the hooligans," demanded local residents. In less than four days, over 1,400 people had signed the petition, which again asked for compensation and protection against "violence, nuisance and damage…" [see LEEDS in *Hooligans*]

Wednesday's hooligan dominance over United coincided with the Blades' on-field decline. Having just missed out on a European spot in the early Seventies, the side slumped down the leagues. In May 1981, United travelled to Walsall knowing that anything less than a point would see them relegated to the Fourth Division. A penalty miss in the last minute saw United down and the pitch invasion by the travelling fans was matched by late-night trouble in Sheffield city centre. Pubs and police cars bore the brunt as thousands of Blades vented their disappointment. Few might have accepted it that night but bottom-league football heralded a renaissance in United's fortunes. Several old players were booted out and a new board with a cash injection entered the club. Within a year, United were back up.

The Fourth Division may not have contained any glamour clubs but there were several northern derbies to be had. In October, United travelled to Bradford, where they were attacked by 100 Ointment hooligans armed with bricks, bottles and baseball bats. In March 1982, an away match at Hartlepool saw trouble before and during the game. The lack of organisation amongst the United fans saw them outgunned in a pub fight and during the game a group of 50 Blades who sneaked into the home end were repeatedly attacked from all sides. "It was to be the most uncomfortable 90 minutes I have ever sat through," recalled Steve Cowens in his book *Blades Business Crew*. The final match of the season saw United travel back up to the North East, this time to clinch the title at Darlington. Over 10,000 Blades made the trip and their sheer strength of numbers saw off not only the locals but also a mob of 100 Middlesbrough who had decided to turn up.

A younger generation of hooligans was emerging at United, but they were generally poorly organised and sometimes too raw to be effective. On a number of occasions they were caught by surprise by home mobs whose ferocity outstripped their reputation. A pre-season friendly in August 1982 saw Lincoln run a surprised and ill-prepared Sheffield mob. "They were so up for it they soon had us backing off, then ran us," recorded Cowens. Thirty-five young Blades had travelled down on a coach expecting no more than a piss-up and were caught off-guard by the Lincoln onslaught.

A month later, the sides met in the League and United this time came prepared. A hundred of their main lads travelled through on the train and literally the moment they came out of the station Lincoln appeared. "They poured across the road at us, with a few glasses and bottles thrown our way," said Cowens. "Then everybody was into them in a flurry of fists and boots, neither side budging." The police finally appeared in numbers and split the warring mobs up. Sheffield were escorted to a pub some distance away but within the hour Lincoln re-emerged armed with bottles, pool cues and glasses.

The clubs were drawn together again early in the following season and like the previous encounters it was a day of violence. Slightly more United hooligans made this trip and again were met by Lincoln at the station, but this was to be only a prelude to the main act. The police divided the mobs but they clashed again in the main shopping centre. "Soccer fan battle 'terrifies' OAPs," ran the headline in the local paper.

Nearly 50 old people cowered in terror last night as soccer hooligans fought a running battle with bottles, glasses and iron bars outside a home for the elderly in Lincoln.

Many had to be led to the safety of an upstairs room as more than 200 rioting supporters turned the lower High Street into a battleground.

'The old people were absolutely terrified,' said Mr Matthew Littlewood, husband of the warden at the home for the elderly at St. Botolph's Court.

Eight people were arrested in the trouble before, during and after the match. A mob of 200 Lincoln attacked United in the Golden Eagle pub, smashing seven windows in their attempt to force their way in. One United fan was cut in the face by flying glass while another was hit in the head with a brick. Despite the numerous incidents spanning several hours, the police later claimed that they had the situation "fairly well under control".

A particularly violent encounter occurred before a Milk Cup game against Barnsley. In one incident, two Barnsley fans were seriously injured after they were attacked by a mob of United fans. Twenty-two-year-old Darrell Round was chased for a mile before he was floored by a brick on the back of his head, while his friend was stabbed and needed emergency surgery. "There were about twenty of us walking together when suddenly about fifty Sheffield fans jumped out from behind cars," Round told the *Sheffield Star*. "They were throwing bricks at us and we just ran for a mile with them chasing us. This brick hit me on the back of the head and I was knocked down. I was terrified. There was nothing we could do but run off. I was lucky, I got away, but some of the others got knifed."

The inexperience of the new young United hooligans was again highlighted with the visit of Cardiff City in February 1983. Despite the Welsh team performing well in the League and so being accompanied on their travels by a large travelling support, United's mob were surprisingly unprepared for this match. When news filtered through that Cardiff were drinking in the Globe pub, close to the railway station, there was only a 20-strong home mob on hand. Unsurprisingly, they faired poorly against an away mob of 150 lads.

In January 1984, United drew Birmingham City at home in the FA Cup. Hooliganism was at its peak and the emerging BBC looked forward to the match with keen anticipation. The Zulus arrived in numbers, with 200 lads travelling up in four coaches while others made their way on the train. Despite the serious threat of disorder, the football authorities and police allowed Sheffield Wednesday to play a cup game at home against Barnsley on the same day, and the first outbreak of trouble occurred when Blues fans went into some Wednesday pubs. As the rival mobs exchanged missiles, a large group of Blades arrived heavily armed. "The first thing I knew of what was to follow was a bicycle flying through the window, followed by a big roar," recounted a Birmingham hooligan in the book *Zulus*. The Zulus tried to get out of the pub but the wave of missiles kept them penned inside. "There was no way round the back, so the only chance was out of the front door, which some tried. There was a lot of brass and memorabilia on the walls – well we were in steel country – like swords, rifles, carriage lamps and so on. It all came off. I remember one lad, a chef by trade, grabbing a wired-up carriage lamp clean off the wall, dashing out the door, bashing some Blade with it and retreating as fast as he went out. It was that kind of day."

An estimated £3,000 worth of damage was done to the pub. The landlord was actually an Owl and was on his way to Hillsborough when the fight erupted, leaving his 21-year-old son in charge. "The Birmingham fans were inside but when the United fans started to fight everything just went berserk," he told the press.

The fighting continued inside the ground and for many young Blades it was one of the most violent encounters they were to experience. The match ended in a draw and there was further trouble at the replay, when a 150-strong mob made the midweek trip to the Midlands and fought before the game. Afterwards the home mob attacked United with bricks but they were kept far enough apart by police for there to be little impact.

Sheffield United's decline in the late Seventies meant that their trip to Leeds in October 1984 was their first to Elland Road for seven years. Three hundred Blades arrived in Leeds undetected and saw off a small home mob almost immediately. Leeds mobbed up in greater numbers up the street but by now the police were arriving in such strength that a major row was averted. Despite a hostile atmosphere inside the ground, heavy policing prevented further trouble both during and after the game. But the Blades had thrown down the challenge and they expected a Leeds response for the home fixture five months later.

In the days leading up to the game, leaflets circulated the pubs of Sheffield, urging the lads out. Over 600 answered the call, gathering in two city centre pubs, but there was little trouble before the game as Leeds slipped in unannounced. The first serious clash of the day occurred outside the turnstiles as 100 Blades attacked hundreds of Leeds fans queuing to enter the ground. Tension grew inside the ground as mob sought out mob and the police quickly surrounded any group they could find. A young Sheffield fan fired a naval distress flare into the middle of the Leeds end, which, added to their team going a goal down on the pitch, raised the temperature further. Some hurled their seats onto the pitch and as away fans began scaling the fences, so did some Blades.

The match finished as a 2–1 home win, then the rivals clashed repeatedly outside the ground. The worst incident took place in the city centre as 300 Leeds attacked the Silks pub. "At a given signal they started throwing glasses, chairs and furniture at a group of local people sitting quietly drinking," the local paper described on the front page of its Monday edition. "Expensive mirrors were smashed, a large window put through and pictures stolen from the walls. As terrified staff, some of them crying, cowered behind the bar, the hooligans looted bottles of spirits."

A serious fight erupted between rival mobs by the Moor, when 150 Leeds confronted 100 Blades. "The Moor was being repaired at the time," said Steve Cowens, "which meant Leeds were able to pick up ready-made weapons, such as steel spikes." The Blades, normally dismissive of the "vandals" and "seat throwers" of Leeds, acknowledged their firm that day. "But for the police we would have struggled," admitted Cowens. "They wanted to know and gained some credit from our lads."

The media, politicians and the police all lined up to denounce Leeds. "We expected bad behaviour from the Leeds supporters and they were atrocious. The majority of the Sheffield fans were well behaved but there was a small minority who caused the trouble." While some pointed the finger of blame at the British National Party, and MP Richard Caborn demanded that Leeds fans be banned from future matches, Sheffield United tried to play down the trouble. "To compare the problems we had on Saturday with the trouble caused at other grounds recently is ridiculous," said United director Derek Dooley. "We had 8,000 supporters from Leeds here and they were disappointed at seeing their team lose. But the damage they caused was trivial and the police did a wonderful job. At no time did anyone come onto the pitch; the game was not interrupted and the match was conducted in a sporting spirit."

Coming as it did only days after Millwall's infamous riot at Luton, the media were in hooligan overdrive. The *Sheffield Star* reported the local police were considering using videos to record disorder at matches in a bid to identify ringleaders. "This is just another weapon to be used against the soccer thugs," a police spokesman proudly announced. "As well as providing important evidence about who is causing trouble, it is a valuable training aid to help us develop new ways of stopping trouble before it starts."

A further two days later the *Star* announced, on its front page, "War waged on soccer thugs." While the article centred on new national measures and the decision to cancel the forthcoming England v Scotland international, there was a local dimension. South Yorkshire Police, the paper noted, had called a "crisis meeting" with the five league clubs in its area "to smash the violent menace which ruined last Saturday's game between Sheffield United and Leeds". The deputy chairman of the South Yorkshire Police Authority promised to "stamp out this terror once and for all".

It was a bold objective but quite unrealisable. The final match of the season, away at Brighton, was evidence enough that hooliganism had not been stamped out at Sheffield United. "Blades in running battles," screamed a newspaper headline after trouble before, during and after the match, including fighting on the pitch. The trouble received less media attention than it might otherwise; on the same day was the terrible fire at Bradford City's stadium and mass disorder at a Birmingham City-Leeds game that led to another fatality.

A bitter dispute emerged in the 1980s with Millwall. It began after 50 Millwall fans stopped off in Sheffield in April 1986 on their way back from a match in Leeds. A fight broke out during which a Londoner was pushed over as he attempted a kick and cracked his head on the pavement. He later died. A month later, as United prepared for an end of season match at Crystal Palace, newspapers were full of tales of Millwall fans preparing revenge. The authorities took the claims seriously and put in place a tight security operation but on the day not a single Millwall fan was sighted. In November 1986, a dozen Millwall fans did stop off in Sheffield again, this time after a match in the East Midlands. An evening of drinking ended up in a fight with 60 locals after a Londoner had tried to rob a young lad at knifepoint. Seventeen people were arrested, including all twelve Millwall fans. According to some sources, no Blade was involved, but this did not stop the local press making the link when the arrests were written up. When nine people later appeared in court, the *Sheffield Star* reported it as a "vendetta visit seeking a clash with Blade supporters".

Whatever, the truth, some Blades did see it as a feud. "Although [the death] was an unfortunate accident, Millwall swore revenge and whenever we met over the next decade it was hostile on both sides," one United hooligan told the present authors.

After the violent confrontations of the Sixties there was a lull in hostilities between the two Sheffield clubs for much of the early Eighties. Differing club fortunes meant the two sides did not play a competitive fixture against each other and as a result rivalries tended to focus elsewhere. It was a fight over a packet of crisps that acted as the spark for several years of seemingly continuous battles. On an October evening in 1985, a small group of Wednesday hooligans, three of them black, entered the strongly United Lansdowne pub. Insults were traded and before long the three black Owls offered out nine white Blades. "The Trio," recalled Gary Armstrong in his exceptional academic work *Football Hooligan: Knowing the Score*, "were muscular and better fighters, but in a brutal outcome they were laid out, with one unconscious from a chest burn (the result of being struck by a distress flare fired by a Blade). One other needed hospital casualty having been knocked unconscious. Blades felt the Trio got what they deserved, for they were older, 'harder' and showing off in a Blades pub. Owls saw it differently, their injuries had to be avenged."

Retribution was swift. The Owls managed to obtain the names of some of their attackers and soon they were being picked off. A Blade was attacked whilst out with his girlfriend at a disco, while in another incident, graphically illustrated in *Blades Business Crew*, Steve Cowens was targeted while he played an amateur football match. Small clashes occurred on a regular basis and then finally the Owls mobbed up for an onslaught on the Lansdowne. The assault was repulsed and the Owls, humiliatingly, were chased all the way back into the city centre.

A week later, 80 Blades gathered in their regular pubs expecting a revenge attack. The three black Owls hooligans walked into the Lansdowne pub and exchanged a few insults before leaving untouched. Outside, the police, who claimed to have been tipped off about trouble, were patrolling in large numbers. After some running around, largely to avoid the police, the two mobs clashed along London Road and the Owls were forced back into a pub. The police moved in and during a search of the pub discovered two crude petrol bombs. Later that evening, a group of 20 Blades caught up with the three black Owls.

The trouble continued over the next few weeks, with small skirmishes in pubs and clubs. Later that season, a testimonial for Tony Kenworthy brought the two Sheffield clubs together at Bramall Lane. There was no major turnout from either firm but at the end of the game the Blades still managed to get a mob of 70 lads together and by chance they stumbled into an equal group of Wednesday. The mobs clashed but by Cowens' own admission the Owls probably got the better of the fight.

With that memory still bitter, another testimonial four months later and at Hillsborough gave the Blades a chance for revenge. There were again about 70 of them. Avoiding the police by walking through backstreets, they hunted for their opponents. But by the time they arrived at the pub where Wednesday's mob had been drinking, their foes had already left. The Blades were not deterred and regrouped after the game. Eventually the two mobs met and in the ensuing fight two petrol bombs were thrown by United fans. The Owls, though more numerous, turned and ran. The Owls had been "done" and the balance of power shifted decisively to United.

It was during this fight that the chant "BBC" went up. After toying with a number of possible names, a dozen United hooligans had met in a pub on London road and discussed possible gang names. Blades Business Crew had already been chanted once or twice and after discussing and rejecting alternatives such as Blades Firm Force and Sheffield United Tricky Crew, it was formally adopted. Calling cards were printed – "Congratulations, you have just been tuned in by the BBC" – enamel badges were pressed with a skull above the two swords of the club crest and songs were devised.

The final game of the 1986/87 season saw United travel to Portsmouth. The home side were already promoted and their fans were in party mood but a 2–1 away was sufficient to incite the 6.57 Crew into three pitch invasions, including one that involved over 1,000 lads hellbent on reaching the away supporters. Even BBC "top boy" Steve Cowens admits to being thankful for the presence of the police dogs that day. A mob of 150 BBC were staying in neighbouring Bournemouth for the weekend and they waited in anticipation that Pompey might come through. They didn't, at least in any numbers, so the Sheffield lads got wildly drunk instead.

The BBC was the best-known mob at United but there were smaller groups around and people who were not attached to any one group but who would come out for big games. One of the nastiest little mobs around was the Suicide Squad, according to Cowens. "They were around thirty-strong. Although they were Blades thugs they liked to travel independently from the rest of our firm. They had some very game lads and took no shit. The only other independent mob that has represented United are the Darnall Massive. They are as game as fuck and when they get together they run from no-one, whatever the odds. The Squad weren't as handy man-for-man as the Darnall lot but they would stick together and dish it out if need be. They all came from Shiregreen, which is another tough area in Sheffield. The Squad were involved in loads of bollocks but it was only the really big games that they would be seen out with the BBC. The Darnall lot are different gravy, game to a man and they stand by each other even when the odds are heavily stacked."

Nineteen eighty-eight and 1989 saw United play Bristol City in end-of-season encounters. The first was a relegation play-off which saw fighting on and off the pitch. City won the two-legged affair but losing in the play-off final sent them down all the same. As chance would have it the final game the following season saw them at home to United again. This time the fortunes were different and Sheffield travelled down with promotion virtually assured. Over 200 lads made the trip and the game was only ten minutes old when fighting broke out in the seats. "We went at their mob in the stand and then steamed down the steps to the terraces below," recalled Cowens in *Blades Business Crew*. "Stewards were knocked out of the way and everyone was bang at it. Two United players, who shall remain nameless, shouted encouragement."

The fighting spread to the pitch and it took police horses to restore order. Later that evening there was further trouble in Weston-Super-Mare, where many Blades were staying for the weekend. "Crazed United fans go on rampage of terror," was how the *Sheffield Star* eloquently put it. "Drunken yobs turned the West Country resort into a battleground for four hours," it continued. The police told the press that the trouble started as gangs of up to 50 United fans roamed the streets after the pubs closed. "It was as if all hell was let loose," one officer said.

A trip to Norwich at the beginning of the 1991/92 season saw many Blades make a weekend of it at Great Yarmouth. As is so often the case with these seaside jaunts, the fun and drinking soon gave way to violence. Two hundred Blades ran amok in a Great Yarmouth pub and there was further trouble when they were refused entry into a local disco. Several people were arrested. At Carrow Road itself, there were just four arrests despite 200 United fans infiltrating the home end.

The trouble between the two Sheffield sides continued unabated. The teams met twice in 1990. The first was a friendly at Bramall Lane that saw 250 Blades gather in the pubs along London Road, whilst their rival Owls Crime Squad mobbed up on a council estate some three miles away.

Gradually the away mob edged closer to United but the BBC were also on the lookout and as the Owls gathered in a pub half a mile away, the BBC decided to strike. The fight was brief but the OCS backed off shortly before the police arrived. Order was restored and the United fans drifted off to the game. Over 200 mobbed up again after the match and made their way to a pub in town where they were ambushed by the Wednesday group, who had missed the game altogether. Whilst the OCS were eventually scattered, there were several United casualties.

With both mobs claiming victory, the scene was set for a midweek cup clash later in the season at Hillsborough that saw a crowd of 32,000. Again there was a mob of 200 Blades though there was no sign of Wednesday before the game. The situation was the same after the game so the BBC claimed the "moral victory". The following season, United's promotion to the First Division saw the first Sheffield derby for 14 years and predictably it was made a midday kick-off. The return fixture saw 22 arrests. Inside the ground a small group of United hooligans got tickets for the Wednesday end and a brief fight broke out.

Whilst there was little fighting during this period, at least at the derbies in Sheffield, the general consensus was that Blades were the bigger hooligan force. There are probably several reasons for this. One, says Blade AJ, was the disappearance of black lads from the Owls' mob. "It's a mystery to me where the blacks went from the Sheffield Wednesday firm. They had some heavy geezers, but they all just seemed to stop going with Wednesday at once. The fact that United had taken over the roost may have had some bearing on matters and the fact that three Wednesday had been hospitalised by a few BBC youth but another rumour was they wanted no more to do with Wednesday because of a few of their firm's move across to the right-wing. Those individuals developed strong links with Chelsea and Combat 18. Whether this is the truth or not remains a mystery to us and only the Wednesday blacks and the right-wingers know the whole truth. Wednesday were without doubt a weaker firm without them. One thing's for sure, Wednesday have few or no black lads running with them now."

United claim that a hotly debated incident in London in 1991 illustrates the spinelessness of Wednesday, who on this occasion teamed up with another football firm to see their hated rivals "done". Before an FA Cup match against Chelsea, a large contingent of BBC were lured out of the World's End pub in Camden by the Chelsea Headhunters and were then attacked with numerous weapons. Some Wednesday faces, whose team was at Arsenal on the same day, were with them. Arguments have since been traded about how "tooled up" Chelsea were and what the outcome would have been if no weapons were used, but it is clear that the Chelsea mob took United by surprise and forced them to run. What angered many Blades as much was the presence of Wednesday hooligans with the Chelsea mob.

During the late Nineties, Birmingham again posed serious opposition to the BBC. AJ remembered one particularly lively confrontation. "They'd left the ground early and headed for London Road. It kicked off as sixty or seventy Birmingham attacked the Pheasant pub. Two United lads were stabbed as the twenty or so BBC came out to confront the Zulus. What Birmingham didn't take into account was the fact that within a couple of minutes a lot more Beeb had run up from the ground and it was game on. To be fair, Brum had a right pop and it was a fight for only the brave or insane, as a few Zulus, especially the Asian geezers with their firm, were carrying. One of them got his just deserts as he got dropped just as Birmingham were about to run and he got captured and volleyed into next week. The fight must have lasted around five minutes. The police helicopter hung above the set-to from start to finish.

"In the return game, United took a hundred main actors down to theirs. They were mainly the over-thirty brigade and included loads of grizzlers. We had a bit of a front-up outside but that United firm was one of the best we've had in terms of quality so I don't think even the Gurkhas would have shifted us that day."

Another regular opponent in more recent times has been Derby County. There were clashes between the two sets of supporters dating back to the mid-1980s but then after a lull there was a further burst of tit-for-tat violence between 2002 and 2004. In August 2002, United's opening game of the season was away at Coventry. A mob of 150 Blades took the opportunity to stop on their way home in Derby, where they fought running battles with police and a similar-sized mob of locals. Several pub windows were smashed in what Derbyshire Police described as "large scale public disorder". Officers arriving on the scene came under a barrage of bricks and bottles from United fans. The trouble came only a day after South Yorkshire Police announced that the August Bank Holiday fixture against Millwall was being put back a day because of the threat of violence, and Sports Minister and Sheffield MP Richard Caborn was quick to say the louts deserved to be banned from the game for life.

There was further trouble a few months later, this time in Sheffield. Over 300 hooligans, from a number of firms, were involved in running battles that lasted well into the night. Derby fans were in Sheffield for a match against Wednesday, while Barnsley hooligans were passing through on their way to Chesterfield. Adding to this pot were Blade fans returning from a game at Forest. A further clash occurred early in the following season when 15-20 Derby hooligans wandered into a 100-strong mob of Blades who were lying in wait for Wednesday. The police claimed that Blades and Owls had organised the fight to settle scores but Derby fans got there first. "We have absolutely no idea why they were even in the city," Chief Insp Andy Eddison told the local press. "It was an appalling incident and was very frightening for the scores of people visiting the city centre and going to nearby theatres. The manager of the Surrey pub was left to clear up a large amount of broken glass."

A new wave of inter-Sheffield violence began at the beginning of this decade. Two hundred Wednesday fans, returning from a match at Derby in February 2000, decided to march through the city centre. Shortly before 8pm, they were met by a mob of 150 Blades. "Some were carrying glasses or bottles and most had their faces covered with hoods or scarves," reported the local paper. "It was apparent that disorder had been arranged via mobile phones." The police were on the scene as United unleashed a salvo of missiles at Wednesday and their presence soon diverted United's attention. "The Sheffield United group then attacked the police," continued the news report. "A police officer was knocked to the floor and kicked about the body and head. He was rescued as more officers got to the scene and he was taken to hospital with a suspected broken jaw. Running fights then took place throughout the city centre."

Later that year there was further trouble, this time at a match at Bramall Lane, which was their first league encounter for seven years. Over 450 rival fans clashed in what both police and press called a riot. Thirty people were arrested as battles broke out throughout the city centre after the game. Over 100 police officers, many in riot gear and using CS gas, were deployed to break up the fighting. "It was the fact that they couldn't get to each other for the organised punch-up which frustrated the fans and sparked it all off," said a spokesman for South Yorkshire Police, who had deployed a further 200 officers to cover the match. "The fans then became highly aggressive towards the police, and officers had to use CS gas and batons to disperse the crowd."

Some of the worst trouble in the city occurred when the two sides met again in September 2002, though this time the fighting involved United and the police. "The men hurled bottles, glasses, stools and snooker cues at officers from inside the Sportsman, in Denby Street, Sheffield," reported one newspaper. "The mob, some of whom had been drinking all day, caused innocent drinkers, including young children, to shelter in the kitchen of the pub while the battle with police took place." The pub was trashed and there was further fighting later that evening in other city centre bars.

Sentencing several men to between six months' and five years' imprisonment, Judge Patrick Robertshaw said that they had "besmirched" the name of football. "Football is supposedly the national game yet all too often its good name is besmirched by the mindless and thuggish behaviour of just such a kind that has brought you into the dock." The police concurred, and said that they hoped that the sentences would serve as a deterrent. While United hooligans were beginning to feel the pressure from the authorities, the dominance over Wednesday became stronger to the point that many of the OCS were unable to drink in city centre pubs at night.

Sheffield United achieved the double over Yorkshire rivals Leeds during the 2003/04 season. Despite being in a lower division, they overcame the Premiership side in both the Worthington and FA cups. The Worthington Cup clash at Bramall Lane, in November 2003, was marred by trouble inside the ground. Over 2,000 seats were ripped up in the Leeds end, while hundreds of Blades came onto the pitch, many goading the away fans in the hope of sparking further trouble. The police were not prepared to take any chances for the FA Cup quarter-final clash the following March, especially when their intelligence predicted a Leeds mob of 350 hooligans making the trip, including 100 from Doncaster. With an estimated 250 BBC awaiting their arrival, the huge police operation, which proved largely successful, was on a par with that for a Sheffield derby game. With increasing police action, the frustrated BBC mob tried a different tactic for the return of Leeds the following season, this time in the league. Accepting that they had little chance of reaching their opponents in Sheffield, a mob of 80 actually travelled to Leeds in the early evening of the Bramall Lane fixture and raided Leeds city centre pubs.

An eagerly awaited fixture was the visit of Cardiff City in September 2003. The Soul Crew had gained a formidable reputation and insults had been exchanged over the internet. "Cardiff's visit saw the BBC turn out the best and biggest firm we have out in years," said AJ. "At an estimate, I'd say it pushed 500. Cardiff had been spouting that they were going to come with a big firm but in truth they brought around fifty lads, with some Desperate Dan figures also filling their coaches. It kicked off after and the plod didn't know which way to turn, as the main group of United hooligans had gone down to meet behind the church on St Mary's roundabout. In the meantime we had it with Cardiff up the side streets and to a man they were up for it. A bit of a slinging match went off until the toe-to-toe started. We never shifted and neither did they so claims from either side were bull. One of their coaches had attacked the Sheaf pub before the game. It's a family pub at the wrong side of the ground from town so Cardiff's internet claim that they had done the BBC in a pub was laughable.

"Credit to them that day, they came, and we've never gone mobbed up to Ninian. We would have definitely travelled that year in remembrance of one of our main geezers, we talked and planned it, but the police made the arrangements that after they'd looked up your arsehole you had to be a travel club member and go on club coaches to gain a ticket. A good day out ruined again." The "main geezer" he referred to was Lester Divers, a local music promoter who was blasted to death with a sawn-off shotgun outside his home on New Year's Day, 2003. A huge contingent of BBC turned out for his funeral and two men were later jailed for his murder, although the precise motive remains a mystery.

The *Sheffield Star* pulled no punches in its account of the trouble at Bramall Lane:

FANS RIOT

Soccer yobs caused some of the worst football violence seen in Sheffield for years as Blades and Cardiff hooligans ran riot [reported the *Sheffield Star*].

Two police officers were injured, one needing hospital treatment, as more than 150 riot officers tried to prevent vicious skirmishes between United and Welsh supporters.

Violence erupted before and after Sheffield United's 5-3 victory at Bramall Lane on Saturday afternoon, with parts of the city centre turned into a battleground.

Police had to call in reinforcements from other forces as the level of brutality reached levels not seen for years.

Five Cardiff fans and one Blade were arrested on the spot while several others were treated for injuries. "The enjoyment of a football match has been marred by the appalling behaviour of a minority who were intent on causing trouble," said the Match Commander, Supt Martin Hemmingway. "The level of violence towards police officers by Cardiff hooligans was extremely high. It was the worst we have seen in Sheffield for many years. My officers did a superb job in ensuring large scale disorder was averted. In the circumstances many arrests were impossible but there will now be a full scale investigation to bring these people to justice."

Not everyone was so impressed with the policing. While South Yorkshire Police promised to scour their CCTV footage to identify more trouble-makers, some were pointing the accusing finger at the police themselves. Cardiff City Supporters' Club spokesman Vince Alm accused the police of failing to protect City fans from attack. He also said officers targeted them and ignored the Sheffield fans, who he claimed started the trouble. There was a degree of sympathy with this view from some South Wales police officers. They were particularly annoyed that several Cardiff coaches were prevented from stopping in neighbouring small towns outside Sheffield, which created unnecessary tension between fans and the police.

The increasing violence connected to Sheffield United eventually caused a reaction from within the police service. By 2002, with fights between the two Sheffield clubs occurring on a regular basis, and with the BBC making themselves a nuisance around the country, the authorities began to act. A huge financial grant was made available to South Yorkshire Police to provide extra resources to monitor the hooligans and increasingly tough policing was introduced. There were also suspicions, never confirmed, that at least one senior figure in the gang was a police informer.

Sheffield United hooligans felt the brunt of this in September 2002 when a clash between Blades and Owls soon turned into the BBC versus the police. Several BBC prominents were imprisoned for this fight, but many regulars in the pub, including some staff, argued that the instigators were the police.

Fifteen months later, and shortly after trouble at home to Cardiff City and Leeds, 150 Sheffield United hooligans were prevented from entering Burnley after police intelligence suggested that there was an arranged fight organised with locals. The Sheffield hooligans were rounded up as their three coaches stopped at two pubs in Padiham, on the edge of Burnley. Many Sheffield United hooligans had already received letters from Lancashire constabulary advising them to stay out of Burnley. "We suspect that there may be some complaint from some of these individuals but we are happy with our intelligence," said Chief Inspector Richard Morgan, who oversaw the investigation. "It was known by the football spotters' officers that these people were a known hooligan element of Sheffield United. They were here for one thing and one thing only, and that was to cause disorder. The public and the genuine fan base of Sheffield United and Burnley have a right to expect that Burnley police will take appropriate action to protect their human rights and make a safe environment to enjoy the game."

The Blades Business Crew is no longer as active as it was. Age, prison and banning orders have all taken their toll. With Wednesday's promotion to the Championship in May 2005, and a re-emerging mob at Hillsborough, it was thought that the tide might swing back in their rivals' favour. However, this did not prove to be the case in the two matches they were to play in 2005/06. Sheffield United hooligans, albeit normally dormant, did turn out in numbers for these games.

In the second of those matches, at Hillsborough in February 2006, one policeman was pulled by his protective helmet, leaving him with neck injuries, while a female officer was kicked and punched by rival fans in the ground after they turned on police who were trying to stop fighting. Police made 28 arrests, 22 in the ground, including three for racist chanting aimed at United striker Ade Akinbiyi. Further fighting broke out after 8pm in Sheffield city centre but police were quick to intervene. Seventeen supporters subsequently received football banning orders, along with substantial fines and other community orders for a range of public order offences, in what police hailed a major success.

"The balance with Wednesday now is how it has been for the last twenty years in Sheffield," said AJ. "They go on about United's lads getting older and one day their time will come, but every time we meet it's the same old story, with Wednesday on their toes often before a punch has been thrown. The BBC has lost a lot of lads to bans and travelling to high-profile games is out of the window but we'll always have enough in the locker to keep Wednesday where they belong on and off the pitch – second. Whether it's five on five, ten on ten or mob on mob, they're off-mans every time. We even ran a mob of eighty of Wednesday's finest with a bit of a rag, tag and bobtail outfit of thirty-five up at the top of West Street. As soon as they see us they are already on the back foot."

In August 2006, two United fans were attacked and stabbed as they prepared to watch a pre-season friendly against Sparta Rotterdam in Holland. Around 400 Blades fans had travelled to Holland to support the team on a pre-season tour and many were drinking in bars when trouble erupted. Some were approached by fans of Feyenoord and challenged to a fight. Some accepted the challenge and violence flared in a bar where other Sheffield fans, unconnected with the trouble, had gathered for a drink.

The Dutch authorities had anticipated the potential for trouble and asked English officers to travel to Holland to help oversee the policing operation. One of them said the two victims had not been willing participants and "were having a quiet drink and offered no provocation but they were set upon and given a beating." One was stabbed to the head and the other to the hand. Both were discharged after hospital treatment.

"The incident marks an ugly start to a new football season, following several years where hooliganism involving Sheffield fans has been successfully brought under control," reported the *Yorkshire Post*, not entirely accurately. "Most of Sheffield's worst soccer hooligans are now the subject of banning orders and controls which mean they have to surrender passports, preventing them from travelling overseas when major fixtures are taking place abroad."

Further reading: *Football Hooligans: Knowing The Score*, Gary Armstrong (Berg Publishers), *Blades Business Crew*, Steve Cowens (Milo Books)

SHEFFIELD WEDNESDAY

Ground: Hillsborough
Firms: East Bank Republican Army, Owls Crime Squad
Rivals: Sheffield United, Grimsby Town, Derby County, Oldham

Denis has been through it all. For four decades he has been in the thick of it, up and down the country, through good times and bad, fighting, as he sees it, for his beloved Sheffield Wednesday. "My first sight of footy trouble was Chelsea in 1967," he remembered. "We went down a week before the cup game for the league clash. There were not a lot there but enough. I was very young then and can remember Chelsea coming round the ground and they got at the back of us, and with delightful angelic voices sang 'Knees up Mother Brown' and came charging into us. I, with many others, was soon on the pitch. There were some game Wednesday lads there, scrapping like fuck but taking a beating. Funny as hell was a lad with a bugle running round the pitch edge hitting any Chelsea he could with it. That was it; at a very young age I was hooked.

"I was at the Oldham riot and went to Leeds when they were by far the worst. I shit myself when a well-known lad at the time said we were going on the Scratching Shed as we called it, but we still went. We also went on the Stretford End and had a go. They were great days when Wednesday were up there with the best, but even when we were in decline on the pitch we had good fun in the lower leagues.

"One of the best for a laugh was York away. We took thousands and we lost three-nil. I missed the game after getting off with a local girl and enjoyed ninety minutes behind the old stand with her rather than ninety minutes of shit football on the other side of the fence. After the game, we went into town and got very drunk. After kicking out time, we walked back to find the bus but none of us knew where we had parked it. As we passed a rather posh hotel, one of the lads, Jeff, who was actually a Blade but always came with us for the crack, went in. We waited, thinking he had gone for a piss, when we heard a rather loud smash. Out came Jeff with this massive vase which looked very expensive, which he smashed over the first car to pass. That was it. We spent the next half an hour doing the hooligan bit on cars and shops, as you did in those days.

"As we walked down the road we saw a hotdog van. The queue was quite big so, for a laugh, Jeff lifted the van off the holding and began to run it down the road with the bloke inside. Fat and everything was flying all over. I still laugh today as I can see the queue, stood there waiting for Jeff to bring it back. That was what it was like in those days. Yes, there were mass brawls and yes, people got hurt, but you had a laugh as well. Today you would get jail for things which in the early Seventies were part and parcel of having a fucking good day out."

The national press has reported hooliganism involving Sheffield Wednesday fans since the mid-Sixties, much of it involving their arch-rivals Sheffield United. In February 1967, Wednesday fans painted threatening slogans on the walls of United's ground the night before a city derby. Fourteen months later, the paper reported gangs of rival Sheffield fans clashing in the city centre, and in September 1968 a United fan was arrested for heading up a large mob hunting for Wednesday fans while waving a bottle around his head. A few weeks later, the paper reported 500 rival fans clashing after a match at Hillsborough.

Sociologist Gary Armstrong's book *Knowing the Score* charts the fortunes of Sheffield United's hooligans over three decades and quotes one Blade on the early fighting with the Owls. "There weren't no segregation and the Ends would be mixed. When we played 'em at t' Lane, we'd get into t' ground early, stand at t' back o' t' kop and start throwing things at 'em as they came in through t' turnstiles at t' bottom. The police usually had to escort 'em in on to t' terraces, then we'd fight on and off throughout t' match … Our famous match was at Hillsborough in 1966. Weeks before at matches, Blades were all singing, 'Don't forget your eggs,' and when we got on their kop, we pelted 'em with hundreds of eggs, they got covered in it! …next season though, it got a bit dangerous. A Blade threw a small tube of acid at 'em, it splattered a few Pigs."

Another rival team whose supporters were to cause trouble at Hillsborough on several occasions was Manchester United and its Red Army. One visit was in 1969, as John, a Wednesday veteran, recalled. "The lads met as usual in the Claymore for a couple of bottles of Newcastle Brown, then we moved on to Hillsborough. About twenty of us met up with the Foxhill lads and had a few more beers in the Park Hotel. About forty of us in total got into the ground and we congregated behind the goal with the rest of the East Bank bootboys. Then there was a sudden surge from behind and about 100 Man United fans waded into us. We took a bit of a kicking, then fought back and regrouped. We exited the Kop at the bottom and went round the back and got behind them. Now it was our turn to have the upper hand and we drove them to the bottom of the Kop. There were not many coppers about, as they are busy escorting fans out of the ground. On the whole it was a good day all round but we lost the game three-one and suffered relegation."

The first Wednesday mob was the East Bank Republican Army, who occupied the large East Bank Kop. The leader of the East Bank was Sammy from the Hackenthorpe estate in south Sheffield. "I can still see him now, held aloft on the East Bank or on somebody's kop during our rampaging days of the mid-Seventies," remembered John fondly. "We would stand him on the crush barrier and everybody would sing in unison that they would 'walk a million miles for one of his smiles, our Sammy'.

"On one away trip to Swansea, the boys stopped off for food in a Chinese chippy and, as always, Sammy was the first to be served. As the rest of the lads queued for their food Sammy was shovelling his down his throat like he always did, and as usual was he making a mess. The man behind the counter asked him politely to take his arse outside because he was putting off his customers, Sammy lifted his head momentarily from his chop suey and uttered the immortal words, 'Fuck off, you Welsh bastard,' to the Chinese bloke serving the food. Well the place just fell about and Sammy continued, oblivious to the uproar he'd caused. Grown men were weeping with laughter.

"Another trick of Sammy's was if you sent him to the bar for the ale, and you forgot yourself and asked him which one was yours, he'd run his sleeve across his nose and mouth, then take a swig, then pass it you knowing full well that you'd say, 'You have that one, Sammy,' and he'd disappear with the rest."

Wednesday had a huge travelling army in the Seventies. For the final match of the 1971/72 season, they travelled to Hull City, a semi-derby game. "There was a great deal of trouble before the match," reported the *Hull Daily Mail*. "One sixteen-year-old boy from Sheffield was seriously hurt in the widespread trouble before and after the game. Fourteen youths were arrested and in one of the worst incidents of hooliganism the city had ever witnessed, skinheads smashed windows, damaged cars and ran wild on Anlaby Road. The trouble began as Sheffield Wednesday fans made their way to the ground for what was Hull's last home game of the season. Hundreds of youths smashed windows, hurled road signs around, tried to overturn a car and battered holes in its bodywork. Police described the situation at one stage as 'terrible', and police dogs were let loose on the crowd." Thirty-six people were ejected from the ground after Hull surged forward in an attempt to get at visiting fans but were beaten back by police. After the game there was further disorder at Paragon Station.

Another Wednesday lad, Paul, remembered the day vividly. "The lads met the Foxhill boys at the railway station and we got to Hull for 11am. We headed into the town centre looking for their mob and ran one or two little gangs. Most of us were tooled up with an array of weapons which included ten-inch-long inner tubes filled with sand, with four-inch nails with flat heads in the middle and tied at both ends. It was easily concealed down your pants. About forty of us got into their end but we were ready and when they came at us the tubes were out and we backed them right off. We inflicted some serious damage and it lasted a good ten minutes before the coppers broke it up but not before we had them scrabbling to get onto the pitch away from our onslaught. The police then turned their attention to us but we waded into the coppers and they were not up for it. We then tried to make a solid retreat and mingle with the rest of the Wednesday following but a couple of the lads got nicked."

Two years later, the visit of Manchester United caused national media headlines. It was, everyone agreed, one of the most violent days of football hooliganism up and till that point. The facts speak for themselves: there were 113 arrests, 60 people injured and a Red Army contingent of 20,000 out of a crowd of 35,000.

"The Manchester United game from 1974 was the only time I can remember anyone swamping the East Bank and causing mayhem," said Tony Cronshaw, a veteran Wednesdayite. "Me and my mates travelled to the match but gave the Ozzie Owl Club a wide berth, not that we didn't want to go and have a drink but we got chased around town as soon as we landed in Pond Street, all because my mate wouldn't take his scarf off. There were thousands of the bastards all over the place. To put it into perspective, our previous home gate had been 12,373 versus Fulham. This crowd would be 35,067.

"Eventually we got onto the East Bank and were pinned in the bottom corner. We numbered around a couple of hundred. Some Owls had been chased into the South Stand but the Mancs were all over the shop. To make matters worse, we went three-one up and that really pissed them off. I was only nineteen and new to the game but a lot of Wednesdayites became legends that day and even when United invaded the pitch these lads were undeterred. The police finally brought the situation under control but not before there'd been about 100 arrests and at least sixty got injured, including one Manc who suffered a fractured skull, so there was some Wednesday resistance.

"Our club secretary called for those convicted to be birched, but it was all right for that twat sat in the directors' box with a blanket over his knees, he was not in the firing line all afternoon. Forget the birch, those lads deserved a medal of honour for battling so bravely against overwhelming odds."

There was further disorder at Hillsborough involving Manchester United fans before and after their FA Cup semi-final match there against Leeds United in April 1977. Local residents were furious as Manchester fans ran amok through their streets, smashing windows and damaging cars.

A petition was soon circulated demanding greater police protection at future high profile matches.

Wednesday once again travelled to Hull for the last away of the season in April 1975 and once again there was considerable trouble, though not on the scale of 1972. There were 15 arrests and a further 80 people were ejected from the ground. Most of the arrests happened when the supporters left the ground at the end of the match. "At one point, well over 100 Sheffield supporters left their end of the park and ran across the field to where the Hull City fans were standing," said Chief Insp Gordon Beam. "The rival fans then engaged in fighting."

"I was dressed to the nines in my baggy jeans and dockers on my feet, with my silk scarf around my neck," said Tony. "We travelled by train and as we left Midland Station it seemed that everyone from Sheffield 6 was heading east. Our train pulled in behind that massive terrace that housed thousands, but it was quite clear from the off that Wednesday were all over the place and the Hull fans were finding it difficult to come to terms with the fact that this side that had been glued to the foot of the table all season had brought such a following.

"The coppers on the side terrace were finding it difficult to keep order and their helmets were flying right, left and centre. Unfortunately for me I missed most of it because by 2.30 I'd had my collar felt and was being cautioned under their main stand. Once they'd took my name I was out of the ground with the rest of the Wednesday fans who'd been shown the door, and I can remember having a little altercation with some Hull fans who were trying to fathom out which part of the ground would be safe for them to enter, because Wednesday had swamped the place. These were glorious times to be a Wednesdayite, but not for the on-field activities."

Wednesday finished bottom of the division and were relegated, along with Cardiff City and Millwall. A visit to Southend was their first game in the Third Division, an unattractive fixture for everyone except the Wednesday troublemakers. "Rampaging football fans brought mob law to Southend at the weekend as they blazed a trail of terror through the town," said the local paper. "The countdown to the violence began at 5am on Saturday when the first Sheffield fans began arriving in Southend. By lunchtime they had formed into gangs and were charging up and down the High Street, knocking shoppers flying, shouting and swearing. The first battle took place outside the Sutton Arms in Southchurch Road. Wednesday fans enticed Blues supporters drinking in the pub out into the street and a fight started. One youth was taken to hospital when a bottle was smashed over his head."

Damage ran to more than £400 in broken glasses at sea front pubs alone, at least half a dozen people were taken to hospital and 17 people were arrested and charged. The Sheffield fans were relatively well-behaved during the game and it was left to home supporters to cause most of the trouble. Southend supporters invaded the pitch in an attempt to get at Wednesday fans. The local paper recorded the events in extraordinary fashion. "There were amazing scenes at Roots Hall on Saturday as the half-time whistle blew. It was the signal for a pitch invasion by hordes of young fans who leapt over the wall and started an ominous-looking charge. But Southend police were ready for them and, after a couple of splendid rugby tackles had brought down one or two rowdies, they were effectively sat on. More officers with dogs rounded up the majority of the others and a few of the intruders were frogmarched out of the ground." Chief Insp Terry Rand said, "I wish the parents could have been down here to see what their children do at these games. They would be shocked."

In early 1976, Wednesday was drawn away at Charlton Athletic in the FA Cup. Owls fans travelled down in their thousands and it turned out to be one of their biggest fights. "We'd travelled by an aptly named coach company that went under the name of Sheffield United Tours which we just called the SUT," remembered Tony Cronshaw. "We booked to go with them because they were stopping in London until midnight, and you know how northern boys love a night out in the smoke.

"Before the game everyone was guzzling down the ale and having a good time. Inside the ground, Millwall turned up but they did not have the numbers to trouble the EBRA and the fighting didn't last too long. After the game it was a different story. We'd lost and all hell broke out outside the ground. There were running battles all over the shop, plus the police came under a barrage of missiles, cars were overturned and windows smashed. The trouble lasted for ages and it took forever to get everyone on the coaches. We finished the night off drinking with some Geordies who had been to QPR. It was the worst act of violence and vandalism I've witnessed in over thirty years." Charlton insist that Millwall were not involved that day and that it was they who had the better of the fight, at least after the match.

The mid-to-late 1970s saw Wednesday's hooligans gain a decisive advantage over their United rivals. They had greater numbers, were better organised and had one main lad, a black ex-boxer and fearsome fighter, who was feared by most Blades.

"During my days we didn't have many dealings with the Blades, but when we did we always had the upper hand," said Cronshaw. "In a County Cup game around 1976, the lads met in the Claymore and we'd a tidy mob together. At about seven o'clock, we moved on to Bramall Lane and just as we got to the ground the police pounced. Quick as a flash, to a man we started chanting, 'United, United.' They immediately shoved us towards the Kop and we waited until we were all in before running up those steps to the left hand end of the Shoreham. Even Blades waited with us because we'd told the dummies that a mob of Owls were due anytime. Once we were all in, we showed our true colours and the Reds shit it. We ran across the Kop at the Blades and it was funny really but our mates from our local who supported the Blades were all on their front line. It was weird trying to kick and punch while trying not to connect with one of your pals, even though he was a Blade. After that it was over in a matter of minutes, with most of the Reds legging it, and we all pissed off into town after the game and finished up in some nightclub, red and blue together. Weird but it was like that in our day.

"During the 1979-80 season when we massacred them four-nil at Hillsborough, they made no show, as usual. The return game at the Lane saw at least 5,000 Owls camped on the Shoreham and there were numerous arrests. The Blades say to this day that the Owls were behind the railings, but those were the blokes with kids. If Wednesday were hiding that day, how come there was so many people being dragged out of the Kop?"

Tony went back to Bramall Lane in 1993, where he and 40 others got tickets onto the South Stand. "We sat towards the Kop end and even at half-time when we went for a drink, nothing happened. I was well past my sell-by date by then but it was a good mix of young and old with some very tasty individuals. We watched the game peter out to a one-all draw, then leisurely strolled out of the ground. It was no big deal but I wonder what would have happened if some among us had not got such a fearsome reputation."

Fighting between rival gangs became a norm on Friday nights in the city centre in 1979. A mob of up to 40 Blades who had met up during a pre-season tour in Switzerland began gathering on Friday nights for drinks in town. Their presence was quickly clocked by Wednesday fans, who began mobbing up themselves in response. Fights would break out in pubs and streets and were a regular occurrence for 18 months. The United mob was sometimes joined by a group of Rotherham Blades, who had their own personal feud with two of the main Wednesday faces.

Another chance for a regular scrap was the traditional Christmas Eve drink-up in Sheffield city centre. It was a long established tradition that the factories would close early, allowing their workers to change and get into town by mid-afternoon for what was normally a heavy session. As football rivalry increasingly dominated city centre life in the late Seventies, so the respective supporters would use the festivities to face each other down, often around the Christmas tree at the top of the Fargate Shopping Precinct. As revellers sang Christmas carols, the gangs would alter the words of "Mary's Boy Child" to who really "ran away" on Boxing Day. Fights would inevitably follow. By the early Eighties, the weekly rucks began to die out, partly because some of the protagonists got to know one another, sometimes through criminality, and also because leading figures began to drop out. The lull would not last.

The 1980/81 season proved to have a very violent beginning. It kicked off with a home match with Newcastle, where 14 police officers were injured after being attacked by visiting fans after the game. Wednesday fans were largely well behaved, otherwise "we would have been in real trouble," admitted a police spokesman. The police described the trouble as "one of the worst examples of lawlessness we have seen in this country for many years". The scenes provoked an intensive debate about hooliganism and the rule of law, with calls for tougher policing and sentencing. The chairmen of both Sheffield clubs, Rotherham and Barnsley all agreed to meet the South Yorkshire Police Chief Constable to "discuss strategy concerning supporters" at future matches.

Tighter policing caused a backlash amongst Wednesday fans only a week later, during the club's match at Notts County. Five thousand Owls made the short trip down but were put in a small enclosure, many having to stand behind a pylon. "Incompetent," railed Joe Ashton, local MP and big Wednesday follower. "The situation was ludicrous. The Wednesday supporters were crammed into our part of the ground like sardines. Other parts were so empty you could have played the match on them. I honestly believe that chief constables have got together on matters like picketing and soccer crowds, and that they panic when they get more than a few dozen people in place. It seems as if they won't be satisfied until all games kick off at nine o'clock in the morning and most people remain in bed."

Policing football was about to become a lot more controversial as Wednesday travelled to Oldham three weeks into the new season. Days before the match, Wednesday chairman Bert McGee wrote to *The Times* complaining about police tactics of herding away fans into small pens. "It is my view that this particular policy of the police which seems to be becoming prevalent throughout the country is mistaken and dangerous. The reasoning is easy to understand, but the excessive crushing now being practised is leading to nothing more than trouble and more trouble."

His words proved depressingly accurate and the local paper ran the headline "Wednesday's Day of Shame", after scenes of bedlam completely overshadowed the game. Lumps of concrete and bricks were hurled at police by travelling supporters as violence erupted within minutes of them reaching the stadium. While most Wednesday fans were crammed in to the Rochdale Road End, others infiltrated the home Chadderton End and within minutes were fighting with Oldham fans. "We have never seen anything like this before," commented one of the senior officers on duty. "We had more police there than I can ever remember having before."

The spark for the trouble was the sending-off of Wednesday's Terry Curran for an alleged assault on Oldham's former Sheffield United star Simon Stainrod. The Oldham player fell to the ground clutching his groin in agony, having scored a few minutes before. Curran remonstrated with the referee, and as the away crowd grew ever angrier he was joined on the pitch by manager Jack Charlton. Dozens of Wednesday fans began climbing onto the fences while others collected makeshift weapons to use against the police, who were fighting to keep them off the pitch. The referee ordered the players off the field after they and the police were bombarded with missiles, including lumps of concrete. It was another 20 minutes, during which there was an emotional appeal from Charlton to the fans to behave, before play resumed.

"The pitch invasion that followed was just the half of it," remembered Glyn, another Wednesday fan who was active during this era. "The whole of the Greater Manchester police force on duty that day fought openly with the lads on the away end behind the net. The side terracing, which was full of Wednesday, went berserk, smashing up the steps to launch concrete at the sad excuse for Oldham fans, who were shitting themselves, huddling in the centre of their own kop. I, along with my mate, was pushed to a fence at the front of the kop as the kids were being escorted out of the gates on to the pitch. I distinctly remember smiling with pride as the stones and concrete pinged off the steel barriers as we ducked underneath."

The violence was not as straightforward as portrayed in the press. Curran's sending off was the spark, but the venom was more aimed at what some fans considered excessive policing. "The trouble had been brewing long before because of the way the police were handling Wednesday's away following," recalled Tony. "At Bolton they'd penned us in like animals and kept us in after the game. Worse was to follow at Notts County, when we were penned in like sardines when there was an empty terrace to our right. Oldham was just the last straw.

"We travelled on the club-sponsored Inter City Owl. This was not like the old soccer specials that got smashed up, the club ran them well. When we got to Manchester we were again herded onto buses and charged for the privilege, so we were not in a very good mood when we got to the ground and quickly found a nice little boozer to drown our sorrows. The lads entered the Chadderton End but we just didn't have the numbers and the damned fences were a nightmare. When we got onto the open terrace we could see that Wednesday were everywhere. Oldham in their wisdom had been doing some building work and had left the rubble lying around and anything that could be thrown was launched at the police. Even 'God' himself, Jack Charlton, could not put an end to it. Lots has been written about why the trouble started but Curran's sending off just lit the fuse that had been ready to spark all season.

"When the police eventually got us on the buses back to the station, they were ready for a bit of instant justice as they made us walk through them to board the train. They didn't half put the boot in but we'd had more fun than them so we never reacted."

Supporters, police and players all came under the spotlight. Oldham's chief of police blamed Curran and Stainrod for the injuries to four of his officers and demanded tough action be taken against them. "They must bear the responsibility for what happened," he said angrily. Others lined up to add their condemnation. The Lord Mayor of Sheffield described it as a "tragedy" for the city. "It is an absolute disgrace that a lunatic fringe should bring discredit to Sheffield," he said. The chairman of the city's promotional committee said that the events would not encourage business and tourists, while Jack Charlton, who himself came under criticism for his outburst at the referee, remained defiant and blamed Stainrod for his theatricals.

Wednesday chairman McGee stuck with his criticism of policing as the FA disciplinary committee agreed to meet to discuss action. He said police tactics were "making hooligans out of decent people" and was backed up by his manager, who said, "Cage people like animals and they'll behave like animals." McGee argued that instead of punishing all supporters, the police should focus their energy on targeting hooligans. He advocated the photographing of the crowd so troublemakers could be identified, and called for fans to point out hooligans. He did, however, refuse to extend his criticism to the police in Oldham whom he described as "exemplary".

The Oldham riot proved to be a defining moment in the history of violence at Wednesday. It brought them national notoriety and shame but the scenes were never to be repeated. Some fans were obviously ashamed at the severity of the fighting at Oldham while others simply called it a day and stood aside for a younger generation of hooligans.

"As the 1980s dawned, the rules were changing," said Paul, one who remained part of the mob when many called it a day. "Trouble involving the EBRA became less and less as the old legends of S6 settled down and seemed to outgrow the violence of their youth. The likes of Tommo, Fat Sid and Black Colin disappeared, to be replaced by a new breed and a new culture; the football casual. It was a culture that didn't sit easy with the old guard at Hillsborough, and many, but not all, drifted away. Across the city, however, the casual look was taking off, and the old donkey jackets were being replaced by Sergio Tacchini and other designer labels."

One event more than any other that symbolised the decline of Wednesday's firm was beamed into the nation's households in 1985 in the TV documentary *Hooligans*, about West Ham's Inter City Firm. The programme-makers followed the ICF up to Sheffield where, according to the footage broadcast, a small London group easily ran a much larger mob of Wednesday close to the train station.

Wednesday veterans are still incensed by the documentary. It was bad enough that they were shown to be on the back foot, fleeing far inferior numbers, but, they contend, it was completely untrue.

"We met in town at the Old Queen's Head," said Paul. "A small mob of fifteen or so West Ham came in early doors and we were out and into them. If you watch the documentary you see that small mob walking down toward the pub; they then cleverly edit to the High Street footage, and then back to see a group disappearing behind the Howard. Anyone who knows Sheffield knows that it couldn't have happened like that. The mob hiding behind the Howard was the ICF who got legged from the Old Queen's Head.

"We then headed up to the Bell on High Street, and had a good 100 or so in there. Nowt seemed likely to happen, so most of us, me included, wandered down to the Muff Inn. Shortly afterwards, someone brought a reinforced ICF mob of about forty-five back up to the Bell, and we were down to about thirty. There then followed what appeared on the telly. Interestingly, if you watch that clip you will see at least three Blades with our lot. Most told me that they were very unnerved to see a cameraman with their mob. After the match, we mobbed up at the top of Leppings Lane, a good 150-200, or so it seemed. The ICF came bouncing up and there was a bit of handbags before the OB got in, pushed us back up toward the Park Hotel and rounded up the ICF outside Hillsborough Park. At no time did we 'scatter' like that mong on the TV suggested."

What was unquestionable was that the balance of power within Sheffield was shifting from Blue to Red. This did not occur overnight, but by the mid-Eighties the signs of an upsurge in Blades violence, combined with a decline in the Owls' fortunes, was becoming more apparent.

"When I first came on the scene in 1984, sightings of Blades in town were very rare," said Paul. "The old guard still around showed nothing but disdain for the young Blades coming through, but things were changing. A testimonial at Bramall Lane in May 1986 for long-serving United defender Tony Kenworthy gave the up-and-coming Blades mob, soon to be calling themselves the Blades Business Crew (BBC), a chance to show Wednesday that the tide in Sheffield had turned. It didn't work out that way, and, in a major clash after the game at the Peace Gardens in Sheffield a smaller Owls firm totally routed the United young bucks. It would be months before we got another glimpse of this new firm. The events of the Peace Gardens allowed us to rest easy in our beds knowing they were no threat.

"A cold October night in Manchester in 1986 saw the birth of the Owls Crime Squad (OCS), and the EBRA was consigned to the history books. A small firm of us travelled to Maine Road to watch a League Cup tie between Sheffield Wednesday and Stockport. None of us were older than twenty-one. We breezed past both Stockport and Manchester City that night, and a belief in our invincibility was beginning to grow. In fact, during the 1986/87 season we travelled extensively and scored some major results at places such as Nottingham Forest and Liverpool, although a minibus full of us did come unstuck at QPR. We were really enjoying ourselves, but sadly the season ended in May, and that's when the wheels started to come off.

"By 1987 the zest was fading. The BBC was making lots of noise in town, and our turnouts started to dwindle. Some difficult nights on West Street ensued over the next couple of years. The BBC had, apparently overnight, become a bigger, better organised mob, and they loved to flex their muscles against our ever-weakening firm. A pre-season friendly, again at Bramall Lane, in August 1989 gave us a chance to get things back together. We didn't have a big firm out that day, about seventy, but it was wall-to-wall quality. Poor organisation, however, saw us overwhelmed before the match at the Earl of Arundel pub, and it was a measure of the quality we had that day that we were bitterly disappointed to take second against around 200 BBC. A far better showing after the match saw us gain some revenge when forty of us ambushed the BBC at Silks.

"Away from this, though, we were struggling, and to be honest it was only the Stocksbridge Owls that held the line for us on West Street week in, week out. No matter what any Blade says, we were out every week, home or away. They inflicted some grievous damage on us at times, but we never quit, and I think that laid the groundwork for much of the rebirth the OCS underwent in the late Nineties. We never got any respect for what we did in the late Eighties, and that to me is wrong. The BBC by then was a very strong firm, easily top ten, and for fifteen to twenty of us to constantly put ourselves out there every week took some doing. It was not all one-way traffic either. We scored a few morale-boosting results against the odds, especially the night that the BBC's famous leader, 'Nudger', took a kicking and was heard to scream, 'I'm Wednesday, leave me.'

"The sad thing for me about United was a total refusal to give us any respect. A match at Hillsborough in 1992 saw a huge, resurgent Owls mob run the BBC ragged in Morrison's car park close to Hillsborough Corner, but many of them even refuse to accept that happened, despite the fact that some of their major players were involved. No firm is invincible and we all have bad days at the office, but they refuse to accept it. I have the greatest of respect for BBC faces such as Steve Cowens [author of *Blades Business Crew*], but none at all for those within the BBC who used it both as a vehicle for their criminal activities and to indulge in wanton violence and bullying, even of their own firm members."

The 1990s were barren years as far as hooliganism was concerned at Wednesday. The club was doing well, with a number of Wembley finals and good league finishes. In the Sheffield hooligan world, there is consensus that the BBC was dominant, though it was never one-sided. In April 1991, Wednesday beat Manchester United by a single goal in the final of the League Cup and in the same season were promoted back into football's top flight. The mood of optimism and excitement at Ron Atkinson's emerging side was dented almost immediately when the manager decided to switch to Aston Villa. "Judas," read a huge banner hung outside the ground. If that was not bad enough, Villa were Wednesday's first visitors of the new season.

Everyone knew it would be a high-risk game and the day before the match the police announced that an officer had been assigned the job of minding the ex-Owls manager. The police preparations were helped by the 1991 Football Offences Act, which had come into force a few days before. The new law made it a criminal offence to "chant indecent slogans" and "run on to the pitch without good reason".

Tensions ran high on the day of the game and a large Owls mob clashed with Villa thugs outside the ground before and after the game. There were 27 arrests, but the police were happy that Atkinson's minder was untroubled, despite Villa's 3–1 victory. Atkinson's departure had little negative impact on the team, and in their first season back up they finished third, behind Leeds and Manchester United. This was achieved despite a 6–0 home defeat to Leeds and a 7–1 trouncing at Arsenal. The following season the Owls reached two more Wembley finals but on both occasions they lost 2–1 to Arsenal. Their FA Cup semi-final, again played at Wembley, was an all-Sheffield affair and each club sold 35,000 tickets, though the occasion was overshadowed by the death of an innocent United fan after a post-match altercation in a car park.

One of Wednesday's key figures during this period was Dave Flynn, who through the England and Ulster Loyalist scene formed a close friendship with Chelsea. So tight was this friendship that police intelligence files relating to a leading Chelsea hooligan state that on at least one occasion Wednesday linked up with the Headhunters to attack Sheffield United in London. One allegation levelled at Wednesday's mob in the late Nineties was the emergence of a right-wing political allegiance, to the point where there was a split in the mob and the black members were ostracised. Until then, Wednesday always had a sizeable following of black lads in their mob, though probably nowhere near the number in the BBC. United's firm are adamant that Flynn brought in racist politics, but one Wednesday lad who spoke to us vehemently denied the allegation.

The hooligan fortunes of Wednesday seemed intrinsically linked to their football fortunes, though operating in direct contradiction. The footballing highs of the early to mid-Nineties were soon forgotten as the side stumbled and stuttered in the Premiership. In May 2000, Wednesday were relegated from the Premier League in a season that witnessed trouble at both games against Leeds United. The away fixture, in mid-October, saw a group of 20 Owls attacked by 30 Leeds in a city centre pub. "Glasses, bottles and chairs were thrown during the disorder and as a result several people sustained cuts from flying glass," reported NCIS. "Police attended and order was restored. After the game a large group of Leeds supporters attempted to confront Sheffield supporters but were prevented from doing so by mounted officers." For the home game, a mob of 80 Leeds vandalised a tram taking them to the ground but the real fighting happened well into the evening between the OCS and the BBC and there were eight arrests.

Wednesday's mob might have been in the shadow of the BBC but occasionally could pull on big numbers and this was certainly the case when they played another key rival, Derby County. In 1989, the *Sheffield Star* reported that a mob of 1,000 Wednesday fans went on the rampage after a match in the city. Police blamed "professional" football hooligans for the trouble, during which five mounted officers were injured. According to the newspaper report, "Wednesday's ranks were infiltrated by hooligans from another Midlands club who had picked the day to launch an attack on Derby fans." More recently, a police officer was stabbed trying to separate battling Wednesday and Derby fans.

In early 2001, Wednesday fans caused trouble in Southampton before an FA Cup tie, and a month later, 70-80 OCS attempted to attack local fans at a game in Preston. "Mounted officers prevented a major confrontation and the Sheffield group fragmented before regrouping on the main road and walking towards the town centre," noted an NCIS report. "A

Preston group made it to a nearby public house where they attacked Sheffield supporters drinking inside. Police attended quickly and the Sheffield supporters were removed. The main Sheffield group, numbering 30, made it to another public house. All patrols were then stood down. The Preston group found the Sheffield group and fighting occurred before police attended and eventually escorted the Sheffield group to the train station."

Wednesday were in footballing and financial freefall and there were rumours of near-bankruptcy. In May 2001, the club finished in 17th, only five points off the drop zone. It got worse the following year as they finished just one point above relegation, but there was no saving them a third time when, in May 2003, they were relegated despite four wins in their final six games. Overrun by United in Sheffield, and with key ties against the Manchester United and Leeds mobs apparently long gone, Wednesday developed a new rivalry with Grimsby.

In April 2002, a match on the east coast saw 17 arrests after fighting in Cleethorpes. "Police came under attack from a hail of missiles from Sheffield Wednesday supporters," noted an NCIS report. "There were further outbreaks of disorder at the railway station and two fans were bitten by a police dog." The *Grimsby Telegraph* reported how scores of police officers, some wearing body armour, were drafted in as a series of flare-ups escalated into violence. "Tourists enjoying the bank holiday break in Cleethorpes looked on in disbelief, and young children were in tears as alcohol-fuelled thugs from Sheffield threw missiles and hurled abuse at police officers, police dogs and officers on horseback," it said.

The following year, Grimsby made a show at Hillsborough. One OCS member, Tom, recalled, "The two teams were struggling at the wrong end of the table and embroiled in a relegation scrap. After going to theirs two years in succession and causing mayhem, the word was that Grimsby were going to make a show. They were supposedly going to be turning up on coaches at a big block of flats behind the train station, known as Park Hill. I met a lad in town before heading up and by ten o'clock there were already little mobs of up to twenty walking around. We went in the Bankers Draft to wait for another lad when a few Grimsby started drifting in. We decided to drink up and head off to the meet to tell our other lads that we knew where Grimsby was holed up.

"The boozer for the meet was rammed, so we went to a pub just round the corner in hope of not having to queue for half an hour for a pint. That was also full and we sat down to have a drink and tell the lads the news. Suddenly the phones started going and it became clear a mob of Wednesday had beat us to it. We all started heading down the hill into town and you could see mobs of Wednesday everywhere, twenty in front on the bridge, twenty behind, running down the hill, all trying to get into town where it was going off. As we all leapt over the barrier in the middle of the road opposite where the market used to be, we saw Wednesday lads walking back down. As we mobbed up it became apparent that there had been a few scuffles near the Cannon and that Grimsby had gone in the direction of the Bankers Draft. As we walked up we saw that the police had about forty Grimsby boys outside the Bankers. Apparently they had gone in and yet another mob of ours was in there and these Grimsby had to battle again. This was getting ridiculous, there was a good 150-plus Wednesday with lads arriving every minute.

"After a long walk to Hillsborough and a drab nil-nil draw, the fun could really start. Inside the ground Grimsby had around sixty visible boys, whereas we had at least 150 on the South Stand and 100 on the North Stand. Word was that we were meeting on the bridge on Leppings Lane to give it to these Grimsby boys. It was here that my respect for them grew tenfold. As they came out of the ground, the coppers made it clear they had no intention of doing anything, and should Grimsby wish to get home they would have to go through our mob of 150 standing forty yards up the road. A few Grimsby shit it but about twenty of them walked straight up to us and called it on. They showed serious bottle fronting numbers of almost ten times theirs, but we steamed into them. The sheer numbers were too much for them and the coppers came up and saved them. I have since spoken to a lad who was there and I have nothing but respect for that little mob."

Another recent confrontation took place in Doncaster during a pre-season match. A mob of fifty OCS attacked a smaller group of Doncaster in the Hogshead pub, in the town centre. "They were like a herd of wildebeest stampeding through the bar," remarked manager Denise Howarth. "It was terrifying. I saw one man with a cut hand and another hit by a flying ashtray." There was further trouble when fifty Wednesday fans broke down a gate to enter the ground and rival fans exchanged missiles at the train station after the match. Some time later, six Wednesday fans were dawn-raided by police after video and CCTV evidence was examined. "The message from Doncaster police is quite clear," said Superintendent Adrian Moran. "Come to Doncaster to enjoy the football and behave. So-called supporters who are intent on causing trouble will be targeted by the police and prosecuted. Troublemakers can expect an early morning knock on the door from police."

Twenty-three Wednesday yobs were subsequently sentenced for affray at Doncaster Crown Court in the biggest football hooliganism case ever heard in South Yorkshire. Five were jailed and 15 were given football banning orders after the court heard how they had travelled from Sheffield, mostly in minibuses, and used mobile phones to a confrontation with Rovers in Hallgate. By 8.30pm, only about a dozen Rovers were in the Hog's Head when the group of 50 Owls charged. "Those outside the pub scattered in fear and those inside reported hearing a roar like a deep animal growl," said prosecutor Andrew Kershaw. "The Doncaster supporters realised they were outnumbered and fled through the beer garden and over a wall."

Wednesday besieged the premises with a hail of bottles and stones. There were so many trying to get through the door that they became stuck and others climbed through open windows. The Rovers fans ran into the rear garden and threw themselves over a wall to get away as patio chairs and glasses rained down on them. A party of young women enjoying a birthday drink in the beer garden were terrorised and other customers had to run from the pub as staff were left helpless.

As police reinforcements arrived they were able to set up an ambush in South Parade and detained most of the group, although some were not identified until their pictures were published later in the *Sheffield Star*, as the entire scene had been captured on CCTV. The judge said more of the defendants would have received custodial sentences if there had been any serious injuries.

The Wednesday section could not end without their opinion on the current state of the rivalry with United. The pendulum appears to be swinging back in their favour as a combination of proactive policing and bans take their effect. There is also some resentment about the widespread perception that United have dominated the Owls.

"It's a funny old game sharing a city with another football team," laughed Tom. "However I don't think that other shared cities and towns, with the possible exception of London, share the trouble that we see regularly on Friday and Saturday nights. Whether you're in your local or out in town, there are always pubs that can be labelled as Wednesday or United. It's a rivalry that splits families and often decides who your daughter can bring home and who she can't. It is a tension that very often spills over and ends up messy.

"Unfortunately, because of the level of tension and hatred, sometimes the gloves come off and all unwritten rules go out of the window. I would be quick to add that the majority on both sides are fair and have a certain amount of mutual respect for lads on the other side; however it is the element that are not fair and think nothing of attacking lads out with their women or in lesser numbers that sets our city apart. I have suffered from it, and so have most other lads. I've known lads on their own get turned over by fifteen of the other lot and end up in the A&E for the night. On visits to other towns and cities, it surprised me how you can see mobs walking about singing football songs and think nothing of it. I could never imagine walking through town with ten lads singing Wednesday songs and not getting challenged.

"For the last twenty years the BBC has been the bigger force in Sheffield, but not without a struggle during the last five years. Their lads don't like to admit it, but they have not always had the upper hand. A few years ago they put us on our toes at the Casa Bar, no excuses there, but they forget about the T.P.Woods incident. Ten of our lot walked past and up to thirty Blades piled out to indulge in a spot of bullying. They didn't know it was a set-up, and as they looked round another fifty Wednesday were steaming round the corner right at them. They were then fighting each other to get back in the boozer and didn't come out until a police Mariah pulled up. There have been many different versions of this incident told but the CCTV footage currently doing the rounds does not lie.

"Another more recent incident sums up the scene at the moment. Eighty of us had gone to Hornsea for the game at Hull. A plain-clothes copper in an unmarked car followed a minibus to where our lot were and that was game over before the pubs had opened. We came back to Sheffield and met up in a boozer up Intake [an area of Sheffield]. A few calls were made to the Blades telling them where we were and how many we had, which was around forty. They were at home to Millwall so we expected they would have a mob out. They told us they didn't want to know while we were that far from town, so at around half time we assembled and made our way to the Pump Tavern, a three-minute walk from Bramall Lane in the direction of the city centre. Again we got on the phone to tell them where we were with no coppers in sight and they replied they were too busy trying to attack Millwall's heavily policed escort.

"We decided to go looking for them and set off into town. As we got to the Peace Gardens we spotted around five Blades following us, so we called it on and they declined, telling us to wait for more of theirs to come. Fair enough, so we went in the Brown Bear and again there were no coppers around, but no Blades either. As I popped my head out of the door I saw around a dozen lads at the top of the road. I nipped back in and told one of our main lads that they were milling about and about twenty of us popped out to have a look. As we turned the corner to the Winter Gardens we saw them again, a few young 'uns on their toes straight away with the older lads just slowly walking backwards. We decided they were not worth risking being caught on CCTV for and went back in the pub. If we had steamed them we would have been labelled 'bullies' but because we didn't we were 'shit'. We just can't win with that lot. Anyway we ended up in the Dove and Rainbow and then walked through town to get taxis back up Hillsborough as the Blades didn't seem the least bit interested.

"Once we got back in our main boozer in Hillsborough, some two miles from town, the phones started going and they asked us to go back into town. Why didn't they want us for the two hours that we actually were in town? There will always be little scraps that go either way, be it when ten of us chase their young 'uns down Division Street with a piss-taking chant of 'BBC' or a one-on-one outside a local boozer in the suburbs, but the question of superiority will go unanswered for a long time yet. The OB have seen to that."

In January 2007, South Yorkshire Police issued a press release after an upsurge in disorder. "After a series of minor incidents at local matches, South Yorkshire Police are reminding disruptive football fans to stay away from future matches in the city if intent on causing trouble, or face being banned," it said. "After fans ran on to the pitch at the Sheffield Wednesday versus Sunderland match and minor incidents of disorder at several recent matches, senior officers have emphasised their commitment to support the clubs. At each game police will gather video evidence and will scan CCTV footage for evidence of any trouble between fans. Police will use all methods possible to bring these people to justice, whether they are arrested at the ground at the time or after a post match investigation."

It did not stop a very young gang of Wednesday clashing with Huddersfield fans two months later. The *Sheffield Star* of 2 November 2007 reported the court case that followed:

SHOPPERS were forced to flee as a gang of teenage football hooligans – including four Sheffield Wednesday supporters – clashed in an alcohol-fuelled street fight organised on the internet.

The violence broke out in Wakefield town centre after the teenage football yobs armed themselves with clubs from a nearby golf club as shoppers ran for cover.

Wakefield Youth Court heard the thugs, the youngest of whom was just 15, had organised the fight on Saturday March 24 using internet messaging. Their teams, Sheffield Wednesday and Huddersfield Town, were either not playing or playing away.

Prosecutor Douglas Tomlinson said the youths had met in a pub called Pitchers on Westgate – the town's main street. Despite being underage, they were drinking alcohol. The brawl started when one of the thugs shouted "let's 'ave it," and they spilled out into the street.

Mr Tomlinson said: "We clearly have two groups of opposing supporters. They met for one purpose and one purpose only and that was to fight each other."

District Judge Jonathan Bennett said: "It is abundantly clear to everybody that something was going on here. I am quite satisfied that this was organised violence. The Huddersfield fans and the Sheffield fans chose a convenient location that was easily accessible for both by rail link. It is entirely football-related and happened simply because neither side were playing and in effect they had a free Saturday."

But the judge refused to issue football banning orders against the eight teenagers because he was not satisfied the violence was related to the England under-21s match they had been watching at the pub.

A 16-year-old Sheffield Wednesday supporter, from Bridlington, and a 17-year-old, from Huddersfield, were locked up for four months. Two 16-year-olds, from Sheffield, and two teenagers, from Huddersfield, aged 15 and 16, were given 12-month referral orders. A 17-year-old, from Sheffield, was given a nine-month referral order.

Further reading: *Flying With The Owls Crime Squad*, Paul Allen and Douglas Naylor (Blake Publishing), *Football Hooligans: Knowing The Score*, Gary Armstrong (Berg Publishers)

SHREWSBURY TOWN

Ground: The "New Meadow", formerly Gay Meadow
Firms: English Border Front
Rivals: Wrexham, Telford, Mansfield

The youths looked on with a mixture of excitement and apprehension. Derby County fans were ripping Gay Meadow apart and there was a real risk of a severe beating after the match, but for many watching from the Riverside, this was something new. Derby County were being relegated into the Third Division in May 1984 and hundreds of their fans were determined to grab the headlines. The carnage was the talk of the town and the local schools for the following few days. A couple of the lads even had "Derby Lunatic Fringe" calling cards. It was all exciting, and very soon the Shrewsbury youths would organise themselves in similar fashion.

Organised football violence arrived late in the Shropshire market town. There had been the odd outbreak of disorder dating back to the mid-Sixties but it was essentially random. In March 1966, Shrewsbury Town were instructed by the FA to print a warning to spectators in the next issue of the club programme, following a home game against Bournemouth when a linesman was struck by a stone. The notice warned fans of serious consequences if there was a repeat of the trouble. Three years later, in March 1969, Shrewsbury Town fans were once again in the national news after a referee was struck by a youth during a game.

There were few reports of trouble at matches in the Seventies as the team languished in the Fourth Division. Shrewsbury was rightly considered a nice, friendly family club in a small and relatively prosperous market town. While there was trouble at an FA Cup tie against Aldershot in February 1979, it was the defeat of Manchester City in the following round, in front of a record 16,000 crowd, which drew the attention of the national press. This was followed two years later with the dispatching of in-form Ipswich, who were then riding high in Division One. In many other towns such high-profile scalps would have been followed by mass disorder from losing fans and locals keen to impress. This was not the case with the boys of the Gay Meadow, for whom a news report, especially on the radio, was almost always accompanied by a mention of Fred Davies, the ageing gent who would be dispatched in his coracle to fetch the ball if it was kicked over the stand and into the river. He eventually retired in the Nineties but was forced to return at the age of 75 after his son proved ineffective at reaching the ball before it got swept away by the current.

The Gay Meadow is perched almost precariously on the edge of the River Severn, so making it prone to regular flooding. Between it and the English Bridge, one of seven bridges circling the small town centre, was Wakeman School, which during the mid to late Eighties would transform itself into a police car park on match days for what regularly appeared as overkill for a fanbase so small. The English Bridge once reflected an important psychological underpinning of the town, as less than half a mile away was the Welsh Bridge. Shrewsbury was on the medieval route to Wales and the town had that border mentality.

It is said that a medieval byelaw still exists which allows for the shooting of Welshmen within the town walls by a crossbow after 6pm. When the football casual movement finally caught on in the town, in the mid-Eighties, the name English Border Front was adopted by Shrewsbury's soccer gang.

Perhaps one reason why hooliganism was so late in arriving was because the fanbase did not lend itself to mass disorder. Most of its fans appeared to be older men, or so it appeared to the small groups of teenagers who would gather at the back of the Riverside Stand along with a small hardcore of older lads who were no way interested in the fashion of the Eighties. There was little atmosphere inside the ground, though racist chanting of "Nigger, nigger, lick my boot" was regularly sung at black players of opposing teams. Many of the lads in the town would support bigger clubs, particularly Leeds, Manchester United, Liverpool and Aston Villa. Few young people would follow Shrewsbury regularly and fighting was more normally associated with late night drinking and pre-arranged inter-school scraps on Friday nights.

Promotion into the Second Division in May 1979, with a 4-1 home win over Exeter, brought new challenges to the small club and historical town. Early in the following season, Shrewsbury played host to Chelsea, the first major team to play at the Gay Meadow. A crowd of 10,000 was expected to watch the match but for the police and many local businesses, it was the 1,000 travelling fans which were a cause for concern. In the days leading up to the game there was growing anxiety about potential disorder. "An elaborate police operation swung into action this afternoon to foil the threat of soccer violence as Shrewsbury faced an invasion of Chelsea fans, who have a notorious reputation for trouble," reported the *Shropshire Star*. "Many publicans, anticipating trouble, were keeping their doors closed until the match.

"British Transport Police had extra men on duty at the station and officers aboard the train. From the station the fans were ushered aboard waiting coaches and driven to the Gay Meadow car park where the other visiting coaches were directed to unload. At both points there was a heavy police presence."

The police operation was made all the more complicated because of a dispute over the funding of a short line from the main station to close to the football ground. As an alternative, the police had to organise coaches to ferry those fans arriving by train the mile or so to the ground rather than allowing them to wander through the shopping streets.

The greatest preparations do not always go to plan, as Shrewsbury was left counting the cost of its worst day of soccer violence in its history. Over 60 arrests were made as hundreds of Chelsea fans ran amok through the town after watching their side lose 3-0. A local publican described a mob of between 500-700 fans as "like a tidal wave – an army gone mad".

"Windows of shops and houses were smashed, car windscreens shattered and a do-it-yourself warehouse invaded until the arrival of police reinforcements," reported the next edition of the local paper. "Fifteen arrests were made inside the ground, mostly when police broke up fighting between Chelsea fans and Shrewsbury supporters after some Londoners sneaked into the home terraces.

"The system began to go wrong however at the final whistle. Chelsea fans, incensed at their team's 3-0 defeat tried to get through the police lines and reach Shrewsbury supporters pouring out of the other gates. They were foiled by a massive police presence. Refusing to board the special coaches to take them back to the station, several hundred broke away and ran down the railway embankments towards the station."

Worse was to come. The Chelsea fans had begun to travel home when one died after apparently falling from a train in Buckinghamshire. Twenty-year-old, Terry Burke from Walworth, London, was on the Wolverhampton to London train at the time. A victim of the violence was local lad Ian Turner, who was attacked by Chelsea fans as he was making his way home from a nightclub at 2am on the Sunday morning. "One pulled me down and pulled my shirt off and started scratching me. I was shouting for help but no one came." A picture of his injuries, which included over 30 long cuts, adorned the front page of the *Shropshire Star*.

The first of those arrested began appearing in front of local magistrates on the Monday morning. Robin Onions, prosecuting, told magistrates how between 500 and 700 fans kicked and broke windscreens of cars. He added that one officer, out of the 250 on duty, thought his time was up when the panda car in which he was sitting was overturned. Over 200 Chelsea fans got into Shrewsbury's Riverside End, and within two minutes of the start of the game, fighting broke out. The trouble was caught on police video and Mr Onions explained that few of those involved took any interest in the football. He described the surge through police lines after the game as "a cattle stampede out of a wild west film".

"Chelsea came early, as they always did at the smaller places, and took over the town," remembered one current EBF follower. "Shrewsbury gave a decent account of themselves, though the talk was all about this mob of Cockneys dressed in trenchcoats carrying brollies. They got in the Riverside End and had good numbers in there but Shrewsbury shifted them. It went on all day and most of the night but they never got the walkover they thought they would get." Several of the Chelsea contingent received jail terms.

Three seasons later, there was further serious disorder after the visit of Birmingham City. Any game involving the larger Midlands clubs meant bumper crowds but also growing headaches for the police. Birmingham, Wolves and West Brom would regularly pack the Station End and their allocation of seats. In October 1982, 40 locals fought with an equal number of Birmingham at the Elephant & Castle pub. "It was mental," recalled the EBF veteran.

Another game during this period which saw trouble was the home match against Manchester City in November 1983. "It was very much the same as the Chelsea game. They came in massive numbers but faced resistance that they thought we never had."

But there was no way the Shrewsbury lads could match Derby County in May 1984 for a match that saw their Midlands rivals relegated to the Third Division. Three thousand Derby fans made the journey and there was chaos during and after the game. The Derby Lunatic Fringe calling cards that were littered around town proved too attractive to be overlooked and this one game appeared to be the catalyst for the emergence of a Shrewsbury casual mob. By the time of a pre-season friendly game at Hereford United a few months later, the Shrewsbury lads had gathered themselves together into the soon-to-be-named English Border Front. Almost 200 Shrewsbury lads made the short trip to Hereford by train, and spent much of the time walking around town enjoying the fear they invoked in the locals. "It was a power thing," remembered one. "Most of us were teenagers, with only a few older lads there. You could see shoppers fleeing to escape our path. It made us feel more powerful than we probably were. There was a real buzz."

One of the early Shrewsbury leaders, DM, was then just 18, the son of a former schoolteacher. He loved football violence and soon began running with bigger mobs, particularly in London. A year or so after the EBF was formed, a firm from nearby Telford came into town unannounced on a summer Saturday afternoon. DM quickly organised a mob and by the time the fighting had been brought under control more than 20 people had been arrested. A court was specially adapted so the Shrewsbury defendants, led by DM, sat on one side of the room, with Telford on the other. The majority were found guilty, with many being sent to youth detention. DM, meanwhile, was also beginning to earn a name following England and became close friends with former Chelsea leaders Steve Hickmott and Chris Henderson.

Telford were Shrewsbury's closest rivals, though their non-league status meant meetings were consigned to the Shropshire Cup. A final held in Telford in the late Eighties proved to be a torrid affair for the few EBF who made the trip, as hundreds of the so-called Telford Youth Organisation gathered outside the ground at the final whistle in the hope of getting to the travelling supporters. Some unfortunate Shrewsbury fans were forced to run for their lives in the face of overwhelming numbers. Perhaps as a way of alleviating the humiliation, many EBF lads later claimed that the

Telford ranks had been swelled by Wolves and Birmingham lads, many of whom lived in the new town.

The EBF was not able to cope with many rival mobs who visited during the club's time in the Second Division. Chelsea, Leeds, Manchester City, Stoke and Birmingham were all regularly visitors to the Gay Meadow and these clubs would travel over in the thousands, bringing hundreds of hooligans. In 1986, Shrewsbury hosted Middlesbrough, as they had done for the final game of the 1985 season, and while the previous year the visitors secured the necessary points to stay up, this time a 2-1 defeat led to widespread disorder still talked about by Boro fans. Later that year, it was the turn of West Brom fans to cause trouble when they clashed with police, leaving several injured and arrested. The following year saw Cardiff City fans rampage through town after a last minute goal dumped the Welsh team out of the Littlewoods Cup. [See *Cardiff City* in *Hooligans*.]

Regardless of the numbers some of the so-called main firms were bringing, the EBF were getting stronger and always offered some resistance. It was around this time their biggest turnout was mobilised, 200 for a match in Blackpool.

Shrewsbury's key rivals have long been Wrexham, though a founding member of the EBF once lived in the Welsh town and ran with their "Frontline" gang. There have been a number of serious clashes between the two groups over the years, most of them in Shrewsbury. In the summer of 1987, a coachload of Wrexham fans descended on the town one Saturday evening and before the night was out they were involved in running clashes with hundreds of locals.

"Thirty-seven Wrexham youths were arrested and six policemen hurt," reported one newspaper. "Five officers were taken to hospital with severely irritated eyes, ears and noses after what is believed to be CS gas was thrown. Fighting broke out at about 2am last Saturday, as a group of Wrexham youths on a stag night, clashed with Shrewsbury youths as they left the Park Lane nightclub. A senior police officer estimated that up to 500 youths were involved in running street battles and a black Ford Fiesta car was badly damaged through the rioting crowds."

Tit-for-tat fighting became a feature of their rivalry. "We stopped at Wrexham after going to Chester or Tranmere," recalled Ryan, a leading figure in the EBF. On other occasions, the EBF merely enjoyed going for Welsh targets. "The main one was when the EBF went to a rave in Bangor mob-handed and it kicked off all night."

It was Wrexham, though, who remained top of the hit list and although two of the main lads from the Frontline and EBF are good mates, the friendship stops on match days. "Ask him about 1992," laughed Ryan.

"They came mob-handed and got more than they bargained for. We chased them all over town and I think he still has some scars from that day. They brought 100 on the train and fronted the Castle, the landlord had bolted all the doors and we could not get out straight away but once we were out into them they tried to stand but soon crumbled [see WREXHAM].

"I respect them because they always come but they believe their own hype and claim some ridiculous results. The time five of them attacked the Elephant and Castle with iron bars and cleared the beer garden full of lads is a funny one. They deserve credit for running in and calling it on, as they never had any idea how many lads were in there, but they were lucky as it was about ten – the result they had was fucking up a few cosy couples' evening. They must have shit themselves when five Welsh warriors ran in swinging bats chanting, 'Frontline.' They hit a few and were chased out. One lad was pleading for protection from the police, it was a hit and run attack and they ran alright!

"We took four coaches to Wrexham for one game but the police had us parked up before the pubs were open and in the ground before the fucking groundsman had finished marking the pitch."

Despite the different views as to the outcome of many of the clashes between Wrexham and Shrewsbury, they do agree on one thing: Chester are not in the same league as either the EBF or the Frontline! "They claim some big result at our place one year," sneered Ryan. "Well nobody down here can remember it, but just to even things out we took a full complement up there and they ended up barricading themselves in the Queen Victoria when we tried to force our way in. I don't agree with much the Vile One from Wrexham [Frontline leader Neil Williams] says but I know he is right when he says Chester are not worth a mention."

Any match involving Wrexham and Shrewsbury was heavily policed. The two sides played at the Gay Meadow on 2 January 1993 and though there were some serious fights, the police felt that their operation went a long way to prevent more widespread disorder. A total of 120 officers were on duty for a game, which only attracted a gate of a few thousand, and seven people, including six from Shrewsbury, were arrested.

The 1987/88 season saw clashes during Shrewsbury's away game with Aston Villa. "We did them in the Vines pub," boasted Ryan. The fight hit the national newspapers when 69 Shrewsbury fans were arrested by police after two young brothers were attacked as they sat at a bus stop on the EBF's route to the ground. "The Witton Arms also saw trouble break out and that day it was fifty-odd either side and we came out on top," said Ryan.

Another game that witnessed considerable violence was the opening game of the 1990/91 season when Shrewsbury were host to Bolton Wanderers, one of the biggest hooligan mobs in the lower divisions at the time. "Business as usual," said Ryan. "They brought a good firm, 100-plus, and as they were escorted from the station we charged out of the Rock and Fountain pub and backed then onto the station. They thought it would be a stroll in the park, like many others, but it wasn't."

1990 proved to be a significant year in the history of the EBF, the first time that a large mob of Shrewsbury hooligans travelled abroad together for an England game. It set a precedent for future international tournaments. Several Shrewsbury hooligans were arrested and deported from Italy, particularly after being involved in fighting in Rimini. Over the next few years, Shrewsbury were to earn a surprising reputation as one of the largest firms on the England scene, to the extent that 90 lads went on one trip. In 1993, according to the *Guardian* newspaper, 47 Shrewsbury-based men were deported from Holland in one day during the failed World Cup qualifier in Holland.

"In the early days, firms used to come to Shrewsbury and call us Welsh bastards and we decided to make a point of going to England games to prove how patriotic we are to our country," said Ryan. "We started off by taking small groups but soon were taking fifty or sixty and have taken ninety abroad. Like the papers say, fifty-odd Shrewsbury were deported after one game in Holland, but what they didn't report was that a few flew straight back out there the next day."

It was at the World Cup in Italy that the EBF established links with both Oldham and Newcastle United and this close friendship lasts to this day. The Oldham–Shrewsbury link is especially strong, and they have regularly been to each other's key games. "We all met at Italia 90," said Ryan. "We were banged up with a load of Newcastle when the police rounded everyone up one night. We met Oldham at the same place and made friends with them after we bought acid tabs off them. It's the kind of thing you do on England duty and one reason why we can never remember half the fucking goings on! We have been to Newcastle for some big games, Sunderland, Stoke and Boro to name a few, we were at Stoke for one big battle in the Coca Cola Cup. Some of our lads got sent down for the Oldham–Stoke riots and our lads were at Wrexham and Leeds when Oldham did both the Welsh lot at the Four Dogs pub and the Service Crew at the Viaduct pub a few years ago. We have been to Oldham, Spurs home and away and they have come down to us a few times, no major numbers on either side but good lads from all three mobs have swelled the ranks for key games and we have great respect for each other."

Prior to the 1992 European Championships in Sweden, Shrewsbury and Telford hooligans battled on a ferry, causing the captain to turn the boat around and call the police, whilst the Shrewsbury, Oldham and Newcastle axis saw a united mob of almost 200 lads travel to the 1993 match in Holland. Even for the World Cup match against Wales in Manchester in 2004, the Shrewsbury, Oldham and Stockport group numbered over 100.

Shrewsbury's linking with Newcastle United is described in Stoke hooligan Mark Chester's *Naughty*, though the EBF is dismissed in derogatory terms. An equally scathing account of the Shrewsbury link with Oldham is made in the Wrexham section of this book. It is not just the Stoke football mob the EBF have clashed with; for several weeks they fought battles with a group of Stoke bouncers who tried their hand at running the doors in Shrewsbury.

"Similar to some of the football firms who come here and think they can take the piss these meatheads turned up one night, dressed like Max and Paddy, and started largeing it on the door of the Paradise boozer. One lad went in with his missus and they ended up slinging him out over a nothing incident, so he lamps one of them and they kick fuck out of him. We heard about it, went around and demolished them the same night. The following week, they turned up with fifteen men and it was the same outcome, we battered them and then gassed the pub for good measure. This went on for a few weeks, it was bedlam. They kept increasing their firm numbers and we kept turning up and smashing them; there was no cunt left in the pub, it was just full of bouncers. One night the place got badly damaged in the fight and the landlord had the tape, so we agreed to stop going there if he fucked the bouncers off. It was all over the papers and on Central TV, madness, all because of a few pricks who probably could not handle the doors in Stoke and thought they could earn some easy money."

Away from the troubles in town, another trip abroad saw several Shrewsbury hooligans arrested and charged after a violent clash with North Africans in Berlin as they were making their way overland to Poland. "We had it with a load of ethnics over a row about drugs. In minutes every African, Moroccan, Turk or whatever they were attacked with big kebab knives and pizza cutters. We were with some Newcastle and Oldham lads and it was nasty. Sixty of us were fighting for our lives and one of the locals lost one eye and his other was half-blind after a glass went into his face. Seven of our mob were stabbed, five EBF and two Newcastle. One of our lads spent a year in jail over it, they tried to deport us all but never pulled it off."

By the early Nineties, the EBF was widely known on the rave and drug scene. They would regularly travel as a mob to raves in Stoke, Wales, and across the West Midlands, where sometimes they would do "business" with hooligans from rival firms, but on other occasions there would be fights. Several EBF hooligans were also long-term residents in Ibiza, with as many as twenty joining them at the height of summer. "It was like walking down Pride Hill," one Shrewsbury lad, not a hooligan, remarked after a trip to the Spanish resort in the early Nineties.

The police also took a close interest in the Shropshire mob because of their drug-dealing activities. "They were in and out of Holland every fortnight," one former NCIS officer commented. The West Midlands Serious Crime Squad in the late Nineties ran three informants inside the EBF, with their interest being drugs and other criminal-related offences rather than football. Several EBF followers were to be imprisoned around the country for drugs offences, including one who, in the mid-1990s, was sentenced to almost four years after he was caught near Heathrow Airport in possession of 43 kilos of cannabis.

Their drug link also drew the attention of television's *The Cook Report*, which in 1996 attempted to place an undercover operative close to the mob's leader. Fortunately for the hooligans, the undercover man, a former soldier with twelve years' service with the SAS and 14th Intelligence Company (a specialist undercover unit in Northern Ireland), was unconvincing in the role; he was simply too big and way too hard to have any plausible reason for interest in the Shrewsbury gang. The EBF smelt a rat, and together with a local radio station, who they had alerted believing they were the target of a flawed police operation, went to a meeting with the undercover man wired-up and in the company of at least one reporter.

Unfortunately for the hooligans, the *Cook Report* had been doing extensive surveillance on them and learnt of this, so when the former SAS soldier went into the pub, accompanied by another ex-Special Forces operative who was also a martial arts world champion, they knew they had to close the story before the radio station went public. They were immediately suspicious of a plaster cast on the arm of the EBF leader, which they thought might conceal a recording device. To the man's horror they ordered him outside; he resisted but was given little alternative. While the second ex-soldier stayed in the pub glaring at the others, the EBF man was marched outside, where he was searched, and sure enough a microphone was found hidden in his cast. He was told in no uncertain terms that it was in his best interests not to tell tales. All this was caught on a video camera, hidden in the soldier's jacket. The programme came to nothing but to the *Cook Report*'s knowledge, the EBF kept quiet about the events.

Drugs, and particularly heroin, had a huge impact on the Shrewsbury mob in this period. "Like most firms, drugs hit us badly, and apart from the rave scene we have lost about ten lads over the years to overdoses on hard drugs," said Ryan.

All soccer crews have what they call "bad days at the office" and the EBF are no different. When questioned on their worse day ever, Ryan asked for a pause and joked that he would need another drink before he could carry on. Five minutes later he blurted out "Swansea City away." He then reluctantly went into detail about the worst day of his life.

"It was horrible, one of those days when everyone is supposedly coming and there is talk of 150 getting the train and the reality when you get on the fucker that about 120 of them have conveniently missed it. We went anyway and could not believe how easy it was when we got there. We went in the pub that was supposed to be their main meeting place, we wandered around the town and were dropping our calling cards everywhere, total walkover. As we got up by the ground we saw one lad sitting on a wall and he jumped down and ran at us. It was unbelievable, we were looking at each other thinking who the fuck is this nutcase, when all of a sudden 200 of them were all around us at a T-junction and they kicked the shit out of us. We were running everywhere, and once by the turnstiles we were just jumping in to get away. I went straight over, me and a mate were covered in blood and before we could get ourselves sorted they were into us again – we had jumped into their fucking end. We were battered onto the pitch. On the way home every single one of us had bandages or plasters or stitches, and although we laugh about it now it was one scary fucking day. They turned up at our place with 200 and although it pains me to say it, we rate them as good as anyone."

It was during the early to mid Nineties that Shrewsbury began a rivalry with Millwall, surprising given the differences between the two mobs. "It was all to do with them calling it on with a small mob of Shrewsbury after they played at our place," said Ryan. "We walked past a pub and half a dozen went in and ten main Millwall lads were in there who attacked the Shrewsbury lads. What they never knew was what we had outside, and we battered them. It was their call, we had no intention of going into them until they started. We know we could not match them firm on firm, who can? But that day they called it on and were sorry. There were threats made for months after that they were going to do this and that, but fuck all came of it."

A longstanding rivalry has been with Mansfield Town, and over the years the EBF have had more clashes with them than any other team save for perhaps Wrexham. "Where do you start?" pondered the EBF lad. "In premobile phone years there were some great battles with them. We bumped into them late one night after they came to us. They attacked our mob in the Elephant & Castle pub and there were a lot of injuries on both sides, but as a result both firms respected each other. We would take seventy-to-eighty there and have it, the following season they would do the same, great battles. One paper reported that one clash was the first time CS gas had been used at a match.

"The best fight was on the way home from Wembley after England had played Holland. We were on a coach on the motorway and we overtook a coach full of their lads. You know what it's like when one bus overtakes the other, it takes five minutes to pass and after about a minute it was like, who are those cunts, and you can see them doing the same. Next minute we're both telling the driver to stop in the middle of the motorway but luckily there was a service station near, so we both pulled in and it went off, a mental five minutes. We chased them into the services and they came flying out with a load of workmen's tools, wood and metal poles; the services were being rebuilt and there was gear all over the place. We backed off but there was a skip full of old bits of metal and wood from the demolished café, so we got that and chased them back in, it was like a carry on film, fucking crazy. The police turned up and we got back on the busses and went home, no one nicked, quality day."

In April 1996, Shrewsbury Town made their one and so far only visit to Wembley, this for the final of the Auto Windscreens Trophy. They lost 2-1 to Rotherham United in an awful display from the Shrewsbury team in front of 16,000 of their supporters. For the EBF, it was more than a cup final; it was a grudge match between two firms with a history. "We played them a couple of years before at their place and went there forty-handed. We were in a pub called the Turf, but the police had it surrounded and all the intelligence officers were there and everything that comes with them. The next minute, a mob of lads come down the stairs into the pub and call it on, so we slaughtered them. We thought we would all be nicked but the police just let us get on with it. It was definitely a set-up and when we piled out they were all there and our spotter was clapping us. He told one lad that he had a £10 bet with their spotter that we would do Rotherham. The pub was camera'd up – but the landlord had not turned them on, and only two lads were ever nicked.

"The night before the final, about fifteen of us were wandering about Kings Cross after coming out of some club and we bumped into a mob of them and it went off. We chased them down the road and they called a load of lads out of the B&B where they were staying and we smashed them and the B&B up, even gassed them. In the end the owner came out in his slippers pleading with us to stop and leave them and his scruffy B&B alone."

Shrewsbury Town's playing fortunes were taking a nosedive. After almost a decade in Division Two, the team slipped first into Division Three and then into Division Four shortly after. Even there they struggled, and in May 2000 the team travelled to Exeter for the final match of the season with relegation a serious prospect. The 1,500 allocation for the away end was quickly snapped up, and a mob of the EBF travelled to Torquay the evening before. Fighting broke out with locals and nine people were arrested, including six from Shrewsbury. On the pitch, a 2–0 win secured Town's survival at the expense of Barnet, who slipped into the Conference. It was only to be a short reprieve, as three seasons later, Shrewsbury finally dropped out of the Football League.

There have been many key final Saturdays of the season for Shrewsbury, especially at home. During the mid-Eighties there were home matches against Derby and Middlesbrough (twice) in consecutive seasons where the opposing team arrived facing the drop. These crunch matches were accompanied by some of the worst trouble Shrewsbury has seen. In the early Nineties, Shrewsbury's home game against Northampton Town saw the East Midlands team secure promotion and again there was widespread disorder [see NORTHAMPTON].

In May 2001, Brighton celebrated promotion with a game at the Gay Meadow. The National Criminal Intelligence Service recorded what happened: before the game, a group of 25 Brighton supporters were sighted outside a public house frequented by Shrewsbury fans. There was then an exchange of missiles which was quickly dealt with by police. Close to kick-off, a small group of Brighton supporters were attacked near the stadium by a larger group of locals. Two arrests, one from each side, were made and a four-year-old girl was knocked over, receiving facial injuries.

"At the end of the game there was a small pitch invasion," said the NCIS report. "After the match there were several outbreaks of fighting in the town centre on the way back to the railway station. Police used batons in an attempt to separate the groups. A shop was damaged and missiles were exchanged throughout. Brighton supporters were escorted to Birmingham by BTP [British Transport Police] and then onwards to Brighton. There were six arrests, five from Shrewsbury and one from Brighton."

In May 2003, Shrewsbury had already been relegated to the Conference when they welcomed Scunthorpe United for their final home game. The police were on high alert, as the East Coast team were chasing promotion and intelligence suggested that both mobs would be well represented. More than 100 officers were drafted in, as Detective Inspector Martin Whitelegg, of Shrewsbury Police, said he had reason to believe there may be trouble. "Because it is the last league game that Shrewsbury may see for some time, large numbers may turn up to see that little bit of history being made," he said. "Scunthorpe are at the other end of the table and our intelligence is that they will have quite a large following. That always brings an element of problems. One or two individuals will come here intent on causing problems rather than to watch the football." In the event there were only minor scuffles.

Football hooligan websites were now buzzing with the news that Shrewsbury were in the Conference. While hardly a super-firm, the EBF were still a recognised gang with a reputation on the England scene. For the likes of Aldershot, Hereford and of course, local rivals Telford, it would be an eagerly awaited fixture.

Early in the new season, Shrewsbury played at Aldershot and there were five arrests as gangs met in the street after the game. "Police drew batons and had to use CS gas to disperse the crowds," noted one media report. "It is thought the trouble may have been pre-arranged by hooligans attaching themselves to each of the clubs. Trouble broke out involving 50 to 60 people in gangs outside a pub in Aldershot following Saturday's game, which ended in a 1-1 draw. More arrests could follow."

Two months later, Shrewsbury saw a large police operation for the arrival of Hereford United. Over 100 police were on duty, a significant amount in any context but remarkable for a Conference fixture. Police were even stationed on the A49 to monitor traffic for the arrival of the Hereford mob. "Come to Shrewsbury, enjoy the football but if you cause trouble you will be locked up," warned Detective Chief Inspector Martin Whitelegg prior to the game, which was expected to be an 8,000 sell-out. "Both clubs have some history of disorder. We're putting other measures in place to prevent people coming into Shrewsbury on that day. If they are intent on travelling, we'll legitimately be able to detain them." Whitelegg said there were people from both towns who loosely associated themselves with football as an excuse for violence. "It isn't a spontaneous thing," he said. "It's pre-planned disorder. Our job is to make sure the genuine supporters can come to Shrewsbury." The heavy policing appeared to work and there was little trouble reported in the press.

Whitelegg was in danger of sounding like a scratched record when, in late February 2004, he was warning fans over their behaviour at the FA Trophy clash between Shrewsbury and Telford. Overseeing the £25,000 police operation, which including a noon kick-off, he advised, "Come to Shrewsbury and enjoy the football match, but if you come here intent on causing problems there will be a robust police operation and you will be arrested and dealt with."

West Mercia's tough policing policy might have been proving effective but it was costly and for local rivals Telford it was simply too expensive. The club baulked at the £11,000 bill the police gave them for Shrewsbury's visit to the Buck's Head in early April. Already facing a police bill of £36,000, the club's directors were described as "terrified" at the latest operation. But the police were unrepentant, saying that while they sympathised with the club's plight they had a "duty" to spend public money in a responsible manner. Local residents and traders were fully behind the police, especially as the FA Trophy game between the two, held only a few weeks before, ended with running battles and riot police in Wellington. Seven people were arrested and considerable damage was caused to the Oddfellows Arms, with windows smashed and the curtains set alight. Five pubs decided to close their doors for the match in case of a repeat. "There is no point making a bit of extra cash over the till if you end up having to pay for damage caused by hooligans," said one landlord.

Shrewsbury's hooligans have found it increasingly difficult to operate due to strong police action and the imposition of football bans. At the time of the 2004 European Championships, 20 Shrewsbury fans were banned from the ground, though this dropped the following year. The EBF also suffer from being closely monitored by the police. A recent attempt to book a coach from some distance outside Shrewsbury on the basis of going to a wedding did little to fool the police, who were waiting for them at their destination.

Shrewsbury lasted one season in the Conference before a play-off victory against Hereford at Stoke's Britannia Stadium saw them back in the Football League, with a potentially explosive opening fixture at home to Lincoln City, a club with the worst hooligan record in the league at that time. However, another big police operation prevented trouble, and Chief Insp Whitelegg must have been delighted to tell the press how successful the operation was and his officers had combined monitoring the location of the Shrewsbury hooligans with tracking a group of 40-50 Lincoln and ensuring the two did not meet. In another move to tighten the screw on the EBF, the police and club announced a new initiative in December 2004 to ban suspected hooligans from the Gay Meadow for five years. Police gave the club a list of 30 names who were then immediately banned, with the promise of more to come. The news came after 16 people were thrown out of the ground and three arrests were made during Shrewsbury's home game with Swansea City.

Life has certainly become more difficult for the EBF and Ryan admits this. "Including club and civil bans, we have over forty lads who were very active no longer allowed to participate," he said. "That's half our firm. The bigger firms have forty banned and it does not affect them that much but it has hit us hard. We still take thirty or forty to most games, although they are mainly the younger lot. I would say it is dormant, not dead."

SOUTHAMPTON

Ground: St Mary's Stadium
Firms: Milton Mob, The Warrens, The Inside Crew, The Ugliest Men
Rivals: Portsmouth, Brighton

"Pompey's trip to Cardiff brought another invasion when their entire mob turned up at the Wagon on the way home," recalled Mike, a 40-year-old, semi-retired Saints hooligan. "Once again at the first sign of resistance they turned and ran, but an hour later five of them walked into the pub dressed in blazers and ordered a drink. The only explanation I can think of was they were so embarrassed with the rest of their mob they decided to try and restore honour. This was truly a suicide mission. They were at the bottom of the pub overlooked by balconies and sadly the hand-to-hand fighting was brief before a hail of missiles reduced them to cowering behind a table as chairs bottles and tables rained down on them from those unable to get into the brawl. By the time the police arrived they were led out of the pub in a sorry state, one of them sobbing but defiant, saying, 'You never done us.'

"Most Saints fans would agree that Pompey have a tight and well-organised hardcore, but after that there is little difference between what both sides can put out for a derby game. For the Pompey games, Saints unite in a rare show of what they could be if they did this more often."

Southampton's hooligans are, to an extent, defined by their ferocious modern rivalry with neighbours Portsmouth. But the history of Saints' firms started in the 1960s with the infamous Milton Mob, headed by the legendary "Dougal". Any bigger mob attempting to "take the Milton" was assured a red-hot welcome.

"As the Sixties turned into the Seventies and Saints found themselves relegated to the Second Division, the older brigade retired and in their place sprung up a younger mob who based themselves at the Warrens pub in the centre of the city," said Mike. "The Warrens soon acquired a decent reputation in the division, and as Saints enjoyed a golden spell, winning the Cup and getting to the quarter-finals of the Cup Winners Cup, both the reputation and the numbers affiliating themselves to the Warrens grew.

"This was a time when firms stopped basing themselves in the home end and moved into the away fans' sections, The Warrens located themselves in the Archer's Road at the Dell, and in pre-segregation days, 2.50pm was the time they arrived and trouble ensued. The Warrens had a hardcore of northern soul devotees and would often combine trips up north with visits to Wigan Casino. They were a tight-knit little firm who still stick together today, although with most being in their fifties they are now retired from the scene."

The FA Cup provided Southampton with a number of big fixtures in the second half of the Seventies. Every year there was at least one major clash involving Saints fans. In early March 1976, there was serious bother at an away cup game against Bradford City. "Aggro on the Kop," ran the headline in the *Telegraph & Argus*. Seventy people were arrested in violence before, during and after the match and several people needed hospital attention, including one Southampton fan who was stabbed in the neck. Some of the worst trouble occurred inside the ground, on the Spion Kop, where most of the away fans were standing. The battles in the surrounding pubs were described by the paper as "scenes like a Hollywood Western".

The following season, Southampton were drawn at Forest, then a team emerging as one of England's premier clubs. Nine thousand Saints made the trip, including 1,000 who arrived late on a football special and so managed to get into the home section of the Trent End. The police had been prepared for trouble and with 250 officers on duty they were able to contain it when it flared. Ten people were charged because of the violence, including two juveniles.

Almost exactly a year on from that day, it was the turn of Bristol Rovers to face the Saints' onslaught. With their side losing 2–0 and only two minutes to go on the clock, several hundred Southampton fans stormed the pitch in an attempt to get the match abandoned. Their move was matched by Rovers' hardcore, who poured out of the Tote End to confront their rivals on the pitch. Play was held up for four minutes as fans exchanged punches and kicks in the centre circle, until the sheer weight of numbers caused Southampton to retreat. Rovers fan Chris Brown recalled the mass ruck in his book *Bovver*.

We watched from our lofty vantage point at the back of the Tote with a mixture of anxiety and anticipation. As with most pitch invasions, it started with a trickle, just a few brave-hearted and ardent protagonists. But the trickle increased steadily: from ten their numbers rose to fifty, then a hundred or so.

The first punches and missiles were thrown as they moved menacingly around the track, clashing with an angry knot of Dave Ashley's North Stand boys to our left. Dave and his mates, as ever, performed admirably, but with more and more Saints fans joining the fray, we knew it was time for us to take action. As one, the Tote End tumbled down the terrace towards the pitch. 'Hello, hello, Tote End Aggro, Tote End Aggro!' bellowed a thousand voices. 'On the pitch! On the pitch! On the pitch!' As if anybody needed to ask where we were heading. We tumbled on to the pitch, brushing aside the outnumbered stewards and coppers and piling straight in to the visiting mob.

The greater Rovers numbers routed the Southampton, sending them back to their terrace to delirious chants of "You'll never take the Tote End." Outside the ground there were running battles all the way back to the railway station, battles which Southampton swear they won. The final toll was seven fans arrested, 89 ejected and six police injured.

A fourth big game for Southampton during this period was a home tie against Millwall. The South Londoners arrived in numbers and attempted to occupy the East Stand terracing until a tough mob of local dockers unceremoniously chased them onto the pitch.

The late Seventies saw a series of clashes against Brighton. The rivalry between the two teams has never reached anywhere near the animosity felt towards Portsmouth but in the absence of any games with their bitter enemies, Brighton were a good second best. The opening game of the 1977 season saw Brighton bring a big mob to Southampton only to be attacked on two sides. The return fixture, held on 2 January 1978, saw 26 people arrested and 56 injured, including 14 who went to hospital. "Before kick-off, a handful from the Warrens scaled the dividing fence and backed off the entire Brighton end before the police turfed them back into the away section," recalled Mike. "After the game this was repeated but with greater numbers, as Brighton turned and fled. We wouldn't have any resistance from them from then on, and this animosity has long been forgotten."

The two teams met again early in the following season. The violence of the previous game had forced the police to plough in reinforcements and for Southampton, a feeling of job well done meant few lads travelled. The game passed off relatively peacefully, as the local paper proudly announced. "Day the bovver boys came a cropper."

POLICE 29, YOBS 0 – That was the convincing scoreline as soccer aggro was kept to a minimum at the weekend. New crowd controls stifled all but minor scuffles as thousands of Saints fans flooded into the Goldstone for a local derby. 'If people were expecting trouble from Southampton fans on a pub crawl during the evening they were pleasantly surprised,' said a police spokesman. 'Most were headed home before opening time.'

The worst trouble happened at the Swan Hotel, Arundel, when Southampton fans went through it like the Wild West. Fists flew, glasses smashed and the visitors clashed first with locals and then with police.

The Warrens pub shut down in 1980 and the firm moved to the Lord Louis. It overlooked the railway station, so any firm that ventured into town was quickly spotted. In the same year, a young mob appeared who were more fashion-conscious, which further alienated them from the older Warrens crew. The new group based themselves across the road from the Louis in the Painted Wagon, and before long they formed the Saints' first casual firm: the Inside Crew. The initial suspicion of the younger element dissipated as the Inside Crew proved themselves in battle, and while the Warren mob continued to drink in the Louis, they would often move across to the Wagon for evening entertainment. However, they were never to form one group, with the pub's two levels creating a natural divide. "For a long time neither element mixed much socially, although this would change," added Mike. A few years later, a second casual firm appeared, the so-called Ugliest Men. "They were a little younger than even the Inside Crew and at first they couldn't even get into pubs due to age," said Mike. "They could truly be called the first 'Youth'."

The Eighties also saw a number of better-known hooligan firms taking liberties in the city. Possibly the worst were Chelsea in 1984. During the game, a sole Chelsea fan climbed into the Southampton end and began fighting, then after the match, several hundred Londoners rampaged back to the station. A local school was attacked, as were several cars and shops.

More significantly, the mid-Eighties saw a revival of the Southampton–Portsmouth rivalry, and though the clubs had not played each other for several years it had lost none of the nastiness that had marred previous encounters. They might not be the biggest clubs in Britain or indeed the biggest cities, but the animosity between Southampton and Portsmouth more than matches any other football derby. "It is a clash of cultures, a melange of misunderstanding and mutual loathing between clubs separated by a short ribbon of motorway but who might as well be inhabiting different planets," one journalist recently wrote. Southampton fans are "Scum" or "Scummers", while Portsmouth fans are "Stakes", and the origins of these names have become part of the urban mythology that surrounds the rivalry.

"The popular theory in Portsmouth about the Scum thing," said one Saints supporter and fanzine editor, "is that it comes from the

Southampton Company of Union Men and that there was a dock strike in Portsmouth which was broken by Southampton dockers. This sounds a great story until you realise that up until about the 1980s, the commercial port in Portsmouth was very, very small. It was virtually a quayside. Portsmouth is mainly a naval port and you can't just employ a hundred hairy-arsed dockers from Southampton to march into a Royal Navy establishment, for security reasons for a start."

Mike is the first to say that the strike-breaking explanation is not only inaccurate but it was in fact the other way round. "When Southampton was embroiled in a dock strike in the early Eighties, Portsmouth, because they weren't a unionised port, accepted the short-sea traffic between here and France. And it never returned. But nobody here called them scum for that."

The Southampton name for Portsmouth is "Skates", a term of abuse more commonly directed at Royal Navy sailors. Once the *Ugly Inside* fanzine ran a competition to find a rebuttal for the name Scummers. "The winner of this competition," said Mike, "was the guy who pointed out that, whatever we called them, nothing would get up their noses more than the term Skate."

It wasn't always like that. In 1939, Portsmouth won the FA Cup. That same day, only 4000 fans turned up for a Southampton game, the rest deciding to listen to the Portsmouth final on the radio. At Southampton's next home game, the trophy was paraded around the pitch, to the applause of the fans.

That gentlemanly behaviour was not to last. By the time the two teams met in 1966, rivalry had turned to outright hatred and tensions were only to get worse. The teams have played surprisingly few games against one another but those have invariably been either highly significant or controversial. The 1966 game at Fratton Park saw Southampton run out 5-0 winners, and if that was not bad enough, soon-to-be relegated Portsmouth had to endure their opponents celebrating promotion. Pompey supporters attacked their rivals inside and outside the stadium and that day set a tone that remains to this day.

In 1976, when the teams next met, Southampton again won, this time with a goal in the final minute. It was eight years before they played again, this time in the FA Cup. A coin which felled Saints defender Mark Dennis resulted in several minutes of injury time, during which his side scored the only goal of the game. More recently, Portsmouth manager Harry Redknapp jumped ship to join their rivals, and despite an FA Cup victory a couple of weeks later, Portsmouth fans must have enjoyed the 4–0 rout which all but consigned the Saints to relegation. Redknapp eventually, of course, moved back again.

In 1969, the teams did play in a pre-season friendly on behalf of a former Southampton player John Siddonen at the Dell. The match was anything but friendly, with fighting before, during and after. Portsmouth fans invaded the Milton Terrace and fighting continued 45 minutes after the final whistle. Later that season, a mob of Portsmouth travelled through to Southampton, who were playing at home against Everton. Again there was widespread trouble as a three-way battle ensued. The Saints got their revenge three seasons later when 100 lads decided to skip their team's match in Birmingham for a go at Portsmouth, who that day were entertaining Aston Villa.

"It would be 1974 before Saints would meet Pompey again competitively, this time at the Dell," remembered Mike. "Pompey came in numbers, got onto the Milton End early before Saints fans arrived and although they failed to take the centre, which would have been a great victory, they held firm, with the help of a twenty-yard gap created by the police. Only good segregation afterwards, including possibly the country's first ever police escort back to the train station for the visitors, prevented mass violence." The trouble could have been a great deal worse had it not been for the 315 Portsmouth fans arrested on arrival at Southampton after their train was wrecked. In the disorder that did occur, there were fourteen arrests and a further sixty ejections, though the game was better remembered for the attack on the referee by a Southampton fan.

The return game was played on Boxing Day, which kept trouble at a minimum, and this was pretty much repeated the following season, with the police again in control. Over 200 officers were on duty for the game and that, combined with heavy rain, dampened the atmosphere. However, with the Saints going 4–0 up, 400 Pompey fans steamed out of the Archers Road end and rampaged through the streets back to the city centre. They smashed shop windows, attacked cars, and in one of the worst incidents two gangs fought with chains. Twenty-two were arrested.

Pompey were relegated and the two sides were not to meet again in the League for another eight years, but that did not signal an end of hostilities. In 1978, a small group of Southampton fans travelled over to Portsmouth to link up with Chelsea, who were in town for a pre-season friendly. Portsmouth fans, meanwhile, had taken to attacking Southampton coaches with paint bombs as they passed through the city on their way to away matches.

The 1983/84 season saw perhaps the most intense period of hatred between the two sets of fans, with the low point coming when Southampton were drawn away at Portsmouth in the fourth round of the

FA Cup. "Saints took a well organised firm to Fratton in a fleet of transit vans," recalled Mike. "We had about 200 had tickets for the Fratton End, but the police operation worked and we were kept apart." Before the game the two rival mobs, both numbering between 250 and 300, clashed in Goldsmith Avenue. During the game, some home fans were caught with wire cutters attempting to cut through the fencing dividing them from the away fans. But the real action came after the match, which the Saints won by a single goal late into injury time. A Portsmouth mob of about 1,000 lads attempted to attack the heavily policed Southampton escort as it left the ground. When that failed, they turned on the police. Fifty-nine people were arrested, another 32 ejected, 60 shop windows smashed and six police vans damaged.

It was not all one-way traffic, as Mike remembered. "The funniest incident happened after the game as a dozen or so Pompey fans looking for stragglers fell upon several Saints Youth, not realising they were the scouts. The look on their face as the entire firm charged was a picture. The most serious incidents, however, took place away from the match. Pompey's 6.57 had a good and deserved reputation and there is no doubt that the hardcore were as mad as they come, however the rest were cannon fodder troops blindly told that Saints had no boys and would run at first sight. They would come unstuck on several occasions because of this.

"The first incident took place on May bank holiday, 1984. Pompey turned up at the fair on Southampton Common and waited for us to show. This was in pre-mobile phone days and it wasn't easy to rustle up a firm quickly, but soon the troops were rallied to confront the 6.57. After a brief skirmish, and despite their hardcore standing, the rest ran and were chased through the Common before being rounded up by the police. A revenge mission by rail was planned but was stopped by the police, who had learned of the plot and turfed everyone off the train.

"The next and possibly biggest clash between the fans happened at Fratton in August 1987, and for once Southampton were united and put together a decent firm which combined all the city," said Mike. "On leaving the station they were confronted by a large mob of 6.57, and both mobs broke through the police and met in the road. When order had been restored, several Pompey fans had been stabbed, not a pleasant happening and not one I condone, however it dispelled the theory in many Pompey fans that Saints didn't have any boys."

There was chaos outside the ground as a huge mob of Pompey tried to break through an equally large police escort to reach the away fans. Two distress flares were fired at police and the trouble continued for almost three hours after the match, resulting in 58 arrests, three-quarters of them Portsmouth fans. For the return fixture, word spread around Portsmouth pubs and estates for several weeks that this was going to be the game where the Scummers were to be put in their place. The game had been brought forward to a midday kick-off and 500 police were on duty, many manning roadblocks in an attempt to stop the violent elements from travelling. The operation appeared to work, as the game passed off relatively peacefully. That might have had something to do with the 103 Portsmouth fans detained at 9.40am. Portsmouth were again relegated that season and much to the relief of the authorities the two sides were not to meet again competitively for several years.

The lack of fixtures proved little more than a minor hindrance for the hardcore of both teams. During the mid-to-late Eighties, there were numerous occasions of the two sides clashing at one another's matches. Southampton ambushed 100 Pompey lads who travelled over to the Dell for a reserve fixture during the 1985-86 season as they left the ground. A short time later that same season, a group of 60 6.57 Crew bought tickets for the home end of a Southampton versus Millwall game. Fighting erupted in the East Stand and soon spread to the Millwall fans. There was further trouble after the match and 28 people were arrested.

A cricket game became another backdrop to violence between the two sets of supporters, according to Mike. "After watching Hampshire win a cup at Lords, a large Lordshill firm arrived at Waterloo to be confronted by a similar number of Pompey. Once again Saints won the battle, aided by the bat used to score the winning run, which had been removed from said batsman during a celebratory pitch invasion."

The third round of the FA Cup in January 1990 saw both teams play in the capital. Southampton were away at Tottenham and Portsmouth were at Crystal Palace. The rival mobs lost no time in arranging a meet in the West End. A fight between 100 lads broke out in a pub in Covent Garden, during which a CS gas canister was let off, 50 glasses smashed and several people hospitalised. When the police finally arrived they found several more gas canisters on other fans. Their arrival merely displaced the trouble and another fight between 60 lads broke out a few streets away. After the game, 200 hooligans clashed in another pre-arranged meeting back in Covent Garden. The Saints are convinced that despite inferior numbers they backed off Portsmouth.

It was the rave scene that dissipated the rivalry as lads from both clubs diverted their attention to music. There was even an unofficial truce between the two, something unimaginable for either side even a couple of years before. An FA Cup match in the Nineties passed off relatively peacefully and it was not until a League Cup game in 2003 that the teams met competitively again. Southampton recall a fight outside the Joiners pub which saw Portsmouth "on their toes". According to Mike, "The story was pretty similar to that at the Wagon in 1984. A sizeable Pompey contingent turn up with most believing the hype that Saints didn't have a firm. Upon finding this not to be the case, the majority ran, with only the hardcore standing. The internet buzzed with excuses from the Pompey side of things but the facts were undeniable." There was widespread disorder after the match involving Portsmouth fans and the police and police described it as the worst they had experienced in the city.

"Most Saints fans would agree that Pompey have a tight and well organised hardcore, but after that there is little difference between what both sides can put out for a derby game," concluded Mike. "For the Pompey games, Saints unite in a rare show of what they could be if they did this more often. It dispelled the theory among many Pompey fans that Saints didn't have any boys."

The Eighties also saw Southampton in action against teams other than Portsmouth. Two who the Saints were to fight on more than one occasion were Nottingham Forest and Everton. The opening day of the 1983 season saw a 20-strong firm of Millbrook lads go into Nottingham for a post-match drink. Their presence was detected and by mid-evening they came across Forest's main mob. After attempting to make a stand in the Market Square against overwhelming numbers, they were forced into a great retreat out of the centre, battling as they went. As this was happening, another group of Forest came across the Millbrook van and their sleeping driver and gave both a going over. Several years later a coachload of Forest, led by their legendary hooligan Paul Scarrott, opted for a drink rather than the game but were attacked from two sides by Southampton. While the main Saints mob stormed the front doors, a small group of no more than six lads who had been sitting quietly inside the pub jumped up and caught the visitors unprepared.

Most Everton hooligans active during the Eighties respect Southampton after four years of battles between the two teams. The first occurred at an FA Cup game at the Dell in 1983. At the final whistle Everton piled onto the pitch and chased a mob of Saints out of the stand to the left of the Archers Road end. The following year brought one of the all-time mass riots when, after the FA Cup semi-final at Highbury, there was fighting on the pitch for over half an hour. There were no fences at Highbury and within seconds Everton were joined by a couple of hundred angry Saints. There were over 100 arrests and 70 injured, including ten who were stabbed or slashed. Everton claim to have come out on top that day, although news footage does initially show Southampton fans crossing the pitch to attack them as they were celebrating victory.

Mike calls it about even: "In the 1984 semi at Highbury, the Saints were firm favourites, sitting second in the League. A last-minute goal in extra time from Everton sparked a mini pitch invasion from Everton's end, and a retaliatory charge from Saints. Order was restored for the remaining minute, then all hell broke loose. Both sides were well up for it and hundreds slugged it out on the pitch as police with dogs and horses attempted to restore order. It was perhaps one of the biggest and last pitched battles of its kind as supporters of both sides beat hell out of each other on the pitch and in the stands."

The following season, Everton went to the Dell for a crucial league game and took thousands. With so many fans locked out, the Everton mob managed to get into the home end, and as the Toffees went two-up, Southampton charged up the terrace, though with little success. When the two sides met again in the FA Cup the following year, few Scousers expected a Southampton mob to travel. To their surprise, a sole Southampton fan dressed in a green flying jacket walked into the main Everton pub and announced that he had a firm outside. Everton steamed out and sure enough there was a tidy mob of Saints waiting. The visitors were finally pushed back and fled in two vans, which if were rented would have seen the hirers lose their deposits, such was their condition.

Southampton fans were to hit the national media after another FA Cup tie, this time against Oxford in 1990. "Gang War," declared the headline in the local paper. Thirty-two fans were arrested in rival mobs after running battles and emergency sirens reverberated across the city as the injured were taken away for treatment and the arrested for questioning.

There has been a revival of sorts of hooliganism at Southampton, as Mike explained. "In the mid-Nineties a lot of older lads found themselves being drawn back into football, although the constraints of the minuscule Dell meant that a firm was hard to form, as most seats were taken by season ticket-holders and it was hard to get others in any more than ones or twos. Despite that, most of the Eighties' set usually met for a drink near the ground in the Bedford pub and its vicinity. As the new millennium dawned and Saints moved to St Mary's, a Youth element appeared. However, there were again problems. A new ground meant that it was difficult to base themselves in one pub before games, and indeed the Youth tended to move around a little to avoid detection by the police. The Inside Crew and Ugliest Men still go to games and although some of them are still active, most prefer the pleasures of drink, drugs and women to attempting to batter someone senseless, unless of course pushed."

The most recent high-profile incident involving Southampton saw a firm of Youth arrange a meet with Charlton at Maze Hill train station. In addition to them being routed by a larger group of greatly experienced lads, the fight was caught on CCTV and dawn raids followed. A school teacher from Stafford, in the West Midlands, was identified as one of their leaders, which was surprising as he was not present on the day. Police tracked internet postings prior to the fight to him and calls to a mobile phone belonging to one of the Charlton leaders. David Walker, a married father, who used the nickname "Three Lions" for his internet postings, was described in court as a "bedroom general" and was jailed for two years and subsequently lost his job at an all-boys school in Birmingham. "He was an upstanding pillar of society and one would not think that he was a mastermind of violence from whom the public needs protection," said his barrister.

However, genuine Saints fans who knew those convicted were scathing about the verdicts, and particularly about the sentences, insisting that several of those convicted were not even hooligans and had been in the wrong place at the wrong time.

"The problem with Saints over the years is that unlike neighbours Portsmouth, who were content to all rally under the 6.57 banner, we have preferred, with the exception of the above crews, to be mainly district-based," said Mike. "At most games, traditional Saints strongholds such as Millbrook, Thornhill, Lordshill, Weston and Harefield have all fielded tidy little mobs, but they have all preferred to stay separate, and to seek action in smaller incidents that are less noticeable to the police and in more hands-on, rather than showpiece, events which look good in the paper but in truth have barely a punch thrown.

"With no-one prepared in the main to unite under one banner, territorial differences remain strong and most prefer to travel with small mobs under their own steam and have little brawls with like-minded members of the opposition rather than go in a larger mob where the chance of arrest or unknown colleagues running is much greater. This means that rarely have they united and thus been able to have had the headlines that our near neighbours Pompey have."

Further reading: *Derby Days*, Dougie and Eddy Brimson (Headline)

SOUTHEND UNITED

Ground: Roots Hall
Firms: Southend Bootboys, Southend Liberal Front, CS Crew
Rivals: Colchester, Leyton Orient and Brighton

Every football thug likes a seaside resort like Southend. It's an opportunity for the lads to make a weekend of it, get away and mix drinking with a rumble. And over the years plenty have done it. West Ham, Millwall, Sheffield Wednesday, Brighton, Lincoln and Leicester – to name just a few – have taken advantage of the cheap bed and breakfasts and long seaside fronts to misbehave. Or at least they have tried. The other thing about seaside resorts is that they can breed the sort of person who resents outsiders "taking the piss". It is not unknown for well-known gangs to come unstuck at towns like Blackpool, Brighton, Cleethorpes and Southend.

Stuart Payne was typical of the youths who would be waiting to greet visiting fans in Southend in the 1970s. He was an eighteen-year-old trainee messenger boy when he was interviewed by David Robins in the landmark hooligan study *We Hate Humans*. He was born within spitting distance of Highbury but after his Nan moved out to Southend he began spending more time there until, one day, he too moved. Fourth Division football was more exciting to the young Londoner, defences were weaker, goals were more plentiful and the policing was more relaxed. He began going to watch Southend when he was thirteen, decked out in his crew cut and boots. Before long he and his mates would wander along the seafront every Saturday to see who was in town, and, if the opportunity arose, attack and rob them.

"Thought I was a right little lad," he told Robins, "thought I was a right hard nut. All I knew at the time was that kids with the boots just sang. Then I realised the ideas like to keep your end and fight off all the others. There was one bloke, Ginger, he had a white butcher's coat with SOUTHEND on the back. Then you started walkin' around after them.

"Everyone thinks the Third Division is just a handful of supporters. You've only got to go and ask a QPR supporter or Chelsea supporter, they'll tell them how many Southend there are. Chelsea come down in the League Cup, they all got a kickin', they all run out, before half-time before even a goal was scored like.

"At Southend no one goes down the other end at the start. At the start everyone's up the Southend North Bank. And you see it, it's packed tight. There's hundreds of kids down there cos there ain't no other football team, right out here. When you see where the others [supporters] are going, then you're climbing over walls and fences to have a go at 'em."

The Southend Bootboys came in all shapes and sizes. Keith Summers is the last person you would associate with soccer violence. Born on the upper deck of a bus outside Hackney General Hospital in 1948, he went on to become the founder of the paper magazine *Musical Traditions*. His family moved out to Southend when he was four and before long he became an avid football supporter. While he was at sixth form, in the mid-Sixties, he became "unofficial organiser" of the supporters' club coaches. "There were a gang of about forty of us who went regularly," he was to recall in *We Hate Humans*, "and a right bunch of hard-nut hooligans we were." The weekend punch-up, home and away, was just another part of the day out at football.

Much of the worst early trouble came, inevitably, from visiting London teams. In the days before cheap international travel, thousands of East Enders would decamp to Southend every weekend and football became just another day out. Southend was also a popular Bank Holiday destination for Mods and later skinheads. It all made for volatile and violent weekends.

In January 1976, Millwall came to town. "Terror trail of soccer wild men", ran the front page headline of the local *Evening Echo*. "Southend was reeling today after another rampage of terror by drink-crazed football vandals and thugs. More than 400 Millwall fans went berserk on the seafront and in the High Street after Southend had drawn 0-0 with the dockland club." One Londoner "butted his head through a window". Twenty-nine fans were arrested and another 19 were ejected from the ground. It was the latest in a long list of incidents in the town. The opening game of the season had seen the visit of Sheffield Wednesday and there were similar scenes of chaos as hundreds ran amok.

Southend has also had a long-running feud with Brighton and Hove Albion, and trouble between the two teams dates back over 30 years. In April 1974, 15 fans were arrested after violence at a game in Essex which saw rival gangs exchanging sticks, bottles and stones during running battles. A train carrying Brighton fans was stopped at Rayleigh after more disorder and another 43 were arrested in Shenfield. The subsequent court hearing opened with a strange question for the defendants.

"What do you chaps say has got to be done to stop what you are doing?" asked the chairman of the magistrates.

The accused, fearing custodial sentences, lost no time in passing their own sentence. "Fines," they replied happily. Fines were what they got and off they went.

In April 1976, the two sets of fans clashed again, with one 17-year-old Southend fan being punched several times and stabbed in the back with a stiletto-type knife. Rival groups clashed during the game and police dogs were needed to separate them. Other Southend fans, not involved in the fighting, were injured when Brighton yobs began lobbing half-bricks over a wall into their stand. "Unhappily Southend and Brighton matches have a history of bad feeling among so-called supporters," said Southend United chairman Bill Rubin. "I wouldn't like to point my finger on any one set of fans for the trouble. It appears that they are both as bad as each other." Two youths were later sentenced to a youth detention centre for the stabbing, while a 15-year-old Brighton girl and another boy were fined £15 for possession of the knife that was used in the stabbing.

Much more recently, in August 2000, eleven fans were arrested after one fight. One Brighton fan was arrested running onto the pitch while the other ten, drawn from both clubs, were caught after rival gangs fought it out on a grass verge outside the ground. The crowd was only a few thousand strong but the fixture drew 100 police officers, substantially more than for many Premiership games.

Another mob that clashed with Southend was the Lincoln Transit Elite. The encounter was apparently in revenge for an incident that happened back in 1969, as one Southend lad recalled. "Back in the Eighties, Southend had a firm that could really put on a show when the chance arose. One such occasion was when Lincoln City paid us a visit. Southend started gathering at about eleven o'clock in the Fisherman's Arms and by midday a very tidy firm of about 100 were in attendance. A few spotters had done a tour but Lincoln were nowhere to be seen, so we made a move for the ground at about two o'clock. We took a firm of about 150 into the South Bank but still there was a no show from the Transit Elite. Just before kick-off, Lincoln made their appearance and things went mental. The OB were completely taken by surprise and for five minutes it was toe to toe before the law got in between us. They split us down the middle and started trying to herd the Southend lads down the terracing and back to North Bank.

"About fifty lads managed to stay put but we were well outnumbered. That was when a firm from Shoebury showed up and just steamed straight into the Lincoln lads. This lot were fucking nutters and gave the OB a pounding if they got in the way. We ran Lincoln right across the South Bank and really got on top before the law set the dogs on us.

"Some nasty bastard had smuggled in a bottle filled with sand and a Lincoln lad got it straight in the side of the head. He went down screaming like a stuck pig with blood pissing out everywhere. The OB finally restored order and moved all the Southend out of the South Bank and back to the North.

"After the game, we made our way to the seafront and mobbed up in The Ship. Lincoln had some balls to show up again but they soon regretted it and took another beating, this time with a load of rockabillies joining in. The law finally ran out of patience and belted a few of our lads, then nicked them. The day was over but we had come out on top and Lincoln had taken a serious hiding. Fair play to them, they came at us twice but the lads on show that day were in no mood to fuck about. It was in revenge for two birds getting a slapping off blokes back in 1969 at Lincoln and although it was more than a few years before we had the chance, the payback was well and truly taken."

In September 1991, locals were involved in vicious fighting with Leicester City fans during a visit by the East Midlands team. Two and a half years later, Southend hosted Derby County on the last day of the season. Police allowed both sets of supporters onto the pitch for post-match celebrations but things got out of hand as away supporters were chased away. A pitched battle continued for almost 90 minutes.

In the early Eighties, the Southend mob was called the Southend Liberal Front but a decade later this was replaced by the CS Crew, a name that remains in use today. The CS Crew got their name after Southend attacked a pub of Cambridge United fans with CS gas in the early Nineties. Today, the mob's core is about 40 lads but in recent years it has been known to bring out 100 for derbies against Colchester United. In recent years there have been a number of clashes between the two clubs, with 15 arrests at a pre-season friendly in 2003 and further trouble at a two-leg cup tie in February 2004.

A small Southend mob has always followed England abroad but by Portugal 2004 five locals were on banning orders as even the smaller clubs' firms were targeted by the courts to prevent disorder abroad. It is a measure that undoubtedly works but it will never eradicate the violence that seems to go hand in hand with seaside resorts and football fans.

Further reading: *We Hate Humans*, David Robins (Penguin)

STOCKPORT COUNTY

Ground: Edgeley Park
Firms: The Hit Squad, The Company, Edgeley Volunteer Force
Rivals: Burnley, Stoke, Wigan, Man City
Police operations: Antelope, Whip, Limousine

It was only a few lines in the *Daily Mirror* that would have been probably overlooked by most of its readers, but it was there. A Stockport County away game at Oldham in 1967 had the potential for trouble. The local police and the clubs both issued warnings to their fans – behave or else. What was striking was that the game was still some way off but a fight had allegedly between arranged by rival fans. Stockport County might not have had the most glamorous and well-known hooligan mob around but they have history of disorder stretching back over 40 years.

"I never set out to be a hooligan," recalled "Charlie" (not his real name), a long-time Stockport hooligan who has since turned his back on the scene. "As a kid I loved football. I played until it went dark, then we'd take the ball under the lamppost until we got moved on for pissing people off. I'd read anything football-related and watching it on TV I was captivated by the sight of the Stretford End or the Kop swaying and bouncing, long before all-seater stadiums.

"Growing up in Stockport in the Sixties we heard tales of County taking good followings to away games. We saw some of these lads around our estates, they were not the cool, well-dressed hoolies of today, they were long-haired scruffs wearing army combat jackets and big boots. They looked pretty awesome to us kids and must have been a scary sight piling off trains in their hundreds. I never went to a game in the Sixties but I know a few old boys and they have told me tales about wrecking town centres, smashing shop windows and rioting. One in particular made me laugh: they started a collection in the summer of 1967 to pay fines for the following season and raised the grand total of £42, which was quite a lot in those days. But after a pre-season friendly at Chesterfield, the fines totalled close to £1,000!

"My brother took me to Edgeley Park on a Friday night in 1970. I was just out of primary school, we were playing Barrow and to me it was amazing. No Barrow fans turned up but there were about fifty Man United fans from Salford on the Pop side, an old-style terrace made up of railway sleepers and cinders at the back. The Reds were surrounded by police who in turn were surrounded by County all screaming to get at each other. United fans were singing, 'Champions of Europe,' and the County fans were singing, 'If it wasn't for the coppers you'd be dead.'

"Barrow scored and the United fans cheered and taunted the County fans. I wasn't watching the game, I was gripped by what was going on on the terraces. County fans increased the pressure on the police lines, then we scored and it went mental. There was a big surge from the back, the police lines split and they were at it, fists flying, dust in the air. Even old blokes threw Bovril at the retreating Reds. The police restored some kind of order until County scored the second, then the outnumbered Reds just ran, with a couple of hundred behind them and the crowd opening up in front of them. Ever since that night I was hooked.

"My first real involvement was when I was fifteen. I'd been to loads of matches, I'd sung the songs and joined the chase when the opposition was on the run, but not really been in at the sharp end. On the night in question we played Blackburn at home in the cup. We were Fourth Division and they were in the Second. They brought hundreds and were gathered behind the goal, while the County fans were on the Pop side singing and making gestures. There was no fencing, but for some reason the two sets just taunted each other. I walked into the middle of them with my younger brother and started to wave to my mates; I don't know why, because I'd never done anything like this before. A big gap opened around us and a bloke in his twenties tried to kick me but I grabbed his leg and he fell over.

"The police were on the scene in no time and as they were dragging us out all I could hear was the crowd singing, 'County aggro, County aggro.' It was brilliant. I was a hero. We sneaked back into the ground and got in amongst the County fans and they were all over us, slapping us on the back, and this old nutter, Cod Eyes, said, 'Well done kids, I'm proud of you.' I just said, 'They're shit,' and I was straight back on the front line leading a charge. They beat us that night, but with twenty minutes of the game left they had all left the ground."

The only team that Charlie remembered that regularly came to Edgeley Park during the 1970s was Bradford City. "They were mental and it was always proper hand-to-hand stuff. They only had small crowds and we got to know them well, we were on first name terms and it became a real grudge match." For some Stockport lads the visit of Bradford was the only appearance they would make all season. "We often came out second best against Bradford, which really got to me because nobody else in that division could touch us. So one summer in the mid-Seventies, when the fixtures came out, I checked straight away the two Bradford fixtures. The away game was a Wednesday night and it was the first away game of the season, so I recruited a few lads to get the train with the sole intention of going in their end.

"On the night, forty-four of us turned up and it was a decent enough little crew. We got into Bradford, had a couple of beers near the station and really got ourselves up for it. It was unbelievably quiet, but then again why would Bradford hang around near the station, no-one ever went there. We entered their end in silence and gathered at the back, I'd never seen so many ugly people, but we were in and as soon as we knew we were all in we let out a big 'County' chant and they panicked and were off in every direction. It didn't take them long to regroup though and they were coming at us from all angles. There were people rolling about all over the floor and boots flying in. It took the police what seemed like an hour to restore some kind of order; it was probably about two minutes. They marched us around the pitch to the other County fans, who were loving it and coming out with things like, 'Why didn't you tell us you were going in, I'd have been with you.' Some of these were people I'd tried to recruit weeks earlier."

Wigan Athletic were another side who regularly brought a mob to Stockport but Charlie insists they "always got done". Undeterred, they would still return. There was also trouble at the games in Wigan, when Stockport's hooligans would travel over by train. The moment they emerged from Wigan station would almost always see trouble.

"One night in particular sticks out in my mind," said Charlie. "After the usual off outside the station, the police rounded everyone up and marched us to the ground. There were about sixty of us. One of the lads said to me, 'We are going to get put in the County end.' We both knew that this meant that the evening's fun was over so we decided to get out of the escort and dived into a pub. A couple of minutes later, three more of ours came in; they'd seen us make our move and didn't want to miss out.

"We had a couple of beers and walked to the ground. The home gates were closed so we were snookered and it looked like we had to go in our end. Then one of the lads noticed a window open, so we were in. Inside it was all steamed up – we had got into the changing rooms! Four of us got in no problem and we were waiting for the fifth when we heard a splash. He had fallen into the bath. We walked out pissing ourselves laughing and went through the players' tunnel. Nobody batted an eyelid, so we turned right and walked into Wigan's end. They knew us so well that we didn't have to say or shout anything. They were all over us. We were just throwing punches but were coming under severe pressure. The police were in and nicked the five of us. They would not accept that my mate was so wet through sweat, but could offer no suggestion of their own. They must have been puzzling over that one for ages."

Stockport met their match during a midweek home game against Portsmouth in 1979. Pompey surprised the home fans by not only making an appearance but by getting right into the heart of the home end. As much as Stockport tried, Portsmouth could not be budged. The following season Stockport turned out in numbers for the visit of Portsmouth and while the southerners were heavily outnumbered they still had a go. Stockport once organised a coach to Portsmouth but offered little resistance when the police herded them into the ground.

Matches against Blackpool were eagerly awaited by Stockport fans but with the seaside town in a higher division they didn't meet until Blackpool dropped through the divisions. Their first trip there during the hooligan era occurred in the early Eighties when a Bank Holiday fixture saw loads of lads make the trip. "Every nutter in Stockport went that day and a few Blackpool lads were stabbed," said Charlie.

"Fans in Bank Holiday terror," was how the Blackpool *Evening Gazette* reported the disorder. "Holidaymakers enjoying a day at the seaside were attacked by vicious football thugs armed with razor sharp Stanley knives," it continued. "A Bank Holiday turned into terror as a gang of Stockport County fans went on the rampage. One man was slashed in the face and needed 22 stitches, another was cut in the back and a schoolboy was stabbed in the arm." Two Stockport fans were arrested and later imprisoned for their part in the trouble, receiving jail terms of four and three years each. Most of their victims were holidaymakers, but it meant that Blackpool's Benny's Mob were now gunning for the Stockport boys.

"After that we thought we'd never see a Blackpool fan at Edgeley, but we were wrong, they always turned up," said Charlie. "One occasion that sticks out in my mind is when they turned up in a removal van. It had been going off through the match as a few of us had got into their end and there were a couple of pitch invasions to get at them. In those days the pubs didn't open until 5.30 after the game, so we used to go into a snooker hall to kill time. As about half a dozen of us approached it, the removal van pulled up. The shutter at the back went up and they were all piling out. We ran to the snooker hall knowing we would have a good forty or fifty in there. Everyone charged out holding snooker cues and throwing balls and Blackpool were off in all directions. The van screeched off leaving its passengers behind. I remember a couple of them pretending to queue for a bus but they were recognised and took a kicking."

Another North West seaside town is also remembered for good times and bad behaviour. "Southport away in the Seventies was always a good day or weekend out," said Charlie. "One occasion that sticks in my mind was the trip home on the train, for some reason a couple of kids were throwing light bulbs out of the window. One bloke said, 'That's not how you wreck a train.' He got up and came back with the toilet seat, which he threw out. Another bloke said, 'No, this is how it's done,' and threw his seat out. This escalated to a ridiculous level where every thing was getting thrown out, then a lad called Sammy appeared with a sledgehammer, shouted, 'Look what I've found,' and started to dismantle the train. Before we had reached Bolton the train was totally stripped, there had even been fires and burning seats thrown out of the windows.

"When the train got into Bolton the platform looked like a police convention, there was an army of them and ninety-two got arrested for that. I think a few of the very young kids had pointed a few out. I went to court when a few of the lads were up and I remember one lad telling the judge he threw a seat out because it was on fire. When the judge asked why he didn't use an extinguisher he said they'd all been thrown out. I just want to add that I played no part in that particular incident."

The mid-Eighties saw Stockport hooligans bring national shame on their club after trouble erupted at their defeat to non-league Caernarfon Town in the first round of the FA Cup. Police made 15 arrests as angry Stockport fans wrecked a town centre pub, invaded the dressing room to confront their team's manager, stormed the pitch, held up play for five minutes and kicked down safety barriers in a bid to reach the home fans. Bricks were thrown into the home end and a smoke bomb was let off. County's chairman Josh Lewis claimed that the guilty fans were not true Stockport supporters. "It was a coach party which left Stockport at 7.30am and when they arrived they just drank all day. The troublemakers were in a terrible state. They didn't go to watch football. Half of them have never been to Edgeley Park – it was a day out for the yobs." The home fans were not blameless and the trouble first erupted when a Welsh fan threw a smoke bomb at County supporters.

Trouble occurred regularly during this decade. An end-of-season match at Doncaster Rovers saw rival yobs fight well into the evening. A policeman was struck by a missile as fans clashed inside the ground and when a group of Stockport fans trying to invade the pitch were pushed back by police, they got into the Doncaster end. There was also trouble at a home match against Chesterfield, when visiting hooligans began smashing up the New Inn pub. A Chesterfield fan later had a bottle smashed into his face and during the match some Stockport fans infiltrated the 1,500-strong away end and trouble broke out again. A total of 45 fans were ejected from the ground as seats were torn out and used as weapons and missiles.

A particularly vicious fight occurred at another home game, this time against Mansfield Town. Two people were taken to hospital with serious facial injuries after their coach was ambushed by locals. The coach was one of four heading away from the ground after the game when it was attacked half a mile further on. "It appeared there had been some taunting going on, with people gesticulating at the Stockport supporters whose team had lost," an officer told the press. "But what followed was just senseless violence."

The mid-Eighties also saw the emergence of a rivalry with Burnley, one that remains today. "Burnley are hated by us, the scarfers and even the pigeons on the roof of the main stand," said another publicity-shy hooligan who we shall call "County Lad". "They are vastly overrated in our eyes and they've never turned us over. We've had many battles with them over the years, the worst one for them being at that Yates's in their town centre when some of theirs were slashed."

Hostilities were resumed in the mid-Nineties when the two clubs met in the promotion play-offs. The two mobs clash in Ireland in 1995 at England's ill-fated friendly international. "We terrified them in Dublin, with them shitting it in the queue asking one of ours to leave it, we're all together, that sort of nonsense," said County Lad. This went unseen by the English press, unlike the large Stockport flag draped over the stand from where the trouble began. "Fans who unfurled a Stockport County flag in the riot stand at Lansdowne Road face a total ban from their Edgeley Park ground," announced a subsequent newspaper report.

The Burnley feud was next reignited in Munich during a World Cup qualifier against Germany. A clash between Man City and Burnley fans soon drew in Stockport, as well as Huddersfield and Bristol City. The home game against Burnley in March 2002 saw rival fans clash after the game. Four months later, there was a nasty fight between the two mobs at a Loyalist parade to celebrate 12 July in Southport. Another fight occurred at a Happy Mondays gig at Manchester's G-Mex arena.

Stockport have had mixed relations with their larger Manchester rivals. During the Seventies there was little evidence of the trouble that was to become common in more recent times, especially against City. "I never went in for this thing about hating your nearest team," said Charlie. "They were from our neck of the woods and we had a lot more in common with them than most. A few of theirs from Stockport would come away with us because they knew it would be a good day out, when we played Friday nights a few of us would go and watch City and we got into a few scrapes. They had a small crew and were pretty tight.

"It changed in 1983. We celebrated our 100 years in the League with a match against City and they filled the Cheadle End with about 1,200, mostly lads. It seemed to be passing peacefully, with a bit of banter chanted back and forth, but when the final whistle went they invaded the pitch and headed straight at us. We piled on and we were about to meet head-on when they turned and ran. They had a few game lads who stayed but they were swiftly dealt with and we pursued them through the terraced streets around Edgeley. Their numbers were reducing all the time, while ours seemed to grow. Rumour has it that some actually switched sides.

"Through the Nineties and up to 2002 we met City in League games on a fairly regular basis. County always went into town early and stayed late, and while they brought big numbers to Edgeley they never really brought a firm. One occasion was before a game at Maine Road. Eight of us decided we would have a drink in town and stay away from any trouble. We went in the Thirsty Scholar pub near Oxford Road station and it was full of City. The place went silent and it looked bleak until a couple of their lads came over who I knew quite well, one had shared a room with me for the whole of the 1990 World Cup in Italy. They were sound. They could have wiped us out but as there were only eight of us decided there was nothing to prove by tuning us in. It was going really well when a couple of lads ran in the pub shouting, 'County are outside now!' I just said to the lads, 'Come on, let's get out.' Just as we did there was a County lad aiming a flare gun at the pub door. He saw us and stood there open-mouthed until the police jumped all over him. Loads of them were on the scene in seconds and led County away. I have a lot of respect for City for not taking the opportunity to at least give us a slap."

Recent years have seen increasing friction between Stockport and Man City, and not confined to match days. Thirteen people were arrested and later imprisoned for a combined 25 years after trouble at the City vs County game at Maine Road in October 2001. A clash occurred in Canal Street in Manchester city centre, and though only a couple of people were arrested there and then, a subsequent police operation, Whip, rounded up 14 more from CCTV footage. They included an equal number of City and County hooligans. "Football gangs jailed for 'wild west' fight," headlined the *Manchester Evening News*.

An earlier police operation had been launched in 1998 after trouble involving Stockport County fans away at Bury. Operation Antelope resulted in 16 people being found guilty, with ten receiving custodial sentences [see BURY in *Hooligans*].

Stockport's on-field improvement saw them reach the second tier of football, and that meant matches against bigger teams such as Birmingham, West Bromwich Albion and Stoke City. "Stoke in particular became a real grudge match and it meant as much to them as it did to us," said Charlie. "We went there with about 300 on the train and it went off before and after the game. About forty of us stayed in Stoke on one occasion for about an hour after the game. They knew we were there and came to our pub at least three times and each time we chased them off.

"We by no means had it all our own way. After one home match, it had been going off all day and we had been split up by the police. Three of us were walking through Stockport centre and we came across about forty of them. To give them credit just three of them came over to us and said they were up for an even-numbers do. We thought, well that's fair enough, it's not like we had a choice anyway. We did okay for about ten seconds when I felt like I'd been hit with a hammer. I staggered back and cleared the blood from my eyes to see that I had. I leant back on a wall only to see my two mates with the shirts ripped off their backs. We'd been done fair and square.

"For Wolves away, around 1990, five of us went on the train and got there at about 11am. We went in a pub near the station and were having a quiet drink when the pub started to fill up with likely-looking lads, but they took no notice of us, so I thought, maybe they're not Wolves. I was in one of the toilet cubicles when I heard a couple of them chatting while they were pissing. One said, "Do you think they'll bring any?" The other replied that he'd been speaking to a Wrexham fan who had said, 'They won't bring many but they'll have a right go.' I was sort of flattered but my fears had also been confirmed and we were in a pub that was gradually filling up with them.

"I had a word with our lads and we decided to move on to the next pub, which was only a few yards away. There were about a dozen in this one, but we had to stay near the station as we had arranged to meet some of the lads, who were due in at about 12.30. As the train was due to arrive, the lads from our pub went in to the one we had been in earlier, which must have been packed by now. I went to the door to see what was happening and our lads had arrived – twelve of them! I waved them over and said, 'Get in here quick, that place is full of them,' as I pointed to the other pub.

"At that point Wolves burst out in to the street. Our lads retreated but we held the door, a few pots were thrown but they surprisingly made no attempt to come in even though they must have numbered around sixty. The police were quickly on the scene but only one car. Wolves disappeared, the police came in the pub and I think they were surprised that there was only seventeen of us. One of them said, 'You'd better split into twos and threes and drift up to the ground unnoticed.' Then they left. I couldn't believe it.

"As soon as they'd gone, Wolves started to drift back until there were at least as many as before outside, but they were spread about trying to look inconspicuous. A big black lad came in, he looked like Frank Bruno but harder, came right over to me and said, 'What are you scared of, it's even numbers, come outside.' I said, 'Do you think I'm fucking stupid?' and threw my beer over him. Well there was no point in trying to appeal to his better nature, he ran out shouting, 'You're fucking dead Stockport, fucking dead.' Within a few seconds they were all right up to the pub and a couple of windows went in. There were a few old blokes playing dominoes and they just moved the table and carried on playing.

"We took advantage of a brief retreat by Wolves and went into the pub they had been in earlier. We had just started to get the beers in when the windows went again. The landlord was straight on the phone to the police. We then decided that the only place we could get a drink in any kind of safety was the station, so we made a run for it. Our peace didn't last long as they came back in even greater numbers and again they decided the window was the preferred way in. The big black lad from earlier picked up a blackboard and threw it through the window.

"There was no discussion, one of our lads known only as Cockney just went right through where the window had been and got into them. I was right behind him and the other fifteen were right behind me. We got the better of the initial scuffle and this unnerved them and bolstered us. We kept going in to them until they were on the run. We ran them for at least seventy yards when the police turned up in force.

"They marched us to the ground and as we got there we decided to go into the pub rather than the ground. Wolves were all following the escort and I couldn't believe the police let us go in but none of them followed us in and we all had a drink. We were absolutely buzzing. When we left the pub it was like *Zulu*, there was loads of them. It went off proper this time and none of them backed off. I was in the thick of it when I was just pulled along by my hair; I'd been nicked by a copper on a horse. I was handed to a couple of others who were on foot and taken to a cell inside the ground. In there were fourteen of the seventeen and maybe six or seven Wolves. If we hadn't got nicked I think we would have been kicked senseless."

One of the few occasions that County's hooligans featured in the national press came after a League Cup game away at Notts Forest, when several police officers needed treatment after being caught by CS gas let off by visiting fans. "We went in two independent coaches," remembered County Lad. "The first lot got into Notts around 5pm for a 7.45 kick off. They had been drinking earlier in Stockport and by the time we got there they had been battling in the town centre. The police had turned up to move them on but they were gassed by some of the County lads who had taken CS gas. As we got near the ground, they were being escorted there and behind the police were about 60 Forest. We got in behind them and all hell broke loose. That one went on for about ten minutes. After the match our coaches were escorted from Nottingham all the way back to Stockport."

Stockport hooligans treated games against bigger hooligan firms as their own cup matches and sometimes this led to their visitors being caught off-guard. This was the case with the visit of Birmingham City in the early Nineties. Thirty people were arrested as Stockport fans ambushed their rivals. "I was just a kid," one Birmingham fan remembered. "My first away game was at Stockport County with the old man. I was only thirteen but was brought up on the stories of the Zulus, my dad was a face down the Blues and in my eyes no one could touch Blues. There was banter between the two sets of fans during the game but I wasn't prepared for what happened after. As Blues came out the away end, Stockport had congregated and were waiting for the Zulus. Suddenly they rushed us and the old man tried to shield me and in the end told me to keep out the way. Those that stood were trapped in the stampede of others behind to get away and this caused the problems, as there were not enough to hold the Stockport lads coming at us. The old man was bloodied and said it was just a bad day at the office and these things happen but not to worry, it was part of football."

Another opportunity came against London giants Spurs. "Tottenham away in the FA Cup deserves a mention," said Charlie. "It was 2002 and we went on the train. I knew we would take a few as we had sold our allocation but I did not expect so many lads, we had at least 200 on the early train. We were in London for 10.30 and were met by fifty who had got the earlier train. Seven of us went for a drink near Euston but the others headed straight off to Tottenham. If you've seen a firm of over 200, it's pretty impressive. There were some minor skirmishes but to be fair Spurs could not have expected it and it was probably too early for them as well.

"When we got down to the ground we went in a pub full of Spurs and they were obviously pissed off, they were coming out with shit like they were Man U or City. This is an old fallback for anyone we've embarrassed. I remember speaking to some Bristol City fans in Glasgow before an England–Scotland game and when I told them who I support one of them said, 'We had it with a load of Man City at your place.' When he described the incident, I told him that I was there and could name nearly everyone else that was there and we were all County.

"By the way, that was England's first real show at Hampden, I'll bet there was only 100 lads there that day, there was J from Stoke, H from Chelsea, Harry from Man U, he won't mind his name being used he's been in enough books, and we had at least twelve of the 100. It went off all day and we walked back to Glasgow Central after the match and they couldn't move us, even though they tried several times and there was thousands of them. England's turnout at Hampden after that got bigger and bigger and it's probably just as well they stopped it."

Mobs have come and gone at Stockport, as Charlie recalled. "We had A Stand, which was made up of lads who used to sit behind away fans in the paddock. The Company, they had calling cards which read, 'We go all the way.' When they got nicked they claimed to be male escorts! Quality Street were mostly from a big council estate in Offerton. They were mental but were nicked far too often to last. Now we have a load of young lads known as the EVF, the Edgeley Volunteer Force. They travel a lot but I've never seen them do much due to better policing nowadays. When I arrived at Hillsborough in 2005 they were all being marched away from the ground before kick-off and were put straight back on the train."

Other mobs have included the Hit Squad, so-called after the local press used the name to describe particularly vicious attacks on rival fans in the Eighties. Their biggest turnout was 100 lads for an away game at Preston North End, though on most occasions their numbers were considerably smaller.

County Lad is a big supporter of the EVF. They are, he says, "without doubt the biggest and most unified" mob Stockport have ever had. "In 2004 they took 120 to Sheffield Wednesday and had another thirty already in Sheffield." But even he admits police action has taken its toll. "They are a well-disciplined mob but got absolutely hammered by GMP [Greater Manchester Police]. I had the cunts sat outside my house and so did others on match day. They're very rarely let off the leash but ask Bournemouth about what they're like when they are."

Stockport have long had close links with Chelsea and have also developed a number of friendships with other mobs in recent years, the best known being with Oldham's Fine Young Casuals. The two mobs met at England games in the early Nineties and soon began attending each other's key fixtures. Through Oldham, Stockport forged a lesser friendship with Shrewsbury Town's EBF and some of their older generation are also friends with Blackpool lads.

Aside from their on-going feud with Burnley, trouble has become less common in recent years. There were disturbances in Blackburn in October 2000 after 30 Stockport fans, returning from a match in Burnley, stopped off for a drink. They didn't leave until 11pm and as they arrived at the train station there were clashes with other rail passengers. Four Stockport fans were arrested.

A few months later, 900 Stockport fans travelled down to London for an FA Cup game against Spurs. Among this group was a large hooligan element, swelled by a contingent from Oldham. Back at Euston Station after the game, a fight broke out amongst the Stockport hooligans themselves, with one man receiving facial injuries. "During the trip the escorting police were subjected to threats and abuse and a passenger told the officers that the fans were planning to attack the travelling escort," noted a subsequent police report. "Only the presence of police officers on the platform at Milton Keynes subdued the group."

More recently, a pre-season match against Leek Town saw rival Stockport and Stoke City hooligans clash and five people were arrested in what police said was a "planned confrontation". Pre-match intelligence alerted the police to potential trouble and officers from Greater Manchester Police and Staffordshire Police were on hand for the game. The match itself passed off without incident but as the first half was in full swing up to 30 men clashed in the town centre. "There was one set of fans at one end of Mill Street and another at the other end," the town's former mayor told the press. "As the drink went down, the more trouble there was. The police helicopter was also deployed, which was quite alarming for the ordinary public of Leek, who are not used to seeing anything like that."

With these few incidents aside, trouble is uncommon at Edgeley Park. The police seem firmly in control and many of the main faces are on bans. "There's very little chance of anything happening involving groups bigger than ten or so now," said Charlie. Not that he's complaining. "Times have changed and I actually like it better now, it's great to see so many kids at matches. We were products of our time and if you wanted to travel with your team in the Seventies there was no segregation of fans, it was safety in numbers and I learnt to enjoy it, but I'm glad it's all over."

A blow to both Stockport's pride and to their mob came when the increasingly ubiquitous CCTV cameras claimed a number of scalps after a fight with Man City. According to the *Manchester Evening News*:

On Saturday, October 15, 2005 Stockport County had played away at Shrewsbury Town Football Club. At 6.30pm that evening a number of men had gathered in Branningans Metro, Grand Central, in Stockport for a drink. The group became increasingly rowdy, chanting and singing Manchester City football songs.

Staff then noticed that some of the men began to put on baseball caps and use scarves to conceal their faces. Some of the group began using their mobile phones while walking in and out of the bar and looking through the windows.

The men then ran towards the entrance where they confronted a group of Stockport County fans and a fight broke out during which ashtrays, bins, bottles and glasses were thrown. The County fans then retreated towards the A6, chased by the City group. The fight resumed beside the main road in front of members of the public. Police were alerted but when officers arrived at the scene, the group dispersed and the men ran off.

Twelve people, from Manchester, Stockport and Salford, were later sentenced at Minshull Street Crown Court, Manchester, after pleading guilty to violent disorder. They included a well-known Category C hooligan, Neil Holland, aged 40, from Offerton, who was jailed for four years.

STOKE CITY

Ground: Britannia Stadium, formerly Victoria Ground
Firms: Naughty Forty, Under-5s,
Rivals: Man City

The tension was clear on the faces of those involved in Oldham's largest ever football operation. While the police officers in charge were confident they could maintain order, with Stoke City's hooligans anything was possible. The fax machine clattered. New intelligence was arriving all the time, including the latest on the travel plans of an expected 400 Stoke thugs. The police refused to reveal how many officers they had at their disposal, but the word around the force was several hundred, with over 1,000 in reserve across Greater Manchester. The police and the Home Office, which was liaising closely with them, were determined not to have a repeat of the trouble that had marred Stoke's visit to Oldham almost a year before, when over 400 Stoke hooligans, supported by Oldham's Fine Young Casuals, ran through a predominantly Asian area attacking shops and homes. That proved to be a major contributing factor to the tit-for-tat racial violence that eventually led to the worst race riots for 30 years. The Home Office had demanded that this could not happen again. Oldham, and indeed Britain, could not cope.

The latest intelligence briefing was accompanied by a mugshot of one man, a man who the officer in charge of the operation acknowledged was their main target. Locate and contain him, the officer said, and the police would go a long way to maintaining order. The man in question was Mark Chester, aka "Jasper", who police believed was the leader of Stoke's so-called Naughty Forty. The faxed intelligence briefing contained his expected movements the night before the match and his intended travel plans on the day. The police were keeping a close watch.

Stoke City supporters have long had a reputation for football violence. In 1967 the *Sun* newspaper reported that Stoke fans, many of whom worked in the region's potteries, went to matches with small lumps of clay in their pockets which were then hurled into the ranks of away supporters. Throughout the early Seventies, Stoke clashed with Manchester United's Red Army on numerous occasions, ran amok in towns like Blackpool and Mansfield and were themselves overrun by Leeds United. However, it was only in the Eighties that Stoke began to earn a name as an organised gang, and not until the Nineties, when they were taking mobs of over 700 to Wigan and 600 at home to Cardiff, that the Naughty Forty and their younger mob, the Under-5s, reached the pinnacle of English hooliganism.

Given Mark Chester's role in hooliganism at Stoke City over the years, it seemed appropriate to ask him to contribute to this book. Here is his story of hooliganism at Stoke City.

"The A-to-Z of football hooligan firms in Great Britain," Andy Nicholls explained down the phone. And so he began to tell me, in his effervescent manner, what he was writing and exactly what it was that he wanted.

I sat listening to a man that I have never met before, an Everton lad I should by rights have instantly disliked because of past history. Nevertheless my answer to his request was always going to be yes. That's just the way it is, or at least, that's how it is these days.

I liked the fact that he'd chosen not to just pinch the odd bit of info from my own semi-autobiography *Naughty*. It showed me that he and Nick Lowles, although an unlikely partnership, were intent on building a fresh, fact-packed publication, one that in many minds should have been written years ago.

"Happy days then, fella!" And with that Andy was gone, on a promise of coming to see me at my home the following week. I knew immediately that he knew I would not let him down and would adhere to my promise of help. Just call it a football Thing. You know when you know, end of.

So what do you want to know then? How game Stoke's firm is, or was? That police intelligence claimed Stoke's Naughty Forty to be the most organised and violently active gang throughout the UK in the Nineties? Or that even to this day, despite ID card schemes implemented by the club, widespread banning orders from the courts, and mass over-policing of games, there is a tight hardcore of committed men still fiercely dedicated to defending their distinguished and unblemished reputation, regardless of the consequences?

The city of Stoke-on-Trent, or the Five Towns, as it is sometimes referred to, is in the industrial North West of England, sandwiched between Liverpool, Manchester and Birmingham. Its people hold a strong working class identity, with a unique accent, humour and self-belief. People who hail from Stoke are proud of it.

In 2004, a national quality-of-life survey placed the Potteries last in a list of 376 boroughs across the UK. Labelled a black hole of depravity and social squalor, the city was referred to as the worst place in the country to live. That may be the case, but you can't blame people's surroundings for the fact that a large number of its inhabitants enjoy having a fight at football matches. Stoke might be a black hole now, but during the Twentieth Century its industry supported most of the local population. Many young men had a few bob to go and support their team on a Saturday afternoon, and if the need should arise, have a bloody good punch-up as well. I certainly can't remember it being any different; Stokies just love to fight. As for being labelled the "Arse End of Nowhere" by Experian [who conducted the survey], the lads down the match are actually quite proud of it. Make what you like of that mentality.

I grew up on the Seventies terraces of the Boothen End at the old Victoria Ground. Glam rock was in and fashions evolved mostly around music, Northern Soul being a particular favourite of the Stoke hooligans at that time. Oxford bags, denim jackets and Dr Marten boots were obligatory and most hoolies wore scarves tied round both wrists and lapel badges showing off their allegiance to Stoke City. This, in the eyes of the world, was the stereotypical football lout, and those were the people I chose to watch, follow and eventually emulate. Football hooligans became my heroes and I wanted to be one of them.

From the late Sixties to the mid-Seventies Stoke City hooligans made a mark for themselves across the country as being a tough bunch of game lads who would give you a good go up at their place, but rarely travelled well in numbers. The graveyard in Stoke town centre became infamous as an ambush point, and many big names came unstuck while making their way past it, either towards the ground or after the game heading back to the train station. I can stand testimony to this, as countless times as a boy I witnessed the routing of a Midlands or London firm who had seen Stoke as a great day out and a guaranteed brawl.

Maybe Stoke did seem like a crew that didn't travel in numbers, but to us kids it seemed that at every away game a big gap would open up sooner or later inside the home end and the windmilling would start. This was the fuel that fed the fire for our own rise to notoriety. Although we did not know each other at the time, each of those kids that became the Naughty Forty were being educated individually and collectively by the long-haired bootboys of the Boothen End.

Nobody I know can remember there ever being a gang name for the Stoke hooligans of the formative years. Perhaps because of the geographical layout of the city, people tended to stay in their own areas and travel into Stoke just for the games, defend the club and town and then head back to whichever of the five towns they came from. Certain pubs in Stoke town centre became focal points before games: the Star, the Phoenix and the Gordon, and right outside the away end of the old Victoria Ground, the Victoria pub itself. Each would be full to the brim of fighters on match day, though no collective gang name existed.

Too young to enter any of the hostelries, I and scores of other youngsters would sit on brick walls as voyeurs and take in the spectacle. Remembering the faces of other youngsters, if not striking up conversations, laid foundations for our own gangs a decade or so in the future. In this culture, amongst your peers, to later be able to reminisce about days gone by and be able to prove that you were there or thereabouts from such a young age gave you substance. You were always glad of someone else's confirmation of events, and he was just as glad of your remembrance of him. That kind of talk brought people closer together, like they had shared a common bond of fear and achievement. It is called "male bonding" and being a football hooligan is rife with it. It is without doubt a big part of the passion of our culture.

Many names came to the forefront in the bootboy era. The giant Mark Bentley, an ex-guardsman who many times held the weight of Stoke's hostilities, Tony the Axeman and his fighting partner Minstrel from the town of Leek, Tyrone, a young, lithe black lad who was always on the front line, and Coco, a tall, long-haired, bearded fellow, who would always wear a three-quarter-length brown leather "Lee Van Cleef" trenchcoat, with fingerless gloves to boot, were just a few of the characters I admired, and later befriended.

The late Seventies and early Eighties saw a new volatile trend, not just in the music but in the fashions worn down the match. Stoke became "Punk on Trent" and the young voyeurs were coming of age. The Boothen Paddock now became the new focal point of the Victoria Ground. Gradually from within the restraints of that small piece of fenced-in terracing, the foundations for Stoke's first organised mob were firmly set in blood and grit. The cries from the Boothen End of, "Paddock, paddock, sort 'em out," never rang truer as the likes of Wolves, Arsenal and West Ham all added to their own honours list from inside its confines. The Wolves row of '81 was a particular classic that is still talked about to this day. Those that took part in the defence of the Paddock that afternoon fought a 30-on-30 battle with no police intervention for several minutes, until dogs were used to split up the warring factions. Neither side gave an inch, not one inch.

Amongst those young men that fought so valiantly that day against the Wolves was a character who was about to change the face of hooliganism at Stoke City forever. Like him or loathe him, Wilson was instrumental in the forming of Stoke's first organised mob. The son of a publican, he had a strong "neck end" upbringing – meaning he came from the depths of one of the roughest parts of the city. Pub life saw him grow into a shrewd chancer, rarely shunning the opportunity to earn a few quid.

He started running coaches from his old man's pub, the Glebe, in 1984. At that time, the 20-year-old Wilson was a mould breaker at a local pottery factory, earning the princely sum of £36 a week. Living above the pub, his wages were divided between a tenner for his board, a tenner on HP for his scooter, and £10 a week towards his fine for fighting on a train with some Liverpool fans. Running coaches for Wilson was a great sideline which could earn him up to £400 some weeks. Don't get me wrong – and I am sure he would have you know – first and foremost Wilson was a committed hooligan, and a good one at that. That's how firms are made up, of all different characters from all different backgrounds.

He was relentless in his quest to fill his coaches, earn a few bob, or cement the new firm – whichever way you want to look at it. In no time at all, prominent faces from all over the city, faces that would normally fight each other had there been no suitable outside opposition on the day, were for the first time ever sat side by side. In the beginning it was acknowledgement by a nod and a wink. We all knew from childhood memory that each would make a stand of it. Only now, once together, did the personality clashes take place and the lifelong bonding take shape.

Through Wilson our numbers averaged 100 diehards, with potential to reaching over 300 for the big away fixtures. Now Stoke were ready with an identity. We were called the "Glebe" and the rest was up to us. Travelling on the Glebe left you no option at all: you were either there to fight or you could go and travel on the supporters' club coaches. It was as simple as that, as many first-timers found out.

It was never going to happen overnight. The 1984 season saw the gang take on some formidable opponents. Birmingham City away on a Tuesday night saw two coaches crammed with 75 lads each arrive in the Second City late. The game had already started as Wilson directed the slightly hesitant mob towards the turnstiles of the Tilton Road End, where Birmingham's large hooligan element would be congregated. This was a mob that Stoke had struggled with in the early Eighties, even at home. Getting in amongst them would be character-building if nothing else. Wilson knew this and half thought the Brummies wouldn't expect anyone to show up, especially not in the middle of their own end.

Instructed to pay in through the turnstiles and wait quietly on the inside, 100 of the lads did so, several of the more hesitant younger members being pushed through and paid for by a determined Wilson himself. Once inside, many of the lads would admit that they were, for want of a better phrase, shitting themselves. Adrenalin then takes over you immediately, as well as peer pressure and the will to survive the precarious situation that you have placed yourself in. Going over that first drop on the Big One at Blackpool Pleasure Beach for the first time comes nowhere near this one; at least you're strapped in and no one is going to kick your fucking head in on that.

With no noise, the Stoke mob, stomachs in mouths, headed down the gangway in unison and marched straight into the middle of Birmingham's huge mob. Halfway down the steps they were spotted and a Brummie roar went up, echoing under the corrugated roof. Tightly stood together in the dimly lit gangway, 30-odd long and three deep, the Glebe lads were attacked viciously from all sides. All nerves were now gone, it was survival time. Nobody, not even Wilson, thought for one minute that they would take the Tilton End. It was a show, a game effort that was coming more on top by the second. Every man stood exchanging blows, all trying their best to stay clear of an older white bloke wielding a bowie knife and doing a good job of making a nervous situation all the more fraught.

The police intervened and the weight of the crowd subsided a little as the Stoke lads were directed over the fences and onto the asphalt track alongside the pitch. In the glare of the floodlights and in full view of the rest of the ground, the mightily relieved and also jubilant Stoke mob counted their numbers and hugged each other as they were escorted around the pitch and into the Railway End, amongst the warmth of the 2,000 travelling Stoke fans who were singing the time-honoured number for such occasions: "We're proud of you, we're Proud!"

And that's how the 1984 season continued, week in, week out, home or away, the excitement of the fighting and the bonding gaining momentum. Prominent faces began to emerge: Mark "Miffer" Smith, a bullneck of a character who led the charge more often than not, Cossack, Brasso and Mad Ant Walford, to name but a few. Being in the old First Division gave this new coalition a perfect platform from which to learn and ply their "trade". Taking on the likes of Everton, Man Utd, Leeds and other hugely supported clubs with already established firms was a baptism of fire.

On 15 December 1984 came the biggest test to date. An away day in London saw us heading to Stamford Bridge and the chance to make a name for ourselves against the much feared Chelsea Headhunters. Surprisingly for all of us, the expected huge turnout for this chance of infamy was no bigger than a single 56-seater coach. Most of the occupants were in their late teens or very early twenties. The crew that day lacked experience, but not balls, and so at eight o'clock that morning we departed the Glebe and headed south for the capital.

Ever the earner, Wilson had stacked over 400 cans of out-of-date beer at the front of the coach. Those, combined with dozens of bottles of spirits and bags of amphetamine sulphate, had the coach rocking by the time we had passed Birmingham. Talk was of, "Let's just get to Chelsea and give it our best shot," at least just by turning up and having a go. We would surely gain some respect, if nothing else.

By Northamptonshire everyone was dying for a piss. We pulled onto Rothersthorpe Services. Two stewards pulled us to one side as we entered the slip road. They were concerned that we had not made a prior booking to use the services, and told Terry, our driver, that he would just have to drive on through and rejoin the motorway. Wilson informed the stewards that we only intended to use the lavatories and nobody wanted to go into the cafeteria. They agreed to let us use the toilet which was situated next to the petrol pumps on the way out.

Thankful of a piss-stop the lads uncrossed their legs and stood up in the aisle preparing to jump off as Terry headed past the main service buildings towards the garage forecourt.

, "Eh ar, lads, who the fuck are these?"

Every one of us turned towards a double-decker coach. Across the tinted windows in Christmas spray were the words "Mayne Line", and standing around the coach was a tasty firm of Man City's Mayne Line crew, all of them older than us.

What followed was an unprecedented football riot. The Mancs brought it to us immediately, clapping their hands and laughing as Terry, oblivious to the situation, slowly drove on towards the toilets. Shouts could be heard from within our coach of, "Fuck 'em let's get to Chelsea!" while others shouted, "Let's do the fuckin' scruffs!"

Cossack jumped out of the moving vehicle through the fire exit and ran under the canopy of the garage, laughing and clapping his hands back at the advancing Mancs. Everyone else did the same and the two sides clashed in a brutal encounter. Order was eventually restored after 20 minutes. Two Jaguar patrol cars had obviously called for assistance from nearby Northampton, and spent their time driving in and reversing through the disorder in a vain attempt to persuade both sides to give up the fight. Which neither did. Over £15,000-worth of damage was inflicted on the service station, 97 people were arrested and several ended up in casualty. Brasso received knife wounds to his back. Our coach was so badly damaged that we spent nine hours in custody in two holding cells until a replacement arrived from Stoke to take us all back home.

The Battle of Rothersthorpe for us as a young, up-and-coming firm, sorted out the men from the boys. Structure was beginning to appear, and several personalities were starting to lead the way. All any of us really wanted now was a suitable name instead of the "Flying Squad", a temporary headline adopted by some of the lads from the north end of the city on that very day. Twelve months down the line, a name would find us, but we didn't know that yet.

To round off that fateful December afternoon in Northamptonshire, well, we all thoroughly enjoyed ourselves, and the Battle of Rothersthorpe went straight in at number nine in our all-time top ten rows of the Eighties. Nevertheless, ask any of the lads involved that day and they will tell you straight: we were gutted we didn't have it with the Chelsea Headhunters instead. That for us would have been a proper result.

September 1985, and we were heading for the south coast to Fratton Park, and hopefully a ding-dong with the 6.57 Crew. Portsmouth were another firm that were well established, and there was a slight element of uncertainty amongst the lads for this one, again heightening the excitement. Our numbers at this stage in our history had slightly declined to around 40-60 game lads. We went pretty much everywhere with those numbers, whether it was just a slight hop over the Pennines or a full on slog down to Hampshire.

Three Transit vans were used for this one. We wanted to hit Pompey as early in the day as possible and try to gain the psychological advantage before they showed up with their expected big numbers. Two of the Transits left Stoke at tea-time on the Friday evening and headed to Oxford for a drink with Bamber Gascoigne and his firm, while the other van intended to make their departure after the nightclubs had thrown them out. After a vicious brawl on a petrol forecourt with some local black lads, the third van carrying several wounded members headed south in the early hours.

By 8am, all three vans had made the destination and sat alongside HMS *Victory*, pondering what to do for the next three hours until the pubs opened. Some of the wounded from the previous night's encounter found a landlord outside his pub bottling up and asked if they could wash up in his toilets. He agreed to let us all in his back bar, and as long as we remained respectful he would serve us beer as well. Result! Eight-thirty and we were back on the piss. It didn't get much better than this.

After four hours of heavy morning drinking, we were all slightly disorientated. The suggestion was made that now was a good time to get on the streets and try and take the Fratton Arms, Pompey's main boozer opposite the ground. The vans headed towards the ground and pulled alongside a park nearby. From there the passengers went on foot, leaving the drivers to find a strategically safe place to park the vans out of harm's way. Call us naïve, and we probably were at the time, but we actually thought that an assault on Portsmouth's pub at midday was good timing, at least to get in it and wait – or if it was full, attack it and see what happened.

It was a true autumn day, the sun was out but there was still a slight chill in the air. We upped the pace and psyched each other up on our approach to the Fratton Arms. Adrenalin was pumping so badly it was hurting as we panned out of single file and filled the road. Breaking into a slight jog, we were yards away. This was it now, no turning back. A slight roar breached our buttoned lips as excitement got the better again.

BANG! The mood fell devastatingly flat, and embarrassment curtailed the enthusiasm of our attack. The Fratton Arms up close looked barely open, except for the odd barmaid dusting the pumps. To make things even worse, several dormant Hampshire Police vans, full to the brim with coffee-sipping officers, were parked around the corner. All of us bar the three van drivers were searched and put into the away end terracing. A huge anticlimax, and with over two and a half hours to go to the kick off. All we hoped was that Pompey didn't turn up in half an hour and actually think that we'd showed up early and had gone straight into the ground because we were shitting ourselves.

Talk inside the ground was, "Do you think that they are not out early because they don't rate us?" and, "Bet they would have been out if they were playing fuckin' Millwall instead." Basically we all had a bit of a moan as we sobered up. New plans were drawn. As far as any of us were concerned, we hadn't travelled all that way through the night for nothing. If after the game we were escorted out of Portsmouth by the police, the first chance we got we would turn around and find another route back into the city centre and make our presence felt there instead. We all felt hearty once again.

The game ended with another dismal defeat and we left the ground with the rest of the Stoke following under a heavy police presence. It wasn't looking good. During the game the police had found our vans and drivers and forced them to park up with the rest of the Stoke City supporters' coaches. As soon as we saw where they were parked, it deflated us once again. The day was looking like a non-event on the hooligan front, but the whisper went round: "Just do as we're told, they won't think that we're coming back in and might only escort us out as far as the city limits."

The three vans were filled and we all sat quietly waiting for the coaches in front to move off. The streets were busy as jubilant Pompey fans headed off in all directions, with no sign of a hooligan attack from them. The police looked content with the situation, and still we sat quietly and waited.

"Right lads, when you're ready!"

The fat sergeant with puffy red cheeks appeared in front of our windscreen and beckoned us on.

"Come on Tez, let's fucking go."

Nobody could believe that the sergeant was actually telling us to go while the supporters' coaches remained parked. The mood inside the vans was electric, and we must have looked like a firm of meerkats peering through the windows in disbelief and excitement that the hunt was back on. All of a sudden the day was back in our own hands again and there were still plenty of Pompey on the streets.

Pulling away, we drove slowly in heavy traffic. The sun was warm now and the vans were overheating inside with the sheer desire to cause mayhem – as long as it was with the right people. Signals were being passed from van to van. Some wanted to jump out and walk, such was their impatience. The order was to "keep it tight" and let it happen. It wasn't too long before it did.

With no police anywhere near us, we moved slowly away from Fratton Park football ground. To our right was a huge, open playing field and walking across that field we spied 30 or so of Pompey's boys. Now it was on. None of the Pompey were aware that they were being stalked by three vanloads of blood-curdling loons who up until now had smelt nothing but their own stale farts all day.

The waiting crucified us. Again, signals were sent through the vans to wait, stay put, let them come out of the park in front of us so we could get behind them. It was a gamble to let them come out of the park, because if they had spotted us first we were sitting ducks. If we jumped out of the vans at that moment we would have had to scale a stone wall with a privet hedge, losing the element of surprise and giving them the momentum. They had to come out of the park and not spot us at all for the ambush to succeed.

It worked a treat and all the effing and blinding under our breaths turned into a huge roar as we charged out of the vans and steamed into the rear end of Portsmouth's unsuspecting mob. We had the element of surprise and the upper hand with numbers, and Pompey hit a tactical retreat of 30 or so yards before turning and standing to. Running at full pelt, Stoke piled into the Portsmouth lads with flying kicks and punches, some wielding telescopic coshes. Standing fast, they traded with us blow for blow, the roar of a football row filling the surrounding area. Every man on both sides was in his element; this was what both parties had been wanting all day.

The brawl lasted no more than 90 seconds. Had we all kept our mouths shut and not alerted the police, we may have got another couple of minutes. But charging amongst us with horses and dogs, the Hampshire Police split the warring groups apart, Pompey disappearing over the wall back into the park, us piling back into the vans. It was over, and the smashing of our windscreens by police truncheons brought the hostilities to an abrupt end.

The second unbelievable thing happened in the space of minutes. We feared arrest and a night in the cells, until the fat sargeant appeared once again, gave us all a bollocking and told us to fuck off back up north.

"Of course we will sarge, thank you very much for your hospitality."

The journey home was a cold one with no windows, but none of us cared. The vans were full of conversations about what we'd seen or done. Podge, a 17-year-old, sat alongside me in the front seat. He chuckled as he contemplated the afternoon's events.

"That was a naughty little row that, J. How many of us were there in that street?"

"Forty of us lot," replied Speg from somewhere in the back.

Podge leaned back in his seat, and rubbing his forehead again with a sigh, he replied, "Yeah, the Naughty Forty."

And that was it. Not any of the mass prolonged brawls seen against the likes of Man City, Villa or Wolves, just a brief street encounter with a small number of the Portsmouth 6.57 Crew; it was just a naughty little affair that got us our new name. Those lads that fought together that day, are the original and only true members of Stoke's Naughty Forty.

It's one thing having a name, but a reputation to go with it is another thing altogether. We set out to make history and to take as many scalps as we could along the way. No name or reputation fazed us, not one. To us, our tight knit little firm, which we pronounced "en-four-oh" (N40), was invincible. We based our moral code on trust, love and understanding. The hard knocks to follow brought mutual respect. The next two decades brought us our reputation.

The season 1986/87 saw a new generation of youngsters taking up the baton. Just as we youngsters had followed the Boothen Bootboys up and down the blood-stained streets of Stoke-on-Trent, the aftermath of our exploits were now being mopped up by a small group of fresh-faced 15-year-olds. Calling themselves UFAS – "Under-Five Action Service" – they numbered around 30 and came from different parts of Stoke, and an estate in the north of the town of Stafford. Their appearance at the match at first was shunned by some of the older lads, especially Wilson. We had not been granted acceptance as youngsters ourselves, in fact many of the older heads saw us as a nuisance, in our designer clothes and cocksure manner. Seeing things differently, however, I welcomed the new recruits. To me, sooner or later they would come up against formidable opposition and heaven forbid they might get run or even done. That could not happen, as that would tarnish Stoke's overall reputation.

As much as Wilson pulled his face, I had the last say and the Under-5s were brought in close and nurtured in the correct manner. They became an integral part of the firm while always keeping their own identity, and proved to be a tough bunch of nasty little bastards that played their role well. But they always respected where their position in the firm lay.

By the late Eighties most of us were completely fucked on drugs. Our numbers had been bolstered by the arrival of the Under-5s and during the drug years of Ecstasy and acid house we became even tighter. The black market and rave scene brought new agendas and different fronts to defend and fight on. The early Nineties saw a decline nationally in football-related disorder. It was still going on but less frequently, according to government statistics. Acid house and rave were being pointed out as the main cause of the lull.

Funny that, because as the rest of the nation stood in circus tents in the middle of fields hugging and kissing each other and laughing about the mad old days when the hoolies used to kick fuck out of each other, we took the same drugs as the rest but became more isolated and violent with it. Suspicious of anything and everything, the darkest days of our history began. The decline of Stoke City Football Club itself saw us drop into the lower divisions, where we languished for most of the Nineties.

It was a new platform to assert ourselves from. We didn't bully our way around the smaller grounds, although our numbers were significantly bigger than most. A day out in the capital at say Orient or Brentford to us would mean an early evening trip down the Old Kent Road or the Kings Road looking for Millwall or Chelsea on their return from some fixture out of town. We never left anywhere without leaving our mark, even if we had to wait until the small hours to do so.

Our numbers had begun to increase significantly. Making the news headlines week in, week out drew attention to the N40 and by the mid-Nineties, with the resurgence of the club, we rarely travelled away with anything less than 3-400 boys of all ages. It wasn't quite as simple as it sounds. We didn't just say all of a sudden, "Eh ar lads, anybody that wants to join us is welcome to come along and get stuck in." Everybody was aware that police undercover operations were a possibility, and becoming a bona fide member was probably more difficult now than it had ever been. Nobody was accepted unless they had been introduced via a known and trusted source. It was as simple as that. Any new member would also be placed on probation. They would be watched, and listened to, scrutinised until they were either told to fuck off or accepted as a member. They weren't told of this decision, they eventually just knew it. It wasn't hard: total respect for others, never kick off with anybody from outside of the culture, and 100 per cent love and affection for Stoke City FC. Oh yeah, and never put your missus before the lads.

I used to think – as did many of the others – that I was probably the most addicted of all of us to the culture. From the moment I woke up until the moment I closed my eyes, I would think of nothing else, even dreaming of football violence and the lads. It's fair to say that I was married to the firm.

From the age of the Internet and mobile phone hoolies came another young trailblazer who I am not going to name. Fed on our own exploits, he was but a kid when he witnessed the torching of the Tropics pub in South London, a haunt of the Millwall Bushwhackers. To him, as with many of the others, this was Stoke's Naughty Forty at their best. He wanted nothing more than to be an active member of what he saw as a way of life, not just a phase he was going through.

For simplicity we will give the boy a pseudonym. Coming from a middle class area of North Staffordshire, "Dexter" pulled together a tight mob of around 50 young men, all in their late teens and early twenties. He had a certain charm and charisma, and although vertically challenged, his immaculate turnout and meticulous attention for detail placed him head and shoulders above the rest of a new generation of Stoke hooligans. It wasn't long before he became a valid member of the N40 hierarchy.

Being part of an organised football mob had always had its price to pay. The Government clampdown of the late Nineties gave police new powers to stop and search, and you could be arrested on suspicion of intent without even throwing a punch. It was becoming more and more difficult for any of the lads to get their football fixes. Dexter took to the role naturally, and with a mobile phone full of covert numbers, he remained in touch with fellow hooligans the length and breadth of the country. To beat the police, the firms now had to co-operate with each other, act as lookouts for each other and plan their meetings rather than hunt each other down. For many of the old school, Dexter became a bit of a blessing, taking the weight of organisation away from them and pulling in good numbers of young nutters who, with an audience of their own heroes to perform in front of, went out of their way to do so. Stoke's firm was becoming bigger and significantly more organised and violent.

Certain fixtures determined events, and more often than not the size of the hooligan turnout. Through the Nineties the Stoke mob grew to over 1,000 strong. Many of the old bootboys who had never waned in their own campaigns had smartened themselves up, and along with sons, nephews and even grandchildren, were now part of the one, unified N40. Stoke town centre on match days became impregnable to most visiting gangs, so the police themselves became the targets of frustrations if the match failed to live up to expectations.

On their travels, the N40 took no prisoners. Turning up at some places at the crack of dawn, and leaving sometimes well into the next day, they caused mayhem. Overwhelming numbers would turn up from several different directions, using all manner of transportation. It is fair to say that they were completely out of control, and under the scrutiny of the authorities. It was only a matter of time before something was done with them. With all being fully aware of this, it became all the more difficult to become a member. Any new faces over the age of 17 to turn up would immediately be pulled to one side, taken into a lavatory and quizzed.

"Why start now?"

"Where have you been until this age?"

"Show us the person that's brought you down here."

Unless you were what was called "family" you were not wanted or needed. Everybody knew everybody, and that's what kept it so tight.

The Millennium came and went. For the N40 it was business as usual. Old heads freshly divorced after 16 years of failed marriage were back in the fold, and the youth policy was vibrant and growing. All anyone wanted was the Premiership and a chance to go to places like Tottenham and Manchester Utd – anywhere except the likes of Walsall and Crewe.

Wigan Athletic didn't really fall into the category of must-haves, as Cardiff and Millwall were our main rivals at this time, but Wigan did something that neither of the other two had attempted. They came into Hanley city centre hours after the game had finished. Not Stoke town centre during match hours, where they would have met their maker, but later that night when most of the lads had split up and headed back to their own manors. Take nothing away from the Wigan lads; to turn up in Hanley at night on a match day is still, in the "bottle" stakes, creditable. Hanley city centre is seldom left undefended.

That evening a small, tight group of older Wigan lads had the result against a surprised and complacent Stoke crew. It went off and Wigan kept their nerve. Word went round the city in a rapid fashion and reinforcements arrived from all over the Five Towns, but these days if you're not there when it goes off you might as well forget it, or you will end up in a cell for your troubles.

It is not good for morale being done, regardless of reputation. But it happened and that was that. We had done it to others. It was just a good job that we had still got to play them at their place. All of a sudden, Wigan Athletic away was a revenge fixture. It came later that season, and everyone's promise of turning out was kept. British Rail was chosen as our mode of transport. We weren't going to sneak in through the back door for this one. The order of the day was organised chaos, and 800 determined casuals saw to that.

Crossing Manchester from Piccadilly to Victoria Station in three separate firms during the early morning more than made our point to any observing Mancs. The hoped-for ambush from the Blue half never materialised, even though we knew they were there and watching us. A huge police presence could do little more than monitor our progress all the way into Wigan town centre.

Mass resistance from Wigan was hardly anticipated by any of us. As game as they are, they just didn't have the numbers to contend with Stoke that day. In fact, not many firms would have. Once in Wigan, the Stoke firm was split into three movements, taking over pubs and giving the police a hard time. The threat of mass violence hung heavy in the air, with the younger elements patrolling the streets and monitoring police movements. Had this been elsewhere with stiffer opposition, it would have been carnage.

The first real hostilities of the day came outside the turnstiles of Wigan's end just minutes before kick-off. Thirty Stoke, mostly original N40 with a sprinkling of youth, had it bang off with what could only be described as Wigan's main little crew. It was a proper brawl but Stoke had the result hands down and entered the ground satisfied that battle lines had been drawn. During the game, a small crew of Alsager lads that were serving bans at the time had a mental prolonged encounter in the Bricklayers Arms with some of Wigan's boys. By all accounts it was probably the best row of the day. The pub was completely trashed and closed.

Inside the stadium, hostilities resumed as Stoke hooligans ventured into the Wigan section of the North Stand. The fighting ignited a pitch invasion from the Stoke end of the ground as fellow hooligans ran to their counterparts' aid. For 20 minutes the game was temporarily abandoned by the referee, who removed both teams from the playing field and sent them to the safety of the dressing rooms. The atmosphere remained tense for the rest of the afternoon until proceedings on the pitch were brought to an end.

As 4,800 Stoke supporters attempted to leave the ground, the police decided to hold them back inside for a short period to avoid congestion and more confrontation. This was probably the first real mistake that they had made all day. Below the seated area in the cafeteria and bars, the Stoke fans were told to wait. It was confined and sweltering with body heat and perspiration.

Some people wanted to get home, others wanted to get out and fight. It was inevitable: one wrong remark too many, an unwanted shove with a riot shield, and off it went.

For 15 minutes the Stoke fans fought with line after line of riot police until finally managing to break out of the ground. It was senseless. There were more Stoke fans in the ground than Wigan and it would have been easier to let them out first. The rampage towards Wigan town centre was now a couple of thousand strong. Not just the N40 but all the vanloads of loons that had had enough of being penned in took the opportunity to let the week's bullshit from the factory boss blow big time. Every fucker looked rabid.

Helicopters hovered and sirens wailed. By 6.30 the rush was on to get back into Manchester and give it the Mancs. Wigan was just another entry in the firm's diary by now. I think it is fair to say that if you do manage to get a result against Stoke, enjoy it while it is fresh. Make no bones about it, they will eventually turn up in your manor and put the record straight. Guaranteed.

Before I round things off, I will include the visit to Oldham in 2001. Andy Nicholls deems it relevant, personally I don't. One thing I have got to say is that in all the years that I spent growing up with the Stoke firm, racism was never an issue, so never on our agenda – and I must reiterate that.

The firm that left Stoke-on-Trent by train that day was 450-strong. It was the very last game of the season and a win would see Stoke with a chance of a play-off position. The mood among the lads that morning was, as always, let's get there early and give it the local firm. This particular day it was Oldham's Fine Young Casuals.

En route, newspaper articles were read out and TV news broadcasts recited about an event that had taken place in Oldham earlier that week. An elderly gentleman, a veteran of Normandy in fact – and I am not going to name him as I don't want to disrespect his honour by placing his name on the pages of a book about hooliganism – was returning to his home one evening after watching a local rugby match. Unbeknown to him, parts of the town that he had grown up in, in the country that he had so gallantly defended as a young man, were now no-go areas to white people. For his ignorance of this, he was brutally beaten and kicked unconscious by a gang of young Asian youths. Stomach-churning for most people, to say the least.

As the journey to Oldham progressed, so did the agenda. It's like telling a kid not to touch the bars on the fire; you know he will just out of defiance. Nobody was going to tell Stoke's N40 they couldn't walk the streets of their own country, especially if they were not even from it themselves.

Contrary to previous book accounts, the N40 had no intentions whatsoever of joining up with the Oldham firm. They were still legitimate targets. After an initial encounter in the town centre, however, the locals conceded to the huge Stoke numbers, and were then allowed to follow on with Stoke, acting as guides to the no-go area. En route, residents appeared at their front doors and windows shouting comments of support for what they obviously saw as some form of retribution for their own sad predicament of living under the fear of violence and intimidation in their own neighbourhood.

What followed can only be described as an hour of carnage. After walking through the open-air market and trashing every Asian stall, the Stoke mob exited to a huge baton-charge by waiting riot police. This split the lads into three firms of 150 in each, who then headed towards the no-go area in different directions, obviously being directed by resurgent locals. Each of the firms reached their destinations at different times although only minutes apart, and at different locations. They went berserk; we can leave the scenes to your imagination. The carnage led to a riot after the game, as Stoke fought not only the Asian backlash but Greater Manchester Police as well.

Times have changed a lot, especially for the N40. Stoke's town centre on match day is still impregnable to visiting hooligans, not through the fear of what may lie in wait but the sheer numbers of Staffordshire Police. These days Stoke's a peaceful place. In recent years, the football club along with the courts and police force have worked closely together on combating the problems caused by the N40.

To watch Stoke City play away from home you have to be a member of a "true supporters" club. To gain entry to this and get a match ticket, you have to join an ID scheme, whereupon you are screened by the club and police force. If you have any convictions for violence, not necessarily football related, you are automatically rejected. In essence you are no longer entitled to follow the club you've supported all your life. If you are caught attempting to do so, the magistrates then give you a custodial sentence. Paedophiles do not worry, as none of these restrictions apply to you. You are still free to carry on stalking the playgrounds. Stoke currently have more banned hooligans than any other club in the Football League. This in itself must be a massive relief to the authorities. Obviously a job well done then, eh?

To round things off, I no longer participate in the culture, although if I said I didn't still love it I'd be a liar. All the lads are still in my heart and never fail to be at the end of the phone if needed. Writing *Naughty* filled my veins once again with the thrill and the adrenalin of it all, and brought people back into my life that I had not seen for the best part of the decade that I'd spent retired from the scene.

It wasn't long before, through the lads, I was introduced to the current generation of Stoke hooligans, kids that do not recognise life without the closed circuit television deterrent. "What deterrent?" I hear the old heads say. "It has always been there as far as we are concerned."

Yes, all the old heads have been banned from attending the games. Yes, it is quiet at the moment. But 2005 was the twentieth anniversary of the forming of Stoke City's infamous Naughty Forty, and contrary to what people in power might think, the lads have asked me to say that they have not gone away. And they can assure you that while there is blue English blood pumping through their veins, they never will go away. Each and every one of them is resigned to the fact. It's their destiny.

Stoke, clearly, is one of those places were large-scale hooliganism refuses to die out. Despite Mark Chester and other influential figures retiring from the scene, others seemed determined to carry it on. Early in October 2004, police and stewards were pelted with missiles inside the Britannia Stadium during a match against Queens Park Rangers.

Worse was to come. The Naughty Forty and the Under Fives had always been well-disciplined outfits, priding themselves on targetting only rival hooligans, people who wanted a fight, and also on their knowledge of police surveillance tactics. But in October 2004 that discipline broke down among some of them, with dire consequences. A large number travelled to Manchester on the day of an England World Cup qualifier at Old Trafford and all hell broke loose. Disturbances in the Market Street area quickly spread and the gang ran amok among the Saturday shoppers. Unfortunately for them, much of the subsequent mayhem was captured either on CCTV or on video filmed by police spotters. One member of the gang, a serving soldier in the Staffordshire Regiment, was seen punching people on four separate occasions. A number of the group were jailed in March 2006 at Manchester Crown Court for their part in the disturbances.

In February 2006, another seven men were arrested when police officers came under sustained attack from rival gangs at an FA Cup tie between Stoke City and Birmingham City. Violence broke out in the south-east corner of the Britannia when 200 visiting fans ripped down a length of fencing separating them from home supporters. Uniformed, mounted and dog support officers were attacked by both sets of fans and police were forced to close the nearby A50 trunk road as they dispersed those involved. More people were later arrested in both Staffordshire and Birmingham after police published photographs of people they wanted to question.

"This has been the largest football disorder inquiry in Staffordshire for many years," confirmed one senior officer. It may not be the last.

Further reading: *Naughty* and *Sex, Drugs And Football Thugs*, Mark Chester (Milo)

SUNDERLAND

Ground: Stadium of Light, formerly Roker Park
Firms: Redskins, The Seaburn Casuals
Rivals: Newcastle United, Middlesbrough
Police operations: Crusade

Newcastle United fans, the traditional rivals of Sunderland, were probably the first to discover what an unpleasant place Roker Park could be when they visited in August 1968. At first, the day was theirs. Hundreds of supporters in black and white, mostly teenagers, piled off trains and ran amok in local streets, stealing merchandise from local traders and dozens of glasses from pubs. "I see why the Newcastle fans call themselves the Magpies," said the manageress of one. The Blue Bell, a pub on the route from Seaburn Station to the ground, was badly damaged. Glasses were stolen or smashed, tables broken and used as makeshift weapons and cushioned seats slashed. Many other local pubs reported that they were continually ejecting underage drinkers.

Sunderland fans got their revenge inside the ground. A shower of bottles, broken glass, cans with jagged edges, stones, pennies ground sharp at the edges, and steel darts rained down on luckless fans. Twenty-five people were treated at Sunderland Royal Infirmary, mostly for head injuries, and two were detained. Ambulancemen dealt with dozens of minor casualties at the ground. Other supporters staggered home to patch themselves up. Most of the victims were Newcastle supporters, and one 14-year-old, Ron Richards, who needed two stitches in his head, said, "It was a war. They were like madmen. Every kind of missile was coming down." Seventeen-year-old Elaine Bartram, who also suffered a head injury, told the local paper, "The Sunderland supporters were barbarians. My head had to be shaved and my clothes were ruined."

A *Sunderland Echo* journalist described how the events unfolded. "One of the sickest incidents in a sad day was the cruel cheering as an injured man was carried away, but they got their answer in a defiant Churchillian gesture from his friend. The police, very restrained until then, decided it was time for action and dived into the crowd. But as they fought their way up the terraces they seemed to lose their sense of direction, although colleagues on the touchline kept shouting instructions to them." Defending the fact that no-one was arrested at the game, Supt Norman Bell told the *Echo*, "It is difficult for the police to pinpoint people who throw things in the crowd."

The stunned club promised to root out hooligans and Sunderland AFC Supporters Association pledged itself to an all-out campaign "to uproot trouble-makers and keep them away from Roker Park or any other ground where Sunderland is playing". The Association's chairman, Stanley Lambert, declared, "They are a festering sore on the body of those who follow the team."

Apart from Newcastle, their nearest local rivals of any size were Middlesbrough. Boro fan John Theone, in his book *The Frontline*, describes a visit from Sunderland, or the "Mackems" as they are otherwise known, in the 1971/72 season when thousands got into the home Holgate End and managed to stay there for the entire game. "At the end of the game we met the Mackems in Boot Boy Alley for one hell of a battle – no police, just 2-3,000 going for it good style," he wrote. This battle went down in Sunderland bootboy folklore, and the words of a Boro song "My Old Man said, 'Be a Boro Fan'", were altered to, "We dillied and dallied, then knackered them in the alley."

Another rivalry in the early Seventies was with Sheffield Wednesday, who had a big following with a hard reputation. That meant little to Sunderland's thugs and it was largely one-way traffic, with the Roker boys repeatedly causing havoc among their opponents. In January 1972, Wednesday played at Roker Park twice in 15 days, first in the League and then in the FA Cup. The cup game in particular was bad for Wednesday. "Even though the Owls took a large following, Sunderland smashed up all the coaches and people were cut up bad, some even jumped into the river to escape getting cut up," recalled Tony, a Wednesday fan. Sunderland police made eleven arrests, a similar number of windows were broken, mostly in coaches belonging to Sheffield vans, and a car was overturned. One Sunderland supporter was arrested for possession of a knife and a cutthroat razor in his pocket.

In a twist of fate, a Wednesday fan and a Sunderland fan who were both arrested and charged together in the first January meeting met up face-to-face again in the second meeting. This occasion was very different, with the Sunderland fan chasing his opponent with an axe. Two seasons later, further trouble was reported, this time at a game at Hillsborough. Fourteen fans were to be fined a total of £560.

Chelsea's visit to Sunderland on the opening Saturday of the 1975/76 season, was their first for several years. It was a game awaited by both sets of hooligans and saw a young Steven Hickmott emerge as a Chelsea face with a speech to rally their forces in the face of a huge gathering of Northerners outside the ground. The match saw 25 arrests, all but three from Sunderland, which by no means reflected the intensity of hostility and violence that day.

"Trouble started when a train carrying 800 Chelsea supporters arrived late at Seaburn station, at the same time as a train carrying Sunderland fans from Newcastle," reported the *Sunderland Echo*. "A police spokesman said fighting between rival fans started straight away as they came out of the station. With the help of police dogs and mounted officers, the rival fans were separated to each side of the road and then escorted to the ground. At the ground, Sunderland supporters were put in the Fulwell end and Chelsea fans in the Roker end but fighting between the two factions flared up in the ground and police had to separate them. The trouble started again after the match and at one time Fulwell Road was blocked. Eventually the supporters were escorted by police to the station."

Trouble continued with Newcastle United, both in the League, and, as was the case in August 1979, when the clubs met in a two-legged League Cup tie. The first match, at Roker Park, saw 19 people arrested during trouble at the ground and a further 21 ejected. A police superintendent was hit in the face with a brick. The game was a thriller and ended 2–2, setting up the second leg at St James's Park a week later. A three-page derby match special in the local paper greeted the fans as they arrived that Wednesday evening, and they were not to be disappointed for excitement. Seventeen goals were scored, with Sunderland going through 7-6 on penalties, but there was surprisingly little trouble, with only 3,500 away fans making the trip.

It was to be several years until the two sides met again, but in 1985 they faced off twice in four months. The first match was on New Year's Day, with Newcastle romping home 3-1 winners. There was trouble before and during the match, with the police making 34 arrests. Then at Roker Park in early April, 300 Geordies infiltrated Sunderland's home end. The game was halted briefly while police escorted the mob back to the away end, where they were greeted with applause. Newcastle did not have it all their own way. Amongst the 28 people arrested was 21-year-old George Howard, a Sunderland supporter, who was sent to prison for participating in an attack on a group of Newcastle fans. While he argued in court that he was simply retaliating for a beating he had taken at St James's Park earlier in the season, his cause was not helped by the fact that one of his victims was an off-duty police officer.

A Sunderland home game against Middlesbrough in February 1977 resulted in eight arrests and fines totalling £490. "Traffic was brought to a standstill and women shoppers were cowering in doorways," said Phillip Dyer, prosecuting. As rivals brawled in the city centre, the police intervened with dogs and truncheons. One Sunderland thug was found guilty of punching a police officer in the head, while another was badly bitten by a police dog. Issuing the fines, the Chairman of the Bench said: "It is the responsibility of the courts to see that ordinary citizens can go to the match without their enjoyment being spoilt by the like of you."

Despite having had a huge and unruly away following in the Seventies, for much of the early casual era Sunderland were not known to have a major mob, at least in the eyes of their rivals. "They were a very disorganised bunch," said a Middlesbrough hooligan. "They could've been up there with the best, especially numbers-wise. They tend to draw a lot of their support from the pit villages and towns around the Durham/Sunderland area. I've been there a couple of times with Boro, the last being in 2003 when we were in their seats. There were isolated offs in the ground, nothing major. A couple of times at Ayresome they've come looking for it, notably 1981, there were a lot of fights around the ground and around thirty-five arrests, but don't think they've mustered a decent attempt at the Riverside yet."

The match at Ayresome Park in February 1981 provoked the headline "Violence Bites Boro Terraces", a reference to two Boro supporters who were taken to hospital after being bitten by visiting fans. One, 19-year-old Paul Nayman, required stitches after receiving a scalp wound inside the ground. There were 41 arrests, the bulk being made during the game, but trouble flared up in Middlesbrough long before the game got underway, with police being called to a disturbance in Grand Hotel, in Zetland Road, soon after opening time. "Glasses were smashed and tables and chairs thrown around," a police spokesman said. "There were skirmishes all over town before the match."

Criticism was levelled at the club for allowing visiting fans to occupy terraces alongside Boro supporters, but a club spokesman said it was impossible to prevent the hostile mix. "There is always an enclosure given over to visiting supporters at every game," he said. "The trouble is that anybody who wants to can pay their money and go in at any turnstile. They can go where they want. You tell me how we can control it?"

One hooligan went with a group of 80 of Darlington's Bank Top firm to a Sunderland home match against Millwall, more for a look at the visitors than a confrontation with the home mob. It turned out to be a surreal day. "It was an unusual situation," recalled Andy. "Sunderland thought we were Wall, Wall thought we were Mackems, Darlo being Darlo we wanted to take the lot of them on. The police were confused and stuck us in a paddock next to Wall, then escorted us to the station after the game, with more attention on Darlo than Wall.

"I got to know a few of their lads and they always mention a trip to Cardiff during the 1980/81 season when they claim they took 10,000 down there, with reputedly 2,000 of them being skins."

The first identifiable mob at Sunderland was the Vauxies, who took their name from the local Vaux brewery. They were around in the late Seventies and early Eighties and generally involved slightly older lads, many of whom had been active through the 1970s. Later gangs were the Boss lads and the Redskins, a mob from Washington, a tough satellite town of Sunderland – they copied their name from the American football team from Washington, D.C. The best-known Sunderland firm, however, are the Seaburn Casuals, after the area of the city closest to Roker Park and where many of the lads originate.

Over the years there has been friction between the hooligan gangs of Sunderland and Everton; a rivalry goes back to 1977, when the Mackems were relegated after losing 2-0 at Goodison Park at the last game of the season. An estimated 16,000 Sunderland fans made the trip, at the time one of the biggest away followings ever at Goodison. Despite losing, the away fans believed they were safe from relegation, as their fate rested with another game being played at Coventry. The public announcer gave the good news that Coventry City had won, which meant Sunderland were safe – but he was wrong; Coventry were drawing and were in fact still playing. To make matters worse, the result from Goodison was announced at Coventry and the two sides there played out the final minutes at half pace, ensuring they were both safe but Sunderland were down (the incident resulted in an FA enquiry). When the real news filtered through to Goodison, the Sunderland fans went berserk, rampaging all the way back to their transport.

In 1984, they were back in the top flight and were one of only a few mobs to take the Blue House pub, an Everton stronghold near Goodison. They arrived for opening time, a mix of lads and "beer heads", and it took Everton several hours to muster the numbers for an attempt to regain their base. When they did attack the fighting was intense, and eventually the Blue House was back in Scouse hands.

"The Sunderland fans flooded into the pub at about 11.30 and there was just an explosion after they were taunting Everton fans," said Blue House manager Bob Johnson later. "I am absolutely disgusted – and that's putting it politely – because I am an Everton fan and this trouble was fifty-fifty on both sides."

Sunderland were something of a yo-yo club, up one minute and down the next, so their tit-for-tat with Everton was not a regular occurrence, but whenever the two played, they always showed up. One Christmas in the mid-90s they again turned up mob-handed at the Blue House, but by then it was a fans' pub. After the game, a meet was arranged by the Arkles pub at Anfield, but when 80 Everton turned up at the agreed time Sunderland had vanished.

"There was further trouble in 2001 when news reached Everton that about fifty Sunderland were in the city, swilling ale at people walking past and generally playing up," said an Everton "Category C" hooligan. "After the game Everton went down and mobbed up in the Crown in Liverpool city centre, and they could see the Sunderland firm hanging around by Wetherspoons playing about, so the home mob marched down and after a brief fight the Mackems were backed off past the Blob Shop and JR's, before a few more piled out the side door of Wetherspoons throwing glasses and bottles.

"Everton took them apart and they were chased all the way back up to the Adelphi, where they at last put up a bit of a fight. One Sunderland lad lost his phone and he called the number once police had restored order and Everton hooligans met him and took him out for the night. He admitted they could not match the quality the Merseysiders had out that day. It all turned sour three years later when two lads were sent down for their part in the brawl, which was all filmed on CCTV."

"A pair of Everton FC thugs have been put behind bars for their part in a city centre pitched battle with Sunderland supporters," reported the *Liverpool Echo*. "After an investigation lasting three years, hooligans Mark Hughes and Alan Welsh are in jail for their part in the brawl. They were seen on CCTV footage punching Sunderland fans in Great Charlotte Street hours after the two teams had played at Goodison Park. After studying the film Merseyside police football intelligence officers identified them as two of the key offenders and launched an investigation to track them down."

According to the Everton hooligan, "Up at their place we have always taken decent numbers but it has always been very well policed. It was 100 per cent one of the worst places to go in the late Seventies and early Eighties, and when Everton were casuals all their fat fuckers wanted to tear you apart. It got less intense once they swapped their wool for cotton but was still a place you would get a fight if you wanted it.

"I think Everton v. Sunderland would have been one of our main games if they were any good on the pitch and managed to stay in the same league, allowing them to carry on the rivalry which was evident every time they turned up. They were always getting relegated though, so were never hated in the same way the likes of Middlesbrough were."

The early 1990s saw a new rivalry emerge with Stoke City, another team with a growing hooligan reputation. "In 1993/94, a coachload of Sunderland lads turned up at about eleven in the morning," said Mark Chester of Stoke's Naughty Forty. "It was the right time of the day for them, as we only had about a dozen lads in the Wheatsheaf, which was a well-known Stoke boozer. They claim our lads asked them for an hour to get the lads ready but that is pure nonsense, there was no chance of asking for another hour. We had no lookouts and they were good game lads and piled straight into us. We piled out onto the main street through a fire exit and they filled the pub and smashed it to bits; they put the windows out from the inside! We pulled a few more lads who had heard it go off and totalled about twenty in the street. The lads we had were all decent and we take our hats off to them, they were well up for it and very few firms did what they did that day.

"For the return game we repaid the compliment. After a night out in Blackpool, our coach went straight to Newcastle and we were in the cafes having breakfast at half six in the morning after meeting a couple of minibuses at Scotch Corner. We got a fleet of taxis into Seaburn and went straight into their boozer and seventy of us sat and waited. Before long a few scouts came in and said the place was CCTV'd so to get out in five minutes, but before anything happened a load of big horrible cunts came in and there was a stand-off before the police piled in and cleared them out. We were taken to the ground but loads of us were banned and the police decided to fuck us off and took us back to town. All the way back they were coming at us and you have to give them credit for the effort they put into taking it to us that season." Before another game, police claimed serious disorder was prevented when they intercepted three coaches of Sunderland hooligans *en route* to Stoke.

Sunderland's mob hit the national headlines in the immediate aftermath of the abandoned England international in Dublin in February 1995. Several Sunderland supporters were arrested in the trouble and stories about their involvement in the Seaburn Casuals dominated the national newspapers for days.

Sunderland had a growing name, largely due to their big away following which was always swelled by a hooligan element. A vital promotion game against Huddersfield in the Nineties was a case in point. "While we knew they would bring a mob, we were not prepared for what did come," recalled one Huddersfield hooligan. "We were in the pub from noon onwards, and after an hour two Sunderland lads walked in, one wearing a distinctive CP coat, the one with the goggles. We were chatting to them for quite a while when they said, 'If you lads want it, we will be on the road at two o'clock.'

"As the time was approaching we probably only had about fifty lads out and everybody was looking at their watches, thinking they were not coming. It got to five to and everybody decided to get another pint in. Then a few of us decided to go have a look and see if they were coming on. Bang on two o'clock the Pen & Cob pub, which was visible from our pub, and one below it just started to empty and we saw a swarm of Sunderland coming out of both. As twenty or so Town who were out of the pub were beginning to realise the situation unfolding in front of them, we realised we were going to take a right caning. We did stand, albeit for a limited time, and a fair few punches were traded. In the end we had to realise that discretion was the better part of valour and do one back into the pub. There must have been a good 250 Sunderland on the road that day and we could not handle the numbers."

The increasingly active Seaburn Casuals attracted the attention of the authorities, and in May 1994, a few days before a match with Nottingham Forest, who had become firm rivals due to their link-up with Newcastle, ten fans were arrested at dawn. "Police trying to stop a football hooligan war snatched a pile of weapons, including a replica sub-machine gun and a sword, in a dawn swoop," was how the *Daily Star* reported the arrests. Also found were drugs worth thousands of pounds. "Detectives believe Sunderland fans were arming themselves for a bloody showdown with Nottingham Forest thugs."

Forest's Gary Clarke claims the rivalry began before his firm and Newcastle linked up. In his excellent book on the Forest Executive Crew, he wrote, "I got a hat-trick of nickings up there and have also come unstuck there a couple of times, but Forest have been there and done the business. They once came to Forest 50-handed and 20 of us chased them everywhere. They came down on the last day of the season led by some prick in a poncho who thought he was Clint Eastwood and the police saved them from a massacre. The papers had been full of all this talk about how the Seaburn Casuals were coming down to cause trouble and the free advertising saved me phoning all the lads, we had 300 out and they got well fucked. Our links with Newcastle have just taken the hatred to another level!"

Even bigger raids occurred in March 1998 when 26 alleged Sunderland hooligans were arrested as part of a wider national crackdown before the France World Cup. Many of the arrests were linked to a fight with bouncers in a local pub the previous month, when a military-issue smoke bomb was let off while more than 20 men battled with security staff. Several people were injured, including a woman who was treated in hospital for a head wound, as tables, chairs and bottles flew around the pub. The media was quick to highlight a long list of weapons recovered in the raids, including knuckledusters, coshes, clubs and knives. The net was soon widened and dozens more alleged Sunderland hooligans were picked up for other fights, including away trips to Wolves and Manchester City earlier in the season. By the end of the operation, over 60 were facing charges.

"The vast majority of football fans are *bona fide*, well-behaved supporters who have the best interests of the game at heart," said Det Chief Inspector Dave Hepworth, of Northumbria police after the first raids. "Unfortunately there is a hard core who want to cause disturbances for their own purposes. This morning's arrests are the culmination of a lengthy intelligence-gathering operation going back a number of years. Our aim is to secure the safety of genuine supporters everywhere."

Among the items found in the searches was "extreme right-wing literature". Whilst most Sunderland hooligans were not aligned to any political group, there was strong support for Loyalism, in particular for the Ulster Defence Association. Some of the Seaburn Casuals picked up in the raids were also involved with far-right groups, including the openly nazi Combat 18. One of them was Craig Bond, a former musician with the nazi skinhead band Skullhead, and who had been to prison for political violence.

The high-profile raids were successful in restricting the number of Sunderland hooligans who made the trip to France for the World Cup, but the police's hope of "securing the safety of genuine supporters" appeared to fail when the trial of 15 men for the Sunderland pub fight collapsed after the judge ruled CCTV footage inadmissible. The Crown Prosecution Service issued a diplomatic statement that barely concealed its anger, while the police simply refused to comment. Their costly 19-month operation had fallen apart, but more worryingly for them, several of the leaders of the Seaburn Casuals were now free to return to hooliganism.

Among them was Jason Jamison, the leader of the mob. Less than five months after the collapse of the pub trial, he was among 39 arrested for a ferocious battle with Newcastle that occurred late one March evening on the North Shields New Quay ferry terminal. Likened to "a scene from the film *Braveheart*", the Seaburn Casuals and Newcastle Gremlins battled it out for several hours after Sunderland's league game against Middlesbrough.

Several people were seriously injured, including one who was paralysed. The subsequent court case, which came out of Operation Crusade, heard from one officer how "pool cues, pool balls, ashtrays, CS gas spray canisters, broken table and chair legs and bottles were all found strewn around the battle scene. Knives were undoubtedly also used but none had been left behind in the trail of blood on the ferry landing quayside. 'SAFC' was carved into one of the tables in The Porthole pub." [See *Newcastle* for fuller account.]

"Sunderland had been up for it all day with over 150 lads about town," said one lad who wished to remain anonymous. "Newcastle were giving it the big one on the phone saying they were coming through; the answer they got was, 'Come then.' After a lot of waiting, most lads got sick of it and started to drift away, leaving a hardcore of about fifty-to-eighty from Seaburn/South Shields. More calls followed and the venue was changed, this time to South Shields, only for the Mags to go quiet again. That was it for most of the lads, who decided to call it a night and head off, leaving the thirty. These lads yet again get in touch with the Gremlins and are told, 'We meant North Shields, not South Shields,' so the thirty lads jump on the ferry across the water fully expecting to hit the Mags full-on when they get there.

"When they arrive – nothing. So they have a drink in some bars around the ferry landing, giving it some time for the scum to turn up. After a while they get sick and leave the pub and make their way towards the ferry when the Gremlins come steaming in about 70-80-handed and tooled up with lumps of wood, pool cues, pool balls, chairs and glasses from the pub. They had ambushed the lads on the narrow path towards the ferry, attacking them from the only open side, leaving Seaburn no option but to back off onto the ferry. Once the ferry had started to leave, the lads noticed one lad was left behind and tried to get back for him. On the floor some of the cowards decided to do him some damage, as he was the only one left, and the kicking dished out left him brain damaged. Brave of them, eh?"

Jamison was identified in court as the Sunderland ringleader through an examination of his mobile phone. He had made numerous texts and calls to Graham Russell, identified as the leader of the Gremlins, as well as to several other key people in the Seaburn Casuals. An oil rigger at the time, Jamison was sentenced to four years' imprisonment.

The first few months of 2000 were busy for the local police. At half-time at a home game in late January, a refreshment bar came under attack from Leeds supporters who then attempted to rob the till. Police moved in but they too came under attack and had to baton charge the away fans. At the end of the game a group of 100 Leeds thugs attempted to attack a group of 30 Sunderland supporters but they were forced apart by police. Eighteen people were arrested. The derby against Newcastle in February saw a further 55 arrests.

Then came the fateful ferry fight with Newcastle. Earlier that day,

Sunderland hooligans had already clashed with police after their home match against Middlesbrough. The local paper reported as many as 2,000 Sunderland fans besieging the away exits at the end of the game, with violent clashes breaking out between small groups and the police. "Coins and bricks were tossed at Boro supporters who were being held at the exit gates for their protection and to prevent clashes between thugs," noted the paper. "Although a number of well-known offenders understood to be associated with the Seaburn Casuals hooligan group are believed to have been involved in the violence, some yobs have yet to be identified."

Chief Inspector Dave Hills, of Sunderland City Police, said, "These people are scum for behaving in this way. It's just sheer hatred in their eyes, but they will go into work on a Monday morning and expect to be treated with respect by their colleagues and employers even though they behave in this way. We had trouble after the Manchester United, Leeds, Newcastle and Middlesbrough games. Ordinary fans are getting caught up in it and we want to stop it now."

Sunderland's Football liaison officer, Pc Bruce Hepton, remarked, "These hooligans are sophisticated in that they use mobile phones and the World Wide Web to contact each other and arrange their confrontations. They will even send scouting parties to the preceding matches to check out the best pubs and stopping off points. The vast majority of them don't even go into the match, they are not interested in the football at all." It was through the mobile phones that Jamison's four-year conviction was secured.

In recent years, Sunderland have been one of the more active hooligan firms and there is nothing like a game against Newcastle to bring out the troublemakers. In February 2002, around 200 Sunderland supporters turned on the police, hurling bottles and bricks. Police horses and dogs were injured in the disturbances, which led to 38 arrests. The police were on full alert for the return of the Magpies two seasons later but their best-laid preparations did not stop trouble, though they would argue that it was limited. "There was more OB than there was American soldiers in Iraq," one Sunderland hooligan later wrote on the Internet to a Newcastle fan. "The OB were right on top but if you're honest you know you would have taken a huge hammering due to sheer numbers."

Publicly the police said that they were taking no chances after fighting between Sunderland, Middlesbrough and Newcastle (and Forest) fans had marred England's European Championship qualifier at the Stadium of Light a few weeks before. Tension mounted when Newcastle fans were bussed to the ground, and at one point officers struggled to keep rival groups apart at the Wearmouth Bridge. After the final whistle, there was a 15-minute stand-off between the police and Sunderland fans. Police horses were eventually required to drive the mobs away. In all, 49 people were arrested, most inside the ground. "I think it was the frustration and the animosity between the two sets of supporters boiled over because of the flow of the game," Superintendent Paul Weir told the press. "I think people who normally wouldn't swear or make abusive gestures towards their opposite numbers have decided to do that today."

One of the biggest Sunderland mobilisations of recent years saw 250 hooligans make the trip to Hibernian for a pre-season friendly. Sunderland boast of "taking" the Edinburgh firm during the day, then stopping off in Newcastle on their way home. The Newcastle newspaper reported a clash involving 150 Sunderland hooligans that evening in the Centurion pub, inside the main train station.

By 2003, Sunderland topped the league of arrests with 154, though this was probably due to the numerous arrests at the highly charged England v. Turkey European qualifier and more intensive policing than the number of hooligan incidents involving the Seaburn Casuals. Certainly the local paper and police saw it as a result of their "zero tolerance" approach, while the editor of a Sunderland fanzine also pointed out that with crowds of over 40,000, some arrests were inevitable. By October 2005, 51 banning orders were in place.

Despite zero tolerance and costly intelligence, it is probably the performance of the team that continues to be the main reason that trouble with rival Premiership gangs is limited. Sunderland continue to be a yo-yo club, and unless they show a dramatic and prolonged improvement on the pitch, it seems likely that their rivalries with Newcastle and others will be limited to cup games and the occasional season that Sunderland spend in the Premiership before they fall back among the teams in the Championship.

SWANSEA CITY

Ground: Liberty Stadium, formerly the Vetch Field
Firms: Jack Army, Swansea Youth Squad, Swansea Riot Squad
Rivals: Cardiff, Millwall

"Rows of red-brick-terraced houses, steelworks, docks, a perfect breeding ground for rough, tough aggro merchants. We weren't to be disappointed." So wrote Bristol Rovers hooligan Chris Brown in his book *Bovver*. His description of Swansea, Wales's second largest city, is almost as apt today as it was when he travelled there for a league match in 1972.

Banks of terraced housing still scar the hillsides visible as trains approach the city. While the docks, mines and steelworks have long since contracted, working class life continues to dominate. Swansea is, in many ways, now in the shadow of the capital, Cardiff, but this only makes the hatred towards their neighbours even greater. Whereas once Swansea City, under the stewardship of John Toshack, rode high in the First Division, they then slipped back down as quickly as they had risen. At the same time Cardiff, with the backing of Sam Hammam, rose up through the divisions. Cardiff has benefited greatly from political devolution, while Swansea has largely been ignored by developers and investors. And on the hooligan front, it is Cardiff who have stolen the headlines in recent years; no wonder Swansea hooligans like to wear England football shirts to wind up their bitter rivals.

Fortunately for the authorities, the two Welsh sides did not play each other in the Football League between 1965 and 1980. Instead, Swansea had to content itself with rivalries with Newport County, who they met in league and in cup competitions on a regular basis, and the Bristol clubs. While these matches never reached the intensity of a Cardiff fixture, they were invariably violent.

Under the guidance of former Liverpool and Wales striker Toshack, Swansea began a meteoric rise up the tables, beginning in the 1978/79 season, when they were in the Fourth Division. Over the next few years they were to become, albeit very briefly, one of the leading teams in Britain.

Towards the end of their spell in the Fourth, Swansea played at Wrexham in the quarter-finals of the Welsh Cup. A sizeable number of Swansea fans made the trip to North Wales, but for one coachload their journey ended much earlier in the day, in Ludlow, Shropshire. Their coach, booked in Neath, stopped in a Ludlow café whose owner complained they stole food and drink. The police were called and the fans were all taken to Ludlow police station, where they stayed until 10.30pm instead of watching the game, which Swansea lost 3-2.

In the local newspaper, the owner of the coach company declared that this was the last time they transported football fans anywhere. "We have had trouble before but this is the last time," said Mrs Mair Hopkins. "Enough is enough. They were misbehaving themselves in a café on the way, and continued with this behaviour when they were taken to the police station. According to our driver the police had to call in reinforcements to deal with them at the station. We insisted on a police escort back to Swansea otherwise we would not have brought the fans back. The police agreed to give us an escort or the fans would have still been in Ludlow today."

The 1979/80 season saw them face Cardiff for the first time in the League for 15 years. It was the game both sets of fans had been waiting for but one the police had been dreading. A huge operation was put into place for the first game, in Swansea on New Year's Day, in the hope that it might reduce trouble. And it appeared to work. There were 37 arrests, mostly of Cardiff fans, but the police later reported no major incidents between the two sets of fans. Indeed, the police considered their operation so successful that it was heralded as a blueprint for future high-risk games. The pro-active policing meant repeatedly sending squads of officers into the home end to remove Cardiff fans who identified themselves. This, it was later felt, removed clash points and was welcomed by the bulk of home supporters. Outside the ground, residents took police advice and kept their cars off the streets, thus depriving hooligans of targets and potential ammunition.

A similar policing operation was put into place for Swansea's next home game, the FA Cup tie against Crystal Palace. Once again, the match passed off peacefully, much to the delight to the police. "They were a really jolly bunch," a police spokesman said of the visiting fans. There were only a handful of arrests in a day that saw 150 police officers used. However, Swansea's police knew that the real challenge still lay ahead. "Saturday was by no means a test, the crowd was so good. It will be when teams like West Ham visit the Vetch that the system is truly tested."

A 3–3 draw saw a second replay the following week. The neutral ground selected was Cardiff's Ninian Park and thousands of Swansea fans made the short journey. The trouble-free atmosphere of recent weeks was all forgotten with the news of the death of a Swansea fan during a fight outside the ground. Thirty-one-year-old David Williams was stabbed through the heart after he and two friends were "savagely" attacked by Crystal Palace fans.

One eyewitness to the attack told the press how Williams was an innocent victim. "This crowd of men just set on the men who were walking down the road. They tried to run away, but there was a big fight. It stopped almost as soon as it started and the men drove off, leaving these others lying about. One was hanging over the front garden wall near the lamp-post. One was in the middle of the road and the other was in the doorway." Nineteen-year-old Barry Rondeau was later convicted of the killing.

Easter Monday, 1980, saw Swansea travel through to Cardiff for the return fixture. It had been 15 years and one day since the two sides last met at Ninian Park and there were understandable concerns. "Sufficient arrangements have been made to deal with any trouble that may arise," a spokesman for South Wales Police said confidently. Reinforcements were being brought it from other divisions across South Wales and police promised to search fans as they entered the ground. However, it was possibly the fear of violence that seemed to be deterring many Swansea fans from making the journey. Despite being given all 8,000 tickets for the Grangetown End, only 2,000 had been sold with 72 hours to go before the game.

The best police plans might have limited the trouble but it certainly didn't stop it as rival fans clashed before and after the game. A total of 65 people were arrested, including 14 juveniles, many for involvement in running battles in the streets after the game. One Swansea fan required six stitches after being hit on the head by a stone. There was further trouble in the Canton area as Swansea fans began to make their way home.

The football pendulum was certainly swinging Swansea's way when they played host to their Welsh rivals towards the end of the following season. Swansea were lying fourth in the Second Division, having already qualified for the Cup Winners' Cup through victory in the Welsh Cup, while Cardiff were deep in the relegation zone, making the game more tense than might otherwise have been the case. The end result was a draw but it was good enough for the Jacks, who felt promotion back into the First Division was in their grasp. Off the pitch, the statistics were less pleasant. There were 68 arrests during the day, 29 from Swansea and the remainder Cardiff fans.

Some of the worst trouble came from Swansea fans after the game, when about 100 broke though police lines and threw large stones through windows and at cars in nearby Madoc Street, where Cardiff fans were gathering to make their way home. Hundreds of stones were turned into weapons and it took a good five minutes before the police could restore order.

The police said that elements among both groups were out for trouble. Chief Supt Graham Jones told reporters that there was a Cardiff mob who were "particularly unruly while they were on the West Bank." They broke up part of the terrace and hurled pieces of concrete at policemen and Swansea fans. "Coins were also rained on the policemen and their uniforms were spat upon and the Cardiff fans were an absolutely vile crowd on the terraces," he said. But this changed at the final whistle. "When we escorted the Cardiff fans from the ground they were impeccably behaved. But 200-300 Swansea skinhead supporters decided to blast their way through the barriers in Madoc Street to get to the Cardiff fans. Stones and bricks were being hurled. The Swansea fans took us by surprise. We didn't expect the Swans supporters to come at the police barriers in that way."

Neighbours were understandably shocked and terrified. "These hooligans make you ashamed to say you come from Swansea, they really do," said Roy Nichols, whose bedroom window was broken by a stone. His views were shared by a 77-year-old neighbour who, close to tears, pleaded, "They won't come back will they? Promise that they won't come back." The vandals had attacked her house the night before and daubed "CCFC kill

Jacks" on the wall. "I sleep on the ground floor," she added. "The language they used was disgusting."

The Secretary of the local Residents Association summed up the mood of the community. "I am terrified now, and every time from now on that there is a match at the Vetch we are all going to be terrified again. God help us if they get promoted to the First Division." Local councillor John France demanded that local derbies should no longer be played at weekends. "I wonder if needle matches should not be played in mid-week and, if necessary, before empty stands."

The club itself was defensive but defiant, insisting that it could not be held responsible for the behaviour of its fans outside the ground. "Our responsibility as a club is to exercise law and order within the confines of The Vetch," said chairman Malcolm Struel. "This is what we have done to splendid effect. As far as what goes on outside the Vetch is concerned, that is a matter for the police. The club will certainly not be attending any meetings. Any meetings that the residents want should be with the police or their MPs." He did, however, believe that hooligans "should have their backsides whipped."

A 2–1 win at Bristol Rovers a few days later pushed Swansea even closer to their much-desired promotion place. A few supporters were arrested at the match but it was not on the scale of previous disturbances at Eastville.

Their next home game was against Chelsea, a side whose fans had caused considerable damage when they came down the previous season. This time the police were better prepared and while there were still 37 arrests there was praise from local residents and football fans for the policing of what could have become a highly troublesome match. "The residents were very pleased with the way police handled the situation. The Chelsea fans were comparatively well-behaved because they were carefully and tactfully contained by the police," said councillor John France.

Of the arrests, 20 were Chelsea fans and the remaining 17 from Swansea. One arrest involved an assault on a police officer, another for possession of drugs, two involved wounding and the rest were for public order offences. The police admitted their job had been made easier by the relatively small number of Chelsea fans who had made the trip. There was some fighting inside the ground with the Chelsea fans behind the goal, some wearing nazi regalia, frequently halting play by throwing the match ball to each other and refusing to throw it back onto the pitch. A large number of Chelsea fans, who were not wearing club colours, managed to infiltrate the North Bank, a terrace for home supporters, but they were ejected as soon as they were recognised by police.

Swansea's next game was at home to Luton Town, who were one place below them in the division. A tense draw at the Vetch was played out in front of 21,000 people, the club's second highest crowd of the season. All that was needed was a win at their penultimate game, at Preston North End, for the club to achieve a record of being the first to win promotion from the Fourth to the First Divisions in successive seasons. It was duly secured and Swansea City were in the top flight of English football. Cardiff, meanwhile, had unceremoniously slipped into the Third Division.

Swansea's European Cup run ended with a 3-2 defeat at the hands of the Greek side Panathinaikos, but it was trouble off the pitch that grabbed more of the headlines. Serious fighting between the two sets of fans outside the ground saw 16 Welsh fans appear before a Greek court the following day. Paraded in front of the world's media, ten were jailed for 16 months, though they were allowed to buy their freedom for £800, while the other six were cleared. A lifelong Swansea fan and local businessman, who is now owner of the club, paid many of the fines. While the Swansea fans were quick to insist that they had been the innocent victims and been ill-treated whilst in custody, some were still prepared to praise the police on the street. David Evans, 26, even claimed the police saved him and his mates from being lynched.

"We have been treated like dogs," Evans, from Swansea, told the court. "We weren't even allowed to change clothes to come to this trial looking more respectable. They gave us little food or water. All we want to do is pay for the damage and go home – even though we didn't do it in the first place. I have a wife and baby waiting." He added, "Thank God the riot police came to the rescue. If they hadn't, we'd all have been dead."

Natives of Swansea are often referred to as Jacks, a name derived from the sailors who originated there (though some attribute it to Jack, a famous black retriever dog who saved 27 people from drowning in the murky waters of Swansea docks). The club's football hooligans adopted this tag and became known as the Jack Army.

Swansea did not last in the top flight long and after a couple of seasons were relegated, first to the Second Division and then straight into the Third. Their first game of the 1984 season was away at Millwall, an opportunity few Swansea hooligans were prepared to miss. The police were to later claim that a coachload of Swansea men must have accidentally stumbled into the home Cold Blow Lane end of the ground, though these sorts of "accidents" are unlikely, especially at Millwall. Play was halted for 12 minutes as Millwall fans rallied to expel the invaders and there were even reports of Millwall fans jumping down from the stand into the away mob below. The game – or foolhardy – Swansea contingent of around 40 were quickly forced to flee onto the pitch, but not before two had been arrested and 16 from each side had been ejected from the ground. A group of 100 Millwall then came over the Ilderton

Road end barrier and further fighting followed on the pitch, forcing the players and officials off. Only once the Swansea fans had been removed from the field of play and order restored were the players led out of their dressing rooms, where they had taken refuge, and the game was allowed to resume.

A few months later, Swansea were drawn at home to Bognor Regis in the FA Cup. It was a cold November Saturday and no-one, from the police to the Swansea Jacks, anticipated trouble. They were both unaware that a coachload of supporters following the non-league team were actually the cream of Portsmouth's 6.57 Crew, a few of whom were from Bognor. The game erupted in violence during the first half when this mob attempted to break through police lines to attack Swansea fans. The police held them back but some spilled onto the pitch and the trouble continued. Coins and beer cans were thrown at the police and 20 visiting supporters, most from Portsmouth, were arrested. Some of the worst violence occurred when visiting fans began to fight amongst themselves.

It was described by Inspector Larry Hughes, of South Wales Police, as the worst trouble he had ever experienced inside the Swansea ground. "This group, obviously the worse for drink, just went berserk. We managed to contain them, though they tried to break out on to the field. The lads did a marvellous job." He went on to tell the local press that the trouble was caused by a minority of fans. "The majority of Bognor supporters came up to police after the incidents in the ground and apologised for the way other fans, who aren't regular supporters of Bognor, had behaved."

The mid-Eighties also saw a continuation of the trouble against Cardiff. One home game saw an attempted invasion of the Swansea end by the Soul Crew but this was repelled in violent fashion. There was further trouble after the game when a much larger mob of Swansea hunted their visitors outside the ground. A few years later Swansea caught a mob of Cardiff from Port Talbot, known as the Pure Violence Mob, and literally chased a couple into the sea. The incident quickly went down in local hooligan folklore and "swim-away" became a regular chant at Swansea matches.

It was a very different story when Cardiff came for an FA Cup match in November 1991, the first encounter between the two sides in the competition in 78 years. Cardiff's huge hooligan army travelled over in small groups to avoid the police but it quickly became clear to the authorities that there were hundreds hell-bent on trouble. Tony Rivers, co-author of *Soul Crew*, believes that there were a good 400 Swansea out that day but even they couldn't handle what Cardiff had brought down, and there was serious fighting outside the ground as almost 1,000 visitors ran amok.

"Had I had double, treble or even quadruple the number of officers, this violence would still have occurred," said Superintendent Mel Poole afterwards. Thirty-nine people were arrested, six train coaches damaged and six double-decker buses, which were transporting Cardiff fans from the train station to the ground, had their windows kicked out. The bus seats were then thrown through the windscreens of several passing cars. After the game, hundreds fought pitched battles, many armed with bricks and bottles. The police put the number of Cardiff troublemakers at 900. Of immediate concern to the authorities was the Autoglass Cup clash between the two teams only 72 hours later. "What happened was absolutely deplorable and beyond belief and I will not tolerate a re-run," added Poole. "I will do everything in my power to ensure the tranquillity of the city is not breached. I will not have it spoilt by sub-human animals such as we experienced on Saturday."

The police were determined never to have a repeat of these scenes at any future South Wales derby and for the next few meetings away fans were banned from the respective matches.

Eighteen months later, football riots were again dominating the front pages of local papers, but this time it was because of the behaviour of Swansea fans. On Saturday, 1 May 1993, Swansea travelled to Reading knowing a win would ensure automatic promotion. Thames Valley Police had been told by South Wales Police that no trouble was expected and that those fans who were travelling would be in "party mood". They had also been told that only 2,000 would make the trip, of which only 30 hooligans were expected. Thames Valley Police made their preparations based on this information, and in light of the relaxed atmosphere expected decided to detach 250 officers to cover a hippy festival at Hungerford Common.

The intelligence proved to be complete rubbish. Almost double the expected number of Swansea fans made the trip, including several hundred hooligans, who had obviously not been told about the party. "The football hooligans left a trail of destruction in the town before the game," reported the *Reading Evening Post*. "Windows were smashed, pubs looted and stalls outside shops knocked over as the fans made their way to Elm Park. Terrified traders barricaded themselves inside the stores and allowed frightened shoppers to take refuge also."

One shop owner was forced to place mattresses against his windows to stop them being smashed when the trouble erupted. "It was absolutely terrifying," said the owner of Rod's Discount. "All the old people were being pushed over and the police could not cope. The hooligans were drinking bottles of vodka and wine – it was like a rampaging mob." In a nearby pub, Swansea fans urinated on the kitchen floor after trying to break the stock cupboard. Others damaged the fruit machine and five cases of wine were stolen. The pub owner told local reporters: "We were completely unprepared. There was no warning from police."

There was further trouble during the game, as Reading took a 2–0 lead which would deprive Swansea of their automatic promotion spot. "300 fans tried to get the match abandoned," noted the paper. "The hooligans tore into fencing, pelted players with coins and attacked a tea bar on the terraces. The missiles included slabs of concrete which the hooligans wrenched from the tea bar."

The furious tone of the paper's editorial was matched by local politicians, including Chris Goodall, chairman of the county council's public protection committee, who demanded a full inquiry from Thames Valley Police. "A lot of people of Reading are asking where were the police when we needed them. The answer is they were scouring the country lanes of Berkshire looking for New Age Travellers who weren't even there."

While Thames Valley Police resisted calls for an inquiry, an internal investigation was taking place in South Wales Police. There was a complete overhaul of their football policing and, for the first time, the implementation of intelligence-led policing.

In May 2000 Swansea travelled to Rotherham for a title decider and thousands of Jacks made the long trip to South Yorkshire. There was fighting before, during and after the game, but it was the death of 41-year-old Terry Coles that dominated the headlines. Coles died after being trampled on by a police horse that had come onto the pitch to separate rival fans. A total of 19 fans were arrested. It seemed almost irrelevant that Swansea got the point they required and won the title. An inquest subsequently heard that Mr Coles had been hit with "terrific force" by the horse, knocking him back eight or nine feet, and Swansea City FC subsequently opened the Terry Coles Fund, in conjunction with relatives and friends, to raise money to support his widow and two children.

Promotion took Swansea back into the Second Division, where they were up against a number of teams with large and active hooligan followings. One of the team's first away matches was at Millwall and for the Jack Army it was a must, with posters appearing on walls around the Swansea ground before the team's previous home game. Calling for "no runners", the posters urged Swansea lads to catch the train to London, and about 200 Swansea hooligans took up the call to arms and travelled down by train at 7am. There was a small skirmish with Millwall at a train station but nothing the Met couldn't handle, especially with three lines of riot police on hand to oversee proceedings. The Swansea fans were herded into a large pub around the corner where, much to the landlord's unhappiness, the police could keep a careful eye on them.

Unbeknown to the police, leading Swansea hooligan Andrew Toose, a competition-winning bodybuilder, had slipped out of the pub and nonchalantly wandered into a nearby Millwall pub. Inside there was only a handful of Millwall but that did not stop Toose approaching them and offering them out for a fight. He had no takers.

Word of Swansea's turnout and Toose's cheek quickly spread through the Millwall ranks and by the time the Welsh contingent had been escorted to the ground, a nasty reception committee awaited them. Police managed to keep the two mobs apart but the atmosphere worsened during the game. Afterwards, hundreds of Millwall waited in the hope of ambushing their rivals. Police again managed to prevent a clash but came under sustained attack by the home fans for their pains. There was further trouble on the Underground system as Swansea were being escorted back to Paddington and four police officers were treated for the effects of CS gas after a canister was thrown on a tube. Riot police accompanied the Swansea fans on the train home, but there was still trouble as the train approached Cardiff; the communication cord was pulled and an attempt was made to pile off.

It was proving to be a busy autumn for the South Wales Police's football unit. Swansea hooligans attempted to attack Hull City fans at an early season home game in 2001, taking 120 lads in six minibuses. Phone calls alerted the Hull mob that they were being escorted by police through a housing estate and trouble broke out as 80 Hull tried to break through police lines to reach them, as one newspaper reported:

Gangs of hooligans ran down the street swinging baseball bats as trouble flared between fans of Swansea City and their Hull hosts.

Riot police were deployed as violence reared its ugly head again at a match involving Swansea City. At one point a riot officer was dragged from his horse. But the trouble was prevented from becoming too serious by a major police operation.

Problems erupted on the Great Thornton Street estate in Hull just before 2pm. One woman, who did not wish to be named, described seeing gangs armed with baseball bats and throwing bricks.

She said: "I could not believe what I was seeing but the police soon arrived and within minutes there were police horses and dogs everywhere," she said. There were running skirmishes in various streets on the estate for about 10 minutes. At one stage, police officers in riot gear were pelted with bricks and the mounted officer was dragged from his horse."

One Swans fan said: "Personally, I was glad all those riot police were there. There were about 300 Swans fans and half of them were troublemakers."

Police were stopping cars with South Wales registration plates on the roads leading in to Hull in the hours leading up to Saturday's game, which Swansea lost 2-1.

Some Swansea supporters are believed to have tried to avoid the police operation by arriving in Goole some 20 miles away. It is understood that they were spotted by an off duty officer who alerted colleagues. Humberside Police then commandeered buses to take the Swans fans to Hull.

Swansea fans invaded the pitch at Colchester and disorder was only prevented at Reading after police got wind of their plans. A month after the Millwall game, the authorities had to cope with a home match against Stoke City. "A group of 80 Stoke supporters made their way to a local public house in Swansea," noted a National Criminal Intelligence Service report, which went on to record the presence of 200 Swansea supporters in another pub further down the road.

"There was a great deal of mobile telephone organisation between the two groups. The Swansea group then started to make their way to where the Stoke supporters were. A strong police presence prevented the two groups from clashing. The Swansea group then made a concerted effort to attack the coaches carrying visiting supporters. A large police presence with batons drawn forced them back. The Swansea group were dispersed and taken under escort to another pub, where a police presence was maintained. A decision was made to clear the lane of people drinking and to house them in the pub. Requests were made and warnings given, before the fully protected officers moved to clear the area. At this time missiles were thrown at the officers, batons were drawn and the majority of the violent supporters were cleared from the lane into the pub. Some of this group made their way back to where the Stoke supporters were. The Stoke supporters were then walked under police escort to the stadium. Several attempts were made by the Swansea group to attack the Stoke supporters, but they were unable to do so due to the presence of police."

A little over two weeks later there was even worse trouble with the visit of Bristol City. On this occasion the football police were caught completely by surprise as 200 Bristolians travelled down for the midweek game in the early afternoon. "Riot squads from all over South Wales were rushed to Swansea last night after rampaging soccer fans caught police on the hop," noted the *South Wales Evening Post*. At shortly after 5pm, the Bristol fans, who had been drinking in the city centre undetected, attacked the Potter's Wheel, a pub frequented by Swansea hooligans, causing an estimated £10,000 of damage. Running battles between local yobs and police followed as the Swansea fans sought revenge. The kick-off was delayed by 15 minutes as disorder spread to several other pubs in the area. A coach carrying Bristol fans was bricked, its windows smashed and its tyres slashed as it approached the ground.

There was more trouble after the game and again it was Swansea fans who were to blame. "We took the brunt of violence after the match," said Detective Chief Inspector Tim Jones, head of Swansea CID. "Large groups throwing stones were defying public order. Swansea hooligans were fighting running battles with the police." Two dog handlers were injured as hooligans deliberately aimed missiles at the heads of the animals. At least one of the animals was so badly injured it had to be retired from service.

It seems the police were totally unprepared. "All the indications were that there would be no prominent troublemakers and we expected families to attend the game," Superintendent David Jenkins told the media the following day. He also explained that there had been no arrests, as the police's main strategy was to maintain public order. The local newspaper was unimpressed. "If, as has been suggested, the intelligence system did not suggest there would be any problems, then the system is not very intelligent," noted an editorial. While concluding that the authorities had "a lot to answer for," it did excuse Swansea police if they had not been given the correct information. As a passing thought on local Welsh rivalries, it suggested that some of the trouble may have been caused by Cardiff fans.

Several weeks later, and after extensive CCTV footage was studied, newspapers in South Wales and Bristol carried pictures of 27 people police suspected of being involved in the trouble. "The films were sent to a specialist studio in Cambridge to be enhanced by a firm that carries out work for the National Crime Squad and government agencies," noted one media report.

The Bristol game was the culmination of growing hooligan activity at Swansea, though the media and police interest dampened activity for a while. Older hooligans were returning for the bigger matches but a younger generation was also active. Called the Swansea Riot Squad and sometimes the Swansea Youth Squad, this new mob brought out lads in their late teens and early twenties. The leader of this group was Jason Ryan. Small but squat, he was to be a prominent face at Swansea for the next few years. The Swansea mob, young and old, also began to get involved in the British National Party. A BNP meeting, addressed by its leader Nick Griffin, attracted about 20 Swansea hooligans, over half of the attendance. Among those present were Andrew Toose and Jason Ryan. A year later, 50 Swansea hooligans gathered to watch an England World Cup game and this gathering later became a launch pad for an attack on an anti-racist event in the city.

The return fixture against Millwall, in mid-February, brought everyone back out again. The internet and gossip on the hooligan grapevine notified Swansea of Millwall's intention to seek revenge and the South Wales boys were up for the challenge. A huge police operation was initiated after the Millwall police spotter notified his Swansea counterpart that an estimated 400-500 South Londoners would be travelling by train. South Wales Police, meanwhile, had picked up alarming intelligence of Swansea's preparations, which included the theft of flares and the production of petrol bombs. Careful to protect an informant, the police devised an elaborate scheme whereby a police officer in civilian clothes "stumbled" across the petrol bombs while out jogging. There was to be serious disorder on the day but the introduction of these devices would have made the problems considerably worse.

As anticipated, hundreds of Millwall hooligans poured off a train from London. The two football intelligence officers watched a stream of hooligans, many who had not been seen for several years, emerge from the station. Several Welsh officers simply could not believe the advanced age of some of these fans. In order to avoid a confrontation, the local police took the Millwall group along a convoluted route to the ground. This surprised the 300 Swansea hooligans, who were mobbed up along the expected route. However, word quickly spread that the Millwall escort had been re-routed and a quick sprint across the city meant an ambush was still on. A marine flare was fired into the escort, and another literally blew up a car as it ignited the fuel tank. Worried that the Millwall fans would attempt to break out of the escort, the police began hitting their extendable batons on the ground. "The deafening noise of this, plus the intent it gave off, seemed to do the trick," said one officer. Millwall stayed in the escort and were eventually shepherded into the ground.

Just when the police thought the situation was under control, news filtered through that four rogue coaches of Millwall, containing 200 men, had been spotted on the outskirts of the city. The Millwall spotter appeared perplexed, as he had had no prior intelligence of this. The reason why, it later transpired, was that this group included men in their forties and fifties, men who had been active hooligans many years before the officer came on the scene. Fortunately the coaches were intercepted because when they were searched they were found to contain an axe, Stanley knives, Chinese rice flails, pool balls and an assortment of other weapons.

Trouble flared up inside the ground as the second half got underway. Swansea fans attempted to get at Millwall, while for their part, the away fans tried to climb the eight-foot perimeter fence to attack the home fans. After the game, the Millwall escort repeatedly came under attack and it required dogs and mounted officers to keep the peace. It had been Swansea's largest police operation for a football match, involving 350 officers, and while 22 people were arrested the day was deemed a success. Seven years after Swansea Police had got things so badly wrong for the trip to Reading, they could now rightly claim that intelligence-led policing was having results.

There was one further report of trouble that season, in late April at Swansea's trip to Oxford United. A coachload of hooligans stopped at a pub on the edge of the city, and at about 2pm trouble broke out and they began

Shrewsbury Town fans are watched by police as they gather outside a pub before a game in London. Their hooligan gang, the English Border Front, is well known on the international football scene.

The modern face of intelligence-led football policing: riot helmets, zoom lenses and mini-cameras at a Reading–Millwall match in November 2003.

Stockport County have had one of the more active lower-league firms for more than thirty years. Here they release gas onto the pitch at Caenarfon Town in 1986.

A terrified young fan is trapped on the railing fence after Stoke City hooligans hurl a smoke canister into an Everton section at a game at Goodison Park in August 1983.

Fighting between rival Stoke City and Wigan fans at the new JJB Stadium caused the referee to lead the players from the pitch. Some estimate the Stoke hooligan turnout that day to be their biggest ever.

The North London derby between Arsenal and Tottenham Hotspur in August 1980 and police lead a skinhead in a Fred Perry shirt around the pitch.

A graphic photo of fighting on the terraces at a West Brom match at the Hawthorns in 1982.

From left to right: West Ham faces Cass Pennant and Jela with Gary "Boatsy" Clarke of the Forest Executive Crew and *Hooligans 2* author Andy Nicholls, at a book launch for Hammers hardman Bill Gardner.

West Ham's ICF let off a smoke grenade as they take the North Bank at Highbury in May 1982. An Arsenal fan later died in a clash at Finsbury Park Tube station.

A squad of police with shields and helmets separate Wolverhampton Wanderers and Cardiff City supporters at Molineux on 11 March 2006.

Scenes from a scrapbook: the Wigan Goon Squad kept a photographic record in the Eighties of their many trips and fights. Here is a sample selection over several years.

Members of Wrexham's Frontline caught on CCTV taunting their arch-rivals Chester City outside a pub in Chester. Similar film footage has led to numerous successful prosecutions of football yobs in recent years.

to smash up the pub before police regained order. The Swansea mob was escorted to the ground but left after just 30 minutes. They were rounded up and sent back to Wales.

It was always going to be hard for Swansea's thugs to repeat their exploits of the 2000/01 season. The police were cracking down hard and some of the bigger teams had been promoted. A further problem occurred when the anti-fascist magazine *Searchlight* began reporting on the far-right connections of the mob. It was clear that someone inside the group was talking. Suspicion turned to paranoia after a rumour went round that a BBC investigation was also taking place into football hooliganism. Millwall fans posted messages on the internet that TV cameras had been seen at games early the following season and someone at Swansea believed that they were going to be the focus of the programme. "There was panic within the mob," one Swansea hooligan admitted. "Some were convinced that someone inside the group was talking. To be honest, it paralysed the mob for a while and scared some lads away."

In the past few years there have been fewer instances of trouble involving Swansea fans. Most has involved fighting with Cardiff. In April 2003, two fans were arrested after a train bringing Swansea supporters back from a match in Shrewsbury was vandalised as it arrived in the Welsh capital. Around 250 Swansea fans tried to get off at Cardiff but British Transport Police and South Wales Police were on hand, with several dogs, to prevent them leaving the station to attack Cardiff supporters. Their original train was so badly damaged it was taken out of service.

Clashes between Swansea and Cardiff could occur well away from the football ground and even match days. With both clubs drawing supporters from South Wales towns such as Neath and Port Talbot, there are regular brawls in the pubs and even in workplaces. Towards the end of 2003, 25 Swansea attacked a pub in Neath frequented by locally-based Cardiff hooligans. The fight spilled out onto the street before the police arrived to restore order. A number of Swansea hooligans were sent to prison, including Jason Ryan.

There were arrests and ejections during Swansea's match at Shrewsbury in November 2004 after fighting broke out inside the ground. The local media and the club quickly distanced themselves from the troublemakers, a view shared by the club's Supporters' Trust, in a statement to the media:

> Trust officers as well as many Trust members were present at Shrewsbury and were able to witness first hand the trouble caused by certain individuals who had little regard for fans (from either club) and no apparent regard for the club itself.
>
> The Trust Board would like to publicly announce its support for that condemnation and would echo the many views already being expressed that genuine Swans fans should now move to expose the idiotic element

concerned, at matches both home and away, by bringing the culprits to the attention of police and officials. Furthermore, the Trust Board would ask that the club now actively moves to ensure that such individuals, if identified or convicted are banned for life from attending Swans matches.

...The problem is a cancer amongst our support and needs to be eradicated. Similarly, the element of racism that now also appears to be attaching itself to various factions within the fan base needs to be wiped out. In recent weeks when racist chanting in Spain has made the headlines, Swans fans are also being accused of a racist attitude which insults, via anti English chanting, the bulk of players who make up our current team.

"Anti-English chanting" is not a charge often made at the Jack Army, in fact quite the reverse. In recent seasons, a common gripe by Cardiff yobs towards their rivals has been the display of English flags and songs during games. At one international match in Cardiff, a mob of Swansea arrived by train with the hope of clashing with the Soul Crew, only to be rounded up and returned home. On the platform, much to the irritation of a few Cardiff who had come to look, England songs were sung. Their support for England is partly in response to their inability to follow Wales for fear of being attacked by Cardiff. Such is the hatred that the Soul Crew, who travel in large numbers to away matches, simply won't countenance an alliance, whoever the opposition. A Euro 2004 qualifier in Italy saw serious fighting between first Swansea and Cardiff, and then Swansea and Newport County against Cardiff, which left several people unconscious and a number of rival Welsh hooligans arrested, including Andrew Toose.

An attempted alliance against England shortly before the World Cup qualifier in Manchester in 2004 came to nothing after Swansea hooligans were ambushed as they arrived in Cardiff on their way back from an aborted game at Mansfield to discuss the link-up. "The first Swansea lad into the pub was literally thrown back outside," recalled one Swansea fan. "Cardiff then came piling out and it went off big time in the street. To say that any talk of an alliance was now over was an understatement."

Swansea's move to a new stadium was initially accompanied by a decline in hooliganism, at least amongst its old guard. As with most other clubs, Swansea has seen the emergence of a youth mob, with some of its members as young as 11. Priced out of football, these youngsters gather either outside the ground after the game or on the route away fans leave by, and attack their opponents. The Swansea hooligans were also a lot less obvious on their travels during the 2005/06 season, with clashes restricted to away matches at Southend, Colchester and Chesterfield. Large mob-on-mob battles have given way to small-scale fights involving only a dozen or two hooligans, often late into the evening after the police have stood down.

One large outing was for the LDV final in Cardiff. An estimated 800 hooligans and "thugs" made the trip over to the home city of their fierce rivals. Swansea took over the city centre pubs, and a smaller mob of Cardiff wisely decided against leaving their Canton base. "I have never seen a crowd like it," one Swansea policeman admitted afterwards. "It was a really nasty mob. There were no women and children there, just men."

Whilst violence is no longer as common as it used to be, Swansea have still managed to pull big numbers for the odd game, two of the main outings being to high profile opponents Millwall and Leeds United. One lad who is still active said, "Three hundred and fifty took an early train to Millwall. The police killed it before the game but after we had it with the Bermondsey police trying to get at the waiting hordes. A few lads ended up with Met trophies, including hats and truncheons. The riot police were eventually called in and thought the state that the local OB had gotten themselves in was hilarious. Millwall, as you would expect from them, returned the compliment at ours and once again there were running battles with the police as both firms tried, without much success, to get at each other.

"We went up heavy to Leeds in 2007 and it kicked off everywhere, with one massive brawl erupting on the main car park. It was well documented that the police only got involved when Swansea got on top. Leeds had a quality mob out that day and tried very hard to get to a pre-arranged meet a few miles away from the ground. Not many would have done that knowing what we had waiting for them. Of course there were lads who got a slap and plenty melted, lads were not prepared for what Leeds had and with any firm as big as ours that day you will have plenty of hangers-on, but we did more than enough. Apart from the big games there are always the smaller offs to keep us interested. One was at Port Vale, where a mob of just nine of us trashed their main boozer, then walked into a welcoming committee of about forty. We took a good hiding but took plenty with us."

SWINDON TOWN

Ground: County Ground
Firms: Swindon Town Aggro Boys, Swindon Active Service (SAS)
Rivals: Bristol City, Reading, Oxford United

The history of Swindon Town FC closely follows the history of the town itself: the club was formed in 1894 by the Reverend William Pitt, during a time when Swindon was a mere shadow of the urban centre it was to become. In the pre-WW1 period the club did well, winning the Southern League Championship twice and reaching the FA Cup semi-final twice. Its fortunes declined in the inter-war period and the club was almost relegated from the League on three occasions. Success came in the Seventies as the town began expanding to accommodate thousands of people spilling out from London. They won the Anglo-Italian Cup in 1970 and reached the sixth round of the FA Cup, where they lost 2–0 at home to Leeds United, courtesy of two goals by Allan Clarke. During this period, the hooligan contingent was largely disorganised and made up of smaller groups from Swindon and the smaller satellite towns and villages.

It was in the Eighties, coincident with the massive expansion of high-tech industries across Wiltshire and Berkshire, that the club achieved its best years. From the lowly ranks of the old Fourth Division, it earned successive promotions, and if it hadn't been for financial misdemeanours that led to exemplary punishment, would have gone from the bottom league to the top in four years. But as the town grew and prospered, so did the hooligan mob, which became more centred around Swindon itself.

The first reported violence at a Swindon match was actually the club's Anglo-Italian Cup Final win over Napoli in Naples. After the English side took the lead, Italian fans began to throw lumps of concrete on to the pitch and the game was abandoned with twelve minutes to play. Swindon were still awarded the trophy, but they required the help of tear gas to get through to their dressing room.

The earliest mob in the town was the Swindon Town Aggro Boys (STAB), who were active in the Seventies. Their numbers were drawn, as continues to be the case today, from Swindon and the surrounding smaller rural towns of Chippenham, Melksham, Devizes, Calne, Highworth, Faringdon, Wantage, Newbury, Stroud and even as far as Gloucester. While they all fought as one inside the ground, they were in fact several distinct groups.

A home game against Wrexham in March 1978 saw the away goalkeeper pelted with darts, stones and a golf ball. The referee reported Swindon over the incident which ended with keeper Eddie Niedzwiecki being hit on the head with a lump of concrete. With Football League action against them likely, the club offered a £100 reward for information that would lead to a conviction of the supporter responsible. Club chairman Cecil Green claimed that the club was doing everything it could to remove hooliganism. "We intend to stamp out this thuggery," he said. "[The] incidents were diabolical and we want to make it plain that these kind of people are not welcome at Swindon Town." His stand was backed by the supporters' club chairman Mick Lewis, who added, "We seem to have attracted all of

Swindon's riff-raff and rubbish to matches. But we will back the football club in every way possible to get rid of them. These thugs disgust me and every other decent supporter."

Swindon's key opponents have long been Oxford and Reading, and violence between their supporters was noted in the press from the Seventies. In September 1980, a Swindon match away at Reading resulted in 31 arrests. "Police with dogs moved in to separate rival groups as violence flared up on the terraces," reported the *Reading Evening Post*. The trouble started before the game when Swindon fans tried to get into a home section of the ground. However, police were happy with the day, as the trouble was described as "no worse than any other Swindon-Reading game". Violence became the norm at matches between the two clubs and in 1982 there were another 30 arrests at the fixture.

That same season saw Swindon relegated back to the Fourth Division after a final-day defeat at Newport County. A huge mob of Swindon made the small hop over the Severn Bridge and ran amok in what South Wales police called "mass public disorder". Eight police officers were injured and shop and car windows were smashed. The wreckage could have been a lot worse but for the interception of two more coaches of lads on the M4 motorway after a tip-off from Swindon police. As it was, 51 people were arrested, two-thirds of them Swindon fans. The trouble received little national publicity largely because 3,000 Leeds fans rioted at West Brom as their team was relegated.

The Newport loss was a low point in the club's history but within a couple of years their fortunes had improved. A new hooligan gang also emerged during the Eighties: the Southside Scuffling Firm was named after the area of terracing they occupied. Life in the bottom division brought Swindon new opponents and new grudges. At a match at Northampton, fans clashed immediately outside the ground. Swindon boss Lou Macari wandered out of the players' entrance and straight into a mob of more than 100 SSF chasing the home mob up the street under a barrage of milk bottles. He said it was "worse than a Celtic-Rangers game".

Swindon also clashed with Bristol City fans. Missiles were thrown at police at one game, causing the match to be halted. A loudspeaker announcement at half-time warned that the ground would be cleared and the match finished behind closed doors if there was more trouble.

In May 1986 Swindon were promoted back to the Third Division, and under the managership of Macari, a wave of optimism swept through the club. The new season began well, with a win at Bolton, but two successive defeats saw a heavy dose of reality set in. However, with the fans coining the chant "Lou Macari's Red and White Army", the team went on an unbeaten run of ten games, including nine wins. During their match against Plymouth

Argyle, a fight between rival fans led to the death of 17-year-old Mark Smith, an epileptic. He was part of a 25-strong group of Plymouth fans who had made the journey up in two vans. They met a similar-sized group of Swindon in Gladstone Street, just outside the ground. In the ensuing battle, Mark was hit by a plastic milkcrate and then hit his head on the ground, causing brain injuries. He managed to get to the stadium, where he collapsed and was rushed to hospital. For nine days, doctors fought to keep him alive but eventually his life support system was switched off.

The game at Plymouth threatened to be a bitter event. "The OB and the club did everything to stop us travelling, nevertheless three vanloads of us went for it," remembered Swindon veteran "Stab". "When we unloaded in the car park they came from everywhere. We all grouped up and expected to get a hiding but it never happened. The OB presence was massive and it would be fair to say we would have come off second best if it had gone off. Every game between the two sides since the lad's unfortunate death brought up threats of revenge. It kicked off down there last year and thirty SAS (including a lot of youth) put up a game fight against heavier numbers of TCE [The Central Element – see PLYMOUTH]."

Automatic promotion looked certain as Swindon rose to second in the table with a 4–3 win at Bristol Rovers, but end of season jitters set in and after some poor final games the team slipped to third place and into the play-offs. A 3–2 aggregate victory over Wigan saw a two-leg play-off final against Gillingham. A goal from a disputed free-kick eight minutes from time handed the first game to Gillingham, but a Swindon victory in the second saw the Wiltshire club promoted again. Off the field, Swindon attacked a Gillingham pub, but the 40 arrests that resulted from this incident broke the back of the SSF.

Swindon Town were now on a roll and it looked as though the club was heading for promotion into the top flight, but a play-off defeat at Crystal Palace ended all that and, perhaps more significantly, Lou Macari left for West Ham. He was replaced by Ossie Ardiles and the following season they again reached the play-offs after a final day draw at Stoke, in a game marred by crowd trouble. The point was all Swindon needed, while Stoke City were relegated. The final few minutes was a virtual non-event as both teams obviously feared further crowd trouble.

Swindon defeated Blackburn Rovers in the play-off semi to set up a final against Sunderland at Wembley. The Wiltshire club won by a single Gary Bennett goal but the celebrations were shortlived; financial irregularities saw the club penalised and their promotion blocked. Glenn Hoddle replaced Ardiles as manager and three years later Swindon were back at Wembley, this time securing promotion with a thrilling 4–3 win over Leicester City.

Life in the top flight lasted one season, with the team conceding more than 100 goals. When opposition fans chanted, "Going down, going down," Swindon fans would respond, "So are we." Mercifully there was little trouble during Swindon's solitary season with the big boys. The SSF had been crushed by the arrests at Gillingham and the next generation was lost to the rave scene. "There were incidents with a few sides but nothing involving significant numbers, just small offs in back streets," said Stab. "With the smallish ground, some teams thought they could just go where they wanted. Groups of Tottenham and Man United, amongst others, got slaps inside the ground when they went to the wrong place. We had a decent firm at Southampton at the beginning of the season and ran them near the ground. When we played Man United, Mark Hughes tried to grab the ball from a fan in the Southside for a quick throw but got grabbed by a few lads and got a few spanks for his efforts."

Gradually a new mob did emerge in the Nineties, bringing together a few older faces and some younger blood. The Swindon Active Service was quite different from the earlier STAB and SSF in that it was a tighter knit group who came mainly from Swindon rather than the small towns around the county. Like the other mobs, it performed better away from home, though many of the most amusing and memorable incidents involved very small groups.

"After a game at Derby in the early Nineties, a fifteen-year-old Swindon lad ran up to a few older faces saying he had been chased by four older Derby lads, and was offered a lift by one van load of Swindon," said Stab. "As the OB tried to move everyone on, the same four Derby lads walked past the van making gestures, but as they reached the corner at the bottom of the road ten Swindon spread across their path. Three of them quietly walked past in single file but the fourth bottled it and turned back up the road. Meanwhile, the OB had turned their backs to the first vanload and two lads jumped out to stop the Derby lad. Now this may sound like bullying but nothing was going to happen until the three other Derby lads screeched back up the road in a new top-of-the-range Rover like something out of *The Sweeney*. It spun a handbrake turn in the middle of the road and the fourth lad jumped in. As the back panels got totalled by the two Swindon lads at the top of the road, some of the other ten at the bottom launched missiles through the windows. The driver panicked – understandably – and drove straight into a wall, ripping off part of the wing. Hilarious."

Stab also recalled Swindon's trip to Italy in the Anglo-Italian Cup in the mid-Nineties. "Six lads and two shirts kicked off before the game in several bars, and after the game ran a mob of about forty-five Italians who ended up hiding behind the Italian plod. To avoid any further problems in the town, the OB took the eight Swindon back to where they were staying, twenty miles away, with an armed escort. In the van on the way one of the lads farted nearly causing the driver to crash from the beery smell while a large Cross of St George was hoisted in the back window."

The SAS continued hostilities with local rivals Oxford United and Reading. In September 1998, 19 fans were arrested at the home match with Oxford. In August 2000, Swindon's first away game of the season was at Reading. The home team won 2–0 and a section of Swindon fans booed through the minute's silence in memory of former Reading player and manager Maurice Evans. The referee had to call time on the tribute early because of the unpleasant reaction of some of the away support and there were clashes after the match.

The first few months of 2002 were possibly the most active for the SAS. In mid-January there was a free-for-all at Banbury railway station between Oxford, Swindon and locals. A group of 20 Oxford were travelling back from a game at Rochdale, while a similar number of Swindon were returning from Peterborough. A fortnight later, seven Swindon lads were arrested after trouble at the club's home game against Hereford. Six of the seven were under 25, a reflection of the youthful mob that had emerged.

The Swindon mob had long been in the shadow of Oxford's South Midland Hit Squad, partly through inferior numbers and organisation. "If I was fair," said Stab, "I would have to say Oxford had more major results against us than the other way round. Mind you, they will never admit to being done by Swindon." But, he said, by the turn of the millennium this was changing. "The tide turned to a degree because the firm at Swindon was now a lot closer knit and no longer fragmented. With a lot of new faces and some older ones returning, the old Indian sign that they used to hold over Swindon was no longer there. In recent scuffles, Swindon have more than held their own – indeed the nasty little incident in Banbury between Swindon and a similar number of Oxford resulted in them being routed. On several occasions over the last few years, SAS lads have stopped off in Oxford when returning from games to have a pop with the locals."

When Swindon were drawn away to Oxford United in the FA Cup, the BBC decided to broadcast the game live and the police insisted on a Sunday lunchtime kick-off. It had been a few years since the two firms had crossed paths other than the odd Saturday night visit to each other's watering holes or bumping into each other in a North Oxfordshire market town. "There was no doubt that both firms were looking forward to this to settle old scores," said Stab. "Sunday morning public transport isn't the best in this part of the world, especially when you are trying to move several hundred lads away from the prying eyes of the boys in blue. Nevertheless, a show had to be made and this was the best Swindon firm that had turned out for many a year. This was no group of spotty faced, Burberry clad teenagers but a mob of seasoned veterans, many with a background of terrace antics covering the previous three decades.

"The first train arrived at Oxford just after 10am, with around 150-200 SAS bouncing out of the station hoping for an early morning rendezvous with the SMHS. Sadly, Thames Valley Police were having nothing of it and immediately rounded up these unwelcome visitors to Oxford's dreamy spires. Double-decker buses were laid on to take the SAS straight to the ground, but as the first one was being sent on its way, a group of about sixty SAS managed to break through the police lines and headed into town.

"We thought the SMHS would be around somewhere but all we met was a group of around thirty Oxford, who were soon put on their toes. No other opposition was met before the Thames Valley Police with horses and dogs rounded up this splinter group. By now the next train from Swindon had arrived with another 100 or so lads. Everyone was surprised that Oxford weren't around and later reports suggested they were in three different pubs nearer the ground. The police finally succeeded in bussing all of Swindon's firm to the ground, and as the first one pulled up by The Priory the first signs of the SMHS were seen. Eighty or ninety of their finest came charging out of the pub, and with Swindon beckoning them on it looked like the OB at one stage would lose it, but the police kept control. One of the later buses was detoured via the city centre and came across a group of twenty or so SMHS by the ground, but again the OB managed to prevent anything serious going off.

"After the game, a mob of SAS poured round the back of the stand to get at the SMHS, who were trying the same thing. Once more the police kept on top of the situation. Forty to fifty SMHS attacked the buses carrying SAS on their way out of the car park but with little effect. With the police focusing on the buses, about fifty SAS were left in the car park. Phone calls were made to the SMHS and an invite offered for post-match discussions. For some reason this wasn't taken up in the forty-five minutes that they were left by the ground. As the last of the Swindon were being pushed onto trains at the station, up to forty Oxford made a token attempt to attack the visitors, but it was too little too late.

"In reality very little happened and for the best part of the day the two firms were kept well apart. The SMHS claim to have had in excess of 350 out, and on their day they are capable of pulling those numbers. Swindon showed up with a solid 250 and there is no doubt that had the police not stayed on top of the day then it would have gone off in a big way."

Fifteen Swindon Town supporters were banned from travelling to Asia for the 2002 World Cup and were "named and shamed" in the local press. They included a 16-year-old who had smashed the windows of a coach carrying Bournemouth supporters, two 18-year-olds convicted of disorder at Swindon rail station on the day of a game against Bristol Rovers, a 26-year-old convicted of affray at a Millwall-Nottingham Forest match, a 42-year-old who had admitted hitting a Rotherham fan, and others convicted of public order offences, being drunk at football grounds, or assaulting stewards.

Today the average SAS turnout varies from 20 for a non-event home game up to 100 for a more tasty fixture. Away from home Swindon can put out a tight firm of anywhere between 30 and 80 depending on the game. A firm of 30 Swindon lads travelled to Munich for the England World Cup qualifier in September 2001 and several were caught on film in the vicinity of trouble before the game. In December 2004, Swindon clashed with rival fans at Boscombe when their team was playing at AFC Bournemouth. A group of SAS were drinking at a pub when they were verbally abused by Bournemouth fans. The Swindon mob ran up stairs from a lower level bar and chased the Bournemouth fans through part of Boscombe shopping precinct, throwing kicks and punches.

It led to police raids four months later, as reported in the *Swindon Evening Advertiser* in March 2005:

Seventeen fans have been arrested in the biggest crackdown on Swindon Town football violence ever carried out by the area's police.

The fans, aged between 18 and 44 years, have been arrested in connection with disorder which erupted at the Swindon versus Bournemouth away game at Christmas.

Trouble flared just before kick-off as fans brawled in a busy shopping area near Bournemouth's Dean Court stadium.

The area was packed with Christmas shoppers, who watched in horror as pub windows were smashed and fans traded insults.

Most of the skirmishes which involved around 40 supporters were caught on CCTV cameras. After studying the footage, football intelligence officers from Swindon managed to identify 17 alleged culprits.

In an unusual move, officers contacted all the suspects and told them to attend Swindon police station for questioning. They all reported over two days last week, and were arrested and charged with public order offences.

During the operation, described as the biggest carried out by both the Swindon and Bournemouth divisions, Swindon police worked closely with colleagues in the coastal town, who arrested six fans.

The Swindon supporters were among around 700 fans who travelled to Bournemouth for the game on December 18.

Football intelligence officer PC James Neighbour, of Swindon police, vowed to root out hooligans. "The vast majority of Swindon fans are law abiding, but we want to rid the club of those who act in an anti-social manner," he said.

"This has been a big operation for us, and we have spent many hours poring over the CCTV footage."

The clashes in Bournemouth surprised many. While Swindon's enmity with Oxford United and Bristol City is well known, there is no history of rivalry with Bournemouth.

Swindon does not have a reputation for football thugs. But a number of STFC fans are believed to be members of a hooligan group called the SAS Swindon Active Service.

The group's website features adverts for DVDs containing footage of fights between rival 'firms', hooligan gangs associated to clubs. The worst violence prior to the disorder in Bournemouth happened in 2002 before a game against Hereford at the County Ground.

Three Swindon fans were jailed and three more were given community punishment orders.

PC Neighbour said hooliganism was a way of life for some fans. "Most work hard during the week, and it is a way of letting off steam," he said. Often it doesn't come to blows, they enjoy the buzz of organising confrontations."

By the end of 2005, twelve Swindon fans had been banned from the County Ground after being convicted in relation to the Bournemouth brawl. Certainly hooliganism is not dead in the Wiltshire town.

T

TORQUAY UNITED

Ground: Plainmoor
Firms: Torquay Mental Mob, Bayline Firm, Torquay Youth Squad
Rivals: Exeter City, Hereford United, York City

Another seaside club, another whole heap of trouble. Wolves, Blackpool, Birmingham City and Wigan have been just some of the clubs whose fans have misbehaved in a town at the heart of the English Riviera. Twenty-two miles of coastline, an abundance of cheap accommodation and a pleasant climate have attracted many more football supporters than a club Torquay's size would normally expect. The town has also provided a convenient and probably altogether more entertaining rest stop for fans travelling on to Plymouth, as it found to its cost at hands of supporters from Portsmouth, Bristol Rovers, Leeds and Cardiff. The town even entertained Shrewsbury lads before a crucial end-of-season match at Exeter in the late Nineties.

In the late Sixties and early Seventies, Bristol Rovers were repeated visitors. It was always an unequal contest as thousands of Bristolians descended on the seaside town, swamping the local pubs and taking over the home end. "We took their end – the aptly named Cowshed – no sweat," wrote Bristol Rovers fan Chris Brown, in his book *Bovver*, about a match in 1969. "Christ, even a bunch of one-armed dwarfs could take their end. It was hardly an achievement." The following season Rovers were back and despite the violence at the previous match the club decided to host the game on a Saturday evening. Unsurprisingly, a lot of Bristol fans were drunk by kick-off and there was further trouble well into the night.

In 1978 it was the turn of Cardiff City, whose fans came in their thousands to cause trouble. They began arriving early and there was fighting with locals throughout the day, continuing until the early hours of the next morning.

In May 1984, "SOCCER FANS GO ON THE RAMPAGE" was the front page headline of the *Herald Express* after the visit of Blackpool for an end-of-season Friday night game. "More than 150 Blackpool supporters wreaked havoc at the Yacht public house and broke windows at Macari's ice cream parlour and Claire's nightclub," reported the newspaper. "Four people were taken to Torbay hospital with minor injuries ... The worst incident was at the Yacht on Victoria Parade where glasses, tables and chairs were thrown at walls, forcing the manager, Mr Paul Hurley, to close early at 10.15pm. 'There was a lot of bad feeling going round and it was obvious they had it in their heads to wreck the place,' said Mr Hurley. 'Anyone who was local seemed to be under threat and it could not solely be drink because we had to throw out 50 people who were acting stupidly at 8.30pm. It was very frightening but we had no time to panic.'" Several boats in Torquay harbour were set adrift by the marauding northerners and extra officers had to be drafted in from Plymouth to help.

The violence continued the following day. In all five people were stabbed or slashed with craft knives, one seriously, 61 people were arrested and thousands of pounds' worth of damage was caused. Several Blackpool fans were subsequently jailed for a variety of offences, and two admitted stealing a four-poster bed from the Warren Park Hotel. Throughout the carnage, there had been little resistance from the locals. "They didn't seem to have a clue about football hooliganism, even though at that time it was at its height," remembered one Blackpool hooligan. "I know it's not the toughest area of the country but we would have expected some opposition. The only resistance came from some of the bouncers, although a rock through the window of the main nightclub put paid to them, and with some Scousers living down there, one of whom was badly slashed."

The following year it was Wolves fans who rampaged through the seaside town. Hundreds made a weekend of it in what one newspaper later called "twenty-four hours of violence and mayhem". About 1,500 Wolves fans were involved in the trouble, which was made worse by the absence of segregation in the ground. Wolves fans attacked their rivals in every part of the ground, while throughout the match missiles were thrown at police and smoke bombs set off. There were repeated pitch invasions and at half-time match commander Supt Morley Pull attempted to have the match called off but the referee refused.

In November 1991, the town was similarly overtaken by Birmingham City. There was a weekend of fighting between the Brummies and locals and one clash, in a nightclub, saw bottles and chairs thrown and a local stabbed. There was further fighting over the weekend and sixty Birmingham fans were arrested.

The town clearly has been overrun on a number of occasions but despite the size of the club's support, and the town itself, the lads of Torquay have often been up for a rumble themselves. The first organised firm was called the Torquay Mental Mob. They were active in the late Seventies and early Eighties and consisted of mainly punks and skins, who were both resident in the town in sizeable numbers during this period. "Torquay harbourside witnessed some mad battles in those days," said one Torquay hooligan.

"The most notable was Leeds," he added. "Their mob stopped off at Torquay on their way back from Plymouth and went to a local nightclub, where they caused some trouble. They came under attack from the Torquay mob plus a couple of Scousers and Jocks and got hammered. The other mob that sticks out in my memory was Wolves in 1985. To be honest we got smashed everywhere. They were the best mob I've seen. They ripped up everything and anything that moved."

On a cold Wednesday night in 1987, a new gang was born during a match at Swansea. The casual fashion had caught on around Torquay and a loose collection of 50 or so young lads began to coalesce. They attracted the attention of some of the older hooligans, who themselves were adopting the causal fashion. Together, they decided to hire minibuses, from a firm called Bayline, for the match at Swansea. The mob went into home seats behind the goal and above the home terrace. Their presence caused a violent reaction from the locals but Torquay held their ground, though after the game they had to exit sharply as it seemed the whole of Swansea was waiting for them. The Bayline Firm was born.

During the Eighties the Bayline Firm would regularly take up to 50 to matches against Leyton Orient, Newport County, Aldershot, Exeter and Hereford. Two games against Exeter in 1987 and 1996 stand out in the memory of Torquay lads. The two sides are obviously local rivals, though traditionally Exeter have been the more organised and older of the two mobs. But in those two years Torquay got their act together and, according to them, ran their rivals. "We have always been fairly disorganised," admitted a Torquay lad active in that period, "but when we did firm up, we were always a match for them. The trouble is we just didn't do it enough."

The Bayline remained Torquay's crew until the mid-Nineties when it disbanded, though they did stage a "reunion" at the away game at Bournemouth in 2002. They were to be followed by the Torquay Youth Squad, a name still used today. "The Youth Squad name came in mid to late Eighties, when forty or fifty of us were fed up of firms coming down and taking the piss and decided to do something about it," recalled one of them. "The name isn't rocket science, we were a younger lot than the Bayline Firm and wanted our own identity and thus the Youth Squad was born."

In the late Eighties, Torquay would regularly turn out 60 lads for away games and, if the match was high profile enough, up to 100 for a home match. Their biggest turnouts included 150 for an FA Cup match away at Coventry in 1988, 100 for a midweek League Cup game at Tottenham and between 150-180 for the Sherpa Van Trophy final against Bolton at Wembley. However, their record was the 180-200 who travelled and met at the Greyhound pub, in North-west London, before their Wembley play-off final against Colchester United. Torquay's numbers have been boosted for the higher profile games by the significant numbers of Mancunians and Liverpudlians who live in the town.

"More recently, our biggest turnout was for Yeovil home and away," said the Youth Squad member. "We had sixty out for the away match and more than eighty for the home game. Unfortunately Yeovil didn't return the compliment. We could slate them for this, seeing as it was a first League meeting between the two sides and a local derby, but when we haven't taken anything of note to Exeter in years, who are we to moan?"

Torquay's key rivals are Exeter City, Hereford United and, perhaps surprisingly, York City, though the trouble between the two sides has been confined to games at Plainmoor. "Notice the pattern here?" laughed the Youth Squad member. "Don't have a rivalry with us or end up in the non-league depths of despair!

"In the early Nineties, there was a fight in a town pub with some York lads, resulting in one having his finger chopped off. This odd rivalry with them continued up until a couple of seasons ago, when we were both on the verge of relegation to the wilderness of non-league and played them on the penultimate game of the season. The game ended 2-2 with both our goals resulting in pitch invasions. When York scored a very late leveller, a few of them came on, to which thirty or so Torquay got through the stewards and into them. A couple of the lads even made it into the away end and are still serving bans for it."

Torquay has never made life easy for its fans. For most of the past fifteen years the club has either hovered around the relegation zone of the bottom division or been involved in one play-off or another. In May 1988, Torquay went into the final game needing a home win over fellow promotion challengers Scunthorpe United to ensure promotion. The fixture was marred by trouble after twenty away fans gained access to the home end and fought with locals. One policeman cut his hand on wire fencing after he was knocked to the ground. Six Torquay supporters were arrested and charged while another four picked up were later released.

"This idiot element have been photographed and they will be dealt with," promised club owner Mike Bateson. "Behaviour like this will not be tolerated. A small group seemed intent on causing trouble with the York fans who behaved throughout. They were not a problem."

Torquay lost the game and went into the play-offs against, of all teams, Scunthorpe again. Police requested that the game be brought forward to a midday Sunday kick-off in an attempt to prevent fans drinking heavily beforehand. The match was further complicated when Torquay banned away fans, something they argued would reduce the likelihood of trouble and cut a £5,000 police bill to just £200. Scunthorpe's chairman pleaded with Torquay to allow them to bring a small group of possibly 400 fans down, saying tickets would only be sold to people travelling on organised coaches.

Torquay stood firm until the Football League forced them to back down. "Our view is that the principle of knock-out cup ties should be applied to the play-offs in this respect," a League spokesman told the local newspaper. In the event just 300 terracing tickets were sent to Scunthorpe but police remained insistent that the midday Sunday kick-off stayed. This did not please the Humberside club, whose supporters would have to set off at 5.30am. However, it appeared that the limited tickets, the early start and heavy policing prevented a repeat of the trouble.

A Boxing Day match against Hereford in 1989 probably brought about the end of the Youth Squad for a lot of the lads. Fourteen Torquay fans were arrested during clashes and several were subsequently jailed. "Hereford were drinking in the Fortune of War pub when we walked in," recalled J, another Torquay lad. "It was Boxing Day and an early kick-off. I think there was a bit of banter and I can remember them saying their main lads were coming down and we could meet after the game. We had about sixty out and as soon as the final whistle went Torquay went to the away end and walked straight into their lads, and as you would expect it kicked off. Hereford were soon backed off and the majority of Torquay left to avoid the police. However, a few followed Hereford knowing that Torquay would soon reappear and when they did the remnants of the Hereford were soon pointed out and attacked. All the convictions came from one group of lads attacked getting in to a car."

The town centre had, however, become a tougher proposition than during the Eighties. "In the mid-Nineties Wigan brought a big firm down for a promotion party and were taking the piss in town on the night," said one of the Torquay crew. "Twenty to thirty locals got together and had it with them for about half a mile along the seafront, some needing hospital treatment."

In 2002, a Torquay United home match was the scene of a football fight that had nothing to do with Torquay. On the day that the club was entertaining Bristol Rovers, Plymouth were playing at Exeter. Shortly before the end of the match, with Torquay having taken a 2-1 lead, a group of Rovers left the pitch to confront a mob of Plymouth who had decided to make the short hop down from Exeter. In a short but fierce battle, knives and CS gas were used.

The current hooligan group who follow the club don't go by any name bar simply "Torquay", though some still claim to be Youth Squad. With banning orders against some older faces recently finishing, there has been a new alliance with a younger element in the resort and the hardcore claim they now regularly turn out 40 lads each week. "Soccer firms thinking they could visit the resort on a weekend jolly might find the nightclubs and bars less than welcoming," warned one, as many who had retired from the terrace scene still take offence at "wannabe thugs taking liberties".

TOTTENHAM HOTSPUR

Ground: White Hart Lane
Firms: The Yids
Rivals: Arsenal, Chelsea
Police Operations: Take Off

Frankie Parish was an unlikely hooligan leader. At only 5' 6", he certainly did not have the statue of Arsenal leader Johnny Hoy, and choosing to base himself around the pylons in a corner of the ground rather than in the heart of the Park Lane meant he did not have the authority and inspirational qualities of Chelsea's Mick Greenaway. Yet for all that, Parish was up there with the best, and by the early 1970s ran one of the hardest little mobs on the London football scene.

Hooliganism at Spurs had largely followed the fortunes of the club. During Tottenham's heyday of the early 1960s, their supporters were involved in street fights years before hooliganism became a national phenomenon. But, as it rose elsewhere, it declined at White Hart Lane, so much so that they largely became a hooligan joke by the end of the decade. The team had been overtaken by neighbours Arsenal and much of their fan base had also made the switch. On the terraces their decline was no less dramatic, with Hoy and the Arsenal boys regularly taking and holding the Park Lane End. In April 1970 the core of the Spurs mob was forced to take refuge in a local chemist shop after being chased around Seven Sisters by a rampant Gunners firm, highlighting not only their poor fighting record but also their lack of numbers. Their humiliation was complete when Arsenal took the title with a 1–0 win. By the time the referee blew his whistle and thousands of Arsenal fans spilled onto the pitch, most Spurs fans were already back home.

Spurs fans will cite Arsenal as their main rivals but for their hooligans Chelsea have been their main adversaries over the years. The hostility began at the 1967 FA Cup final when Spurs ran out 2–1 winners. Chelsea took revenge off the pitch at the League game at White Hart Lane the following season, when hundreds of Blues, led by Eccles, infiltrated the home end. When Spurs travelled to Stamford Bridge in 1968 there was further trouble. "Police formed a barrier between two groups of supporters, numbering about 200, trying to attack one another, and bottles were thrown during the match," noted one press report.

Spurs fared better out of London, regularly turning over clubs in the Midlands and the North. In 1969, Spurs fans hit the national headlines after their fans ran amok through a Hertfordshire town after they had earlier been thrown off a train for vandalism. Middle England was shocked that urban violence had been brought to their comfortable communities on a quiet Saturday evening. The newspapers were full of indignation, while the club promised to crack down on the troublemakers. "The directors, officials and players express disgust at the reports of vicious conduct last weekend by hooligans claiming to be supporters of this club," declared the match programme for the visit of Sunderland. "No true supporter would besmirch the proud and honoured name of the club in this way, and we wish it to be known we disassociate ourselves with all persons guilty of such appalling conduct. If any of the culprits are here today we want them to know they are unwelcome on this ground and wherever we play. Stay away – we don't want you."

George Marshall, chairman of the supporters' club, said that it would accept all responsibility for their fans travelling to away matches on football specials. "This seems the only way to restore the club's good name, which was tarnished by people who were not members last week." The club agreed to make fans give their names and addresses when buying tickets, ban anyone caught causing trouble and provide stewards to patrol further football specials.

The disorder also forced British Rail to rethink their travel arrangements for supporters. "We are investigating the possibility of using very old stock with centre corridors, so that the police and railway staff who patrol trains will have the situation under better observation," noted a company spokesman. "We have frequent discussions with the county police and they are to be stepped up so that assistance in considerable strength can be sought if there's a repetition of last Saturday's troubles." Mr Claude Hankins, divisional manager for the region said: "The best solution of all would be for football clubs to charter trains for their supporters, thus accepting responsibility for keeping elementary social discipline. One club, Luton, has already done this with encouraging results."

In a landmark article on young hooligans in the magazine *Time Out*, journalist Chris Lightbown had dismissed Spurs as a leading hooligan force by 1971, but White Hart Lane could still be a hostile place to visit. In August 1971, the Newcastle United team refused to come out for the second half until the referee assured them that it was safe after three of the players had been hit with missiles. Referee Ray Johnson had earlier had to use a loudspeaker to give a warning to "the idiots who are firing missiles at various players".

Another team which regularly experienced trouble from Spurs was Wolverhampton Wanderers. A match at Molineaux in August 1970 saw eight arrests and three stabbings, including one in which the blade missed a boy's heart by no more than an inch. When Spurs travelled up there again for the first away game of the 1972 season, the police were determined not to see a repeat of the trouble. A National Front demonstration was being held in the city, and to prevent fans and protestors from mixing, a heavy police presence greeted the 500 Spurs fans that came off the train. A line of vehicles broke up the travelling army, making it easier for the police to pick out and search people. Yet there was still disorder at the game and eight people were arrested. "It was business as usual," said a police spokesman. "There were one or two skirmishes, but it wasn't too bad."

A couple of months later, Spurs hosted Millwall in the League Cup. On the pitch the visitors were outclassed but off it was a different story. "Long before the game started the rival hooligans had engaged in battles for territorial advantage," noted one newspaper report. "Millwall took over the Park Lane end which is Tottenham's stronghold. Several times the legions of Tottenham followers attempted to reclaim their castle. The police managed to stop a total riot."

By 1972, Spurs were re-emerging as a hooligan force. Arsenal were stumbling and other mobs, such as West Ham and Chelsea, were being affected by the demise of the skinhead era. Spurs had never had as large a skinhead following and there were few of the racial clashes between local white and black gangs that were beginning to engulf Arsenal and West Ham. Under the stewardship of Frankie Parish they began to earn a reputation, even taking the West Ham North Bank in 1972. This was more by luck than planning, but while most of the Spurs yobs gathered in their usual spot in the South Stand, Parish took a mob into the top of the North Bank and caught West Ham by surprise. Parish was pragmatic and always looking to expand his firm's numbers, even to the point of linking up with rival mobs. A trip to Southend in Easter 1971 saw Spurs join up with Arsenal, and Parish even had a direct line of communication with West Ham. By 1972 he was becoming a legend, according to Chris Lightbown.

"Every smoothie worth his crombie has either seen or heard of Frankie Parish," he wrote.

A snapshot of the violent following at Tottenham was also captured at this time by the writer Hunter Davies in his landmark book *The Glory Game*. Davies followed the Spurs squad for the 1971-2 season, gaining access to management, players, club staff and fans alike, and his subsequent chronicle became an instant classic. One chapter, "The Skinhead Special", described a trip on the train to Coventry in the company of a young, aggressive group of fledgling hooligans.

As a species they used to be called skinheads, and still are by the press, but that term was already about a year out of date. Almost all of them had long hair and many of them could have passed for hippies, except for their big heavy boots. The average age was fifteen. They called themselves Smooths, if they called themselves anything ... The term Smooth had come about because of their smoother hair and more colourful clothes compared with the drabness of the skinheads.

The gang, led by a bespectacled but aggressive youth called Tony, said the worst places to visit were Manchester and Liverpool – "It's a long way from the station to the grounds and the police just let you get kicked" – but disparaged other clubs, suggesting Spurs considered themselves a major hooligan force at this time.

Spurs' terrace revival was mirrored on the pitch and in May 1974 the club reached the final of the UEFA Cup, where they were drawn against the Dutch side Feyenoord. It was to be one of the first outbreaks of serious disorder by an English club on the Continent and the beginning of a long-running feud between the two sets of supporters that was to have fatal consequences. Over 3,000 Spurs fans travelled to the Netherlands in the hope that their side would prevail after a 2–2 draw at White Hart Lane, but even before a ball had been kicked there was trouble, with 19 fans arrested after several shops were looted. The night got worse.

"Rotterdam had not been visited by such scenes of violence since the war," reported *The Times*. "More than two hundred people were hurt during the match when Tottenham supporters tore seats from concrete and hurled them at Feyenoord spectators. Before the game the Tottenham crowds had terrorised the town and 22 were arrested. Nine were 'too drunk to stand,' a police officer said. After the game about 80 cars were damaged near the stadium and the Feyenoord club estimated yesterday that £4,000 damage was done to the stadium."

Over 200 people were injured, including 50 who were taken to hospital, and 100 Spurs fans were arrested. Among the injured were five police officers who had attempted to stop the Tottenham fans fighting and throwing seats inside the ground. One was struck over the head with an iron bar. "It was a terrible day," said a police spokesman. "It is the first time we have seen anything like it. They have destroyed a great deal in the stadium." Before and after Feyenoord's 2–0 victory, the Spurs chairman and manager both made appeals for calm over the loudspeaker system.

English clubs had won the competition in the previous six seasons but Spurs returned in shame and in fear of the obvious fallout. Chairman Sidney Wale said that in future tickets would only be sold to "genuine fans", while the team captain said that he was "ashamed of our fans". The British Consul in Rotterdam was forced to visit the head of the local police to express his deepest apologies for behaviour one commentator described as "animal warfare". A *Times* editorial called for more than just apologies, saying that British people needed to be ashamed exporting what had become an all-too-familiar sight on Saturday afternoons. "Given the very serious circumstances of the case, it would seem proper for the British club to make good the damage done. A large cheque will not by itself wipe out the disgrace to the name of British football, but it would at least be compensation for the physical damage. It would, indeed, be a nice gesture if Spurs could assemble a group of their supporters to go over to Rotterdam to help clear up some of the mess at the stadium." A month later, a UEFA committee banned Tottenham Hotspur from playing their next two European matches at home and fined the club 25,000 Swiss Francs, about £3,500.

The Rotterdam violence emboldened the Spurs hooligans and during the next few seasons scenes of disorder were repeated up and down the country, home and away. There was virtual domination over local rivals Arsenal, with Spurs taking the North Bank on three occasions during the mid-Seventies. They gave the Gunners particularly severe beatings, home and away, during the 1976 season.

Spurs were a rated mob in the mid-Seventies, as is evident in the hooligan books written about that era, and were one of the few London teams to take large mobs northwards looking for trouble. Manchester City's Mickey Francis, in his book *Guvnors*, recalls a mob of 100 infiltrating the Kippax shortly before kick-off, while Manchester United hooligan Tony O'Neill attended his first ever away match at White Hart Lane during the 1970-71 season and saw fighting break out all around him. "After the game," he wrote in *Red Army General*, "we came out into a war zone. There was no police escort or controlled movement out, we just spilled into the street to be confronted by thousands of wild-eyed Cockneys." Spurs were one of the few mobs to travel to Old Trafford as a firm in the Seventies and made a vivid impression.

It was in 1975 that Spurs gave Chelsea hooligans a vicious beating in what some West Londoners have described as their darkest day. Leading Spurs that day was a black hooligan, Sammy Skyves, who would become well-known at White Hart Lane.

In May 1977, Spurs lost their place in the top flight of football and like Manchester United the season before, trouble followed Spurs around most of the country during their one season in the Second Division. Nowhere was it worse than at an Easter fixture at Brighton. Violence flared on the Friday night as hundreds of Tottenham supporters took advantage of abundant cheap travel and accommodation to make a weekend of it. Fights erupted all over the town and 51 people were arrested as Spurs fans met local youths in a night of violence. A 17-year-old girl walking in West Street was hit in the face by a brick and in Queen's Road an 18-year-old Spurs fan was stabbed in a brawl between 20 Albion fans and eight Spurs supporters. Labourer Alan Williams, from Brentwood, Essex, was rushed to hospital with a collapsed lung.

"Trouble began as rowdy Spurs fans travelled to Brighton by train last night," noted the local paper. "The seven o'clock train was stopped just outside Victoria as youths ran riot in the corridors and stormed the bar. A frightened passenger pulled the communication cord and the train reversed back into the station where police threw out some of the troublemakers. The rest continued their journey with a police escort after an 18-minute delay. Police also met each train-load of fans at Brighton and searched them.

"More fans arrived by car. A minibus of Spurs supporters stopped at the Duke of York pub in Sayers Common at closing time and tried to storm their way in. Publican Mr Malins barricaded the door and called the police as a window was smashed. There were more clashes between rival fans in Black Lion Street, Queen's Road, Cranbourne Street and Market Street."

The violence on Saturday continued from the night before in what was described as Brighton's "worst ever weekend of soccer thuggery". In total, 91 people were arrested over the weekend and 20 police officers and 85 people were injured, of which 20 needed hospital treatment. Police told the local newspaper that a large group of Albion fans attacked the visiting supporters, scattering them into nearby streets and buildings. At the ground, 29 people were arrested for breach of the peace, three for criminal damage and another three for possessing offensive weapons. A lack of segregation in the capacity crowd led to widespread disorder on the terraces and there were two pitch invasions which caused the game to be held up by 19 minutes.

"Efforts to contain the bulk of the Spurs fans into the north-east corner of the ground failed when early arrivals jumped two barriers into the North Stand, the traditional territory of Albion's heavy mob," reported the *Argus*. "This time they were heavily outnumbered. There was fighting a good hour before the start but insufficient police – although twice the usual number were patrolling inside and outside the ground – were there at that time to enforce segregation. Most were on duty outside. An appeal was made for reinforcements but by then it was too late. It was when the Spurs hardmen attacked from the back of the North Stand that trouble flared. Police moved in as hundreds of Brighton supporters got away from the violence by going on to the perimeter track."

The referee refused to be intimidated by the hooliganism and waited patiently for the police to restore order. "I shall keep the teams here all night if I have to to finish this game," he said.

Spurs' stint in Division Two lasted only a year but this did little to quell the trouble off the pitch. The club's first game back in the top flight was away at Notts Forest and 8,000 Spurs fans made the journey, surprising both clubs and the police. Many arrived hours before the game, catching the police off-guard. Fighting with rival fans spread from the street into the stadium and the kick-off was delayed for 14 minutes as 400 Spurs fans, angered about being separated from the rest of the travelling contingent, poured onto the pitch. "We didn't expect wolfpacks of idiots to be descending on the area of the ground and rampaging some three-and-a-half hours before a ball was kicked," admitted Supt John Yarnell.

Many of the national newspapers reported on a group of nuns being harassed on the train by Spurs fans. Questions were asked in the House of Commons and Nottingham Police were forced to reassess policing at home matches against teams with large travelling support.

Spurs had a liking for the FA Cup and in 1981 and 1982 they won the competition for the sixth and seventh times, then a record. They were a flair side, with Glenn Hoddle forming a creative midfield with the Argentinean imports Ossie Ardiles and Ricky Villa and Garth Crooks and Steve Archibald making a formidable strike partnership. The Cup took them back into Europe, and back to Holland, scene of the mayhem in 1974. In September 1981, Spurs played away at Ajax and the game was accompanied by running battles with local youths. Police told the media that two people had been stabbed in fighting before the match and there were unconfirmed reports that gunshots were heard.

"The fighting left the Zeedijk, a run-down street in the city's Red Light district and centre of Amsterdam's drug traffic, strewn with glass from broken windows and bottles," reported the news agency Reuters. "One black was taken to hospital with knife wounds, and an English fan was also injured but disappeared." Eleven Spurs fans were arrested.

Spurs were unable to win the FA Cup for the third consecutive season but still qualified for the UEFA Cup after finishing fourth in the League. They went on to win the competition for the second time in their history but the cup run was accompanied by further Tottenham violence on the continent. The first incident was back in Rotterdam, where they were drawn against their old foes Feyenoord. Old memories die hard and there were several, on both sides, who appeared keen to carry on the trouble from nine years before.

"Pitch battle," ran the front-page headline in the *Daily Mirror*. "Bomb is seized at match of hate." A crude explosive device was found among home supporters after a battle between rival fans in Rotterdam, which left at least 27 people injured, eleven seriously. The police noted that both Dutch and English supporters "sparked the violence". The homemade bomb consisted of a copper tube crammed with high explosives, leaving police in no doubt that the aim was to kill. "It appeared the intention was to throw the bomb at Tottenham supporters during the game," said the local chief of police.

While mass carnage had been averted, there was still considerable trouble around the match, which Spurs won 2–0. Fighting broke out inside the stadium and several smoke bombs were thrown during the match. Police confiscated a huge armoury of knives from fans entering the ground, though 13 people were still hospitalised, including seven Spurs fans with stab wounds. Another British fan suffered a fractured skull in the fighting.

There was further disorder after the game as hundreds of Spurs fans, in the words of the *Daily Mirror*, "ran riot" on the luxury ferry *Princess Beatrix*. The ship's shop was looted, the lifeboats ransacked and even the navigation system was damaged. The ferry was delayed until a unit of Dutch troops arrived to escort the fans home.

While the Spurs fans received widespread condemnation, they pointed the finger at the Dutch. "They were waiting to get their own back for the trouble nine years ago," said 18-year-old Clive Brooks. "They had knives, blades and razors. We didn't stand a chance. We had to fight for our lives."

The link to the 1974 game was not lost on Tottenham officials. Chief Scout Bill Nicholson, a Spurs legend who had been the club's manager in 1974, said, "Obviously the Feyenoord fans could see their team losing and got the needle." The current manager, Keith Burkenshaw, was more intuitive. "I don't know whose fault it is, our fans or theirs. But there must be memories of the last game nine years ago."

The first leg of the final was played in Brussels, where Spurs drew 1–1 with Anderlecht. However, the game was overshadowed by the fatal shooting of 19-year-old Spurs fan Brian Flanagan. He was shot by an owner of a bar after a group of Spurs fans refused to pay for drinks. A fight quickly erupted, which spilt out onto the street, and as some of the Londoners attempted to run off the bar owner reached for his gun and fired several times. Flanagan was hit in the chest and died an hour later.

This was the worst of many incidents that night. Most of the trouble occurred after the game as thousands of travelling fans spilled out of the stadium. Cars were overturned and bars and restaurants attacked. Two policemen were stabbed and several cars set alight. In another incident, a group of English fans went into a local hardware store and asked for knives, hammers and other tools. When the owner refused, the fans simply helped themselves. Over 100 Spurs fans were arrested and the Belgian bar owner was charged with manslaughter, but he remained unrepentant. "The behaviour of the English fans made me so mad I lost control," he told police.

Sadly, death was not totally new to Spurs fans. A few years before, a Leeds United fan had been killed during a clash between the two sets of fans at a match in London. This began a longstanding feud between the respective hooligan mobs. Another death occurred in 1981, this time of a Spurs fan after a home game against Manchester United. As rival gangs converged on Seven Sisters tube station, someone pressed the emergency stop button on the escalator causing several people to fall and one man was crushed to death and several others injured. Again, it created a great deal of bitterness among Spurs hooligans, particularly towards United's so-called Cockney Reds.

The mid-Eighties saw Spurs overtaken in the hooligan table by the likes of Chelsea, West Ham and Leeds, but they were still a handful for any rivals. They out-thought Birmingham City fans at St Andrews, attacking the home fans in the seats and on the pitch. Twenty-three fans were arrested. "Blues won the game 1–0, but 'the Yids', as their hooligans were known, got the off-field victory that day," wrote Caroline Gall in *Zulus*. "They exploited the Zulus' lack of organisation and planning to turn them over and achieve the best 'result' by any firm at St Andrew's in the past twenty years."

A couple of years later, over 200 football fans were involved in trouble in Nottingham and ten arrests were made. There was further fighting inside Forest's ground when home fans moved into a section of the Executive Stand reserved for Spurs fans; however, police moved in and prevented any major disorder. A Forest fan needed ten stitches in a gash to his chin.

Even by the mid-Eighties, Tottenham's hooligan mob had not come up with a snappy name life ICF, Headhunters or Bushwhackers, though the tag

Soul Firm was briefly bandied around (and eventually appropriated by Cardiff City's Soul Crew). Instead they were simply known as the Yids. This was originally a term of abuse from other fans due to the fact that then-chairman Irving Scholar (and later successors Daniel Levy and Sir Alan Sugar) was Jewish and many of the club's supporters were drawn from north London areas such as Golders Green, with its large Jewish population. Rival fans made up sick songs about "the Yids from Tottenham" being "on their way to Belsen" but the hooligans adopted the name as a badge of pride.

A Spurs home game against Manchester United in 1985 saw them attack a United mob of 150 lads, made up largely of Cockney Reds, from all sides after the game. The away mob splintered, with most running off to escape. United leader Tony O'Neill was caught and by his own admission couldn't remember how many blows he took. Even when they got back to Euston, several torrid hours later, a mob of Spurs charged out of a side street armed with poles and forced them to retreat into the station.

A Milk Cup tie against Portsmouth brought trouble at both fixtures. A large 6.57 Crew travelled to North London for the first leg and so Spurs responded for the return. "Night of Terror," was how the Portsmouth *News* reported the trouble that accompanied the return fixture a fortnight later. "Broken bottles, knives and a metal cosh were weapons left behind by the football fans that soured Pompey's Milk Cup victory," it continued. "After a rampage that left a pub wrecked, cars damaged, windows smashed and Somers Town residents terrified, Spurs supporters dumped their weapons on the steps of a Portsmouth bingo hall."

The Tottenham fans went on the rampage after a pub they were drinking in was attacked by locals. At its height, over 200 people were involved in running battles through the Somers Town district of the city. Glasses, sticks, pool balls and cues were all used as weapons. All the main windows of the Travellers Rest pub were smashed and after the battle the road outside was littered with glass, smashed beer glasses and Christmas decorations ripped from the pub. The Spurs fans quickly turned their attention to the police and 53 Londoners were arrested.

After the game, rioting spread through the streets. "I have never been so terrified in my life," said one young woman, who held a knife in her hand as she cowered on the floor of her living room. "I would have used the knife if anyone had come in." She and her friend were alerted to the trouble when they heard glass smashing and screaming in the street outside. "It looked like hundreds of them out there. We could see furniture and sticks coming flying out of the windows. Then they smashed our window. We were petrified. We went into the kitchen and grabbed a knife. We lay on the floor of the kitchen, cowering down where no-one could see us. We were hugging each other and crying. I was afraid they would come in and rape us."

Spurs fans faced the local magistrates the following morning. Their duty solicitor insisted that they were just "private individuals set upon by thugs," and that the blame should be placed squarely at the feet of Portsmouth fans. "It is a great shame that there is not one person in court who threw a brick through the windows," said John Saulet, acting for the defendants. "It is a pity that the Spurs fans were caught on the receiving end of the sort of reception Pompey supporters mete out to visiting fans." He went on to insist that these supporters had no history of previous trouble and that they had travelled across Britain and Europe in the same coach without any problem. "They always have used the same coach driver and he has said it is a pleasure to drive them around." A compromise was struck and the Spurs agreed to be bound over for a year if some of the more serious charges were dropped.

"Don't blame us, we're innocent," insisted Spurs fans as they left the court. Several told a local journalist that they were quietly having a drink when, for no reason, locals attacked the pub. "The Pompey fans were all to blame," one was quoted as saying. "They were the ones that smashed in all the windows yet we are the ones up in court. It's totally unfair. We picked up the first things we could lay our hands on. We thought we'd better defend ourselves with something. Wouldn't you?"

The FA was quick to intervene, though only to clear Portsmouth FC of any blame for the trouble. The club could only be considered responsible for disorder inside the ground but as it had already banned 105 spectators, its record was considered good. The club, however, did agree to ban from Fratton Park for life anyone successfully prosecuted for the incident.

In 1987, Spurs were heading for another FA Cup final when they drew Watford in the semi-final at Villa Park. There was little trouble between rival fans but the presence of the North London firm was too much of an opportunity for the Zulus to overlook. Acquaintances on both sides ensured that a meet was arranged for close to Snow Hill station but the arrangements did not stay secret, as the police were camped opposite with the camera rolling. Blues boasted of victory in the short but fierce encounter, with two Spurs fans receiving stab wounds. The fight was to form a large part of the police evidence during the subsequent Operation Red Card trials against the Zulus.

By the late Eighties, the hooligan stock of the Yids was growing as more established and once-active mobs at rival clubs were declining. They were one of the few London mobs to be spared the police operations that hit many of the capital's gangs, including Millwall, Chelsea, West Ham, Arsenal and Charlton Athletic. The changing fortunes were most sharply seen in Spurs' relationship with their old-time rivals Chelsea. "Ten mad minutes as

Spurs and Chelsea go to war," ran the backpage headline in the *Evening Standard*, following Spurs' away match at Stamford Bridge in October 1992:

> The match, say police, passed 'peacefully and without incident' – but on the streets outside, rival fans went on the rampage as a pitched battle raged outside a Chelsea pub.
>
> In just 10 minutes of street fighting they caused damage put at thousands of pounds when they wrecked a pub, damaged cars and shattered windows.
>
> The violence erupted as 200 Chelsea and Spurs followers gathered in the area of the Ifield Tavern in Cathcart Road, just minutes from Chelsea's ground.
>
> Rampaging fans grabbed iron bars, wooden pool cues and bottles as the fighting blocked the pavement at 1.50pm.

Spurs were up for it that day, indeed the confrontation had been planned for some time. Trevor "T" Tanner, a relative newcomer to the hooligan scene, was emerging as the Spurs leader, and had carried out a recce of the Earls Court area a fortnight before the game to sort out possible meeting points. On the morning of the game he met his men in The Continental, with several other pubs taking the overfill. The word went out to move at 1.30pm.

At the appropriate time they filed out onto the Chelsea streets and made their way towards the Ilfield Road, home to pubs frequented by Chelsea's hardcore. Greeting them was a home mob of 150 to 200, many armed with makeshift weapons acquired from the pub. Spurs attacked and within moments debris littered the street. "It spilled out on to the street when Chelsea fans inside the pub gave chase," one eyewitness told journalists. "They came out with pool cues, stakes from saplings in the street, anything they could lay their hands on. They even ripped a bumper off a car to use as a weapon."

Spurs, however, claimed the "result" and lost little time in rubbing Chelsea's noses in it. Chelsea did not have to wait long to hit back and fired their opening salvo at Spurs' home game against QPR, whose hooligans had a close relationship with the Headhunters. The game passed off peacefully but two hours after the game a mixed mob of QPR and Chelsea attacked a small group of Spurs drinking in a North London pub on the Tottenham High Road. Spurs claimed they repulsed the attack, despite being up against 80-100 lads. A week later, Chelsea returned. This time there was a tidy group of 30-40 Spurs drinking in the Bull, half in anticipation of a repeat attack. Sure enough, at 8.30 that evening a Chelsea mob, numbering about the same as the previous week, appeared. "This time we were ready," recalled Trevor Tanner – and the attack was repulsed.

Each meeting between Spurs and Chelsea was now a grudge match, with

Trevor Tanner making it a personal mission to crush the West London wide-boys. In March 1993, Tottenham played away at Stamford Bridge and their mob met up at Kings Cross at eight in the morning. Their destination was the Three Kings pub close to Gloucester Road tube. Their opponents appeared before the bulk of the Spurs mob had arrived at the pub, but against far superior numbers Tanner and his team, who had armed themselves with much of the pub's furnishings, piled out. A flare fired by a Chelsea hooligan ripped into a nearby car, setting it alight. Spurs threw their bottles, chairs and pool cues before chasing their attackers down the road. "No excuses, giving it to them at 11.30 in the morning in their manor," said Tanner. "Enough said."

The euphoria was shortlived. Within minutes of the fight the air was buzzing with the sound of police sirens. Seemingly from the woodwork, police swarmed around the streets, picking up Spurs fans. Five weeks later dawn raids netted more hooligans, including Tanner himself. He would receive a three-year jail sentence for his role in the violence. Unbeknown to him and the other hooligans, NCIS had received details of the meet from an informant and their video specialist was in the building opposite. Fearful of the accusation that they allowed violence to occur despite prior knowledge, the police later claimed that the information was not specific and that their presence was more of a coincidence than it actually was.

The Spurs mob was earning a name for itself, both with other firms but also with the authorities. "Spurs thugs 'worst in the capital'," noted a headline in one London newspaper. "The Football Intelligence Unit said Spurs' hooligan element is the best organised, and provokes the greatest number of incidents, of any of the capital's clubs," the article continued. It listed trouble at Tottenham's home match against Feyenoord, in the Cup Winners Cup, numerous clashes with Chelsea and other confrontations with Millwall, Arsenal, Manchester United, Sheffield United and Middlesbrough.

Shortly before Euro 96 began, a number of Spurs hooligans were dawn raided as part of Operation Take Off, a police task group set up after clashes after the Arsenal v Spurs game earlier that season.

One especially sickening confrontation came on the night of an England international at Wembley. "Bloody trail after horror machete attack on soccer fans," ran the newspaper headline. "A mile-long trail of blood marked the route taken by four soccer fans after they were attacked with machetes."

The trouble erupted after a group of Derby County supporters began drinking in a Tottenham pub on the night of the England versus Argentina match. A fight broke out inside the Bank pub shortly before kick-off and soon spilled out onto the street. The victims were chased down a street before being found by police collapsed in Tottenham High Road. They had been brutally slashed with machetes and suffered appalling injuries. The attack on the four fans was treated by police as attempted murder. "We had a mile of blood from the pub to Tottenham police station," Detective Inspector Simon Thomas told the press. "It took me twenty minutes to walk it. It was absolutely horrific."

The Spurs mob were again in the news after trouble at their club's FA Cup quarter-final at Manchester City. For many of them the fixture provided an opportunity for a weekend away, and in the North West that meant Blackpool. About 70 Spurs arrived in the seaside town ahead of their Sunday fixture and it wasn't long before the free-flowing beer turned into mayhem as they clashed with a small group of Man City fans late on the Saturday night. For the game itself, the Spurs mob had agreed to rendezvous in a quiet pub in Moss Side. The short hop to the ground proved uneventful but inside the stadium was very different. As the London club took an unassailable lead, home fans reacted with fury to some Spurs fan celebrating behind them in the Kippax executive boxes. They egged on Tanner and his Spurs thugs, who then clashed with their rivals and then the police and stewards on the pitch.

"Blues' day of shame," was how the *Manchester Evening News* reported the disorder. Thirty-seven people were arrested inside the ground and another 20 ejected. One City fan was stabbed in the back, while in a separate incident a home fan attempted to kick out at Tottenham's goalkeeper. For City's groundsman, Stan Gibson, it was all too much. "I feel like packing it in. I have been with this club for thirty-three years and I'm sickened by what those morons did."

Arsenal's burgeoning trophy cabinet during the Nineties, coupled with Tottenham's football stagnation, led to increased bitterness between the two sets of fans. Spurs' hooligan element was considerably more powerful than the Gooners but there were several nasty clashes between the two sets of supporters. In November 1998, a match at Highbury saw 25 arrests after a mob of Spurs attacked an Arsenal pub. Later that season there was trouble in Leicester as 150 Spurs fans stopped off in the city after their FA Cup match at Barnsley was postponed. After first drinking in Sheffield, they made their way to Leicester where fighting with locals led to eight arrests. A few months later, Spurs fans attacked the police after they were prevented from attacking a van driven by a Leeds United supporter. Numerous missiles were thrown at the police by a large group gathered outside the Bank pub.

One particularly nasty incident came at an FA Cup semi-final between the two North London rivals at Old Trafford in 2001. "I got the firm to meet in Wetherspoons in Manchester on the Saturday afternoon," said Trevor Tanner. "Arsenal were supposed to show at six o'clock. There was a big kick-off outside against Sheffield Wednesday, who got battered, but no show from Arsenal. Next day there was a big clash near Salford Quays, but the day will always be remembered for what happened in a hotel bar. Forty Arsenal in there called it on with fifteen Spurs. The Tottenham were big hitters who more than held their own until Arsenal called for support from another pub nearby. Forty more of them came in and absolutely battered the fifteen Spurs. One main lad was in a really bad way, smashed up on the floor, yet they took photographs of him while people were waiting for an ambulance and later put the image on tee-shirts. They will never be forgiven for that."

But it continued to be against Chelsea that Spurs' most consistent trouble occurred. A clash between rival gangs in 1998 just off Oxford Street saw several Chelsea fans imprisoned [see CHELSEA in *Hooligans*]. In February 2000, the Metropolitan Police arrested 80 football supporters as a preventative measure before the two sides met at White Hart Lane. According to the Met's own website, "officers visited the Park Hotel Pub in Willoughby Lane, Tottenham, where away supporters had congregated. Searches were conducted in the pub and a number of offensive weapons were recovered. These included a meat cleaver, CS spray and various knives (believed three)."

Later that day the police arrested 80 Chelsea fans in order to "prevent a breach of the peace". More weapons were found, including a baseball bat and flick knives. Chief Supt Steven James, the officer in charge of policing the match, said, "Early intervention by police prevented serious violence as it was quite obvious that the away supporters were intent on causing serious injury. The carrying of such lethal weapons is outrageous."

In January 2002, a man was stabbed in a fight between rival hooligans outside West Kensington tube station. According to a police report, "A small group of Tottenham also attacked Chelsea fans at Victoria Station." Inside the ground Jimmy Floyd Hasselbaink was hit by a coin and a bottle was thrown at Les Ferdinand. When the sides met at White Hart Lane two months later, rival hooligans fought outside the ground and Tottenham fans hurled stones and smashed a coach window as Chelsea left the area. Two men were stabbed and a policeman suffered a broken foot. Coins and missiles were thrown inside the ground.

Trevor Tanner, in his recent book *Tottenham Massive*, boasts that Spurs were London's leading hooligan mob in recent years. Certainly they appear to have been dominant amongst the capital's Premiership sides and the pasting they gave Chelsea early in the 2005/06 season seemed to confirm this. Their strength has also been acknowledged by other mobs around the country, including Birmingham City.

"On our return to the Premiership in 2002, Spurs brought their best firm to St Andrew's and somehow got out of the away end while the game was on and made their way round to the main stand, where a lot of our lads sit," recalled one hooligan in the book *Zulus,* "but the Old Bill intervened before anything happened. Spurs had done their homework that day and knew exactly where to go." The return fixture saw a large Blues mob travel down to London but strong policing kept rival fans apart. "I hate to admit this ... but the Yids can put a good firm together and are probably the best to come out of London in the last few years," added the Birmingham hooligan.

The same year saw Spurs clash with Middlesbrough's Frontline, arguably one of Britain's leading hooligan mobs at the time. "They turned up at our place and I've got big respect for that," said Trevor Tanner. "They are a main firm." However, their ultimate test came in July 2001, when the strange decision was made to play a pre-season friendly at Millwall. For both it was a chance to claim the title of top mob of London. Tottenham arrived at South Bermondsey station over 200-handed. Millwall were also in the area and for a brief minute or two the bottom end of Jamaica Road became a battleground. A police officer later reported to the BBC journalists making the *Hooligans* series that the fighting was so intense, and involving hundreds of men in their thirties and above, that the Met's surveillance team simply ran off. The police managed to round up the Spurs mob but they then became the targets, as bricks, bottles and fists were directed at them.

The rival mobs were eventually herded into the ground but the gates were opened five minutes before the end of play. Spurs seized this opportunity and piled out in the direction of the home end. The police quickly moved in but there were several small skirmishes before the away fans were successfully taken out of the area. For Spurs, the day confirmed their dominance.

Yet some rivals claim to have found Spurs wanting. In 2002, Tottenham Hostpur played a Worthington Cup final against Blackburn Rovers at the Millennium Stadium. For Cardiff's Soul Crew it was a chance to test themselves against one of the Premiership's finest. The home firm mobbed up on the Saturday evening after learning that Spurs were making a weekend of it. However, in the event 80 Spurs hooligans opted for the safety of Swansea for the Saturday night entertainment and only headed into Cardiff on the day of the game. A few months later, hundreds of Soul Crew travelled to White Hart Lane after the two teams were drawn together in the same competition. Whilst heavy policing prevented wide-scale disorder, there was sporadic fighting across North London.

And in October 2003, after a high-profile game against London rivals West Ham United one newspaper carried the following report:

> Ninety-three West Ham fans have been arrested after violence before and after a London derby football match.

Police arrested the fans before the Hammers' Carling Cup clash against Tottenham Hotspur at White Hart Lane, north London, on Wednesday.

They were called at 15.08 GMT to a Tottenham supporters' pub, The Cockerel, on Tottenham High Road, after reports of a large group causing trouble.

The pub suffered "extensive damage" and a number of West Ham fans were later arrested at nearby Northumberland Park for criminal damage and violent disorder.

Police said "skirmishes" continued throughout the afternoon and evening on the High Road and at least two other pubs were damaged.

There were some injuries and one man, who is not thought to be seriously hurt, was taken to hospital.

Scotland Yard said there was no trouble inside White Hart Lane, although two people were arrested and eight ejected for drinking and vandalism offences during the game which started at 1945 GMT. Police are now examining CCTV footage to "find any other perpetrators".

Gary Lee, the owner of the Cockerel, told BBC London: "I'm surprised at the police. They are usually on the ball but I think they were caught on the hop. At one point there were just two WPCs in the middle of it all and I felt sorry for them.

"But I don't understand how 150 football fans can go from one side of London to the other without being noticed."

For nearly 40 years Spurs have been one of Britain's hardest hooligan mobs. While they might not have had the media attention of others, especially in London, the respect shown to them from other gangs over several decades is a clear indication of their presence.

Like many of the bigger firms, the Yids found that European football was increasingly the outlet for their violent tendencies. In August 2006, four people were injured during a brawl involving 80 fans after Tottenham's 1-1 friendly draw against Borussia Dortmund. Dortmund police said one English fan was hospitalized with a head injury after bottles and chairs were flung in an Irish pub in the city. Seven Germans were taken into custody, along with two English fans and a Dutchman. All were later released. About 50 English fans got into a shouting match with Germans in the pub, triggering the brawl, according to Dortmund police captain Werner Ruhoss. "The majority involved were English," Ruhoss said. "It's hard to say who provoked whom."

Three months later, Spurs fans rioted in the German city of Cologne ahead of a midweek UEFA Cup match against Bayer Leverkusen. A group of about 80 fans smashed up the interior of a pub, causing damage costing 5,000 euros, and also damaged a car. One English supporter was hurt in the incident. Visiting fans often gather in the pubs and bars of Cologne before making the short journey to the industrial city of Leverkusen for a match.

Perhaps the most violent incident in recent years, however, was, at the time of writing, still the subject of a police inquiry. According to the *Evening Standard* of 12 March 2007:

At least 10 people were stabbed as hardcore soccer violence erupted in the streets of west London.

Drinkers fled as running battles broke out between about 40 thugs carrying knives, baseball bats, wooden clubs embedded with nails and hockey sticks.

The riot began last night outside the White Horse pub in Parsons Green, known as the "Sloaney Pony", following a dramatic FC Cup clash between Chelsea and Spurs.

Police believe it was either a prearranged fight organised over mobile phones and the internet or Tottenham hooligans had ambushed Chelsea fans "in their own backyard".

One witness said: "It was pandemonium, I've never seen scenes like it. It was a battlefield in the middle of Fulham's smartest area on a Sunday evening. I was on Parsons Green itself having a quiet drink with friends – nothing to do with the football.

"Suddenly there was a lot of loud shouting and screaming and we saw a huge mob fighting outside the Sloaney Pony, smashing each other with baseball bats and anything they could get their hands on. People were fleeing in all directions, it was chaos."

Police initially arrested 34 men, including seven who were taken to hospital. The oldest was 52.

Further reading: *The Glory Game*, Hunter Davies (Sphere Books), *Tottenham Massive*, Trevor Tanner (John Blake)

TRANMERE ROVERS

Ground: Prenton Park
Firms: Free Library Boys, Tranmere Stanley Boys.
Rivals: Wrexham, Port Vale, Stockport County

Tranmere Rovers fans have never had it easy. Called Scousers by many and "woolies" (woolybacks, or sheep) by the Scousers, they can't win. Not only does their small club live in the shadow of two of the biggest clubs in British football, but given their proximity to Liverpool, being called Scousers is a label their proud followers hate. They are quick to point out that Birkenhead, the town where Rovers resides, on the Wirral, has a Cheshire postcode and is not affiliated to Liverpool in any way.

For those unaware of Tranmere's location, it is an area of Birkenhead which is a short ferry ride across the river Mersey or a five-minute jaunt through the Mersey Tunnel. In the opposite direction it is a fifteen-minute journey from the Welsh border. Over time Rovers have struggled to stem the flow of potential fans to Goodison or Anfield, and for years the majority of home games were played on Friday nights in an attempt to attract fans to Prenton Park.

Whilst many from the area do follow Everton or Liverpool, the hooligan mobs of the three clubs have clashed repeatedly for many years and there is a genuine hatred between Birkenhead gangs and Scouse football mobs. For years, Birkenhead youths were terrorised while waiting for transport back across the river. But these hassles, rather than act as a deterrent, seemed to encourage Tranmere's mob to make a stand against the Scouse thugs, and even today trips home from away games via Lime Street Station can result in violence on the streets of Liverpool when the mobs bump into each other.

The first hooligan crowd at Rovers was a collection of local hard men, dockers and general bootboys who, like most clubs' followers, defended the home end from infiltration rather than going looking for trouble. And trouble was not hard to find. "There were good and bad days," said one veteran Rovers lad. "In those days there were some tasty firms around in the lower leagues, and the likes of Sheffield Wednesday, Port Vale, Bolton and Hull City would always try their hand at taking the Cowshed End. For some reason Hull always seemed to get a good hiding and they were unlucky really, as we always pulled a top mob out when they came to town."

"What people don't realise is that Birkenhead, although situated on the Wirral, is a tough fucking town. Yes, the Wirral sounds very nice with its little Tory villages and upmarket areas like Parkgate and Neston, but in reality Birkenhead is a million miles away from all that, and the Woodchurch and Ford estates in the Seventies and Eighties were amongst the biggest and most run-down in Britain. Some firms came to town thinking Birkenhead was actually a posh area of Liverpool and many had changed their minds by the time they were on their way home."

Shaun Tordoff, in his book *City Psychos,* confirmed that Tranmere was indeed not what the Hull lads had expected: "It was our first game in Division Three and at a place we only knew to be somewhere near

Liverpool. In the ground, scuffling broke out on both sides of the fence and briefly spilled on to the pitch. We were three-one up and all sitting and lying across the terracing as the pre-match drinking and hot sun took its toll. In the dying moments and with the exit gates open, a mob of Tranmere showed themselves.

"Bursting in through the exit of the covered end, about 100 of them appeared, armed with sticks and rocks. Led by oldish blokes in their late twenties, they were well organised and knew exactly what to do. They laid into any City fans they could spot, bricking others and punching anyone between fifteen and thirty in what seemed like a well rehearsed attack."

It was indeed a well rehearsed attack. At the time, policing at Rovers games was virtually non-existent as crowds dipped below 2,000, but within that sparse following was a band of thugs who were to take Tranmere up the hooligan ladder as the Eighties arrived. The decade brought football violence into everybody's front room as it nearly brought the game to its knees.

Around 1980 the older fighters started to take a back seat and leave the sorting of terrace issues to youngsters who were coming through the ranks thick and fast. With Liverpool being so close, it was a nap that the changing face of football fashion would find its way across the Mersey long before it was exported further afield. The older skins still turned out for the big home games and local away matches but a young firm of "scallies" were soon regarded as top dogs at Prenton Park, and for the next ten years they were at the forefront of all the major disturbances involving Tranmere.

Awaydays, by the highly regarded Liverpool novelist Kevin Sampson, is a fictional account of a mob of Tranmere hooligans called "The Pack" and is believed to be based on a real hooligan gang at the club in the Eighties. One of the lads who regularly went with the real "Pack" was Steve who, although born and bred in Birkenhead, was an Everton supporter. Nevertheless he became addicted to the thrills of watching lower league football and the ease at which the hooligans could go about their business.

"With Tranmere playing the majority of their games on a Friday night, many kids from Birkenhead and the Wirral watched Everton or Liverpool on a Saturday as well as Rovers," said Steve. "It was a nightmare for us at times, as gangs of Scousers used to hang about Lime Street and pick off us 'woolies' as we were making our way home. That station has seen some nasty incidents over the years. I would say Liverpool were the worst for it, but Everton had their share of twats as well until they realised that the lads who watched them from over the water came in handy at away games when the Scouse numbers needed backing up.

"Both Liverpool and Everton lost good lads because of the bullying and many like myself ended up watching Rovers full time in the end. In 1980, there was a huge change at Rovers, older lads took a back seat and a younger, more violent posse attached themselves to the club. These lads were all into the gear – clothes, not smack; well, most of them – and the music, the pubs and the fighting went hand in hand with being part of the mob. We were normally only about thirty-strong but for some games we pulled 150, which for the lower leagues was decent.

"All the main lads were mates and there was very little in-house fighting, which made us solid as a unit. Carl Power went on to become one of the main faces at Rovers for years but good lads like the Robinson brothers, Hughey, Harris, Paddy and many more made up the firm which went on to become the Free Library Boys, which was the name of a pub near Hamilton Square we used to all drink in.

"Before long we were the ones handing out slaps at Lime Street, and revenge for years of snide attacks was sweet on many occasions when we bumped into mobs of Scousers on our way home from an away game. Soon there was real hatred between us and the Scousers, as at last they woke up to the fact that there were three firms on Merseyside.

"The rest of the country had not sussed us out though and we were constantly branded Scousers everywhere we went. The chant of 'You Scouse Bastards' used to make us laugh and sometimes the likes of Rochdale would sing, 'If you all hate Scousers clap your hands,' and we would all clap and join in. The thick fuckers looked at us like we were daft. It was at this time that we all started singing, 'Don't be mistaken and don't be misled/We are not Scousers we're from Birkenhead/So you can fuck your cathedral and your Pier Head/'Cause we are not Scousers, we're from Birkenhead.' It was spot on, especially when we were on suicide missions around the Crown and the Yankee by Lime Street after consuming too much cheap cider on the way back from wherever.

"During these crazy days, we went to most away games. It was all we had, a shit job all week and Tranmere at the weekend. Clothes were important at the time and shit games were missed so you could splash out on something you had seen over the water the week before.

"Local games were always the best, we went to them all and very rarely came unstuck. Rochdale, Chester, Wigan, Wrexham were all relatively easy for us, although it was a bit on top one year at Rochdale when they had a load of Man City boys with them. We ended up fighting them in every part of the ground, as you could walk right around it. We ended up in the seats and they got the result but only thanks to the rent-a-mob they had with them. Stockport was another who always turned out for us, 'You Scouse bastards' again, Man City again. We are not fucking Scousers; how many times you thick bastards? Anyway, they were not having it and every time we went there we were guaranteed mither.

"Wrexham came one year and caught us out. We were holed up in the Black Horse thinking it was the usual no show from the sheepshaggers when a load of lads ran in saying they were on their way up from Rock Ferry. By the time we got it together the bizzies had it all wrapped up but the Welsh lot managed to get in the seats and at least had a go. Afterwards, we had welcoming parties at all the stations but the British Transport Police were with them. It was the first time they ever showed by train and they got credit for that, but we had been going there and taking the piss for years, so it was about time they showed.

"Port Vale was not far away and we have every respect for them. They gave us problems from the Seventies right through to the Nineties. One season we went in the upper seats and one lad was taunting them below and someone said, 'These cunts will climb up here in a minute.' We took no notice but minutes later loads of them were scaling the walls to get at us and a few of ours jumped into the paddock to get away and were never trusted again.

"Another game that it came bang on was at Bury. The game got called off and we ended up staying there on the piss. It went off with some United fans and we gave it them. In the end, the town was out for us and about 100 of them chased us all over. After the re-arranged game, we were walking back to the car park when a fucking van pulled up and it was the United lads with a gun. 'We're gonna shoot you Scouse cunts.' There was no time to tell them we're not Scouse, it was offside and pray the fucking thing is not loaded.

"With most of the home games being on a Friday night, very few firms not from the North West turned out massive numbers in those days. Bristol City and Wolves were an exception. City brought a decent mob more than once and one season Wolves took the Carlton Pub on Borough Road before we could get near them. It soon went off and the pub was totalled. With the help of some old fellas who took offence at the Wolves lot fucking up their boozer, we battered them out of there. There were casualties on both sides and it was described as a bloodbath; we were loving it, and had come of age. By the ground, young kids were running to us shouting that Wolves were in the Prenton, so we attacked that as well. Eventually, bizzies from Liverpool were drafted over to restore order. We had finally made them realise that even though we were Division Four, we were bang at it.

"Sheffield United were another lot to come in numbers. They arrived at 10.30am with two coachloads of pure boys. To this day only a few have done that. We were drinking in Spud Murphy's, and as the day wore on the

Blades split into small numbers and we were battering them all over town. By the time they got it together by the ground it was too late and we had done enough. Inside they had another shock, they brought a firm into the Main Stand seats but we had a few hundred in there and they shit themselves. Over the years only Hull City came in that stand and came anywhere near to taking it.

"Cup matches were always a buzz. We got Chelsea one year and they brought 2,000, including 500 lads, in the stand, which was as good as we had seen. We became the Tranmere Stand Boys briefly, but the name never caught on and soon some called us the Tranmere Stanley Boys, which was as close to a firm name as we ever got.

"Bolton were another lot to turn out a full squad for a cup match and it was one of the nastiest mobs to come to Rovers. Before the game, a good Tranmere lad was slashed by them and it went off before and during the game. Only the drafting in of the flat caps [police] from over the river prevented a riot afterwards. After the lad was slashed we went mental and chased a mob of them all the way to the ground. The joy was short-lived as the game finished in a draw and at the replay we came across a huge mob of at least 400 of them. We got dicked 4–1 and they still wanted to kill us but the bizzies saved the day.

"In the end we started to get undercover police with us and it sort of fizzled out. As with most clubs, those mid-Eighties were the best ever for the lads, but the drug scene was always big in Birkenhead and soon most were going to raves or earning money from pills and the football was no longer the most important thing in their lives."

Another well known Rovers lad, Jeff, was born an Evertonian but became involved with Tranmere on a fairly regular basis from about 1980 to 1985.

He was of the view that the journey to Tranmere for an away team could be quite misleading.

"If you come in from the South, along the M53, and go to the ground via Bebington, the image is of green fields, rather prosperous upper middle class homes, all in all a very pleasant area. If teams came in from Liverpool, and the M62, the image of Birkenhead was very different, with dilapidated buildings and poor housing. Birkenhead is historically a ship-building town, and with that comes its own brand of toughness.

"Tranmere's lads came from various estates around Birkenhead, including the Ford and Woodchurch, both of which featured on national TV at the time as examples of some of the worst estates in the country. There were others such as Prenton, Rock Ferry, New Ferry, and North End. Estate rivalries meant the firm was always a bit fragmented. The gang I got involved with came from Prenton and became known as the Apaches.

"There was also the Tranmere Stanley Boys, who were what they sounded. They had a few who were willing to use blades, it was just the way it was. The Apaches were based in a pub called the Swan. From the outside it looked a very decent stop-off for away fans, well decorated with a large beer garden. But as anyone from Prenton knew, most weekends trouble brewed, and some away fans were caught unawares.

"Around 1982, Tranmere were due to play Chester City at Sealand Road on the Easter Bank Holiday. That was a banker for all of us. Train into Chester, all day on the ale, on to the game, then last train back to Birkenhead. When we arrived at Rock Ferry station there were about 100 Tranmere and we all got the regular train to Chester. At the station we checked the first few pubs on the street, looking for any Chester, but there were none to be seen. As we didn't feel threatened we decided to split up to get served quicker in the city pubs. The plan was to meet at the top of the road by the ground half an hour before kick off. No-one had phones in those days. I was in a group of ten and didn't see any Chester all the time we were out on the ale.

"We got to the corner as arranged but the other lads were nowhere to be seen, nor were Chester. We decided this was crap, and most decided pay and go in the home end. A couple declined, so we were left with seven or eight who were well up for it. We simply walked up to the turnstile, said nothing, paid our money and we were in. The crowd was up to about 3,000 and we could see Tranmere had about 1,000.

"As the teams ran out, Chester started singing. We immediately responded. Most of those we had mingled in with weren't Chester's lads, so they went very quiet. At that moment we noticed a big mob of about fifty Chester coming from the side. Here they were. We knew we'd get battered, but we'd made a statement and had to follow it through to the end. We did take a bit of a battering, but we all stood until the police got in between us. As was the custom in those days, we didn't get thrown out, but marched around the touchline to the away end. I can still remember the round of applause from the Tranmere following as we bowed and saluted, albeit looking a bit bruised and bloodied. After pats on the back from the rest of the lads, the accusations flew about where the rest of the mob had been.

"Another decision was taken to get back into the home end just before the game ended, but this time with the full 100 or so. The police were useless, and as soon as the gates opened Tranmere walked round the back of the main stand and straight into the home end. Chester came at us, but we had twice as many as them now, and as they took a battering they legged it across the terracing and out of the opposite exit. We had taken their home end, a classic objective back in those days. Outside, Chester were over by the industrial estate, gesturing and bouncing, but the police came and rounded up the stragglers. We knew we were back on the train home. No night out. Game over.

"While not the greatest of travellers, Tranmere were very decent opposition on their own patch. One team who got more than they bargained for was Chelsea in the first leg of a cup tie at Prenton Park. This was a big one. Many lads were in town or round the ground very early. I was up for this as I had never been fond of Chelsea; Everton and Chelsea had a few good battles over the years.

"We were in the chippy ordering chips and curry when we heard the London accents walking past. We had a look, concluded they were lads and got out into them, curry and chips in hand. They gave us a few verbals, then bang! My hot curry and chips was in one lad's face. Not pretty. He went down holding his face and I gave him a bit of a half-hearted kicking in the ribs for good measure. The other lads put up a decent enough fight but they got off eventually. The lad got picked up and complained he was blind. I didn't give a fuck and just said, 'You're all going to get the same later.' It was just the way it was. It was war.

"We headed to the ground and saw a double-decker bus full of Chelsea. They all looked very handy and up for it. We lobbed a few full cans of Coke at the windows and put a few through, which shut them up for a bit as they dodged the flying glass.

"We decided to go in the Main Stand for this, made our way near to the segregated part and it went off immediately. Chelsea were very capable, but I think they were a bit surprised at what we had. It was a good effort from us. We certainly gave as good as we got. At one point we thought we were going to get them running, but being the experienced crew they obviously were, they kept tight and didn't run.

"For my troubles I took a cracking blow on the bridge of my nose that split it right across, blood everywhere. I didn't go down, but I was out of it from then on in. I've still got the scar to this day.

"I didn't go to the away leg; Tranmere's following was pitiful, I believe. I was told the side opposite the big Main Stand where all the Chelsea lads used to go was full for the return and they were baying for blood. I like to think it's because we gave them a good fight and they needed to put the upstarts back in their place.

"Mostly Tranmere were aged late teens to mid-twenties. A very young crew indeed, these days probably called Youth something or other. But that didn't come into it in those days. You were either good enough or you weren't, end of story. We knew we couldn't compete with some outfits like the big Yorkshire teams, the two Sheffields, or Bradford City, although I saw

Bradford get run ragged in the car park one season. These teams would come and take over the place. Out of a gate of 6,000, literally 5,000 would be Blades or Owls. They all seemed like big monsters from the mines.

"One time we had a bit of a do with the Blades in one of the pubs near the ground and thought that maybe this year we might be able to get a result. But in the ground it was different, they were everywhere and we were probably thankful for the police line. One funny thing I remember from a game with Wednesday was the exchange of verbals. There were all the usual songs, 'We'll see you all outside,' 'You're going home in a fucking ambulance.' Then, as we got closer to them, an older, particularly nasty-looking bunch of Wednesday started singing, 'You're going to get your fucking botties smacked,' which kind of put us in our place. Still in our teens, with the casual look, we must have looked like a bunch of wankers to them. Although we did manage to put the odd lard-arse on his backside, we never got the better of the two Sheffields, I'm afraid.

"Two other mentions should be to Blackburn Rovers, and Portsmouth. These are the only two clubs I ever remember taking the Tranmere home end, the Cowshed. And to do it on a Friday night gets much respect. Who'd want to travel from Portsmouth to Birkenhead on a Friday?"

The Nineties at Tranmere were similar to many other grounds around the country, non-eventful apart from the odd flare-up with a local rival or big cup game. Wrexham were one of the few who kept it going and turned up a few times when others didn't bother. One Tranmere lad was slashed at Wrexham and there has been bad blood ever since.

"The Nineties were shite," declared one lad just released from jail for a hooligan-related offence. "Tranmere became a family club, money was invested and the ground smartened up, whilst on the pitch we went up the leagues and gained a reputation as a good lower league cup team. Like at a lot of places, though, lads who had retired became bored and started showing up at the odd game and it went full circle. Younger lads latched on and before we knew it we had a decent firm again. There was probably only a hardcore of fewer than fifty but for a decent game we pulled over 100 and two years running on Boxing Day we took top mobs to Huddersfield and Blackpool. Huddersfield deserve a mention, as their black lad came into the boozer and fronted our full mob. He was battered but he is one game or stupid bastard."

The relationship with the Big Two across the Mersey has always been strained, although both Everton and Liverpool have played prestige friendlies to help Tranmere's financial plight over the years. Everton and Tranmere's mobs fell out in the late Eighties, with a few violent clashes at summer friendlies. The arrival of Peter Johnston on the scene meant there would never be allegiances between the two clubs again: Johnston was the multi-millionaire owner of Park Foods, a Christmas hamper empire, who bought Everton FC despite being the owner of Tranmere and a season ticket holder at Anfield. He then took Everton to the verge of bankruptcy and relegation, and on the final day of the season only a draw at home to Coventry and a Bolton defeat at Chelsea saw Everton stay up. A banner at Anfield read, "Mission Complete, Agent Johnston We Thank You," and although he was soon replaced as the major shareholder, his term at Goodison still haunts the club.

"We hate the fact that people have us all down as Scousers," said another Tranmere lad. "We have our own identity and never were a firm who would attempt to hang on to the coattails of Everton or Liverpool, as some of the smaller Manchester-based clubs do with City and United. There are some very game lads who live this side of the water who watch Everton and Liverpool and we have no problem with them, but the sly cunts from across the pond are not worthy of a mention. Liverpool were the bullies late at night, picking us off after a night out. Everton lads seemed okay, but one year they came here for a pre-season came, fronted a boozer called the Carlton and we could not live with them. No shame in that, but why then slice lads up for the fun of it? That lot were fucking evil.

"A few years later we picked off a small mob of them and they were chased for ages, but I will admit we missed our chance when we drew them at their place in the FA Cup a few years ago. Tranmere beat Everton three-nil at Goodison, but despite it being their first visit there for thirty years it was a poor show by the away mob. Fuck knows why, but we just never pulled it together that day. For years it had been an uneasy truce between us and then the slashing changed it all and we hated them. We got the train across, got off at Central Station and a few went up to Wetherspoons for a nose. Within minutes they were chased back. Everton had a decent mob out and we did not try very hard to get it on. They claim that after the game we disappeared. What can I say? We did. Late on we called it on over here but to be honest it was too little, too late and to this day we still argue about why we fared so poorly. We drew Liverpool in the next round and that also went off peacefully. They had fans all over the place getting spat at and slung out, but apart from a few bouncer-type blokes who fronted it in our stand, they had no mob to speak of that day."

The Tranmere mob hit the headlines in 2005 when a sizeable number of their firm were jailed for an incident which a few years earlier would perhaps barely have warranted a two-inch column in the *Liverpool Echo*. After a home game against old rivals Wrexham in September 2003, the two mobs agreed to meet up in Chester after the match to sort out their differ-

ences. It was a foolish plan, as police had been monitoring both mobs'
movements, and when the Rovers lads arrived in Chester the police
swooped and block-arrested them all. Football intelligence officers were
ecstatic when it was discovered many of the lads had left text messages on
their phones indicating that the trouble was planned and the *Echo* took
delight in reporting the dawn knocks.

> This morning officers raided homes across Wirral and parts of Cheshire after
> a lengthy undercover operation to identify hooligans.
>
> At around 7am, one police team pulled into the affluent Polden Close, in
> Ledsham, Cheshire, to arrest a man believed to be at the forefront of the
> violence.
>
> The 33-year-old suspect answered the door at his £200,000 detached home
> in his shorts and was led away in handcuffs. He hurled abuse after answering
> the door.
>
> His cars, an Alfa Romeo and a Citroen Picasso, parked on his driveway,
> were also searched.
>
> Similar operations were carried out across the area. They focused on
> Tranmere, Prenton, Rock Ferry and Birkenhead.
>
> Officers also seized mobile phones believed to be used to organise hooligan
> battles and paperwork relating to violence.

After a lengthy court case, the *Echo* again put the minor skirmish on its
front page.

> A gang of 31 football hooligans have been jailed for plotting violence at a
> football match between Tranmere Rovers and Wrexham in 2003.
>
> Merseyside Police learned of the organised fighting before the game after
> reading messages on websites used by hooligans, Liverpool Crown Court
> heard. Judge Brian Lewis said it was an organised attempt to cause large scale
> violence. The gang, most of who lived on the Wirral, were sentenced to a total
> of 31½ years in prison.
>
> Officers from the Merseyside, North Wales and Cheshire police forces
> acted before the match to control any violence and managed to prevent serious
> disorder at the Prenton Park ground, the court heard.
>
> Trouble did break out on a train after the match, however, as Wrexham fans
> headed home. Violence also broke out in Chester city centre after the game.
> Police said many of the men had planned to meet before the game at a local
> pub, the Prince William near Green Lane.
>
> Officers had tracked several text messages sent between the conspirators,
> including one that read, 'Wrexham, they're bringing 200 or more. Can't wait.'

Judge Lewis said many others who were involved in the fighting had not been tracked down, which was worrying, knowing that football hooligans are still active.

'Tranmere Rovers has always enjoyed the highest respect and reputation not only in the local community but in the wider football world,' he told the convicted men as he sentenced them.

'It has become a family club in the truest sense and you have besmirched that with your criminal activities. The courts must send out a message that organised violence of this nature will not be tolerated.'

Five described as key figures were jailed for between one and two years and all were banned from attending football matches for up to six years. In truth, barely a punch landed in the incident, but the sentences handed out reflected how hard the authorities were cracking down on hooligan gangs. The irony was that the "mass brawl" claim and a magazine description of the firm as "third-string Scousers who frequently give bigger clubs a bloody nose" were likely to have upset those convicted at least as much as the sentences.

"The convictions and the six-year banning orders decimated the firm," admitted one veteran. "Thirty-odd banned would kill off the best of firms but at Tranmere it has hit even harder. There are a few left and they are a game bunch of young lads, but they are out of their depth at most places and I know a few who took a slap from Bolton at Lime Street after getting a bit lippy. Still, they have a go."

One of the 31 jailed still can't believe how so many people ended up being sent to prison for such a non-event. "I got fifteen months for basically fuck-all," he insisted. "I was at the very front of that mob in Chester and not one single punch was thrown. Okay, before the Wrexham lot left Tranmere there were a few slaps handed out and they were backed off on to the train at Rock Ferry, but at Chester, nothing, not even handbags. I wish we had gone right through the fuckers, the jail would have been the same."

Further reading: *Awaydays*, Kevin Sampson (Vintage)

W

WALSALL

Ground: Bescot Stadium, formerly Fellows Park
Firms: Street Enders, Junction 9
Rivals: Shrewsbury, Port Vale, Chesterfield

Largely ignored by their bigger Midlands rivals, Walsall nevertheless have had decent mobs dating back from the early Seventies. While they have never had the numbers of Wolves or Birmingham, they have, on their day, turned over many a top firm.

The first mob at Walsall in the Seventies were known as the Street Enders after the Hillary Street End behind the goal where they stood at the old Fellows Park ground. There were never any specific leaders, they were a motley crew of local lads looking for a fight. Ian, a seasoned campaigner from the town, remembered, "I saw many off-the-field events, but one that springs to mind was turning over the Blades [Sheffield United] at Fellows Park in the early Eighties after a four-four draw. They came mob-handed but after the game we ran them ragged in the streets outside." Other famous Walsall battles include going after Birmingham, again in the streets after a match, and chasing the visitors over the old bridge in town. However, it was not all one-way traffic. A match at Blyth Spartans saw some old Newcastle faces complement the locals and take Walsall. "From kick-off until the final whistle, Blyth kicked the fuck out of us," said Ian.

"The Street Enders travelled to away games by coach or special train. If it was by coach then it was invariably Dawson's Coaches, which in contrast to the official supporters' coaches, run by another coach company, was fairly lax. The regular driver of the main coach was Harry. He was a good laugh and got on well with everyone. As all the nutters were getting on board, he would stand by the side asking if anyone had any beer, almost tongue in cheek. 'No,' came back the reply as all and sundry climbed aboard with Party Sevens and massive carryouts of Younger's Tartan Bitter.

Harry didn't give a fuck really. Everyone would get pissed up and burst into a chorus of the old Sham 69 number 'Hurry Up Harry'."

There was no real leader of the Street End but several well-known lads who made up the core of the away travel led it collectively. Among them were Mad Derek, Growler, No-Teeth Pete, Big Paddy, Bobby, Barry, Piano, Keithey and Hazeldine. "Yata was another well-known face back then," said Ian, but he was better known for leading the singing in the Street End in the Seventies and early Eighties. If one bloke could be considered a Walsall legend it was Beechy, who was considered the hardest man in the town during the late Seventies and early Eighties, and is still occasionally spotted at big games.

Fighting would occur most weekends but none of it was organised. Home matches against Bristol City, Cardiff, Portsmouth and Millwall were always lively. Cardiff and Bristol City would take over much of the town but Millwall often came with only 200 fans, though every one would be a fighter in their twenties, thirties or even older. One game against Millwall, in 1981, saw a police officer kicked unconscious and a write-up in the *Sun*. Derbies against Port Vale often saw trouble as passions flowed over. Back in the days of the Street Enders, Port Vale were Walsall's main enemies, though this rivalry has diminished in recent years.

The casual fashion was slow arriving in Walsall and up until 1983 the lads would be a mixture of punks, skins, rockers, rude boys and bootboys. It was a diverse collection of individuals who co-existed fairly amicably.

Two away games at Wigan were among the most explosive of the period. On 26 April 1980, Walsall played their last away game of the season in the Lancashire town having already secured promotion to Division Three. With Walsall losing, tempers flared on the terraces, the perimeter fence was smashed down by away supporters and a pitch invasion followed. Fighting broke out on the pitch and Walsall even climbed into the Wigan end and ran the home fans up to the halfway line. The game was stopped for several minutes as police moved in to restore order. "Thirteen Walsall supporters were arrested as Wigan police had to use dogs to restore order as fans threw bottles and bricks," reported the *Express & Star*. "Fifteen others were ejected from the ground."

Wigan followed Walsall up two seasons later, and four days after Christmas, 1982, the Midlanders were once again travelling up the M6. "One of my mates from the Beechdale pub organised a West Midlands double-decker bus for the trip and it was obvious that it would end up in chaos," said Ian. "And it did. The bus arrived in Wigan with every-one pissed up and fighting broke out in the town centre, with traffic being brought to a standstill. The police impounded the bus and made around fifty-five arrests. This story featured on the national *Nine O'Clock News*."

Portsmouth are one firm who always travel well and for two or three years running they went into the Street End for a ruck. In one incident, in 1981, a Pompey lad even threw a metal *shuriken* kung fu star into the home crowd. However, when they came back the following year, Walsall were ready, as Ian recalled. "A group of fifteen Beechdale, all dressed in black berets, made an attack on the Laundry End where the away supporters were and steamed straight into Pompey with a big cry of T-H-E W-A-L-S-A-L-L! The Old Bill had to separate the two sides from hand-to-hand combat as the rest of the Pompey lads came across the terracing, and the Beechdale lads were thrown out."

Two of the most fearsome mobs ever to visit Walsall were Sheffield United and Chelsea. The Yorkshiremen arrived in October 1982 with a score to settle. The last time the two teams had met, at Bramall Lane, Walsall had avoided relegation but in doing so sent United down. A large chunk of the 16,000 crowd erupted, with some fans even attacking some Walsall players on the pitch. One player who refused to be intimidated was winger Mark Rees, who took off his boot and gave the Sheffield lads a bit back. After the game, police vehicles were overturned and officers injured.

With the memory of that game still clear, Ian and the lads arrived in town that October morning with some trepidation. "I went into the town centre with a couple of mates and realised my worst fears had come true. Sheffield United were 250-plus by eleven o'clock – and it got worse. By noon they had taken nearly every pub and their numbers had risen to 400. Walsall had never seen anything like it before or since. They were well dressed too, in a sea of bright colours: Pringle and Lyle and Scott knitwear, Adidas cagoules and Fila and Sergio Tacchini tracksuit tops. This trainer-clad army of lads were taking the piss.

"The local plod gave them a hard time though. Walsall Police rightfully have a reputation as cunts who take no shit, and they enjoyed cracking a few heads with truncheons and even set a dog loose on some lads in one pub after they refused to leave the premises. It ended up biting several of the Yorkshire lads. But our mob of fifteen was no match for this lot."

The other big visit during this period was at the Milk Cup tie against Chelsea in October 1983. "Chelsea came in the old Street End in big numbers but Walsall gave it to them really hard. If anyone tells you different, it's a lie. They just came in from the back and started shouting, 'Chelsea,' and the game was held up for around twenty minutes."

The local paper not only reflected on the trouble but the aura that surrounded the London club.

An 'undercover operation' by Britain's most notorious football thugs brought terror to the terraces at Walsall's Milk Cup glory tie against Chelsea.

Members of the London team's blue army of followers infiltrated the Hillary Street section of the ground. The section had been reserved for home supporters at last night's match.

While the teams prepared to take the field, violence exploded as hooligans charged into terrified men, women and children – sending them spilling on to the pitch for safety and delaying the start by two minutes.

Today, Supt Barry Downes, who organised the massive police operation at the match, slammed 'irresponsible' Walsall people who helped wreck the elaborate plan to segregate the rival sets of fans.

The drama happened just before the start of the match. Some police – many drafted in from neighbouring divisions – had shepherded thousands of travelling Chelsea supporters from a fleet of coaches, cars and trains into the Railway End of Fellows Park.

But despite the precautions, a number of London fans got into the Hillary Street end and began brawling. Police made 28 arrests before, during and after the game – 26 involving Londoners – and ejected 23 fans from the ground.

By the early Eighties a new mob had emerged at Walsall called Junction 9 after the motorway junction near the ground. Most of the lads came from the Pleck area and complemented a larger but looser alliance of lads from Bloxwich, Walsall and Coalpool, who did not operate under a single name but rather were known under groups banners such as Coalpool Youth and the Bloxwich Lunatic Firm. Junction 9 had to be dragged kicking and screaming into the casual age, as some insisted on wearing their donkey jackets for some time. The new casuals were in their late teens and the main mob during this period was still the non-casuals from Beechdale. Turnouts varied according to opponents, club success and time of year. For a few big games Walsall could get out a mob of 200 lads. The casual component of this was always a minority, nothing more than a score for normal Saturdays and maybe up to 60 for big games. The Walsall scene was not helped by infighting. "Coalpool Youth would fight both Bloxwich and Beechdale lads and Brownhills also had problems with Coalpool," said Ian. "It wasn't really until the away game at Shrewsbury 1988 that Walsall, Bloxwich, Coalpool and Brownhills mobs all got together for the first time."

In the early Eighties, Bristol City emerged as a main rival. At 63 miles away, it was one of City's closest games and the relatively small support for Walsall usually meant that visitors could attempt to swamp the ground. In May 1988, the two teams were drawn together in the two-leg play-off finals. In what was to be one of Walsall's greatest nights, it was the actions of the fans that dominated the headlines the following day. "Two police vans were overturned and 44 football fans arrested as violence marred Walsall's stunning 4-0 victory over Bristol City," reported the local paper. "The ugly incidents cast a shadow on the club's proudest day which saw them book their place in the Second Division. Today, Walsall's head of police called on football chiefs to seriously reconsider the whole idea of play-offs after revealing that yesterday's game cost a total of £116,000 to man."

The same year saw an incident at another local rival, Shrewsbury Town, which was to receive national publicity. During a fight after a match in October 1988, 17-year-old Shrewsbury fan Steven Clarke collapsed and died of respiratory failure. A Home Office pathologist was brought in to investigate the circumstances of his death and the police arrested nine Walsall fans in what they described as a "possible murder investigation". Two of them, including the person who led the Walsall firm that day and a man who was later charged with manslaughter, described the events for this book. Both gave their accounts on condition of anonymity, so we have called them Mr X and Mr Y respectively.

Mr X: "I had decided to try and get as many of the lads together as possible for this one as it was the first meeting at Shrewsbury in over ten years, and the response was excellent. Coach travel was ruled out, as the police were likely to capture us, so I decided the service train would be best for the short hop. Word was put out and all the relevant personnel were duly recruited. It had come to my attention that some of the Coalpool Youth mob were intent on joining our ranks for the day and this worried me, as there had been problems between them and both the Bloxwich and Brownhills lads in the firm. However everything was okay on the day. We all stuck together and from that day onwards the in house fighting ceased and friendships were forged.

"The Walsall, Bloxwich, Brownhills and Coalpool lads met up at Wolverhampton train station and caught the local service to Shrewsbury. There were sixty-three of us altogether and everyone was in top form. We arrived in Shrewsbury around eleven bells and only one solitary policeman at the station. The look of horror and disbelief on his face as we bounced off the train and onto the platform was priceless.

"We came out the station, headed towards the town centre and plotted up in the Royal Exchange. The beers flowed and we settled in. Some of ours went off spotting but came back with nothing to report. After around an hour and a half we decided to move on and went in search of another pub. Old Bill were around now and followed us to another venue. We only had one drink and one of our lot had noticed we could get out the back of the pub without being seen. Pints were downed and out the back we went. Meanwhile out front the riot van, dog handlers and the rest of the boys in blue were blissfully unaware we had slipped away.

"We came out the back, turned right and walked down the road. A right turn was made down an alley and as I emerged onto the street I was confronted by a big lad around the same age as me. 'C'mon,' he roared, hands out-stretched. I instinctively kicked out at him and went to throw a punch but before I had pulled my hand back, an arm came over my left shoulder like a missile and struck the lad. As the rest of our lot came out the alleyway, Shrewsbury bounced across the road. We were into each other and it was game on.

"Most of the Shrewsbury legged it after the first few blows went in but about six of them stood and went straight into us. One of their lads, with dark hair in a wedge-style cut and a navy hooded jacket, was doing very well. He was dodging and weaving in and out and getting in some good punches and none of our lot could get near him. You could hear the sound of fist smacking against flesh but it was coming well on top for them with so few numbers.

"Shrewsbury were forced onto the back foot as more of ours poured out the alley. The lad in the navy jacket beat a retreat and several of us gave chase, led by me. 'Stop him, stop him,' I shouted at the top of my voice. He was getting away and punishment needed to be administered quickly. He was too quick for me and just as I had almost given up hope of catching him, from nowhere came one of our lads, Pompey, who brought the Shrewsbury lad to the ground with a rugby tackle Bill Beaumont in his heyday would have been proud of.

"As they both tumbled to the ground, I swung a kick at the enemy and heard the dull thud of trainer making contact with its target. Pompey and myself administered a few kicks to him and I thought about chucking him in the nearby river. He was on his jack, though, as his mates had long gone and he didn't deserve that after such a spirited display.

"As we both walked away he got up, shouted, 'Come on then, you wankers,' and gestured for us to go at him! Cheeky fucker, I thought and ran back at him but he was off. That was a game display and credit also to the other five or six Shrewsbury who stood."

The police finally caught up with Walsall and, under heavy escort, marched them to the ground where they watched a boring 0-0 draw. After the game, the Walsall were herded up to the railway station, but not before a few managed to break their escort. Free from the police, this group of six soon came across five Shrewsbury lads.

Mr Y: "One had a motorbike helmet in his hand and swung it at me. Instinctively I raised my hand in self-defence and the helmet wedged on my arm, as the visor was open, so I swung it round and hit him on the head with it. Punches were exchanged but the Shrewsbury lads scattered. The group continued toward the station but literally bumped straight into another gang of about six Shrewsbury lads on a walkway above the railway station.

"Again it went off and punches were exchanged from both sides and a big lad, who I now know was Stephen Clarke, was steaming into me. I threw punches back but most missed, while his seemed to all make contact and he was getting the better of me. The police were quickly on the scene and both sides ran off. We lost one of the lads and ran round the corner and bumped into more Shrewsbury, around fifteen this time, and had to leg it again. We saw a police van up the road and so headed that way, as we figured their lads would not give chase when they saw it. As we drew level there was an officer on his radio and he stopped us and told us to get in the van, as we were all nicked."

The cause of Steven Clarke's death was initially unknown and the handful of Walsall fans were held over the weekend. Most were charged with minor public order offences but Mr Y was charged with manslaughter. This was later dropped after a Home Office pathologist decided that Clarke's death was due to natural causes. The Walsall man was, however, fined £500 for his part in the earlier fight with the lad with the motorcycle helmet.

Walsall's hooligan following has always been smaller than it might otherwise be because many casuals who live in the area follow bigger local sides such as Wolves, Aston Villa and West Brom. Indeed, sometimes these casuals will join up to help out their hometown mob.

"This doesn't happen by chance," said Ian. "Many of us know each other as we live and drink in the same areas." Peterborough were attacked during a match against Walsall and were quick to claim that the perpetrators actually supported Wolves. "There were five Wolves lads and eight Walsall who were having a drink together because they are mates when they heard of Peterborough's presence, simple as that," said Ian. "It was nothing to do with them getting on the mobile and calling Wolves for help, as some have said. Several of the older Walsall lads, including me, are very good mates with some of the older Wolves lot and have known each other years. As the two teams have rarely played each other over the years, there is no hatred for some of us – that seems to be reserved for the singers and youth mob."

With Walsall gaining promotion to the First Division in the late Nineties, and the appearance of younger hooligans at the club, this mutual respect turned to rivalry, though more from Walsall's viewpoint than from their neighbours'. Local derbies have become an opportunity for Walsall's new youth firm to put one over on bigger opponents and there have been clashes with both Wolves and West Bromwich Albion. At an early season fixture at home to West Brom in 2001, a small group of young Albion tried to drink in Walsall town centre but were soon told to move on by a larger mob of Walsall. The home mob were less confident against a group of thirty "big hitters" in the stand and so kept their distance, but after the game the initial young West Brom group, with a few additions, walked back into a Walsall pub. On seeing over thirty home lads, however, they turned and headed straight back out. A few minutes later a larger group of West Brom attacked the pub.

"There was a charge for the door as the pub emptied and we steamed straight into them," said Ian. "Some of them seemed surprised and obviously thought we would bottle it. A few of them stood but most backed straight off to the other side of the road and were on their toes. The ones that stood got whacked and backed off too, except for a big lad who was wrestling with one of our well-known lads but coming off worst for it. One of ours threw a firecracker but it hit a road sign and bounced back across the road and landed back in our mob, exploding by my mate's foot.

"Glasses and bricks were exchanged and we advanced across the road towards them but they were still backing off. There was a brief Mexican stand-off, with us in the middle of the road and Albion on the pavement opposite us, with insults and missiles getting hurled and then the familiar sound of sirens in the air. Plod were quickly on the scene and both sides went in opposite directions.

"We went back in the pub but only stopped about thirty minutes and then headed in small groups into town. As five of us got outside the pub, one of the Albion lads from earlier was across the road on his mobile. 'Stay there lads, stay there,' he said. He was obviously calling up the troops for a rematch. We had no intention of staying to get shovelled in by bigger numbers, as most of our lot had already either gone into town or gone home. A couple of hours later, a mob of Albion attacked the Fullbrook pub and seriously injured a Walsall lad who was out with his wife and kids and assaulted several others. None of these people were anything to do with Walsall's mob and weren't even present at the off earlier.

"No big result is being claimed by us here, as most of ours are well aware that had we bumped into the thirty Albion who were in the main stand, things would probably have been different. Certainly Walsall's firm is no match for any of our neighbours' mobs in full flow. They can all turn out 200-300 easily, whereas sixty or seventy is a good show for us. Just goes to show on your day, though, if you underestimate the opposition you can and will come unstuck sometimes."

The Walsall Casual Elite was formed for a cup game at Sheffield United in the early Noughties and made up the major part of two coachloads who attacked the Blades. A more recent clash was against Wrexham, a week after an England v Wales World Cup qualifier. By 9.30am, 45 lads had met for the trip and decided to catch an early train to avoid police. Their plans were in vain as they were spotted changing trains in Shrewsbury. Walsall were not finished, however, and jumped off the train a couple of stops before Wrexham. However, they were conspicuous by their presence and their bus journey into town received a police escort. A strong police presence prevented the two mobs getting together and even the burning of a Welsh flag in the doorway of a pub could not provoke trouble.

Frustrated but restless, the Walsall mob played up on the train and in Shrewsbury as they clashed with the waiting riot police. By the time their next train pulled into Wolverhampton they were met by the most senior officer on duty in the town that day, who had decided that he did not have enough officers to cope with the situation and ordered Walsall to continue on to Birmingham. The Walsall lads reacted furiously and there was further trouble on the train, including the assault of several police officers. At Birmingham New Street, a huge police operation took the lads off one by one to be photographed and issued with Section 60s. Under a heavy police escort they finally made their way home.

"Although we didn't really have a chance to get at Wrexham – although they didn't try and get to us – all in all it was a good day and a decent turnout," said Mark, a well-known member of the firm. "Wrexham have since said that this is one of the best turnouts they'd seen at their place for a few years, it was certainly better than what they bought to Walsall for the return game, when they stayed in Birmingham prior to the game, then went straight to the match and straight back."

Walsall FC owner Jeff Bonser subsequently threatened to ban the group from the Bescot Stadium. "They left a trail of havoc behind them," he complained. "The train was trashed, they caused bedlam in a Wrexham public house [and] local police were forced to use dog handlers to prevent them leaving the train at Shrewsbury. Once at the ground, they threw coins at police and opposing fans. At half-time they left the ground – this shows how interested they were in the match – and went to a local pub to wait for Wrexham supporters to arrive."

There are, of course, two sides to every story, and a well-known Wrexham thug gives a different slant to that account in his firm's chapter.

WATFORD

Ground: Vicarage Road
Firms: Rookery/Watford Boot Boys, Watford Away Raiders (WAR),
    Drunk and Disorderly Firm (DDF)
Rivals: Luton

Watford has been put on the hooligan map in recent years by Dougie and Eddy Brimson, two brothers who from the mid-Nineties have written a string of popular books on football hooliganism, including *Everywhere We Go* and *Derby Days*. This has not necessarily bolstered the reputation of their town's hooligans, and "Who the fuck are Watford?" has become a common riposte. In truth, Watford has always had a mob but they have largely been sidelined by the club's determination to build a "family" image.

Many northern mobs view Watford as a London suburb and more particularly as Tottenham Hotspur's hooligan nursery. But lads at Watford are clear about who they are and who they are certainly not. Theirs is a small town which has had a surprisingly good football team over the past 20 years, and that success has caused its own problems as the club has often been pitted against those from larger towns and cities.

"In the Seventies and Eighties, as hooliganism emerged, Watford were predominantly a lower-division club, mixing it with the likes of Southend, Oxford, Gillingham and Brentford," said Gary McCall, a long-time Watford lad. "We always had good crowds for the size of the town, and there was always a feeling that we were better than our level. The home terrace, the Rookery, though not big, was well respected as a decent skinhead end in the early Seventies, and very few teams at that level would turn up at Watford with a mob. Notable exceptions were Norwich in 1972, probably the biggest away turnout in their history, 18,000 for their promotion game, and Plymouth Argyle in their 1975 promotion season."

Watford would also travel during this period. In 1969, the sending off of two of their players at arch-rivals Luton Town led to a pitch invasion. The same season saw Watford fans involved in disorder at Swindon. Three years later they were fighting on the pitch at an FA Cup game at Oxford; in the ensuing battle a wall collapsed, though no-one was seriously injured.

"When Graham Taylor took over in 1977 and began a period of unparalleled success for the team, it was tremendous but ultimately led to marginalisation for the hooligan element," said McCall. "During the promotions from the old Fourth and Third Divisions in 1978 and 1979, Watford generally averaged the biggest home crowds in the lower divisions and took thousands away each fortnight, with at least 200 boys. In this golden era of football violence, Watford tried to take the home end at almost every away game, with majority success. Watford fans even stood and traded with West Ham in the FA Cup 1978, earning respect at the time but paid back with a humiliating takeover of our ground when we met them in the Second Division twenty months later."

Watford took 7,000 to the West Ham game and a few months later a similar number made the journey down to Bournemouth for a promotion match. The Hornets took over the town. "This, in essence, was the problem for the firm at Watford," said McCall. "Whilst major players at a lower level, cutting it at a higher level was always difficult for a club and town of our size. In 1982, we were promoted to the top division for the first time ever. This coincided with a major effort by Taylor to rid Watford of the previous hooligan element and a move towards the family club, which is how most younger fans will know Watford."

The hooligans saw out the Second Division in style with a trip to Derby County for the last game of the season. Watford were out to party while Derby were battling relegation. There was fighting inside and outside the ground, including a punch-up on the pitch, but Watford admit they were well outnumbered.

Watford's hooligans might have not been welcomed by the Taylor administration, but they did not disappear completely. Most of their fights during the early Eighties involved Midlands clubs, especially Villa, West Brom, Coventry, Leicester. Perhaps it was because these clubs did not quite have the confidence to take it to the big teams in the capital, but they always put in an appearance in Watford. Conversely, few London clubs ever brought mobs to Watford, probably because they thought of themselves as too big and superior for the satellite town. One exception was Arsenal, though this might be because many people have linked Watford to Spurs. Watford lads will never forget the match against Arsenal in 1984 when a major face came in the Watford end and got put on his backside.

Watford's progress into the top division coincided with emergence of the casuals and, as at many other clubs, there was a definite split between the older Seventies faces and the fresh faces. "The younger lads took the clothes very seriously and those that still go today have maintained that stance," said McCall. "In the Eighties the presence of Punch, a very good clothes shop in town, was a large influence on the football lads, as the owner sought out not just the top labels such as Armani but also lesser known Italian and French labels as the initial sportswear-based casual look moved onto a more dressy style."

The club's rise continued in the First Division and in the first season at the top level they qualified for Europe. It was to be the club's only foray abroad and the Watford lads made the most of their away fixture at Kaiserslautern in September 1983. Over 5,000 fans made the journey, with trouble breaking out across France and southern Germany. There was further fighting inside the ground and two Germans were stabbed.

The following season, Watford played Birmingham City in the quarter-finals of the FA Cup. Watford took 12,000, among them were a tidy mob, but faced a far bigger army of Zulus. "Birmingham had every lunatic under the sun out that day," remembered McCall. "A rogue Watford coach was stopped in city centre and the lads jumped off and had a toe-to-toe with a pub full of Blues until the Old Bill intervened."

Watford developed a good cup reputation during the Eighties and a tie and two replays with arch-rivals Luton were lively, while there was also trouble during quarter- and semi-final matches against Liverpool, Tottenham and Plymouth during this period. In April 1987, Watford played Spurs in an FA Cup semi. "We lost four-one in a match in which we fielded a wine bar owner in goal," said McCall. "However, the main talking point here was the Watford coach that stopped in Solihull after the game. Drinking in the Snooty Fox, they encountered a number of Birmingham Zulu main faces, and after a bit of a build-up things got out of hand. After backing the Zulus, and any other locals who wanted to join in, up the road, Watford turned on the arriving Old Bill and proceeded to fuck them back down the high street. Street sealed off, major incident, coach eventually impounded, several major players returning home via train. Bizarrely it went almost unreported in the national press because Spurs fans had apparently been involved in a food fight elsewhere. However, Zulus in the know will vouch for the turnout that night."

Another cup game is fondly remembered by the Watford lad. "It was the late 1980s and Notts Forest hammered us three-nil at ours in the fifth round of the FA Cup. To make matters worse, the game was live on telly. After the game, Stuart Pearce bowls into the social club under the stand to meet 5 blokes he obviously knows since he is from Kingsbury, local to Watford. He is standing next to seven or eight of us, holding one of those knee-length puffa coats that were all the vogue with football teams back then. The bloke nearest to him sets light to one of the strings hanging from it. After an initial period of success the flame goes out, but five minutes later smoke starts pouring out of his coat. Neither Pearce nor his crowd notice it, but soon as it was really smoking, one of his crowd points it out and Pearce throws his coat on the floor and starts jumping up and down on it. Then some fella I've never seen walks up and throws a pint over Pearce and says, 'There you go mate, you were on fire.' Cue his mates going for the bloke, us stepping in, and Pearce as peacemaker. There were lots of chests puffed out and the moral is, if you've just pissed all over a team on the pitch, don't go into their supporters' club bar ten minutes after the whistle, because that's really taking the piss."

By 1988, when Watford were relegated, many of the faces that had been active during the previous decade had either started following the action at bigger London clubs or had become disillusioned with Taylor's family emphasis. The next couple of years were quiet, the only exception being Oxford United on a couple of occasions. Being located close to the M25 orbital motorway, the burgeoning rave scene saw an endless stream of parties within easy reach, and as with other mobs during the period, a number of lads turned their attention from football. "Early parties around Edgware, Kingsbury and Elstree were particularly memorable, and one of the top lads was well-connected with the Harrow firm that were major players in the early days of the scene," said McCall. "Some lads did take a break from football at this time, and followed raves like Sunrise, then later the likes of Full Circle and Boys Own. But despite the trend towards baggy flares, Wallabies and Kickers, a small number of Watford lads stuck with a smarter look based around designers such as Paul Smith, John Smedley and Nicole Farhi. Shops that became popular with main lads around this time included Shop 70 – good for Massimo Osti, especially Stone Island coats – near Great Ormond Street, and Paradox in Islington. The Duffer of St George was also popular with its retro, acid-jazz look, back in the early days when it was just a London label in D'Arblay Street. During this era, clubs frequented by lads from Watford included High on Hope, Stomp at Dingwalls, Bournemouth and Southport Soul Weekenders and Garage City when it was at Bond Street."

Watford were not known for taking big groups away with England, but 25 made the trip to Germany for the European Championships in 1988. They were a mixture of older lads and younger casuals, most on their first trip abroad with England. Almost as soon as they got off the train at Frankfurt, they were invovled in fighting, some of it reported on the front page of *The Times* the following day. The trouble began with Italian restaurant workers but soon involved locals and then the police. Later that evening, the Watford group joined with Bristol City against American G.I.s stationed in the area.

The trip would also be remembered for the exploits of one Watford man. "During a stay in Heidelberg, it turned out that many Irish fans were based there," said McCall. "After an 'entertaining' night, the police sealed off the street where the Watford lads were drinking and gave about 100 Irish supporters an escort past us. Later that might, one of the Watford crowd, drunk and confused, ended up at an Irish party back at the hotel. As they do, the Irish were having a big sing-song. A couple of the Irish lads sang some rebel songs, and then jokingly invited our friend to sing. He took the mike and sang 'God Save the Queen' to the whole room. Then for good measure he knocked out one of the IRA-loving tools, dragged him out of the venue and urinated on him."

After several quiet years, the Watford lads began to regroup in 1993. Fewer in number but tighter-knit and more clued-up, this new mob was adapting to increased police surveillance and the emergence of the football intelligence officer. The core of the group, numbering 40-50, used the Wine Shack in Watford as its base. "This group differed from many football groups of lads in that everyone was genuine friends, who socialised together outside of football, went clubbing together and so on," said McCall. "Drugs were very prevalent, and although you could never claim that Watford as a town was awash with drugs ahead of the big cities, this was definitely one of the first football mobs where *everyone* was on the packet back in 1995."

The following year, Watford clashed with Sheffield United an hour after the two teams met at Vicarage Road. This fight later received an extensive write-up in *Blades Business Crew* by Steve Cowens, who said the Sheffield contingent consisted of lads from his pub and his Sunday League football team, while the Watford group contained a sizeable number of Tottenham. Watford, for their part, say there were only three Spurs supporters with them and insist the group they attacked were hooligans.

"A small group of twenty-five Watford turn up at a pub where twenty-five BBC are drinking," insisted McCall. "A couple go in to have a look around and quickly come out and confirm they are in there, along with celebrity supporter Sean Bean. One of theirs appears at the door and tells Watford to fuck off and come back when there is enough of them. He's invited out and all the Sheffield pile out. With the momentum, they back Watford ten yards up the road. A couple of Watford who had gone around the back of the pub walk into the middle of them and it goes of again. After a minute there seemed to be a lull and when it goes again Watford, with the help of a picket fence, run Sheffield back in to the pub, which then had every window trashed with limited resistance. With no Sheffield coming out and sirens getting louder, Watford do the off in dribs and drabs. When there are three left, Sheffield come out and chase them in to a house, which then gets a window broken downstairs."

The claim of a Tottenham link has repeatedly been levelled at Watford but this is something they deny. Yes, they say, a few Spurs had been over to Watford on a couple of occasions but never numbered more than five and this came about because they were in the same group of friends as some Watford lads.

The declining fortunes of the club meant that they once again played local rivals such as Reading, Leicester, Luton, Northampton and Brentford. However, Watford were no longer known as a travelling mob and mainly stuck to home matches, continuing to use the Wine Shack as a base. One away match attended by the Watford mob was a cup game at Scarborough in 1995. There was no trouble but 100 Watford made the trip, including some older faces who decided on a weekend away. Most spent the Friday night at the Grand Hotel in York, where they took over the Piano Bar, entertaining the pensioners in long-term residence by taking turns at the piano. A couple of lads even tried their hand as stand-up comics.

The same season saw Watford play away in the cup at Crystal Palace in what is remembered as "the day of the cake". According to Gary McCall, "One of the lads brought a hash cake along to the pub and a good few of us over-indulged. After, in town, three or four Palace lads tried to front a half dozen of us with planks of wood. Through the haze of the drugs, the Watford lads laughed hysterically as they fronted and chased the Palace lads up the road. One Palace guy tried to run into a pub, unfortunately the door was locked so he went straight through the plate glass and was hanging trapped in the widow. One of our lads was so out of it he tried to hit the guy with a lump of wood; sadly in his messed up state he had picked up a piece so long and thin the effect was rather like whipping the guy rather than battering him."

At around the same time, Watford came unstuck against Millwall. A feud had begun when a Millwall face travelled to Watford to link up with some Oldham fans he knew from England games. Oldham were attacked near the train station, which set off a chain of events culminating in Watford "calling it on" with Millwall. When the two teams next met a fight was arranged for long after the game. Millwall were in the Bedford Arms and Watford in the Southern Cross, about 100 yards away. At an agreed time, the two mobs came out of their respective pubs and met halfway. After an even start, Millwall ran Watford back into the pub, which they then proceeded to demolish. Gas was let off and a number of Millwall were arrested.

The following year Watford returned to Palace, this time in a couple of limousines. "Mountains of charlie, lots of paranoia," laughed McCall. "Maybe we had good reason to get worried, because when we arrived at Palace, the Old Bill were on us straight away. The limo got spun, we got refused entry and then they tried to stop and search us."

Relegation in 1996 saw Watford renew hostilities with Luton. With both mobs acutely aware that the police would have this high-risk fixture under tight control, a provisional meet was arranged for St Albans. To reach there undetected, 25 of the Watford mob bought tickets for a "scarfers' coach" run by a local pub. The coach departed several hours before kick-off and the driver agreed to stop in St Albans, where they were joined by a few Watford spotters who had been searching for Luton. There was no sign of their opponents, so the lads returned to the coach and set off for Luton itself. They left the coach a short distance from the ground and made their way on foot. Almost immediately they came across two males who, after enquiring who they were, told them to stay put while they "got their mob".

Then one of the two Luton lads, who appeared to be only five feet tall, shouted, "Fuck it, let's go now Watford!" And with that he bounced over the road, to the horror of his mate. Watford were caught unprepared, with most of the mob up an alley having a piss. Three lads went to meet the challenge, and to escape a beating the Luton lad turned to run, the rest of the Luton mob appeared and it "went off". Before long, however, the police, who must have been following the home mob, got in between. Skirmishes continued along the route to the ground and the police blocked an attempt by Watford to get into the home end. The visitors were marched around to the away end, held outside the ground for 30 minutes, then forced onto a coach and out of town. Unaware of this, Luton were as mystified by Watford's disappearance after the game as they had been surprised by their appearance before it.

The Watford mob are generally not held in high esteem by many others, which annoys their lads. As a result they take greater delight than many would in "turning over" a rival firm. In 1996, Watford clashed at home with Reading. Initially, the Berkshire mob were in triumphant mood when Watford were locked into their local pub by the police while they strutted around the streets. However, almost two hours after the game Reading were attacked in another pub by 25 Watford, causing some of them to scatter. It was later reported that the Reading football intelligence officers were a little upset. One was heard to comment, "But we thought Watford were a bunch of girls," to which a Watford officer responded, "Yeah, but who's the girls now then!"

Two seasons later, Watford travelled to Bristol City for a promotion decider. Their hooligans hired a coach and plotted up in the Hole In The Wall pub, just out of the centre. Before long an equal number of City turned up and a knock-down, drag-out brawl ensued that some swear lasted for ten minutes with no police around. Both sides exchanged bottles and glasses and when they ran out they engaged in intensive hand-to-hand fighting. "It could easily have gone either way," said McCall, "but finally City got the upper hand. The row was ferocious, with the age of most players averaging thirty upwards. There was incredulity on both sides at how mad it had been, and afterwards a mutual respect between major players on both sides.

"Watford ended up with one badly hurt in hospital. To be fair I think both sides were a little shaken up at the level of violence. A call from the Bristol in the ground after said, 'We are sitting here shaking our heads, still can't believe that you have brought that firm here.' He expressed concern for our lad that was hurt – they thought he was dead – and reckoned ours was the best firm at Ashton Gate since Millwall a few years before."

For as many as ten Watford lads, the Bristol game marked the end of the road. The level of violence at that fight, combined with increased police activity and in-fighting amongst the group, led some to drop out of hooliganism, fearful of prison sentences. Trouble has erupted at the odd Watford game since, such as the play-off finals against Bolton, but incidents have been few and far between.

That was until they were drawn at home against Luton Town in the League Cup in September 2002. For some odd reason it was decided to make the game police-free. The two clubs were bitter rivals and there was trouble in town throughout the afternoon. Even when fighting broke out on the pitch, it took several minutes for the first police to arrive. However, with Sky TV broadcasting the game live there was enough footage around to see a number of people jailed and banned [see *Luton Town* in *Hooligans* Vol.1].

That game effectively signalled the end of Watford's firm. A young mob has emerged since, the Drunk & Disorderly Firm, but they lack the experience and muscle of the older lads. "Most of the older lads from the Seventies and Eighties days take kids of their own now," concluded McCall. "Football has changed a lot, not necessarily for the better, and many of us miss the old days. But you never know when a big cup game or a local derby will bring out certain old faces."

Further reading: *Derby Days*, Dougie and Eddy Brimson (Headline)

WEST BROMWICH ALBION

Ground: The Hawthorns
Firms: Clubhouse Mob, Smethwick Mob, Section 5
Rivals: Wolves, Stoke City, Aston Villa, Sheffield United

"The situation is really critical," Inspector Fisher told the local magistrates. "It is fast approaching the situation which could turn into a serious disturbance where someone might get killed. It is as serious as that."

West Bromwich Albion had just entertained Manchester United in

October 1969, in a game marred by violence. "Bottles, stones, coins and other missiles were hurled during an unhappy hour before the game even started – and the casualty list mounted to alarming proportions with four people being taken to hospital for treatment," reported the local paper. The list of injured grew as queues formed outside the first aid tent. One youth was in danger of losing an eye after being hit by a flying penny.

"Some of the crowd chanted, 'Munich, Munich, 58' – an obvious reference to the tragic air disaster which killed eight United players – and this incensed the Manchester fans," continued the newspaper report. "But they, too, aggravated the outbreak of skirmishes at the Birmingham Road end by deliberately gaining access to the section of the ground normally the stronghold of Albion support – despite appeals from police to keep segregated."

The corridor between rival fans was fifteen feet but this proved inadequate as rival fans exchanged insults and missiles. Despite the level of violence, there were only six arrests. One 18-year-old Albion fan was sent to a detention centre for three months for assaulting a police officer and using threatening behaviour, while a youth described as a United "cheerleader", 17-year-old Martin Doyle, of west Manchester, was fined £30. "The crowd was in an ugly mood and there were a number of scuffles," said Insp Fisher. Doyle was waving his fist and shouting, and everyone around him was doing the same. Doyle was then taken out of the ground but by then the mood was extremely ugly, added Fisher.

Albion's chairman launched a fierce attack on those responsible. "The lunatic actions of a minority of terrace hooligans [are] threatening to ruin the reputation of Albion fans, last season voted the best behaved in the First Division," he ranted. "We will hit the troublemakers so hard and often that they will realise it's a waste of time coming to the Hawthorns. We have taken positive measures to stop hooliganism by doubling the police force for home games. The club intends to back the police all the way. We are sick of the minority groups who are spoiling the enjoyment of the genuine supporter." He was equally furious with away fans trying to enter parts of the ground normally reserved for home fans. "We went to a lot of trouble to advise them to keep away from this section of the ground. There would not have been the disturbances had they all gone into the Smethwick end."

What made matters worse was that this trouble happened only days before the club was up before the FA for a pitch invasion at a home game against Liverpool only a few weeks before. Albion fans twice stormed the pitch to remonstrate with the referee and show their displeasure after the visitors equalised in the third minute of the injury time. As the referee walked off the pitch at the final whistle, he was punched in the face. The defiant ref, Keith Walker, defended his decision to play extra time. "I added time on for second-half injuries and for gamesmanship by Albion players who deliberately wasted time in the closing minutes. I am the sole judge of timekeeping and I have a completely clear conscience."

The first pitch invasion occurred immediately after Roger Hunt had equalised, with one supporter carried off by police after he was seen standing directly in front of the referee, pointing angrily at his watch. The man was an unlikely yob, as he was pictured in the local paper wearing a suit and tie and appeared to be in his forties. The second invasion happened when the referee blew for time literally seconds after Hunt's goal.

The Manchester United game was followed a week later by the short trip to Wolves, West Brom's arch-rivals. There was regular trouble at the Black Country derby and the clubs, police and local newspaper feared the worst. "To all Wolves fans: Do Behave!" pleaded the front page of the *Express and Star* on the Tuesday before the match. The appeal came from Wolves chairman John Ireland, who added, "This nonsense of football hooliganism has got to stop. The good name of the club is at stake and we would like to think that our supporters will not let us down on Saturday. To those people who are thinking of coming on Saturday's game to make trouble I would ask them to please stay away and make room at the ground for those fans who genuinely want to see the game, but who are afraid to come because of what might happen."

There was one piece of good news for Albion in the lead-up to the Wolves match, when the FA cleared the club of responsibility for the pitch invasion against Liverpool. The FA decided to listen only to the complaint by the referee that he was spat at and punched. Club chairman J.W. Gaunt was relieved but warned that supporters were still on trial. "The fact that spectators came on to the field was not brought up due to our excellent record." But he added: "Because the commission showed leniency yesterday does not mean they will do so again if our supporters repeat this silly offence."

The following day the local paper announced that 33-year-old fitter Ian Brown was convicted for assaulting the referee. He was fined £25 and ordered to pay £10 costs and was banned from the Hawthorns. The guilty man was a long standing season ticket holder who had supported the club since childhood but was so incensed by the extra time that he leapt out of his seat, immediately behind the directors' box, to confront the ref.

Meanwhile police announced a major operation for the derby game the following day. Each division in the West Midlands force was ordered to send a detachment to Wolverhampton and a new radio system was introduced to link police inside the ground with patrols outside. On match day police were out in force early in the morning, and with a crowd of over 50,000 expected, special busses were laid on to bring West Brom fans directly to the ground.

Despite the huge operation, more than 20 people were arrested as hundreds of youths fought running battles before the game. In one fight a policeman was knocked to the ground as he attempted to stop 300 people fighting. "Trouble started brewing before the match," reported the local paper, "when crowds of youths were involved in clashes as they roamed Wolverhampton town centre. Before the match started, 15 people had already been arrested. A further seven arrests were made in the ground, but a police spokesman described the crowd as being generally 'very well behaved indeed'." There were more disturbances after the game and West Brom fans damaged a train, repeatedly pulling the communication cord, tearing down curtains, throwing cushions through windows, smashing light bulbs and breaking windows.

Local derbies were always highly charged. A home game against Aston Villa in the late Seventies saw a policeman "kicked senseless" by hooligans. He was forced to leave the force because of his injuries after 30 years' service. Almost two years later, he received £67,000 damages, a record amount of compensation at that time for football-related injuries. The media reported that the money meant he and his wife would be able to buy a bungalow in Devon.

The first organised gang at West Brom was the Clubhouse Mob, who were active in the Seventies. Around the same time another gang, the Smethwick Mob, would ambush rival fans coming off Rolfe Street station, "particularly when the big mobs were due such as Blues, Villa, Wolves, United and the Scousers," recalled Carl, a WBA hooligan. "One ruck with Man United around 1982/83 saw Albion waste the Red Army boys outside the Red Fort pub on the High Street. Man United had been there the year earlier and had a good result but they came unstuck against big numbers of the Smethwick Mob the following season. It was a row which meant people around here stood up and took notice of the Albion firm once again after the Clubhouse firm was taken apart by the police."

The Smethwick mob was followed by Section 5, the name still used today and a play on the fact that many football-related charges come under Section Five of the Public Order Act. The mid-Eighties saw them clash with Birmingham City's Zulu Warriors, though there are very different accounts of the trouble. "There have been times when, from Albion's point of view, they've taken it to Blues and given it to them big time," claimed Glen, one of the older WBA faces. One such occasion was in

1985 at home. The away fixture, earlier that season, had seen a big battle outside the Old Crown pub in central Birmingham. West Brom attacked the pub, but according to them, 100 Zulus inside were soon joined by another 300, many armed with blades, hammers and CS gas, coming down the street. It was a one-sided contest which left some West Brom fans seriously injured and many others nursing more minor wounds. For their part the Zulus say there was no-one in the pub when it was attacked and their mob who arrived down John Bright Street was only 100-strong, but they admit one of the WBA leaders was "done with a hammer".

A leading West Brom hooligan, Cola, later recalled in the book *Top Boys* how they got their revenge a few months later: "We were well prepared, plenty of gas; we all chipped in and got some flares from a local boat shop. We heard Blues were in West Brom at the Lewisham pub. They came out and showered us with bottles and glasses, so we opened up with the flares. It was like the parting of the Red Sea as the rocket-like flare went through the middle of them Zulus. Then we went into them, each mob was about 150-strong. It was mental. Blues were probably one of the best firms in the country at the time and we wasted them." The Zulus openly admit they lost this encounter – though they dispute the numbers involved – and say it was the first time any of them had been sprayed with CS gas in a football fight.

Glen recalled another row, this time a League Cup game at St Andrews in 1986. "Albion and Blues clashed on the McDonald's ramp in the city centre. Albion were able to run the Blues mob after a little but nasty row."

Another fearsome mob who came to West Brom was Millwall, for a midweek cup game. Seventy South Londoners went into the home end and ran amok, even causing mayhem in the executive boxes. For the return leg, only two of the five coaches that left the Black Country arrived unscathed. The other three were either hijacked on the services or ambushed and smashed up close to the ground as they went under bridges.

West Brom were sitting pretty at the top of the Second Division the day Everton came to town in the third round of the FA Cup. The Baggies were full of confidence, having won their previous match 4–0 at home to Shrewsbury, and for Section 5 it was a chance to test themselves against one of England's nastier firms. "Fan may lose eye after attack," ran the headline in the local paper after the teams drew. A hundred West Brom fans threw stones and other missiles at transport carrying away fans, and the injured Evertonian was one of seven people caught in a minibus as it was attacked by brick-throwing yobs. Once all the windows had been put through, lighted paper was thrown in and as the terrified passengers stumbled out they were kicked and punched remorselessly. "It seems that this mindless minority suddenly turned like a pack of wild animals," said Chief Supt Keith Pemberton. "We hope that all genuine Albion fans will be as appalled as we are at what went on and help us find the culprits."

The game ended in a draw and therefore a replay at Goodison. It would see one of the most savage and chilling revenge assaults ever perpetrated at an English football ground, carried out by a blade-wielding youth who was leader of a Liverpool gang known as the Country Road Cutters. He hunted down an Albion fan after the game and later gave an account of what he did, and why, to author Andy Nicholls in the book *Scally*: "The chase was over and he was finished, the dimly lit cobbled streets had become his prison and were soon to become his graveyard ... His fate had already been decided a few days earlier when his crew had attacked a minibus of Everton supporters, yes, supporters, not hooligans like me, just lads who went to watch the match, and that is out of order. They blinded one bloke; lost his eye, he did, when they smashed a brick into his face when he tried to fight back ... I ran at him in a frenzy, and slashed, and just carried on slashing really, slash after slash, through his clothing. But I couldn't get my target – I wanted his eye ... I tried to prise his fingers back from his face but he was a strong lad and he was not giving an eye up that easy."

The Baggies lost the replay and their season petered out, as they finished ninth in the table, a disappointing 27 points behind Division Two champions Chelsea. The following season the team finished in 20th position, just three points off relegation. A year later, in May 1991 West Brom travelled to Bristol Rovers once again staring relegation to the Third Division in the face. Four successive 1–1 draws had kept them out of the drop zone only on goal difference, but a draw against Rovers and a win for Leicester City saw West Brom relegated and their fans riot.

West Bromwich Albion fans fought pitched battles and smashed shops during a drunken rampage [reported the local paper].

They ran amok in Bath and Weston-super-Mare in some of the worst scenes of soccer hooliganism this season.

In Bath, dozens of police reinforcements had to be drafted in as more than 200 drunken Albion supporters ran riot through the centre of the city on Saturday night.

At the same time another group of 40 Albion fans caused more than £12,000 damage after smashing shop windows in the main High Street at the holiday resort of Weston-Super-Mare.

Eighteen people were arrested, 13 from the West Midlands. It took police four hours to regain control of the historic city and many pubs were forced to close to prevent further chaos. However, this policy appeared to backfire, as the fans thrown out of several pubs rampaged. Albion's chairman was horrified. "I absolutely deplore what went on and we don't want people who do these sort of things as supporters. I am sure that the people who have caused this trouble are not Albion supporters."

The draw at Bristol Rovers sent the Baggies into the Third Division and away from most of the teams with the larger mobs. There was one exception, Birmingham, and the two teams met at the Hawthorns in late October 1991. There were 19 arrests and another 30 were ejected after fighting broke out inside the ground when the Zulus had got into the home end. In further trouble outside the ground, a bus window was smashed and a young girl had to be treated by an ambulance crew after being hit by a firework. There was also more violence away from the eyes of the media.

"The Blues were holed up in the Hen and Chickens pub in Oldbury on their way back to Birmingham celebrating another easy derby day win," recalled Glen. "Albion must have been belled for them to turn up, as it's not an Albion haunt on match days, only really frequented by Albion lads on a Friday night when it was open late hours. The Albion lads turned up in a couple of vans armed to the hilt with bats and chains and really went to town on the place. Fortunately for the Blues inside, the bouncers took the worst of it before the police turned up."

Within a couple of seasons at the lower level, West Brom began to turn around their fortunes. A fourth-place finish, with a league-topping 88 goals, saw them into the play-offs, where they first beat Swansea and then Port Vale. An 8-0 FA Cup win over Aylesbury had been the highlight of a high-scoring season. Off the pitch, there were fierce battles with Stoke and Burnley, though recollections of this latter game differ greatly.

In the autumn of 1992, West Brom travelled to the Lancashire town to find the locals out in force. Rumour spread through the Burnley pubs that their visitors were drinking near the ground, and the Burnley Suicide Squad set off in pursuit. Several minibuses were attacked, with visiting supporters being dragged out and beaten. Some West Brom fans in a nearby pub were also attacked. "The West Brom lads picked up pool cues but they were soon snatched from them," recorded Andrew Porter in his book *Suicide Squad*. "We had the pool cues now and we used them well. The police steamed in the front door and we disappeared through the side door. Burnley were all over the street, banging every West Brom fan they could see. There was so much fighting going on the police lost control. After the game it was the same scenario, the Brom lads being picked off for fun and the ambulances kept busy."

Porter describes further trouble at the return fixture the following March. Two hundred Burnley made the trip and while they were soon rounded up by police and escorted to the ground there was fighting inside and at the end of the match. Thirty-two people were arrested, 14 from Burnley and 18 from West Brom. The local police commander described it as the most serious disorder of West Brom's season. Yet when asked about it, the West Brom lads were dismissive. "Nothing to write home about," said P, one of their "youth" lads currently serving a lifetime ban from The Hawthorns. "Maybe big for them. Albion are not bothered with them as far as I am aware."

There was no ambiguity about West Brom's rivalry with Stoke City, and during the 1990s the gangs clashed repeatedly. "Whenever we've played them, home or away, there's been aggro," said Glen "In my time I've seen Albion going into the Smethwick End at the Hawthorns mid-Eighties and kicking off with Stoke and the whole terrace just opening up with the Albion lads in the middle calling it on. As they were escorted around the pitch they were clapped by the Brummie Road End.

"Most trouble at their place took place on the old car park outside the main stand and on the way to the train station, when they would appear from nowhere. In 1992, when they beat us 2-1 at the Hawthorns, it kicked off crazy down Halfords Lane by the canal bridge leading to Smethwick. There were 100-plus on either side and I couldn't give the honours to anybody as there were too many bodies flying about to see who came out on top. During the game they had lads in the paddock and when Stoke scored they came onto the pitch taunting the Albion, only to be dragged back into the stand, where they were severely dealt with. One guy dived into the stand on his own, only to be caught by a flying headbutt by one of our black lads, England Bernie, and thrown back onto the side of the pitch.

"A couple of hours after the game, a mob of Albion were in the Throstle club having a drink when a mob of around fifteen Stoke bounced in shouting, 'We're Stoke.' The Albion at the bar showered them with bottles and followed them outside, where it kicked off for a second or two. The Stoke lads got chased up the road towards the Hawthorns pub, where they vanished into their vans as quickly as they had appeared. Earlier in the day, two vans of Stoke were attacked near the motorway island coming towards the game and a small off at the Hawthorns pub saw a Stoke lad kicked unconscious.

"Another clash with Stoke came after the England game against the Republic of Ireland at Lansdowne Road in 1995. A mob of around forty Albion travelled over there and, after the exploits of the game, clashed with

Stoke as they were boarding the ferry home. Seventeen Albion lads got nicked during the day and returned as heroes, as you might imagine. More recently, Albion travelled up there only for the game to be cancelled due to high winds. Between eighty and ninety Albion were put in the boozer opposite the station. They were playing up, robbing and generally picking the place apart. Stoke said they would come to Albion but the police were everywhere along the way and it was impossible to meet. Albion then went on to Wolverhampton and holed up in their boozer, the Prince Albert, and belled Wolves, who were playing at Anfield, and told them they would wait for them to get back. Unfortunately after a row between some younger Albion lads from Oldbury and Tipton in the pub, the police turned up in over-the-top numbers and baton-charged them out of the boozer towards the Metro. Another forty older Albion then turned up from the station heading for the Albert, only to be shipped back to Bromwich town centre.

"The last row with Stoke came after an England game at Old Trafford. Albion and Oldham were at it in a city centre pub and it spilled onto the street, where Stoke arrived and put themselves in the row, as they have lads who know a few Oldham after their exploits over there following the race riots." Weeks after the game, police raided homes in Staffordshire, Oldham and West Bromwich.

Football fortunes brought West Brom together with Wolves on a regular basis from the mid-Nineties onwards and there was hardly a game where there wasn't serious disorder. In early September, 1993, louts clashed as West Brom attacked a coach carrying their rivals home from a match at the Hawthorns. Wolves fans threw seats out of the windows and in a separate incident a £14,000 car was written off. Fifteen people were arrested, with the police adding, "Tensions obviously run high during this type of match and some problems were almost inevitable."

Eighteen months later a policewoman was hit on the head with a snooker ball as officers made 17 arrests during another match between the two sides. Wolves fans smashed up a toilet unit inside the ground and Albion fans caused similar vandalism, badly damaging a coach which had brought Wolves fans to the Hawthorns. Police had thought they had catered for every eventuality, bringing 29 coaches into West Bromwich under heavy escort and without trouble, but a spokesman said, "It was hard to plan for the thirtieth coach, that we knew nothing about and which obviously brought the Wolves hooligans into town. It was that coach which was damaged."

In August 1995, more than 100 rival fans were involved in running battles outside a pub in Coseley, Dudley. Two people were treated for minor injuries and a further two were arrested. The fight happened two hours after the final whistle of the Black Country derby. When the two teams met later in the season, twelve people were arrested for a number of incidents after the game. "One fan was hit over the head with a bottle and a pub was wrecked," reported the local paper. "Bottles and sticks were used to smash up the bar and pub windows causing more than £2,000 damage. A gang also broke windows at the Wagon and Horses pub, Lewisham Road, near the Hawthorns before the match. Albion fans threw coins at Wolves fans in the ground and there was also a fight at Junction 1 of the M5 between gangs after the match."

There was more trouble during the 1997/98 season. "Drunken Wolves fans armed with baseball bats and car locks had to be locked out of a Baggies supporters' pub after Albion's derby victory," the *Express and Star* reported in September 1997. There was an equally depressing report of the match at Wolves the following February:

Soccer thugs armed with CS gas and pepper sprays, bricks and bottles clashed in Wolverhampton as pre-arranged violence erupted in the town centre.

They fought and hurled missiles at each other before and after the derby match between Wolves and West Bromwich Albion.

Dog handlers, mounted police and scores of officers armed with batons were drafted in to tackle the crowds as the force helicopter circled overhead.

Police today condemned the thugs as 'animals' and said violence was organised by about 100 hooligans.

There were 27 arrests and several people were taken to hospital, including a police officer set upon as he tried to administer first aid to a fan, and another officer sprayed with CS gas. "We could see these animals coming to cause trouble, which enabled us to nip it in the bud," said Chief Inspector Tom Duffin, in reference to the use of CCTV cameras and the force helicopter.

At a time when hooliganism was on the decline across the country, there was no let-up in the Black Country violence. An NCIS police report of the Baggies home game in October 2000 was grim reading:

A group in excess of 100 Wolves supporters were met by police and escorted towards the ground. At this time there were various reports of disorder in close proximity to the ground resulting in one Wolves supporter being knocked unconscious. This disorder was quickly dealt with by police.

The Wolves supporters were kept under escort and taken towards the ground. On route, a group of 80 Albion supporters attempted to confront them but police kept both groups apart. The Albion group had to pass the rear of the Wolves stand and attempted to break into the ground via the exit gate; police again prevented this and the group then moved off to their end of the ground. Due to this provocation the Wolves group attempted to break free from their escort but were prevented from doing so and then entered the ground. During the match a number of Wolves supporters attempted to come onto the pitch but police and stewards prevented this.

At the end of the fixture the Wolves group and the Albion group walked off in the same direction. Disorder broke out between the two groups, now numbered in excess of 100. During this altercation a Wolves supporter was slashed causing serious injuries to his right wrist, which required hospital treatment. Officers using batons eventually separated both groups. Following the game a CS gas canister was recovered from the Paddock area of the ground (this was the section of the stadium occupied by the Albion supporters).

Ten fans were arrested, including two in their forties and four in their thirties.

NCIS staff were busy again for the return match at Molineux Stadium, when a large group of Wolves hooligans fought with police before the game. A short time later, a coach carrying Albion hooligans was damaged as it approached the ground. There were nine ejections from the ground and, in the words of NCIS, "considerable hostility" between rival fans during the match.

"Following the game, serious disorder occurred at the bottom of Camp Street as fans clashed. A Wolves group had moved in from the concourse along the Ring Road towards Falkland Street and officers were deployed against this group, who retreated into the city centre. Disorder took place at Falkland Street, but officers at the scene dealt with it quickly and an arrest was made. At 8.30pm officers at Wednesbury identified a group of Wolves supporters. One was arrested for causing damage to a public house. The group numbering approximately 40 people travelled by Metro back into Wolverhampton, and there was some friction between them and the officers escorting."

A couple of months later, there was mass disorder in Blackpool as hooligan gangs from West Brom, Wolves and Birmingham all clashed. Locals and holidaymakers were forced to flee as dozens of hooligans battled it out in the seaside resort. First West Brom and Wolves supporters fought, then Birmingham City fans became involved. "Approximately 300 people from Wolves and West Bromwich clashed near a public house," noted the annual NCIS log. "At least one person was stabbed, possibly up to three, and there were numerous injuries to others who refused to go to hospital."

The ferocity of the trouble is remembered by one Albion hooligan.

"Funnily enough it didn't involve our lads but our beer monsters in Blackpool," recalled Carl. "Wolves turned up on a beano, though they were playing at home, knowing Albion were travelling in numbers, and when Albion's beer monsters got wind of sixty to seventy Wolves down the road they all piled out of the pub and attacked the Wolves mob, who were most of their main faces. The Albion numbers were roughly 100 but they came unstuck against this Wolves mob and that was that. Albion's mob actually turned up an hour or so later by train, all geared up for Wolves, only to be told what had happened. Obviously the main players were pissed off with the barmies, who by all accounts were told not to get involved with the Wolves mob."

Arguably the worst trouble in recent years between the two close rivals occurred in October 2001, when the teams met at the Hawthorns. That was certainly the view of Chief Supt Bruce Gilbert, who was in charge of policing the match. "There was a hardcore of vicious fans from both sides who were just out for trouble," he told the press. "At one point Wolves fans smashed down the gates to get into the Smethwick End. Albion fans, and that included men in their forties, were spitting on the Wolves directors sitting watching the game. It was quite shocking and disgusting." He described the violence as the worst he had experienced between the two clubs. There was further trouble at Midland Metro Parkway Station.

Around this time, another clash with Birmingham saw Albion's mob swelled by a younger element who were fast becoming a headache for the club and local police. "About 1999 a load of us younger lads had begun to get involved" said one. "As always, it is difficult to get accepted by the older lot, and that is particularly evident at Albion as they have always had internal problems with each other, so when a load of Youth lads start latching on, a certain amount of shit was thrown our way, but we stuck at it and have gained respect from most of the older lot. The first time we clashed with the Zulus was in 1999, there were forty-odd of us in some pub down a side street and suddenly there were bricks and bottles flying into us from everywhere. Soon the OB turned up and took us to the ground.

"After the game, Albion mobbed up under the stand and when we got outside there were over 200 of the cunts waiting for us. We ended up getting marched to Snow Hill, which is a fair walk, and all the way they were trying to get at us and the police were struggling to stem the attacks. They had a black lad with them who used to come with Albion and it went off briefly at Snow Hill before they got us away from the place in one piece. The older lads were unfazed by it all but for the younger lads it was mental. But rather than put you off, it was the kind of day which made you crave for more."

Whilst local derby clashes saw the most trouble, it was another Bristol game eight years after the riots in Weston-super-Mare that made national news, though this time it was a home fixture against City. The match was designated police-free and the absence of officers contributed to fighting between rival fans at half-time. At the height of the trouble, more than 100 people were involved and the second-half was delayed for 13 minutes. Police were rushed to the ground but it had been left to a handful of brave stewards to get themselves between the gangs.

Many ordinary fans were furious at the violence and the lack of policing and hundreds left the match early. One was Ray Johnstone, who left halfway through the second half. "I had my six-year-old lad with me and I was worried about what was going to happen at full-time," he told his local paper. "I just could not risk it – it makes you sick to have this happen again."

The following season saw a new rivalry emerge, with Sheffield United. In March 2002, there was serious disorder in the ground after their league match was abandoned; Sheffield United had been left with only six players on the pitch, after three had been sent off and two went off injured. West Brom fans were furious at the Sheffield United boss Neil Warnock, who they believed had engineered this situation for his club's benefit – they were losing heavily at the time. Fighting on the pitch continued in the streets outside.

West Brom's rise into the Premiership temporarily ended the local derbies with Wolves, but Birmingham City and Aston Villa were both in the top flight. And it was against Villa that West Brom appeared to have most trouble. In December 2002, two gangs of about 15 people each fought each other after the game at Villa Park. The battle happened at the Square Peg, in Corporation Street, over two hours after the match finished. "It only lasted about two minutes, but it seemed to go on a lot longer," said the pub manager. "They were shouting at each other, egging each other, yelling 'come on' and things like that. They seemed to know exactly where they were going and who they were looking for. No-one wore any football shirts but many of them had pin badges on."

"Football thugs run riot," was the huge headline after clashes between West Brom fans and Aston Villa in August 2004. "Scores of football hooligans armed with baseball bats and iron bars battled with riot police," reported one paper. "Eight supporters were injured and 12 fans arrested as up to 80 people confronted each other outside the Uplands pub in Oxhill Road, Handsworth. Thugs rampaged through the streets in a running battle lasting half an hour, before riot police managed to regain control." The fight is considered by at least one Villa hooligan as one of the "best" he has been involved in, though the Baggies apparently broke an agreement not to arrive with weapons. The police videoed much of the trouble and several dozen people were later arrested, with most receiving between six months' and three years' imprisonment.

Such football banning orders are finally decimating many gangs, as one Albion "youth" member bemoaned. "No doubt us younger lot have missed the boat, but we still had a go and have had some decent days out. Forty youth went to Stoke and got off at Stafford hoping to get a bus into Stoke, where they had only thirty waiting for us. The police pulled us and stuck us on a train to Stoke and kept us in some pub by the station. At two o'clock, we heard the game had been called off, so we got off to Wolverhampton, as they were on their way back from Liverpool. But during the wait, as happens with the younger lads, a mixture of strong lager and heavily cut powder resulted in an in-house brawl and long before Wolves arrived we had been sent home by the police.

"Two games with Cardiff saw us earn some stripes from the older lot when we turned out a few youth for a Friday night game at Ninian Park. We took a good firm, a few minibuses and a coach of older lads from Tipton. A load made it there early although the bus arrived late, which was a pity, as a mob of their youth attacked the Walkabout Bar, where we were drinking. After the game, we had a good sixty and Cardiff were trying to get at us big time, as they were pissed off we had shown and gone into town, but the police managed to get us onto the coach. Before we got out of the place the windows came in and it was a long, cold trip home on a Friday night.

"For the return game we met up early and met in the Hargate, about 200 good lads. The main Cardiff mob were pulled by the OB and we ended up by Motorway Island waiting for the coaches to come through, and hit them hard. There is a video of the police trying to stop us attacking them and although we know it was not the main Cardiff mob they were fighters. Considering our age and numbers we gained respect for not letting the Welsh lot walk to the ground on show as they think they can do everywhere else.

"During the last three years I know personally of six different dawn raids being carried out on the Albion lads. I am banned for three years and many of the lads are banned for life from the Hawthorns. But still the youth come together. There are not the numbers of a few years ago, and if we are honest we have not travelled well. Recently less than twenty had a cracking row with large numbers of Walsall, who done us in the end, but believe me, once the bans are up in a few years we will be back."

Further reading: *Top Boys*, Cass Pennant

WEST HAM UNITED

Ground: Upton Park
Firms: Mile End Mob, Teddy Bunter Firm, Inter-City Firm, Under Fives
Rivals: Millwall, Manchester United, Chelsea
Police operations: Fulltime, Tiger

West Ham United were treated to a baptism of fire by the visit of Manchester United on the final Saturday of the 1966/67 season. United's exciting team needed a point to take the First Division title, but the warm glow surrounding football since England's World Cup triumph eleven months before was about to be shattered by the travelling Red Army of over 20,000 supporters. Football hooliganism had been growing for some time in the north west of England but this was the day when it was exported to London. The match was played out between the two most colourful teams of their generation, yet it was the violence that was to dominate the post-match coverage.

"Soccer's Day of Shame" was how the *News of the World* reported the disorder.

> Trouble started before the kick-off. While many in the 38,000 crowd chanted hysterically for the Manchester team, one fan ran the length of the pitch, pursued by policemen.
>
> He dived into the crowd behind the goalmouth, knocking four or five people to the ground. He was arrested.
>
> With the match under way, the trouble mounted at each successive goal. The rowdies were everywhere. Bottles were hurled in the North stand. Supporters behind the West Ham goal lashed out with banner poles.
>
> The 80 policemen on duty at the match broke up fights, made a dozen arrests, saw 20 more people off to hospital, many with blood streaming down their faces.

There was further trouble after the game as hundreds of Manchester United fans went on the rampage in East London, clashing with West Ham fans as they did so. Sections of the Underground was forced to close for over an hour, and one mainline route was also suspended, as the mayhem extended to the public transport system.

The press saw this as a seminal day in football disorder in Britain, coming as it did on the same day that 39 people were arrested at an Old Firm match in Glasgow. "For years we have despised the Latins for their hysterical and violent behaviour," said the *News of the World*. "In 1967, the

British fans are themselves held in disgrace by the rest of the world. It is a sad comment, but will Britain have to introduce barbed wire, water hoses and ditches round the grounds to keep the hooligans – though in a minority – under control?"

A changing football culture had been occurring at Upton Park for several months before the Man United game but it was that match that gave it direction and purpose. The previous season had seen the formation of the North Bank "end" as the place for young supporters to gather, as the post-Mod period brought younger, more violently inclined fans onto the terraces. The North Bank Enders were often young gangs, many family orientated. Following the United game, many of these gangs became determined to prevent their end ever being overrun again. With the exception of Chelsea in 1968, it wasn't.

The West Ham fans were also beginning to export their violence. During the following season, there was hardly an away match that did not see some disorder from Hammers fans. An early indication was the opening game against Sheffield Wednesday, where three East London youths found themselves before the bench on the Monday morning. "This is the start of the season, and I give you fair warning," said the magistrate. "If this behaviour persists we may have to think about sending some people to prison. We are going to fine you heavily as a warning to others. It is disgraceful that in a civilized society you should behave in this way. We are determined that there should be order in the ground, or there is a danger of people being killed."

In the 1967/68 season, all of West Ham's games around London saw trouble. They encountered little resistance in the capital, but trips further afield proved more dangerous. Wolverhampton Wanderers was one of the worst, as was an excursion to Sheffield United when an attempt to infiltrate the home end ended in a spanking for the Londoners. Other grounds proved easier to stamp some East End authority upon and Stoke were surprised when hundreds attacked the home end, where West Ham claim to have fought for the prize of a huge wooden cut-out of the FA Cup. A trip to Southampton saw the town and ground overrun by West Ham without a punch being thrown.

It was relatively easy in the pre-football intelligence days for the gangs to cause trouble on their travels, but the London police were soon wise to the Hammers' reputation and in the autumn of 1967 banners were banned inside Upton Park, as the poles were being used as weapons. Their mob had no single, identifiable leaders but remained a number of little localised gangs who could call on larger numbers of lads who may not have been specifically interested in football. This was particularly the case for games against Arsenal, who were West Ham's key rivals during this period. For one match to Highbury in 1969, seven lorry-loads of Barking and Ilford gangs made the trip simply for the fighting.

One prominent hooligan element at Upton Park was from the Mile End Road area and from the mid-Sixties onwards was largely made up of skins and bootboys. As the decade drew to a close, new mobs formed from the Harold Hill and Collier Row areas, where people from the old East End were being rehoused, and together they became known as the Mile End Mob. Insular and prickly, they trusted no-one and refused to mix even with other West Ham fans.

An away match at Ipswich in November 1968 saw trouble in the ground and a train wrecked on the return to London. It proved to be the final straw for the club, which issued a warning to the North bank in its match programme:

> **So you have done it again.** Not only did the behaviour of some of you at Ipswich make us feel thoroughly ashamed, but the result of your train-wrecking activities on the way home was seen by millions of people on Television. It must have filled them with utter disgust.
>
> **Why do you do it?** If you consider yourselves to be supporters, then quite frankly, yours is the kind of support that both the game and this Club can well do without.
>
> As we understand the term, a **supporter** is one who is proud of the Club and its record, proud of the team, and so proud of its reputation that he would do nothing to tarnish it.
>
> Until you disgraced us with your presence two or three years ago, West Ham supporters were voted by British Railways as the best-behaved travellers in the game, **and they still are – apart from you.**
>
> A very few of you are the ring-leaders, and we know who you are. So far you have exercised your 'authority' in the very worst possible way, with your punch-ups, obscenities, and train-wrecking. Why not be different from the rest of your kind up and down the country? You could just as easily use your influence to bring this about?
>
> Why cannot you follow the example of your seniors? Why cannot YOU be jealous of our reputation? **Why cannot YOU become known as the best-behaved young supporters in the country?** You would undoubtedly get just as much publicity – probably more!

The club might have been mystified as to why the North Enders acted like they did but others were not. Chris Lightbown wrote an extensive piece for the London listings magazine *Time Out* on the London ends in 1972, where he gave his explanation: "To get an idea of the North Bank, West Ham, visualise Alf Garnett, and multiply it by 5,000. They are, by turn, witty, courageous, cowardly, bigoted, loyal, friendly, insular, open, honest and prejudiced. What other End would sing: 'We shall not be moved' as '…just like the team that is going to win fuck-all, we shall not be moved'? It happened at West Ham two years ago. What other End would take 4,000 to Stoke for a League game, fight for the End, split for the pub before half-time, and jog back home and South like honky kings, having heard that they had lost the match 2-1. West Ham August 1968."

Although well intended, the warning issued in the club programme fell on deaf ears and only highlighted the hooligans' actions to many who had previously watched in awe at the rampaging youths. Many of them now wanted a piece of the action.

In Micky Smith's *Want Some Aggro?*, which covers the early West Ham hooligan years, he claims the Hammers fought off all comers at Upton Park and often took the fight the length and breadth of the country long before other clubs had established a hooligan reputation. Smith asserts that after the Manchester United game that made national headlines, it was rare to see away fans at West Ham, and very few visiting followers had lads looking for trouble. Nottingham Forest were one of the first mobs to come by train but took a beating, while Bristol City turned up seemingly unaware that the place was "moody" and somehow lived to tell the tale. Stoke did the same and although they came with low numbers were rated as showing plenty of "bottle".

Around this time, Chelsea went on the North Bank well before kick-off and claim to have taken it. West Ham say the police saved them but agree they were outfoxed by Chelsea coming in so early and 500 strong. Arsenal brought large numbers but stayed in the South Bank, so West Ham infiltrated the away end for the first time. This was the beginning of a trend of end infiltration and in 1969/70 the first segregation was introduced in the South Bank for a game against Newcastle – though the Geordies gave as good as they got.

Between 1968 and 1974 West Ham's hooligans came off second best away to Newcastle United, Man United, Everton and Derby County. At the same time, however, they took the North bank at Highbury, battered the likes of Wolves and Leeds at home and infiltrated the feared Shelf at Spurs for the first time. Weapons began to make an appearance and rivals were becoming more aware of why the East End's reputation for toughness was justified, but the sheer weight of numbers against foes like Chelsea and Arsenal was sometimes too much for them. Around this time clashes were occurring all over London as various firms waited for each other to arrive back from away games.

Nineteen seventy-five saw a change in fortune on the pitch and some silverware arrived when West Ham won the FA Cup for the first time since 1964. The cup run included the defeat of Arsenal in the quarter-final, when once again West Ham's support on the North Bank remained there throughout the game. Ipswich Town were beaten in the semi to clinch a final against London rivals Fulham, captained by ex-West Ham hero Bobby Moore. The final was never going to make news off the pitch, despite talk of Chelsea or Spurs teaming up with Fulham, but the West Ham fans still managed to shame themselves after their 2–0 win when hundreds spilled onto the Wembley turf and spoiled what should have been the customary lap of honour by their team.

The following season began with running battles outside Wembley at the Charity Shield game against champions Derby County. There were also serious in-house skirmishes throughout the game in the West Ham end. By now very few teams brought an away following looking for trouble, such was the reputation West Ham had built up at home. The *Liverpool Echo* reported that a special train from Lime Street had to be cancelled when only fourteen Liverpool fans turned up prepared to face the gauntlet of a day out amongst London's finest.

Manchester United were the exception. After a riotous season in the Second Division, they once again turned up at Upton Park – but found the reception a lot hotter than at most lower league grounds. It had taken eight years for West Ham to exact revenge on United for their previous humiliation, and they were ferocious in their attacks. "Hammered," was the headline in the *Sun* in late October 1975. "The day the terrace terrors were hunted like animals." There was certainly no disguising the glee from the *Sun* journalist at the thought of the Red Army being battered. "For once they were on the receiving end in a mass punch-up which halted Saturday's soccer match in London for 17 minutes. And as West Ham officials began an inquiry into the violence, United's fan club Chairman David Smith said: 'I hold them totally to blame. Admittedly, we have a few idiots but the mood of the West Ham fans was evil.'"

The trouble erupted when hundreds of West Ham fans stormed the away end, forcing the visitors onto the pitch. "We were outnumbered and hunted like animals," moaned one United fan to an unsympathetic media. The authorities came under severe criticism for the lack of segregation inside the ground, but the club said that while it could separate fans coming into the ground there was little they could do once inside. Manager Ron Greenwood made the mood worse when he declared at the post-game press conference: "For heavens sake, let's talk about the match not the incident. You are football reporters."

His comments received a stinging rebuke from sports columnist Frank Clough. "Wrong, Mr Greenwood. We are journalists first – and we report the news. When 102 are hurt, when 132 people are ejected, when 38 are arrested, when some are likely to be charged with carrying offensive weapons, when a great match is held up for 17 minutes, that is news, Mr Greenwood."

From the early Seventies, the shadow of Millwall worried everyone – except West Ham's hardcore. The two clubs had never played each other in the League but the prospects of a meeting increased as Millwall's performances improved. What was not in question was the animosity felt between East and South East London and the violence associated with both teams. In 1972, West Ham travelled to Millwall for the testimonial match of former player Harry Cripps. While the game might have been a friendly on the pitch, there was nothing but hatred off it.

The match was played one evening and the Teddy Bunter Firm, which included the redoubtable Bill Gardner, probably the number one terrace legend, linked up with the Mile End Mob for the journey south of the river. It was unusual for the two to meet up before a game but they knew they would face unprecedented hostility. The Mile End Mob broke into a railway workmen's hut to arm themselves, and West Ham's first clash with Millwall saw their opponents scatter almost immediately. "It was before the game and after the game that saw the real action," remembered Bunter in the book *Top Boys*. "Good firm, Millwall, for a testimonial. But if it was a league game, West Ham would have had more boys out. But we didn't need no more than the Mile End/Teddy Bunter firm that night. I reckon there was a good 100-200 West Ham there. I've never seen a firm so tooled up as that night." Bill Gardner, in his no-nonsense manner, simply described it as "unbelievable, the worst violence I have seen in all my years of going".

It was to be another five seasons before the two clubs finally met in the League, by which time both sets of fans were even more notorious. The game was set against the added backdrop of the death of Millwall supporter Ian Pratt, allegedly at the hands of West Ham fans after two mobs had clashed on the Underground system a couple of years before. Millwall's home game immediately before the trip to Upton Park saw the distribution of at least 1,000 leaflets urging revenge and even carried a picture of the dead fan. "We have not forgotten you West Ham," read the leaflet. "This is the day we have been waiting for, for over two years. This is no ordinary ruck. They killed a Millwall fan. Every one we do is for Lee."

The *Stratford & Newham Express*, the local paper that covered the West Ham area, urged its readers to "Stay Cool!" on its front page. "Hammers fans will be under severe provocation to indulge in a terrace war with Millwall on Saturday – and the immediate area surrounding the ground will inevitably be a battlefield," it went on. "The Den menaces have declared war by circulating a leaflet vowing revenge for the death of Lions fan Ian Pratt – but the battle cry for a punch-up had already been sounded … by West Ham North Bankers. Right from the time late last season when Hammers lost their First Division status, the 'we hate Millwall' chants have sounded from the Upton Park terraces. And this season as the match drew closer the volume of threat increased. So both camps are in the mood for bloodshed."

Sports editor Jim Gains ended with a plea to the fans: "Think before you act, and put the club – whose colours you supposedly wear with pride – first. Just remember this: It is more courageous to turn your back on trouble than to charge into it fists flailing."

The police and club agreed to segregate fans inside the ground in an attempt to minimise the trouble. "We trust that our fans will recognise that the club could be penalised if they misbehave," said West Ham chairman Reg Pratt. "We hope they'll behave in their usual orderly manner, even under provocation." A few miles away, a similar message was being sent out by Millwall boss George Petchey, who urged his club's own hooligans to stay away. At Millwall's previous home game, fans had run onto the pitch, which, according to the boss was "the last straw as far as I'm concerned. And then came that leaflet, this gist of which is neurotic. We are well organised for the West Ham game but I would ask both sets of supporters to behave. We're aware that the game is being set up for those supporters who want trouble, but why should they want to fight?"

While the authorities and clubs were becoming increasingly anxious about the game, some residents and traders refused to be intimidated. "We didn't close for Hitler and the doodlebugs and we certainly won't close because of the Millwall match," said local greengrocer Harry Mansfield, whose shop was directly opposite the ground.

"Match of Hate," was how the local paper reported the game. "70 arrested as teenage soccer thugs go to battle." The paper claimed that the violence would have been far worse if it had not been for the substantial police operation. Over 500 police were on duty around the ground, and there were dozens of dogs and mounted officers as well as aerial surveillance. In addition to the 70 arrests, a further 69 people were thrown out of the ground.

"The massive police presence stifled most of the fans' violent intentions but the worst cases of premeditated violence came from the Hammers' fans," reported the paper. "About half an hour after the ground and streets had been cleared of West Ham supporters, police escorted Millwall fans to Upton Park station. As the police-protected fans neared the Queens Road market about 500 Hammers' fans laying in ambush attacked and tried to burst through the police cordon, but mounted police quickly chased the troublemakers off." The police admitted they came close to losing control at times. "These fans are like wild animals and I'm afraid in situations like this you have to treat them accordingly," said a spokesman.

Hooligan fashion was changing and by the 1979/80 season the now infamous Inter City Firm, or ICF, was born. The nucleus was a group of young lads, led by his own admission by one Andy Swallow. He and his friends were becoming increasingly fed up with the older lads taking charge even though the younger generation were causing at least as much damage. The skinhead fashion of shaven heads, tight jeans, flying jackets and boots marked the older faces out as easy targets for the increasingly aggressive policing. Casual clothes were adopted and the scarf and ten-hole boot were replaced by the ammonia-filled Jif bottle and the craft knife. Over the next few years Swallow, Grant Fleming and Micky Ramsgate, to name just three of the prominent ICF leaders, were to change the face of football hooliganism. The ICF was born when these three met in an East London flat one night. They made some badges and, as Swallow once said, "the rest is history."

The mob hit the streets with an away match at Villa Park. The huge Holte End had been an unwelcome venue for many a visitor over the years but its reputation held no fear for Swallow and less than 100 others, all aged between 15 and 18 years of age. They sneaked into the Holte in small groups, then with ten minutes to kick-off, covering their faces with makeshift balaclavas, they treated the Holte End to the first ever chant of "ICF". The home end was in chaos for a couple of minutes until the Villa fans realised their end was occupied by teenagers with West Ham hats pulled over their faces with eye holes cut out. The police reacted quickly to take out the visitors but the fledgling ICF had arrived. Back in London their numbers swelled to 150, and they chased Millwall after having given the older West Ham generals cheek all day. "Not a bad first day for the firm" was how Andy Swallow later summarised the events of the ICF's first day on the road.

That same season, a large West Ham firm made the long trip north to Newcastle. Rival mobs battled outside the ground and inside and darts and other weapons flew into the away end. These type of objects, dubbed "missiles" by the authorities, were then regarded as the norm at many grounds, and the press gleefully printed pictures of any fans being taken to the first aid room with darts sticking out of their heads. But that day

515

Newcastle brought a new meaning to the word missile when a petrol bomb exploded among West Ham fans sparsely congregated on the terracing. Not surprisingly it caused uproar within the ICF ranks. One commented that they were fair game for anything thrown at them but a petrol bomb could have hit women or the few children who were there to watch their team play. That made it personal.

After the game the Hammers mob managed to escape the local police, who were for once sympathetic to them given the horrific attack they had witnessed. A huge mob of ICF managed to scatter hundreds of Geordies at the train station before the police decided enough was enough and sent them back on the first train heading south. That was not the end of the matter though; on the train revenge attacks were plotted, as Newcastle were due to visit the capital in the next few days to play QPR.

West Ham announced that Newcastle United fans would be banned from the return game at Upton Park but did not anticipate the ICF's determination to hand out their own retribution for the petrol bomb attack. As usual, they did it in style. Arriving early in west London, the ICF holed up in a pub near Loftus Road and soon were being bought drinks by QPR fans who were told they were under no threat – Newcastle were the only targets. Before long a huge mob of Geordies came bowling arrogantly down the road. An equally massive firm of lads in golf jumpers blocked their way, and at first the Geordies were unfazed, as in their eyes it was "only QPR". Then West Ham announced themselves, and fear spread into the Newcastle ranks. Those who didn't run were beaten. At the same time, QPR manager Tommy Docherty arrived, and when told what was happening, exclaimed in bemusement, "We're not playing West Ham though!"

Even Newcastle lads remember the petrol bombing incident with regret. "Every trip to London after that was murder," said John Sharp, a veteran Newcastle supporter. "No matter where we were playing, West Ham would turn up and cause murder with us."

Around this time the ICF had their first clash with Cardiff City, and while the Londoners claim to have "taken the piss" before the game by chasing the Welsh firm across town, it was also the game when many of the lads realised that undercover police were beginning to show them some interest. This would manifest itself several years later in a major police operation.

The ICF took their football violence seriously – very seriously. Dour and unsmiling to the outside world, they played on the reputation of the East End as a close-knit place both impenetrable and unwelcoming to outsiders. They realised the value of the fear factor long before most other soccer firms, as well as the importance of organisation. Yet despite the uncompromising reputation of their fans, West Ham United was a club that neutrals seemed to love, with their passionate crowds and attractive football. Bobby Moore, Geoff Hurst and Martin Peters had provided the backbone of England's World Cup-winning team and in the late Seventies this mantle was passed on to Trevor Brooking, a true footballing gentleman. After the Hammers won the FA Cup they went on to lift the European Cup Winners' Cup. But another bid for the same trophy, this time in September 1980, brought the club totally the wrong sort of publicity. A 3–1 defeat away at the Spanish club Castilla was overshadowed by highly-publicised misbehaviour off the pitch.

"Night of Shame," ran the back page headline in the *Daily Mirror*. "It is beyond reason that a human being can travel so far, supposedly in support of his club, and before the echo of the first whistle of a potentially memorable evening has died away start to urinate from a balcony on to the crowd below," noted the *Times*. "The police troops, accustomed to incidents in the capital, waited before acting and then did so with fearsome authority. But, with an uneasiness hanging in the humid air, peace did not last long. After the interval trouble flared again, batons were wielded and waves of fleeing spectators could be seen scrambling across the distant terraces."

The club was in hot water as UEFA ordered an investigation. Manager John Lyall insisted that they had done everything they could to minimise trouble but this was not good enough for the football authorities. There had been a fear of disorder before the game and the club had sent a warning letter to everyone who had applied for tickets. What they couldn't cater for were those who travelled independently. While Lyall wanted the guilty fans to be locked up for "a long time", others blamed the Spanish. "Our directors on the spot insist that newspaper reports which said that West Ham fans were to blame for the trouble were totally untrue," said a spokesman for Knight, Brown Travel, the travel agents who had organised the trip for the Hammers' fans. "The Spanish police just stood by and watched while the Spanish fans harassed the West Ham supporters. Those West Ham fans who attempted to defend themselves were arrested. West Ham fans were being antagonized and after the match the police violence was unbelievable." An American living in Madrid, when interviewed by the *Mirror*, backed this account. "The police went in batons flying," he said, "and at some stages were hitting out at everyone. I saw seventy to eighty people injured. One looked in a bad way and I also saw a girl attacked. The police were wild."

The authorities were not listening and West Ham was ordered to play the return leg behind closed doors. They were knocked out of the competition and the club also received a ban, though it was later rescinded on appeal.

West Ham's long-running terrace rivalry with Arsenal dated back to the late Sixties, when the two clubs had arguably the biggest mobs in London. The mid-to-late Seventies saw that drop off as Arsenal's mob declined and football results took West Ham out of the top flight. However, hostilities were resumed with a vengeance again in the early to mid-Eighties and quickly spread from the football grounds to London nightclubs. West Ham took the North Bank on numerous occasions during the late seventies and humiliated the North Londoners when the clubs met in the FA Cup final at Wembley. However, the most infamous battle was in 1982, another day when West Ham went into the North Bank. The match will be remembered for the death of a young Arsenal fan who was stabbed to death near Finsbury Park station shortly after the game. Despite the killing, some West Ham hooligans still brag about that day, which saw a smoke bomb let off in front of the Gooners in the North bank. "To us, it was like Christmas," said Terry Sherrin, one of their top boys, in Cass Pennant's *Congratulations* ... "Arsenal were all coming through in spluttering groups, not knowing where the fuck they were. They just got battered as we picked them off at will." Arsenal were run off their North Bank and were then taunted with the chant, 'Thank you very much for the North Bank Highbury, thank you very much, thank you very, very, very much.'"

The day's events are remembered differently by Arsenal. To them, the ICF were the ones who were turned over, hit from left and right on the terraces before taking shelter behind the police lines to the Gooners' chant of, "We thought you were hard, we were wrong, we were wrong." Said one, "Bloody ICF, spent all their lives trying to avoid the Old Bill, I bet they were glad of them that day."

Two West Ham fans were charged and later acquitted of the stabbing murder, in what one judge described as a "dreadful conspiracy of silence on the part of everyone". With little prospect of ever finding the person responsible, the judge said the case had disclosed "in vivid and depressing detail" the "trend towards anarchy among football louts". Several people were convicted of trouble at the game but all on lesser charges.

The cases brought the ICF into the spotlight, as the police and media revealed an organised conspiracy behind growing football violence, but it also highlighted a lack of knowledge about modern hooliganism. "The ICF gang of 500 toughs has been responsible for outbreaks of violence during the past three seasons," said the *Times* in a bizarrely inaccurate story in August 1983.

> They descend on grounds and have brought disgrace to the game by creating as much havoc as possible.
>
> ICF members recruited mainly from the ranks of London-based clubs,

have their own 'calling cards' printed to leave in the pockets or on the bodies of their viciously beaten victims, 'Congratulations. You've just met the ICF,' they proclaim.

Most of the thugs claim to be West Ham United followers, but they have teamed up with others to form the ICF, whose sole intention is to disrupt and spark battles at first division games. They try to remain faceless, travelling by Inter-City trains, and shunning the regular football 'specials' or coaches. Teenaged or in their early twenties, the ICF contingent, beer-swilling big-spenders, hold regular meetings to plan their campaigns.

Many ICF members wear the long blue or brown coats favoured by warehousemen. They also wear peak caps or trilby hats, reinforced with wood or metal. Some carry rolled umbrellas with finely sharpened points to use as swords.

Typically the report was way off the mark, although they had finally discovered that hooligans no longer wore knee-high bovver boots and butchers' coats. What neither the *Times* nor any other newspaper knew was that much of the trouble at the Arsenal game was caused by a younger mob of West Ham hooligans, the Under-Fives. "We had a really good mob and we went into Arsenal's North Bank," recalled Djelal Ispanedi, better known as Jela, one of their main faces. "We met up at Canning Town and went to Highbury Corner. Everyone got into the North Bank without being detected until we actually let off an orange smoke bomb. We was so well organised and there'd be different groups of us. We had so many police round us, we really took the piss that day."

The Under-Fives respected no-one: not the older ICF, not the police and certainly not away fans. They were known to carry weapons and would regularly rob their opponents during a fight. Out of season many would go into the West End with a view to robbing people coming out of clothes shops. "If we saw other fans that had just got the clothes, like the hooligan uniform – we used to have Pringles, Filas – and you see someone standing out like a hooligan, we'd just set upon them, and really ruin them, beat them up, nick their money, nick their clothes, and make sure they knew who we was," said Jela.

"We would know where lads from other firms worked and meet them on pay day and attack them, taking their wages. We'd go down Petticoat Lane on a Sunday and in a nutshell rob anyone resembling a football lad of anything they had that we took a fancy to. In the end, lads from other firms would tag along, especially some of the younger Arsenal lads, and we were a nightmare on the streets, in shops or at concerts. Anyone was a target if they had the gear on."

The Under-Fives were East End youths who the senior West Ham thugs initially deemed too young to tag along with the main hooligans. The youths saw this as an insult and soon had 20-30 members out to prove their elders wrong. "We used to mob up outside and always tried to get into the away end at Upton Park," said Jela. "When I started going, I was only nine or ten. My first away game was a night match at Liverpool. All the lads had a whipround for me and off we went. The Scousers had lads my age looking for trouble and tooled up and we thought, we'll have a bit of that, and from then on we were known at West Ham as the Under-Fives. We could pull about 100 for some games and we caused some damage. Like the Scousers, we had our share of blade merchants and if the Under-Fives got you, you were in serious trouble. We were handy back-up for the ICF at some games, as we caused some damage, and soon we were going our own way and thought, fuck the ICF, we're okay on our own.

"The following year we went to Liverpool and all the Under-Fives got off at Edge Hill and walked all the way to Anfield. We were attacking Scousers all the way and tried to get on the Kop, but we blew it when we kicked off in the queues outside and the OB put us in the away end. I remember all the lads sitting on the terrace doing the boat song [Oops Upside Your Head] dance, singing, 'We are ICF, we are ICF.'

"Eventually we went off the rails a bit and it was pure violence, not just West Ham, that attracted us. We went to a big London five-a-side tournament at the Wembley Arena and caused murder, we had it with any fans who wanted it. We were young and loads thought we were easy pickings but we did them all in.

"One time we were on the train heading north and the lines went down on the train and we piled out of the station to see a few coaches parked up. There were no drivers about so one lad, Readie, started the fucking thing up and off we went, a coachload of Under-Fives on the road to nowhere. It was a short trip, Readie lost control after a minute or two and ploughed through some poor cunt's hedge and the coach ended up in the front of their house. We just got off and walked into town, which was somewhere near Luton – and they were playing Arsenal. When the police turned up we all started singing, 'Arsenal, Arsenal,' so they got another coach and took us to the ground and put us in the Arsenal end. No-one paid, they wanted us off the streets. It was madness and we kicked off straight away with the Gooners. The OB kept us there all game, segregated from Arsenal and Luton.

"One good trip was in 1986 when about twenty Under-Fives flew to New York and went overland to the World Cup in Mexico. Most lads that age were at scout camps and in Margate with their mums and dads but the Under-Fives were years ahead of their time, as that trip proved."

Jela's time as a football hooligan was shortlived. At the age of twelve, barely out of junior school, he was nearly killed in a fight at Epping Country Club.

"One lad had his twenty-first at the club and we all went down. There was a big fight and someone hit me across the head with an iron bar. I was in hospital for over a year, in and out of comas, had to learn to talk and walk again, so after that I kept my head down for a few years. By the time I was well enough to go again the rave scene had knocked the back out of the firm and everyone was into making money, not fighting at the football.

"The core of the mob stayed together and still meet up and have a drink after some games, but like any of the older lads will tell you, ICF or Under-Fives, those days in the Eighties were unbeatable and to try and carry it on would be impossible."

Another rivalry formed in the early Eighties against the redoubtable Zulus of Birmingham City. In October 1981, the two sets of fans fought on the pitch at St Andrews and there were thirty arrests. Two seasons later, Birmingham travelled to London and 236 Blues were picked up after rampaging through Euston Station. Despite that, a mob of 70 Zulus still made it to East London, where they battled far superior numbers of ICF.

The biggest clash between the two occurred in February 1984, when the sides met at St Andrews in the FA Cup. Trouble kicked off inside the ground after a penalty put Birmingham 3–0 ahead. Hundreds of West Ham fans streamed onto the pitch in an attempt to halt the game. The police restored order but with five minutes to go, West Ham managed to break through a 50-strong police cordon and fights broke out all over the main stand. Trouble continued outside the ground and a police motorcyclist was hit in the face with a brick. The final tally was 30 injured and 109 arrests, 32 inside the ground. "Give 'em a taste of the birch," Birmingham manager Ron Saunders demanded. "If you have a wild dog you don't stroke it, do you?"

West Ham's firm that day was impressive, and in hooligan memoirs several top players in the ICF recall it as one of their best days on the road. Hundreds made the trip to St Andrew's and the mob was so big it was split onto two trains, although before the match was relatively peaceful. Andy Swallow took a firm into the home mob's seats while Taffy, another main face, pulled a masterstroke and, after claiming to be a steward, allocated a block of seats near the dugout to a huge mob of Londoners. When Birmingham went 2-0 up, a mini pitch invasion turned into a massive free-for-all and at 3-0 many more West Ham left the ground and re-entered the Home Kop. At one stage, City defender Noel Blake was forced to defend himself with a corner flag, and it was well after 5pm when the game finished.

The Zulu Warriors had a slightly different view of this match and while acknowledging that the ICF were faster off the blocks, they insist that they were more than up for trouble themselves. "We had a decent mob in the Railway End that day and they came on to the pitch after we scored, they were right up for it," remembered one in the book *Zulus*. "Blues had it with them on the pitch and most of the action was in the Blues' third of the pitch. I remember some people would not come out of the Kop, there were fences around it but still, I thought West Ham had a better show because not enough Blues came out of the Kop to take part. They brought it to us for as long as it took the police to get it under control and they kept bringing lads over from the main stand where some Blues lads were. It was one-to-one fighting and the match was stopped."

"Blues were going wild trying to get to West Ham," insisted another. "We wanted them. We'd had enough of them Cockneys bashing everyone all the time. We assumed they were all NF, we had such hatred for them."

There was further trouble between the two sides in 1986, though this time the Zulus insist that the ICF were "annihilated". About 50 West Ham were at New Street Station when the Zulus top boy and a few others wandered into view. West Ham gave chase but unbeknown to both groups a much larger mob of Birmingham was heading in their direction at the same time. "We chased them off the station, bashing them all the way," recalled one Zulu.

While fixtures between West Ham and Millwall were limited thanks to the varying fortunes of the teams, their fans repeatedly clashed, often on the London Underground. In February 1984, during one of the most violent confrontations, West Ham claim to have had the upper hand albeit with the help of a couple of vans that had been filled with weapons. Three hundred Millwall were on their way to Sheffield when a much smaller mob of ICF called it on. Millwall thought it was their lucky day until they were just yards away and realised the extent of the ICF weaponry. Millwall fled back into London Bridge station, where a petrol bomb was thrown at the Bushwhackers as they tried to regroup and save face.

Weeks earlier West Ham had come unstuck at Millwall when they attacked the home firm after stopping off at the Den on their way to Crystal Palace. After chasing a much smaller mob of Millwall, the ICF lost their usual organisation and were sent packing, much to the dismay of many of their main faces who were in the ranks that day.

That same season, Millwall also battered a firm of 50 ICF who were unfortunate enough to stumble across the full complement of Millwall at Bank tube station in an incident one of them described as "horrible". One West Ham fan was left fighting for his life after being stabbed through the chest with a knitting needle. Later that night the hunted became the hunters when a 300-strong mob of ICF attacked Millwall at Kings Cross.

In August 1985, the ICF once again made national headlines thanks to their unlikely appearance on a Thames TV documentary entitled *Hooligans*. Producer Ian "Butch" Stuttard somehow managed to persuade the firm that it would be a good idea for him to follow them home and away, giving certain individuals semi-celebrity hooligan status. Stuttard did his best to portray a well-drilled hooligan firm who were prepared to take on and defeat all comers. However, the film footage did not always show West Ham at their "best". One game against Manchester United clearly showed them in disarray on the streets surrounding Old Trafford, whilst other footage showed them fleeing Victoria Station in London, purportedly from the police but to this day Chelsea claim they were the ones doing the chasing.

No doubt it seemed like a good idea at the time and the lads were more than happy to appear in paisley silk shirts and Wham-style mullets of the time for their ten minutes of fame. Today some of the things said on film, backed up with clear video footage, would be the foundations of serious jail sentences, but in 1985 it merely brought them into the sights of the police and authorities. The film gave the ICF almost folklore status, with a style and organisation that more than matched the raw brawn of Harry the Dog and his Millwall comrades in the equally famous *Panorama* documentary of the late Seventies. The programme makers also gave the first serious insight into the men who made up a modern football gang. The nucleus of the gang was put at 150, swelling to 350-400 for big games. Interviews with 141 of the core people found that 32 were unemployed, 14 were bouncers, twelve were ticket touts and ten were rock musicians. The remainder were drawn from a wide range of working class jobs, from market traders to soldiers, dockers to lorry drivers. When divided by social class, all but ten were skilled or unskilled manual workers.

Over seven million viewers watched the documentary on its first screening and soon the rights were sold all over the world. Today it still sells well through the internet hooligan market, though most of those who feature on it probably wish it would go away, particularly the Manchester policeman who in full view of the cameras falls on his backside trying to boot a fleeing hooligan.

Aside from Millwall, West Ham's most intense rivalry over the years has been against Manchester United. As described, in 1967 the Red Army took over Upton Park and taught the Hammers an unpleasant lesson, while eight years later revenge was obtained. Following the latter match, West Ham United banned Manchester United fans from Upton Park. The rivalry was no less intense in the 1980s, when the two mobs clashed on several occasions. In more recent years the hostilities have been continued through the written word, with both sides publishing accounts of earlier fights that vastly differ. In what is a widespread gripe at several West Ham hooligan books, Manchester United lads mock the one-sided nature of their accounts, while Bill Gardner is on record as saying he was prompted into collaborating on his own book because of what United had said about him.

The first big disputed clash occurred when the two sides met in a FA Cup match at Old Trafford in 1985. Whereas West Ham claim to have taken the battle to the "Mancs" all day, footage on the *Hooligan* documentary seems to support the Manchester claim that they came out on top throughout the day. Eddie Beef, a well-known Manchester face, has no doubts. "How the fuck can they claim anything apart from the fact that they came looking for it and then came unstuck? Watch the film, which was made by one of them; they don't take a forward step all through it. They get done in and the best bit is when the ICF kid is saying that 1,000 United turned up and 300 West Ham went toe-to-toe with them at the exact time the film shows them scattering. Pure comedy."

Another clash between the two mobs that received massive publicity was on a North Sea ferry in August 1986. Fans from both teams, plus others from Liverpool and Everton, were heading to the Continent for pre-season friendlies and ended up on the same ferry together. As the boat was halfway to Hook of Holland, a fight erupted, which at its height involved 150 people. "A stairway and panelling on the boat were described as 'running with blood' at the height of the fighting," said the *Evening Standard*.

According to the newspaper the fight began when Manchester United fans took their revenge on West Ham fans for a stabbing at a clash between the two sides the previous season in which 16-year-old Eddie Collins was left fighting for his life. "We decided to take revenge for what they did to Eddie," one United fan told the press. Admitting that they outnumbered the East Londoners five to one when the two groups began to exchange insults, he added, "They were taunting us about the 1958 Munich air crash. They had their arms out like aeroplane wings and they were wriggling them and singing, 'One slippery runway'.

"At first we were going to ignore it but then somebody remembered what happened to Eddie Collins at Plaistow. We tried to pile up the stairs but they were throwing everything down at us. They even ripped the maps off the walls of the boat and threw them down, they were belting us with fire extinguishers, they turned the fire hoses on us and they were slashing at us with

Stanley knives. Our lads were stabbing at their legs through the banisters. We smashed some display cabinets and threw glass paperweights back at them but we just couldn't get up those stairs. They stood their ground because they knew if they retreated they'd be massacred."

The ship's captain ordered his crew to lock the fighting fans in the bar while he turned the vessel around and headed back to port, where the police had been alerted. When the boat arrived there were 100 officers on the shore, who made 14 arrests. Another 110 fans were put on a train and escorted back to London. At least one of the Manchester contingent would serve a lengthy jail term for the affray.

West Ham fans immediately gloated about their achievement in holding off the much larger mob of Manchester fans. "We're proud," said one, "it's one up for London." The West Ham leader was identified in the press as "Taffy Harris", a man, the *Evening Standard* claimed was known and feared across London. The paper painted a graphic picture of the West Ham boss, who "with his breath stinking of stale beer, curled his lower lip to reveal the initials of the Inter City Firm tattooed inside". According to the paper, Taffy told their reporter, "That's what it's all about. The Inter-City Firm have made their mark again. Now we might change our name to the Inter-Boat Firm. We gave them a bloody good hiding. Despite being outnumbered ten to one we didn't give an inch. They came at us with knives and bottles. I got hit in the face with a cider bottle. But they got more than they bargained for."

The Manchester contingent on the boat inevitably have their side of the story, though they are quick to praise the West Ham stand. "Let's just say they got lucky," said one. "When it went off, they were on the top deck and we had to get up the stairs to them. The lads they had were top drawer and did as well as anyone could have at holding that top deck. But to say they done us is a joke. At times we were inches away from them, the boat was rocking and they were firing water hoses and fire extinguishers at us as well as slinging anything that was not screwed down. Had we got on that deck there would have been people killed, it was pure hatred, and they were very lucky. Game, yes, but they had to defend those stairs for their lives.

"It was a bad time to get nicked for football violence. We were in jail with lads banged up for the Heysel Disaster and once a week helicopters would land at the jail and they would be taken back to Belgium. At the time we even felt a bit sorry for them but eventually they did five years less than me so I should not have lost any sleep over the cunts."

The publicity surrounding the *Hooligans* documentary made the ICF a household name, so when the Metropolitan Police began to organise their response to growing panic over football hooligans, they were always likely to be a target. By August 1986, six police officers were undercover in the ICF in what became known as Operation Full-time, which culminated in a series of dawn raids in January 1987 and the arrest of 26 people. Fifteen months later, the trial began at Snaresbrook Crown Court of eleven men accused of organising violence at West Ham between 1980 and 1986. Among the accused, who all pleaded not guilty, were Cass Pennant, Andy Swallow, Bill Gardner and Ted Bugby.

The prosecution alleged that these were among the ICF ringleaders who organised violence and travelled on inter-city trains to avoid detection. "Their avowed object was violent confrontation whenever and wherever they could find the opposition," said Mr Vivian Robinson, QC. He went on to claim that the men would meet up before matches to arrange their "angles of attack" and that when trouble did start they would shout instructions to their followers. On one occasion the undercover police overheard the hooligans arranging to get weapons for "a bit of back-up".

The arrests and trial were accompanied by the usual razzmatazz in the media. Lurid pictures of weapons discovered in homes, including kitchen knives, were put on display and the heroics and bravery of the undercover officers were discussed at length. Unfortunately the trial did not go according to the script. Proceedings were stopped after a defence solicitor began to question the validity of some of the evidence. The defence enlisted the help of a retired Home Office forensic scientist who concluded that varying pen pressure in the policemen's logs proved that they had not all been written at the same time, as the police claimed. The suspicion was first raised by the number of staple marks on a photocopied sheet, with some having several while others from the same log had none, and then when handwriting appeared to "flow" too easily from documents written after events from notes on cigarette packs and programmes. "There was no crossings-out and it seemed too smart," said the expert.

The case collapsed and the defendants all walked free, proclaiming their innocence. "The police framed up innocent people and it has been proved in court today," said Bill Gardner afterwards. Andy Swallow told the *Sunday Times* that he knew that police had infiltrated the gang. "We would have been stupid to cause trouble with the police watching us," he added.

The collapse of the ICF trial coincided with the emergence of the rave scene and these two developments played a significant part in the demise of the ICF and the move by some into more murky money-making ventures. One such was Andy Swallow, whose bold antics at Villa Park many years before had given birth of the ICF and who had more recently been acquitted in the Full-Time trial. He swapped East London for Essex, where he ran a market stall selling clothes. Before long he was mixing with Tony Wilson, an East End DJ, and together they began hosting after-hours parties. Over the May Bank Holiday, 1989, Swallow launched Centre Force, Britain's first acid house pirate radio station. Over the next few months it would direct thousands of young people to raves across the South of England.

"Centre Force was instrumental in fostering the sense of community which illuminated the summer of 1989," says Matthew Collin, in his book on acid house, *Altered State*. "Its rattle and hiss a constant background, whether at home or in the car, it shot static and sparks through the drab cityscape. The combination of off-the-wall DJ babble and superlative music was unprofessional, unpredictable, and completely inimitable, and not only made the station's owners the biggest players on the East End scene, but set the blueprint that all house pirates have followed since."

The rave scene and the undercover operations, as well as the attention brought by their own reputation, hit the ICF harder than any firm at the time. While in more recent years mobs like Stoke and Cardiff bemoan the number of banning orders and police pressure they have suffered, West Ham were all but wrapped up ten years before some firms were even heard of.

Upton Park remained a dangerous place to visit and on occasions they could still pull out huge numbers away, like the 400 who witnessed Paulo DiCanio pass the ball past a comical Barthez in the United goal during an FA Cup tie. "That mob was untouchable" said one Mancunian, "but they were there for the show, not the fight." But they were no longer invincible – if they ever had been. Never was this brought home more starkly than on the so-called Night of the Balaclavas, when a contingent of Manchester United heaviest hitters hit the streets around Upton Park clad in a job lot of full-face balaclavas and dressed all in black, looking for all the world like a paramilitary death squad. It was the kind of stunt of which the ICF themselves would have been proud.

West Ham, and particularly the Inter-City Firm, were arguably the top hooligan gang of the early Eighties. They took the football fashion to a new level of style and flare, pioneered calling cards and subtle methods of travel, and had an organisation and toughness that surpassed just about every other firm around. The Full-Time trial and changing fashion ended the ICF as a major force, but for some, it stayed in the blood. When Cardiff City went to Upton Park in 2003 for the first time in twenty years, the Soul Crew were up for a fight. They overran a West Ham mob that was only a shadow of its former self. Several West Ham were arrested and later convicted for trouble during the day, including five men aged 35 or over.

Judge Georges Khayat, QC told them, "Society is sick and tired of people who choose to turn to violence to the detriment of other street users." For almost 40 years, judges up and down the country had been saying exactly the same things to some of the very same people.

At a game in the 2004/05 season at Wigan, a huge mob of West Ham stopped off at Manchester and roamed the streets unopposed, an indication that although not as active as they were, they are still about, and still prepared to settle old scores with "liberty-takers" if the chance arises.

Hundreds of people were involved in the violence ahead of the Uefa Cup match between the Hammers and Palermo in September 2006. Trouble flared at about midnight in the city's Teatro Massimo with rival groups of supporters hurling missiles at each other. Riot police battled with supporters for more than an hour before eventually putting West Ham fans on three buses. "Bottles, cans, glasses and chairs were thrown by both groups," said a police spokesman. "It was a huge battle which took more than an hour to control." Twenty West Ham United fans have been arrested and another six injured.

Further reading: *Want Some Aggro?* Cass Pennant and Micky Smith (Blake Publishing), *Congratulations, You've Just Met The ICF*, Cass Pennant (Blake Publishing), *Good Evening Gentlemen, The Name's Bill Gardner*, Bill Gardner with Cass Pennant (Blake Publishing), *Altered State*, Matthew Collin, with contributions by John Godfrey (Serpents Tail)

WIGAN ATHLETIC

Ground: JJB Stadium, formerly Springfield Road
Firms: Wigan Thieves, Wall Gang, Vulture Squad, Goon Squad
Rivals: Bolton, Oldham, Burnley

It had been a long time coming. After 34 disappointing seasons being refused admission to the Football League, Wigan Athletic were finally granted their wish on Friday, 2 June 1978, beating Southport in a re-vote. It was the end of one chapter of 56 years as a non-league club, under a number of different names, and the beginning of a new one. Twenty-seven years later, a 3–1 win over Reading secured second place in the Championship and automatic promotion into the Premiership.

Their non-league status did nothing to prevent hooliganism at Springfield Road. As early as 1967, the *Times* reported that the club had been ordered to issue notices around the ground as a warning about further trouble, and not long after their arrival in the Football League they made national headlines at an FA Cup game against Altrincham in 1980, when a policeman was led away injured after being hit in the head by a dart. A picture of the officer appeared widely in the press.

While the town's sporting focus was its mighty rugby league team, nevertheless a hardcore of hooligans attached themselves to the football club. During the late Seventies, Wigan's first casual mob, the Wigan Thieves, was born. "The Wigan Thieves were a nasty mob of sly bastards who fought with anybody, even our own lads if they thought there was something in it for them," said Mick, who has been part of the darker side of events at Wigan Athletic Football Club for three decades. By 1981, the Thieves had transformed into the Wigan Wall Gang, or Wall Boys. "They got the name due to the fact that they used to congregate at the top of Wigan where a long benched wall was situated," remembered another lad who watched the club rise from semi-pro status to the Premier League.

"Around this time a younger group of smooths was organising themselves and were named The Vulture Squad – a reference to the fact that they would allow the Wall Boys to steam in first and the Vulture Squad would descend on any stragglers or people who had been brought down, usually relieving their opposite number of trainers, jackets and jewellery," he added. While the Wigan Thieves and the Wall gang would now be in their late thirties to early forties, the Vulture Squad would be mid-to-late thirties.

The more infamous Goon Squad was an offshoot of the Wigan Wall Gang and took its name from the David Bowie song "Fashion", which contained the lyric, "We are the Goon Squad and we're coming to town." According to a Goon Squad member, "A few loonies who liked a scrap got together, and the main lad Suddy, who liked Arsenal at the time, made the name up." Suddy was David Sudworth, who was also regularly in the news-papers for his National Front activities. He went on to become a prominent NF organiser during the late Eighties, sitting on the party's national executive committee. By the Nineties he was a renowned hooligan and was prevented from boarding a plane to Dublin for the friendly in 1995, and later banned from travelling to England matches altogether.

Wigan were new to league football but their gang was soon giving as good as it got. There were numerous clashes with Blackpool during the early Eighties and the fierce resistance displayed by the Latics earned them admirers. "My favourite fights in the early Eighties were with Wigan," said Benny, leader of the Blackpool hooligans during this period. "They were a good mob, like us, and we had some great rows." [See BLACKPOOL in *Hooligans*] Sometimes the Wigan lads would arrive in the resort for a bank holiday weekend, leading to three-way brawls between them, Blackpool and the Leeds Service Crew, themselves frequent visitors to the seaside.

Another mob impressed with them was Hull City. "We had three memorable matches in the Eighties against Wigan," recalled Hull ex-hooligan Shaun Tordoff in his book *City Psychos*. At one, a Hull coach drove into the town past the rugby ground. "We saw a mob of young casual dressers who gestured at the coach as we went past," wrote Tordoff. "This was my type of match, as we seemed evenly matched. We were predominantly in our late teens and early twenties, rugby league had cornered the older market. The Wigan lads seemed the same age." However, on this occasion the Yorkshiremen were tactically smarter and a short time later ambushed the advancing Wigan crew as they unwittingly passed the pub where the Hull lads were holed up. "They took a hiding, and I'm sure the element of surprise had a great deal to do with it."

The numerous run-ins with Blackpool were nothing compared to the intensity of the hatred reserved for Bolton Wanderers, who Wigan hooligans regard as their main enemies, and during the Eighties most games between the two clubs saw trouble. "The rivalry with these is pure hatred. In the early Eighties I think we came off second best against them, other lads disagree but I think they definitely had the upper hand at that time," admitted Mick. "As the years went by we got better, their numbers dwindled and we were on top. The battle at the Market Tavern was the one they don't like bringing up, they were scared to death in there and that day was proof they could not cope with us anymore and the tide of local supremacy had turned."

The Market Tavern incident occurred in March 1986, and was described in one newspaper as "some of the worst scenes since the club joined the League eight years ago". The reporter was unclear as to what exactly triggered the violence, but what was uncontested was that Wigan hooligans launched a barrage of tables, bottles, glasses and chairs at the Bolton mob inside the pub. There were 20 arrests and numerous other incidents, the worst of which was the stabbing of 23-year-old Bolton fan Andrew Greenwood. His family insisted that he was having a quiet drink in the pub when the violence erupted.

There was another stabbing when the two clubs met again in Wigan 17 months later. "Ugly scenes between rival fans marred Wigan Athletic's first home game of the season," reported the *Wigan Evening Post*. A 22-year-old Bolton fan was slashed with a trimming knife, leaving a wound that required nine stitches, after being attacked by a large group of Wigan supporters. Four fans, two from each side, were arrested on the day, though none for the slashing.

Differing playing fortunes kept the two sides apart for much of the Nineties and when they did meet the trouble seemed to have passed. Bolton's firm of more recent years was a mere shadow of the one that had terrorised lower league clubs up and down the country, and though Wigan's promotion to the Premiership brought the two teams together again, little happened at the game at the JJB, despite internet threats and posturing.

"They brought a pitiful forty-five to our place for what they tell us is their biggest game of the season," said Mick, disparagingly. "Word went around that all their main lads were still in Bulgaria after a UEFA cup match. Whatever, forty-five lads is a poor show no matter where the rest are claiming to be. There is bad feeling still between us after a busload of them came to Wigan on a stag night and one lad was killed. It went off in some pub and they got back on their bus when one poor lad strayed too far and was kicked to death on King Street. No-one wants that to happen and four lads got six years each for his manslaughter."

Both sides were capable of sly moves. "One of the funniest fights I saw there was when we fronted a pub at their place," said Mick. "They wouldn't come out and we were bouncing outside calling it on. The doors opened and a lad walked out on crutches, saying, 'Leave it out, I'm fucked.' Anyhow we let him limp past us and got ready to steam the pub when the crafty twat throws one of the crutches to his mate and they wade into us with them. To this day that bloke is respected by us."

There has been surprisingly little trouble over the years with Wigan's other close neighbours, Preston. "They have got decent lads but if they are honest they could not compete with us," stated Mick. "We have no major axe to grind with them, unlike Bolton." A Preston old-timer begs to differ. "They hate us much more than we hate them," he said. "This is based on us always discounting them as they, in our opinion, are still a non league-club. How times change, eh?"

One firm who do have Wigan's respect are Oldham, much of which stems from a ferocious ruck between the two mobs in Ashton, several miles from Oldham. "We went up in taxis," recalled one lad. "It was all arranged and it was a 'mare. There were forty-odd of us heading there, but as we were pulling up, Oldham were picking us off. They had their Hibs mates with them and basically steamed us. The year before we had gone there and smashed them in a pub called the Blue Bell, we had thirty of our finest in there and they bowled in expecting to thrash us but they were turned over big time. That was a wake-up for them and they had a full squad out for us the year after. It was like a riot zone, respect to them that night they did us fair and square." Several lads from both sides were dawn-raided by police for this fight.

The 1998/99 season saw Wigan in the same league as Manchester City and over the course of the campaign there were serious clashes between the two. Wigan travelled to Maine Road for an evening league game and for the Goon Squad it was a night to forget. "It was a scary night," said Mick. "That place was horrible. We had a decent firm there and came out at the end but in seconds their black firm, or the Moss Side lot, were all over us. One good Wigan lad took a hammer straight in his face. There was not a copper in sight and they were bombarding us with fireworks. The place was evil."

Wigan scraped into the play-offs on goal difference, which meant a semi-final contest with City, who finished third. The first leg was at Springfield Park at what was to be Wigan's final game at the old ground. There were clashes outside, eight people were arrested and one Man City fan was rushed to hospital after being struck on the head by a brick.

The Latics travelled to Maine Road for the second leg after a 1–1 draw at home. "We took it to them all the way," said Mick. "A big firm of Young Goons backed them off before the game. That firm of 250 was quality and City knew it."

A City lad concurred. "The Wigan firm that day was very impressive," he said. "They took us by surprise with what they brought and backed City down the big road outside the ground. By the time we got it together the coppers lost it, with even horses being pulled over by Wigan, and the City lads gave them some respect after that one."

Mick laughed. "What else can they do but respect that fucking mob, it was mental. We just stood back and let the young 'uns do the damage, we weren't needed at all that day." Success off the field was not matched on it and a 31,000 crowd saw City win by a single goal.

The following season brought a high-profile clash with Stoke City on the day football remembered the legendary Stanley Matthews. Just moments after the large crowd observed a minute's silence, fighting broke out inside the JJB. The incident received national condemnation, but its origins were in an earlier clash when Wigan travelled to the Potteries.

"We went there with mainly the younger mob but they had had their heads in the nosebags all day and were lawless," recounted Mick. "We were in one pub and got the call to go to meet Stoke, who had 100 down the road. Their copper came in and said, 'You're going to get killed,' but then our spotter came in and said, 'You lot will do okay here.'

"We bounced out and the younger lot were flying through the TAG [Tactical Aid Group] to get at Stoke. It was mental. Today they would be throwing five years at you but that day they were just bouncing truncheons on heads and letting us get on with it. Stoke took the hump at us showing at their place and that triggered the mass invasion of them the season after."

Literally hundreds of Stoke hooligans travelled to Wigan in three large groups; best estimates put the figure at about 800. They had a few skirmishes with small groups of Wigan on their arrival but as the size of the Stoke mob became clear the home mob melted away. "Their firm was awesome and very few mobs would live with them that day," admitted Mick.

"Thirteen people were arrested after an outburst of disorder at Wigan's JJB stadium on Saturday," reported the local newspaper. "Eight Stoke fans and five Latics supporters were held after fighting broke out at the match which marred the memory of Sir Stanley Matthews. More than 100 fans battled across the pitch and Stoke fans surged forward from their stands minutes after kick-off – just moments after a minute's silence. Fighting continued after the game when Stoke fans were asked to remain in their seats – a large number attacked police officers, many of whom received minor injuries."

The referee was forced to take the players off the pitch and police reinforcements were rushed to the ground. There was a ten-minute delay before the officials could restart the match. "The behaviour of these fans involved in both incidents was absolutely disgraceful," said Supt Ian Harrison. "They clearly came to the stadium with the intention of causing problems which is something I find particularly sad on a day when we are honouring a football icon of Sir Stanley Matthews' stature."

Some Stoke City fans have claimed that Wigan supporters broke the minute's silence and this sparked the first trouble. It is a claim strenuously denied by the Wigan hooligans. "That is bollocks," said Mick. "About six or seven Stoke lads came into our seats and it went off just as the silence was starting. It was a fight that got everyone going, not disrespect to Matthews. The other thing is they invaded the pitch to get at us; well, they never tried very hard, as we were in the seats across from them and they did not try too hard to join us. In saying that, they had a fantastic turnout that day. We had our usual seventy up for it but the numbers they had that day could not be touched."

It had already been a busy few months for Wigan's Football Intelligence Unit. In late November, there was trouble when they hosted Lancashire rivals Burnley. "There were confrontations between Latics and Burnley fans before and after the game," reported the *Wigan Evening Post*. Its front page carried a large photograph of Burnley fans, surrounded by police, goading their rivals. Further trouble inside the ground was only prevented by a large and visible presence of stewards and police, who at one point were stretched to the limit to hold back Burnley fans as they surged forward to attack the home crowd.

The trouble at this game warranted a write-up in the annual NCIS log. "This derby match saw Burnley take a travelling support of around 6,000 to Wigan, with about 200 lads, who settled down in the Moon Under the Water pub in Wigan city centre. A large police presence prevented any trouble and the Burnley mob is escorted to the ground. A few incidents take place inside the ground as Burnley fans try to gain entry to the Wigan stand but police restore order. After the game some Burnley lads escape their police escort and are involved in a pitched battle with a mob of Wigan lads. All kinds of weapons and missiles are used before police again restore order. Burnley lads are then put on the train home, but get off in Preston but trouble there is prevented by a heavy police presence."

There was further trouble at the return fixture, held in mid-February, when 100 wigan hooligans travelled through. They clashed with almost 200 Burnley, who later turned on police when they intervened. "Shame," was the single-word headline in the Wigan paper. "On a day of what should have been a celebration of football, as Ian Wright made his debut for Burnley against Latics, 300 fans clashed to show the ugly face of the 'beautiful game'," said the paper.

A visit to Millwall has always been a daunting prospect for any fan. In January 2001, the Goon Squad fought with the home fans at London Bridge Station before the game. After a couple of scuffles inside the ground, 15 Millwall fans were removed from the Wigan end. Afterwards, a mob of 100 Millwall attempted to attack the Wigan escort but were beaten away by police. Frustrated, some of the Millwall mob ran ahead and simply bricked the escort as it went by. A Millwall crew travelled to the game at Wigan but there was little show from the locals.

Other fights in more recent years have been with Wolves and Coventry. Wigan battered Wolves after a clash in a branch of the discount store Matalan, close to the JJB Stadium. "It was twenty against thirty," recalled one lad. "It was a dark night and it happened very quickly. They were gobbing it before the match, so afterwards Wigan got a few older lads together, followed them out the ground area and as soon as they were on the Robin Park retail park, made themselves known. Wolves were up for it but couldn't handle the sheer venom of the Wiganers. They were soon on their toes and were chased into Matalan. Trolleys and bins were used to scatter them all over the shop and the fighting lasted for about ten minutes, but when you're in the thick of it, it seems like half an hour. The police arrived and knocked the fuck out of a few Wigan and Wolves lads. Most Wigan just walked off into the dark and that was about it. One of Wolves' main lads was robbed by some young kids with knives. I was never sure if they were from the Matalan fight or just scallies, but anyway, they took his wallet and coat."

Several people were nicked by police but the case was eventually thrown out of court because the 15-minute CCTV footage, which was supposed to form the basis of their case, was blank. This was a relief for a couple of the Wigan lads as they were already on charges.

There was a further clash with Wolves as the Goon Squad travelled back from a weekend in Bournemouth. A group of 50 Wiganers, including about 20 hooligans, were on their way home when they bumped into Wolves at a train station. "Some older Wigan lads recognised Wolves from the Matalan fight and started to mouth off," said Mick. "About 200 were ready to come charging across the lines when a train pulled in and blocked them in. One hundred or so Wolves charged over the bridge and it kicked off.

"A few Wigan, about half the group, didn't want to know, but the other twenty stood and traded blows for five minutes. No one was badly hurt, though there was a few bits of blood here and there but nothing serious. The police rolled up and rounded us up in a corner with them sticks with balls on the end. One funny thing was one Wigan lad, a big fucker, hid in a phone box. He let all the Wolves run past him, then was going to run at them from behind but got sussed by OB and got called superman for weeks – what was he going to do, change into his tights, et cetera, et cetera."

Wigan's last major confrontation was with Coventry city a few years ago. Two of the older Goon Squad lads were having a stag night, resulting in three mobs travelling down to Coventry for a day on the piss rather than seeking a fight. But as the beer flowed, old habits died hard. After the match, the Wigan lads went off in search of their rivals and were joined by some banned lads from another team who in turn rang Coventry and arranged a fight. The end result was a badly wrecked pub and several arrests and convictions but, insisted Mick, it was "one of the best days out in ages".

Wigan's form fluctuated during their first fifteen years of league status. Promotion was invariably followed by relegation and *vice versa*. In May 1993, Wigan was relegated to the bottom flight. Their poor form continued in the following season, finishing 88th in the Football League, just four places off relegation to the Conference. The ship was steadied the following season and Wigan finished mid-table. Their second half of the season was markedly better than the first and optimism returned to the club. In 1996, they missed out on a play-off spot by just two points but twelve months later a win against Mansfield saw them win promotion as champions, pipping Fulham on goal difference. The club's fortunes improved enormously and in May 2003 they were promoted again, this time with a record 100 points, 14 clear of their nearest rivals. They won an incredible 29 games during the season and lost just four.

On Wednesday, 29 October 2003, Wigan played host to Middlesbrough in the League Cup. The distance and fact it was a midweek fixture did not stop a Boro mob from travelling and on that night they proved too much for the Goon Squad. "They battered us," said Mick. "We arranged it and they did not disappoint. We only got about forty there at the time it went off and they came into us, 100-odd, all their main faces, and battered the fuck out of us.

"They turned up in minibuses and firmed up in a boozer we call the Balk. We were in touch and told them we were on our way but they did not bother waiting and stormed down Darlington Street right into us. Only about ten stood and two lads were on the deck. Fair play to Boro, they picked them up and dusted them down and told them to clear off. They had heard we had a top firm and said that was why they came with such a big mob, as they thought they would need it. The truth is they never did, as we were poor that night."

After only two seasons in the second tier, they were promoted to the Premiership for the first time. Under the stewardship of Paul Jewell, backed by the considerable financial investment from club chairman Dave Whelan, the Latics were motoring, but as they did so the pressure grew on the authorities to crack down on the Goon Squad. "There is too much OB now," said one lad. "We also have a grass in the camp and the police know most of our moves. There's currently a massive police clamp-down and civil cases are being slapped on loads of the lads, especially the younger lot. It seems we are not going to be given the chance to punch our way through the Premiership, but despite what the so called major pundits said about our one season in the top flight, it looks like we may be here to stay!"

The Goon Squad have been a tough mob who have earned a decent reputation over the years throughout the non-league circuit and lower divisions, but they are now finding that this sort of behaviour is not tolerated in the top league of football. "It's like that film *National Lampoon's Animal House* when the lad has a devil on one shoulder and an angel on the other advising him what to do," summed up one hooligan. "We have still got a tidy firm but the police presence with us is crazy. Do we enjoy days out at places we only ever dreamed of watching our club play at, or do we carry on as we did in the lower reaches and end up on certain bans? We took great numbers to Everton but were wrapped up all day by the police, ended up on the piss and saw us win, unbelievable day, but some still say it's better going to the likes of Huddersfield and Carlisle, getting dicked four-nil but smashing the locals all over their town."

WOLVERHAMPTON WANDERERS

Ground: Molineux
Firms: Temple Street Mafia/Mob, Subway Army, Bridge Boys, Yam Yam
  Army
Rivals: West Brom, Birmingham
Police operations: Growth

It was a fitting game to open the new season. Wolves, dominant in British football for much of the Fifties, hosting Manchester United, the club of the Sixties. Both had recently been underachieving, but both were still huge teams. Between 1954 and 1960, Wolves, led by the famous Billy Wright, had won the League Championship three times and finished runners-up twice, while in the mid-Sixties United had collected two League titles and the European Cup. Now it was 1970, and Wolverhampton was about to witness one of the most violent days in its history.

As was typical of any Man United game, thousands travelled to the Midlands, some arriving in Wolverhampton as early as 7.30am. Sporadic fighting was kicking off everywhere but numbers were still small. As the morning progressed, so the advantage swung towards the home supporters who by and large were older and more experienced than United's early arrivals. Fights broke out in pubs, in the middle of streets and in the frightening subway network in the city centre.

The Reds already in Wolverhampton knew that a special train was due to arrive and moved to the station to meet it, while Wolves headed there too to repel them. Up to 300 United fans fought a rearguard battle outside the station against even larger numbers of Wolves. They were losing but help was on hand. The first train came in and 600 Reds, the hardest of the Red Army amongst them, came pouring out. From that moment the tables were turned and Wolves were sent running. A triumphant Manchester mob ran through the town, smashing shop windows and damaging cars as they went. In Queen Square, 100 Man U cornered a crowd of Wolves and demanded they hand over their scarves. They refused and fighting commenced. Trouble flared again as a mob of 250 Reds confidently marched through the subway network towards the ground.

Suddenly, as if from nowhere, hundreds of Wolves were all around them, punching and kicking out at their unwelcome guests. "There were people lying on the floor getting a kicking, people standing toe-to-toe trading kicks and punches, you were fighting someone in front of you and taking whacks from behind and all the time fear kept you on your feet," wrote United face Tony O'Neill in his book *Red Army General*. The brawl ended as they spilled out of the subway into the daylight, but soon recommenced, with neither side giving ground. "Thirty-one arrested as fans go mad," declared the local paper, whose editor was particularly annoyed that one Man United fan decided to steal the keys of several newspaper delivery vans.

It was to be the start of a difficult few months for local police. A fortnight later, 20 fans were arrested after fighting at Wolves' home match against Everton. A fortnight after that, 17 were arrested for trouble before and after a Midlands derby with Notts Forest. The court heard how Wolves attacked the away coaches with bricks, then the same weapons were used by Forest on home fans. At the end of October, 38 were arrested after trouble at another Midlands derby, this time against Coventry City. Taking ends was fashionable at the time but it mystified the local paper, which ran the headline, "When the soccer fans changed ends…" The article went on, "Trouble flared up at the Molineux Ground on Saturday when groups of rival fans on the North and South banks decided to change ends. They met in the middle of the pitch and soon more than 100 fans were involved in a clash. Loudspeaker appeals were made in a bid to restore order. Police brought down fans with rugby tackles and escorted them from the ground."

The Wolves mob's first pub was the George, and it became a target for rival fans. Manchester United tried but failed to take it, as did Stoke and Chelsea. In fact, the only mob who managed to clear Wolves out of the George would be West Ham's ICF. The George was also the home of the Temple Street Mob (or Mafia), Wolves' first identifiable gang. The name came from the lads who used to hang out at the Rollerdrome and Catacombs in nearby Temple Street. By the mid-Seventies, the TSM was beginning to earn a reputation, which came to a head after 50 of its followers occupied the home end at Stoke City in the 1975/76 season. A mass brawl saw many Stoke fans stabbed. In the following days, most of the TSM were rounded up by police and several sent to jail. It was the TSM's finest battle but also their last, as it signalled their break-up.

In 1976, Wanderers again hit the national headlines after 50 arrests at a match at Blackpool. "Gangs of Wolves fans rampaged through the resort before the kick-off and the referee had to take the players off the pitch during the game after missiles were thrown from the terraces," reported one newspaper. The George continued to be a focal point, and in 1977 a new mob emerged called simply the George Lads. Some were TSM veterans, others just Wolves fans up for a ruck, and most were from the Scotlands, Bushbury and Fordhouses areas of the city. It was as the George Lads that Wolves tried to defend themselves when Chelsea arrived in early May, 1977. The game should have passed off peacefully, as Chelsea fans were banned from travelling away at the time because of earlier crowd trouble. But if there is one thing Chelsea fans are good at, that is being resourceful, and on match day well over 1,000 of them were in the ground, most in the Wolves North Bank. Despite the ban, the police had prepared for the worst and had 500 officers on duty, but there was still so much trouble before, during and after the game that Supt Roy Mellor called it "the worst afternoon of violence at Wolves this season". Seventy-six were arrested and 23 hurt.

Chelsea face Steve Hickmott later recalled the feeling of dread as the London mob entered the infamous Wolves subway on the way to the ground. However, once they had survived the home onslaught in the subway, they carried out an all-too-familiar tactic of slipping into the home end in small groups. The roar went up from Chelsea leader Eccles and the North Bank, according to Hickmott, was cleared.

A week later, Wolves travelled to Bolton for their last game of the season. With them already crowned Division Two champions, the event was supposed to be a celebration. Ten thousand made the trip, but trouble broke out inside the ground resulting in 34 arrests and 42 ejections. The George Lads continued the tradition of attempting to take away ends, travelling to matches in what was known among the group as "the monster coach", and Bolton was no exception. They arrived in time for the pubs to open and were soon fighting anyone in their path. "Hooligans battled with fists, beer bottles and glasses in the town centre," reported one newspaper, which went on to complain that some clubs might now ban Wolves fans from attending at their grounds. "It's all right to go on to the pitch and express delight at winning the Second Division championship with a couple of points to spare, but to deliberately bait, chase and strike down home supporters is just plain crazy," said the paper.

After the Bolton game, hundreds of Wolves fans went on to Blackpool, where they were involved in running battles with Manchester United supporters. One man was sentenced to three months' imprisonment for throwing bricks at opposing fans, and two other Wolves fans were fined for possessing offensive weapons, bricks and a paving stone. The following Monday's *Wolverhampton Express and Star* reported the largest fines dished out for football-related violence, a whopping £400 in the days of £35 a week wages.

Molineux always gave opponents, on and off the pitch, a hostile reception. Former Wales keeper Dai Davies recounted the horrors of playing a Youth Cup fixture there in front of 15,000 fans. "My world fell to pieces as I came up against crowd violence," he said. "I had my back to thousands of Wolves supporters, most of them skinheads, and I was the butt of non-stop taunting, curses and spitting. Pennies, pieces of glass and rocks were thrown at me and, because of my lack of experience, it all left its mark on me. I felt every taunt, and I could not, dare not, look up into the crowd each time the ball flashed past the goal into their midst. Three goals were scored past me, and I was to blame for each of them. For the only time in my career I felt lonely, afraid and sorry for myself."

The lads from The George mixed football and music, and took violence to both. The TSM attended skinhead gigs in Birmingham and clashed with locals. In the late Seventies, Brum skins came to Wolves and fought with the George Apprentices (a short-lived mob comprised of youngsters who drank in the pub) before an Angelic Upstarts gig. Only three songs had been played before fighting erupted, and police dogs were brought out to clear the dance floor. The *New Musical Express* blamed the National Front but it was really Birmingham v. Wolverhampton. Six Wolves lads went to the next gig on Upstarts' tour, in Nuneaton. There they not only had to contend with Birmingham skinheads but also had the band calling for the blood of the Wolves fans from the stage. Wolves hoped to travel mob-handed to the next big gig in Nuneaton, this time featuring the Cockney Rejects, but to the disappointment of many, it was cancelled. In the early Eighties, the Wolves Subway Army also fought at a Jam gig, whose concerts always brought out football firms.

By the end of the Seventies, it was only a matter of time before a new group emerged at Wolves which harnessed both the football and casual culture, and in 1980 the first Wolves casual firm was formed. It began as a small group of up to 20 lads in their late teens, led by Roger Quintyne and Ray Hickmott, who were soon joined by Gary Johnson, then just 17 and from the tough Lowhill estate. Together they formed the Subway Army, named after the large underpass below the town's ring road. The group contained a mixture of black and white lads and soon usurped the George Lads, in numbers at least.

Between 1980 and 1982, the Wolves hooligans were at their peak, though the team was in a slump. The club was relegated in May 1981 and though it was to return to the top flight two years later, this was to be a temporary respite from long-term decline. Most games saw the Subway Army pull together 80-100 lads and the George Lads another 50. On the odd occasion, the Wolves mobs could total 500 lads.

The first game of the 1980/81 season saw Wolves travel south to Brighton. "We sat in a Tipton pub on a warm Friday afternoon as we waited for the minibus to arrive," remembered one Subway veteran. "There were seventeen seasoned Wolves fans there. A dozen were teenagers emerging from the late 1970s punk scene and beginning to warm to the new casual culture, with clothes somewhere in between. Another five older lads had become disenfranchised by this new wave of youth culture and wanted to prove that they were still up for the crack and could put on a good show, albeit clinging to the Seventies fashion.

"By five o'clock, the posse had increased to thirty. The newcomers were a mixture of tatters boozed up on the money from their early graft and local thieves who perceived Brighton as a shoplifter's paradise and easy pickings. The sudden growth in numbers meant that we needed an extra van. Our prayers were answered by the arrival of a hired twelve-seater and a stolen bread van with no windows, a roller-shutter door and a driver with more car convictions than anyone in the West Midlands. Something told me that this was not going to be an ordinary away day.

"The twelve most sober and organised boarded the twelve-seater and the rest piled in the back of the bread van, without any protest and in no order. Off we set, a total of six miles to the Dog pub on the Hagley Road. Some wanted a piss, others were thirsty, but all wanted the Brummies to know who we were – hence the first brawl. Ironically it had nothing to do with football. One of our lads, known for his paranoia, thought some office bloke was staring at him aggressively, so he decided to move his gaze to the other side of his face. The locals didn't take too kindly to this and bottles, chairs and glasses exploded all over the place. Coppers soon arrived and nicked two of our lads who had jumped over the bar to raid the till. Happy with their catch, they forced us back on to our transport and paid no attention to the bread van. We set off again, with Paranoid promising a revenge trip to the Dog in the near future. As he worked as a bouncer back in Dudley, we knew he probably would carry out his threat. It was only 6.30pm and we had already lost two and a couple of others were carrying injuries.

"The trip down to London was dominated by talk of the fight and our hatred of Brummies. We comforted ourselves with the thought that they would never take a trip to Tipton; no-one thought of the fact that they probably had no reason to. Soon after midnight, and after what seemed twenty-five piss-stops, we arrived in London. Having gobbled down the large amount of pre-packed food stolen from the motorway services, some of the more refined members of our entourage wanted some proper food, so we decided to stop at a Greek fish shop in Holloway. One by one, we carried out food back to where the vans were parked. Suddenly, one of the lads bowls out of the fish shop while another jumps over him and back into the shop. Within seconds he falls back out with a Spurs fan on board. They roll about like two spoons huddled together in some sexual act. We realised it wasn't when two more Spurs fans came bounding out and jumped straight in, feet first. Chips were flying everywhere so we all decided to pile in, leaving the Spurs fans flat out, with the Greek shop owner shouting abuse at us. His wail was silenced by Paranoid, who was still going on about the office worker in Brum. Not wanting to lose more of the group, we quickly boarded and drove off.

"It wasn't until we reached Brighton that we realised we had left a lad behind, probably still queuing for his chips. It was five in the morning. Some tried to sleep off the effects of the drinks while others passed the time chatting about past encounters. I tried to explain the new casual culture to a couple of the older lads but they were dismissive. They believed that no new organised firm could ever achieve what they had done at the likes of Bolton, Exeter and Man Utd. One lad was convinced that the Subway Army were ponces in their casual wear and if they ever came to Tipton they would be destroyed. The strange thing was that throughout the entire journey no-one had mentioned football. The Brighton nudist beach was the preoccupation of many.

"At 8.30 we decided to split up. The thieves waited for the shops to open, some went off in search of the nudist beach while others explored for a place to buy beer that early in the morning. As planned, we reassembled back at the vans at 12.30, from where we found a small, back street pub just off the main drag. The thieves showed off their spoils and the pissheads complained about the weakness of southern beer (though that didn't stop them sinking gallons of the stuff). I never found out if the group found the nudist beach; I felt I would be considered a pervert by asking.

"We hadn't been drinking in the pub long when Paranoid shouted that he had seen Brighton and vowed to give them a bit of what the Brummies got. I had just hit the jackpot on the bandit and earned £20 and I was sitting on a table outside the pub with a dozen of the others when twenty Brighton ran towards us. These weren't naturists or gays but game lads. All hell broke loose. The battle lasted three minutes, long enough for a few of our lads to require hospital treatment. Paranoid got nicked after he steamed out of the pub only to take his anger out on a copper. He was last seen screaming and kicking as he was bundled into a police van.

"It was now 2pm and we made our way to the ground, preferring the local bus to our own transport. We were only twenty-strong, having lost a few to the police, some to the hospital and others missing in action, but vengeance was in the air and we were going to get it. We disembarked the bus half a mile from the ground and no sooner had we got off than we saw five Wolves lads having a toe-to-toe with fifteen Brighton. As we ran across the road to join them, another twenty Brighton appeared and then, apparently from every direction, more Wolves joined the fray. It was going off all around us. The Old Bill arrived and most vanished, leaving behind only the odd Wolves and Brighton who had taken a slapping.

"The police rounded up about 200 Wolves and escorted them to the ground. We lost two-nil and there was a bit of trouble in the Brighton end and an exchange of missiles between both sets of fans as we were leaving the ground. One Wolves took a brick on the back of the head, which in turn led to a charge by other Wolves lads.

"The Tipton lads managed to find each other and made their way back to the bus. We managed to squeeze in a few drinks at the pub where we'd had the fight earlier and set off home, minus the bread van and two more lads who decided to stay. From a total of thirty lads, only fifteen made it home. This was nothing new. Most trips out with the Tipton lads ended this way."

In the 1981/82 season, there was serious disorder away at Stoke City. Before the game Wolves went looking for Stoke, while during the game a group of 30 from Rugeley got into the home end and kicked off, then after it, 60 Subway Army mobbed up with 30 lads from Gornal and Kidderminster to await the Stoke response. Wolves' cheek had obviously riled Stoke, and boys, "shirts" and beer monsters came roaring out of the ground to exact revenge. By the time the police restored order, Wolves were taking a beating but their pride was intact.

For many Subway veterans, the highlight of their escapades was taking Leeds United outside the Peacock pub opposite Elland Road in September 1982. Heavily outnumbered, and mostly lads in their late teens and early twenties, the Subway Army ran what many thought to be one of the main mobs at the time. The euphoria was not to last long, as internal divisions brought an abrupt end to both the George Lads and the Subway Army. For a number of years the two groups co-existed but tensions were never far beneath the surface, and following the Leeds game, the Subway decided to sort out their differences physically. They arrived back on two coaches shortly after 8pm and headed straight for the George. Newspapers report as many as 50 being involved in the trouble, which soon spread out on to the streets and in the ensuing melee 18-year-old Subway lad Ian Edwards was stabbed to death. The Subway had not expected the George lads to be armed and awaiting their arrival, and were taken by surprise.

Police immediately began an investigation. Fifty detectives were put on the case and over the next few days interviewed dozens of people they believed were connected to the Subway Army. They soon discovered an "armoury" of weapons, including sharpened screwdrivers, hidden under the seats of two of the coaches that took the Wolves mob to Leeds, and also found what they believed was the murder weapon. Police frogmen also discovered an axe that had been dumped in a canal close to where Ian Edwards died. Yet 48 hours into the investigation, the police had failed to identify a single person who had been on the coach that Edwards had caught to Leeds.

While the town was shocked at the inter-gang violence, the Subway plotted revenge, and a short time later attacked the George lads again outside the Connaught Hotel. One man suspected of involvement in the death of Ian Edwards was slashed across the face outside the Red Lion pub and a week later the pub was wrecked completely.

The police came under further pressure three days after the murder when a local magistrate criticised their tactics in handling the Subway Army. At a Regional Police Authority meeting, Captain John Haydon told the Chief Constable of West Midlands Police, "The police had them marked and taped and knew of their existence and may have anticipated trouble from these people. The fact that their activities were tolerated or even condoned worried me deeply."

The Chief Constable defended his officers, and while he expressed concern at the rising gang warfare in Wolverhampton, he stressed that the police could not arrest people for just belonging to a gang. However, stung by the magistrate's criticism, he ordered a full report into the Subway Army, while the chairman of the Police Authority promised a crackdown on their activities. The police were backed by Ian Edwards's father who, four days after the murder, made a public appeal for his murderer to be identified. "I appeal to those people to look to their conscience and good sense to come forward and tell the police who did this to my son," he said.

Six days after the murder, 25-year-old Sean Gallagher was charged with Edwards's killing. Fearing reprisals, the dark-haired defendant appeared at his first hearing flanked by 15 detectives. A week later, 15 more people were charged with involvement in the fight, including Roger Quintyne, the leader of the Subway Army. Just like the Temple Street Mafia before them, a court action was to signal the end of the Subway Army and the George Lads.

The early Eighties saw regular clashes between Wolves and Birmingham City. There was no love lost between them and their history of trouble dated back to the early Seventies. On two occasions during the 1982/83 season, Wolves even travelled to Walsall when the local team was hosting the Blues. There was further trouble during the following season, with Birmingham travelling to Wolverhampton and having an almighty tear-up in a car park close to the station. A large Wolves mob travelled into Birmingham for the return fixture and camped up in the Toreador pub, near the market. One of Wolves' main faces was actually the cousin of the Zulu leader, and while they were chatting amicably outside the pub, making arrangements for a meet later in the day, a group of forty young Zulus approached. Their leader initially calmed the situation – until his cousin launched a bottle in their direction and then it all went up. Every window in the pub was smashed as the Zulus launched a barrage of weapons at the building and the Wolves hooligans threw other weapons out.

Wolves won promotion back to Division One with a home win over Newcastle United, but as hundreds of home fans swarmed on to the pitch to celebrate, away fans flooded out of the South Bank for a confrontation. Police later claimed that their swift action prevented more skirmishes but 51 people were still arrested. Former Subway leader Gary Johnson recalled the match as one of the most violent he could remember at Wolves. "There was fighting going on all around town," he remembered in *Terrace Legends*. "They came mob-handed. There were fucking loads of them. It was like us kids fighting grown men but we did them in the end."

The club's return to the top flight was to last only one season and their relegation in May 1984 signalled three consecutive drops, ending in the old Fourth Division for the beginning of the 1986/87 season. Worse still, the club was on the brink of financial collapse, with debts rising to £2.5 million, and was forced into administration. Wolves fans reacted to the deepening crisis by becoming more violent, and this went beyond the small hooligan core to the point where it engulfed much of the fan base, at least away from home.

The demise of the Subway Army left a void soon filled by Dave Powers, better known as "Fingles", and his lads from Darlaston. He organised a coach to away matches which would pick up at various points around Tipton and before long his transport became a magnet for those looking for trouble. "They were great fun and we used to have a right laugh," recalled Gilly Shaw, in his book *Running With a Pack of Wolves*. "Fingles would sit at the front, just behind the driver. He was like a strict teacher and we were like naughty schoolchildren sitting behind, pulling faces. We would have all sorts on the coach, beer monsters, hooligan wannabes, and out and out headcases."

A new mob, the Bridge Boys, had been formed in 1984 but at its core was just 50 lads. It brought together elements of the defunct Subway Army with younger Wolves fans. It was less organised and more of a loose alliance, but on its day could pull out 500 young men. While it helped resolve some of the internal problems that afflicted earlier mobs, it brought its own difficulties by way of police infiltration.

Three days before Christmas in 1984, Wolves played Leeds United at Molineux. The animosity of the earlier encounters had not been forgotten and during the game 50 Wolves hooligans invaded the pitch in the hope that Leeds would meet them for a battle. The match was briefly halted as police moved in quickly and several arrests were made. Wolves chief executive Eric Woodward said, "I can only imagine this incident had something to do with the reputation which Leeds fans have. We don't want a similar reputation ourselves which is why I am so disappointed and annoyed." Unfortunately for Woodward, his fears were soon to be realised.

Wolverhampton Wanderers hit rock bottom when they were relegated to the Fourth Division, but hope springs eternal, and a new management took over the club. Birmingham City chairman Ken Wheldon came in as an adviser and he brought with him Jack Harris and Dick Homden, the latter taking over as chairman of the club.

Three months into the new season, Wolves played away at Torquay and for hundreds of the club's fans it offered a weekend away at the seaside. Unfortunately, more than a few got carried away and fought throughout the day. "Mayhem – 30 Wolves fans face court," announced the *Express and Star*. "Police were overwhelmed as they tried to contain rampaging mobs who tore through the resort, terrifying shopkeepers and residents. The police were so overwhelmed by the sheer numbers involved – around 1,500 Wolves fans – that they were only able to arrest a few of the troublemakers. There were reports throughout the day of large numbers of fans trying to buy sharp objects and weapons."

The problem was made worse by the ground not having proper segregation, so Wolves fans mingled and clashed with locals in every stand. Throughout the match, missiles were thrown at police and smoke bombs set off. There were repeated pitch invasions, and at half-time the match commander attempted to have the game called off, but the referee refused.

Wolves won 2–1 but the result was forgotten amid the fallout from the violence. Twenty fans went before the Torquay magistrates and the club threatened to ban them from Molineux for life, while admitting enforcement would be difficult. The first to receive a ban was Christopher Deeley, fined £300 for threatening the referee. Postal worker Karl Spicer was fined £500 and bound over to keep the peace for two years for running on to the pitch and punching the home captain. He was on the sick from work at the time. While Wolves mulled over the implementation of identity cards,

Torquay United demanded the match be replayed and described the fines as too lenient. In the end, few were given life bans but the club did ban fans aged under 18 from supporters' club coaches and decided against putting on any official transport for the away fixture at Bolton, a club with its own hooligan problem.

Five months later and new chairman Dick Homden must have cut a dejected figure when he stared at more depressing headlines, this time after Wolves fans misbehaved at Southend. "What more can I do?" he asked after news filtered through of the trail of destruction left by supporters. "We've tried banning people from supporters' club coaches, we've made admission to the John Ireland Stand ticket-only, and we've withdrawn concessionary admission rates. If anybody has the answer I'd be delighted to hear it."

Homden's comments came after Wolves had lost a crucial Friday-night promotion clash, effectively ending their chances of going up. More than 400 Wolves fans rampaged through the town, causing thousands of pounds' worth of damage. Police trying to round them up came under a hail of bricks and bottles. Shop windows were smashed and people in pubs terrorised as Wolves fans went hunting for targets. Even before a ball had been kicked, Wolves caused trouble. A special train bringing 2,500 fans down from the Midlands was vandalised and the violence spread to the town almost as soon as they disembarked. Violence intensified after the game as disappointed Wolves fans vented their anger on the town. The police eventually managed to push the Wolves mob down to the seafront but it was 2am before the peace was restored, and only after the use of police dogs and horses. Specially chartered coaches were required to collect the marauding Wolves fans.

Wolves' final away game of the season took them back to Devon, this time to Exeter. Their club had no chance of going up but thousands of supporters decided to take advantage of the bank holiday fixture. Hundreds travelled down on the Saturday and decamped in nearby Torquay and Paignton, but trouble flared as drunken and boisterous Midlanders spilled out of pubs and clubs at closing time in both seaside towns over the following two nights. In one incident, Wolves fans attacked a couple paying for petrol. While some threw bottles at the man, others surrounded the woman, who was fortunately locked in the car. One even asked her if she had ever been raped. "It was a frightening experience," Julie McGovern later recalled. "At first I thought that they were just kids but some of them were grown men." Her husband rushed to her rescue on seeing a mob surround the car. "There is only one way to describe these people – animals," he said. The game passed off relatively peacefully as extra officers were drafted in to prevent any further outbreaks of violence.

If the Wolves board were happy to see the end of one season, they must have wept when it was announced that the club's opening game of the following season was at the Football League newcomers Scarborough. As was now the norm with Wolves' seaside matches, hundreds made a weekend of it, many without tickets. They were packed tightly into the ground – perhaps too tightly to be safe – but that was no excuse for what happened during the half-time interval. Wanderers fans ripped down the security fence that was supposed to keep them off the pitch, wrecked the new toilet block at the back of the stand and overturned the refreshment bar. As police moved in, they were pelted with bricks, lumps of concrete, beer cans, bottles and pieces of metal torn from the stand. The trouble spread to the roof of the ground, on to which dozens of Wolves fans had clambered. Television captured 23-year-old Andrew Charlesworth falling through the thin roof onto the terrace below. Fortunately for him he only suffered a broken arm and a ricked neck, though he claims that he was beaten and mugged by home supporters after he landed.

With the violence escalating, the ref had little choice but to take the players off before a ball had been kicked in the second half. Wolves manager Graham Turner and his opposite number, Neil Warnock went onto the pitch and appealed for calm. The trouble subsided and the match resumed, but the damage had already been done. Fifty-six people were arrested on the day, with more identified and charged later in the year.

Strong headlines littered the front pages of nearly every national newspaper. Reports were accompanied by demands for action against the hooligans who had now been involved in four seaside riots within a year. As the FA ordered an investigation, the club took steps unilaterally by announcing that with immediate effect all Wolves supporters had to supply the club with their names and addresses before being allowed to buy a ticket for away games. In doing this, Wolves became only the second club in Britain, after Leeds United, under such ticket restrictions. It was also reported that Wolverhampton police intended to use video cameras at home games to identify troublemakers by publishing their mugshots. Supporting the new CCTV system at Molineux, Chief Superintendent David Ibbs said, "Our task is to identify the ringleaders and troublemakers and bring as many to court as possible." The local paper also asked readers to identify the culprits. "Shop the Yobs!" it declared.

Chairman Dick Homden called for a league-wide ban on away fans and the introduction of a membership scheme. "I thought it was terrible when

Luton imposed their ban on away supporters, but now I believe it is the only way that we have of stopping the trouble," he said. Scarborough, meanwhile, were unmoved by the cries of horror from Molineux and demanded £10,000 from the Midlands club for the damage caused. Wolves refused to pay, claiming that Scarborough should have had adequate insurance to cover the costs, a response that hardly won the club many friends.

Four days after Scarborough, Wolves were at home to Northampton Town. There was no trouble and Ibbs even described the behaviour of the 6,000 crowd as "exemplary". At half-time, Homden and Derek Greaves, managing director of shirt sponsors STAW Distribution Services, made an appeal to fans. "If we work together we can be the best supported club in the country," said Homden. Greaves was more blunt. "We'll go nowhere if you behave like scum. If you are not, then prove it."

The FA fined Wolves £5,000 and banned their fans from six away fixtures starting from the beginning of September, but the club, fearing a repeat of any trouble, decided to implement the ban immediately. In truth, the ban benefited the club and financially damaged smaller clubs reliant on the bumper crowds that came with a visit from Wolves, who had easily the largest support in the division. Hereford and Notts County were just two of the clubs that were expecting their biggest gates of the season but had to do with their smallest. Carlisle's chairman claimed that the ban cost his club £6,000. "We were expecting 2,000 Wolves fans and we were looking forward to having them here," he said.

With no sign that the club's hooligan problem would improve, West Midlands Police launched Operation Growth. Standing for "Get Rid of Wolves' Troublesome Hooligans", Growth was an undercover operation involving eight officers, who, over a period of six months, ran with the Wolves hooligans. One of the undercovers was Dick Shakespeare, a life-long Wolves fan, who would later go on to work for the NCIS football unit. The officers were drawn from the West Midlands force, West Mercia, Staffordshire and the British Transport Police.

The result was the largest round-up of football hooligans anywhere in the country. In March 1988, 66 people were arrested in Wolverhampton, Shropshire, Staffordshire and Warwickshire. Among the items displayed for the media were a butcher's knife, other knives, jewellery stolen from a shop in Wolverhampton, hooligan scrapbooks and "Bridge Boys" calling cards. Of those arrested, all but one was later convicted. Forty received immediate or suspended jail sentences for a series of charges, including assault and conspiracy to riot. The judge also imposed five-year bans from all Football League grounds.

The raids and subsequent convictions had an immediate effect, with arrests at Wolves matches dropping by two-thirds. Not only had many of the Wolves ringleaders been taken out of circulation but the severity of the sentences, coupled with paranoia about on-going police operations, brought organised hooliganism almost to a halt. The raids also coincided with the emergence of the rave scene and improving fortunes for the club on the pitch.

In 1988, an FA Cup run saw two away ties at Wigan and Bradford City, and on both occasions the Wolves mob had a hard time. Operation Growth did nothing to prevent 300 lads travelling on the train to Wigan, where they met a very hostile reception from the moment they landed. "Each pub and social club we passed attracted groups of locals who would shout abuse at us and taunt us," recalled top boy Gilly Shaw. "If it wasn't for the Old Bill being there, there would have been murders." There was serious disorder during the game as the police tried in vain to prevent the locals attacking the visitors.

The trip to Bradford was no less difficult, and for this one there was only a small mob of 50 lads. They searched in vain for the locals before the game but were ambushed as they approached the turnstiles. "They were real geezers, not a young lot, just proper men," added Shaw. Worse was still to come, as on their way home they decided to stop off in Derby, whose team had been playing Chelsea at home. They spotted a handful of locals and soon disembarked their coach, only to see a mob of 250 lads waiting up the road. "They destroyed us big time," admitted Shaw.

After a couple of years of inactivity, a few began wanting action again and a new mob coalesced around Gilroy "Gilly" Shaw, a man of Romany heritage from Wednesbury in the Black Country. He claimed that an incident where he helped rescue people from a burning building saved him from serving time after being arrested during Operation Growth. Shaw held things together with a small group during the barren years and by 1989 was leading a new, young mob called the Yam Yam Army. The group took its name from the Wolverhampton accent, often mimicked by Brummies: "Yam daft, yam thick, yam wrong." While the Subway Army had drawn most of its support from a narrow Northern section of the city, and the Bridge Boys from Wednesfield, the Yam Yam Army attracted younger lads from across the city and neighbouring towns. Older Wolves hooligans are sometimes dismissive of the "clueless kids" in the Yam Yam but admit that they are game. The Wolves mob of the Nineties became prominent on the England scene and took large mobs to most games.

The Yam Yam Army continued hostilities with their close rivals. An early encounter came in 1989 when young Wolves hooligans attacked a pub holding 70 Stoke. During the game, a mob of 150 Stoke broke on to an empty terrace to confront Wolves. The return fixture, at Stoke, saw Wolves running a tidy firm of 40 Stoke with hardly a punch being thrown. Mark Chester, of Stoke's Naughty Forty, described this as an "unprecedented humiliation" in his book *Naughty*. Stoke wanted revenge and the following season 60 of them broke away from their police escort to hammer 100 Wolves. "They weren't prepared for the ferocity of Stoke's aggression," remarked Chester, with some satisfaction.

Wolves' main rivals remained West Bromwich Albion and Birmingham City, and over the past few years they have clashed several times. In January 2000, 60 fans came to blows after Wolves stopped off in Birmingham on their return from a match at Walsall. A far more serious clash occurred on April Fool's Day, 2002, when the two fought outside a pub two miles from Birmingham's ground. One hundred and twenty Wolves, under the leadership of Shaw, arrived on a double-decker shortly after midday. Calls were made to Birmingham and the waiting began. At 1.30, a mob of 50 Zulus came up the street. Wolves steamed out of the pub to meet them armed with anything they could remove from the bar. From the opposite direction, a 100-strong Birmingham crew appeared. Battle commenced. Pool balls, cues, bottles and glasses were exchanged and flares lit up the sky. Once the missile stocks had been exhausted, it was toe-to-toe fighting for as much as 20 minutes, an almost unheard of battle in the modern hooligan era. Given the intensity of the fighting it is not surprising that there were severe casualties, the worst being a Wolves fan who was left in a coma after being struck on the head with a brick. A Birmingham fan was later imprisoned for four years.

It was Yam Yam leader Gilly Shaw's most memorable fight. "It was on a par with anything seen on our TV screens from somewhere like Northern Ireland," he said in the book *Terrace Legends*. "Three lanes of traffic were brought to a standstill with car windscreens smashed and cars damaged. Glass and prostrate bodies littered the streets. People were getting knocked to the ground and stayed down. Some were unconscious. The street was alight with coloured smoke and flames from the flares. They'd get run and backed off a few times, but then they'd come at us again from another side. But we held strong, we battered them."

Birmingham, unsurprisingly, have a different take on the day and indeed, on the Wolves mob of today. "Before the days of Gilly, Wolves used to have a decent firm," recounted Wally, a well-known Birmingham face, in the recently published book *Zulus*. "I have a lot of respect for the old Subway boys, unlike the shower they have got down there now."

Six months after the Birmingham clash, Wolves were in the news again after mass disorder with Stoke. A pre-arranged meet saw hundreds of Wolves and Stoke hooligans clash in Stafford hours before the tea-time kick-off in Stoke. Outside the ground, police confiscated knives and fireworks from fans entering the Britannia Stadium and it took 100 officers, many on horses, to separate rival fans. On three occasions Stoke fans attempted to invade the pitch. Twenty-six people were arrested in what the press dubbed Stoke's "Day of Shame".

On the England scene, Shaw and a sizeable group of Wolves formed an alliance with Plymouth's Central Element and together made up one of the largest contingents following the national side. A looser alliance was formed with Stockport County, who in turn were linked with Oldham, who had a close relationship with Shrewsbury, who had a link with Newcastle. There was also a brief link up between a few Wolves and Chelsea but this did not last long and caused a split between the white and black lads in the Yam Yam Army because of Chelsea's racism.

The Yam Yam Army might have been able to raise numbers for local derbies but struggled against the bigger London firms. This was clearly shown in a midweek game in November 2001 when Millwall selected Wolves as one of their few outings that season. Two hundred of Millwall's older lads caught a lunchtime train from Euston, to the complete surprise of the police, who had not predicted the Londoners would travel. By the time the train pulled into Wolverhampton, a Yam Yam welcoming committee was being held back by police. Millwall strode purposefully out of the station and swept aside their police escort.

Onlookers appeared shocked as middle-aged Millwall fans pulled baseball bats from their coats and steamed into a clearly frightened Wolves mob. Two Wolves lads were stabbed and others scattered as fast as they could. The internet was buzzing for the return fixture as Wolves promised revenge. However, it did not materialise as Wolves brought no more than 30 lads down on a coach which was escorted to and from the ground.

In May 2002 Shaw was featured in the BBC *Hooligan* series, though he was given another name and had his face blacked out because he was at the time facing criminal charges. The club immediately banned him from the ground. It was not a new experience for the Yam Yam leader; he received a suspended sentence as a result of Operation Growth but was still banned from Molineux for five years. He miscalculated his ban and returned to the ground a week before it expired, only to be met by a grinning Dick Shakespeare, one of the undercover cops involved in Operation Growth. Shaw received a further five-year ban after trouble at a match in Stoke.

Wolves were eventually promoted back into the top flight of English football after an absence of 19 years. Shaw later revealed in his autobiography how the Wolves mob were eagerly awaiting the chance to meet some of Britain's more famous hooligan firms. In reality, many had seen better days, and Wolves may not have been the attraction they once were. Manchester United barely took a mob there, but there was serious disorder at home games against Liverpool, Everton and Spurs. Wolves only lasted a season in the Premiership, but for the soccer hooligans the second tier of football is often the real battleground anyway.

For a home game against Cardiff City, Wolves had a mob of more than 500 out and there was serious trouble after the game, both at the ground and in the nearby coach park. A cup game against West Ham saw Wolves arrange to meet their London rivals out of town but a no-show from the ICF meant there were only isolated fights, including two stabbings, in the town centre.

In January 2004, Wolves were drawn at home to Millwall in the FA Cup. Many of the Yam Yam were still smarting from the onslaught they had faced a couple of years before and a good turnout was guaranteed. However, for the infamous South London fans, Wolves were actually a sideshow, as the real action for them was a pre-arranged fight with Leeds, who were playing the same day at Birmingham City. Wolves tried to attack the Millwall escort but the police were out in force and Millwall were not desperate to get involved.

In October 2004, a Wolves gang attacked innocent bystanders in a rampage through the West End of London. They approached a small group of young men standing outside a Tube station and were caught on CCTV punching, kicking and butting their victims after a game at Upton Park. Two years later, 14 of them, aged between 18 and 44, appeared before Southwark Crown Court variously charged with violent disorder and affray.

The court heard how street camera operators first noticed the gang congregating near Charing Cross, before barging their way through crowds of shoppers to Leicester Square. Some were seen wrapping scarves across their faces or pulling hoods over their heads. Only a handful of those arrested, including family men with children, had actually been to the match. The CCTV pictures showed two victims being booted repeatedly in the head as they lay on the ground. Others, seen trying to back away from trouble, were hit. "The video footage was truly shocking," said Judge Paul Dodgson. "This was a Saturday evening, a time when Leicester Square was packed with people." Some pleaded guilty while the remainder were convicted by a jury. They were given sentences ranging from 16 months in jail to community service and most were banned from going to any football match for six years after their release from prison.

Despite high-profile police operations and many banning orders, it seems that Wolves still manage to churn out lads willing to fight, and firms from other clubs still look at Wolverhampton as one place they might still find trouble. This was certainly the case when Bristol City turned up in force and took a Wolves stronghold, the Rothwells pub, soon after it had opened its doors at 11am. Gilly Shaw, while impressed with the Bristol turnout, was not so impressed with their quality. "Give them credit, in 2007 not many firms will land early doors with two hundred lads and fill your main boozer," he said. "But if you're going to do that, surely you could go the extra few yards and come out of the fucking pub when we arrive? Once our lads heard they were in there, about a hundred went to shift them but apart from throwing a few bottles and glasses the Bristol lot declined to take up the offer and come into the street. There were just three police officers outside so it was hardly a case of being kept in by the riot squad. It was an impressive show but nothing more, they were all over the place like ants but wasted a great chance to make a name for themselves."

In 2006, the club arranged a pre-season "friendly" against Den Haag, home to one of Holland's most notorious hooligan mobs, and Gilly and his mates saw it as a trip too good to miss. "Only a few went out there and as always we all got nicked. Before the game we had it with about eighty of them with no OB in sight and later we left the game early and bumped straight into a mob of them outside and we done them fair and square. Within minutes, eighteen of us were locked up and held over night. We had to pay for new flights home. This was, shall we say, funded by currency which may not have been one hundred per cent legal!"

West Brom continue to be Wolves' main rival and one recent clash between them saw Shaw receive yet another banning order. "They had played Villa and we were at Coventry and met them in a place called Darlaston," he said. "The police were soon onto it and about forty were nicked, although only about a dozen were charged, me being one of them. In court they used my book as evidence and that helped them to convict me, although more damage was done by one of their main lads who I won't name, we'll just call him Johnny the Grass. He told the police I ran out of the pub spraying CS gas at them which was bollocks, but they believed him and I was lucky to get away with a suspended sentence but was also hit with another three-year ban. The Grass made it all worthwhile though. CCTV footage showed him punching the wall in temper, yet when interviewed he was bragging that the damage to his hand was caused by my teeth!"

Further reading: *Running With A Pack Of Wolves*, Gilroy Shaw with Martin King (Headhunter Books), *Terrace Legends*, Cass Pennant and Martin King (John Blake Publishing)

WREXHAM AFC

Ground: The Racecourse
Firm: Frontline
Rivals: Shrewsbury Town, Chester City, Oldham Athletic

Neil Williams has been looking forward to this interview for a long time. He sits impatiently in a dreary corridor, body slouched, legs wide apart, and can't wait to tell his story. Perhaps it is the recognition of his terrace exploits, or simply that he just can't stop talking about hooliganism. An hour later, as we sit in a pub in Mold on the Wales/Cheshire border, he bumps into an old Wrexham face. "I'm being interviewed for a book," he grins. His friend nods in approval. Recognition indeed.

For many years, Williams was leader of the Wrexham Frontline; in fact it is fair to say that he *was* the Frontline. While no gang firm is one person, it is widely accepted that the Frontline would not have achieved half of their "successes" over the years if it hadn't been for the leadership and drive of Williams. He is simply obsessed by football violence, and within minutes of meeting him you are bombarded by tales of Wrexham's exploits over the years.

"To be honest I don't really care about the football," he admitted when asked when he first attended a match. "I'm not one of these people who knows the names of every player or who cries when my team loses, because I really don't care about it. I'm only interested in the violence. Of course I want our team to do well but only because that means bigger matches and bigger Wrexham firms."

Williams began going to football when he was 14 years old. "It was Port Vale at home, but there was no trouble," he said, bringing the conversation quickly back to his favourite subject. It wasn't long before he did see trouble, and was instantly captivated. "In the early days there were not many of us who were real Wrexham fans. Most of the lads at school supported other teams, Liverpool, Man United, Everton or Leeds. That's changed now but only because the Frontline has brought some pride into supporting Wrexham. We are now only Wrexham."

The early years were simply about having a go and trying your luck. "Me and my mate would go away and just try to get in their end," he said. He gives the impression that they were just two barmy loons, and perhaps they were. "You knew you would get a kicking but we were young, we didn't care. That's just what it was like in those days." He mentioned several occasions when he would get a beating before being escorted around to the Wrexham, only to try again a while later. Wrexham were disorganised and it was every man for himself. This was twenty-five years ago, or thereabouts. Williams can't remember; dates are not his thing.

"Me, little Mike and a few others would go on the supporters' bus and go in the home end. The home lot would go, 'These cunts are here again, same few as last year!' The supporters' club banned us in the end and we started taking our own coach or minibus and it grew from there. Once the casual thing started we were as good as anyone in the lower leagues. We had the lull, the same as everyone but today we are one of the most active."

At home, when Wrexham would gather in the old Kop, there was trouble at most games. The most memorable for older fans was the visit of Crystal Palace. They, together with Brighton and Mansfield, topped the division, with Wrexham one point further adrift. Palace came and won 4–2 and their fans kicked off. They were Cockney skinheads in their thousands and it was a mob never seen before or since.

Wrexham lost to Mansfield three days later and there were expectations of more trouble, but the game passed off peacefully, and although Wrexham lost and stayed down, the following season they were promoted with a side which is still legendary today. The likes of Mickey Thomas, Bobby Shinton, Billy Ashcroft and Dixie McNeil put Wrexham on the map with their giant-killing cup exploits and won the division title after thrashing Rotherham 7-1 before a full house at the Racecourse.

The Frontline was formed in about 1983/84 by a group of lads in a pub, who wanted to keep up with the then-current trend of all the main firms having names. An earlier name attached to the hooligan element had been the Turf Bar Boys, a group of less than 20 who regularly went into home ends at away games and were barred from the pub adjacent to the Wrexham Kop due to their violent tendencies.

Wrexham claim that they were the first firm to take the name Frontline, arguing they had sprayed it all over the towns of the lower divisions at least a year before the more notorious Frontline of Middlesbrough adopted the title. "Without a doubt we had the name first," said Williams proudly. "We played somewhere and saw [Middlesbrough] graffiti saying 'Redcar Casuals', when we had been the Frontline for at least a year. They may have had a bigger mob over the years and may be better known but they nicked our fucking name – fact! Don't get me wrong, they are one of the best in the country, but fuck them, I don't care who they are, we had the name first."

In those days, the Frontline could pull about 200 for a decent away game, with as many as 250 going to Rochdale by train in their heyday, but numbers were swelled by many younger, impressionable members who were into the clothes scene more than the violence. "We are only half an hour from Liverpool and when I was in school used to go with a few mates and see what the scallies were wearing. Sometimes I'd go to Liverpool and stand on the Road End just to clock what was in and then go into town before the match had finished and try and find a certain item. Soon it caught on and we ended up with all the young ones in the area tagging onto us, which at the time did us no favours, but the good thing is that twenty years on sixty of them are still at it and form our hardcore. Our firm now is far better than those early days. Some days we'll have no one out but for some games it will swell to a good 150."

Many of the early clashes were with nearby Tranmere Rovers. The first was in the 1982/3 season and "they fucking terrorised us. They were in the seats behind us and simply terrorised us. They came at us after the game, loads of them and I got off in a car and the rest got chased for miles, not odd little bits of running, full fucking stop to the station."

A year later Wrexham travelled to Birkenhead in a double-decker bus but after they parked up they were bricked by small groups of locals. "I remember chasing them into some street and one lad ran into a house and we chased him inside. It wasn't his fucking house and a couple got nicked for breaking and entering!

"At the ground we went straight into the seats. It was a decent mob of ours but they were game and it went off all over the stand. A couple of flares were fired, it was at its height then and probably our best night at their place." That didn't stop another vicious brick barrage after the game.

"After that night it was a big game for us, but for some reason they never bothered with us as much as we did with them. They came to ours in 1987 and got a result, they slammed us on a bank holiday Monday, early, and they attacked the Talbot pub. Tranmere did the business that day but a few got cocky and later two were slashed in isolated incidents."

The rowing with Tranmere became so intense that local police had to appeal to the magistrates to impose stiffer sentences. After one fight at the Feathers pub in Wrexham, rival gangs threw bottles, chairs and glasses at each other. "I've never seen anything like that in my life before," said the landlord. "One minute everything was calm, the next all hell broke loose." He suggested that the only solution was to ban football supporters from coming into town, or closing pubs on match days. The assistant manager of a local clothes store shared his despair. "It's about time something was done, many people just won't come into the town centre when a match is on for fear of being beaten up or worse," he said.

"Banning football supporters from the town centre is far too impracticable and wrong," a local police spokesman told reporters. "The solution is far stiffer sentences to discourage a repetition of incidents. If the magistrates came down hard, I'm sure many would think twice before having another go."

It is hard work getting Williams to remember anything, but when he does it is hard to shut him up. "Wolves were rivals in the early Eighties," he recounted. "They were shit then and we could pull out mobs of 200-300 at home." For one encounter, in 1985, Wrexham took at least 150 to Wolves; it could have been 2-300, but Williams can't quite remember. "We arrived late, so late that their mob had gone into the ground. We steamed any group we could find in the Mandle Centre. That's what you did back then. It didn't matter if they were their firm or not, we were young and any group of lads were considered fair game.

"In one of the fights a local is downed but rather than being left alone one of the Wrexham boys strides over and slashes him. Another Wrexham lad walks over and, pointing at the Wrexham tattoo on his forehead, sneers at the victim. When the victim is later led by police onto the Wrexham coach to identify his attacker, all he can remember is the tattooed loon. The man gets five years and what is worse his wife dies in a house fire while he is inside."

Did Williams try to get the real lad to own up? "A few people asked me to do that, including the lad who was put away. But what could I do?" He broke into a laugh. "I certainly wouldn't own up if some lad got sent down for something I've done. 'Yeah, here I am for my five years'. Everyone was gutted for the lad who got the jail, especially when his wife died and he was banged up, going through all that, but the problem is between him and the fella who had the knife."

"Rampaging fans," was the headline in the local paper. "A 'LUNATIC fringe' of more than 100 Wrexham hooligans went on the rampage in Wolverhampton's shopping precinct and left a teenager needing 40 stitches for a slash wound from a craft knife. The Wrexham gang terrified shoppers, smashed a window in an empty shop and stoned cars."

There was more fighting when Wolves arrived for the return fixture. "It was a huge game for us and everyone was out. Hundreds. Every corner had groups of Wrexham, every pub was packed. There were a lot of youngsters but then everyone was in those days. Wolves came with the mob, Millsy, Pixy and the Bridge Boys, but we backed them back into a pub. It was a result." Williams knows everyone and everything to do with soccer violence. "I got to know the Wolves lads and went down there a few times."

Williams also carries the telltale signs of many a battle. His head is heavily scarred and he has suffered numerous broken bones. His worst beating came at the hands of Shrewsbury, or the "Wurzels", as Wrexham like to call them. "One year we went there with a top firm and fronted their pub but no-one would come out. I knew they were all in there and was screaming for every-one to stick together but lads started to drift off looking for other

Shrewsbury who were more up for it than this lot in the pub. I knew it was their pub and I knew their lads were in it and a few of us carried on shouting at them to come out. They were clever bastards; as soon as they saw that the majority of our lot had moved on, the doors burst open and they steamed into us.

"It was well on top and the few of us that had stood there were chased, with two of us ending up inside a garage where the blokes were working on cars as we ran in. I picked up an exhaust pipe and my mate got a wheel lever and these mechanics were shouting at us, wondering what the fuck was going on. The Shrewsbury lads piled in and caned us. My head was opened up and they put something across my back. Once they left, we made it to the ground and then I collapsed and was in hospital with concussion and broken bones in my back. I was in fucking agony for months with it.

"We got revenge when we stopped off there on the way back from watching a game at Hereford. We were in a car and pulled up near their boozer. I had a nose around the back and saw the beer garden was full of them. We decided to give it a go and grabbed some wood and a few bits and charged into them. They were in panic thinking there was a coachload of us and we smashed them into the pub before getting off. The police came and then they saw the five of us and wanted to kill us. Too late, we were off home, job done."

Being a hooligan for almost thirty years takes a serious toll on one's career, family and relationships. "I live with a girl now and we have a young son. Even though I rarely go now, the hassle I still get from the police for stupid things related to my previous ban upsets us all. I got done for breaching the ban and we both know I had not been through the fucking door all night. She is sound about it all, knows all about my past but it still pisses us off. I had one relationship with a girl who was in university; she ended up with me as well as a degree in chemistry! We bought a house and were thinking of getting married, but after I was getting nicked all the time and I went down, it fucked it all up and we went our own way. Some girls will turn a blind eye to it and some love the fact that you are well known all over the country. Strange creatures.

"My mother despairs over it. If ever I need a bed for the night I know not even to knock on my parents' door. She makes me welcome when I take the little lad there but that's it. Three years ago they raided her house and turned the place upside down when they tried to pin a conspiracy charge on me. It was a disgrace, turning a seventy-year-old pensioner's underwear drawers upside down; I had not lived there for ten years. That was when she decided it was best if I stayed away, as we were all convinced I was being followed everywhere and it was not fair bringing the hassle to their place at their age, even though I didn't have as much as a pair of socks still in the house."

Williams has been arrested over a dozen times for football-related offences, charged with conspiracy and dawn-raided twice, but remains undeterred. "At the end of the day it's pride in your town. I don't give a fuck how they get on on the pitch but if any mob came into this town I would do my utmost to defend it. It really was as simple as that."

Some of the most violent clashes have been between the Frontline and Oldham, and hatred between the two groups exists to this day. "It all started at a pre-season friendly when they turned up at a night game about twenty-five-handed and we ran them from McDonald's in town right to the ground. The next year, they came with about seventy and got in the wine bar. They wouldn't come out so we were going in in twos and threes trying to get them out.

"A season later they had met some Hibs on holiday and some Shrewsbury, and all this joining up shit started, and they done us at home, which was all our own fault. It was the first game of the season and Wrexham had eighty in the Egerton waiting for them and then we phoned them and told them to get to the Four Dogs out of town. Wrexham caught a local double-decker bus to meet them with the idea of getting to a pub nearby called the Acton, supposedly to get tooled up and take it to them.

"As we drove past on this big daft bus, a few Oldham saw us and they all come piling out. Lads try getting off, but this fucking bus driver is having none of it. Some of our lads pulled open the doors while others were screaming to leave it and get off further up the road. About ten got off and were getting slaughtered, bottles, glasses, the lot going at them. A few more managed to jump off as the bus hadn't stopped, lads upstairs were kicking out the windows and trying to get out and help the lads who were getting slaughtered by fifty Oldham with a good dozen Hibs with them for good measure, all tooled up.

"By the time we get up the road and this fucking hero driver had stopped, our lot had been done and the police were there. Oldham drank up and fucked off home with a police escort and didn't even go to the game. It was a nightmare. I remember going home at five o'clock gutted. We were all arguing among ourselves, in-house fights were breaking out, all that nonsense. It was one bad day at the office."

As hard as Wrexham tried to get even, they failed, but as Williams said, it wasn't for the want of trying. It looked like the Frontline would never get revenge for the Four Dogs massacre, but in 2002 they were given an opportunity when Oldham called on a meet in Manchester while the game was being played in Oldham. Williams and his firm had waited four years for the chance to settle the score, and he excitedly took up the story.

"We were told to get to some pub in Piccadilly at three o'clock, when the match had kicked off, and all the police spotters would be up at the ground thinking it was a no-show from both mobs. We got the train and waited in Warrington to save bringing ourselves to the attention of the Manc police, as United were at home and we were taking no chances. We got in this pub and soon a couple of faces came in. I knew them from the Four Dogs incident but they said they were nothing to do with Oldham anymore, they were now part of the Manchester United-Hibs-Oldham alliance, or whatever.

"They told us to wait, as Oldham's firm were holed up in another pub, thirty-odd of them, and were waiting for a few more cars to arrive. They were full of crap, saying if Oldham were getting done they'd help them but they didn't think it was going to work out that way, and so on. There was about fifty of us in this pub and we were pissed off with them by now, we would have had a couple of hundred if this had been organised the year after we got done at home but loads fucked it off thinking it wasn't going to happen.

"By now the lad's phone was going and some United were leaving their match to come for a nose, main lads and a few Cockney Reds. They turned up and said the same thing, they just wanted to watch and told us we had to take it to Oldham now. We told them we were not arsed if they did join in but they were adamant they were just observers. The Man United lads told us the pub was called the Edinburgh Castle, some back street dive in Ancoats, and fair play to them it was a perfect venue, no CCTV, perfect.

"It was strange, we set off on this march and on every corner was a Manc pointing us in the direction of the pub. On the way we were picking anything up we could find for the attack, as we knew we would face an onslaught when we got there. We got to a crossroads and there were ten United on the corner watching. Only a few of us knew who they were and it nearly went as loads were ready to steam into them. That moment, about ten Oldham came from behind this factory unit slinging bottles and as we went towards them another thirty-odd came down the side street at us. It was fucking blinding, it was what we had waited four years for, there was none of the usual bouncing about, we just went straight into this thirty and they turned in seconds and were off. All our ammunition was hitting them as they tried to get back into this pub, they were stuck in a bottleneck and about ten escaped but for the rest there was no hiding place.

"The first one to stand at the pub door got cleaned, sparked out, as they tried to fight us off but then every window in the pub went in. We were screaming, 'Get in the pub, get in the fucking pub,' but waited a moment for the usual barrage of bottles and glasses – but it never came. We thought they had got out of a back door so went in slowly and we could not believe it, the back door didn't exist and they were spread out, breathless, picking up a few stools. Normally it's the kind of situation you would walk away from, as they were fucked already, but the Four Dogs was the same for them and they mercilessly battered the few that were trapped off the bus, so we thought, fuck it.

"Basically we destroyed them. Lads were ripping the beer pump handles off the bar and whacking them, every chair in the pub got smashed over them. One of Stockport's main lads with them was knocked out. It was stopping and we were outside ready to go when someone would run in and start it off again. They were well and truly slaughtered, hiding under tables, locked in the toilets, pleading with us to leave them, there was no fight left in them. No police were coming; it was like a ghost town. All you could hear was bits of glass falling from the wrecked windowpanes with the curtains blowing in the wind.

"Eventually we heard sirens and left sharpish. One of the United lads told us later that it was the best he had seen for ten years and when the police turned up with paramedics they were slapping lads across the face trying to revive them. It was job done and on the way home I remembered how bad I had felt after they had done us four years earlier, but I'll tell you what, if I had been with them in Ancoats I would never, and I mean never, fucking go again. It was that bad for them."

Wrexham's closest opponents are Chester City, but the Chester of today are no match for the numbers of Wrexham. "But for the fact they reside a few miles away, it would be a nothing game, they are very poor. They have a few decent lads and I respect a few of their older lot from years ago, but as a firm, no respect. They have never had a result against Wrexham and I have been going for twenty-eight years. They make a big thing of the Welsh-English factor but to us they are nothing, just an irritant really, and ninety-nine per cent of their lads will tell you they can't get near us. They claim a result here and there since the Seventies but I have been at them all and even when the games have been postponed the fucking Pools Panel would not give them a result against us."

In December 1997, Wrexham were drawn away at Chester in the FA Cup. The match was played on a Friday night and it spelt trouble for both mobs. "We were drinking down by the river and if ever there was a police set-up, this was the best ever," said Williams. "They came in and made us all leave, ushered us up to the centre and then pushed us down the Rows to near the Victoria, where Chester were mobbed up. On the Rows, were police filming us coming up and the police behind us were pushing us towards Chester. That would never have happened on a Saturday when there were hundreds of tourists about; they were trying hard to get everyone nicked. A few obliged but it was a nothing incident."

Over 20 alleged hooligans were arrested and the case came to Chester

Crown Court the following September. The prosecution explained how a handful of police desperately tried to prevent disorder between over 100 Wrexham hooligans and 50 Chester. "It was frightening," said Sgt Mark Chesters. "When I turned the corner into Watergate Street, the sky was full of bottles and glass, and the noise was tremendous." Many of the defendants, including Neil Williams, pleaded not guilty. Giving evidence, Williams did not deny being there but claimed not to be involved in any trouble. The jury believed him and he was cleared, along with several other men.

"My funniest moment was when we were all in the stand against Chester and two lads unfolded a huge England flag in the middle of our Kop," says Neil. "The whole Chester end erupted and we could not get near the Kop from where we were. They stood there, arms out, calling for Wrexham to come at them, knowing the police would be there in seconds and they were soon to be heroes. Well no police fucking saw them and some bloke called Alan just walked up to them and knocked the pair of them clean out with two hits. The St John lads had to stretcher them off the Kop and the Chester end was silent. It was without doubt the funniest thing I have ever seen at the match."

Cardiff City are a different prospect. "We have had some right rows against them. In the Eighties we slammed them at home a few times. Our main lot bumped into them early one morning and steamed them, they had much bigger numbers but one of our lads pulled a blade and they crumbled. They were diving over the counter in McDonald's and running into shops, no mention of it in their book though! A few years later, twenty of us met in Yates's early on and suddenly the police brought their firm in and left them with us. One copper went, 'There you go lads,' and walked outside. They could not believe it, and the place was eerie, all the police outside with cameras, excited to fuck. Macca [a main Soul Crew face] came over and we all agreed it was a set-up and they let us do a swift one.

"In reality we never took what we should have done there. We got battered on one trip, a Welsh Cup final on a Sunday. Forty of us turned up and they could not believe it. Afterwards hundreds attacked us, as they do at Cardiff, and it was not pleasant. Three police were laughing at us, going, 'You're gonna die in a minute.' They respected us for that and since that day I have been mates with a few of them."

The Frontline travelled extensively across England, visiting most groups whatever the reputation and odds. Sometimes their mob was just 20-strong but they still travelled, but on other occasions they could raise 250 with ease. In 1986, it took over 100 police to quell fighting at Wrexham's away match at Crewe. Some fans climbed on the roof of a social club to stone people leaving the ground. Wrexham yobs were blamed by one Crewe councillor, who demanded that the club ban away supporters in future.

Two years later 60 rival fans mixed it before a Wrexham home game to Burnley, while in 1990 there were clashes in Blackpool before a league game. Over 800 Wrexham fans made the trip to the seaside resort, including two coachloads of supporters who claimed to be on a stag weekend. Two pubs were wrecked in the trouble as rival fans fought running battles along the promenade. Blackpool's football intelligence officer said he was disgusted by the violence. "We spotted the Wrexham Frontline troublemakers. One of them was seen with a Blackpool fan and they were obviously organising fights. We are talking about organised crime and we have a police officer who is still unconscious." It may have gone some way to alleviating the memory of a humiliating Boxing Day game in the early Eighties when Blackpool took a huge contingent to North Wales and overran Wrexham.

A year later, 16 Wrexham fans were arrested after rampaging through Halifax town centre. More recently, in 1997 extra police had to be called in to deal with a series of pitch invasions during Wrexham's FA cup tie at Peterborough. A total of 27 people were arrested, most being Wrexham fans. And after one trip to the North-west, a newspaper reported, "Wrexham fans are in disgrace following violent scenes which saw a policeman hurled down steps in the side's league clash with Rochdale. Mayhem erupted during the vital away game with the Lancashire side and 14 fans were arrested as fighting broke out between rival supporters."

Williams is proud of their record. "People say we only mix it when we have the numbers. That is nonsense. Is it our fault we have a bigger mob at games? We have been on a hiding to nothing at places and still had a go, all over the country.

"People laugh that we say we have 100 banned but very few clubs would still be at it with the lads we have had banned. Laugh all you want but the proof is there, we have got loads banned and still we compete. That is rare today and only the bitter cunts out there will question our reputation. We can't compete with the like of Stoke or Millwall but we have had a go with them. Millwall took a slap in town, forty of them got slammed. Full firm, no chance, but if that kind of number come across us we will do them. Wrexham went to Stoke for an arranged meet and we turned up, the police got onto it but Stoke said, 'Fair play, you came, very few others have.'"

Over the years, Wrexham have travelled extensively abroad to follow their national team. During the Eighties the combined North Wales contingent formed the main group at international matches, but by the Nineties Cardiff had begun to travel in huge numbers. It was put to Wrexham simply: join us or fuck off.

"They had serious numbers and relationships were strained," said Williams. "It all went off in Belgium when we steamed them in Brussels and sixty-odd Wrexham were deported. They won't agree with it, as they don't like the fact they were done, but they were and there were main faces in the mob we put on their toes. After that it died down a bit and today both mobs mix okay when Wales play. At home games they put up with large followings of North Wales lads as long as we don't overstep the mark. No-one is that stupid, as the numbers they have down there are awesome at times. But Wrexham do not go down there and hide."

The Frontline are not afraid to travel for a fight, even when at home, if some mob insists on sitting off away from Wrexham. "There have been a few cases when the lads have got on a bus or train to take on another mob who would not come into Wrexham. Wigan were the perfect example and they were taken to bits when they called it on in some pub on the outskirts of Chester after refusing to come to us. They thought we would not turn up and when we did they still thought they would do us but they got a good kicking and every time I speak to them the numbers they had that day keep dropping. In about three years they will claim to have had minus-eight lads there."

Wrexham's poor league performance has meant games against the big boys have been few, usually cup games or chance meetings. "We got turned over by a huge firm of Yids [Tottenham] when we were on our way to Oldham once; we went into a pub in Manchester and their full firm terrorised us. A mob of Arsenal came unstuck at Wrexham a few years ago, as did a firm of Liverpool recently. We went to Manchester United in the cup and did okay and they played us in a Cup Winners Cup game and did nothing of note when we had a few hundred out."

A highly disputed clash was in 2002, when 200 Wrexham clashed with 50 Everton and came out on top. "Everton say it was not their firm but they were lads and very game lads too," said Neil. "They stood and fought for ages but our numbers were too great for them and we did them. Just before kick-off, a trainload of their so-called faces turned up and bounced about but by then we were wrapped up with police. If the ones we had it with were not the main lads, they were game, so it was hardly a bunch of barmies." The Merseyside team also came for a pre-season game with 40 lads and fights broke out outside the Horse and Jockey pub. "It was proper toe-to-toe, no cameras, no police and no fucking about. We have had both the Scouse firms here and Everton are miles better."

In the past few years, a new generation of hooligans has emerged. Initially they took orders from their elders but have since become more independent. "We have come forward a hell of a lot, and started going our own way if the older lot don't fancy it for whatever reason," said one youth. "The banning orders and more intense policing have restricted the opportunities for trouble but there are always a few matches a season where Wrexham still turn out in numbers. "A couple of seasons ago we managed firms of sixty at Stockport, sixty at Oldham, seventy at Tranmere and Walsall and about 150 at Chester, which included some very game old-school lads." Huddersfield came out on top in one recent encounter and others they have tangled with include Oldham, Walsall and Port Vale [see *Port Vale*].

Huddersfield Town get most respect off the youth "after the mob they brought to us at the end of last season. It was a really tidy mob who came on top when it went off after the game." Others include Oldham, Walsall and Port Vale after the big clash several years ago [see *Port Vale*].

Neil Williams is confident that there is life without him at the Frontline. "They are on the rise again," he asserted. "There are loads of young lads who have started going, booking their own coaches." That has had a knock-on effect among some of the older lads, who are now starting to show again for some games. "It will never be like the mid-Eighties when we had mobs of 2-300, but people tell me we still take a firm of sorts to most games and can pull good numbers for the big games. The younger lot are lawless, the mob is not as good as it used to be but they don't seem to give a shit about the police and are as game as fuck. I was having a drink with some mates in Birmingham one Saturday and they turned up on their way to some game in the Midlands and it nearly went off with the Zulu mob I had met. They would have done the Wrexham lot, they were old-school Birmingham, all blokes, but the young Wrexham lot were not bothered."

Neil says he has finished with hooliganism, but his addiction is evident to anyone who meets him. And while his gang have moved on, they still seem to rely on him. His services to the Frontline are also acknowledged by the younger generations. "All the youth lads at Wrexham know Neil and respect what he's done over the years," said one. "Even if they haven't seen what he's done, they've heard about it. I think there would still be a Wrexham Frontline without him, as I don't think one person makes a complete mob, but I don't think half the battles over the years would have been organised without him."

Williams' importance to the Wrexham was emphasised by an aborted trip to Manchester for a recent England v. Wales World Cup qualifier. Oldham, looking to avenge the "Ancoats massacre", had been in touch and were looking for Round Three. They had called upon old allies Shrewsbury and Stockport and a meet was set up on the day of the match. Wrexham, buoyed by their previous success in Manchester, were happy to oblige.

"Everyone was up for it and I told people we had three coaches booked," said Williams. "They never existed, I just wanted everyone out and then we could get there by train, bus, who gave a fuck as long as we were there. The police got wind of it and they nicked me the night before the game for some daft drive-off from a garage a year before and I was remanded for a week, though they never even charged me. People turned up at the arranged departure point, no coaches, no chief but a couple of hundred Indians. It was a fuck-up and in the end no-one went as a mob. I was gutted."

When banned from the Racecourse and on a full exclusion order from the courts Williams was jailed twice for breaching the FBO and can see little light at the end of the tunnel when quizzed about his return to the terraces. "I have had four breaches altogether and when my ban was up I was surprised there was no civil one to follow. I have had community service, probation and jail but in the past it has never stopped me going. I'm a family man now so things are different." He smiles and adds, "Honest!"

In May 2005, the Frontline attacked Huddersfield fans outside Chester railway station. The two teams had played at Wrexham that day and later a Welsh mob gathered in Wetherspoons in Chester before heading to the Beehive in Hoole, where the landlady overheard a conversation between them about a fight. Another member of staff heard someone on their mobile phone saying the Huddersfield fans were on the train and heading for the Town Crier pub. The fracas occurred in and outside the Town Crier just before 9pm. A camera pointing at the pub showed about 20 Wrexham fans arrive and push their way in, forcing the Huddersfield fans back inside. Punches were thrown and a chair was hurled through the window. Two Wrexham fans then jumped out of the window, one falling so badly he broke both his ankles. A total of 19 men were subsequently charged with a variety of offences. Three were sent to prison, while others were given community sentences and fines.

The 2006/07 season was one of gloom for Wrexham on the pitch but the team's poor displays saw a resurgence of the Frontline. With a handful of games to go, the team was in serious danger of being relegated from the Football League. As the town rallied support to keep them up, the firm reformed. Mickey was one of the lads who had seen it all before but he was impressed by the numbers that turned out for crucial games.

"Early on in the season we had the usual suspects at it and larger numbers of Mansfield and Telford came unstuck against a small but ruth-less mob of veterans and youth lads," he said. "At Telford one of theirs was slashed and another knocked clean out when thirty locals tried it on with less than a dozen of our lads and at Mansfield twelve of our lads, mainly youth, searched high and low for their firm before finding them and backing them off despite odds of two-to-one against. By the time we looked like going down, plenty of old lads had returned and we took over a hundred to Shrewsbury and Walsall. Derby in the Cup saw well over two hundred lads on duty. Shame that when we got to the arranged meet, Derby told us they were still in bed!"

There is no doubt that Wrexham are one of the more active firms in the lower leagues. At the start of the 2006/07 season, 48 Wrexham fans were on football banning orders, the highest number in their division, and the Welsh club also had the highest number of fans arrested, something the Frontline's founder member would once have been proud of. However, when two goals at the end of the last game of the season saw Wrexham stay up, and thousands invaded the pitch to celebrate survival, one of them was indeed Neil Williams. Maybe he really has given up his life of hooliganism and begun following Wrexham for all the right reasons.

y

YORK CITY

Ground: Bootham Crescent
Firm: York Nomad Society
Rivals: Bury, Scarborough, Shrewsbury Town

On first impressions, the York mob has more similarities to an Italian Ultra group than an English football firm. The York Nomad Society (YNS) was formed in 1981 as an alternative to the club's official travel club. Their first coach was to Peterborough, the second to Lincoln, and their customers included a motley assortment of punks, skins and beer drinkers. It was well organised, with membership cards, a bank account, an answerphone booking service and one of the first football fanzines, *Terrace Talk*.

The YNS was initially to be called the York Nutter Squad, but the organisers had to rethink when it came to opening a bank account. The group wanted to retain the YNS initials, so the York Nomad Society was born. There was even "The Scheme" where lads paid a couple of quid a week into a separate bank account and if they got arrested during the season The Scheme would pay the fine.

Pressure from police led to coach companies refusing to take the group, so they started using vans and trains more often. This hampered their organisation, but not their enjoyment. "The biggest thing about the YNS has always been a bunch of good mates having a good time, never mind how shit the team is or what pressure we get from police," said one York lad. "This will never change."

Fundraising for the football club is also a big part of the YNS, and once they paid almost £1,000 for an advertising hoarding on the halfway line at Bootham Crescent, as well as supporting various other events by way of numbers and hard cash. In the mid-Eighties, the YNS organised a Christmas party which was attended by the club's manager and players. It caused some embarrassment to the club, as they were unaware until it was too late that the main entertainment was provided by local strippers.

More than 1,000 people have been official members of the YNS since its inception. The largest turnout on official YNS transport was 144 on two coaches and a minibus to a fixture at Hartlepool in the late Eighties. The group can still muster up to 100 lads for a big name, but normally their numbers are around 20-30. Ages range from young lads in the mid-teens to veterans in the mid-fifties.

Obviously only a small proportion of that 1,000 were up for fighting, but as time progressed and the club and police cracked down on their independent travel, the fighters become more prominent in the diminishing group. Whilst never hitting the headlines in the way other Yorkshire hooligan gangs did, the York lads have had battles over the years and recall disorder against Doncaster Rovers, Chester City, Stockport County, Stafford Rangers and Macclesfield Town.

The Macclesfield game was probably the worst. Clashes took place throughout the game and on the pitch after the final whistle. Who won the fighting is disputed, with the York lads keen to point out that Macclesfield were bolstered that day by a number of Manchester City hooligans.

Probably because of its rail connections and because it is such a pleasant place to visit, York has attracted large mobs from other teams. In 1985, police launched a huge operation to prevent major trouble at the home game against Bradford City. Working off information received from police in Bradford, officers were stationed at every turnstile with metal detectors to search fans on their way into the ground. Dozens of weapons – from flick knives to razor blades, chains and even a metal scribing spike – were confiscated and many more were discarded by away fans well away from the stadium on hearing about the police action. This did limit the trouble, though inside the ground Bradford fans fought with police.

A year later it was the turn of Sunderland fans to run on the pitch and attack home supporters, and the following season, York City played Bolton Wanderers at Bootham Crescent in what was their final home game of the season. Bolton brought a mob of more than 150 and there were clashes all over the city centre. Not all these fights involved equal numbers. In one case, three YNS were making their way to the ground with four young York lads, none older than 15. At the top of the road, they bumped into 15 Bolton and, despite an attempt to take shelter in a paper shop, they got pasted. Five York were actually behind the counter as they tried to fight off their attackers, who managed to grab hold of one and smashed a number of bottles over his head. Police arrived from the ground in numbers to save the rest from an equally nasty hiding.

The Bolton group were rounded up, handcuffed, and forced to sit on the shop floor waiting for the York lads to point them out. Then, without a word, the police walked out of the shop, giving the home lads a couple of minutes to exact revenge. "The police just walked away and let us have a few free shots," remembered a YNS veteran. "Yeah, it was a bit low, but when you saw the lad with loads of blood pissing out of his head, who cares? The young lads went to hospital with the injured. I went to the game and rallied the troops."

Five Bolton went into the home end and were soon the subject of local attention. It wasn't long before they made their escape on to the pitch. At half-time, Bolton began kicking off in their end. As police rushed to the away end from all over the ground, a group of 30 Bolton entered the home terrace and fought running battles throughout the interval. Mounted officers were sent in but it was several minutes too late. It was a lesson to both the home firm and the police that the main players in the hooligan world were becoming organised.

In the Eighties, York played Liverpool twice in the FA Cup. The first game was at York and the locals mobbed up and clashed with Liverpool at the Lendal Cellars pub after the game. Not wishing to be humiliated, Liverpool put on a show for the replay and more than got their revenge. There were other fights during this period at the George pub in Scarborough when playing Darlington away, while games against Stockport always seemed to result in crowd disorder.

York's key rivals, however, are Bury, and fans of the two clubs have had a number of clashes over the years. The origin of this feud dates back to 1993, when the two sides met in the first leg of the play-off semi-final. Before the game, a group of City fans, a mixture of lads and scarfers, were walking past the Pack Horse pub near their ground when Bury came out and it kicked off. City were heavily outnumbered and took a pasting. During the brawl, a woman from York was knocked to the ground and her leg was repeatedly stamped on. When one of the City lads went to help her he was knocked unconscious and his head was stamped on by the same group of Bury. The woman, who was in her early twenties, was taken to hospital where it was found she had multiple fractures of her leg, requiring an operation to insert pins. The lad had a broken cheekbone and a smashed eye socket, which meant surgery and a "Phantom of the Opera" mask similar to one worn at the time by Paul Gascoigne.

"Regardless of anyone's take on the incident," said one York lad, "they will always go down as cowards in our book. Forget the lad who had his head stamped on, and don't bother with the wrong place at the wrong time chestnut, any hooligan mob who repeatedly stamp on a girl lose the right to exist. The cunts should have served time for what they did that day."

The return leg passed off quietly despite an impressive York mob. Payback was exacted the next time York travelled to Lancashire as 50 lads made the trip. They stopped in Rochdale, where someone had the bright idea of dressing up as women to make it easier to avoid the police and get into Bury's main pub. The sight of 50 lads queuing in Age Concern to buy hats, handbags and dresses was something to behold, but the plan worked a treat.

"The plan worked like a dream," said one York lad who was there. "The coach pulled up round the corner from the pub and we all just wandered in. I think the pub staff thought we were students. On a given signal, we went to work and the pub and its occupants were given a good hiding. We chased them outside into the fists of more City who'd been waiting in the opposite pub, the Spice of Life. We all mobbed up again down an alley near the ground and I remember hearing a rallying cry from one of our lads. 'Right lads,' he said. 'Dresses off, it's serious now!'

"After another game, Bury launched a pool ball through a window of the pub that was the scene of the disgusting attack on the girl a couple of seasons earlier. All the City lads had left for town by then as it was about half six and, true to form, the ball hit a girl in the head. It kicked off as the Bury escort was making its way to the station. To be fair to Bury, they did stand and have a go and looked the part in a battle that was described in the paper as 'like the OK Corral'. But they eventually came off second best.

"Since then it has been relatively quiet between us. Thirty York travelled to Bury the following season for 5pm on a Tuesday and were unopposed all night. Later on in the season it was quiet once again, Bury deciding not to travel, citing Euro 2004 being on the horizon as their excuse. The following Saturday they took a coach to Yeovil and had a few arrests."

About this time, a rivalry began with Shrewsbury and another York lad has good and bad memories of spats they had with the English Border Front (EBF). "In February 1993, around fifty of us arrived in Shrewsbury on the train and wandered into the first boozer we come across. The landlord however, refused to serve us, explaining it was not our fault, but to do with 'the local idiots, they attack any large group that comes in'.

"Our first mistake of the day was the decision to split into smaller groups in order to get served. Ten of us went for a drink in the Elephant and Castle, unaware, until it was too late, that the bar and pool room was full of EBF, meaning we had to fight our way back out of the bar, still in search of our first pint. The day continued in much the same way as it had begun, with little scuffles breaking out until we had a chance to re-group, at which point the trouble stopped.

"York won promotion that season via the play-offs at Wembley, so we didn't renew acquaintances with Shrewsbury until March 1995. We made the trip in a couple of minivans and a car and headed straight for the Elephant and Castle, which to our surprise was empty. Someone decided it would be a good idea to leave a load of calling cards in the pub.

"The following season, we travelled down in a minibus and one of the lads left his jacket in one of the pubs we'd been in before the game. After the match, we went back to collect it but hadn't counted on thirty Shrewsbury coming at us down a hill, assisted by one group coming across a field, and another coming up the hill. We all managed to get back in the van, but had to fight them off from inside the van as we couldn't get the doors to lock. Finally, we managed to pull off the great escape, or so we thought, as it quickly dawned on us that the road we'd 'escaped' down was a cul-de-sac. A drive back through the Shrewsbury mob that qualified for a land-speed record followed, and finally we were on our way."

There have also been occasions when the YNS was simply in the wrong place at the wrong time, as when they bumped into the Chelsea Headhunters at the Flying Scotsman pub, near Kings Cross Station. "This was my first visit to this pub and from the very first glimpse it didn't bode well," explained one YNS veteran. "We had been to Brentford and on the tube back the other lads said that it was traditional to stop there just for one drink. As we got to the corner, you could see faces in the window not looking too welcoming. After pleading to everyone to think again, as it wasn't looking good, I was accused of being paranoid.

"It was frosty walking in and a number of them were heard to ask, 'Is this them?' As we went round the far side of the bar my mate said, 'Right then, what you having?'

"'I don't think you're getting a drink,' I responded.

"'Why not?'

"I pointed at the mob across the bar. The largest beast amongst them shouted, 'Outside Everton.'

"'We're not Everton, we're York,' I answered proudly and to absolutely no avail. It went off – bottles, chairs, all sorts went flying in our direction. It was one of those horseshoe-shaped pubs with one exit/entrance and anyone who attempted to make the door was beaten back with bottles and chairs. The whole place was totalled, beer pissing out of every smashed pump, bar staff with slop buckets over their heads to stop the debris hitting them, naked strippers running around screaming.

"As we had just arrived, we had to rely on what they were throwing to give it back with interest. A chair was about to go in Chelsea's direction but the bar staff tried to stop it being thrown. 'It will antagonise them,' they argued.

"This attack by Chelsea went on for ages without police interference.

"After the first exchanges, they stood outside and fired off all their ammo. I said the only thing we haven't had is the kitchen sink. Cue a big green wheelie bin right through the last remaining window. They started running back in for more things to throw. Eventually we heard the police sirens, so it was time to catch our train back to York, picking glass out of our hair for two hours."

As with most clubs, within the ranks of hooligans are terrace legends. At York icon status goes to a one-legged former grocer called Terry Exelby, known as XLB to the lads. XLB is a name familiar to many fans who have followed York or England over the past 30 years. His exploits include being the first person to be arrested at the Mexico World Cup, this after he was plastered all over the local paper saying he was going to be an ambassador for England. He got drunk on the plane, wouldn't put his cigarette out, climbed into the overhead lockers and then assaulted the cabin crew. The plane landed in Texas, where he was arrested by the FBI and led off the plane in irons. The story made all the national papers. The *Sun*'s headline read, "First Mexico Arrests – A one-legged Englishman and four legless Scots!"

The paper reported, "It had to happen, but so soon? Five British World Cup fans have been arrested before even arriving in Mexico. One of them, a one-legged Englishman, was said to have endangered the flight from Gatwick to Houston, Texas, while the other four, all Scots on the same plane, 'drank their way across the Atlantic!'"

Another story which will be told for many years to come is of the dramatic "shark" incident in Yugoslavia, when XLB came out of the sea, with just the one leg of course, and proceeded to shout, "Shark! Shark!" causing mass panic among people on the beach and hysterical laughter among the York lads present.

XLB stopped going to City games for a few seasons for one reason or another, but eventually reappeared and was soon up to his old tricks. The most memorable was at Oxford United, where at half-time he made his way to the catering kiosk and its unsuspecting staff, ordered 88 bottles of Carlsberg and then handed them out to anyone who was passing. The bloke behind the counter said reasonably, "That'll be £202.40, please sir." XLB replied, "I've only got a tenner," and hopped off into the crowd. He also has to be the only fan in the world to use his false leg and crutch as a weapon.

The York Nomad Society continue to exist and develop and a new generation of lads is currently coming through, while many of the old faces will turn out for bigger games. The 2005 New Year fixture at Scarborough saw a mob of 80 make the trip. However, such large turnouts are rare, with or without the appearance of one-legged Terry.

In April 2006, a dozen people were arrested when York yobs fought with Halifax Town before and after their Yorkshire derby, bringing the city centre to a standstill. Riot police had to be brought it and a dozen people were arrested, most from Halifax. A group of 200 away supporters were escorted from KitKat Crescent to the station after the match.

And in October 2006, trouble erupted at York City's away fixture against Oxford United. "Hooligan havoc as 100 clash," declared the *Oxford Mail*. A pre-match encounter took place at the Blackbird Leys pub in Oxford and the local football intelligence officer, Det Con Huw James, called it the worst he had seen for at least two seasons. He told the *Oxford Mail*, "Up to sixty supporters from York City were found to be drinking in the Cowley area and they made their way to the Blackbird Leys area where it was clear to police that a pre-planned meeting with Oxford United supporters, also known to the police, took place. It appears bottles, glasses and other items have been thrown between the groups. Prior to the end of the game, a number of known York City fans left the ground and went to the Priory pub where it's alleged a number of them smashed a window." After the game, police officers escorted the "trouble element from York" to their coaches and then escorted the coaches out of the city to the A43.

Football liaison officer Dc Steve Norman, one of the first officers on the scene, said, "When we arrived on the scene we were confronted by two groups of football supporters. They were all up for a fight. It was only because we had our batons out that we prevented them meeting each other. We had to use force."

Officers on the ground alerted the police helicopter, which flew above the scene recording what was going on below. At least nine York City fans were subsequently convicted of involvement.